Conquering The Impossible:
Justice

By

Carol Higgins

Printed by Charlesworth Press.

Original Cover Design by Tony Black.

Multimedia Technology by Tony Black.

ISBN-13
9781919633312

DEDICATION

For my beautiful sister Donna, son Jake & daughter Ella.

"CONQUERING THE IMPOSSIBLE: Justice" contains QR codes which are links to optional extra content such as scanned documents, colour photographs, and even video segments which were submitted as evidence for the trial.

I would have liked to have included all of the documents and have full colour photographs like in my first book, but this would have vastly increased the printing costs and made this book (with its vastly higher page count) prohibitively expensive to my wider audience.

For readers of the paperback edition, you may use the QR code scanning feature of a smart phone or similar device to access these extra features.

If you are reading this title as an eBook, the QR codes themselves will serve as links, allowing you to tap or click on them as is applicable to your device.

ABOUT THE AUTHOR

Carol Higgins (54) grew up in a violent and dysfunctional family in Denby Dale, West Yorkshire, where she was psychologically, physically and sexually terrorised by her incestuous father. As a result she left school with no qualifications and was later diagnosed with complex PTSD.

Forced to leave the family home to live on her own at 16, Carol moved to live alone in a cold rented house on Stanhope Street in Barnsley. She recalls her thoughts from the first night she spent in that cold, high second-hand bed, wrapping her arms around herself, saying "Pretend you're in a bed & breakfast." She then realised she had never been in a bed & breakfast and had only been camping with her family while growing up. From this point she was on her own.

Working in a sewing factory for eight years, Carol's supportive colleagues were the force that kept her going through her lonely home life, and they felt like one big happy family through the bad times.

During this time, Carol met her future husband, with whom she had two children. This marriage came to an end after Carol helped her ex-husband build a successful business.

Divorced and bringing up her two children alone, Carol gave her spare time to work with the elderly and children in schools and as a youth worker, soon enrolling on adult education courses.

Until as recently as 2014, Carol did not know that she was dyslexic, a diagnosis that helped her realise why she had struggled all of her life, particularly in school, work and college. She has consistently refused to live life as a victim and became the author and publisher of her first book in 2015.

Carol lives in Ackworth, West Yorkshire, where she is a keen fundraiser for numerous charities. Only eight months after she underwent 9 hours of surgery to remove the tumour that threatened her life, Carol climbed Mount Kilimanjaro to raise money for a charity close to her heart.

Carol now uses her own experiences and voice to stand for social justice and advocate for those whose own voices have been silenced. She raises awareness about the taboo subjects of familial rape of children and incest and encourages others to speak out. She believes the truth will set you free and she fights to change attitudes and laws. Child incest is rife and not enough is being done about it.

ACKNOWLEDGMENTS

My wonderful children, Jake and Ella, for giving me the best love and support one could ever wish for (and pain). For telling me "how it is" and being "straight John Bull!" I am sorry I am not the easiest person to live with. We have grown through brilliant and difficult times and it is our love and patience that has bound this book together.

My late beautiful sister, Donna, such a gentle and honest soul. She taught me unconditional love and continues to inspire and guide me with her innocence and bravery, long after her passing. Her daughter Millie continues this inspiration with her positive and fun-loving attitude.

Graham Geddes for being the family I never had and great friend. He is definitely the force who has guided, advised and listened to me for over ten years. His support and wisdom have given me the courage and confidence to challenge the establishment and to conquer my fears. He believed in my ability to become an author and spent countless hours with me when writing my first book. He has given me moral support throughout the writing of this second book.

Lisa Thorn for being a valuable friend since 2014 when we worked together on my first book. For helping me to write the second book, editing, proofreading and dedicating her time to make it possible. For being with me through good and bad times and without the love and compassion she has shown me, this book would not have come to fruition. She has helped me to break down the walls of a hard heart put there by my parents and replaced it with a softer one.

Anthony Black, a great friend since 2015, where would I be without him? He has been my rock, a gentle and kind soul. He has dealt calmly with all the challenging tasks I have thrown at him and taught me patience and kindness. His technical knowledge has been invaluable in designing and curating this book.

Alison Booden for being a true friend and personal assistant through the making of this book. Proof-reader, organiser, giver of wise advice, emotional support and encouragement.

Bernie Nyman from BM Nyman & Co, IP and Publishing Lawyers. For the professional and legal advice on publication, support and encouragement beyond our professional relationship.

For friends who supported me in court and witnesses who bravely testified in the trial.

Facebook friends and others who have supported me on my various social media platforms, encouraging me to persevere and continue fighting for truth and justice.

Thanks to the people who kindly donated to my GoFundMe page, which went towards the cost of obtaining the Trial Transcripts (£5,450.00).

Thank you, I have been truly blessed by the universe for introducing me to all these lovely people.

INTRODUCTION

My motivation in writing and publishing this book is to highlight failings of the justice system, particularly of South and West Yorkshire Police and the Crown Prosecution Service. I wish to use my experiences to raise public awareness of the taboo subjects of familial rape and incest and to support other victims who have been sexually abused by a parent. Identifying how predators like my father groom, terrorise abuse and rape children will enable society and the authorities to recognise the signs and ultimately lead to their earlier prosecution. It took thirty-five years to bring my father to justice and in the process, I was labelled a liar and a slag, dismissed by the authorities and made to feel worthless. There was no deterrent for my father and he relied on my silence and the unwillingness of people, including the police, to countenance that he could rape his own child to protect him. I am sure that if this has happened to me, it must have happened to many others. It must not be allowed to happen again. It is my literary and journalistic responsibility to assist in breaking the silence, this is key to preventing children's lives being ruined and destroyed. The reproduction of the trial transcripts, various items of evidence and recordings of conversations within this book are for the purposes of breaking the silence and raising awareness. My hope is that a more effective national deterrent and prevention strategy can be developed to safeguard children.

Society needs to realise that child incest is like putting a nuclear bomb under the family. Picking up all the pieces is virtually impossible. However, there is hope for victims to survive and thrive given the right environment, tools and loving support. It requires courage to reach out and ask for help to heal your broken heart. I hope my story will help and I want to show that if we stand together, we can overcome adversity. It takes courage for us all to stand up for what is right and to challenge a what is wrong in a failing system. I have been inspired by reading books by great leaders who bravely spoke out to try and make the world a safer place for our children. I also want to inspire others to choose a path to healing and to believing that they can make their dreams come true and conquer the impossible.

The Kingdom of God belongs to the children.

INDEX

Page no.

Prologue 1

Monday 14 January 2019

Diary 9
Preliminary matters 21
Jury Sworn In 35
Charge to the jury 35
Judge's address to the jury 35
Opening speech on behalf of the prosecution by
Mr Hampton 48
Diary (continued) 62
Video evidence of Carol Denise Higgins 84
Diary (continued) 99

Tuesday 15 January 2019

Diary 102
Video evidence of Carol Denise Higgins 105
Diary (continued) 135
Witness testimony of Carol Denise Higgins 137
Diary (continued) 216

Wednesday 16 January 2019

Witness Testimony & Examination of Jean Voss 218
Cross Examination of Jean Voss 251
Re-examination of Jean Voss 276
Letter from Carol's Mother, Jean Voss 277
Witness Testimony & Examination of Carl Higgins 280
Cross Examination of Carl Higgins 288
Witness Testimony & Examination of
Paul Appleyard 294
Cross Examination of Paul Appleyard 307
Diary 315

Friday 18 January 2019

Cross Examination of Paul Appleyard (continued) 317
Re-Examination of Paul Appleyard 329
Examination of Hilda May Graham 333
Cross Examination of Hilda May Graham 338
Examination of Julie Clarke 342
Cross Examination of Julie Clarke 351
Examination of Carron Ward 354
Cross Examination of Carron Ward 357
Statement of Ena Whittle 363

Monday 21 January 2019

Preliminary Matters 366
Examination of Diana Judith Thorpe 367
Cross Examination of Diana Judith Thorpe 370
Examination of Diane Louise Croft 376
Cross Examination of Diane Louise Croft 380
Re Examination of Diane Louise Croft 384
Examination of Alex Wilson 385
Cross Examination of Alex Wilson 429
Re-Examination of Alex Wilson 436
Diary 459

Tuesday 22 January 2019

Preliminary Matters 461
Examination of Elliott Appleyard 467
Cross Examination of Elliott Appleyard 498
Diary 547

Wednesday 23 January 2019

Examination of Sarah Thomas 549
Cross Examination of Sarah Thomas 555
Prosecution Closing Speech 558
Defence Closing Speech 574
Summing Up 598

Thursday 24 January 2019

Preliminary Matters 619
Summing Up (Continued) 620
Deliberation 665
Summing Up (Continued) 668
Verdict of the Jury 682
Diary 687

Friday 25 January 2019

Reading of Carol Higgins' Personal Impact Statement 689
Sentencing of Elliott Appleyard 701
Diary 710

Epilogue 715

PROLOGUE

"PEACE TO THE WORLD, I AM A CHAMPION!" I shouted with exhilaration and fulfilment, as I stood on the top of Leeds Crown Court steps. "Justice has been served finally after thirty-five years! That Beep Beep Beep is in prison as we speak!"

As a child I was always surrounded by violence and fear and every time I pulled the dried out wishbone from the chicken after Sunday dinner, I would wish for "peace to the world." I still wish for the same.

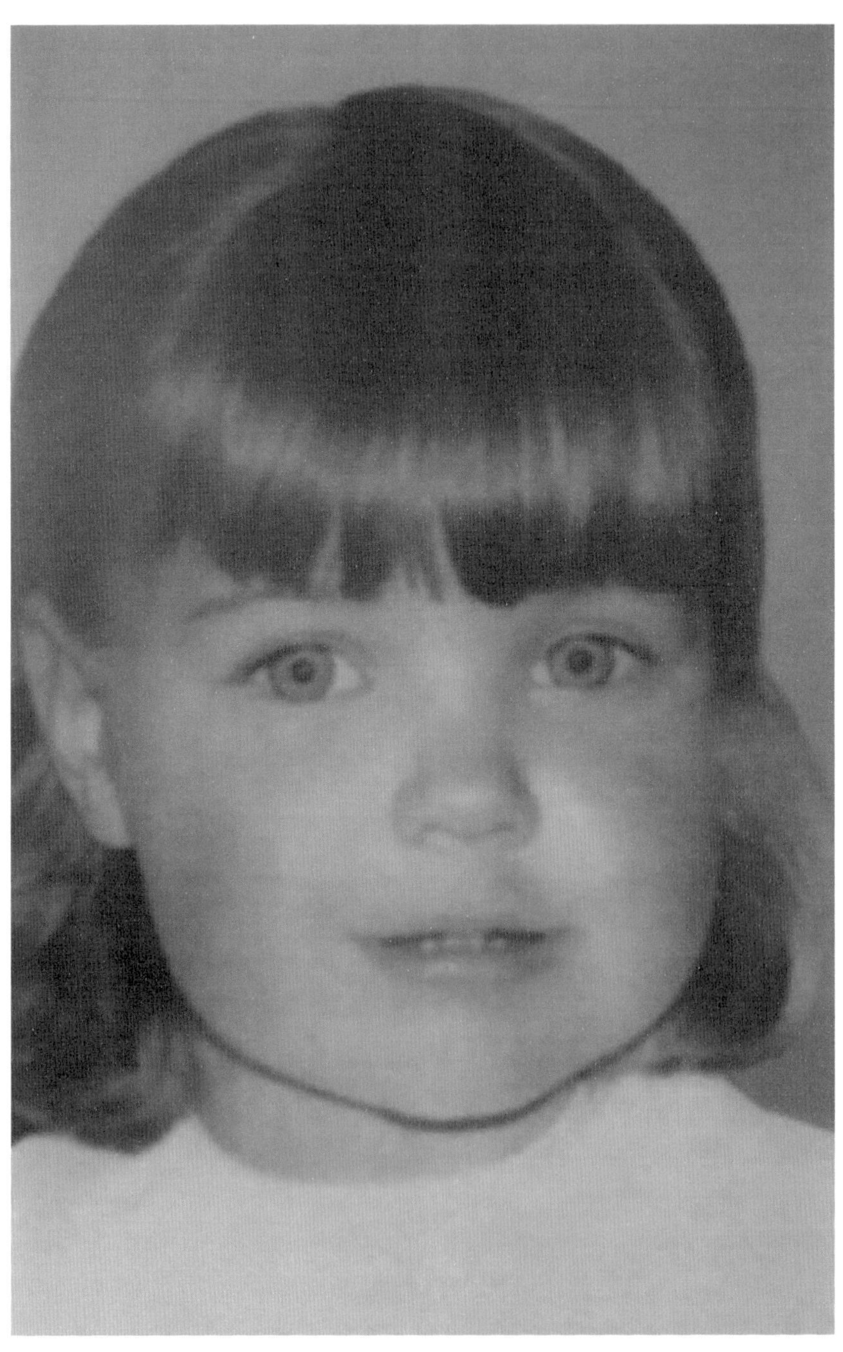

The only surviving picture of me as a baby (age unknown)

IN THE MATTER OF POTENTIAL CRIMINAL PROCEEDINGS
IN THE CROWN COURT AT LEEDS

REGINA

-v-

ELLIOTT APPLEYARD

APPENDIX 4: PROPOSED CHARGES

No. T............

INDICTMENT

IN THE CROWN COURT AT LEEDS

THE QUEEN -v- ELLIOTT APPLEYARD

ELLIOTT APPLEYARD is charged as follows:

Count 1

STATEMENT OF OFFENCE

INDECENT ASSAULT, contrary to section 14(1) of the Sexual Offences Act 1956

PARTICULARS OF OFFENCE

ELLIOTT APPLEYARD between the 22nd day of April 1980 and the 23th day of April 1982 indecently assaulted CAROL HIGGINS (NEE APPLEYARD), a girl under the age of 13 years.

[Specific]

[Occasion where the defendant kissed the complainant like she was his partner, age 11-12]

30

Page 1of the Indictment against Appleyard

Count 2

STATEMENT OF OFFENCE

RAPE, contrary to section 1(1) of the Sexual Offences Act 1956

PARTICULARS OF OFFENCE

ELLIOTT APPLEYARD between the 22th day of April 1982 and the 23rd day of April 1983 raped per vagina CAROL HIGGINS (NEE APPLEYARD), a girl under the age of 16 years.

[Specific]

[First Occasion of vaginal rape, aged 13]

Count 3

STATEMENT OF OFFENCE

RAPE, contrary to section 1(1) of the Sexual Offences Act 1956

PARTICULARS OF OFFENCE

ELLIOTT APPLEYARD between the 22th day of April 1982 and the 23rd day of April 1983 raped per vagina CAROL HIGGINS (NEE APPLEYARD), a girl under the age of 16 years.

[Specimen]

[Repeat offending of the same kind – vaginal rape, aged 13]

Count 4

STATEMENT OF OFFENCE

INDECENT ASSAULT, contrary to section 14(1) of the Sexual Offences Act 1956

PARTICULARS OF OFFENCE

ELLIOTT APPLEYARD between the 22nd day of April 1982 and the 23th day of April 1983 indecently assaulted CAROL HIGGINS (NEE APPLEYARD), a girl under the age of 16 years.
[Specimen]
[Repeat offending of the same kind – requiring complainant to perform oral sex upon him, aged 13]

31

Page 2

Count 5

STATEMENT OF OFFENCE

INDECENT ASSAULT, contrary to section 14(1) of the Sexual Offences Act 1956

PARTICULARS OF OFFENCE

ELLIOTT APPLEYARD between the 22nd day of April 1982 and the 23th day of April 1983 indecently assaulted CAROL HIGGINS (NEE APPLEYARD), a girl under the age of 16 years.

[Specimen]
[Repeat offending of the same kind – requiring complainant to masturbate him, aged 13]

Count 6

STATEMENT OF OFFENCE

INDECENT ASSAULT, contrary to section 14(1) of the Sexual Offences Act 1956

PARTICULARS OF OFFENCE

ELLIOTT APPLEYARD between the 22nd day of April 1982 and the 23th day of April 1983 indecently assaulted CAROL HIGGINS (NEE APPLEYARD), a girl under the age of 16 years.

[Specimen]
[Repeat offending of the same kind – placing his fingers in the complainant's vagina, aged 13]

Count 7

STATEMENT OF OFFENCE

RAPE, contrary to section 1(1) of the Sexual Offences Act 1956

PARTICULARS OF OFFENCE

ELLIOTT APPLEYARD between the 22th day of April 1983 and the 23rd day of April 1984 raped per vagina CAROL HIGGINS (NEE APPLEYARD), a girl under the age of 16 years.

[Specimen]

[Repeat offending of the same kind – vaginal rape, aged 14]

Count 8

STATEMENT OF OFFENCE

INDECENT ASSAULT, contrary to section 14(1) of the Sexual Offences Act 1956

PARTICULARS OF OFFENCE

ELLIOTT APPLEYARD between the 22nd day of April 1983 and the 23th day of April 1984 indecently assaulted CAROL HIGGINS (NEE APPLEYARD), a girl under the age of 16 years.

[Specimen]
[Repeat offending of the same kind – requiring complainant to perform oral sex upon him, aged 14]

Count 9

STATEMENT OF OFFENCE

INDECENT ASSAULT, contrary to section 14(1) of the Sexual Offences Act 1956

PARTICULARS OF OFFENCE

ELLIOTT APPLEYARD between the 22nd day of April 1983 and the 23th day of April 1984 indecently assaulted CAROL HIGGINS (NEE APPLEYARD), a girl under the age of 16 years.

[Specimen]
[Repeat offending of the same kind – requiring complainant to masturbate him, aged 14]

Count 10

STATEMENT OF OFFENCE

INDECENT ASSAULT, contrary to section 14(1) of the Sexual Offences Act 1956

PARTICULARS OF OFFENCE

ELLIOTT APPLEYARD between the 22nd day of April 1983 and the 23th day of April 1984 indecently assaulted CAROL HIGGINS (NEE APPLEYARD), a girl under the age of 16 years.

[Specimen]
[Repeat offending of the same kind – placing his fingers in the complainant's vagina, aged 14]

Count 11

STATEMENT OF OFFENCE

RAPE, contrary to section 1(1) of the Sexual Offences Act 1956

PARTICULARS OF OFFENCE

ELLIOTT APPLEYARD between the 22nd day of April 1984 and the 23rd day of April 1985 raped per vagina CAROL HIGGINS (NEE APPLEYARD), a girl under the age of 16 years.

[Specimen]

[Repeat offending of the same kind – vaginal rape, aged 15]

Count 12

STATEMENT OF OFFENCE

INDECENT ASSAULT, contrary to section 14(1) of the Sexual Offences Act 1956

PARTICULARS OF OFFENCE

ELLIOTT APPLEYARD between the 22nd day of April 1984 and the 23th day of April 1985 indecently assaulted CAROL HIGGINS (NEE APPLEYARD), a girl under the age of 16 years.

[Specimen]
[Repeat offending of the same kind – requiring complainant to perform oral sex upon him, aged 15]

Count 13

STATEMENT OF OFFENCE

INDECENT ASSAULT, contrary to section 14(1) of the Sexual Offences Act 1956

PARTICULARS OF OFFENCE

ELLIOTT APPLEYARD between the 22nd day of April 1984 and the 23th day of April 1985 indecently assaulted CAROL HIGGINS (NEE APPLEYARD), a girl under the age of 16 years.

[Specimen]
[Repeat offending of the same kind – requiring complainant to masturbate him, aged 15]

Count 14

STATEMENT OF OFFENCE

INDECENT ASSAULT, contrary to section 14(1) of the Sexual Offences Act 1956

PARTICULARS OF OFFENCE

ELLIOTT APPLEYARD between the 22nd day of April 1984 and the 23th day of April 1985 indecently assaulted CAROL HIGGINS (NEE APPLEYARD), a girl under the age of 16 years.

[Specimen]
[Repeat offending of the same kind – placing his fingers in the complainant's vagina, aged 15]

Count 15

STATEMENT OF OFFENCE

RAPE, contrary to section 1(1) of the Sexual Offences Act 1956

PARTICULARS OF OFFENCE

ELLIOTT APPLEYARD between the 22th day of April 1984 and the 23rd day of April 1985 raped per vagina CAROL HIGGINS (NEE APPLEYARD), a girl under the age of 16 years.

[Specific]

[Final Occasion of vaginal rape, aged 15]

URN: 13KD0601916

35

Page 6

Diary: Monday 14th January 2019: Day 1

The Queen V Appleyard. The indictment should have said Carol V Appleyard in my eyes. The Queen was prosecuting my father, Elliott Appleyard, on fifteen charges, five counts of rape and ten indecent assaults, including oral sex, digital penetration, sexualised kissing and masturbation. I was angry because the indictment did not reflect the reality of the violence I had suffered from birth. In 2016 when I asked my therapist, Melody, from the Well Women Centre why I could not stop crying, being angry and feeling worthless, she said it was because I had been terrorised as a child. I was shocked to hear such an extreme description because I had never recognised the violence and rapes as abuse, I had always seen it as normal behaviour. The indictment did not acknowledge the grooming and sexualisation of me from birth moreover the rapes and indecent assaults had occurred far more frequently. My Barrister, Queen's Counsel Mr Peter Hampton, explained that we stood a more realistic chance of conviction on these specific fifteen charges for which we had evidence. I asked Mr Hampton why Appleyard was not being charged with incest. He replied that incest carried a lesser charge than rape because it implies that the child is complicit. I asked, "How can a child be complicit?" He said, "That's our law." This not only upset me, it made me fume. Once again the shame and guilt flooded back and I felt like I was somehow to blame, a familiar feeling that I have struggled with all my life.

I slept quite well last night after watching 'Les Misérables' and 'Dancing on Ice', although while ironing my blouse for court, I felt impatient and at the same time angry that Appleyard had put me in this situation, by pleading 'Not Guilty'. I awoke feeling strong and full of energy but simultaneously apprehensive. I flexed my muscles and balled my hands into a fist. I started jumping up and down like I had when I stood on the summit of Kilimanjaro, five years earlier. I was mentally and physically preparing myself for the fight. My day in court had finally arrived 35 years after first reporting the rapes, in 1984, to South Yorkshire Police.

I stood impatiently at the bedroom window watching for the police to arrive. At 8.00am a male and female officer pulled up in a small black car to take myself and my partner, Del, to Leeds Crown Court. I had requested protection from West Yorkshire Police for my journey to Court on several occasions. I lived in fear of Appleyard, I knew he still had his shotguns. He and his wife, had recently threatened "I'll fucking have ya" to me at a car boot sale in my neighbouring village. Rather than protecting me the police were allowing him to lodge an harassment charge against me and had gathered evidence which had gone to the CPS. My trust in the police had been shattered by the lies, manipulation, bullying, intimidation and attempts to pacify me. DI Thorne's actual words to me during the investigation were "I don't know how to pacify you anymore, Carol."

Harassment Phone Calls

Unsurprisingly, the police refused protection, saying they did not have the resources. Eventually, as I was genuinely scared that I would not make it to court, I had to ring the CPS to ask them for help. I felt Appleyard would do anything he could to stop the trial going ahead. I was reluctantly granted two days protection.

The driver drove sporadically, speeding up and then driving really slowly but not allowing other cars to pass. The way he was driving gave me the impression that he thought he owned the road and he was being arrogant and impatient, an attitude that I had experienced a lot from West Yorkshire Police over the years. The officer told me he did not realise their route was taking us back past Normanton Police Station where they had set off from. I found this amusing because once again, the incompetence was evident.

"I'll fucking have ya," he said. For many years he'd fooled everyone into thinking he was a loving father, including me.

NOT PROTECTIVELY MARKED

WEST YORKSHIRE POLICE

ALLEGATION OF HARASSMENT

Name:	Carol Denise Higgins	Date of birth:	23-04-69
Address:			
Postcode:			
Description:			

An allegation of harassment has been made against you:

Details of alleged conduct (specific actions that are cause for complaint):

It has been alleged that between the months of April and July 2017 you have repeatedly posted comments on a social media site making unfounded allegations against Elliott Appleyard. These comments have been of an offensive and harassing nature towards Elliott Appleyard, who has found the comments to cause him considerable harassment, alarm and distress. The many comments that you have made are a course of conduct which you know or ought to know would cause Elliott Appleyard such harassment, alarm and distress and must cease immediately.

Any further comments posted by you of this nature about Elliott Appleyard, on any social media sites, will render you liable to arrest and prosecution.

An excerpt of the document alleging my harassment of Appleyard.

14th January 2019 – Day 1

It took ages to navigate through the busy rush hour traffic in Leeds and looking through the window at the bright sunny day and people going about their normal business was a welcome distraction from the small talk going on inside the car. We eventually arrived at 8:55am.

Witness protection suggested we enter via the back door, but I refused as I had nothing to be ashamed of, or to hide. I was determined to enter through the heavy rotating glass doors and completed the security checks which reminded me of airport security. One of the police officers had already told us to report to the witness desk situated on the ground floor. Nobody was on the desk so we went to the court listing board and found that we were due to attend Courtroom Seven. Seeing my father's name up there made it feel real, like finally he was actually facing justice. As I turned from the board I saw my father walk through the security check, the man who I had feared for so long.

All I ever wanted was a loving daddy like any normal child. Instead, he had left me questioning "why me, why did this have to happen to me, why do I have to be the one without a loving family?"

I looked at him and he avoided eye contact with me. I was shocked to see him dressed in his best hunting gear, wax jacket, fawn trousers, a fawn shirt and walking boots, instead of a suit. To me this felt like another expression of his arrogance. His stocky build, thick neck with that tell-tale tattoo of a swallow and his oversized scary head brought everything back to me. His demeanour and his confident smirk were designed to intimidate. I had been told that Appleyard asked one of his neighbours in the run up to the trial to look after his little black book of names and evidence, saying "If I go down, I'll take twenty coppers down wi' mi." Make of that what you will!

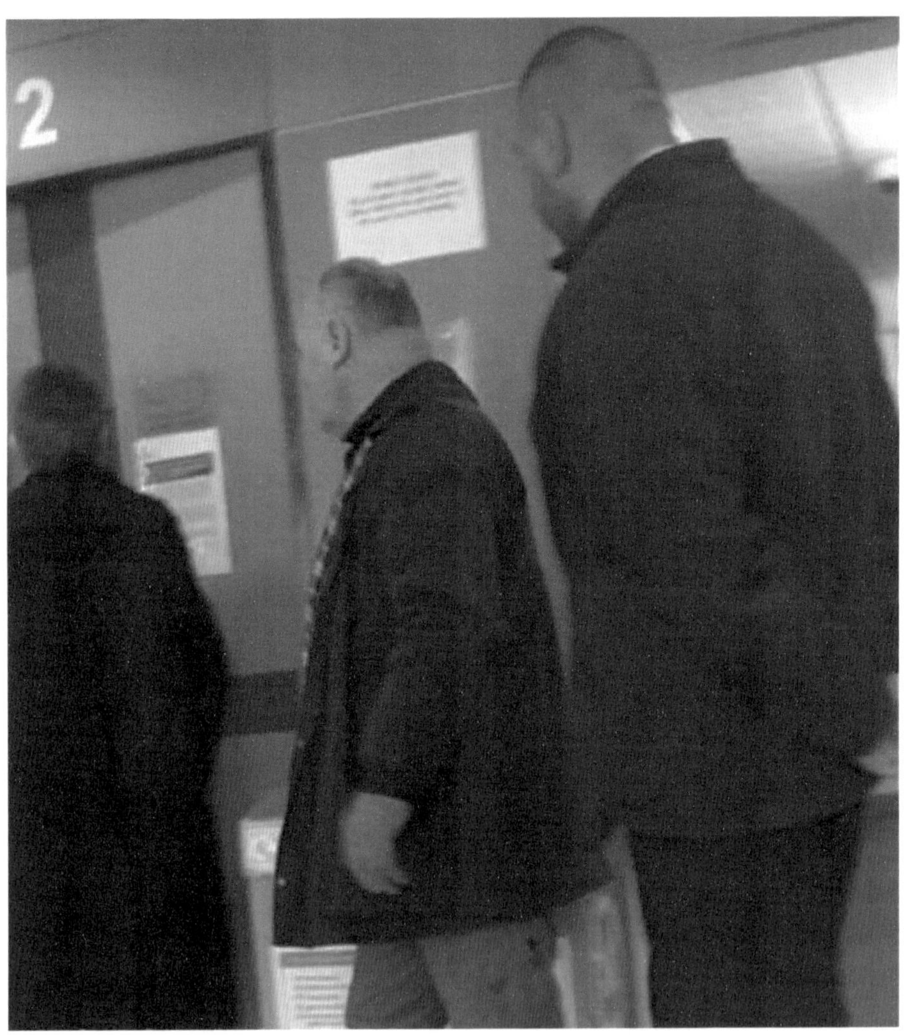

Appleyard being escorted into the Huddersfield Magistrate's Court on the first day.

I was born in Huddersfield St Luke's Hospital on 23/04/1969.

I felt my heart beating quicker and my legs began to shake, I once again felt the nervous fear of his brutal power which he obviously still had over me.

Meanwhile, a lady had come to attend at the witness desk. We checked in with her and she guided us to a consulting room where we would be meeting my barrister, Mr Hampton and his assistant from the CPS, Mr Smith.

I have a good memory of when I first met my barrister and his assistant in his chambers in 2018. He had kindly welcomed me, we had sat round a large table and the first question he had asked me was, "What is it you want from me Carol?" I replied, "I just want you to be straight John Bull, (meaning I just want you to be straight up and truthful), that's all I have ever wanted." He replied, "You will get that from me, Carol." I had been relieved and thanked him. I showed him a thick brown folder of medical records and a blue folder which contained evidence of the years of medical referrals to rape crisis and other services, in addition to healing and therapy work I had undertaken. As a result of my successful Victim's Right to Review in 2018 I had asked DI James Bellhouse on the phone whether he had given my medical records to the CPS. He told me that he had put one in from 1987. I told DI Bellhouse that I had obtained my medical records from my GP at a cost of £50 and I had seen them. Why was he only putting one record in? DI Bellhouse was annoyed and asked me "Why have you gone and got your medical records, Carol?" I had no faith that DI Bellhouse or previous investigators had passed the entire file to the CPS before the decision not to charge my father in 2017. In fact, Mr Hampton said he had not seen the records in this format before and advised me to hand them into the police in a sealed envelope and ask them not to open it. He would not be allowed to take them directly from me, they needed to go through the usual legal channels. Despite the fact that I had signed three separate disclosures allowing the police to access my medical and counselling records, they

Brown Folder

Blue Folder

had clearly not passed these on. Mr Hampton knew nothing of the blue folder of therapy notes, either. The investigating officer, PC Alex Wilson, had continually refused to take it in 2015 as he believed it was not actual evidence. I was so angry and frustrated that he did not see it as evidence, even though DC Brear, DI Thornes and DI Green agreed it was. In 2017 DI Thornes had questioned why I had not given the blue folder in as evidence before, even though I had repeatedly tried and had even taken it with me when I gave my video statement. Mr Hampton told me to bring the folder to him on the morning of the trial. I finally felt that somebody was listening and actually taking the blue folder seriously after years of banging my head against the wall.

My support worker, Laura, from the charity Independent Sexual Violence Advise Centre, (ISVA) had arrived in the courthouse and together we entered the small, secure consulting room. Already present were DI Bellhouse, the investigating officer currently in charge of my case, and DS Wilson, previously the PC investigating my case and presently the overseeing officer. After preliminary greetings, Mr Hampton gave me a briefing of how the day would proceed. He explained that Judge Rodney Jameson would be outlining to the jury what would be expected of them and sworn in.

He would be highlighting the importance of the jury being continually mindful about the details of the case and how it should never be mentioned to anyone, including other members of the jury and that it could jeopardise the entire case.

Next he would give an explanation of the charges that Appleyard faces. This would take time and Appleyard would be in court throughout. I wouldn't be allowed in court today because the jury would be shown my edited video statement.

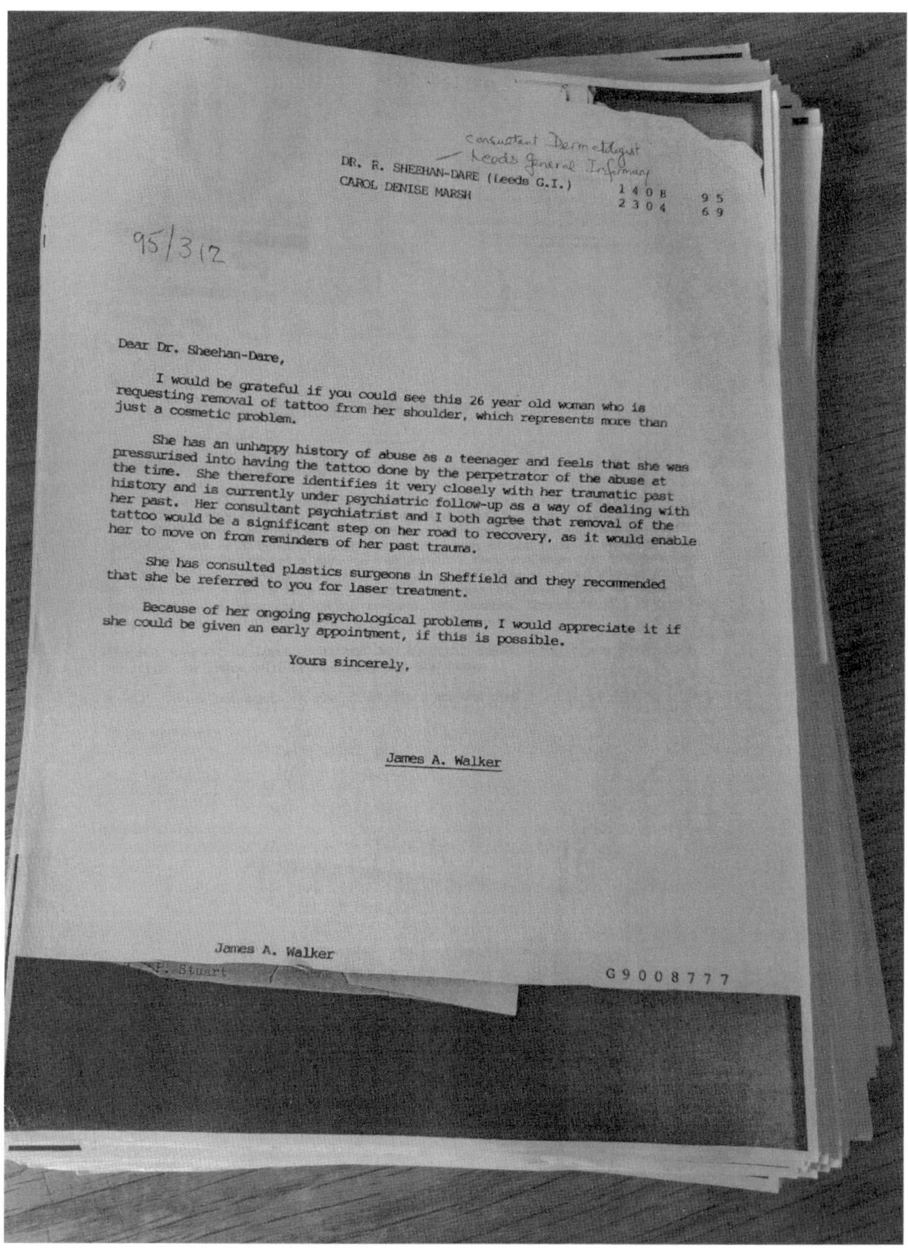

Consultant Dermatologist
— Leeds General Infirmary
DR. R. SHEEHAN-DARE (Leeds G.I.)
CAROL DENISE MARSH

1 4 0 8 9 5
2 3 0 4 6 9

95/312

Dear Dr. Sheehan-Dare,

I would be grateful if you could see this 26 year old woman who is requesting removal of tattoo from her shoulder, which represents more than just a cosmetic problem.

She has an unhappy history of abuse as a teenager and feels that she was pressurised into having the tattoo done by the perpetrator of the abuse at the time. She therefore identifies it very closely with her traumatic past history and is currently under psychiatric follow-up as a way of dealing with her past. Her consultant psychiatrist and I both agree that removal of the tattoo would be a significant step on her road to recovery, as it would enable her to move on from reminders of her past trauma.

She has consulted plastics surgeons in Sheffield and they recommended that she be referred to you for laser treatment.

Because of her ongoing psychological problems, I would appreciate it if she could be given an early appointment, if this is possible.

Yours sincerely,

James A. Walker

James A. Walker

G9008777

The 28 documents from the Brown Folder

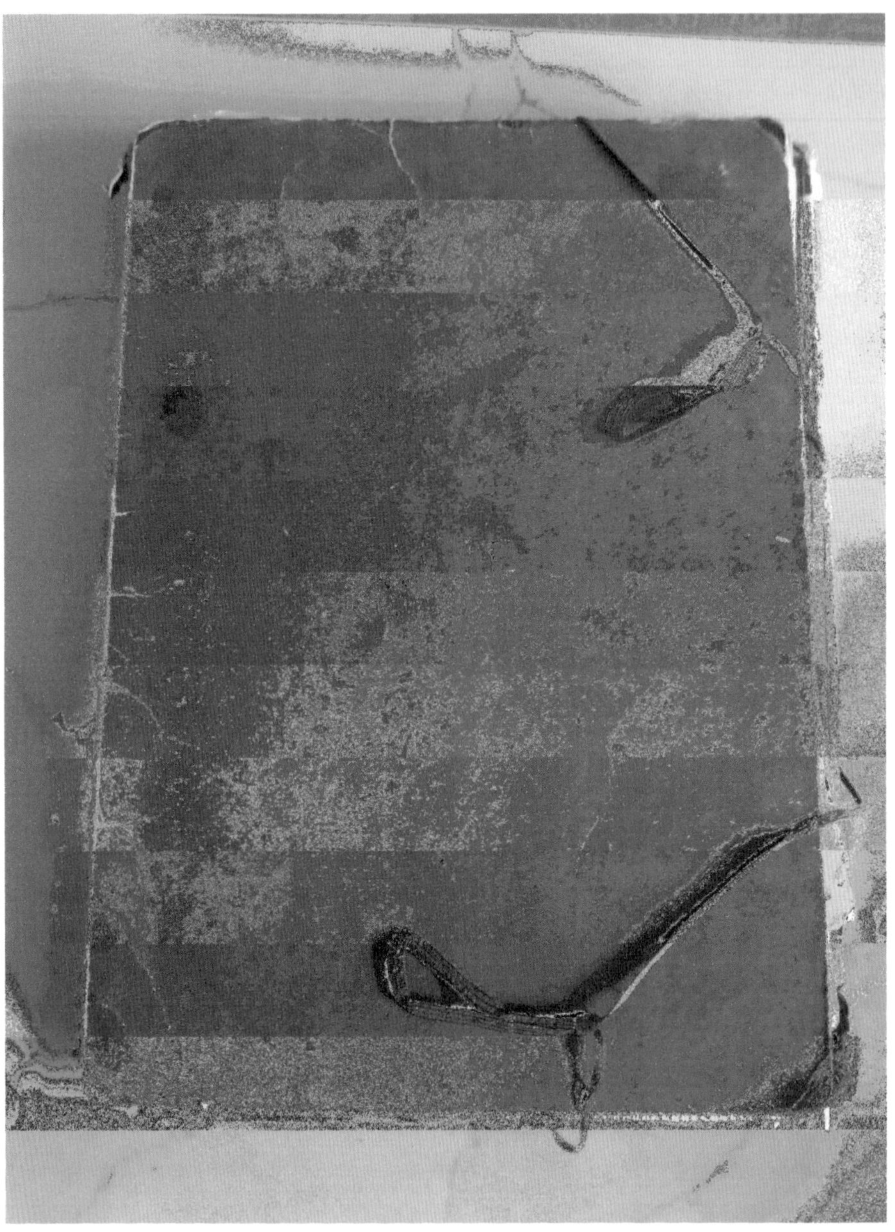

The blue folder, which held the evidence of my therapy sessions.

In fact, I was given the opportunity to go home because I wouldn't be allowed into the court room until I was called to give my evidence tomorrow when I would be the first witness on the stand. Mr Hampton told me not to tell the jury that my father was a police informer. I said to him "Does that mean the police are going to get away with a cover up?" DS Wilson rolled his eyes and puffed out loud and Peter replied "No, but that is a separate case. If the defence asks you if he's an informer, tell them."

After the meeting a member of staff had to get a code to let everyone out. I didn't want to go home and Laura asked me to stay in the room with her after everyone had left, because that's what everyone usually does during proceedings. I did not want to stay in the room, I was interested to see what was going on and be in the public space, outside the courtroom. There was no way I was going to be trapped in a room like I was scared or had something to hide. Laura and I parted company, agreeing that she would be there to support me in court tomorrow.

Del and I climbed the stairs, walked through the double doors and were surprised to see a large, open assembly area with the courtrooms situated on the external walls. The space was carpeted and furnished with black leather-look seating arranged outside every court entrance. There was a central seating area where people waited for their day in court. We found Number Seven Courtroom and sat outside on the soft, comfy chairs watching young men and women pacing up and down, or sitting anxiously waiting for their names to be called. I remember some of the female barristers looking attractive in their high-heeled shoes and immaculate make-up and some of the male barristers looking tall dark and handsome, both with their wigs and long black gowns. I admired how professional they appeared and appreciated their dedication to upholding the law, carrying their bundles of documents as they went about their business. We waited, not knowing whether the trial would start today, or if my father had changed his plea to guilty. The usher came out of the courtroom calling for Elliott Appleyard, but he was nowhere to be seen. The officers on my case,

DI Wilson and DI Bellhouse were stood at a distance from me in case they were needed to take further statements from witnesses or to carry out additional directions from Mr Hampton in the course of the trial. I shouted across the floor to the officers, "Where is he, do you think he's done a runner?" They both stood there, arms outstretched, shrugging, saying, "We don't know where he's gone." I asked the usher about the confusion as to Appleyard's whereabouts. Andy, an old school friend had just come out of the Court and heard our conversation. He said that Appleyard was in the courtroom. Andy's family knew our family because they had lived on the next street and had witnessed his bullying antics over the years and seen the way Appleyard had evaded justice.

At that moment I took the opportunity to say to the usher, "Would it be ok if my partner went into the courtroom?" to which she replied, "Yes that would be ok, as long as he doesn't tell you what's going on." I immediately turned to Del and told him to "Get in there now!" I still don't understand how the usher could not have known that Appleyard was in court. What a relief, panic over, he hadn't done a runner!

IN THE CROWN COURT AT LEEDS Case No. T20187160

Leeds Combined Court
1 Oxford Row
Leeds, West Yorkshire
LS1 3BG

Monday 14 January 2019

Before:
HIS HONOUR JUDGE JAMESON QC

R E G I N A

- v –

ELLIOTT APPLEYARD

MR P. HAMPTON (instructed by the Crown Prosecution Service) appeared on behalf of the Prosecution.

MR T. STOREY appeared on behalf of the Defendant.

PROCEEDINGS

Monday, 14 January 2019

(Transcript prepared without the aid of documentation)

(10.34 a.m.)

MR HAMPTON: May it please your Honour, I appear to prosecute together with my learned friend, Mr Smith.

JUDGE JAMESON: Yes.

MR HAMPTON: My learned friend Mr Storey and my learned friend Mr Yates appear on behalf of the defendant, Mr Appleyard.

JUDGE JAMESON: Yes.

MR HAMPTON: Your Honour may have seen at 04A a witness list or batting order.

JUDGE JAMESON: I am not sure that I have but I probably should have done. Anyway, I am sure it is there.

MR HAMPTON: Well, no, I could have emailed it to your Honour. I apologise. There is a not too ambitious but realistic timetable for day one.

JUDGE JAMESON: Yes. I was wondering – I've seen the ABE interview is about three hours long and it may well have been edited, I don't know.

MR HAMPTON: It is one hour 30, or one hour 40, dependent on a ruling Mr Storey and I would invite your Honour to make.

JUDGE JAMESON: Right, okay. Well, we will need to deal with that, obviously.

MR HAMPTON: Fairly promptly, yes. In terms of issues we wish to raise if we may at this stage...

JUDGE JAMESON: Yes.

MR HAMPTON: ...we feel we should inform your Honour that there are matters that would normally be covered by s.41...

JUDGE JAMESON: Yes.

MR HAMPTON: ...but have been deliberately left in the video. It relates to the complainant saying that she was sexually active at the time and had a boyfriend who was older than her. The material serves the purpose of both parties: firstly, the defence would wish to cross-examine that the love bites referred to in the evidence came from a source other than the defendant.

JUDGE JAMESON: Yes.

MR HAMPTON: We would have no objection to that. Secondly, it provides part of the explanation as to why the complaint in the 1980s was not pursued at the time because the police basically said such material would be used to blacken him.

JUDGE JAMESON: Yes, well it has occurred to me. I mean, obviously I don't know all the details of all of the unused material. I'm conscious that there is a very large quantity of unused material.

MR HAMPTON: Yes.

JUDGE JAMESON: I obviously do not have any of it.

MR HAMPTON: No.

JUDGE JAMESON: I am rather assuming that because where I am fortunate, the court is fortunate in having if I may say so more than competent counsel on both sides that you would have reached sensible accommodation about the approach to all of those matters. Obviously if there is anything outstanding – there is obviously one matter –

MR HAMPTON: Yes.

JUDGE JAMESON: But anything that is outstanding I really know nothing about at all so you will have to help me with all of that, but I am entirely confident that you will have reached sensible conclusions about matters where you are agreed, so...

MR HAMPTON: We have reached agreement and we just wanted your Honour to be aware.

JUDGE JAMESON: But anyway, thank you very much for telling me. It's helpful to know.

MR HAMPTON: The next point: your Honour will give the usual directions about only considering the evidence in the case and no media reporting or social media. In this case as your Honour has already referenced, there is a large amount of unused material relating to activity on social media by the complainant...

JUDGE JAMESON: Yes.

MR HAMPTON: And perhaps others. We'd ask your Honour to particularly emphasise that direction in this case.

JUDGE JAMESON: Yes, I will.

MR HAMPTON: Thank you. We would ask your Honour, unless your Honour wishes to raise any particular issue at this stage, to consider aspects of the transcript that the defence object to at this stage.

JUDGE JAMESON: Yes, certainly.

MR HAMPTON: So that we know which version of the video we can play.

JUDGE JAMESON: Yes.

MR HAMPTON: Could I hand up a transcript to your Honour which has page numbers listed and the relevant passages are highlighted in green.

JUDGE JAMESON: Certainly. (Same handed to judge) Thank you. Right, so page 38?

MR HAMPTON: Page 38 is the first reference. It is highlighted in green at the bottom of that page.

JUDGE JAMESON: Yes, so let's have a look. So, what context are we in at the moment?

MR HAMPTON: She's describing in detail the alleged abuse of oral sex.

JUDGE JAMESON: Yes.

MR HAMPTON: We say, the Crown say, that although it may be perhaps a little crude in its description, it is very relevant detail to what she recalls happening, and in a case where the defence will be that this is all fantasy, really, we say the detail is all important.

JUDGE JAMESON: Yes, right. Do you want me to take it passage by passage then? It might be more helpful, I suppose.

MR HAMPTON: There's two ways of doing it. Your Honour can retire and read the whole of the passages or we take it passage by passage. I am in your Honour's hands.

JUDGE JAMESON: Well, what I will do, I will just find out, I think, passage by passage what Mr Storey's concerns are unless he feels it is easier dealt with in one global submission. I don't know. Mr Storey, what do you think is most helpful for you?

MR STOREY: I am content to do it either way, to be perfectly honest. I'm obviously aware that your Honour hasn't...

JUDGE JAMESON: Let's have a look at it bit by bit, shall we?

MR STOREY: Certainly.

JUDGE JAMESON: What's...

MR STOREY: Well, the passage that is in green, 38 over to 39, in fact, is contained within a larger section which your Honour can see from – I assume that the document you have is the same as ours – that has been redacted by agreement.

JUDGE JAMESON: Yes.

MR STOREY: It's a large passage of discussion between the officer and the complainant which don't really touch in large part on any of the issues that the complainant herself alleges until this section where the officer makes an observation, not a question: "Discussing it like this, it brings it all back to the front of your – the front of your mind, doesn't it?" and then there is that three-line, again, observation by the complainant...

JUDGE JAMESON: Yes.

MR STOREY: ...before over on page 49 she goes on to again describe as best she can her thoughts about it. This is all material that has been covered previously by the complainant in her interview and it comes at a time, as I say, where the prosecution concede that the conversation before and after these passages is irrelevant or repetitious and certainly need not go before the jury in any event, and I would simply submit that this falls within that same category, and, to a large extent, as your Honour will hear when we look at the other sections, similar observations apply.

JUDGE JAMESON: Yes, well that's why I wondered if it might be easier to deal with it just as – it's really your concern is what, simply that it's repetition?

MR STOREY: Well, it's repetition. The next section that is highlighted in green is at pages 47 to 48...

JUDGE JAMESON: Yes.

MR STOREY: ...where she refers to it becoming a Screw Fix safe and it's not entirely clear what she means by that but she appears to almost engage in – I hesitate to be too demeaning – but to call it, perhaps cod psychology, trying to rationalise for herself why she has done things in the past or why certain things have happened to her, whether of her own volition or because of counselling that your Honour won't be surprised to learn she has undertaken and had the benefit of over, I think, many years.

JUDGE JAMESON: Yes.

MR STOREY: And the passage at page 48 concludes with, again, comment rather than question from the officer, "Until you were 15 and couldn't take it any more", and so it doesn't follow the usual question and answer process that these ABE interviews arguably should follow. Would you just allow me a moment to check something with my learned friend?

JUDGE JAMESON: Yes.

MR STOREY: Thank you. Forgive me, your Honour, I turned over the page 51 and seen another section in green.

JUDGE JAMESON: Yes.

MR STOREY: I concede I don't recollect why I was objecting to her observation about things being pitch black.

JUDGE JAMESON: Yes.

MR STOREY: That is my error, and I've missed that. I'm sorry. But the next section that I was aware we were going to be discussing was page 61 to 62 and again a larger section here.

JUDGE JAMESON: Yes.

MR STOREY: 61, 62 and 63, in fact – in which she is asked a question, "Did he ever speak about the future?" and she goes on to describe that he did speak about the future with her before, effectively, again repeating material that she's already described happening previously. I don't, I concede, think that I am sure I know what relevance conversations about the future might be to the question of whether he did what she says he did to her, but repetition, I would say, doesn't need to be in, really.

At page 62 she starts to theorise that she had been groomed by him from birth, effectively. Again, there is no evidence to that effect other than her theory that that is what took place, based perhaps on what she's been told or discussed in her counselling sessions, I know not. But again, her theories about that, with respect, are not really relevant to the question of what the defendant is actually said to have done to her when she was in her early teens. And similarly, the passage over at page 62 is a recitation again of what happened – I am sorry, page 63 – a recitation again of what happened to her the last time that she says she had any sort of sexual contact with the defendant, evidence that she's already recounted at some length earlier on in her interview, so I questioned why it was needed to be repeated at that point in the interview towards the end of its duration. Again, scattered within this, observations that could be described as cod psychology where she's trying to work out for herself and to give voice to her thoughts about why he's done this and why she's behaved as she has, so I would submit arguably not really matters for the jury to consider given that what's in issue here is whether certain physical acts took place or not.

And that really is all I can say, I think, in relation to those passages. I'd asked for them to be redacted or deleted and the prosecution declined that request.

JUDGE JAMESON: Yes.

MR STOREY: Hence raising it with your Honour now. If it's not clear from what my learned friend Mr Hampton has already said, two versions have been prepared…

JUDGE JAMESON: Yes.

MR STOREY: …one with those sections in green and one without them.

JUDGE JAMESON: As we are – I won't, of course, take my eye off the ball that you are presenting, inviting me to judge, but while we are on the subject of transcripts, is it proposed that the jury should have them? These are very long interviews. I think it is going to be pretty difficult for them to concentrate on them without, frankly.

MR HAMPTON: Yes. I wasn't going to make that proposal having watched the video.

JUDGE JAMESON: Yes.

MR HAMPTON: It has been very clear to me when I've watched and heard it, and I don't see the need at the moment.

JUDGE JAMESON: You do or you don't?

MR HAMPTON: I do not.

JUDGE JAMESON: You do not. So, you would suggest that the jury don't have transcripts?

MR HAMPTON: Personally, if the quality of the video is as it was when I viewed it in this room, I'd rather them concentrate on viewing the witness.

JUDGE JAMESON: Yes, all right.

MR HAMPTON: In fact, I take your Honour's point. It's a long one, but there will be a break and jurors do have the capacity to follow without a transcript.

JUDGE JAMESON: Yes.

MR HAMPTON: It's very clear audibly.

JUDGE JAMESON: Well, if that's your position, then I am not going to interfere with that unless Mr Storey takes a different view.

MR STOREY: No, thank you.

JUDGE JAMESON: No, all right. Well, I'll just give them the usual explanation then that they won't be getting transcripts and why not.

MR HAMPTON: Yes.

JUDGE JAMESON: But inviting them, of course, to let me know immediately if they are struggling at all following what's been said.

MR HAMPTON: Yes, please. Thank you.

JUDGE JAMESON: Yes, okay, right. Well, anything more then on the point about…

MR HAMPTON: In terms of these passages, can I very quickly, in relation to each passage say why we say it is relevant?

JUDGE JAMESON: Yes.

MR HAMPTON: It's not wholly repetition because she gives detail about the oral sex.

JUDGE JAMESON: Well, I mean if the ground is – I'm sorry to interrupt you repeatedly, but just so that we know where we're going…

MR HAMPTON: Yes.

JUDGE JAMESON: If it is repetition, really, I think the grounds that Mr Storey advances are two: firstly, repetition and I won't be able to judge that without reading it rather more fully, I fear, but secondly, he submits that some of it is essentially theorising, but I am not entirely clear, given what I understand and I don't of course have his intimate knowledge of what his tactical approach will be but from what I do know I'm not entirely clear that I understand why he wants that out. I would have thought it was rather grist to his mill, I would have thought, but…

MR HAMPTON: Yes, well, be that as it may, we say they are important passages in there, including explaining why she didn't want to go into a children's home, which may answer why she didn't flee immediately.

JUDGE JAMESON: Yes.

MR HAMPTON: Page 39.

JUDGE JAMESON: Well, I have to say I am struggling to see why any of this should be excluded.

MR HAMPTON: So are we, and that's a starting point.

JUDGE JAMESON: And even if it is repetitious, that is not necessarily a ground of itself for excluding matters and again, it may all be part of a picture that the defence want to exploit in any event.

MR HAMPTON: Yes.

JUDGE JAMESON: I have to say it seems to me that if I am misjudging the situation then I would much be grateful to be told at the outset because I don't, as you know, have access to all of the unused material, but I do have access to all the various judicial comments that have been made about the way the case has developed, representation and so forth, so I am conscious that there is a great deal of unused material and I am conscious, at least in a broad sense, of how it's likely to be deployed.

It seems to me that this really is going to be one of those cases where fine judgments about the precise – whether for example one particular matter falls to be determined under s.41 is likely to be subsumed into a much larger overall picture that both counsel are going to follow as to the way things are done, and if, in essence, a huge amount of background material is going to go in, and rightly go in…

MR HAMPTON: Yes.

JUDGE JAMESON: I don't criticise that for one moment – then on the face of it unless there is a very clear and obvious reason for editing bits out of the transcript to add to the ABE interview, then I am not really inclined to do so.

MR HAMPTON: Thank you. We'll prepare the longer video to be played.

JUDGE JAMESON: Yes, all right. If you want me to give a more considered judgment having actually read my way through all of the material to think about the point on repetition, I will, but on the face of it I really don't think repetition is going to matter hugely in the case.

MR STOREY: No, I am quite content that your Honour has dealt with it thoroughly enough, thank you.

JUDGE JAMESON: All right, fine. We'll go for that one then. Now, are we going to get on, do you think, to having the complainant called today?

MR HAMPTON: No, we've specifically arranged for that not to happen.

JUDGE JAMESON: Right.

MR HAMPTON: I hope your Honour doesn't mind that. We thought that this case was best served by assuring that she had a clean start in the morning.

JUDGE JAMESON: Well, that was very much my provisional view of it.

MR HAMPTON: Yes.

JUDGE JAMESON: Good. So, essentially then today it's a question of swearing in the jury, my address to them, your opening, playing the video?

MR HAMPTON: Yes.

JUDGE JAMESON: Stop.

MR HAMPTON: Yes.

JUDGE JAMESON: I agree.

MR HAMPTON: Thank you. We between us would appreciate if your Honour would allow us perhaps 30 minutes just before the jury are empanelled. I think there are one or two matters we need to just discuss.

JUDGE JAMESON: Yes, certainly. So, now, in other words?

MR HAMPTON: Yes, please.

JUDGE JAMESON: Yes, of course.

MR HAMPTON: And if we could reconvene at...

JUDGE JAMESON: Half past 11?

MR HAMPTON: Quarter past 11, please. It will give time for your Honour to address my opening and some of the video.

JUDGE JAMESON: Well, is that enough time for you? It is less than 25 minutes. You can have until half past if you need it.

MR STOREY: In fact, I think the request from the second row is for more like half past 11. Your Honour won't appreciate that as I understand it, the complainant has brought...

JUDGE JAMESON: I don't need to know. It's all right. If you want half past 11, half past 11.

MR STOREY: It will certainly assist my learned friend's junior.

JUDGE JAMESON: Okay, that's fine and if you need more time, just let me know. I understand very clearly that this is not the easiest of cases to deal with. It requires a lot of thought and I would be very grateful for all the help you can give me in the appropriate approach so that I can make proper rulings and fair rulings as we go along if I have to. So, yes, of course if you need time you may have it. Okay, well, we'll aim for half past 11 then. I'm asking if we can get a completely first week set of jurors because we're obviously going to need pretty much all of our fortnight. Do you think there's a serious risk of going beyond the fortnight?

MR HAMPTON: I think Mr Storey and I both think it can be completed within the two weeks.

JUDGE JAMESON: Yes, okay, good. Okay, thanks very much.

MR STOREY: Your Honour, the defendant has attended on bail. May he be readmitted to bail?

JUDGE JAMESON: Of course, yes, absolutely and at all adjournments hereafter until any further order if necessary.

MR STOREY: Thank you very much.

(Short break)

MR HAMPTON: Your Honour, thank you for the time. We're ready for the jury empanelment.

JUDGE JAMESON: Good. Do you want to give them a list of names…

MR HAMPTON: I have that to hand.

JUDGE JAMESON: Excellent, I will tell the panel that that will be happening, and when I talk to them, once we've got our jury empanelled, just one query. The cross-examination of the complainant, is that going to be over a video link or…

MR HAMPTON: No, she'll come into court. There will be special measures.

JUDGE JAMESON: With a screen or…

MR HAMPTON: No.

JUDGE JAMESON: Just as is?

MR HAMPTON: Yes.

JUDGE JAMESON: Okay, fine. Thank you very much. Right, yes, jury panel, please.

(The jurors in waiting entered court)

JUDGE JAMESON: Good morning, ladies and gentlemen. Welcome into this particular courtroom. What we are about to do is to select 12 of your number to be the jury to try the trial that is about to start here in this court. Obviously, it's important that those who are involved in the trial don't have any knowledge of anybody involved in the case or likely to be mentioned in the case or the events that you are going to hear about, all 12 of you will be hearing about and will be trying. So, what's going to happen now is that Mr Hampton, who is prosecution counsel, is just going to read out to you a list of names and any other material that he and Mr Storey, who is defence counsel, think is relevant for you to know. So, if you would be kind enough, please, to listen carefully to the material that is about to be read out to you now, if you recognise any names or anything else, wait until the end and then let me know if you would, please. Yes?

MR HAMPTON: The jury will be examining events that occurred between 1980 and 1985 at the family address of the Appleyards at 26 Gilthwaites Crescent. That's in Denby Dale, West Yorkshire. You may also hear about a village called Upper Cumberworth, which is somewhere between Denby Dale and Shepley. And the complainant at that time was called Carol Appleyard. She would have been 12 to 15 years of age. She is now called Carol Higgins and she is now 49 and she penned a book called Conquering the Impossible. The defendant, Mr Elliott Appleyard, who sits in the dock, would have been in his mid-thirties in that timeframe. He is now in his early seventies.

There were other members of the family: Donna Appleyard, now deceased, Paul Appleyard, a brother, and a lady called Margaret Jean Appleyard who called herself Jean Appleyard, now called Jean Voss. Other witnesses you may hear from include a Karl Higgins, Steven Marsh, Ina Whittle, Carron Ward, Joanne Frankland, Diane Croft, Julie Clarke, Deanna Thorpe, Hilda Graham, Janet Appleyard and Sarah Thomas.

JUDGE JAMESON: Thank you very much, Mr Hampton. Mr Storey, anybody you want to add to that or...

MR STOREY: No thank you. They've already been incorporated.

JUDGE JAMESON: They have probably been incorporated already. Right. Anybody have any concerns about any name? Yes? All right. Do you just want to have a quick word with my – two possibles.

MR HAMPTON: Mr Storey has helped by reminding me that Carron Ward was once called Carron Garside.

JUDGE JAMESON: Yes, okay. (Brief discussion with associate) Okay. One of our potential jurors knows somebody called Karl Higgins. Any more details you could give about this Karl Higgins?

MR HAMPTON: Only this, that in the 1980s he was resident in the Penistone area of South Yorkshire near Barnsley.

JUDGE JAMESON: Yes, so he would have been around in the 1980s, so he is going to be at least what, in his...

MR HAMPTON: In his sixties, I would have thought.

JUDGE JAMESON: In his sixties, perhaps? No, not that one. Good. All right, well quite right to raise it. Now, there's a gentleman at the back, if we can just – a slightly anomic concern. I'm not sure I understand it so I'm just having it checked. All right. Our potential juror is a bit concerned that somebody might have written a book about...

MR HAMPTON: Yes, I mentioned that...

JUDGE JAMESON: You did.

MR HAMPTON: Carol Higgins, I did – had authored a book called Conquering the Impossible.

JUDGE JAMESON: Right.

MR HAMPTON: That is probably what the concern is.

JUDGE JAMESON: Yes, right. Well, our juror knows something about that so that's best to, I think, ask him to stand by.

MR HAMPTON: Indeed, yes.

JUDGE JAMESON: Yes, thank you very much indeed for mentioning that, sir. We won't call you. We'll just check your name and we'll take your card out. Sorry to get you standing out in the light of all the time. (Discussion with associate) Right, okay. One of our potential jurors used to work with a Carol Garside. Anything more we can say about this Carol Garside?

MR HAMPTON: We are talking about a Carron Garside.

JUDGE JAMESON: Carron?

MR HAMPTON: Carron yes.

JUDGE JAMESON: Carron, not Carol. So, could be Carron.

MR HAMPTON: Doing my best to remember her background, she would be in her mid-forties, early fifties now.

JUDGE JAMESON: Yes.

MR HAMPTON: Again, from the Denby Dale area.

JUDGE JAMESON: (Discussion with associate) No, okay. Well, it was a Carron Garside and it was about 20 years ago and the potential juror doesn't unhappily know really much about where she came from, so there is a possibility.

MR HAMPTON: Yes.

JUDGE JAMESON: That will get us down to 13, Mr Storey. That still satisfies the random selection test, unless you have any concerns. I mean, we can try and get some more if you would wish.

MR STOREY: The bar can be conducted at 13. I'm obviously aware that it is not ideal, but there we are.

JUDGE JAMESON: Yes.

MR STOREY: I am not going to seek further delay.

JUDGE JAMESON: I think it will be sufficient if we simply bring ourselves down to 13 and select our 12 from them. Right, thank you all very much indeed. Well, we won't ask those two members of the panel to answer the questions. Yes, right.

(Jury sworn)

THE CLERK OF THE COURT: Members of the jury, you are all sworn. Your Honour, may the remaining jurors be released?

JUDGE JAMESON: Yes, certainly. Thank you very much.

(The jurors in waiting left court)

THE CLERK OF THE COURT: Members of the jury, the defendant, Elliott Appleyard, is charged on this indictment which contains 15 counts. He is charged with 10 counts of indecent assault and five counts of rape. To this indictment he has already pleaded not guilty. It is your charge to say, having first heard the evidence, whether he is guilty or not guilty to each of the 15 counts on this indictment.

JUDGE JAMESON: Thank you. Do sit down, Mr Appleyard. Right, ladies and gentlemen. Well, you are now our jury so welcome to this court. I think you are all in your first week, am I right? So, nobody has been involved in a trial before? No? Okay.

Right, well what I am going to do now, I'm just going to talk to you for about 10 minutes or possibly a little longer just really by way of introduction to what's going to happen so that you can have a fuller understanding of essentially what you can expect to happen, what you can expect of us and what we expect of you during the course of the trial.

This is a trial that counsel tell me is likely to last most of the length of your fortnight's sitting. We expect it to finish within that fortnight without any problem and without the necessity to rush or to take any shortcuts, so we hope very much that everything will be comfortably concluded within the fortnight, but it will take most of it, we think. As you've heard, there are allegations, sexual allegations now looking back some significant time into the past, and in due course, when I give you written directions about matters, which I will do – I'll say a little bit more about that in due course – I'll give you some directions about the difficulties that may arise as a result of the passage of time since the matters that you are going to try take place, but just in general terms, as a statement, you may think, really, of the blindingly obvious, obviously when people are looking back to events, whatever the events may be and whatever the rights and wrongs may be of the allegations that you are going to have to try, that when people are looking back at events that took place now a very long time ago, of course, there are certain difficulties that will arise in recollection and there are difficulties for anybody who has tried, in the circumstances, particularly if there are not, for example, dates put on individual allegations and very often in cases of this nature there aren't. And, of course, it's very difficult or may be very difficult for somebody in those circumstances to be able to say, "Well, I can tell you exactly what I was doing on that day and it wasn't what I am alleged to have done". You very probably won't be able to do that. So, it's all fairly obvious stuff, I'm sure, but just bear in mind that these are going to be matters that you hear about that took place, or are said to have taken place, a significant period of time ago. So, obviously, just bear that in mind as you listen to all the evidence as it goes on.

Well now, how is the trial going to progress? Let me tell you as much as I can about that now. The first thing to say is that you and I are going to try the case together. We each have our roles to play within the trial process but those roles are quite different and it's probably as well that I just say a word or two about what they are from the outset.

My role first. My role is to preside over the trial, to help counsel as best I can to put the evidence before you efficiently and expeditiously and above all to ensure that the trial is scrupulously fair to everybody involved in it. That's my job, principal job during the course of the trial, but I am also the judge of the law. That's my area of responsibility, so if there are any issues of law that arise during the course of the case, and it's entirely possible that there may be, it will be my job to hear submissions about that, make rulings, if necessary.

If that happens – as I say, I don't know whether it will, but if it does, you usually get to take a break. Now, one of the problems that we have with this particular court is that it really doesn't have a proper room outside, a fact of which I am very well aware. So, I hope all counsel will bear in mind, and I'm sure they will, that if we ask you – if I need to ask you to step outside, I am quite happy for you to be outside for two or three minutes, but if it's going to be longer than that, then I'm not prepared to ask you to mill about outside where there isn't proper facilities for you. You will probably need to go back to your jury retiring area. So what I'm really saying is that in this court there is no adjournment between a maximum of five minutes and a minimum of 15, so if counsel can bear that in mind, I'd be very grateful.

At the end of the trial, my job as a judge of the law is to sum the case up to you. That has two elements, the summing-up. The first is such legal directions as you will require in order to reach your verdicts. Now, that will be done in writing. I'll give you a document. I'll take you through it and explain it all to you. Don't please, be concerned that you are going to be overwhelmed by complexities of law in this case. There will be some law; there always is, but it's not going to be, I think, overwhelmingly complicated. It will be important but it will all be set out in writing and I'll take you through it, so don't, please, be worried about that. That will all become very straightforward, and if at any stage, even when you are in retirement considering your verdicts, you have any concerns about any legal direction, don't feel that you're on your own; you are not. You just send me a note and I'll have you back again and explain anything. So, don't please be worried that at any stage you'll be left on your own wondering and not absolutely clear as to what the law is. You will be absolutely clear about it so everything will be fine. Don't, please, worry about that.

The second part of the summing-up is to remind you, at least in summary form, of the evidence that by then we will all together have heard. Now, again jurors who haven't been involved in a trial sometimes, for entirely understandable reasons, are concerned, "Well, are we going to be able to remember the evidence properly when the time comes to make judgments about it?" The answer is that I can very confidently assure you, yes you will be because the whole process is designed to be essentially user-friendly, by which I mean jury-friendly, so that you can follow it. We'll go at a pace where you will be able to take the evidence in and remember it and you will be astonished, I think, when you find just how much of every detail you do remember when the time comes to discuss it. And, of course, counsel will have addressed you about the evidence during the courses of their addresses to you and I, as I say, will be summarising it for you. And again, the same applies. If, when you're in retirement, there's a conflict of recollection and somebody says, "Well, I think this witness said that", and somebody else says, "Well, I'm not sure. Was it that or was it this?" Nothing could be simpler. If you can't sort it out, send a note and we'll have you back and counsel will have notes, I'll have notes of the evidence and we'll remind you of exactly what was said. So, again, don't be concerned about that. The whole process is designed to make your task as straightforward as possible.

Right, so what is your task? Well, it is to be the judges of the facts. So, as I'm the judge of the law, you are the judges of the facts. In other words, you are actually the real judges in the case.

How do you make judgments of the facts? Well, you do it by listening to and watching witnesses as they give evidence and, in due course, when you've heard all of the evidence and in the light of the various arguments that will have been advanced on both sides by counsel, you will decide what you accept and what you don't, and in this particular case, as I understand it, there is going to be a pretty head-on clash as to what did or did not happen many years ago between a father and his daughter. And that is really the essence of the case.

And it's for you to say what evidence you accept and what you don't and what conclusions you draw from the evidence that you do accept. That's also a very important part of any jury's task.

So, that's your job. I want you, please, to be relaxed as you do it. So, unfortunately this is a court that can get rather warm. I would love to tell you there's something I can do about it but there isn't. I can complain, we can all complain, but nothing will happen. I don't know how bad it will get, not too bad, I hope, but if any of you do start to flag a bit, and you need a break, just let me know. More particularly, if you've got a jacket on or a sweater or a scarf or anything and you want to take it off because you are getting warm, just do it. Don't please feel you need to be remotely formal about this or ask permission or anything like that. Just make yourselves comfortable and, as I say, if you are starting to flag, let me know.

Now, what about our sitting hours? Well, you probably know about this. I'm sure it's all in the documents you get but just as a quick reminder, we'll sit on now until about one o'clock or thereabouts, take about an hour and five minutes or an hour and 10 minutes for lunch and then we'll sit on until about quarter past, half past four, something like that. Tomorrow morning we'll start again at half past 10 and sit on in that way.

That means essentially that what we are aiming to do is two roughly two-and-a-half hour sessions, one in the morning and one in the afternoon. Those of you who work or have worked will think that doesn't sound like very lengthy hours. Can I tell you why we sit what may appear rather short hours? There are really two reasons. The first is that as you sit and listen to the evidence you will find it's quite long enough. It's actually pretty hard work concentrating on evidence for longer than that. Secondly, in many cases, and this, I think, is probably a pretty good example of it, there is an awful lot going on when you are not in court. Counsel and, indeed, I have got quite a lot of work to do, both before you come and after you go to try and make sure that we use your time productively and efficiently when you are here. So, that's why we sit those hours.

I have to tell you now, we don't always, with the best will in the world, achieve perfection in this regard and it may well be that there will be times when things just aren't quite ready for you and you may need to take a break. If that happens, will you bear with us? Everybody will be doing their best to minimise that and to get on as quickly as we reasonably can, but things on the whole tend not always to run perfectly smoothly, but we'll do the best we can, all of us, to ensure that your time is properly used.

I think what we'll do is see how the evidence progresses. Some evidence is much more difficult and demanding to follow than others and it's not possible, really, to pre-judge how that's going to go. I'll just keep an eye on things. If we can sit through full half-day sessions, I'm going to aim to try and do that because that way we keep momentum going and the case will progress smoothly. It's not always possible to do that. Sometimes it isn't even desirable. Sometimes if the evidence is hard work, it may be that we will all just need a break, as simple as that, so I'll try and keep an eye on that. But equally, if any of you feel that you do need a break, don't hesitate to ask for one for any reason, whether it's because you simply need five or 10 minutes just to get a breath of fresh air and recharge yourselves before we carry on, or whether it's because you need to go to the loo. I mean, don't, please, be embarrassed if that arises. It happens all the time. I don't want anybody sitting there and wondering how long is this going to last. If you need a break, just ask for one and of course, we will take one, but if we can press on, we will. We'll see how we go with that.

I think so far as practical matters, that's pretty much it, but I've got to give you a couple of directions now and these are legal directions, and because the law is my responsibility you must therefore please apply these directions faithfully. You won't know this because this is your first trial, but in fact these directions are not specific to this trial; these are directions that all judges give in every trial, so they are general directions, and I'll tell you what they are and I'll explain very briefly what their reason is because I always think it's helpful for you to have that in mind.

The first direction is this. Please don't discuss the evidence that you are going to start hearing, probably this afternoon, with anybody outside your own number, so that is the 12 of you, and please when you do discuss it amongst your own number, only when you are all together, so not in twos and threes. For example, if a couple of you take the same bus home this evening or if two or three of you go out for a sandwich on a lunchtime or whatever it may be, don't be discussing the evidence then when there's just a few of you. It's a collective decision that we are looking for ultimately, so please only discuss it when you are all together. And also, of course, only when you're in private, so that really means in your retiring room.

Now, the reason for that is really an intensely practical one. There is, in fact, a duty of confidentiality but that's not really the real reason behind it. The real reason is a very simple and practical one. When you get home this evening, or if you telephone anybody at lunchtime, for example, you are bound to be asked by your nearest and dearest, "Have you got on a jury?" Well, by all means say "yes", no problem so far, but you know what the next question's going to be, don't you? It's going to be, "What's it all about?" and of course if you then start to say, "Well, actually, this is what it's about and this is what we've been told", human nature being what it is, whoever you are talking to, with the best intentions in the world, will have an opinion about it and it won't be a very helpful opinion, of course, because they won't know anything about the case. The only people who will, will be you, but in order to ensure that there is no chance even of subconsciously you being influenced by anything that you hear other than in this courtroom, we give that direction. So, it's as simple as that. When the case is over, if you are still interested in talking about the evidence that you heard, you are entitled to do it because the evidence is, after all, given publicly. What I think you are never allowed to speak about is the discussions that you have had within your jury room. I think you've probably been given directions about that, but the actual evidence, if you are interested in talking about it when the case is all over, you are entitled to do that but not, please, until it's all finished and you've returned your verdicts.

The second direction is this. You have all just either taken an oath or affirmed that you will return true verdicts according to the evidence, and it's just a good idea to just pause for a moment and think what that actually means. True verdicts, of course, the verdicts that you regard as the right verdicts, and that's easy, but "according to the evidence", well, that again isn't really a very complicated concept but it's worth just underlining because of course what that means is the evidence is what you hear in this courtroom and nothing else. So, that's what you return your verdicts on. We have what we call an open system of justice, which means that it is a matter for counsel on both sides to put before you all the evidence that they consider relevant to the decisions that you will ultimately have to make, and it's their decision to do that as to exactly what is called and what is not. We rely on that, and from your point of view, and this is the second direction, you must not, please, be tempted to supplement the evidence that is placed before you by any inquiries of your own. Now, I don't suppose any of you live very near Denby Dale or would be remotely interested in going there but sometimes if there's a more local address that's relevant, people might think, "Well, I might just pop round and see what the street looks like". Don't. We always have to say to people, "Just don't do that." If you need to be told something about an address or physical or geographical relationships between one place and another, we rely on the evidence to tell us that.

But much more importantly than that is this. We all know now that we live in an internet age and we all know that if we want to know anything about more or less anything, you go on to Google or whatever your search engine of choice may be and you put in your search term and you will find out the best refrigerator to buy or who is doing cheap flights to Tenerife in August, and reams of information will come out. Now, I don't know what, if anything, is out there on the internet about this particular case. I think and I believe from what I have been told by counsel that there probably is quite a lot of material, particularly on social media about the case. Don't be tempted to find out what it is, for very obvious reasons, if you think about it. What people post on social media tends to be what they believe and whether that has any relationship to reality is very often questionable one way or another. There may well be motives for people to put forward one point of view as opposed to another. None of it will be evidence. None of it would be guaranteed to be accurate or helpful. Some of it might be positively unhelpful, so it really is very important that you don't please, try and make any sort of an inquiry about this case in any way but most particularly by internet research at all because if you did do that and read something, unless you were unwise enough to tell one of your fellow jurors and they reported it back to me, nobody would ever know what you had found out and you might be being influenced by something that neither counsel on either side would know what it was, and it is critical to maintain the integrity of our jury system that everybody, the prosecution and every bit as importantly, for obvious reasons, Mr Appleyard himself, can be confident that whatever decisions you ultimately reach have been reached as you have all either sworn or affirmed on the basis of the evidence and nothing else, and the evidence, of course, is what you hear in this room. So, that is direction number two. Do forgive me. (Coughs) I think I am past the infectious stage so I think you are all right.

So seriously does Parliament take the integrity of the jury system that they actually made it a criminal offence for jurors to research the facts of cases that they are trying. I am obliged to tell you that. I always hate to do it because it sounds like a threat and it's the last thing it is. What I am actually wanting to do is make sure that we do it right, but nevertheless that is the situation so for goodness sake don't be tempted to do that. Trust the advocates. We are exceptionally fortunate in this case that we have extremely able advocates on both sides. I can tell you that is not always the case but it is in this case. So, we will trust them to put before us all the relevant evidence.

Okay, now one thing I need to tell you about the way that the evidence is going to be put before you. There are a number of different ways in which evidence can be put before you. The principal complainant in this case, her evidence has been pre-recorded, or at least her evidence, as lawyers call it, "in chief", her evidence for the prosecution. This is entirely normal. Don't please think that anything unusual has happened in this case. It hasn't. In this sort of case where allegations of sexual natures are made, it is now absolutely normal for complainants to be video-interviewed by trained police officers and that's what's happened in this case. So, after the adjournment we will all start at some point to watch the recording that was made of the complainant's evidence in this case. You will watch it on this screen here. I am told by counsel that the quality of the recording and most particularly the quality of the sound is good. Fingers crossed, let's hope it is. If you have any difficulty hearing it, please let me know.

It will very early on become apparent to you, as you are watching it, that there are transcripts of it, in other words a complete transcript of what the witness said, and it will become apparent to you that counsel have got them and I've got them but you haven't, and you may well think – and if I was you I think I almost certainly would think, "Well, hang on a minute. Wouldn't it be helpful if we had a transcript of this as well?" I just want to explain to you why you're not going to have transcripts. There are really two reasons for this. The first is because experience does tend to teach us that if you have a transcript, it's terribly difficult to tear your eyes away from it. You start reading and that's not what I want you to do because you have to make very important judgments about what you believe and what you don't, what you accept and what you don't in this case and you do that with all witnesses, whether they appear live in the witness-box or whether they appear by pre-recording in exactly the same way by watching and listening and making judgments rather than simply by locking on to a transcript, so that's one reason.

The other reason is a fundamental reason of fairness and it's this. I don't of course at this stage know whether Mr Appleyard will give evidence or, for that matter, call witnesses. That will be a decision for him to take in consultation with his lawyers when the time comes, but if he does, you won't have a transcript of his evidence. You'll just hear it the once so it wouldn't obviously be right for you to have one side in writing and not the other, so that's another rather important reason for the way that we do it. It isn't intended to make your life more difficult or to make it a memory test and, as I say, we'll do, all of us, counsel and I, our utmost to make sure that it isn't a memory test by reminding you of what's been said, but that's the reason for you not having transcripts. Very rarely, but it does sometimes happen, if you really can't follow and can't hear what's being said, please let me know because if we have to have transcripts, it can be done. It's not ideal, but it can be done. So, do let me know if there's a problem. Otherwise, treat it like evidence because essentially that's what it was when it was being given. It's just live at the time, not live now. So, treat it like any other evidence. Treat it like live evidence. It has some disadvantages, it must be said, in that, for example, I can't pause and say, "Right, just a minute, I just want to make sure that I've understood what you've said". It goes at the pace it goes at because it's a recording. However, that difficulty can be largely overcome by this fact, that the complainant, when her recording is finished, will come into court, into the witness-box. If there are any further questions that the prosecution need to ask her to clarify any matter, they can do it and cross-examination will then take place in the conventional manner here in court. So, that's how the evidence is going to start but it will then carry on fairly normally. There may be other ways that I'll need to give you explanations about a witness as to how evidence is being given a bit later on but let's see how that goes. I'll give you further directions if I need to as we go along.

So, that I think is that. If you want at any stage to take a note of anything, you have got the wherewithal to do so. Don't feel that you need to. You absolutely don't. There's no requirement on you to make any kind of a note at all. I have to have a complete note of all the evidence so that I can remind you of it but of course it doesn't matter if I've got my head down in a book taking a note. That doesn't matter because it's not for me to make judgments about the evidence. That's your job, not mine. If you do want to take any kind of a note, can I just ask you to keep it pretty short? Don't, for goodness sake, try and write down everything. That would completely deflect you from the job that you are really trying to do, but if you just think, "Hang on a minute, that might be important", or a time or a date or something that just strikes you that you might want to make a note of, by all means do that. that's fine, but don't, please, try and keep a verbatim note of everything that's going on.

Right, I think that's it. I'm sorry I've been talking rather longer than I meant to but there we are. There's just one final thing I want to say to you and it's this. The vast majority of trials in our courts progress if not perfectly smoothly at least without any significant problem and I have absolutely no reason to suppose that this won't be one of the vast majority, but just occasionally something does happen that a juror or sometimes jurors are concerned about, sufficiently concerned about, that they think that the judge needs to know about it. I always find it rather difficult to know how to give an example of this and so the only way I can do it is to give the only example that I can recall that's happened recently to me which was – or at least in my court – which was a couple of jurors going home on a bus together and it just so happened that there was a couple sitting in the seats immediately in front of them who knew the defendant that they were trying, knew he was on trial and were discussing the rights and wrongs of the case. They weren't doing it maliciously. They'd no idea they'd got jurors sitting behind them and they were just having a chat, but the jurors were worried that they might have heard something that they shouldn't and very properly they reported that back to me. I made some inquiries, discovered that actually there was no problem and on we went. But that's just an example. So, it could be that, it could be anything. I mean, anything that concerns you, if anything does, wherever – in court, out of court, on your way to and from court, even at home or even in your jury retiring room, anything that concerns you that you think I ought to know about, it's very straightforward. Write a note, give it to our usher, it comes to me and if it's a problem I can usually sort it out. So, if you need to contact me, that's how you do it. You probably won't, but if you do, that's what you do. Good. That's quite enough from me. Right, Mr Hampton, do you want to make a start?

MR HAMPTON: Yes, thank you, Your Honour. Members of the jury, the case you are to try over the next two weeks and which I have a duty to introduce to you now centres upon Carol Higgins, a 49-year-old lady who alleges that her father, the defendant, Elliott Appleyard, sexually abused her three decades ago in the early to mid-1980s when she was aged 12 to 15 years. I together with my learned friend Mr Smith will present the prosecution evidence to you. Mr Appleyard, who is represented by my learned friend Mr Storey who sits in the same row as me, and my learned friend Mr Yates.

Mr Appleyard is now 71 years of age, if I have my maths right. At the time of the alleged offending, he would have been in his mid-30s. The prosecution case in a nutshell is that the defendant manipulated, groomed, controlled and eventually oppressed his daughter, Carol, she being his natural daughter, at a time she was entering puberty and that he began to seriously sexually abuse her at a time she was vulnerable and felt abandoned by her mother, who was living elsewhere.

Carol Higgins, then a child – of course she had the name Carol Appleyard at that time – became conditioned to comply with this defendant's perverted sexual demands of her. This culminated in him, say the prosecution, raping his own daughter as well as other forms of abuse. The Crown's case is that the defendant was violent within the family home and the other members of the family were fearful of him: that is Carol, her siblings and the defendant's wife, Mrs Appleyard.

This defendant enjoyed a sense of entitlement and treated Carol as his own property to do with what he wished. When she was around 13 years of age, circa 1982 to 1983, the defendant took her and had his nickname, Sam, tattooed upon her shoulder, the name Sam on the top of a rose with the name Carol tattooed underneath. This, say the Crown, was not an act of affection towards a 13-year-old girl but a stamp of ownership. The defendant did the same with his son, Paul. He, too, was tattooed. Carol Higgins as an adult would later have the defendant's physical mark upon her surgically removed.

On 2 November 2015, just some three years ago, Carol Higgins provided a full account to the police of the abuse she suffered at the hands of the defendant. She was 46 years of age then. That account, as you have heard, was video recorded and you will see and hear an edited version of that interview, a version agreed between the defence and the prosecution having taken out irrelevant or repetitive material. Accordingly, you will notice that at times the footage will appear to jump and you will see the top counter go from one time to another which is not sequential. That is simply editing of material that has been cut due to its irrelevance to the matters you must deliberate.

As you've heard, the video will stand as the complainant's evidence just as if she was in court with me asking her questions and the defence will then have the opportunity to cross-examine her after the footage has been played.

This opening address to you, which I hope will take us to around one o'clock, until lunch, is not evidence. It is simply a method of introducing the evidence to you, hopefully identifying what the real issues in the case are and giving you an outline, a context, of what the evidence will be.
It is important that you bear in mind at all times that it is the prosecution who bring this case and the prosecution who must prove this case by making you sure of Elliott Appleyard's guilt. The defendant need prove nothing to you.

So, an outline as to the facts of the allegations there.

Carol Higgins was born to Elliott and Margaret Jean Appleyard, now Jean Voss, on 23 April 1969. She is today 49 years of age. By the age of eight she lived with her parents, her brother Paul and sister Donna at 26 Gilthwaites Crescent in Denby Dale. Donna was the eldest by a year. Carol was the middle child and Paul was a year younger than her. So, Donna, Carol, Paul with a year in between each, roughly speaking. In fact, to assist and by agreement, can I hand to you a photograph that has been produced as part of the investigation which shows the children together. The best we can date this photograph is the early 1980s. One between two, please. It's something of a tradition here. (Document handed to the jury) So, the eldest, Donna, to the right in the white dress; Carol the middle child, to the left in the black and white jumper; and the younger brother, Paul wearing the fashions that remind us of the decade we are going to be examining. There you have the three children in and around the early 1980s.

Donna had special educational needs. She also suffered from ill health, epilepsy. It seems that because of the combination of these factors, she would spend long periods of time away from the family home in children's homes. When she would return, Donna would tell her younger sister Carol of the bullying she suffered at those institutions. This terrified Carol and she was very scared at the prospect of entering any such environment, and this fear, you'll hear from her video evidence, stayed with her throughout her childhood and throughout the period of the abuse.

Carol's first recollections of her father are that he was abusive, physically, and when she was a small child, he would beat her with a belt or belts as punishment. It seems that he had one or two that he would use to inflict physical punishment. He would also strike her and her siblings around the head. On occasions, he would intentionally make as if to strike her causing her to flinch in fear and then simply scratch his head. Even allowing for the fact that this behaviour with knowledge occurred in a different age, when looked at in the round we ask you to conclude that the defendant's behaviour amounted to nothing less than physical and emotional abuse. It provided pre-conditioning to what was to develop into sexual abuse.

Carol recalls that Mr Appleyard was also violent towards her mother and on occasion would threaten her with weapons. That relationship between Mr Appleyard and Margaret Jean – who seems to have called herself Jean – was unstable, chaotic and marked by violence and threats of violence. Carol recalls that her mother threatened to leave and indeed did leave the defendant on a number of occasions, but she would always go back to him.

The beginning of the sexual abuse occurred when the complainant was aged around 11 to 12 years old. The defendant was in the habit of sometimes inviting the children to accompany him on walks collecting scrap metal. When Carol turned 11 or 12 years old, the defendant manipulated that arrangement to ensure he was alone with Carol. He would speak to her about adult matters on these walks, such as his relationship with her mother. She recalls a specific occasion when during one of these walks, he sat her down and kissed her. This was not as a parent would kiss a child but as adults would kiss. It was indecent, it was sexual. It is represented by the first count on the list of charges you are to face. This is probably a good moment to hand that document to you now. (Documents handed)

Again, it is six for the members of the jury and one for his Honour. So, again, one between two, please, members of the jury. I hope you now can all see a document entitled, "Indictment". There is no magic to that word. It's another way of saying "charge sheet". These are the counts, charges, one through to 15 that you will decide upon in due course.

You will see that it tells us where we are, the Crown Court at Leeds, and the parties, the prosecution or the Queen against Elliott Appleyard, Mr Appleyard being charged as follows: count one, indecent assault contrary to s.14(1) of the Sexual Offences Act 1956, that piece of legislation in force as of 1980, and that between 22 April 1980 and 23 April 1982 he indecently assaulted Carol Higgins, nee Appleyard, a female person, that specific count to represent the specific occasion it occurred, the occasion when the defendant kissed the complainant like she was his partner aged 11 or 12. I will come back to giving some assistance, I hope, with the law in due course but that count reflects the incident I've just told you about.

Carol recalls that the defendant went on to kiss her on more than one occasion and also gave her love bites, and more of that later. But after this incident on the walk, Carol told her mother of the kiss. As far as she recalls, this was reported to social services. Shortly after, her mother told her that she was leaving the defendant and would be taking her, Carol, with her. Her siblings, Paul and Donna, were to remain with the defendant. The two of them, Carol and her mother, first moved to a friend's home in Cubley, near Barnsley. The circumstances were such that they had to sleep on a bare mattress placed upon bare floorboards with blankets upon them. A little later they moved to another home. This also belonged to a friend of Jean's and this was in Penistone near Barnsley, and Carol recalls moving from Shelley High School to Penistone Grammar School. This second home was the home of a lady called Linda Wadsworth.

As part of this case, the police have made inquiries with the relevant social services and educational departments but have failed to obtain any documentation relating to the family during this time period no doubt, you may conclude, due to the passage of time. However, it seems that no action was taken back then by social services with the family or involving Mr Appleyard.

Life was not easy at the Wadsworth's. Looking back, Carol takes the view that the mother was somewhat liberated after leaving Mr Appleyard. She was living her own life. She was out a lot of the time and Carol began a consensual sexual relationship with a younger man who was slightly older than her, but she missed her mother and she missed the attention of her family.

It came to be that she bumped into the defendant in Barnsley market. He offered her gifts, bought her some clothing. She was persuaded to return to the family home. He presented himself now as being a normal father and she felt reassured. She believes she was around 13 when this occurred. However, she had not been back at the family home for long when the defendant would begin play fighting with her and again this was not normal, parental play fighting. Again, it was sexual and he would leave her with love bites. Carol recalls that the sexual abuse became very much more serious during this phase in her life. She recalls Mr Appleyard taking a trip to America and whilst he was gone, her mother Jean took the opportunity to collect some furniture that the defendant had previously refused her.

Again, whilst he was away, the children, Carol and Paul, decided to throw a party for their friends. The defendant was furious about what had occurred when he came home. This prompted Carol – we ask you to conclude clearly, a vulnerable and troubled child – to self-harm. She cut into her wrist using a knife. Her brother made her father aware of what she had done. Carol recalls she was about 13-and-a-half years of age when this happened.

That evening Carol recalls the defendant telling her she was too
disturbed to sleep alone and that she would have to sleep in his bed. He uttered these words as he tended to her physical injuries, and with the benefit of hindsight you may conclude in due course that it was cold, clinical manipulation of a vulnerable child. Carol's reaction to this was what you would expect of a child. She was simply relieved that he was no longer angry at her and there had been no physical punishment. So it was that she ended up in his bed.

Carol recalls the abuse began that evening with him tickling her lower stomach. He then touched her breasts and vagina. She recalls him going to his drawer and a bedside table and removing a condom from it. He then had vaginal sex with her.

Count two, rape, the first occasion of vaginal rape, aged 13, a specific incident as seen from your indictment. A vaginal rape. After he had finished, Carol recalls asking him what her grandfather would think of what he had just done. The defendant replied with these words, "Don't worry, sweetheart, he wouldn't say anything. He believes the same as me that fathers should break their daughters in like the Indians do." Memorable words, you may think, from a father to his own daughter, a recollection, a detail of recollection not an invention.

Carol recalls from that time simply having to get on with life as if it was normal once this had occurred and she describes the abuse as becoming an everyday occurrence thereafter and counts three to six reflect what occurred thereafter.

Count three, rape. All of the rapes are vaginal, repeat offending of the same count. It is reflected in this specific count, a number of occasions all rolled up into one count to keep the indictment to a manageable number of counts, when she was 13.

Count four, an indecent assault. The defendant compelled the complainant to perform oral sex upon him when she was 13, again a specimen count.

Count five, compelling the complainant to masturbate him when she was 13, and count six, indecent assault, he placing his fingers into the complainant's vagina on a number of occasions when she was 13 years of age.

Those were the forms of indecent assault. I will just pause outlining the facts just for a moment and address briefly, but I hope helpfully, an issue of law that will be fully addressed by his Honour at the end of the case. In relation to the indecent assaults on the indictment, in law it is irrelevant whether Carol consented or not because consent is not a defence given her age at the time, 11 to 12 years of age on count one. She was 15 at the oldest.

It follows that if a man kisses his own daughter in a sexual way, he is in fact guilty of an indecent assault, even if she agreed to it. There is no requirement that force is used by the defendant. The law does not require a complainant to be dragged kicking and screaming, and this perhaps will come as no surprise to you: in law, Carol was a child and the law is there to protect children. However, and in any event, the prosecution case is that Carol was not truly consenting to any of this behaviour be it categorised as indecent assault or a rape – this behaviour from her own father, whether it was sexual kissing, vaginal sex or the other forms of sexual conduct on the indictment. There is a term often used in cases involving sexual offences, and that is "grooming". It is not a term of the art. It can take many different forms. It involves the perpetrator building an emotional connection or trust or oppressing the victim. Groomers may be male or female. They can be of any age. The prosecution's case is clear. The defendant's behaviour in this case towards Carol amounted to a classic form of grooming. His offending amounts to cynical and manipulative behaviour of a child, his own child, designed to achieve his own sexual gratification. He groomed her. For example, he effectively oppressed her through violence. She feared him. She witnessed the physical abuse meted out to siblings and her mother. She knew he possessed weapons. He knew she was vulnerable and troubled. The serious abuse began when she had self-harmed. The very nature of a father/daughter relationship – this was the 1980s; he was an imposing man – she could not question him. He bought her gifts to persuade her to come home. She was effectively brainwashed into believing, as time went on, that what followed between them was normal. She had a distant relationship with her mother and the defendant knew this.

Given Carol's age at the time, for rape to be made out, you must be sure that she did not consent to have sexual intercourse with the defendant. The prosecution case is that Elliott Appleyard – sorry, is that Carol, when she had sex with Elliott Appleyard, was not exercising genuine free choice at the time this activity occurred. This was not consensual sex.

In assessing that issue, you are entitled to take into account the disparity in age, the manipulation of the child by the adult and the dynamic of the relationship, as I've just set out to you.

The prosecution do not have to show violence or the threat of violence. Nor do the prosecution have to prove that the complainant told the defendant, “No”.

There can be different forms of rape. Effectively, the Crown say this was submission by a child to her own father and that, in law, does not amount to free consent. That context is all important. Put simply, if the child had had free choice, she would not have agreed to have sex with her own father.

In any event, consent is not an issue between the parties. The defence do not say that this was simply incest. The defence case is that this alleged behaviour never occurred, or anything like it. In simple terms the issue for you is whether this was rape or it didn’t happen at all.

Back to the facts. There came a time that Donna went to live with her mother and Carol and Paul remained with Mr Appleyard. There were divorce proceedings ongoing and questions of who would have custody of the children. Carol recalls a conversation with an employee of social services who told her that if she were to change her mind over who she wanted to live with again, i.e. by deciding she wanted to go back to her mother, she may well end up in a children’s home. That thought terrified her. So it was that she remained with her father and Paul at the family home and the sexual abuse continued.

She recalls the family, the defendant, herself and Paul, attending a meal at a Chinese restaurant when he had obtained legal custody of the two of them. Some legal correspondence and documentation produced by the defendant when he was arrested and interviewed indicates that this was around April 1984 and Carol would have been 14. She recalled that the defendant’s abuse of her carried on for around another two years. That’s reflected by counts seven to 14 and you’ll see, counts seven, eight, nine and 10 deal with identical sexual abuse of vaginal rape, forced oral sex by him, requiring her to masturbate him, digital penetration of her when she was 14. Counts 11 to 14 identical abuse when she was 15. So, the abuse reflected per year.

Through the course of this she recalls an occasion in the kitchen when Paul, her brother, saw his father "snogging", in her words, the complainant and she wondered how her father would manage to brush things under the carpet, but it seems he did. She recalls in her video-recorded interview how the defendant would come back from the pub on an evening. She recalls being asleep in a foetal position, was pretending to be asleep, in fact. He would come into her room and shake her, tell her to come on, but she knew what he wanted and she'd be led into his bedroom and there he would vaginally rape her.

He would also make her read pornographic stories to him from magazines and masturbate him. He placed her mother's engagement ring on her finger. He treated her as his, his wife. He told her such behaviour was normal with his friends and their daughters. She recalls him saying that if she got pregnant it would be an albino baby. She would be kept home from school and would complete the housework that Jean had previously been responsible for whilst the defendant would tend his land before coming home.

When they had sex, she dare not complain, and sometimes made noises to pretend that she liked it and on occasions she did not, the defendant would complain. He became angry and aggressive, accusing her of not wanting sex. She had no choice, in effect, but to accept the role the defendant directed she should take.

She recalled that the defendant took sexual photographs of her including her pretending to commit a sexual act using a hairbrush. He kept these pictures in a tin box. He also penetrated his teenage daughter using the handle of that hairbrush.

Throughout the period of the abuse the defendant recalls – sorry, the complainant recalls – the defendant would make her perform oral sex upon him. She recalls that he was very smelly. She recalls conversations akin to the following occurring. He would say to her, "Who loves you, baby?" She was conditioned into replying, "You do" and he would reply, "You'd better believe it". If she didn't comply, he'd simply repeat the opening words until she did. She would perform oral sex upon him until he ejaculated.

Throughout the period of the abuse the defendant would also make Carol masturbate him. This would happen three to four times on a weekly basis. Throughout the same period, he would also regularly digitally penetrate Carol. He would do this roughly and give her no pleasure but would leave her feeling bruised and hurt.

At some point during the abuse Carol reported to a friend, Diane Croft, believed to be around 1982 to 1983 that her father was sexually abusing her. Diane recalls that this was at a time when Carol was living with the defendant, her brother and Donna. She recalls Carol's mother had moved out. Diane recalls Carol telling her that her dad was messing about with her, touching and kissing her. That's back in 1982, 1983.

The two teenage girls reported it to Diane's parents but clearly the Crofts did not know what to do with that information and Carol was to receive no help through that route.

The abuse ended when Carol was 15 years of age. On this occasion, the sexual abuse had been ongoing for around two years. The defendant vaginally raped Carol, following which they argued and Carol just asked him to leave her alone. He beat her whilst she was laid on the floor crying. He called her pathetic and kicked her in the stomach. When he went to the pub, Carol left the house and caught the bus from Denby Dale. There was no contact from her with him for some months thereafter. She bumped into her mother and her new partner, Karl Higgins, on the bus, and Carol complained to her mother about the sexual abuse at that time. Carol recalls her mother speaking to her father on the phone about this and the defendant stating, "You can't prove a thing".

Carol was encouraged by her mother to make a complaint to the police which she did. Carol's recollection is that at that time, at around 1985, she provided a 17-page statement to the police regarding her complaint. Her memory is that she was subject to intimate forensic examination at the time, but again there has been an inquiry by the investigative team in this case who have failed to recover any original paperwork relating to that investigation again, no doubt, due to the passage of time.

The past is sometimes a foreign place. They do things differently there and this was the 1980s. Carol recalls being advised by the police that her brother was too young to provide any corroborative evidence. Further, she was told that there would be an examination of her previous sexual history, that this would be used against her, that her name would be blackened and she would be called a liar. In her words, "I'd be made out to be the biggest slag going". So it was that any official complaint at that time to the police was not maintained by Carol after the receipt of the advice from the police.

By the age of 16, Carol was no longer with her mother. She was living alone and working at a machinist's, SR Gents in Barnsley. Her mother had asked her to leave home by that stage. At that time the defendant's then partner arranged for Carol to meet her in a café in Barnsley. This woman introduced herself as Janet and she asked Carol about the abuse. She then told Carol that the defendant was upstairs, a fact that hadn't been revealed before the meeting, and asked if she would like to meet him. Carol agreed as she was too scared not to. She asked why the defendant had sexually abused her and he told her that it was because he loved her as a person rather than a daughter.

In later years Carol reported the sexual abuse she suffered to the police and in particular she did so in 2005, 2012 and 2014. No prosecution was brought on those early occasions. You need not speculate as to why. There will be other evidence in the case. You will hear from other members of the family, Jean Voss, Carol's mother, and Paul, her brother. Sadly, Donna Appleyard passed away some years ago post these events. She is no longer with us.

You will also hear from friends and neighbours of the family from the relevant time who witnessed interactions between Carol and the defendant which may now well be regarded as supportive of Carol's allegations.

The defendant was arrested and interviewed regarding the allegations on 21 February 2015 and 8 December 2016. He denied the allegations. He indicated that he believed the allegations may have been as a result of peer pressure by Carol's mother upon her. He recalled being arrested and interviewed in the 1980s following Carol's complaint to the police. He produced documentation relating to his divorce from Jean in 1984. He said it was Carol and Paul's choice to have tattoos, they had chosen the designs they wished.

So, in terms of issues for you to have in mind throughout the evidence and by way of conclusion, the defendant denied that anything like the offending occurred at all. There is no question of consensual sexual contact. You must examine the detail of the evidence and determine whether you are sure that the defendant sexually abused Carol as alleged and as reflected in the indictment. The prosecution submit that having considered the totality of the evidence presented by the prosecution and defence in due course, you will be driven to be sure of Carol's allegations. That concludes this opening address.

JUDGE JAMESON: Yes, thank you very much indeed, Mr Hampton. Right, ladies and gentlemen that is a convenient moment to take a break so shall we gather together again at 10 past two and we'll make a start at least on the playing of the video recording.

MR HAMPTON: Yes, please.

JUDGE JAMESON: Right. Thank you very much.

(1.01 p.m.)

Diary: Monday 14th January 2019 (continued)

At 1.00pm the Court broke for lunch. People who had been sitting in the public gallery and the Queen's Counsel came out of the courtroom entrance, the jury left through another exit. Present in the public gallery had been BBC Look North, the Huddersfield Examiner, journalists from other media agencies, my friends Glad and Dave, Del and Andy. I was surprised to see that Appleyard had no friends or family supporting him. Not even his current wife. I believe the reason is because he does not want her to know the truth and he has lied to her.

Del and I went to a lovely Bistro in the centre of Leeds and had posh kebabs. Del couldn't tell me anything that had happened in the courtroom, though he was able to tell me the jury was made up of eight women and four men. The jury hadn't watched my video but were going to watch it after lunch.

After lunch we returned to court, through the security checks, climbed to the third-floor canteen which had closed down where we purchased two coffees from a vending machine. We took them back to the first floor assembly room, fully intending to sit where I had before, only to see Appleyard slumped in the exact same seat. He glared at me with hatred in his evil eyes, his face contorted. Our eyes locked, he was trying to intimidate me as he always had, gauging how much power he had over me. The look on our faces said it all. We stared at each other for what seemed like minutes. Neither one of us wanted to give in. It gave me great satisfaction to see him turn away. The once fearsome man appeared broken, dejected, his brazen confidence shaken. At this instance I felt no more fear. "This is war. Let the battle commence!" I was ready to fight for justice now, more than ever. It felt surreal, like it had happened in slow motion, almost as though no-one else was in the room. Once the spell was broken I glanced across the room and saw Glad and Dave who had watched our interaction. As I approached them, they said in disbelief, "We saw that." Everyone then returned to the public gallery, leaving me on my own once again. I retook my seat and texted my brother to let him know what had happened so far today. I tried to read my book, written by Joanna Trollop but I couldn't concentrate. I went through the messages on my Facebook page and thanked people for their support. There were hundreds of messages and this gave me renewed determination.

In July 2017 my father thought he had got away with his crimes. I had reported him on five separate occasions, 1984, 2005, 2012, 2014, and 2015. Investigations were opened and not pursued, due to the evidence no longer being available. My seventeen-page statement, forensic evidence and social work records had been lost or legally destroyed – burnt along with everyone else's from the 1980's, so DS Barnes informed me. The police refused to take another statement from me until 2015. DI Thornes told me over the phone in 2017 that he had seen on a log report from the CPS on the police computer that the decision not to charge in 2005 had been due to them questioning my credibility about my sexual activities in 1984. He said this was "the biggest hurdle they could not get over." In another telephone conversation that same month DI Thornes said it would be unfair to charge the suspect because he had previously been investigated in 1984. He said that this was "the biggest hurdle they could not get over." Which was it? The CPS lawyer Sarah Nelson, decided not to charge Appleyard in July 2017, saying that it would be an abuse of process. During the meeting with DI Thornes and DS Wilson when they delivered this decision to me, I asked if they had believed that my dad had raped me and they both said yes and conceded that I had been given a poor service in the past. I was absolutely furious and angrily shouted at them, "You are still giving me one now."

I obviously disagreed with the CPS decision. My father had been left free on the street to continue raping children. I immediately exercised my Victims Right to Review (VRR). In January 018 the decision not to charge Appleyard was overturned by CPS. They said the decision was flawed and that a prosecution would be in the public interest. CPS lawyers Elizabeth Jenkins and Claire Walsh had even told me in a meeting before the decision was overturned that abuse of process was no longer used. I believe that Mr Hampton played a big role in re-opening the investigation. During one of our consultations today I had asked him why he had taken on my case and he replied that he believed me and my video statement was plausible. He instructed the police to carry out one hundred and fifty further actions to gather the evidence which I believe should have been gathered in the first place. This is what led to my father being in court today.

Ms Carol Higgins

For delivery by hand

Our ref: 13KD0601916/SEN/CH
Please include this reference in all communication

5 July 2017

Dear Ms Higgins

My name is Sarah Nelson and I am a lawyer working with the Crown Prosecution Service (CPS) in the Rape and Serious Sexual Offences Unit.

I received a comprehensive file from West Yorkshire Police regarding the report of rape made by you in 1984 and 2005 and then more recently in 2014. A male was questioned by the police in connection with your allegation.

Although I realise that you are aware of the identity of that male, I am unable to name him in this letter due to legal restrictions.

In making my decision I have carefully reviewed the case by applying the Code for Crown Prosecutors. This guides me when I make decisions about prosecutions. The CPS does not decide whether a person is guilty of a criminal offence, but makes a fair and independent assessment about whether the case should be considered by a criminal court.

I have decided that there is not enough evidence to bring charges in this case, as I do not believe that there is a realistic prospect of obtaining a conviction. I am writing to explain why I made that decision.

In his interview the male denies any activity of a sexual nature. This means that the evidence in the case is 'word against word'. The police looked for further evidence capable of supporting the prosecution case. The police did not provide me with any direct evidence but there was some evidence which could be used to support the account you have given. There are no eye witnesses to the actual allegations.

Crown Prosecution Service

Crown Prosecution Service, Yorkshire & Humberside, Greenfield House, 32 Scotland Street, Sheffield S3 7DQ
www.cps.gov.uk

Page 1 of the letter from Sarah Nelson explaining the decision not to charge Appleyard.

However, in addition to looking at the evidence that I have been provided with I have to take into account that the evidence gathered during the police investigations in 1984 and 2005 is no longer available. The prosecution would be obliged to show that the male could have a fair trial. Given the lack of evidence from both investigations, I have concluded that the prosecution could not establish this and that the court would stop the case as an abuse of process.

I realise that providing your interview to the police will have been a difficult experience. Nothing within this letter is intended to leave you with the impression that you have not been believed.

I have informed PS 6496 Alex Wilson, the officer in the case, of my decision. I hope that he, or a colleague on his behalf, will be able to bring my letter to you in person, so that they can answer any questions that you may have.

Under the CPS' Victims' Right to Review Scheme you can ask for a review of my decision. If you would like further information about this or would like to discuss my decision, please contact the Victim Liaison Unit by on calling on 0114 2298862 between 09:00 and 17:00 Monday-Thursday; or between 09.00 and 16.30 on Friday; or by e-mail at Y&H.VRR&Complaints@cps.gsi.gov.uk; or in writing to CPS Yorkshire and Humberside, Greenfield House, 32 Scotland Street, Sheffield S3 7DQ.

A request for a review should normally be made within five working days of the date of my letter. However, requests can be made within three months of this date. An early request allows for a prompt review by a prosecutor who has not been involved with the case and, where appropriate, the case to be (re)started as soon as possible.

If you would like a more detailed explanation of my decision, I would be happy to meet with you to provide you with as much of my reasoning as I am able. I should emphasise that the purpose for this meeting would be to explain and not revisit my decision

If you think that such a meeting would assist, please inform the Victim Liaison Unit (contact details above) and arrangements will be made. If you would like to bring someone with you, please let them know.

More details about the Code for Crown Prosecutors and your rights under the Code of Practice for Victims of Crime can be found in the leaflet which I have enclosed with my letter and on the CPS website at www.cps.gov.uk .

I appreciate this may not be the outcome you wanted but I hope this letter helps you to understand how my decision was made.

Yours sincerely

Sarah Nelson
Senior Crown Prosecutor
Rape and Serious Sexual Offences Unit
CPS Yorkshire and Humberside

Decision Meeting

Alex Wilson Lying About the Decision Meeting to Say it Was an Update

Page 2 of the letter from Sarah Nelson with a link to the recording of the meeting.

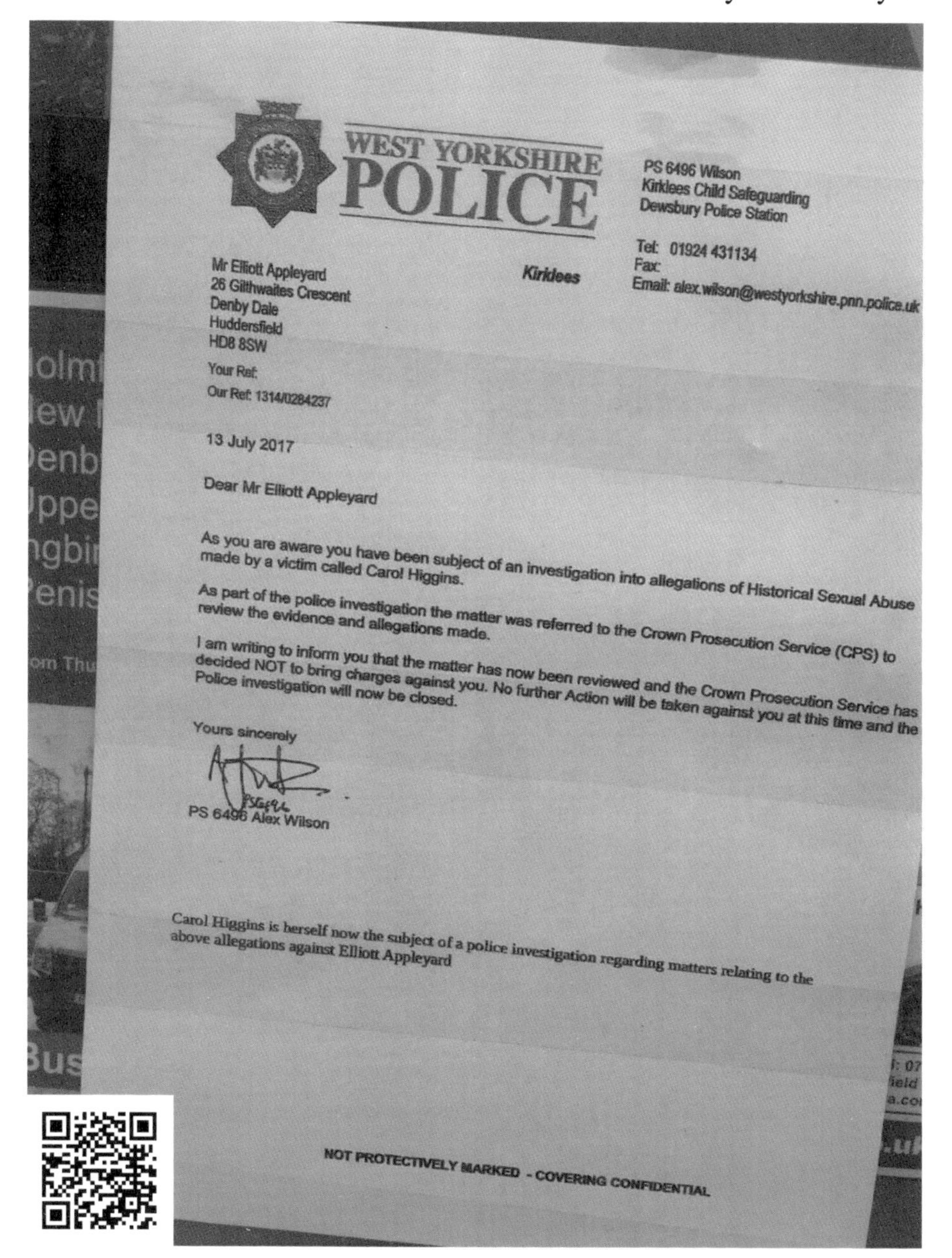

WEST YORKSHIRE POLICE

PS 6496 Wilson
Kirklees Child Safeguarding
Dewsbury Police Station

Tel: 01924 431134
Fax:
Email: alex.wilson@westyorkshire.pnn.police.uk

Kirklees

Mr Elliott Appleyard
26 Gilthwaites Crescent
Denby Dale
Huddersfield
HD8 8SW

Your Ref:
Our Ref: 1314/0284237

13 July 2017

Dear Mr Elliott Appleyard

As you are aware you have been subject of an investigation into allegations of Historical Sexual Abuse made by a victim called Carol Higgins.

As part of the police investigation the matter was referred to the Crown Prosecution Service (CPS) to review the evidence and allegations made.

I am writing to inform you that the matter has now been reviewed and the Crown Prosecution Service has decided NOT to bring charges against you. No further Action will be taken against you at this time and the Police investigation will now be closed.

Yours sincerely

PS 6496 Alex Wilson

Carol Higgins is herself now the subject of a police investigation regarding matters relating to the above allegations against Elliott Appleyard

NOT PROTECTIVELY MARKED - COVERING CONFIDENTIAL

Thornes Call

Written by Alex Wilson and appended by Appleyard in a different font. I reported this to Alex Wilson but he was not concerned and did nothing.

Carol Higgins

Ref/13KD0601916/SEN/CH

26/07/2017

Please find below a list of questions that I have made regarding the CPS decision that I disagree with, which is to be reviewed by another CPS lawyer. I understand that some, if not all of the points I will raise below in my request for a review, will need to be addressed by the police as well; for this reason I have also lodged a complaint against West Yorkshire Police and this is currently with their Police Professional Standards Department. Whilst reading this list, please also refer to the following documents enclosed:

"Chronological dates of investigation" compiled by myself, Carol Higgins, for MP Jon Trickett, Chief Constable Dee Collins, Chief and Crimes Commissioner Mark Burns Williams, Safe Guarding Office Stuart Piper (Enc 1)

List of fifty two questions compiled by DS 5888 Penny Morley and DI Truelove from West Yorkshire Police Professional Standards Department. (Enc 2) These were derived from the Chronological dates of investigation above and a six hour interview, which Penny Morley said highlighted systematic failings and which necessitated her sending the case to the IPCC (she said in a recorded phone call it would look "dodgy" if she did not).

Below is a list of information I believe to be missing from the file given to CPS in 2017 by WYP:

- **17 – page statement from me made in 1984**
- **Forensic evidence from me in 1984**
- **Details from original investigation including evidence of arrest of Appleyard in 1984 or any other year**
- **Three page incomplete, unsigned draft from me made in 2005 and submitted to CPS, according to DC Strafford**
- **Police and CPS file from 2005. The only reference I have been provided by the police for this is VN/05/33129.**
- **Decision letter from the CPS in 2005 with their decision not to prosecute Appleyard. I was informed by DI Ian Thorne's in 2017 that this decision was based on my alleged sexual activity and the assumption that Appleyard was previously arrested in 1984. Ian Thorne's informed me that he based this on information he "saw on file" in 2017. I never received notification that it had gone to CPS in 2005 , neither did I receive a decision letter from them. Where is this file Ian Thornes viewed? Did Sarah Nelson see this file?**
- **Letters from Jordan's solicitors from 2012 (Encs 3,4,5,6,7,and 8) and any record I approached the police in 2012 directly.**
- **Crime, reference number and data I reported to Sonya Strafford, Philipa Write, DS Barns and Sergeant Sewell in 2012.**

1

Page 1 of my Victim's Right to Review

- **Details of two years of counselling with Dove House (from approximately 2013)**
- **Seven page, signed statement I made at Normanton police station in 2014. This statement was passed on to Sonya Strafford in 2014, by the interviewing female officer.**
- **Written signed statement from Carron Ward nee Garside in 2014, taken by Sonya Strafford.**
- **Police file from 2014 containing any additional statements gathered by Sonya Strafford (including Garry Mannifield, Paul Appleyard and Jean Voss).**
- **A letter from Sonya Strafford dated 10th October 2014, no reference or crime number, stating the matter was investigated in 1984 and there was insufficient further evidence to take the matter further (Enc 9).**
- **My book titled Conquering the Impossible:Making the Dream Come True written and published by Carol Higgins. (Enc 10)**
- **Medical records from 1987 to 2015 (Enc11)**
- **Letter from my mother, Jean Voss, dated 1993 confirming her knowledge of the abuse. (Enc 12)**
- **Written, signed statement taken from Carron Ward in 2015 taken by Alex Wilson.**
- **Information about therapeutic work with additional organisations such as Rape Crisis from 1987 to present day, which continues. (Enc 13)**
- **A list of witnesses Alex Wilson provided on 9-9 2016. (Enc 14)**
- **Proof of evidence receipts (Enc 15)**
- **Recorded decision meeting 10-07-2017 (Enc 16)**
- **Subject access form sent 7-03-2017 (Enc 17)**
- **Subject access form sent 8-08-2017 (Enc 18)**
- **Attached video statement 1 and 2 (Enc 19)**

The following are a list of questions and key points which I need to be addressed as part of this Right to Review process. (I have also enclosed a list of questions compiled by Sergeant Penny Morley, Police Professional Standards for DI Thornes and Alex Wilson to answer regarding the investigation, Enc 20, as some of the questions are similar).

Question One
Why were there only 3 dates considered by the CPS (and two discounted, 1984 and 2005 due to the files allegedly being legally destroyed?) In total there should have been 5 dates when I reported the rapes by my father Elliott Appleyard over 34 years. In the decision letter from CPS, dated 05/07/2017 that I received on the 10/07/2017 Sarah Nelson stated that she had been provided with a comprehensive file from WYP regarding the reports of rape made by me in 1984, 2005 and more recently in 2014. I would like to argue that the file provided by WYP to CPS in 2017 was not as comprehensive as it should or could have been. Not only is the evidence from 1984 and 2005 allegedly "no longer available", (my seventeen-page statement, forensic evidence or any documentation to show whether Appleyard was investigated or arrested), there was also no mention of me reporting the rapes in 2012 and 2015. I

actually approached the police on the following dates: 1984, 2005, 2012, 2014 and September 2015.

Question Two
If the statement I made in 1984 at Penistone Police Station, the forensic evidence I gave at Huddersfield Police Station and any other information about the investigation in 1984 is "no longer available" why does this count against my case and why would it result in an abuse of process to the suspect?
Have the CPS requested information with regard to the forensic evidence, was it destroyed, lost or conveniently omitted?

When I gave my statement in1984, my mother asked the police what would happen next. They informed her that Appleyard would be arrested and taken to Kirkburton Police Station. My mother and I never knew whether this actually happened and were never officially informed whether he had been arrested. The day after I gave my seventeen page statement, I was taken to Huddersfield Police Station for internal forensic evidence to be taken. Approximately three weeks later an officer came to my mum's house and said that they had searched Appleyard's house but no evidence was found and no further action would be taken. No documentation, crime number or reference number was ever issued to me or my mother in 1984. Where is the forensic evidence taken from Appleyard if he was ever arrested?

Key point
In 1984, when I made my 17 page statement, on the same day a policeman warned me that if the case went to court I would be made out to be the biggest liar in the courtroom and my sexual activity would be called into question by Appleyard's defence lawyer. The policeman also said that my character would be blackened and I would be dragged through the mud. The officer asked "could I handle that"? I replied, "No I couldn't". I felt ashamed because at the age of 13, I had lost my virginity. I had slept with someone in a house in Penistone, where I had been lodging with my mum. He was much older than me, about 19 but I still didn't want him to get into trouble if it came out in court. I was told by the police that because my case had not reached court, it could be investigated in the future, when my brother was older and no longer a hostile witness (because he was still living with my dad), whereas if it had gone to court and been tried and thrown out, there would be no chance of opening the case in the future. Following this information I still had hope that my dad would be brought to justice. Is this the reason why no statements were taken from my mum and my brother in 1984? Is this also the reason why my credibility about my sexual activities was questioned in 2005 and my case supposedly thrown out by CPS?

Question Three
Alex Wilson and Ian Thornes stated in the recorded decision meeting (Enc 16) when asked on the 10th July 2017 "what evidence do you have Appleyard was arrested in 1984? They both replied, "There is no documented evidence that Appleyard was ever arrested in 1984". In the next breath they said there is a log on the police computer from 2005 (Sarah Nelson does not appear to be aware of because she says any evidence has been legally destroyed from 2005) stating that "the information is that Appleyard was arrested during the original investigation" because I had told previous

investigating officers in 2005 that I thought he had been. In the decision meeting Alex Wilson said this may have been misinterpreted or misunderstood, rightly or wrongly by the investigating officer. I have never said to Strafford or any investigating officer that I have known for certain that Appleyard had been arrested. How would I know whether he had been or not? No crime number was ever given to me or my mother in 1984 and we received no verbal or written notification in 1984? Just because my mother was told they were going to arrest him, does not mean that he ever was. Alex Wilson informed me that during the current investigation my mother Jean Voss gave a statement saying that Appleyard had been arrested; my mother denies saying this, because she genuinely does not know if he was or was not arrested in 1984. Alex Wilson and Ian Thornes said that the hurdle that CPS could not overcome in the 2017 investigation was that Appleyard had already been arrested and investigated in 1984 and it would be abuse of process to charge him. (Enc 26). Sarah Nelson states, that it is because there is no evidence from 1984 or 2005. Surely this must be viewed as hearsay and not evidence? Has Appleyard actually ever been arrested? Did Alex Wilson ask Appleyard and where is the actual proof he was? Appleyard has never been to court before or been tried or formally recorded as not guilty. According to Martin Hawes from CPS in a lengthy recorded telephone conversation on 31.05.17, this should not be a hurdle to looking at the case again, because it had never been to court. Furthermore, did Alex Wilson not ask Appleyard if he had ever been arrested or investigated in 1984 during the course of his voluntary attendance at Dewsbury police station in 2015 and what was Appleyard's reply?

As I understand it, you are basing your decision not to prosecute Appleyard on the assumption that he was arrested and investigated; however, as Sarah Nelson points out, there is no documentation to prove this. After researching and learning that the "abuse of process" is very rarely used, I wonder why it would be applicable in this instance and why this would mean Appleyard could not have a fair trial. If the evidence is only "word against word" because there were no witnesses and because Appleyard denies any activity of a sexual nature, legally why would Appleyard's word have more significance to a jury than my word as a victim? How can a victim ever get justice if this is the case? And when are there ever any witnesses to the rape of children or historical child sexual abuse?

Appleyard's friends are contacting me on my Amazon book review site, Conquering The Impossible, Making The Dream Come True, stating that I am lying and he has never been investigated or arrested in 1984 or any other time. Appleyard has told them this himself.

If Appleyard had been arrested, then surely there should be a crime number from Kirkburton police or at the very least, a log on a database, or has this been conveniently destroyed as well?

Question Four

Sarah Nelson says there is no evidence from 2005. However, Ian Thornes says he has seen a log on the computer saying that CPS lawyers threw my case out in 2005 because they "questioned my credibility about my sexual activities." Where is the evidence of this CPS decision and a record of who made this decision and what was it

4

based on? Alex Wilson is also aware of a reference from 2005, which he gave me to enable me to fill in my subject access form (VN/05/33129). (Enc 17). Why was I not given a crime number in 2005 and can CPS make a decision on a case without a crime number?

In 2005 I went to West Yorkshire Police to report historical sexual abuse. I spoke to Child protection officer, Sonya Strafford who said that there were no statements or internal forensic evidence from 1984, because they had been lost. (At a later date, 2012, she said they had not been lost, they just could not be found. I was informed by a DS Barnes that my statements were not lost and that they had been burnt along with everybody else's from the 1980s.) In an effort to recall what I had put in my original 17-page statement, I started drafting a new statement at home, as requested by Sonya Strafford. I wrote three pages which Sonya Strafford took from me in order to see if I was writing the right sort of things, as far as I was aware this was a draft and not an actual statemen. I was devastated when she telephoned me and told me she had sent the three-page draft to CPS because it was far from complete. Where is this incomplete statement?

No statements or evidence were gathered from my family or other relevant witnesses. I don't believe that Appleyard was interviewed in 2005 and if he was, where is the transcript? I do not believe that the case was thoroughly investigated in 2005 and if my draft statement was the only piece of new evidence, the evidence would not have been strong. I wonder how the case would have got past the RASSO gatekeeper, as since 1986, this would have been a requirement under the law. Who would the RASSO gatekeeper have been at that time? Was it Ian Lawrence?

Alex Wilson gave me the reference number in 2017 (VN/05/33129) relating to my accusation in 2005? Did Alex Wilson pass this reference number on to Sarah Nelson? If he did, why has Sarah Nelson said that all evidence from 2005 has been legally destroyed? Alex Wilson stated in the recorded decision meeting (Enc 16), that every piece of evidence I gave to him, had been sent to Sarah Nelson, including historical evidence. Would I be able to find out what evidence Sarah Nelson received?

Question Five

I have documents showing that I approached WYP in 2012 through Jordan's solicitors (Enc 3,4,5,6,7, and 8). These documents were provided to Alex Wilson by me for the investigation in 2015. I also spoke to Philipa Wright, Sergeant Sewell, DC 5621 Sonya Strafford and DS Barnes from the child protection unit in 2012. I have details of dates of when I spoke to all of the aforementioned people. Was this recorded by the police and were these documents included in the file and viewed and considered by CPS in 2017? I doubt that they were because the date is not listed in Sarah Nelson's decision letter.

Sonya Strafford told me in 2012 that unless I could find another victim of Appleyard, that no case could be opened. I found my cousin Tony Brearley,(female) she confirmed to me that she was sexually abused by Appleyard. According to Alex Wilson, Sonya Strafford had interviewed Tony Brearley in 2012. Was a statement taken? If so, where is it? Why did Alex Wilson refuse to interview this vital witness in

5

2017, when he knew she was a victim of Appleyard? His reason was that she had already been interviewed by a female officer, Sonja Strafford in 2012. If this information was passed on to the CPS, why wasn't the 2012 investigation included in the Decision made by Sarah Nelson? She stated in her decision letter that there were no direct witnesses. Why?

Were the letters sent to the police in 2012 from Jordan solicitors passed on to the CPS? I also gave Alex Wilson a copy of "My Story" which I wrote in 2012 and sent to ITV This Morning (Enc 23) . According to Alex Wilson all information regarding the case was passed to the CPS. Why was none of this considered by Sarah Nelson? Was she aware of this evidence?

Question Six
I asked Alex Wilson, the investigating officer, when completing my Subject Access Forms on the 07.03.2017 for the crime numbers relating to these dates. He told me that there was only one crime number ever recorded and that was from September 2015, this is the crime number 1314/0284237. He has subsequently informed me that this crime reference number was in fact generated in 2014 on an audit trail and he reopened the case in 2015 with the same number. I don't understand why it was generated in 2014 because I was never provided with this crime number in 2014. There was not even a crime reference number on the letter, dated the 10th October 2014 sent to me by DC 5621 Sonya Strafford, WYP, with the decision not to take this matter any further at this stage (see Enc 9). I feel that this information perhaps explains why my 2017 CPS decision letter does not mention me approaching the police in 2015. However, it does not explain why 2012 is not mentioned.

How far does the audit trail go back? When my MP Jon Trickett submitted a second Subject Access form (Enc 18) on my behalf, the only evidence that I received back was my video statement from November the 2nd 2015 (Enc 19). Where is the rest of the evidence for which I have receipts (Enc 15) such as recordings of BBC radio interviews, medical records, my book Conquering the Impossible, recordings of my brother, Paul Appleyard and my mother, Jean Voss and Ian Thornes (Enc 21) other items of evidence relating to the case?

Question Seven
In 2014 I once again reported historical child sex abuse to the Child protection unit in West Yorkshire. I went in one Sunday morning to Normanton police station where after a five hour wait I made what I thought was a 7 page statement to a young female officer. Sonia Strafford contacted me saying her supervisor wanted more evidence. She told me to send it in the post. I refused to send names of witnesses through the post and asked her for a meeting. She agreed that I would go to Dewsbury station to take in the letter my mum wrote to me in 1989 (Enc 12) stating she knew I was being sexually abused by Appleyard. I also took names in of other witnesses, Carron ward who has now given a statement saying Appleyard asked her when she was 15years old, "As thi father broke you in yet?"

My brother Paul Appleyard was telephoned by Sonia Strafford in 2014 and asked if he had seen Appleyard rape me? He told her he saw Appleyard kissing me properly and saw us in bed together many times. She replied to me that this is not evidence as my daughter kisses my husband and gets into bed with him. I asked her if she read the 7 page statement Id given to the young officer I was made to wait five hours to give and if she would use it as evidence. She replied, "It's not a statement as such because a crime number hasn't been given". No reference or crime number was issued regarding the complaint. A letter was sent to me after I requested it by DC Sonya Strafford (5621) stating, sadly as this matter was investigated in 1984, there is insufficient further evidence from the above enquiries to take this matter further at this stage. I enclose the letter with no crime number from 2014 (Enc 9). It also states in the letter that "Jean Voss has written proof that she knew her daughter was being abused." "Jean Voss was aware, however she was aware in 1984 when she took you to the police station." What difference does it make whether she knew in 1984 and 2014 – why should this be a reason for her evidence not to be taken into account? The bottom line is that she knew the abuse was happening.

How could Sonia Strafford relate back to 1984 when there was no actual documentation or crime number relating to this period, when she had told me already that the file had been lost?.

Question Eight
Why did Alex Wilson inform me at the decision meeting that the 7 page statement was omitted from the file sent to the CPS in 2017? Is the CPS aware of this signed statement?

Question Nine
Why was no crime number or reference number issued by Sonia Strafford in 2014 and why are Alex Wilson and Ian Thorns saying my case was opened in 2014 when I have the letter off Sonia Strafford to prove she said no case would be investigated or crime number given? (Enc 9).

Question Ten
I reported Historical Child Sex Abuse for the fifth time in 34 years on the 04/09/2015 naming Appleyard again for the years of beatings, grooming and rapes he subjected me to from a baby because the police wouldn't bring him to justice. When he raped me for the first time, I was thirteen; this was in 1983.

I asked him, "What would Granddad say if he knew what you have just done?" He replied, "Don't worry he believes the same as me, that fathers should break their daughters in like native American Indians do".

This rape continued nearly every day from this point on for nearly two years

I have been informed by Alex Wilson (see Enc 14) that written, signed statements were finally taken in 2015/2016 from my Brother Paul Appleyard, my Mother Jean Voss, Hilda Graham, Karl Higgins, Garry Mannifield, Steven Marsh, Deanna Thorp, Carron Ward, Ena Whittle, and Julie Clarke. Have they all been submitted to the CPS? I would also like to know whether my 4 hour video statement from November 2015 has been included (Disc 1337-1443, Enc 19)?

Were recorded conversations relating to the case, containing relevant evidence from Jean Voss, Paul Appleyard and the investigating officer Ian Thornes dated 18/05/2017, 20/05/2017 and 26/05/2017 forwarded to the CPS (Enc 21)? Did Alex Wilson give my letter, which I wrote in 1985, to the CPS (Enc 24)

I identified the above named people as important witnesses for my case. Below is a brief overview of information given to me by Alex Wilson about what each statement covered in addition to what I believe was covered in these statements:

Paul Appleyard – Confirmed to Alex Wilson in 2016 he witnessed sexually abusive behaviour by Appleyard toward Carol, that he had seen them kissing passionately and often together In Appleyards bed, with Carol in just her underwear. Paul confirmed that Appleyard had both Carol and Paul tattooed with his pseudonym, Sam. Has the CPS got this statement with regard to the statement that Paul had witnessed intimacy between them?

Paul Appleyard in 2014 informed Sonya Strafford in a telephone conversation that he witnessed Appleyard kissing me passionately and in bed often together. Sonya remarked, "My daughter kisses my husband and gets into bed with him". She disregarded this as evidence and refused to include it as evidence (Enc 9) No statement was taken. Was this information made available to the CPS and If so were questioned asked. Why can't it be ascertained if Paul was spoken to in 1984?
Why didn't the police ask him?

Jean Voss – Confirmed that Carol had informed her that Appleyard sexually abused and raped Carol. She took her to Penistone police station and reported it. This is when I made my seventeen page statement. Carols mum confirmed she had reported her concerns to social services and removed Carol from the family home in 1983. Also confirmed comments made by Appleyard about fathers "breaking their daughters in". A letter dated circa 1993 confirming that she knew Appleyard was raping her was written to Carol by her Mother and was passed onto Alex Wilson. Jean also confirmed other incidents of violence. Mum took me for a pregnancy test. Jean Voss can confirm she called Appleyard on the night I told her to confront him about the abuse. His reply to her was, you can't prove a thing. Has the CPS got this statement and letter (Enc 14)?

Hilda Graham – Alex Wilson told me that Hilda gave a good statement confirming that she had heard an argument between Appleyard and Jean Voss about Carol having to be taken to have a pregnancy test. I stayed with Aunty Hilda when Appleyard went to America. Has the CPS got this statement?

Karl Higgins – Alex Wilson told me that Karl gave a good statement confirming that the night Carol ran away he witnessed carol disclose to her mother that her father had been sexually abusing her.

Garry Mannifield – Alex Wilson told me Garry gave a good statement confirming that he had been told by retired Sergeant, Brian Fearnley that he had seen on police file my original statement from 1984 with an accompanying letter saying that they needed to be destroyed as they were an embarrassment to the family. Gary said that

8

this was said to him by Brian Fearnley after Garry had been beaten up by police officers and put in the cells for calling Appleyard a Peadophile. Brian Fearnley informed Garry that it was his boss who sent the officers out to his home in Denby Dale to beat him up. He also confirmed that Appleyard had pointed a gun at him because Garry had called him a paedophile; this resulted in the whole village being cordoned off whilst armed units responded to the incident. He also confirmed that he was told by Diane Croft that when Carol was 15 years old she had told Diane that Appleyard had been having sex with her. Has the CPS got this statement? Why wasn't Appleyard arrested for threatening someone with a deadly weapon?

Steven Marsh – Alex Wilson told me Steven gave a good statement confirming that he was my ex-husband and the impact the abuse had had on me and our 15 years of married life together. He also confirmed that Carol had had counselling and therapy over the years and that he had also accessed counselling and support for male partners of survivors of sexual violence. Has the CPS got this statement?

Deanna Thorp – Alex Wilson told me that Deanna gave a good statement confirming that she is Carol's cousin and that she had witnesses an occasion where Appleyard and Carol had come downstairs together and were both half naked and dishevelled. She said that this had made her think that they had had sex. She also confirmed that when Carol was around 14 years old she had told Deanna that her dad was having sex with her. Has the CPS got this statement?

Carron Ward nee Garside – Alex Wilson told me she gave a good statement. Carron was my neighbour when I was a child. When she was fourteen my father asked her the question, "As thi father broke you in yet?" She also confirmed that whilst on a camping trip whilst brushing her teeth she dropped tooth paste on her t-shirt (chest area) Appleyard said something along the lines of "has he missed your gob?" She also said that she saw Appleyard acting as though I was his girlfriend. Carron gave a full one page statement to Sonya Strafford in 2014 giving full details of what she had witnessed. However, the in letter from Sonya Strafford in 2014 (Enc 9) Sonya wrote that Carron "cannot remember any inappropriate behaviour between Elliot Appleyard and Carol". Where is this statement from 2014? I feel that this statement is crucial to help build a case around the statement I gave to the police in 2015 and help to corroborate the abuse committed by Appleyard. Has the CPS got this statement? A further statement was taken from Carren Ward in 2015/16. Have the CPS got this statement?

Ena Whittle – Saw Appleyard holding Carols hand and treating her like a girlfriend, Appleyard confronted Ena about this and his behaviour toward Carol. Ena also said that she noticed big love bites on Carol's neck and thought that Appleyard wouldn't allow other boys to do that. Has the CPS got this statement?

Julie Clarke – Alex Wilson said Julie gave a good statement. Julie confirmed that she knew Carol from the age of 16 years old and that she used to work with Carol. Julie also said that she used to accompany her weekly to Sheffield Rape Crisis so Carol could access support. She also witnessed me collapsing in Barnsley market when I saw my dad. Julie also witnessed the tattoo on my back and the removal of it. Has the CPS got this statement?

Question Eleven
Have additional statements been obtained from the following people and submitted to CPS? Jane and Harry Innes, Janet Appleyard, Julie Garside, Reece and Alan Morley, Diane Croft, Mr Brocklesby and Brian Fearnley, Tony Brearly , Jim Pipkin and Jess, who was Appleyards girlfriend at the time?

I believe these questions are justified because, I feel strongly that any omissions from the case file would ultimately affect the decision made by the CPS. I have been informed that only ten out of the above named witnesses gave statements to WYP during Alex Wilson's investigation. Have the CPS received nine signed and dated statements plus a video statement from myself in 2017? He also informed me that he had provided all of the above names and it might be possible that CPS would request statements from those who had not already provided one. I understand that some of the witnesses approached were afraid to come forward as official witnesses in support of the case. However, I would like to know whether the following people were included in the file provided by WYP or not. I have included a brief bit of information for each witness, informing you of why I feel their statements could provide additional corroborating evidence for this case.

Jane Innes – Witnessed physical abuse towards me by Appleyard as a baby, punching me in the chest to stop me from crying. She was willing to give a statement, but Alex Wilson refused to take one. He informed me that he spoke to her over the phone and Ian Thoms suggested he take a statement from her, as this would build a picture of the behaviour of the accused. Why was there only a phone call made and no statement taken? Was this telephone conversation made available to the CPS?

Harry Innes – Started a petition in Denby Dale village twenty years ago for Appleyard's guns to be taken off him. The reason for this was because of an incident involving Appleyard, when he pointed a gun at Garry Mannifield and threatened to kill him, this was because Gary accused Appleyard of being a Paedophile. This resulted in the village being cordoned off by Armed Response Police and the evacuation of the local school on Gilthwaites Crescent.
This incident was witnessed by neighbours and many people in the area, although no action was taken against Appleyard, it left many people in the village in fear of their lives. This was the reason the petition was sent to the police. The response from the police was to return the guns to Appleyard that they had previously confiscated. Why was no statement taken from Mr Innes or people in the village who witnessed this incident?

Janet Appleyard (Appleyard's current wife)– When I was 17 years old Janet asked to meet me because Appleyard had asked her to marry him, she was concerned about information she had been given concerning the sexual abuse and rape of me by my father. We met in a café and I told her of the abuse. After a 2 hour meeting with her she told me that my father was waiting for her and did I want to see him. I said yes. I met him and I asked him why he had raped me? He replied, "I'm sorry, it's because I loved you as a person, not as a daughter. My brother Paul Appleyard who lived with Janet and Appleyard, told me later that he had heard them arguing about me. Appleyard stated that it was me, who came onto him, but he rejected me and this was the reason that I was accusing him of rape. Was this information passed on to the CPS?

Julie Garside – Julie was another victim of Appleyard, Wilson stated that there was no point in interviewing her because Sonya Strafford had interviewed her in previous years, there is no statement to this effect, was she interviewed, was a statement taken from her, if not, why wasn't she included in the investigation? (Jean Voss, nee Appleyard can confirm this). Wilson agreed to speak to my mum about this, and then changed his mind. He could not proceed, unless instructed by the CPS. Who was leading the investigation the police or the CPS?

Alan Morley – Informed me that his stepson, Reece, had a girlfriend called Sue and that she had been raped by Appleyard about 20 years ago. Were Reece and Alan ever interviewed by Alex Wilson. Why wasn't this girl found and asked to give a statement?

Diane Croft – When I was 15, I told Diane that my father was having sex with me and I had to get away. Alex Wilson informed me that he had gone to take a statement from her, but she refused to give one because she was frightened of Appleyard and what might happen to her. He said in a recorded telephone conversation with me that he had been to talk to her on three occasions to try and persuade her to give a statement. He said he would go back a fourth time. He admitted that she did confirm to him that my conversation with Diane did take place. Wilson stated to me that although no statement was taken, he would be able to confirm this once in court. Was the CPS made aware of this?

Ian Brockelsby – Confirmed to Alex Wilson that I was beaten as a child; he stated that it was common knowledge in the village that I was being abused by Appleyard, but fear of retribution prevented any intervention. Why was only a telephone call made to Mr Brockelsby, instead of a full written statement? Was this conversation included in the file passed to the CPS?

Brian Fearnley – told Alex Wilson in 2017 that Appleyard had made his life hell all the years he had been in the police force. The reason being was that Brian Fearnley had confiscated Appleyard's guns after the incident on Gilthwaites Crescent twenty years ago involving Garry Mannifield. The guns were returned to Appleyard. Appleyard continued to harass Officer Brian Fearnley and reported him to his sergeant over 20 times. Sergeant Penny Morley from police Professional Standards told me in 2017 she had seen this on the statement Alex Wilson had taken from Officer Brian Fearnley in 2017. Brian Fernley told Garry Mannifield that he had seen on file my original 17 page statement from 1984 and with it a letter stating that the statement needs to be destroyed, because it is an embarrassment to the family. Was Fearnley ever asked about this by Wilson and was this information passed on to the CPS?

Tony Brearley – Is Appleyard's niece, she was also a victim of Appleyard. Tony admitted to me that she was raped by Appleyard as a child and abused over a period of time. Alex Wilson refused to interview her because Sonya Strafford had allegedly interviewed her in 2012. I asked Alex Wilson and Ian Thornes if it would be possible for her to be interviewed by a female officer with regard to the current investigation.

Wilson and Thornes agreed, but then decided that because she had been interviewed in the past there would be no point. No statement was taken, what happened to the audit trail of the interview with Sonya Strafford in 2012? Is the CPS aware of this? (As I pointed out to Wilson, Jean Voss would have confirmed the sexual abuse). Why did Wilson wait for instruction from the CPS with regard to taking a new statement? Who was leading the investigation the police or the CPS?

Jim Pipkin – A penfriend of Appleyards who he visits in Dallas Texas and who he went on hunting trips with. It was on his return from his first ever hunting trip in 1983 that Appleyard first raped me. My brother and I both told Alex Wilson that we believed Appleyard and Pipkin were part of a paedophile ring. Why were their computers not seized? Why wasn't this man investigated? Why were other prominent individuals who had association with Appleyard not investigated? Was the CPS aware of the connection between Appleyard and Judge James Pickles and the land Appleyard rented off him? How much of this information was passed on to the CPS by the police?

Jake Marsh – Ella Marsh – My son and daughter, made a request to Alex Wilson if they would be allowed to make statements concerning the impact that the abuse I suffered as a child has had on my life and on theirs. Wilson informed them that if the CPS required impact statements from them, then they would be allowed to do so. Wilson yet again deferred to the wishes of the CPS,
Did the CPS consider this?

Jess - What enquiries were made to locate Jess, who was my father's girlfriend in 1983 when he was raping me? I feel she was an important witness to this case as she witnessed Appleyard giving me love bites and play fighting with me and behaving inappropriately towards me. She lived on Green Road in Penistone. Wilson informed me Appleyard had no recollection of her but my mother Jean Voss can confirm that Jess was his girlfriend at the time. Wilson said he couldn't find her, but the CPS would ask for this information if they needed it,
Was the CPS made aware of this and did they request further enquiries to be made?

Question Twelve
Was Appleyard questioned about the tattoo I was forced to have at the age of fourteen with his pseudonym on it?
What evidence was forwarded to the CPS with regard to this tattoo? If nothing has been provided I would be happy to provide photographic evidence to support this. Indeed, I offered to provide this to the police carrying out the investigation; however, I was informed that it would not be needed.
Was the CPS made aware of this?

Question Thirteen
When I made my video statement at Normanton Police Station in November 2015, I told the interviewing officer Helen Brear specifically about a large tin box.
Was the tin box containing items Appleyard molested me with, sexy underwear, a Polaroid camera, a white handled hair brush, pornographic magazines and Polaroid photographs he took of me ever considered to be searched for by the police, when the

12

decision to invite Appleyard in for a voluntary interview was made. Why did Wilson tell me he had missed this important information but after watching the video statement for a second time he confirmed that "yes you did mention the tin box". Alex Wilson informed me that because an alleged search was made of Appleyard's house in 1984, when nothing was found, it would be highly unlikely that they would find the tin box now. Why was I told by Alex Wilson that Appleyard didn't meet the criteria for search or arrest, even though I gave evidence of the tin box in my video statement? I would also like to know why Appleyard's property was not searched in an attempt to locate the above-mentioned items or why his computer was not seized.

Question Fourteen
During the 2015 investigation I reported, once again, that my father had subjected me to physical and emotional abuse, as well as sexual abuse. For example, I told Alex Wilson about Jane Innes witnessing Appleyard punching me as a baby. I told him in my video statement (Enc 19) about Appleyard making me bend over the sofa without my pants on and him violently whipping me with a thick, black leather belt. It was so painful I could not sit down. I was also beaten about the head regularly and was witness to my brother and sister being beaten as well. I also told Alex Wilson and Sergeant Brear about Appleyard holding guns to my mum's head and threatening to slash my mum from her vagina to her throat with a machete. Appleyard also shot my dog in front of me. Alex Wilson told me that he was investigating child sexual abuse, not physical abuse, so this wasn't relevant. Surely this is just as relevant and builds a picture of Appleyard's character and motivation and the fear that he constantly instilled in me?

Question Fifteen
Sarah Nelson stated in her decision letter (Enc 25) that the police did not provide her "with any direct evidence but there was some evidence which could be used to support the account" which I gave. What is this supporting evidence? Why can I not view the CPS file to reassure myself that all available evidence has been put to CPS?

Question Sixteen
One of my main concerns is the fact that the CPS are supposedly an independent legal review process that determines whether an individual will be charged or not. According to Alex Wilson an agreement was made between the Child Protection Unit and the CPS to gather evidence because my case is complex and is not being treated like any other case. According to Alex Wilson the CPS have continually issued instructions as to what statements to gather. Is this true?
If this is the case then how can the CPS review a case in a non-judgemental way, when the CPS has ultimately directed the investigation?.

Alex Wilson informed me, that he had interviewed Appleyard with a solicitor present for the third time and put to him the question, did he rape me over a 2 year period. Appleyard denied this. Wilson informed Appleyard that 12 people had made statements against him and gave Appleyard the names of the witnesses and informed Appleyard about the content of the statements. Wilson stated that he was obliged to

13

do this under the Pace Act and It was Part Law. Appleyard responded by saying that all these people had a vendetta against him and I had told them what to put in their statements. I have not seen any of these people except my brother and mother in over 34 years. So how could I have influenced any of them?

I understand that in summary your decision is based on the fact that all evidence from 1984 and 2005 has gone missing. That the 22 witnesses who were willing to give statements, only 11 were actually taken. Because there were no eye-witnesses, no action could be taken. Exactly what evidence has been used to come to this decision?

I am contesting this decision based on a number of points, that I truly believe have either been omitted or disregarded for whatever reason. I don't feel that my case has been handled fairly from the very start and I feel like I have been lied to and misled and the process has not been transparent or considerate towards the victim. This experience has left me with a complete mistrust of the police and I believe that the actions of the investigating officer have contributed to the CPS making, in my opinion, the wrong decision. I have for many years tried to bring my abuser to justice, I have maintained and stand by my allegations. I can only be honest and speak the truth.

Yours,
C Higgins...

LIST OF ENCLOSURES

1 Chronological dates of investigation

2 52 questions compiled by DS 588 Penny Morley and DI Truelove from West Yorkshire Police Professional Standards

3-8 Letters from Jordans Solicitors

9 Letter from DC Sonya Strafford 10th October 2014

10 Conquering the Impossible:Making the Dream Come True

11 Medical Records 1987-2015

12 Letter from Jean Voss 1993

13 Information about healing and therapeutic work, counsellors, psychologists, Rape Crisis etc

14 List of witnesses Alex Wilson provided 09.09.2016

15 Receipts for evidence from police

16 Recording of decision meeting 10.07.2017

17 Subject Access Application 1

18 Subject Access Application 2

19 Video statement Disc 1 and 2

20 Copy of e-mail questions from Penny Morley

21 Recordings of Paul Appleyard, Jean Voss and DI Thornes

22 BBC Radio Leeds and Radio Sheffield interviews

23 "My Story"

24 Letter written 1985 by Carol Higgins

25 Decision letter from CPS

26 Hurdles to overcome

Ms Carol Higgins
To be delivered by hand by the police

10 January 2018

Our ref: [redacted]

Dear Ms Higgins

VICTIMS RIGHT TO REVIEW

I am writing to you as the prosecutor dealing with this case following your request for a formal review of the decision not to bring charges in the case in which you were involved.

Having carefully considered the case papers provided, and applying the Code for Crown Prosecutors, I am of the view that there is sufficient evidence for there to be a realistic prospect of conviction and that a prosecution is in the public interest.

I have therefore concluded that the decision taken not to bring charges was flawed and that a prosecution should be brought against [redacted] for the offences listed in the attached schedule.

I am grateful to you for drawing this matter to our attention. It is through direct contact such as this that we are able continually to improve our service to the public and to bring offenders to justice. Communicating with victims and witnesses is very important to us and I hope that in reaching this conclusion you will feel that I have listened to your concerns and taken into account your representations.

We will now make the arrangements for the accused to be summonsed.

I anticipate that in future you will be kept informed as to the progress of the case by the prosecuting team and the Witness Care Office.

If you have any future enquiries as to the progress of the case please contact DS [redacted]

Yours sincerely

[redacted]
District Crown Prosecutor
CPS Yorkshire & Humberside

Crown Prosecution Service INVESTORS IN PEOPLE

Crown Prosecution Service, Victim Liaison Unit, Crown Prosecution Service, Yorkshire & Humberside, Greenfield House, 32 Scotland Street, Sheffield S3 7DQ
Telephone 0114 2298862 between 9am – 5pm Monday – Thursday and 9am-4 30pm Friday
Email Y&H VRR&Complaints@cps.gov.uk
Web www.cps.gov.uk

CPS letter overturning the earlier decision not to charge Appleyard

(2.13 p.m.)

JUDGE JAMESON: Right, ladies and gentlemen, well, I think we're going to make a start on the evidence now, which will involve the playing of the recording of Carol Higgins, as she now is, which I think is going to last about----

MR HAMPTON: The video which Mr Smith will introduce in a moment is 1 hour, 40 minutes.

JUDGE JAMESON: All right.

MR HAMPTON: So we were going to seek, with your Honour's leave, to find an appropriate moment about 50 minutes in----

JUDGE JAMESON: Yes.

MR HAMPTON: -- to have a 10-to-15-minute break.

JUDGE JAMESON: I think that's a sensible idea. Yes, okay, thank you very much. Yes, Mr Smith.

MR SMITH: Your Honour, this video was taken on 2 November 2015, when the complainant was 46 years old.

JUDGE JAMESON: Yes.

MR SMITH: And, as my learned friend just said, it last an hour and forty minutes. We'll try and stop it halfway through for a short break.

JUDGE JAMESON: Yes, all right. Thank you very much.

Video Statement (Part 1 of 3)

Video Statement

DC YVONNE BREAR: Are you warm enough Carol?

CAROL HIGGINS: It's a bit cold in here.

DC YVONNE BREAR: Are you cold? Yeah? I can turn it up a bit.

CAROL HIGGINS: I think shock keeps you a bit cold though, don't it?

DC YVONNE BREAR: Yeah. Right, see if that comes up a bit. Right. I'll just go through introduction and then people watching this video know where we are, date, time and things like that. So today's Monday the 2nd of November 2015, and the time by my watch is 10:55 in the morning, and we're at

Normanton Police Station in the video suite. I'm DC974 Brear and I'm normally stationed at Dewsbury Police Station, that's where I work out of on the, erm, child safeguarding unit. And then in the monitoring room we've got, er, PC6496 Alex Wilson. Um. You've met Alex before?

CAROL HIGGINS: Yeah.

DC YVONNE BREAR: Okay. Erm. So we're here to talk about something that's happened to you, that's why we're here. Erm. And as I said before, if you need a break at any point just let me know and we can have a five minute break, a 10 minute break or we can finish for today and come back another day, it's not a problem at all, okay? (CH – "Yes") Don't feel like we need to get everything out today. (CH – "Yes") Erm. The only thing that I must remind you is that everything that you say today must be the truth. Now, I'm not doubting anything that you say but I have to say that to everybody that I speak to, okay? And with little children, we go through a little explanation, truth and lies, I don't need to do that with you, you're an adult, okay? Erm. And just when you're talking, I may have my head down sometimes just taking notes and that's just because when people are giving me all that information, I can't remember it all, so if there's something that I think is pertinent and we need to come back to, I'll make a little note of it, and then that just reminds me to come back to it later. (CH – "Yes, okay) So if I've got my head down, I'm not ignoring you, I'm just writing a few notes, okay?

JUDGE JAMESON: (Confers with clerk) Right. Okay. Sorry, is this something that--- you spoke to somebody about this, did you? Yes, all right. Is it just today?

JUROR: Yes, just today.

JUDGE JAMESON: Yes, all right, but you won't be able to come back, presumably, after you've left.

JUROR: I could (inaudible).

JUDGE JAMESON: Well, it depends how-- you won't know how long you're going to be, do you? No, all right, okay. Well, we're going to have an early day. We'll just do about 35 minutes. So if we rise at 2.50, that's all right, is it? Yes, okay. We're just going to have to rise at 2.50. Okay. If we can break it at that point. Right. Sorry, it's just our juror has a medical appointment and there we go. So we'll just have to take a break and we'll have to stop, I'm afraid, at 2.50, so we won't get very far but there we go. So we'll get about 35 minutes in. Yes.

Video Statement (Part 1 of 3, continued)

CAROL HIGGINS: Okay, yeah.

DC YVONNE BREAR: So in your own time Carol…oh, you give me your name and your date of birth please?

CAROL HIGGINS: Yeah. Carol Higgins, Carol Denise Higgins, 23rd of the 4th 1969.

DC YVONNE BREAR: Okay, Carol. So in your own time, you go right back to the beginning and start from where you think is best and you tell me in as much detail as you can remember, er, what you've come to talk to me about today.

CAROL HIGGINS: I don't know where to start to be honest. I thought I would be starting from when I actually thought I understood he started abusing me but I understand now that he was abusing me from being a baby and planned to have sex with me as an adult. The reason I believe this is because of the things he said to me when I become a teenager but he said to - I found out that he said to friends, has your father broke you in yet and other things. I feel that he had a plan now to groom me whereas I didn't know that at the time, do you know what I mean? When I've heard that he was violent to me when I was a baby and I've gone back to Denby Dale after 31 years, and a girl Jane - since she told me that she babysat for me, and that when I was crying as a baby, he got his hand and his fist and he went like that on my chest, so it winded me and shut me up. So, I just know and I know he's been violent to me as a child. If I wet bed, if I was naughty, he had two belts—a thin belt and a thicker black belt, it wasn't thin, and a thick black belt and he used to, depending on the severity of my punishment he used to hit me with that. I know that we were always flinching because he'd hit me around the head and he'd joke, and sometimes he'd walk past me and he'd scratch his head and I'd think he were going to hit me but then he laughed, do you know what I mean? That kind of thing, but I didn't know that was all part of him getting power over me, these are things I have recently understood really.

What happened was, when I was growing up, he used to take me for walks, we used to go collecting scrap metal and breaking into skips, council skips and finding things to weigh in or to sell on the flea market, in Barnsley flea market, we used to take it there. Then the walks got where he didn't used to ask my brother anymore to come, he were just asking me, so I were like 11, 12-year-old, and he'd just ask me. I used to wonder why he'd just ask me but I think my mum never said owt because she wanted to keep the peace, I'm not sure. And one time he took me, he took the dog and he shot the dog in front of me. And he sat me down on broken pipes, Naylors Pipes at - like a scrap yard for broken pipes and stuff and he sat me down on there, and I think I were about 11 I think, 12. And he started kissing me.

He used to talk to me all the time about him and my mum falling out, and I know he were a very violent man, he used to hold guns to my mum's head and machetes and things like that, so they were always arguing, and he used to make me feel quite adult because - and important because he were telling me things and my mum would be telling me stuff on her side and then he'd be telling me stuff, and we went on these walks all the time. And then he'd hold my hand and stuff but even though he used to hit me a lot as a child, I didn't know any different and I just thought that he really like loved me, and.

So he'd take me for walks. And this one time he started kissing me properly, proper kissing me. And I didn't know what to do about it. So after a few time - I don't know if it happened a few times, I told my mum. I told my mum when I come home from school that he were kissing me properly like a boyfriend girlfriend kiss, and then... And I begged her not to tell him because I was scared of what he were going to do. And he come down the street this one day and I were telling her on the front doorstep, sat on front doorstep but she must have told him because the next thing I knew I were at school, Shelley High School where I went… Two social workers came to see me and asked if I'd go up into the staff office, something like that and they had a meeting with me, and asked me about him kissing me and I said, yeah, he was. We already had social workers in our lives, Pauline, somebody called Pauline and a man called Mr Sykes, but I'm not sure if they were the men - if they were the ones who came to see me, I can't really remember.

And then from that going to Shelley High School and from that happening, a few days later my mum told me that she were leaving my dad but she wasn't taking our Donna and Paul with me, that's my handicapped sister and my brother, just me. But she took me before as well when I were younger, she just used to leave them all with my dad if she ever left him and she'd take me. And she once took me to a place in Huddersfield in Newsome, a battered wives home. And she denies this but I know she put sleeping tablets in my cocoa and in her cocoa, because I get halfway down drinking and she just started crying and saying, "Don't drink it, don't drink it." Because I've got a feeling my mum knew what would've happen to me, now I'm working it all out. Anyway, so this is why I'm saying, she took me a few times before she'd left him, always gone back to him though, she always went back to him.

So this time she took me to a place called Penistone and she'd met these people on the CB radio. So after me telling her about my dad kissing me, she took me out of the house after the social workers have been to the school and then we went to live up in Cubley on Angela Pottle and this man's - her husband's floorboards, they gave us a mattress, and we slept on the bare mattress on these bare floorboards and some blankets and we slept there. And then she got me into Penistone Grammar School, and after staying there a few months, we got kicked out, and we went to go and live at Millhouse Green with a lady called Linda Wadsworth. She had a son called David Wadsworth who was a teenager. My mum had got a newfound freedom so she used to go out all the time and leave me on my own. David Wadsworth, he had sex with me in this house we was at but he didn't force me or anything but I wasn't a virgin, and.

Like somehow a contact was made between me and my dad because I was left on my own all the time and because nothing had been said about him kissing me at school or no other social workers have mentioned it, my mum had never mentioned it. This one time my mum threatened to take an overdose at this Linda Wadsworth's house where we were staying in this little single room with bunk beds, and I'd seen my mum taking many overdoses in my life, I'd come home from school and my mum would take many overdoses, I'd see my dad hanging from the rafters and stuff like that, and I just - I just couldn't take living with my mum anymore. And because nothing had been said about my dad, I guess I'd forgot about the kissing, you know, it happened that time, I guess I forgot about it. And my sister and my brother were still living at Denby Dale as well, and I met him on Barnsley Market and I met him with my boyfriend David even though he were a lot older, the boy from the house. And I remember my dad not liking David, how he were interacting with me like a boyfriend girlfriend. But then I went to live back home. Oh, he bought me a pair of jeans and a bikini, something like that, because my mum even says to me to this day what a price you paid for that pair of jeans, but I didn't know what were going to happen, and he would've just been like a normal dad, like, you know, being nice to me.

And so then I went back to live back home. And then so me, Donna and Paul were back together as a family then. He were going out with a girl called - my dad were going out with a girl called Jess, Jessie from Penistone, all her family lived there. And then he started play fighting with me and giving me love bites when he were play fighting with me, and I didn't used to like it, I felt really uncomfortable with it but I couldn't - I didn't tell anybody about it. But Jess actually saw him play fighting with me and giving me them. I don't know where she lives now, her family might still live in Penistone.

Anyway, that started happening. And then it went around—and then he went to America, he went to America on his first ever hunting trip to kill deer. He's got a friend called Jim Pipkin, I think he's in a cult against black people or a paedophile ring, you know, with this Jim Pipkin, I remember him being friends with him, writing to him, pen pals when we were younger, and this other guy from Philadelphia. So he went to America and he's come back from his hunting trip. And then my mum took half of the furniture. I had a wild party with my brother, we got a key cut, before we knew we were going to have a party when he went, like teenagers do, and my mum come and took half of furniture because he wouldn't let her when they split up, let her take half of it. He said he'd rather saw it in half.

So that happened and then - so when he come back from America, he were absolutely fuming, fuming. And he went around to the phone box, he wanted some questions answering from when he come back, and he went around to the public phone box to phone his girlfriend Jess who lived at Penistone to say he was back. And in that time, I got the knife out the drawer and I started cutting my wrist. I've never done it before but I started cutting my wrist and my brother got me and took me and dragged me around to the phone box and then brought me back around. My dad got out of the phone box and brought me back around home and he started bandaging it up and saying that it's okay, it's not too bad for you to get stitches or for you to go to hospital. But you're too mentally disturbed for you to sleep by yourself tonight. So he said you'll have to sleep with me in my bed. Still never thought anything about it, I just thought he's not angry with me anymore and I'm going to be okay.

And so I went to bed that night and I went to sleep him cuddled up to me, and then I woke up and I felt this tickling here and, you know, when your belly goes in like that, so I didn't know what he were doing and then he started touching me in places and then turned me over and got a condom out of his side of the drawer cupboard and then he had sex with me. And then when he finished having sex with me, I just said to him - I'm not even close to my granddad, dad's dad, I didn't know my grandparents from my mum's side. And so I said to him and I don't know why I said this, and I went, "What would my granddad say if he knew what you've just done?" And he says, "Don't worry sweetheart, he wouldn't say anything, he believes the same as me that fathers should break their daughters in like the Indians do." I thought, "Right." I didn't think nothing about it. I can't remember if I got back in my own bed or just stayed there all night.

I got up next morning, I can't remember getting up the next morning, I just got on as normal, doing things as normal I think. I must not have gone to school, I don't think, because I will have had the bandage round my arm, I can't remember, but I just know it could become an everyday occurrence. I'd get in my bedroom, our Paul were living at… Oh, at this point, Donna had gone to live with my mum. Donna had gone to live with my mum, so. It were just me and Paul living at home. My dad had gone to get custody but he went to court to get custody of us. He went to court to get custody of us, legal custody of me and my brother. And then Mr Sykes, the social worker, came to the house and said to me, "It's obvious you've been to live with your mum once and it hasn't worked out and you've come back to live with your dad. It's obvious you can't make your mind up who you want to live with. So if you change your mind again, you will go in a children's home." Because he were emphasising that I couldn't make my mind up who I wanted to live with.

So at that point, that's when my dad went and got custody of us and went to court. And we'd come out, I remember we were going for a Chinese to celebrate or something like that in Barnsley, and the sexual abuse carried on from then. I think he were still going out with Jess, his girlfriend. I remember Paul… I know Paul saw him kissing me in the kitchen one Sunday morning, he come downstairs, Paul, and my dad were full on snogging me like a girlfriend and I think he'd seen us in bed as well that morning but nothing sexual and my dad had to explain and try and you know, work out, you know, I know it's, like it were nothing or something like that. Because I used to try and keep it from Paul, I try and hide it from Paul, the fact that he come in from the pub on a night out, and he'd come into my bedroom and I'd be like laid on my side, wanting to be asleep and pretending to be asleep, and I'd be in foetal position and he'd shake me and say, "Come on." And I'd be quiet because Paul would be in the next bedroom and I didn't want Paul to know, so I'd go into his room and he'd have sex with me, and he'd also - he'd had rude magazines and he used to make me read the stories in the blue pages to him and masturbate him and things like that.

He put my mum's engagement ring on my finger, and he tried to tell me that it was normal what has happening, a lot of his friends had incest, had relationships with their daughters and lived as a married couple. He told me that if I had or if I ever got pregnant, it would be an albino baby. And he would keep me off school to do the housework and the chores that my mum would normally do and he'd go and tend his land, what he used to rent off farmers. And he'd come home for his lunch or something, and this one time he had me lay done in front of the fire and to have sex with him. He made me go upstairs and get the condom out of his drawer and masturbating while I put the condom on, to get him hard, to put the condom on, and then laid me down in front of the fire. And the fire, log fire were burning my leg but I knew it would be over quick if I just kept quiet. And sometimes I used to pretend I was enjoying it and make some noises just so that it would be over quicker. And this one time, I couldn't stand for the, you know, you want - the fire were burning me too much, so I said my leg's hurting and he got really angry and had me - he's saying, "You're only fucking saying it because you don't want to have sex, because you don't want to do it." And I'm saying, "No, no, no. No, I do, I do, I do." So, there was never any screaming and shouting saying get off me or anything, I just accepted this as my role, it's just something I had to do.

He used to take photographs of me, he had a tin box. And in his tin box, I knew, I knew for the fact it were gone because when I made statements when I were 15, I made 17-paged statements to Penistone Police Station. I told them then, that he had his tin box and he had pictures. I don't know, a polaroid camera, and he had pictures of me. He used to get me to dress up in sexy underwear and like have hairbrush and pretend I were doing sexual acts with this hairbrush and he used to make me act out doing things. But he kept these things in a tin metal box and I just… and that will have gone, he will have hid that somewhere. And I remember thinking that when I told them about that back in the day. I don't know, he used to chat to me like a girlfriend. He told me to call him Sam even though his name were Elliott, I never heard his nickname before, Sam, and he said that his friends called it him when he were a child and I never knew that, but I've got a tattoo on my right shoulder that I have had removed that he took me for when I was 13, and it says Sam on the top but it's gone now, I've had it removed, and it said Carol on the bottom with a rose in the middle.

So basically, he wanted us to live together as man and wife happily ever after, so I just… I think I lived with him like that for about two year. But obviously not, because he didn't want Paul, do you know what I mean, so my brother. So it wasn't out in the open, it was like you know, sneaking about doing it but I never wanted Paul to know because I wanted to keep what bit of family we had left together.

DC YVONNE BREAR: When you talk about him, you said his name is Elliott, what's his full name?

CAROL HIGGINS: Elliott Appleyard.

DC YVONNE BREAR: Okay. And growing up, when you were growing up, where was it that you lived? I know you said you moved out with your mum and things but what was the family home?

CAROL HIGGINS: We lived at number 8 Gilthwaites Crescent and that were a two-bedroom house. So me, and Donna and Paul used to all share a bed then, or share a bedroom I mean. Me and Donna shared a bed and Paul had a single bed I think. But then we moved further up to number 26 Gilthwaites Crescent because that was a three-bedroom house.

DC YVONNE BREAR: And do you remember how old you were when you moved there?

CAROL HIGGINS: I think I were about eight, I think I were. And I don't remember any of the babysitters then. When Jane tells me this and my cousin Tony tells me that she used to babysit me when I were little and I know he's abused my cousin Tony, his niece. She used to babysit for us but I don't remember her. Because she used to say I liked my cuddles. Well, she once said this when I tried to contact her a couple of year ago, she said I remember you liked your cuddles and I couldn't remember kind of being a child down at number 8. I remember the violence, I remember the belt and having to bend over on the settee and lifting my nightie up and we didn't wear pants for bed anyway because sometimes it'd be when I'd had a bath but I never had - I'd have to - but if I had pants on I'd have pull my pants down when he used to beat me, he made me bend over and do it. I suppose I didn't think that was sexual until… Because it just seemed normal to us, that's what were normal.

So we moved up to number 26. I remember when I were at that age. I remember my sister Donna went into a children's home and she had grand mal epilepsy and she was slow, she went to a special school called Lydgate at New Mill. She couldn't even learn properly so she was slow, you know, backwards. And my mum said she told me that she moved her there because of my dad's violence and because she couldn't cope with her illness, with her disability, but she said it was down to my dad's violence as well. I don't know. I know my mum, like I say, he used to hold guns to her head, double barrel shotguns, because he used to have farmer's rights for shooting. And she once had a sexy dream or something and he dragged her downstairs and ripped her nightie off and he had this big machete and he held it to her vagina and he says, "If you don't tell me who it is, who are you talking about, I'm going to slit you from the vagina straight up right up to your neck." And she was screaming and crying and I saw her just pee herself, she got no clothes on, she just peed like a cow peeing in a field, I remember this pee gushing out of her and him saying. She's shouting, "Phone the police, phone the police." And he said, "You get upstairs or else I'm going to do the same to you." So we never. I know I never phoned police on that but it were just continual violence in our house.

If my mum went to supermarket, he used to time her how long she'd gone and accused her of shagging somebody if she weren't home by a certain time and stuff. I remember when I went back to live with him, this blue bikini that I'd bought off the market, I used to just - I used to watch the Dukes of Hazard on TV and I used to like the girl on it and she used to wear a bikini and I were a teenager and I wanted to look sexy, and I remember wearing this bikini, putting it on and sunbathing at the back garden. And his field where he rented, there's a ginnel where I lived on number 26, there's a ginnel down the side and he used to always walk up and down that ginnel to get to his field, and he could see our house from there. So he'd see me sunbathing with this bikini on, and he ripped it, you know, he said get in the house now and he's got the bikini off me and burnt it in the fireback, and.

And that was obviously then I'd realise that was, you know, his jealousy, so he was jealous of me as well, I couldn't go out with my friends. If I were out with my friends in the village, if he drove past in his van, he'd watch me. If I'd be in the cricket field with my friends or something and he'd send my brother down and said, "Me fatha wants you now." And then he'd - I'd get home and he'd say, "You can't go out now." And then he'd go out to the pub, my brother would be there, but then he'd come in from the pub, and he'd come in my bedroom and he'd get me, and he'd get my arm and take me into his room and he'd have sex with me. So, everything just felt like normal, it was just a normal routine to do that, I don't know, I must've - I don't know how I'm supposed to describe it.

DC YVONNE BREAR: How old is Elliott now?

CAROL HIGGINS: I'd say - I don't know, about 67, 68 maybe. I don't know.

DC YVONNE BREAR: And do you have contact with him?

CAROL HIGGINS: I haven't had contact with him since the day I left, I left. He'd been beating me and calling me pathetic and sexually abusing me for about two year. And then the night I left, I was crying and asking him to stop, and I was on the floor, I was shaking, and he was saying, "Get up, you're pathetic. Get up." And he were kicking me in the stomach, and I just thought that's the last time, even though I'd been threatened that I would go in the children's home if I did say something, I was 15, and I thought, and it was, I just couldn't take anymore. So when he went to the pub that night at Denby Dale Pie Hall, I got on the bus from Denby Dale Salvation Army steps and I got on the bus to Penistone. And when I get on the bus, my mum got on the bus with Carl, her boyfriend at the time, and she'd gone to live at Thurgoland then. And when I got on the bus, she says, "What are you doing here?" I told her everything that my dad had been doing to me, about the abusing, and she said, "Where is your dad now?" And I said, "He's at Denby Dale Pie Hall." So she phoned him and they brought him to the phone and she says, "Our Carol, she's here with me now and she's told me everything." And his first words were to my mum, "You can't prove a thing."

And then my mum wanted me to go to the police and then make a statement but I didn't. I felt partly to blame for what had been happening and I didn't. But I went a week later. And I went a week later and they took a 17-page statement off me. And then they took me to Huddersfield Police Station and I had forensic tests, internals and putting pubes and things like that, giving them pubes and I were bleeding internally and they had me jumping up and down on blotting paper. I think they thought I were miscarrying, I don't know. Even though I told them that he'd always used a condom. And so then they told me that my brother would be classed as a juvenile witness and that if it went to court that my name would be made mud and blackened, and I'd be made out to be the biggest liar going and that I'd be made out to be the biggest slag going.

DC YVONNE BREAR: Who said that, sorry?

CAROL HIGGINS: The police officer said that if it went to court, that this is how they would blacken my name and he said that they would. And because I'd had sex before, I felt guilty and ashamed, and I didn't want that lad to get done, David, because he didn't rape me. He was older, I think he was about 17 or something like that, maybe 19, I don't know, but I were reaching out for affection at that time, and it just didn't feel like rape. But I think that's what my dad thought, that's why now looking back, that's why he were angry when David were in Barnsley and shopping with me because he didn't like him being that familiar because he obviously knew that he wanted that role to break me in, so. And I'm sure I think I told him as well. I think I told him in Barnsley bus station that I had sex with him, so he knew that he wouldn't be actually breaking me in. I think I did.

But he used to also make me have oral sex with him and, you know, he stank, he were vile, he were dirty. But he used to say, "Who loves you baby?" And "you better…" And I used to have to say to him, "You do," and he used to say, "You better believe it." And if I didn't say, "You do," and he used to repeat it. Really, I was just complying to everything that he would ask of me really.

DC YVONNE BREAR: So you lived at home with your mum, your dad, your sister Donna and Paul. What age difference is it between you, Donna and Paul?

CAROL HIGGINS: Exactly a year. So I'm the middle one. Paul is the youngest. So I'm 46, so Paul would've been 11 or 12 at the time. I remember it being 12, 13 and then 13 and 14.

DC YVONNE BREAR: Okay. And you said that when you moved to this second address, there were three bedrooms there. So who would be in what room at that house?

CAROL HIGGINS: Paul would be in his own bedroom. And me and Donna used to share a double bed in this double bedroom because of Donna's fits as well, epileptic fits, I used to take care of her if she had fits in the night, I could hold her down so that she wouldn't fall out of bed, so we shared a double bed.

JUDGE JAMESON: I think that looks like a suitable moment. Yes, all right. Right, well, sorry, I'm afraid that was rather a short afternoon, ladies and gentlemen. That was unexpected but, anyway, not to worry. If there are, obviously, needs for anybody to be away, don't hesitate to say because, of course, we'll adjust our sitting hours around but if I could have a bit of notice, it would be helpful and then we can perhaps try and sit a little bit earlier or something like that but, anyway, not to worry. So that's it for today, I'm afraid. So thank you very much indeed for your attention thus far. We'll come back to this tomorrow morning. Half past ten all right for everybody? Okay. Remember please the two directions about not talking about the evidence and not making any enquiries of your own and I hope the appointment goes well and I hope you all have a good afternoon and evening. See you all tomorrow morning, half past ten. Thank you very much.

(The jury left court at 2.47 p.m.)

JUDGE JAMESON: Right. Well, I hope that doesn't throw timing out too much but I don't think there's much I----

MR HAMPTON: No, well, it's----

JUDGE JAMESON: -- can do about it, I'm afraid.

MR HAMPTON: I'm sure it's not a problem. It's nice for it to not to be the Bar for once. Nice for it to be the jury.

JUDGE JAMESON: There we are. All right. Right.

MR HAMPTON: Mr Storey and I are working on whether there can be an agreement of some witnesses, so we're actively trying to----

JUDGE JAMESON: Good. All right.

MR HAMPTON: -- shorten where we can.

JUDGE JAMESON: Well, if there is anything I need to do, tell me about it tomorrow morning.

MR HAMPTON: Certainly.

(2.49 p.m.)

Diary: Monday 14th January 2019 (continued)

Only thirty minutes passed before proceedings ended for the day. Del told me that one of the jurors had passed a note to the court clerk who passed it on to the Judge. It read that she had an appointment with her doctor, which she couldn't miss. The Judge played my video statement for half an hour then court finished for the day because of this woman. I couldn't believe it, all that time and money wasted for everyone.

After the court had emptied Glad and Dave came to say goodbye and said Appleyard was shaking his head all the time he was watching my video statement.

The police should have escorted Del and I back home as arranged but we were told by the police we would have to wait two hours before they could get a car to us. They suggested we get a taxi and claim it back through the expense system. Instead, we walked to the train station, trying not to feel too disappointed, focusing on the positives from the day. At least the case had started.

When we arrived at Fitzwilliam station I had to walk home through the woods and fields in my high heels but was glad of the fresh air. When I got home Laura from ISVA called to tell me the police wouldn't be picking me up until 10.00am because the Court might be delayed. This added more stress. What if it wasn't? I would be late, plus the public gallery might be full and I wanted Del to be present. I knew that the police would only be providing two days protection, despite my fear. To reduce further stress I was advised to call security to arrange disability parking outside the court for Day Three. I have a blue disability badge due to having low anterior resection syndrome (LARS) as a result of 9 hours of bowel cancer surgery. Making my own arrangements to get to court and not having to rely on the police helped me to feel more in control but the anxiety and fear that something or someone would stop me from getting there remained.

Back home it's hard to rest my mind, I'm exhausted and need time to think and relax. Friends have been calling to see how I have got on but I can't answer because I had been told that talking about the trial could jeopardise the case. Apart from that, I have no energy left. However, someone sends me a message saying that my story was in the Barnsley Chronicle, which sends me into panic because my barrister had told me that under no circumstance should I go on social media to tell my story anymore or speak to the press during the trial. I try to contact the press to tell them not to report anymore, I manage to speak to a reporter from the Huddersfield Examiner who puts my mind at rest that what had been written was normal court reporting and would not jeopardise my case.

I get into bed and am surprised to see a big, bright lone star shining outside my window, I know it is Divine intervention and I call it the "Star of Justice." Before the trial, on New Year's Eve 2018, I turned the Premier God Channel on the TV. The presenter said "there is a lady just tuned in and she is taking her dad to court in January for incest and she needs to know she is going to be alright." I knew this was me. Just like I know the star is for me.

Diary: Tuesday 15th January 2019: Day 2

I woke before the alarm which I had set for 6.00 am. The bath I had last night while listening to Beethoven's Concerto NO 4 by the Vienna Philharmonic Orchestra seemed to help me relax, but it was short lived. Last night I had a nightmare that I had arrived at court and the Judge was waiting to start proceedings but the police had not provided all my evidence. He said the trial could not commence without it. I begged him to allow me to go and look for it, he told me to hurry up, if I was not back in half an hour, he would dismiss the trial. I was running through a huge building, the police headquarters, frantically searching in and out of offices, in filing cabinets and on desktops for the rest of my evidence. Thankfully I must have found it because the trial continued. The nightmare did nothing to quell my anxieties.

I am still angry that the lady stopped court proceedings yesterday at such short notice to go to the doctors and worried she has set the whole case back. Only eight days have been scheduled for the trial, this might not be enough time to get all of the witnesses into court.

I should have been going into court at 10.30 am to give my evidence, but instead the jury have to listen to the rest of the video statement. One and a half hours left then I go in at twelvish. Laura said the police car isn't picking me up until 10.00 am which is cutting it a bit fine. What's more, because lots of people are coming today, I'm worried Del won't get a seat.

I prayed and read my Bible, as I do every morning, I'm now onto Psalm 74. Sonja and Jan sent messages saying Jesus loves me. This made me cry, as I often do when people show me empathy and compassion or give me a compliment, I am not used to a show of affection. I find it hard to accept, nobody has ever cared about my feelings.

15th January 2019 – Day 2

I remember the look in my dad's eyes yesterday as we stared at each other and I recall his evil anger, furious because I didn't back down. This triggers my PTSD and I start to purge uncontrollably. The evil he had put inside me needs to come out. I cough, choke, gag, retch uncontrollably with tears in my eyes, it is draining. I struggle to breathe, trying to stop myself from being sick but the vile feelings want to come out. I have lived with these extreme physical and emotional reactions throughout my life. At times I have wanted to pull the floorboards over my head and just disappear. One time I got down on my hands and knees on my landing and shouted out "Please God, help me, I can't take any more." All of a sudden, I felt like I was no longer on my floorboards. I was a big white horse with powerful wings soaring through the sky. I could hear the sound of my wings flapping. My stomach lunged as I looked down on the expanse of the Earth below. It was such a feeling of peace, escaping from reality. I later read in Revelations that a single white horse signifies victory, I believe there is something greater than me. My son Jake and I were both sitting on the settee chatting one evening when I heard a voice saying "beware of the steps you are taking." I looked at Jake in disbelief and said "did you hear that?" He looked at me and said "Yes," and repeated what I had heard. We were both in shock and once again felt that there was something bigger than us out there. We questioned what it could possibly mean, beware of what?

My spiritual journey started when I was thirty-two years old. I felt alone and heartbroken that I could not make my marriage work. I had left my husband after fifteen years and was raising our two young children on my own with no other family for support. Both my family and my husband's had thrown me into exile because I would not "do as you are told!" I had been surrounded by manipulating, bullying controllers who were making my life hell. I was looking for love and often in the wrong places. One Valentine's morning I was drawn to go to church. The sermon being given by the Pastor was about the way husbands should love their wives and the way wives should love their husbands. I listened with tears streaming down my face, stifling sobs. I was barely able to stand, wanting to fall to the ground on my hands and knees. I was thinking "Why haven't I ever been taught this?" I was hearing for the first time what love is and Jesus was the one who was teaching me. My newfound Faith gave me the hope and strength to carry on and still does to this day.

Waiting for the police to pick us up is frustrating because I am scared we are going to be late. I'm tired before I get there. Waiting, waiting, waiting. Thirty five years of waiting. That's all I do! Yesterday I waited outside the courtroom all day, I hope I get to take the stand today without further hitches. I keep checking my phone as hundreds of Facebook friends send wishes of support like, "I hope the bastard rots in hell" and "You've got this Carol, stay strong." I had been forced to be loyal to my father as a child by harbouring his vile secrets. Now is the time for me to break the chains and set myself free by telling my truth. He will not get away with the years of suffering he has put me through and now this. Making me out to be a liar and a slag.

9.00 am, still waiting for the police to take us to court, I can't stand to hear the voices on the telly, I feel so angry and tearful. I hate going through this, it's the hardest mountain I've ever had to climb and it makes me feel sick and tired, totally violated.

We eventually arrived at Leeds Crown Court at 10.30am.

Tuesday 15 January 2019

(Transcript prepared without the aid of documentation)

(10.37 a.m.)

JUDGE JAMESON: Welcome back, ladies and gentlemen. You had, I think, your leaflet yesterday, either yesterday or this morning. At some point, read it if you would, please. It's really no more than a written record of what I was saying to you yesterday but the latest practice is that you have to have it in writing as well, so you've got it. Don't read it now because we are going to crack on with the evidence, but at some point when you have a convenient moment, if you just read your way through it, thank you very much. Yes?

CAROL HIGGINS

(Continuation of video evidence played)

Video Statement (Part 2 of 3)

Video Statement

DC YVONNE BREAR: And what age were Donna when she went into the children's home?

CAROL HIGGINS: I'd say she were about 13. I'd say she were about 13 because I remember they went on a school trip to, a trip to France from there. And she didn't know how to use, and she would be on her period that week they were going. Because of her disability and her slowness, she didn't know how to use Tampax because I remember my mum trying to explain. I went up and I showed Donna how to use it, I tried to show her how to use a Tampax, but, because I remember her coming back and all her clothes were covered in blood because she never really got how to use it, she were too slow.

DC YVONNE BREAR: And did she stay in the children's home from that age?

CAROL HIGGINS: No, she went into 2 children's home - she went into one in Holmfirth and then she went into one in Dewsbury, Coombs Hill, and she were there for quite a long time I think, maybe a year or so. I know she were abused in that children's home, she used to tell me there were a girl called Veronica who used to bully her. And there weren't a lock on the bathroom door, and she said they used to put, tried to push soap inside her, lads and that. So the threat of this me going to the children's home, do you know, it absolutely petrified me.

DC YVONNE BREAR: Yeah. And you spoke earlier about the time that he took you on the walk and he kissed you properly the first time, you said you were about 11 and then…

CAROL HIGGINS: I think I were about 12 more like, yeah.

DC YVONNE BREAR: Okay, so about 12. And then you've told mum about that and then that's when the social workers have come and seen you at school, but nothing really happened. And is it after then that mum took you and you lived at these other addresses and then you returned back to dad's care?

CAROL HIGGINS: Yeah.

DC YVONNE BREAR: And how long do you think you were away from dad's care when you went with mum to these other addresses?

CAROL HIGGINS: About eight month I'd say, six, eight month, six month. It's hard to remember. But when I went back to my mum, she did say, when I went back, "When you came back to me, when you'd have enough of being an adult, when you'd had enough of being treated like an adult, you came back to me. What the hell did you expect me to do about it?" And because she said that and she said to me - because I went back to live with my dad after that time, about eight month period, six, eight month when he bought me a pair of jeans and she said, what a price you'd paid for that pair of jeans, I feel like somebody knew. She knew what were going to happen to me, and they expected me to know what were going to happen to me. To me, that's what it sounds like. And I didn't know what were going to happen to me. When I cut my wrist, I didn't know what were going to happen to me, I didn't know when I went back there. I had forgot about the kissing. I honestly did not know what were going to happen to me, and I wish she'd have told me, she'd have known and she had an inkling no doubt.

I wish she'd have told me because then when I went there to live with him, he used to poison me about my mum, and I used to call her a slag when we used to see her at weekends on the time when I used to go and see her. And I used to be angry with her but he were poisoning me against her, and I know that now, but I didn't know that at the time. And even though I didn't want to live with her, it would've been better to live with her than to have, continued living there with all that happening. But I didn't know and I believe that somebody knew.

DC YVONNE BREAR: Yeah. And that's just through comments your mum said to you, you think she knew that it was going to happen, yeah.

CAROL HIGGINS: Yeah. And she'd call me a drama queen all my life and told me that what a price you've paid for that pair of jeans, God Almighty if she'd known why in the fuck didn't she tell me?

DC YVONNE BREAR: Tissue.

CAROL HIGGINS: She used to say, "Look at you, you're always looking in the mirror, you always liked fancying yourself." Now I know I were looking for some kind of - in myself, I were just looking for some kind of, I don't know, security, some love, something that I knew, familiar, I don't know, that felt - it's like, maybe, I don't know, I don't know why. I didn't know why my mum would be jealous or that's how it felt like. And I played the role, I actually, you know. He also said to me, "You're going to end up having 12 abortions…," he used to call me a slag and he said because how I used to dressed, but all of my friends wore short skirts at that age when I was at school and I used to have my hair at different colours with a short crew cut or something like that or all to one side. And he used to say to me, "Look at you, you're going to end up like your cousin Tony. You're going to end up having 12 abortions by the time you're 18." Well, Tony, she were my cousin, I used to think she were bonny and I used to look at her and think she got a lovely figure and stuff like that. I only found, I didn't know at that time that he'd been abusing her, I found out that afterwards. But to me, that tells me if he's been saying that, that she's had terminations to him and this is his niece that he used to take home and have sex with her over the Thorpes from Denby Dale to Skelmanthorpe in his van and I think that's where it's happened.

DC YVONNE BREAR: When Elliott was in a relationship with Jess, did she stay over at the house?

CAROL HIGGINS: Yeah, she must've done because she lived at Penistone. So he were angry with my mum still with divorce, from leaving him, but he met Jess. But, yeah, and then he were doing that to me as well. But, yes, she must've stayed over, yeah.

DC YVONNE BREAR: Do you remember a surname or any of the family's name?

CAROL HIGGINS: No, I just know her family used to live on Green Road in Penistone. I can see her mum's face but—and she had short blonde hair, chubby-ish woman with glasses but he'll know who she were obviously.

DC YVONNE BREAR: And how old will she be about now (overlapping conversation)?

CAROL HIGGINS: I'd say she was a bit younger than him, so I'd say now she must be about 65 I'd say - no, about 60. About 60 I'd say.

DC YVONNE BREAR: And you said that she will have seen the play fighting where he's giving you the love bites?

CAROL HIGGINS: Yeah.

DC YVONNE BREAR: And whereabouts would he give you those love bites?

CAROL HIGGINS: On my neck so people could see them.

DC YVONNE BREAR: And what about when you went to school, did people comment?

CAROL HIGGINS: I just kept quiet. If somebody said who's your boyfriend, I just - I can't remember what I said. I never told anybody. I never told anybody. I just know that I felt like a slag and that people, boys, wouldn't be interested in me because they think I've got somebody else or, you know, because I've got these on my neck. Yeah, go on.

DC YVONNE BREAR: No, were you going to say something then? I don't want to cut you off.

CAROL HIGGINS: Yeah, but it's gone out of my head now.

DC YVONNE BREAR: Sorry.

CAROL HIGGINS: It's gone out my head. Yeah, go on.

DC YVONNE BREAR: So, when, you were about 12 when this kissing happened, and then you've gone off with mum six, eight months, which is when you've met this David Wadsworth.

CAROL HIGGINS: Yeah.

DC YVONNE BREAR: And then you've met dad in Barnsley bus station with him.

CAROL HIGGINS: Yeah.

DC YVONNE BREAR: He's bought you the jeans, you've got this bikini. And then how soon was it before you returned home to dad?

CAROL HIGGINS: I'd say about maybe two or three week, a few week, I'd say a few week, because I was still at Penistone Grammar School and I were still meeting up with friends in Penistone. And my brother were living with my dad at that time, and our Donna was. And I keep going to tell you something and it's gone out my mind again. So it were a few week that I rang my dad and said I want you to come pick me up I want to come back and live with you. Like I said, my mum had found her new freedom and she were off on her own and, you know, a lot of time. People were saying did you know your mum were slag of Penistone and things like that, so. I weren't getting the attention that I really wanted from her really.

DC YVONNE BREAR: So you've returned back to dad's house and was Donna living there then?

CAROL HIGGINS: Yeah.

DC YVONNE BREAR: Okay. And then you spoke about the incident where you've got the knife and dad's been at the phone box and you've got the knife and you cut yourself, your brother's taken you around to the phone box and that's the night when he first raped you? That day, sorry, how long was it before you were living back at dad's to that incident happening?

CAROL HIGGINS: If I've gone back there and he's waited while I've…? It's got to have been maybe about two month I think, something like that. Roughly about I think. It were about two month.

DC YVONNE BREAR: Okay. And…?

CAROL HIGGINS: Another thing that I just want to remind you before I forget. When I was 16 and I went to work at SR Gents and I got my own house because my mum kicked me out at 16. His wife were, Janet who he's with now, were going to, he met her after I'd left, after I'd left, and she asked me, or she's told me, she rang SR Gents, and they said there's a number here, this lady wants you to ring her. So I didn't know who she was, so I rang her, and I said what do you want? She says "I'm Janet", she says "I'm about to marry your dad but I've heard that things have happened, and I want to know if it's true before I do marry him." And I said, "okay," I said, "but only if you're prepared to believe me," I said "because I'm not going to waste my time if you're not." So she said, "yeah, I do, I will believe, I will believe you, I want to meet you."

So we met in a café in Barnsley this Saturday morning, I went to this café and we were talking for about two hours. And I didn't know this but for some reason when I finished talking to her, she asked me loads of questions about what had happened and I told her, and she says to me your father's upstairs in the café, do you want to see him? And I thought to myself, oh, God, I remember thinking that's a quick yes or no, you've got to decide here, so I just went, yeah, okay, I will, because I was scared of him. Anyway, I saw him, because I'd always, if I used to see him in Barnsley market, I used to nearly collapse and hyperventilating, nearly be sick and I'd - do you know what I mean, I couldn't control how I felt. So when she said that, I thought, yeah, I'll see him, I don't know what I was going to achieve but I'll see him. Anyway, she went into the café and he come out, so she wasn't there then and we sat on these red seats on top of Barnsley Market and I said to him why did you do what you did? And he said to me then, "I'm sorry, it's because I loved you as a person and not as a daughter." So he's gone from the first time telling me, you know, he broke me in because that's what Indians do, break their daughters in, to then saying to me he was sorry. But no witnesses there, saying that it's because he loved me as a person and not as a daughter.

DC YVONNE BREAR: And that's when you were 16?

CAROL HIGGINS: That's when I was 16 and that was the same time as meeting Janet, that she wanted me to, so then he's gone back home, Paul was still living there at that house with my dad before he come to live with me in my rented house. And Paul's heard Janet confront my father about this and Paul said he'd heard my father say to Janet because I'd come on to him and he denied me, I'd come up there with these allegations of rape, and that's how it's all come about that why I'm saying it's because I've come onto him and he's denied me and this is why I'm saying all this, and my brother said he heard her say that. He heard, yeah, him saying that. But I don't have a relationship with - I've heard this once years and years ago, so I just thought, you know, that our Paul remembers all these. I can remember being told it.

DC YVONNE BREAR: You spoke about the first time it happened which is when you cut your wrist, that was the first time, and then you said that it's happened on a number of occasions where he's had sex with you, oral sex. He's got you to dress up in sexy lingerie, photograph you. How often…?

CAROL HIGGINS: Read magazines to him, masturbate him.

DC YVONNE BREAR: Yeah, masturbate, and how often would these incidents happen, say on a weekly basis?

CAROL HIGGINS: I'd say three or four times on a weekly basis.

DC YVONNE BREAR: And would that always happen when he'd been to the pub?

CAROL HIGGINS: No, sometimes it'll happen during the day when Paul was at school and I was told to stay at home and school bobbies would come to the house wondering why I wasn't at school. He put the ring on my finger, why are you treating me like a wife? And he'd hit me then and then he'd like expect me to make liver and onions like my mum and stuff like that, and if it wasn't made the same, he'd get angry, and.

DC YVONNE BREAR: Yeah. How old were you the first time it happened?

CAROL HIGGINS: That night when I cut my wrists?

DC YVONNE BREAR: Yeah.

CAROL HIGGINS: I'd say I were 13, 13 and a half, yeah.

DC YVONNE BREAR: And you said that it stopped when you 15 which is the night…

CAROL HIGGINS: I think the love bites started when I were 12 and the kissing and stuff, and I think that started maybe when I were 13.

DC YVONNE BREAR: And then it stopped when you were 15 and that's because you left that night when you got the bus and met your mum on the bus?

CAROL HIGGINS: Yeah.

DC YVONNE BREAR: And you said that he always used protection when it was ...?

CAROL HIGGINS: He said that if I got pregnant, it would be an albino baby.

DC YVONNE BREAR: Okay. Was Donna ever in bed with you, because you shared a bed when he's come and woke you up?

CAROL HIGGINS: No, because Donna had gone to live with my mum at that time. Donna gone to live with my mum. Donna's not here anymore, she committed suicide.

DC YVONNE BREAR: Right, I'm sorry to hear that.

CAROL HIGGINS: Yeah. And I don't know if he's done it to Donna or not.

DC YVONNE BREAR: Okay. So Donna went to live with your mum and then is it from your mum she went in the children's home?

CAROL HIGGINS: No, it was before when we were all together as a family together before the love bites started and that. What did you just say then? Was it before…?

DC YVONNE BREAR: About her going in the children's home. Because you said she went to live with your mum for a bit. So was she with mum and then where, to the children's home?

CAROL HIGGINS: No, we was all together, that's why my mum put her in because we were all together in a violent family and she says - she told me one time the reason she put Donna in the children's home was because she couldn't cope with her disability, with her epilepsy because of my dad's violence. And then when Donna was in the children's home, so there were me, Paul, my mum and dad living at home, I remember awful - I thought Donna was my real sister all my life, and I didn't know that she's really my half-sister, that my mum was pregnant when she met my dad. She were pregnant with Donna when she met my dad. So he told her on the phone that he wasn't her real dad and I remember that breaking Donna's heart because she didn't know that, and he told her that when she were in the home over the telephone.

DC YVONNE BREAR: Right. And then you spoke about two incidents that you can remember where you think that Paul, your brother saw your dad kissing you in the kitchen and then once in bed?

CAROL HIGGINS: I don't know if he saw him kissing me in bed but I know he used to see us on a Saturday morning when Paul were playing out, he'd see us in bed. But you see, we used to have play fighting with my mum and dad in bed and things like that, us growing up. So I don't know if he just saw it as that.

DC YVONNE BREAR: And did he ever say anything to you when he saw your dad kiss you in the kitchen?

CAROL HIGGINS: And I remember Paul being really upset and confused, and I remember being - I were upset and confused that he'd seen it because I tried to keep everything from Paul. And I remember my dad getting flustered and panicking, and how he were trying to explain that kind of thing, what had happened, so, I can't remember how it got resolved, and I just remember it being, God, how is this going to...? How are you going to hide this one? He managed to somehow. But he can't have hidden it completely because Paul's got children of his own and he won't let them nowhere near him. He says, "Once a paedophile always a paedophile." So even though - I don't know what he's seen, I don't think he's seen us have, you know. And, you know, intercourse, whatever, it's disgusting.

DC YVONNE BREAR: And you said that you told your mum about the kissing incident when you were about 12 and then two social workers came and spoke to you about it. And then you didn't tell anybody about any of the sexual abuse up until the point that you left and that was your mum that you told?

CAROL HIGGINS: No. I think before I left, I think I told a girl called Dianne Croft who were a friend of mine back then, but. And I think her parents, I told them. But, but nothing was said. And I guess I imagine now just nobody wanted to get involved and they knew my father. My father were a bully of the village. People used to call him 'has been' and he were known for being an aggressive violent man, and I imagine people just wanted to mind their own business and keep out of our business, I don't know.

DC YVONNE BREAR: So you told Dianne Croft, a friend?

CAROL HIGGINS: Yeah, just before I left.

DC YVONNE BREAR: Was she the same age as you?

CAROL HIGGINS: Yeah.

DC YVONNE BREAR: And her parents as well?

CAROL HIGGINS: I think so, yeah.

DC YVONNE BREAR: And then Paul's seen the kissing incident? And then you spoke about your cousin Tony, she'd seen some violence towards you that you don't remember when you was a baby?

CAROL HIGGINS: No, that was Jane Ibotson who saw the violence. So Jane was the babysitter and so was my cousin Tony was a babysit - I can't remember them being babysitters but, yeah, Jane had witnessed him being violent to me as a baby, yeah.

DC YVONNE BREAR: Okay. And when this violence happened when you were younger, do you remember how it was with your brother and your sister?

CAROL HIGGINS: He was violent to them as well, aggressive. And he used to say he used to beat us and say if you carry on - shut up crying or I'll give you something to cry for or rua for, so I just know he were violent with all of us.

DC YVONNE BREAR: Are you all right to carry on or do you want a break?

CAROL HIGGINS: Yeah, no, I'm okay, yeah.

DC YVONNE BREAR: So then you said that when you left, you were on a bus you saw mum and then you disclosed to mum everything that had been happening, and she wanted you to report it to police?

CAROL HIGGINS: Yeah.

DC YVONNE BREAR: But you didn't at that time, it was a week later when you gave a 17-page statement. You went to Huddersfield police station and had a medical?

CAROL HIGGINS: Yup.

DC YVONNE BREAR: And what happened…? That you're aware of what happened with that investigation?

CAROL HIGGINS: I don't know. I know they didn't investigate, they didn't take a statement from my brother or my mum, I know that hadn't been done. And I told you they said to me that my name will be made mud and dragged through court and my name would be blackened and I've been made out to be a slag and things like that. As far as I know, they arrested my dad, took him to Kirkburton Police Station, this is what I've heard. Forensics went into his house, took a forensic test of his sheets, bedroom, stuff like that. Nothing was found. My dad's told them that I used to sleep around with numerous lads and stuff, and that it just - and that they've let them go and it were my word against his. So it's never been investigated properly because Sonya Strafford's kept telling me that it can't be reopened because it's been investigated, but it hasn't because when they told me that at Penistone Police Station about my name being dragged through the court and could I handle that, and I said no. They said because it'd never been sent - gone to crown prosecution, if it had gone to CPS crown prosecution and I had lost the case, it can't be brought back. But because it hasn't, there would always be a chance in the future because they had his statements as well, and Paul wouldn't be then classed as a juvenile witness that I could bring it back in the future. So I have always kept, you know, that I would be able to. And then when I have tried to, on numerous occasions, I've had different excuses for the reason - poor excuses for reasons not being able to.

DC YVONNE BREAR: Okay. And what are the other occasions that you've tried?

CAROL HIGGINS: Ten year ago, well, it'd be longer than that now, when I lived in Cockerham Avenue in Barnsley. I phoned and reported historical sexual abuse, and I think I spoke to Sonya Strafford at that time, and she looked into it and got back to me, and said that the statements have been lost and the forensic evidence as well. And I was really, really upset then. And I said is there no way I can start compiling my statements again, and she said no, and I said please, and so she let me, she says okay then. So now I know it were just to appease me, it must've been because she didn't pull me in to do it, she let me do it at home, I started doing it, remembering like I'm telling you now, so, and I wrote so much in it, and then I rang her up and I said "I've started doing them, is this the kind of thing that you want?" So I met her for the first time and she come to my house and to pick them up. I hadn't finished them. I knew I got a list as long my arm to write about, but, and I just started with it. But I wanted to know if that was the kind of thing she wanted. So she didn't read it when I gave it and she just took it and went. So then I got a phone call, I remember exactly, and I was on the front lawn, and I got a phone call saying that she'd given the evidence to CPS what I've just written and that there wasn't enough for it to go to court and that the door would be closed on it forever, and I were crying, I were heartbroken, I'm like, "You're joking, you're joking. You can't do this to me. It's not complete, I told you it wasn't complete. You've got to let me do this." And now I'm fuming because she'd done that anyway, she was, "No, that's it, that's it." And she put the phone down on me, she wouldn't come and tell me to my face or anything like that, so I were absolutely fuming, so then I had to start to carry on and accept what I've been told. And then about five years ago, I was around at my friend's house and I were talking about it again, and I just said at that time I need to do this again, I need to ring the police and tell them again. So I phoned them again and I think that was Sonya Miller again, Sonya Strafford, I keep calling her Miller, again. And she said that unless I got another witness, and it'd happened to somebody else, I wouldn't be able to go forward with it because the statements have been lost, because there's no - and I'm like, well, other people bring historical cases, you know, who haven't made statements from years before but she said - and because she says the case has already been investigated, this is what she kept emphasising to me, and that's what I'm telling you, it hasn't been investigated. So then I went on the hunt looking for my cousin Tony because I knew he done it to her. So I phoned my cousin Les, this is his sister - Tony's brother Leslie, my cousin Les, and I found him and he found Tony, he gave me Tony's address and I rang Tony, I got her number on my phone but she said she'd already - she has got bipolar and she'd already the year before gone to court through some sexual assault case and it'd been thrown out, so, and she wasn't prepared to go through none of that again, so then it was - the door was closed on me again. And then I've been - Sergeant Sewell, Philippa Wright and Sergeant Sewell, and another sergeant, I've got it written down here. They were part of the investigation I think the time after that that I brought it because I brought it - I tried to bring it not last year, the year before, there's so many times I'm getting them mixed up, I've got dates on here.

DC YVONNE BREAR: If you want to get your dates out, that's fine.

CAROL HIGGINS: These are, (muttering) amongst all of 'em. But they then turned it around and said that I haven't got enough evidence. So this is when... Because Tony wouldn't be a witness, you know, she wouldn't say that he'd done it to her, so that closed the door on that one again. So then I tried again, I've got some things here. And, then, I think it was the year before last, 10th of the 1st 2012, but then I brought it back. It was last year, I came, I sat here for five hours and made a statement.

DC YVONNE BREAR: Last year?

CAROL HIGGINS: Last year as well, but Sonya Strafford said that statements counted for jack shit because there wasn't enough evidence then. So she said that because of the statements being lost, I can't bring it forward, then she said I can't bring it forward because I need another witness and I haven't got one, then she said I can't bring it forward because I haven't enough evidence, so then I gave her Carron Garside's name and my mum and my brother, and she's apparently phoned them and told my brother when she said that - I mean, I've told her that my brother had seen him kissing me, she said that her husband kisses their daughter and gets into bed with them, and that's not classed as evidence. When I give her the letter last year that my mum wrote to me saying that she knew, it states in there that she knew that I was being abused, she's saying that's not evidence. When I said about Carron Garside she said she's been to see her, that's not evidence. So she closed the door on me again.

DC YVONNE BREAR: Okay. Who is Carron Garside?

CAROL HIGGINS: Carron Garside, Alex Wilson has been to take a statement from her, she was my next-door neighbour when I were growing up. And Ena Kilty, she were my next door but two neighbour down, from growing up, so, they're recalling seeing the love bites and the violent, you know, violent behaviour towards me and his abusive behaviour.

DC YVONNE BREAR: And just what's your mum's name?

CAROL HIGGINS: Now she's called Jean Voss. Margaret Jean Voss. So you should still have that letter from last year that she wrote to me, that states as well that she knew he were having sex with me, raping me.

Mum's Letter

DC YVONNE BREAR: Okay, I can't comment because I don't know anything about the previous times that you've reported it but I'm sure Alex knows.

CAROL HIGGINS: I called the police department, my dad had sex with me when I was 12 or 13, I did it because I cannot let go of the fact he tried to make me his wife or fiancée by putting my name and my mum's engagement ring on my wedding finger. This was a while after he had sex with me. It's somewhere, I've got that somewhere. I've got here, 12th of the 1st 2012 at 4:00, Philippa Wright called me back after leaving her a message to let me know what was - to leave a message an hour before to call me to let me know what progress is being made. So that were back 12th of the 1st 2012 at

Normanton Police Station. Sergeant Sewell called said she'd called my mum and Paul, he sent a DI from child protection unit, an inspector to review everything, awaiting answer. So I know it's being done on - I forgot about that time, well, I haven't forgot, but. This is a letter from October 2014, I asked Sonya Strafford to write down evidence why it couldn't go to court, proof and that's what she wrote me, I wanted it in writing.

(no dictation)

CAROL HIGGINS: So that's them two files that I have, you can see that's one time and that's a separate time. And then I think I've got from 2005, them reports. Now, Sonya Strafford I think, told me, kept telling me that my statements have been lost, my original statements.

Sonya's Letter

DC YVONNE BREAR: The one from when you were 15?

CAROL HIGGINS: When I were 15. But I made a statement in here, last year as well so there should be some from there, but DI Mick Brown or I've got PC Jackson, I've got mixed up there, told me not to live in hope that they'll be found he says because "they've been burnt love," that's what he said to me.

DC YVONNE BREAR: Right. I don't know about that.

CAROL HIGGINS: Yeah, he said they've been burnt but then - I've left my pad at home, I've got some names on there. I've been told that there's a man, I forgot his name now, and he's an ex-copper, and I forgot his name now, I know Ena's mentioned him I think or. And he saw, it was about 16 years ago, he saw my statements in the archives at the police station, and Elliott Appleyard's step-daughter Pauline, she used to be in the police, at Dewsbury Police Station, she used to work there. She lives in America now, she went there seven years ago I've been told. But I've been told DI Farnley they call him I think, Brian Farnley, this guy, Furnley, Farnley, who used to be in the police. He went and arrested Gary Mannifield because my father phoned the police because Gary Mannifield had supposedly been calling my father names and a paedophile and that, so he used to - because I've been told that my - that he's a copper's nark, that's how I've had it described to me, that my dad's a police informer, he's been a copper's nark for years, that's what I've been told, so every time he phoned the police and somebody above in CID or summat, would be always protecting him obviously, would send policemen out and these policemen beat Gary Mannifield up and took him and arrested him for apparently calling my father a paedophile, and he got beat up, did Gary Mannifield, by loads of police at this time, and Gary Mannifield is saying you're protecting him, I don't know, how can you protect him? I dress my kids in the morning, not undress them, like this and he knows what he is. And Brian Farnley has recently said all these years, Gary I believed you when you told me what he said and he said he saw my statements at the police station and that it said there was a letter with them saying something about them being embarrassment to the family and they need to be removed or they're going to be removed. But if you interview Gary Mannifield, he will be able to tell you that whole story. I don't exactly know what happened.

(11.25 a.m.)

MR HAMPTON: Your Honour, I've just asked Mr Smith to pause it simply to offer your Honour and the jury the opportunity of a break if you feel it's wanted at this stage. We are about halfway through.

JUDGE JAMESON: Yes, well, I think probably that is a good idea because it is quite warm in here, so...

MR HAMPTON: I think your Honour is in the jury's hands.

JUDGE JAMESON: Yes, all right. I'll make a note of where we are. I think we'll take 15 minutes, ladies and gentlemen, just because it isn't that easy taking in a constant account like this. It's much easier when we do get on to questions and answers. So, we'll take a few minutes or thereabouts, so come back in, perhaps, at 20 to 12. Let's aim for that. It's a little bit over. I think that's probably better. Right.

(Short break)

JUDGE JAMESON: Yes?

(Continuation of video evidence played)

Video Statement (Part 3 of 3)

Video Statement

DC YVONNE BREAR: And who is Gary to you?

CAROL HIGGINS: Gary grew up on the same street as me, so.

DC YVONNE BREAR: And how old is Gary?

CAROL HIGGINS: About two year older than me I'd say, or three year older than me. And his mum's Ena Kilty as well, who Alex has taken a statement off as well, so that needs investigating with Brian Farnley about my statements as well.

DC YVONNE BREAR: And he's an ex-DI?

CAROL HIGGINS: Yeah, or an ex - what's one below a DI?

DC YVONNE BREAR: A DS.

CAROL HIGGINS: So I don't know but I knew he was in the police force.

DC YVONNE BREAR: Okay, so ex-police officer Brian Farnley?

CAROL HIGGINS: Yeah, yeah.

DC YVONNE BREAR: Okay.

CAROL HIGGINS: He's seen my statements. And he lives at Skelmanthorpe.

DC YVONNE BREAR: Okay. Over the years then, who, I know, I don't know if you've discussed it with different people but who have you spoke about what happened?

CAROL HIGGINS: I've had counselling for all my life, I went to Rape Crisis every Friday afternoon in Sheffield from Barnsley when I finished work at SR Gents. I used to get a train to, to Sheffield and go there every Friday, and then, that'd stop for a bit if I felt okay, and I was 16 so I remember social workers used to come to my rented house sometimes, and, um, and talk to me. I went to the doctor's once and the doctor told me that it were my dad he felt sorry for, um, not, and he needed counselling not me, oh, weird, that were when I was searching - and I think it weren't long after that somebody put me in touch with Rape Crisis in Sheffield. Erm. I've, er, seen Glenys Braylsforth. If you get my doctor's reports, you can see there I've got psychiatrists, counsellors with medical reports going back all my life, having to have intervention just to keep me above water really to stop me from going under. I've just got lists and lists and lists of different counsellors that I've had to go and see for that, whether it'd be through church groups, Dove House, I used to go to Dove House in Wakefield.

DC YVONNE BREAR: Were these referrals before?

CAROL HIGGINS: Barnsley Hospital through my doctor's, I used to go to Barnsley Hospital, I used to go Keresforth Centre. Erm. Um. Castleford Hospital. I've just, I've been going to my doctor's, I've been diagnosed with post-traumatic stress disorder, um, yeah, they know that I suffered with this all my life. Yeah.

DC YVONNE BREAR: And I know you just spoke about there, er, the PTSD suffering with that. How else has this affected your life?

CAROL HIGGINS: (sobbing) I don't know, it's just disabled me most of the time. It's just. It's hard for me to value myself. I've tried my best. I feel just angry every time I've gone in to see a counsellor, they can see I'm just consumed with anger, anger. Just like my daughter found out when she - because she found a letter that I'd written when I were younger, this is my blue folder that I keep everything in, that helps me, ya' know, (sobs) if I write things down it helps me and I just… It's devastated my life because it took my f, my father away from me, I wish somebody on the street had done it to me because then I would've still have my parents to, ya' know, to look after me and I've brought myself up on my own. Every morning even now I wake up scared because I've got nobody to catch me when I fall or anything, you know what I mean, I've got no family. (Crying) I look at other people and they make me jealous because they've got families, and on top of not having a family and grieving for a family, I've got this vileness inside me that I just want to - if I can get my hand inside out, just pull it all out, and it will never go away. (Sobbing) You just don't understand what it feels like, so, I just want to get inside, just get it out, and then fucking gone once and for all. And I don't even know if this court, this goes to court if that's what will happen but I need to stop feeling like this. I've got to stop feeling like this. He's took my whole life away from me, from what he's controlled and forced into me, I feel like I will never know what I would be if he hadn't done all that things to me. Every day I smile, yeah, I smile but it's all a fake a lot of it. I don't know who I am.

DC YVONNE BREAR: Do you take medication?

CAROL HIGGINS: No.

DC YVONNE BREAR: No, and have you ever been prescribed medication?

CAROL HIGGINS: Yeah, I took Prozac for 12 year and I took it, and as soon as I got divorced, I put it in the bin and I tried to manage without it, and I tried to get through without it. I don't, you know, they call them happy pills and I've been to the doctors for years on and off and they've prescribed them, they tried to gimme masses of tablets but then, ya' know, then when I get home I've just got this, I'm adamant I'm not taking them anymore and I don't take them anymore.

DC YVONNE BREAR: And relationship wise then since this, has it affected relationships that you've had?

CAROL HIGGINS: It has affected relationships I've had, yeah. Saying that, I were married for 15 year and I ended that, and I ended the relationship with Duncan that I had for 5 year after that, and I ended the relationship with, ya' know, I've ended all the relationships, um, because I see something, and I don't trust they're not going to hurt me, I think they're going to hurt me, so what probably people might see as like something they can - a disagreement or they don't like, I see as a big red warning light and that's it, you're going to hurt me if I carry on. Or, er. As, um, as far as my sex life it… I don't know if it's normal, my sex life really. Um. I want to be normal. I, er, feel like some of the things he's done to me has deeply engrained into me and I feel ashamed to some of them things, for… I don't know if that's normal or not or whether I'm just, like, if everybody else has them feelings. I feel disgusted but, and I feel ashamed for liking it as well sometimes. And then I feel like why don't I like it sometimes as well. It just, it changes all the time. I'm not with anybody at the moment. Um. The reason that this has come about this time is because my ex-boyfriend, he came down at quarter past 12:00 that night and he wanted to see me, talk to me, he didn't want the relationship to be over, and I was adamant that it was over, and he hit, um, my daughter's boyfriend, headbutted him, so the police rang me and said do you need any support with victim support? And I said, yeah, I do actually because this has triggered, ya'know, it's brought a lot back for me, and thank god they've picked up on it this time, ya' know, and this has made my inroad this time for hopefully getting it dealt with.

And I do, I want closure, I don't want to take this to my death bed, and I feel like I will take it to my death bed if I don't get the justice I deserve. And, erm. Because of my counselling, it's made me realise, like, ya' know, why me, and I owe them for all these years but now one of the ways I looked at it was if I saw a girl my age in the playground and she'd been violated the way I've been violated, would I think that she deserved it? No, she doesn't deserve it, just like my daughter wouldn't deserve it, or my son if somebody ever did anything like that to them.

DC YVONNE BREAR: And how has it affected you with your children?

CAROL HIGGINS: Erm, I think you're better off asking them that. They're okay because as I said when she read it, she read one of my letters in there, she says don't feel bad that I know about it now, that it's going to affect me and I'm going to be damaged from it, she says if I know, ya' know, the fact that I know now, or when I'm near what, 33, she says, ya' know, I'm old enough to understand this, don't feel like you've damaged me in anyway, she said and you deserve a gold medal, not just for what you've gone through, she says but for concealing it from me, and so they feel, they think I've concealed it, but now they can kind of understand from the past why I've got drunk sometimes and why I've behaved in the way that I have and why I've got angry and upset in the way I have, so, and they said they underst', that I'm glad because at least now we understand, ya' know, why you are like you are sometimes, what they've said. And Ella is training to be a vet surgeon, so I think what I've done with Jake and Ella has been difficult but I've wanted to give them everything that I haven't had and, you know my mum brought a lot of men into our lives and, and put them first and I haven't done that, although I've had relationships and ended them, I've never lived with anybody else since I've got divorced in 15 years, and I didn't want anybody to ever do to my kids, you know, I've had big issues with trust.

DC YVONNE BREAR: Yeah.

CAROL HIGGINS: And not being trapped and controlled, I've got big issues about being trapped and controlled because I don't think, because I've always tried to please and do things to keep the peace. I'm not very good with my boundaries with myself and consistent with them, so.

DC YVONNE BREAR: Is there anything else that we've not discussed that you think you need to tell me?

CAROL HIGGINS: I'm sure there's lots of things.

DC YVONNE BREAR: Yeah. I don't. You know. If. If more things come to you later, erm, after today, we can arrange another video, it's not a problem.

CAROL HIGGINS: I don't know if Paul remembers this but, um, but when he were raping me, we went to Sweden on a boat trip, on like a booze run or something like that, we went to Sweden and Paul were there, we got these pictures of Paul on this ship. And in the cabin, I remember Paul banging on the door to get in and my dad were having sex with me up against the wall of the cabin inside and Paul not being able to get in until he's finished, and, ya' know, there's loads of times he had sex with me that if I think back I can remember times, but.

DC YVONNE BREAR: Yeah.

CAROL HIGGINS: I know you probably going to want more, ya' know, if it's going to court. I just feel myself light-headed, I just feel dizzy.

DC YVONNE BREAR: Yeah. Do you want to have a…? Shall we have a little break and then see if there's anything else comes to front of your mind that you want to discuss today?

CAROL HIGGINS: Yeah.

DC YVONNE BREAR: And if there isn't, it's not a problem. And it comes later, like I said, we can arrange to come back, it's not a problem.

CAROL HIGGINS: I feel like I'm holding it all in and I don't know… (sigh) I don't know if this feeling of like, I feel like I've got this massive scream, like I want to scream on top of my voice inside. I feel like I really, really, really want to scream on top of my voice and let all this stuff out. And I don't know if it's because of all these other times that I've tried, and I don't know even after all this it's because it's going to actually happen, because Motteshaw, says to me, Ian, Motteshaw I could do this and it might not even still go.

DC YVONNE BREAR: But all we can do is try. All we can do is try and go through all the motions, speak to all the people, get all that evidence together, and then Ian Motteshaw look at it and review it from there. And I can't promise you today that this is going to court and Alex can't, but all Alex can do is try to do that for you, yeah? So every little inquiry, every person that you spoke to or you think might've seen something or been aware of something, we can go speak to. And obviously you're getting upset now, it's understandable, discussing it like this, it brings it all back to the front of you, front of your mind, dun't it

CAROL HIGGINS: It does, it's vile I can feel his knob in my gob, do you know what I mean? Everything I can feel, I can taste every smell. None of it ever goes away. None of it ever goes away. And the fact that that man is still there being able to do that, ya know, perpetrate it, do all that and the things he's done before and he's fucking got away with it, and he still sat there, and the suffering he's put me through all these years. Now, it's just, no wonder I feel stressed and I feel like I've got chains wrapped round me and I feel, like, it wouldn't sit right with anybody because it's not right, it's wrong. And how many times he tried to dress it up and make me feel like it were normal because, ya' know, that his friends did it with their daughters and they lived happy as a man and wife. I were confused. I didn't know what to think of it, if to fight it, if to agree with it, if to go along with it. I didn't know what to do and it's not, that I'd had enough being treated like an adult, it wasn't nothing to fucking do with that, it was survival at that time. I didn't know what else to do, I would've been put in a children's home, I couldn't go back to live with my mum I've been told and it weren't right, I didn't like it anyway, I just didn't know what to do. (Sobbing) And the fact that, ya' know, she thinks that I fucking, ya' know, enjoyed that place, the entrapment. All these things, the things that I'm never been able to relax and move on and be totally happy with my life because they think that about me like I'm a little slag. I'm not a fucking slag, I were a child. And my parents, even though my mum says she believes me, she must've known, she must've known.

DC YVONNE BREAR: What contact do you have with mum now?

CAROL HIGGINS: I don't, I don't, because of that, and she says when I have, when I have seen her in the past and we tried to be friends and that, I can't because she says I'm living in the past, and when I get drunk I can't help get angry with her about it, the things that she said to me. I cannot get over the fact that she says when you been, when you said you'd had enough of being, when you'd had, when you come back to me, that's what she says, "When you come back to me because you'd had enough of being treated like an adult, what the hell did you expect me to do about it," so…I can't get over it, even now as I'm talking to you, it makes me dizzy, the extremity of it all, the fact that she can actually think that I wanted to be part of that. I don't understand her. And she says I'm living in the past and then until I stopped living in the past we can't have a relationship but I can't help but living in the past until it's dealt with.

DC YVONNE BREAR: Yeah, and you've had some closure.

CAROL HIGGINS: I can't, no. I don't see my brother. Ya' know. He's arrogant. He fell out with me before with something a few year ago, er, about an affair he had with this woman, and he, er, he makes out, he thinks I've told his wife and I haven't told his wife, his wife phoned and told me about it, and I just said I'm sorry and she didn't answer, she says, ah, well, you just confirmed that it were true now because I didn't really know and I'm like, oh, God, do you know, what I mean, and my brothers there "I wouldn't do that to my worst enemy" and I'm never going to speak to you again, can't do owt about it. So, I don't have anything to do with any of them. My mum would like me to have a relationship with her but only on her condition that, sorry (reach for a tissue), that, you know, that I don't bring the past up. I've got letters here that, um, that my mum's written to me in the past about things, ya' know, she kicked me out at 16, telling me that… um. Well, she kicked me out because she had an affair while she were married, that she was seeing somebody else, Karl, at the same time and he made her choose between him or me because I couldn't stand the fact that - because Higgins is where I got my name from my mum's secon', no, third husband. I've got letters here. This folder here is all my letters that I've written to my dad when I were younger or things that my counsellor have told me to use, to learn about forgiveness, sex cases. It's just everything that I've used, ya' know, I've written to help me get over, trying to help me heal from my abuse. So this is everything in here, I don't know if you want…

DC YVONNE BREAR: Well, when we're finished today, in here, we'll, we'll have a look through it all, me and Alex, and then see if Alex wants some copies of anything that's in there. Okay?

CAROL HIGGINS: Yeah, yeah. I know I did have the letter from my mum, um, so I'm hoping they still got it from last year because I didn't take a photocopy because I took it in as evidence, er, sexual abuse, (reads from a letter), just to let you know, this is like people and doctors, professionals who have put me in touch with counsellors and things like that over the past.

DC YVONNE BREAR: So if the referrals have been made through your doctor, they should have a list of who you've spoken to.

CAROL HIGGINS: Yeah.

DC YVONNE BREAR: So again when we finish here today, we'll get you to sign, um, a form that allows us access to your medical records.

CAROL HIGGINS: When I was 13 (reads from a document).

DC YVONNE BREAR: What's that, sorry?

CAROL HIGGINS: That's just something I've done when I was 13. My counsellors told me to do some letters then, this is a letter about you're not here because I feel too disgusted to write to you, that's what I wrote to my dad about my feelings, about growing up and things like that years ago. This is from my mum. I think it needs to be gone through.

DC YVONNE BREAR: You keep all that together and then we'll have a look through all that when we finish.

CAROL HIGGINS: And then I've got these things in here. And, then, obviously I don't know if you've read that but that's my book, that's how it's all come about the second time, I've written a book about it.

DC YVONNE BREAR: Right, no, I haven't.

CAROL HIGGINS: Well, that's in my epilogue about it, in the back, and that's why I think all the witnesses have come forward from reading my book, that can relate to things that I've put in here.

DC YVONNE BREAR: And does Alex have a list of people that have come forward to say.

CAROL HIGGINS: He's been, he took statements off two of them already. Yeah.

DC YVONNE BREAR: Is there anything else at this point?

CAROL HIGGINS: No, but I wouldn't want to rush off, do you know what I mean, because in case …

DC YVONNE BREAR: No, no. All I'm going to say is, is if we conclude, I'll just pop and see Alex and see if there's anything that he needed to ask right now. And then we'll pause it, well, we'll conclude this interview now, we'll go have a seat out there and have a drink and have time and then if there's anything else comes to the front of your mind, we can come back in and start.

CAROL HIGGINS: Because going through this might help me as well?

DC YVONNE BREAR: Yeah. And we'll go through that out there and then if there's anything else, we can come back in if you feel up to it today and discuss some more if there's anything that you've remembered. And if, and if not and like I said it comes later on that you remember, we can come back another day, but we're not just going to finish it and run off and that's it today. So I'll just pop and see Alex and see if there's anything he just wants me to mention before we finish now and then we'll go sit out there and have a look through all that. All right?

CAROL HIGGINS: Okay, yeah.

(DC Yvonne Brear leaves the room)

(no dictation)

(Carol sits and waits for the officer to return. She sits pensively, looking down to the right).

DC YVONNE BREAR: (DC Yvonne Brear re-enters the video suite) This door's heavy.

CAROL HIGGINS: Has he taken the video off?

DC YVONNE BREAR: No, it's still running.

CAROL HIGGINS: Because I know Carron Garside told me that Julie Garside, her sister, she had a baby at sixtee', at 15, she had a baby at 15 and it were born dead, and I know… and um. And she never, ever told me who that baby, she never told anybody who's baby it were. Now, my mum found her brother, my Uncle Ken when we were all living at home together as a family through a salvation army, and I've not seen him for 20 years, something like that, and he came to stay with us, and, but this is my mum's brother, my Uncle Ken. And I remember then going up the village for a drink in Denby Dale and then all hell broke loose, police come and everything, and my Uncle Ken were being taken to Huddersfield Hospital, he'd been beat to a pulp, literally they've had to revive him, the ambulance men had to revive him, by my dad because him and Julie Garside were kissing in the public toilets, these outside the toilets in Denby Dale, you know villages used to have these toilets, they were in there, and because he were kissing, my dad's dragged him out and beat him to a pulp. Now, I believe now it's because he was jealous and because he used to be having sex with Julie when she were younger. Now, Carron told me this when I had my book launch on the 16th of August, but nothing else, she's not, nothing has been mentioned since. But I think he were having under aged sex with her sister as well. So I know like Tony Brearley my cousin, his niece, she was another one who was, but I believe or else he wouldn't have beat him up now that that's the reason he was jealous because he was having under age sex with her.

DC YVONNE BREAR: And how old was Julie in comparison to you?

CAROL HIGGINS: I think Julie were not much older than, well, she were, maybe about three or four years. She used to babysit for me I think as well. It seems to be like it with our babysitters, because Tony used to babysit for me, but I think Julie, she might deny it but I think Julie Garside needs to be questioned, Carron's sister.

DC YVONNE BREAR: Okay. Alex just mentioned when I went through about, er, just going over the disclosure witnesses. Obviously you've spoken to counsellors over here. But just to clarify, at the time that this abuse was happening, apart from that, sorry, the girl that you said, the friend, did you say Dawn?

CAROL HIGGINS: Dianne Croft.

DC YVONNE BREAR: Dianne, apart from Dianne and her parents, and then you told your mum when you left, was there anybody else that you spoke to?

CAROL HIGGINS: I know when I gone on the bus, this is how everybody knows in the village I think because when I got on the bus, all my friends who I used to knock about because there were people from Shelley and different villages visit, ya' see, because when you go to school you meet friends from all over, so all my village friends who I used to knock about with, they were all on the bus and they said where are you going? And I told them I were leaving, that I were being raped my dad. So I know I told everybody on the bus, my friends.

DC YVONNE BREAR: Right. And do you remember their names?

CAROL HIGGINS: Erm. I don't know, if Susan Cocking, erm, Nicola Wommersley, Susan er, Susan Cocking, I think she were on the bus. I don't know if Dianne Croft were on the bus, a lad called Tucker, erm, because sometimes we're different people in different groups you all come in together, so, erm, that's a few names that I've remembered so far. But I'm wondering if that's the reason why it's gone around the village and Dianne because apparently before the book came out, everybody's known for years because I left at 15 but there's been no evidence, so now my book's come out and I've written about it, everybody is like dawning now, ah, that's, you know, it was true, it wasn't just a rumour, do you know what I mean, it has actually happened. But I, ya' know. I could try and make a list of the people, Susan Cocking I think she was on the bus, I think Nicola Wommersley. Er. I think maybe Joanne Franklin might have been, I can't remember. Er, Mark Tucker. Erm. Arr, Prance. A ginger haired lad called Prance because he went out with Susan. Er. I can't really remember any more of them. Yeah.

DC YVONNE BREAR: Well, I'm going to leave it there just for now and we'll go have a seat out there. And then, erm, we'll go through that stuff that you've got and then possibly come back and speak a bit more.

CAROL HIGGINS: I'm trying to remember if there's anybody who I would've told during that time. There's only the tattoo artist who put my tattoo on, but he lived in Barnsley, but that's not about that, that were underage, wasn't it, the guy that put my tattoo on.

DC YVONNE BREAR: Do you remember his name?

CAROL HIGGINS: No. No. I just know that he had the shop, the tattoo shop in Barnsley and it was above the railway crossing or where the railway crossing is in Barnsley there was a bus station, it were above there so I'm sure it could be found out back in the day, but. I suppose that's evidence of what Sonya Strafford said that she's looked into it and there's no evidence that social services were ever involved in us lives. That's what I've been told, so, that's going to be a ghost story really, everything is going to have gone in't it, all the evidence from back then.

DC YVONNE BREAR: I don't know because I've not made those inquiries and I don't think Alex has yet but they are avenues that he needs to go down.

CAROL HIGGINS: It's. it's. I can't believe I ain't told anybody in that two year, I can't believe that I hadn't told anybody. That's how tight, compact, do you know what I mean, that's…? I can't believe, I must've told somebody. But I'm sure my mum knew. Maybe that's maybe that's why she knew, maybe she didn't know I was going back to him maybe that's how she knew, but, like that's why she said that when you had enough of being treated like an adult. Maybe she, she knew but I denied it to her or something like that. I don't know. Because she, I once thought I were pregnant when I went to her house and I says I think I'm pregnant, and I honestly thought it was his, and he told me it would be an albino baby, I were frightened to death and she said to me whose is it, and I told her a boy I were going out with but it wasn't, I weren't, I weren't allowed any boyfriends. I used t', I remember going out with Jason Coverdale a boy at school and he were lovely and I wanted just to be normal and have boyfriends like my friends did, and, er, then Paul would come up and get me and said my dad wants you if he saw me hanging out, you know, at shop corners with him or something like that. And so then, you know, and then he'd finish with me because I never ended up meeting up with him because he got that much tight reins on me, ya' know, like controlling how long I went out for or who I went out with or where I was. It were always like within two minutes my brother would be there saying my father wants you home, so he were watching me, do you know what I mean, every time I went anywhere. But I can't, I can't think of anybody else who I've told.

DC YVONNE BREAR: Okay, that's fine. And if you does, if you do remember anybody, if you just let, let us know.

CAROL HIGGINS: It seems a big thing to think that I've gone from telling my mum from him kissing me, and then that's gone to school, social workers has spoken to me, then school spoken to me, school had obviously been aware of it, and now so that's where I were open at that bit, then I've gone, forgot about all that, come back, and that's when it's all become closed tight, do you know what I mean? It's almost become screw fixed safe, do you know what I mean? It's become tight, and I've done everything to kind of, to protect him and keep his secret but maybe it were to protect myself because I didn't want to go in that children's home. He says "and you can't go back and live with your mum because you've been to live with your mum once and now you've come back here, it was obvious you can't make up your mind of who you want to live with", so it just become, tight fixed. No outlet.

DC YVONNE BREAR: Until you were 15 and couldn't take it anymore.

CAROL HIGGINS: Yeah, yeah. But I know next door neighbours used to see him holding hands with me and treating me like a girlfriend. That were weird, do you know what I mean, the way that I kind of, went along with his game to keep peace as well. I kind of went along with it that every time he said, "oh, who loves you baby?" I knew when I used to say, "you do," and he used to say "you better believe it." I knew I didn't want to go along, and he, it's hard to explain, do you know what I mean, how you, you accept it and you go along with it, I'm not screaming and shouting when I'm doing it, but, yeah, that, that was the trapped black box I were in, I couldn't get out of that place.

DC YVONNE BREAR: But you were a child.

CAROL HIGGINS: I was a teenager. I don't understand why I didn't kick and scream and just get out of there.

DC YVONNE BREAR: Right, Carol. I'm going to finish it there for now and then we'll go sit out there and have a look through all this. Okay? And then we'll come back.

CAROL HIGGINS: I'd love to know who his other friends are, who live normal together as man and wife, that he kept telling me about. It happens though, dun't it? It happened.

DC YVONNE BREAR: Carol, do you want me to do that or do you want to carry on?

CAROL HIGGINS: Erm. No, I need a wee as well.

DC YVONNE BREAR: Okay, all right then. So we'll, we'll finish it there for now. We'll have a, have a break, have a look at that and then we'll come back, all right?

CAROL HIGGINS: Yeah, okay.

DC YVONNE BREAR: So the time by my watch is, er, 20 to 1:00. I'm going to finish it there for now. So if you'll bring those out, we'll have a bit of a break- (audio cut)

MR HAMPTON: That is the conclusion of the video.

JUDGE JAMESON: Yes.

MR HAMPTON: Can I call Carol Higgins, please?

JUDGE JAMESON: Yes, certainly. Do you have some questions first, or what?

MR HAMPTON: There are two very brief matters by way of amplification.

JUDGE JAMESON: Thank you.

Diary: Tuesday 15th January 2019 (continued)

I was due to take the stand at around 12.00 noon, by which time the Jury would have watched the rest of my video statement. Before I went into court my support worker, Laura, from ISVA asked me if I wanted to wait in a private witness room next door to the courtroom. The room was very small and surprisingly had an ensuite toilet and a sink. Laura made me cups of tea as we chatted about how we liked to shop, dress, and about the food we liked to eat. She was trying to keep the conversation light-hearted to take my mind off the intensity of what I was about to experience. I know her intentions were good but I was beginning to feel frustrated by her chatter because I needed to focus, concentrate on the task ahead and compose myself. I didn't want to be rude to Laura and ask her to leave me on my own but I really needed to be alone. Afraid that I was going to lose my composure, I told her that I needed to use the toilet. I didn't really need to, but I needed a few moments to myself to gather my thoughts and calm my racing heart. I sat on the toilet and prayed to God to give me the strength and courage to stand in front of the Judge and jury to speak my truth.

The usher soon came and escorted Laura and I into the courtroom. I stood in the witness box, Laura sat on a stool beside me, I barely noticed that she was there. Conflicting feelings flooded back as I glanced across at my father, sitting with crossed arms full of defiance. This was the man who told me he loved me and who I believed loved me until I ran away aged 15. Now he was calling me a liar and a slag. But look what he was putting me through by pleading "Not Guilty." I felt a little nervous and my hand shook as picked up the glass of water to quench my dry mouth. I was intent on telling my truth rather than the version of the truth that my father wanted everyone to believe. In 1984 he had challenged me to "fucking prove it." Now I had the opportunity to do so and I was not going to waste it. I was determined to take my power back and stood strong and confident in front of the Court.

I took the oath, choosing to swear on the Holy Bible that the usher gave me, rather than the affirmation, and repeated after her, 'I swear to tell the truth, the whole truth and nothing but the truth'.

(12.12 p.m.)

CAROL DENISE HIGGINS, Sworn

Examined by Mr HAMPTON

Q Could you give us your full name, date of birth and age, please?

A Carol Denise Higgins, 23/4/1969, and I'm 49.

Q Thank you. And how should I address you? Miss Higgins, Mrs Higgins, Miss? What would you prefer?

A Miss Higgins, please.

Q Miss Higgins. Now, you're very politely turning towards me, which makes sense because I'm asking you the questions, but could I ask you, please, so that the judge and jury can hear you clearly, just to turn towards the members of the jury?

A Yeah.

Q So you're faced on with them. Keep your voice nice and loud, as it is now...

A Yeah.

Q ...and aim for that back wall.

A Okay.

Q We've had the opportunity of seeing your video interview with the police so I just have two very brief matters to ask you about, Miss Higgins. First of all, can I show you a document that we've all seen, please? Can I just ask if you recognise it, first of all?

A Yes, I do.

Q As I understand it, this is a document you produced to the police?

A Yes.

Q Thank you. Could you tell us what it is, please?

A It's a picture of me, our Donna and Paul, me brother and sister.

Q And to make sure I've identified people correctly, could you tell us, left to right, who's who?

A Left is me, and in the middle it's my brother, Paul, and, to the right, it's my sister, Donna.

Q Thank you. Now, doing the best you can, can you help us with what kind of timeframe we're dealing with with this picture? When does it date back to?

A I'm 15 in that picture.

Q Yeah.

A And Paul must be 14 or 13. There's over a year - I think Paul might be 13 in that picture, 13 or 14.

Q Yeah.

A And Donna must be about 16 because there's just over a year between us all.

Q Okay. Are we talking somewhere around the mid-80s?

A Yeah.

Q Okay. Next matter, we've heard you talk about a tattoo that you had.

A Yes.

Q Again, just try and... just face straight on to the jury.

A Yeah. Sorry, it's cos it's...

Q It's okay. I won't take any offence.

A Yeah.

Q It's normal to speak to somebody who's asking you questions...

A Yeah.

Q ...and you'll be face on, but this is rather unique circumstances, so face towards the jury.

A Okay.

Q Thank you. Where was that tattoo?

A On my shoulder, here.

Q And what exactly did it say or show?

A It showed a tattoo of a rose, it was about that big, and then there was... it said, "Sam" at top, which was me dad's name, and it said, "Caz" at the bottom underneath it.

Q Caz?

A Yes.

Q And Caz was? Who was Caz?

A Well, no doubt me, short for carol.

Q Okay, and Sam?

A My dad's name. I didn't know it was his name at first cos they call him Elliott but he said it was a nickname that he used to be called when he was younger.

Q Thank you. Are you able to tell us - again, we've seen your video - to the best of your recollection, when it was you had that tattoo removed or covered?

A I... the tattoo, the process, I saw an advertisement in the Yellow Pages for tattoo removals at a tattoo shop in Rotherham so I went to it and it were... I didn't... I thought it was just a tattoo shop where you had them put on and so I asked, "How are you gonna do it?" and he says, "We would go over the tattoo just a small area at a time with an empty needle but deeper than what we would do if you was having a tattoo so it would break the skin below it and then we'd put acid pen on it and that would bubble the ink out and draw it out".

Q So that's the method?

A Yeah.

Q Could you help us with when you actually had it removed, doing your best? If you can't, then just feel free to say so.

The photograph I presented to the Court. My brother's tattoo is circled in red. This evidence was rejected by PC Alex Wilson.

The scar left behind by the removal of my tattoo, also ignored as evidence by PC Alex Wilson.

A I started having it removed when I was about 17 years old.

Q Seventeen, thank you, so we'd be in and around the late 1980s?

A Yes. I remember because I met their dad when the kids... my children's dad when I was 17 and he were 19 and I was going out with somebody else at the time and it was when I was going out with him that I started the process cos I used to stick to the bedding when I slept in their spare bed.

Q How long did the process take, roughly?

A About six years, and then, when I went to the doctors, he says to me, "You should have come to me. Because of the reason you had it on, we would have been able to let you have laser", so he started with laser treatment on it then at Leeds General Hospital.

Q So that was later on?

A Yeah.

Q So it's been a fairly ongoing process?

A Yes.

Q Thank you for that. If you just wait there, there'll be some questions from my learned friend who represents Mr Appleyard.

A Okay.

Cross-examined by Mr STOREY

Q Miss Higgins, as you've heard, I'm going to ask you some questions. Again, as Mr Hampton has said, it'll be easier for you and for the ladies and gentlemen of the jury if you look towards them although I am asking you the questions directly.

A Okay.

Q Don't worry about offending me. I won't take offence if you don't look at me...

A Okay.

Q ...when you're answering my questions. All right? Is it fair to say that you hate your father?

A I hate what he's done to me but, no, it's because he's loved me that it's hurt me so much what he's done because I loved him.

Q This is a prosecution that you've pursued for many years, isn't it?

A Yes.

Q You've been looking forward to having your day in court for a long time now?

A I wouldn't say I were looking forward to it. I've worked towards getting my day in court for justice.

Q You've been quite happy to publicise your keenness to have your day in court, haven't you?

A Only because I didn't feel like I was being listened to. I've tried a lot of years to get justice. I made a statement when I was 15 to the police.

Q Would you agree that you could be said to have orchestrated a vendetta against him?

A Definitely not.

Q You certainly tried to publicise your allegations widely both online and in the area where he lives, haven't you?

A Only the last... and certainly not where he lives, I haven't publicised it there, but on... I went on social media because I wrote a book about me climbing Kilimanjaro after I'd been battling bowel cancer and my book, part of my book, me epilogue on me book, is a brief history of me childhood abuse and I promote me book about me climb up Kilimanjaro and that is part of my book, so that's why. It's not just... I've not promoted it purposely because of what me dad's done to me. I've promoted my book.

Q You have visited places where he frequents, the area where he lives?

A My friends live in them areas.

Q Have you tried to turn local people against him?

A No.

Q Have you organised petitions calling for him to be kicked out of Denby Dale?

A No.

Q Have you expressed views on Facebook about what should happen to him?
A Other people have expressed views and I've just like liked what they've put.
Q Have you expressed views?
A I feel that he should be brought to justice, yes.
Q Fairly extreme views?
A What do you mean? Such as?
Q Paedophiles should be hanged?
A I haven't put they should be hanged. I believe that paedophiles should be hanged, yeah.
Q You do believe that?
A Course I do, for what they do to children.
Q Do you want money from him?
A No. I want him to pay for what he's done by going to prison.
Q I want to go back to a time when you were living as a family in Denby Dale. It's right, isn't it, that the relationship between your mother and father was not great?
A Absolutely.
Q There was a lot of arguments? There were a lot of arguments in the house, within the family?
A Violence and fights.
Q There were a lot of arguments within the house, weren't there?
A Yeah.
Q Do you remember what those arguments were about?
A Jealousy, me dad's jealousy a lot of the time, not trusting my mum.
Q Is it that he felt she was having affairs?
A I don't know. They used to... he used to accuse her, "Where've you been?", timing her when she went to the shop and things.
Q How much were you aware of what was going on, the dynamic between your parents?
A I saw me dad with a machete to her vagina once when she was in the kitchen and he were accusing her of having a dirty dream about somebody else.

Q What did you know of the state of their relationship?

A I know that it was really bad where neighbours had to phone the police but the police wouldn't get involved in domestics and they'd take his guns but they'd bring 'em back, his roaring, just heart-rendering arguments. It were just violence. It were like, urgh, really, really bad all the time, aggression all the time.

Q Did you ever discuss any of this with your mother?

A Yeah. Me mum used to talk to me about how bad me dad were and me dad used to talk to me about how bad me mum were. Me mum used to take me away to battered wives' homes. She used to always take me but not me brother and me sister.

Q Did you discuss matters in the family home with your siblings, with Paul or Donna?

A Donna had special needs. She went to a special school. She had out-of-control epilepsy. She was very immature in her brain, so not so much. Paul, it was a bit... a bit like a... I felt like he were more on me father's side in a way. He was younger. He... Paul... his dad was his hero.

Q Your mother left several times, didn't she?

A From me being a little girl, she's left and gone back, yeah. I wouldn't... I don't know if it was several times but certainly a few times.

Q Yeah. Well, by "several" I just meant a number, more than once. I'm not suggesting a specific number to you. I don't imagine you can help us with how many times, can you?

A Probably... I probably remember about three or four times that she took us.

Q And did she take all three of you with her?

A Not all the time, no. The times I remember her taking... I was too young. I know she's said she's taken us all when we were younger but I only remember her taking me.

Q Were you ever made aware by her of what made her return after those periods away?

A She said he always found where she was. He used to look wherever she ran away to and hid in refuge places. He'd always find her and she felt forced to go back.
Q We know that in the 1980s, and I'll come on to this in a bit, you and your mum left and you stayed for a bit with a friend on their floor, a friend of your mother's, when you ended up in Penistone?
A Because I told her that he'd been kissing me properly.
Q I said we'll come on to that in a minute, but I'm just asking you to think about that period when you and your mother left. Did he ever find you and her then and force her to go back?
A I don't know if he found her or not but I know she didn't go back.
Q If he had found where you and she were living, you'd probably remember that, wouldn't you? Do you think?
A I know he did find her cos I think they once had an arrange... they once met at a pub called the Monkey in Thurgoland.
Q You've told us about your sister, Donna, and the difficulties she had to some extent.
A Mmm.
Q Did that... was that something your parents, so far as you can recollect, found it hard to cope with?
A Me or me parents?
Q Your parents, from what you saw?
A They seemed to cope all right with her, but then one day it was told that Donna were going to a children's home because... I was told it was cos they were finding it a struggle to... me mum was finding it hard to deal with her disability and because of the violence that was happening in the house but then I was later told it was because she wouldn't mix with people her own age, but that wouldn't be possible anyway because she... she had a simple mind.
Q But she ended up spending large chunks of time, I think, in care homes?
A No, not large chunks of time.

Q No?

A She spent one... I think she went to a care home when she was about 13 at, I think it was Holmfirth, and then she went to Combs Hill at Dewsbury, as I recall, where I was told she was sexually abused in there. They wouldn't let her have a lock on door cos of her... because of her epilepsy.

Q But you don't think she spent large periods of time away from the family home?

A No. It were probably about, tops, a year, something like that. It might not have even been that long, I can't remember, not large... not when we were growing up, definitely not, and I know when she was in the children's home, me dad rang her when they'd had an argument with me mum and told her that Donna wasn't even my sister, that he'd got... that she... that he wasn't her dad and Donna was devastated because she'd always believed that Appleyard were her dad and she were upset cos he told her over phone that she wasn't while she was in care.

Q Your father worked, didn't he?

A No, he was always on sick, getting caught... we used to get social workers coming in with food parcels, Mr Sykes, and giving him backhanders out of his back pocket. Me dad always got... got done for being caught up ladders doing jobs for people on side. He was always on the sick when I were younger.

Q He worked in the building industry, didn't he?

A No, he didn't.

Q That's the reality.

A He was always on the sick. He got... I think... yeah, he was always on the sick. He did jobs for farmers and things like that and helping 'em bring taties in and things like that on Derek's farm up at Denby. He were always doing odd jobs for people.

Q What was the nature of the sickness that meant that he was always on the sick?

A I don't know, I don't know. I just know he kept getting shopped and that's why we'd have no food and... we would have food but he'd make us take the food out the cupboards, put them into boxes and put them upstairs so... so that when social workers come, he'd open the cupboard doors and say, "Look, we've got no food", so they'd bring us food parcels and give 'em a backhander, £5 out of his pocket. He were playing 'em like a fiddle.

Q Are you sure that's the truth...

A Yeah.

Q ...Miss Higgins and not something...

A Absolutely.

Q ...you've just invented?

A Yeah. I... I filled the boxes. Course I'm sure. I saw the social workers come in with packages and there were times we did used to go shopping to supermarkets. It wasn't all the time.

Q He'd go out to work and get home at half-past five, six o'clock, wouldn't he?

A No, he would not because a lot of time he'd tend his land that he had round on the next street so he just worked now and again for people and they were backhanders. It wasn't a... he wasn't employed by anybody. He wasn't employed by anybody. Who did he work for? I never knew he was, and that's all the time I were growing up.

Q Your mother looked after the family home? That's right, isn't it?

A And me, yeah.

Q Donna, I think you said, was at a special school because of her difficulties? Is that right?

A Lydgate at New Mill, yes.

Q And you and Paul were at school presumably more locally?

A Yeah. Me mum used to keep me off to do housework a lot of time as well and me dad... me dad... I used to go and tend me dad's land with him, work on it, washing turnips, mountains of turnips, we used to pull 'em up and I'd have to wash all the mud off and... in the shed that he had where he had geese, he used to rear 'em and things like that. He had allotments. He rented land off a farmer. I'd have to pile 'em all up and it'd be freezing cold in winter. I used to be always on his land helping him. He didn't have a nine to five job. He never has done.

Q You would spend time with your mother instead of going to school? You've just told us that?

A Some of the time, not all the time. I still did spend some time in school.

Q That was something your father didn't approve of, wasn't it?

A No, cos he used to keep me off. He used to... if I weren't at school, I'd help me mum and then I'd have to go and help him.

Q Any help you gave him was after school hours or at weekends, wasn't it?

A No, no, definitely not.

Q Because one of the things he'd get cross about and chastise you for was skiving school, wasn't it?

A No, no. Skiving school? I've only ever skived school once and that were when I were at Penistone. I weren't living with him then and I didn't think it were worth doing it after that cos it took more effort trying to hide.

Q When I said "skiving", I meant because you weren't attending school.

A Pardon? What did you say then?

Q When I said "skiving" a moment ago...

A Yeah.

Q When I said your father was not pleased about you skiving, I meant your father wasn't pleased that you weren't attending school, was he?

A No. He was pleased. He kept me off school to help him and he's never showed any kind of unhappiness that I haven't been at school. I've never known him tell me off for not going to school.

Q Because there were times when he'd ask you whether you'd been to school or not and you'd tell him you had when you hadn't?

A No, I wouldn't, no, not at all. I can't remember... I don't even know what you're talking about.

Q Did he tell you that he'd heard you during the day with your mother talking to people on the CB radio which you had at your house?

A Me mum used to talk on the CB radio, yeah, she did, and when he... when she saw him coming in from... from where he'd been, if he'd been working on land up at the farm or on our land, she used to turn it off quick so he wouldn't know she'd been on it, but he got the CB radio fitted in the house. He used to go on it as well.

Q Yeah, but he learned, didn't he, that you...

A He had one in his van. He had an aerial on his van. He had a CB in his van.

Q Didn't he learn that you had not been at school because he'd heard from the CB aerial in his van that you'd been on it during the day?

A Yeah, that's probably one of times that I didn't go to school, maybe one... yeah, that me mam... me mam used to keep me off and do housework; I might have done. My handle were Paper Lady at the time.

Q Wasn't that something that made him cross, that you had not been to school when you should have been?

A I don't know, I can't remember, cos he used to keep me off that much. He knew I weren't... I didn't... I left school with no grades. He knew I didn't go to school a lot, consistently.

Q You told the police and you've told us that there was a time when he held a shotgun to your mother?

A Yeah. They used to argue and he had his guns and he used to point 'em to her and she used to scream horrifically and sometimes the neighbours heard it and so the police would come and the police would take the guns.

Q How much of that do you actually remember yourself?

A I remember it like it's there happening in front of me now, and then the police would come and me mum would be hysterical and they used to say that they couldn't get involved in domestics.

Q And how much do you recall...

A And he used to keep the guns in the living room and just lent up. They wasn't in no cases, they wasn't in a bag, they weren't in a case and they were just leant up in the corner of the living room and he used to make bullets in his bedroom. He got a load-all and the guns was always there to hand. He didn't have to go in a case for 'em or anything. They were just always there.

Q What do you remember the arguments being about that you say led to him producing a shotgun?

A Jealousy. I don't always know what they were about. I were upstairs or they... I'd... they'd come in... or he'd come in drunk or they'd been out together and... and they'd be just... we were brought up where there were just murderous rows going on all the time.

Q Is this something that somebody's told you happened?

A No. I experienced it, never not experienced it. It were part of me life growing up, living in fear of him, and he used to belt us as well.

Q Well, can I suggest that what he did so far as you were concerned was not belting you but sometimes give you a clip round the ear if he was cross with you, Miss Higgins.

A No, no, no. What he did to us were violence. It's like... he used to nearly knock my head off. He used to make me flinch all the time. He had a thick leather belt, about that thick and one about that thick and it was still thick like that, and he used to make me bend over that settee with my pants down and with my nightie up or summat and he used to whack it, whack, whack, and I could be crying and that and then he'd tell me to stop crying else he'd give me summat... and I'd have whelps and even school reported to 'em, you know, "Why have your kids got bruises on their legs?" and him and me mum made 'em give a public apology to... through... through the Huddersfield Examiner to say that, you know, we fell down a lot or something like that.

Q So are you saying your mum was hiding it as well as he was?

A Hiding what?

Q That he was beating you with a belt?

A Well, she didn't used to stop it and she used to beat us with slippers and wooden spoons, but she... yeah, she knew he were doing it cos I even heard somebody once say that me mum had said to 'em, "He... he's at it again. He's hitting 'em again".

Q Did you ever tell your teachers at school what was happening?

A No.

Q Did you ever tell a friend at school what was happening?

A About the... about the belts?

Q Yes.

A Not about the physical violence, no, cos I thought it were normal. I thought every child got hit.

Q Did you ever see a doctor around that time about anything at all?

A No.

Q There was never an occasion when he held a firearm of any sort to your mother, was there, in reality?

A Yeah, yes.

Q Nor did he ever hold a machete to her?

A Yes, yes, he did, and she stood there, and I remember - she's a large lady, me mum - and she pee'ed herself like a cow, it just gushed out of her, and I... start watching through the bannisters in... on the stairs steps and we had blue Artex in the kitchen, we had no central heating, and I watched it happen.

Q You told the police that, when you were younger, your dad would go out collecting scrap?

A Yeah.

Q How often do you say that happened?

A It were part of us lives. Nearly every day we'd go over to Naylors, over fields, over woods. He'd pinch pipes, big aluminium pipes and we'd take a piece of scaffolding over with us so it fitted through the tunnel and him maybe at one end and me and our Paul would be other and we'd pinch it and climb, scramble down the broken pipes. Us legs would be buckling, it'd be that heavy, and he'd take it to a place where we could...where he would beat it up, fold it up, put it in back of van, truck, and then he'd take it to scrap yard. We used to nick copper wire, used to burn it in back garden where we used to live and that. He were always nicking stuff, nicking stuff out of skips and out of council skips. I used to go with him when it were dark for long walks over fields to where they was.

Q Paul and he were, is it fair to say, closer than you were to him when you were younger?

A I never really noticed that he was really. I just felt it were more like it were my job to help me mum more and it were Paul's job to help me dad more.

Q And Paul was happier than you were to go on these walks when you might find bits of scrap?

A No, we were both happy to do it. We just had to do as were told. We just... he said, "You're coming, you're both coming", and we used to go, both go.

Q The family had dogs, didn't it, that had to be walked?

A We always used to take dog. He used to have like a duck whistle. He used to train 'em with cos he used to take 'em out hunting with us, with him. He used to go hunting on his own with John Amelia and that in early hours of morning and sometimes in daytime he'd take us for walks over fields.

Q And one of the dogs that the family had was called Sam, wasn't it?

A Yeah.

Q Was that a Springer Spaniel?

A I think he was, yes.

Q And you were close to Sam, the dog, weren't you?

A Yeah.

Q Now, you told the police that there was an occasion when he shot Sam, the dog?

A Yeah.

Q You weren't actually present when that happened though, were you?

A Yes.

Q Isn't the reality that that dog was shot because it was worrying sheep?

A I... he told me it were cos it had epileptic fits and I'd never seen it have a fit.

Q Well, it was a dog that he and you, I suggest, knew full well wasn't well?

A No, I didn't know it wasn't well.

Q And that was worrying sheep?

A No, I didn't... I wasn't aware of that at all.

Q And that was why it had to be shot.

A No.

Q That's the reality, isn't it?

A No, that is not the reality at all.

Q And it's something you were told about in the family by your dad, not something you witnessed or experienced, is it?

A No, no. I remember when he shot the dog. There was a big broken pipe, we were at back at Naylors, and he sat on there and he started kissing me properly, snogging me.

Q Again, I suggest, Miss Higgins, that that never happened. There was never any snogging between you and your father, was there?

A Yes, all the time. He treat me like his girlfriend.

Q You told people he would use the phrase, "Who loves you, baby?"

A Yeah.

Q Kojak? That's right, isn't it?

A I don't know if it was. I don't... I've never heard that before. I'd only ever heard him say it to me.

Q You've never heard of the television programme, Kojak?

A Yeah, but I've never really watched it. I didn't know he said that.

Q Did you not watch it when you were children?

A No, not that I remember.

Q Is that not where that catchphrase comes from?

A Well, it's the first time I've heard of that. He's told me, and he used to say, "Who loves you, baby?" and sometimes I wouldn't answer and he used to repeat it, "Who loves you, baby?" and I used to say, "You do", and he used to go, "You'd better believe it".

Q Isn't that the sort of thing that people would often say in the late 70s, early 80s?

A No. It's what he said to me, holding my hand, going on walks and that and treating me like his girlfriend, like I were older, and that's when I... I once...

me mum told me she were gonna call me Rebecca and me dad told me he called me Carol after an ex-girlfriend he had...

Q Do you remember when it was...

A ...on one of these walks.

Q Do you remember when it was that your mother left and took you with her?

A I remember sitting down on front doorstep when I were about, I think I were about 13, and telling me mum that he'd been kissing me properly and I didn't... I felt uncomfortable and she told me about leaving him. I think she were gonna leave him anyway. It were another time. I mean, she'd already left and just took me and left Donna and Paul there before in past but gone... but gone back and she said she were leaving him and that's when... when we left to stay with the people who she'd met on the CB radio and then... oh, before we... before I left, social workers came to Shelley High School and asked me to stay behind after school and go up in the office and speak to them and I did and they asked me about him kissing me proper because me mum must have phoned social services and... and then... then, after that, she... we left, she took me, and then nothing else were ever mentioned about it and then I weren't having a good time at Penistone and Donna and Paul were still with me dad and I went back to me dad's and that were the first time he raped me when he come back from America.

Q So you think your mother left when you were about 13?

A Or 14.

Q Do you remember what time of the year it was?

A No. It weren't snowing.

Q But you can't say whether it was summer, spring, autumn or winter?

A No.

Q And it's not the case, in reality, that you and your mother left because of anything you'd said to her, was it?

A (No audible response)

Q When you had the conversation with the social workers at school, were any members of the teaching staff there?

A I can't remember. There might have been a lady, who were our head teacher called Mrs Binliner (sic) or somebody, I think they called her.
Q Was anything said about the police becoming involved at that stage?
A No, not at all.
Q Or at least not that you were aware of?
A Not in front of me.
Q And I think this is when you ended up staying at Linda Wadsworth's house? Is that correct?
A No, not straightaway. This is when we ended up staying at Angela Pottle's and David Pottle's house up in Cubley.
Q And how long were you there for? Do you remember?
A Maybe a few month.
Q And did you go from there to the place in Penistone where Linda Wadsworth lived? I just want to make sure I've got the sequence of events right.
A Yeah, we got thrown out, I think. Me mum got thrown out.
Q From the Pottles' house?
A Yeah.
Q And why was she thrown out?
A I don't know, for her behaviour with men, I think. I don't know.
Q Were you still with her at that time?
A Yeah.
Q And did you and she then move to Linda Wadsworth's house?
A Yeah.
Q And do you remember how long you were there for?
A I don't know, a few month maybe.
Q And was it whilst you were there that you formed a relationship with Linda Wadsworth's son, David?
A Yeah.
Q And he was older than you, wasn't he?
A Yeah, and he didn't live there all the time. He used to live in Bradford and he used to come and visit his mum.

Q Okay, and you were still what, 13, 14?

A I'd be about 14, I think, yeah.

Q Okay, and he was what, 19?

A I think he were about 17. I'm not sure.

Q Right. I think you said in your book that he was 19?

A I've put 17 or 19. I couldn't remember how old he were because he just felt older than me.

Q And how long did that relationship last for? Do you remember?

A No. It weren't a proper relationship cos I remember him going out with other girls my age from Mill House and girls... we always used to hang about together so it weren't like a proper courtship.

Q But was that all whilst you were living at his mum's?

A Yeah, and then I went to see me dad in Barnsley market and he came with me and he were acting about and he got me arms and he went, "I must, I must... you must, you must improve your bust", summat like that, and me dad went mad and then I think he sent him home and then me dad had me on me own then and then he took me to the bus-stop, bus station in Barnsley, and he'd asked me if I'd had sex with him and I told him that I had had sex with him, so he knew I wasn't a virgin and... and I got the bus back to me mum's and not long after that I went back to live with me dad but I didn't know what he were gonna do to me.

Q Can I just ask you how, in relation to that trip to Barnsley, how... how it was you came to meet your dad in Barnsley? Had you been in...

A We'd arranged to... we'd arranged to meet up cos he bought me a pair of jeans as well. We'd arranged to meet up.

Q Was it the case that you felt, whilst you were with your mum staying at Linda Wadsworth's house, you weren't getting things like clothes and stuff like that?

A I weren't getting a lot of attention. I weren't thinking about clothes. Clothes didn't matter. I had clothes so I didn't... no, I had clothes. It were a case of not having enough love and affection from me mum.

Q Presumably, your dad bought the jeans for you because you'd asked him to? Is that right?

A I don't know whether he'd offered to buy me 'em or I'd asked for them. I can't remember.

Q But you must have arranged to meet him, do you think? Is that right?

A Yes, somehow. I can't remember how the arrangements were made but, yeah, cos we had no phone. It were public phone box if anybody used anything, any communications.

Q And so this would have been what, when you were about 14? Is that right?

A I think so, 13 or 14. I can't really remember.

Q I think you said a moment ago it was a little while after that meeting that you moved back to your dad's?

A I think so, yeah.

Q Okay, so...

A I can't... again, I can't remember the... cos I was at Penistone... I'd left Shelley High school then where I used to go to when I lived with me dad and when I'd left with me mum she got me in Penistone Grammar School and then it were when I were in that school I went back to me dad's.

Q So by this time you must have been absent or living with your mum away from your dad's home for quite a few months?

A Mmm.

Q Maybe as many as eight or 10, do you think?

A Yeah.

Q And what led to you deciding to return to your dad's?

A Cos I just felt like me mum were never in and I were on me own all time and I missed Donna and Paul.

Q Had you seen them whilst you were away with your mum?

A Not really.

Q Had you spoken...

A Not a lot.

Q ...spoken to them at all on the phone or anything like that?

A At some point but I can't really remember. I must have done. I can't remember if Donna were in that children's home at that time but I don't think... I think she were already back home.

Q Again, do you remember the time of year it was when you returned to your dad's?

A I just know that me mum and dad were gonna get a divorce and me dad went and got custody of us, court custody of us, and then me mum apparently she went and... he said he were gonna take us to America and me mum went and made us a ward of court so he couldn't take us out of country.

Q Well, you won't remember the date on which your dad was given custody of you by the court, will you? We've been given that information, so if I was to tell you that it was in April of 1984...

A Right.

Q ...would that help your memory about dates?

A No.

Q No, okay.

A I just know when he went and got custody of us we went for a Chinese meal afterwards to celebrate the fact he'd got custody of us.

Q Okay, but you'd been back at his house for a few months by then, hadn't you?

A No, I wouldn't say a few month.

Q Well, what would you say then?

A No, maybe a couple of month.

Q Okay, not very many though?

A No.

Q All right.

A Maybe, I don't know.

Q But once you were back at his house, is it the case that you and your brother were given chores to do?

A We've always had chores to do.

Q Tidying the house, washing up, washing?

A Always had it to do. I used to come home from school and the first job I had to do when... before they've split up were make me mum and dad's bed. I used to wash me mum's false teeth for her. She used to send me to scrub 'em. I've always had to do loads of jobs in house, make tea. They both used me as a slave.

Q Your dad was quite keen that you did your chores rather than went out to hang around with your friends, wasn't he?

A No. Well, yeah, if I did my... I'd do me chores and then I'd be out with me friends and then I'd hear him shout me if I were up in rec or me brother would come and get me and then I'd come and like... I'd be like, "What, what have I done now? I've done me jobs", but he... he'd make an excuse saying I hadn't done it properly or summat and then I'd get leathered for it. He didn't used to like me going with me friends.

Q He didn't like you hanging around with older boys, did he?

A I didn't hang around with older boys, except for when I lived at Mill House and he used to hang about... I were hanging about with people my age from school then as well. There weren't loads of older boys hanging around with us.

Q You told us that David Wadsworth was older and he was part of the group you hung around with?

A Yeah.

Q Were you not hanging around with older boys?

A But he were ... how would he know that I was hanging about with him? He's on about Denby Dale, he didn't like me hanging about with older boys. I hung about with everybody my own age from school at Denby Dale and at Penistone I hung about with everybody my own age. Just cos David were older, it didn't mean everybody else were.

Q You hung around with people with people who had a range of ages, didn't you, in fact?

A Well, we were all at same school, between 14 and 16, summat like that.

Q There was no walloping, was there, when you were called back in because he didn't like you playing out?

A Yes, yes, there was when I were younger and, as I got older, if our Paul told me that me dad wanted me home now, it wouldn't be a wallop, no, it would be rape, he'd get me in bed. He'd go to pub that night and he'd come home and he'd get me in bed or he'd keep me off school and get me on front rug or something. He didn't hit me so much when I were older but he did sleep with me.

Q Well, again, it won't surprise you to hear me say that never happened at all, did it?

A It happened all the time. The first time he did it, and I said to him, "What would me grandad say if he knew what you'd just done?" He says to me, "Don't worry, sweetheart, he believes same as me that fathers should break their daughters in".

Q You told the police that you had love bites on your neck?

A Yeah, and... yeah, and one of his girlfriends, Jess, saw him play... he were always play-fighting with me and I remember one time Jess actually seen him give me them love bites when he pinned me down in front room, but he always tried to make out as if it was in a playful way.

Q Weren't the love bites from boys who you were hanging around with like David Wadsworth?

A No, no. I wasn't living with him at that... I wasn't going out with David at that time. I'd come back to live with him when this was happening. I was back in Denby Dale.

Q But you hung around with boys in Denby Dale as well, didn't you?

A Not who gave me love bites. A lot of boys wouldn't go out with me because of the love bites. They thought I was with somebody.

Q You told the police that he started giving you love bites when you were 12?

A Well, I'd say more like 13.

Q So you were 13 in 1982?

A He started kissing me when I were round about, I'd say just about 13.

Q 1982?

A Something like that, I'd say.

Q Is that right? When you... you were... 1982 was when you turned 13? Is that right?

A I don't know. I can't remember. I'm not very good at working things out.

Q April 1982, I'm being... it's been confirmed by Mr Hampton. April 1982 is when you turned 13. All right?

A Right, okay.

JUDGE JAMESON: Can you just choose a convenient moment?

MR STOREY: Your mother hadn't left home by that time, had she?

A I don't know. I don't know. There was that many times coming and going. I don't know what dates she left and when she come back.

MR STOREY: That's probably as good as any, your Honour, thank you.

JUDGE JAMESON: All right. Thank you very much indeed. Right. Well now, Miss Higgins, I'm afraid we're going to have to take a break at this stage, so we'll come back at 10 past two.

A Okay.

JUDGE JAMESON: Okay? So could you be back for that time, please?

A Yeah.

JUDGE JAMESON: Thank you very much indeed.

A Okay. Thank you.

JUDGE JAMESON: Right, no need for you to stay in the witness box now, so if you'd like to step down. Thank you. Right, ladies and gentlemen, 10 past two. Thank you very much indeed.

(Adjourned for a short time)

JUDGE JAMESON: Yes?

MR STOREY: Thank you, your Honour, thank you, Miss Higgins.

Q I think you said before we broke that it was probably eight to 10 months that you were living with your mum in a couple of places away from your dad?

A I think so.

Q Okay, but it's right, isn't it, that even when you were away from your dad, you kept up some perhaps minimal contact with him?

A No, not for a long time and then after a long time that's when the contact started. That's when... I hadn't seen him for a long time when I saw him on Barnsley market and...

Q Right.

A ...he bought me them jeans.

Q Can you help us any more with what you mean by a long time?

A Probably a few month.

Q Okay, but the...

A I can't...

Q The reality is you and your mum were living somewhere where you were sleeping on people's floors, effectively?

A On one person's... well, we went to her house and she didn't have any carpet in the bedroom and... and she probably wasn't expecting us and she found a mattress for us to sleep on and the people who she'd met on the CB radio, she'd become friendly with 'em.

Q And again you moved from there, as we've said, to the Wadsworths' house and, again, you were staying at someone else's house, weren't you?

A Yeah. She... she used to rent a room out to lodging... lodgers...

Q Yeah.

A ...and so we were her lodger and we shared a single bedroom with bunk beds in it.

Q Okay, but you and your mum didn't have any easy access to money or the means to buy clothes and things like that, did you, at that time?

A I don't know. I just know that I always had clothes on me back and me mum used to have a club in catalogue. I was... I was... I never... clothes was never an issue for me.

Q But you... is it right that you would at times during that what you've agreed might have been eight to 10 months you were in contact with your father either by phone or by going back to his house, the family home, on odd occasions? You... forgive me...

A It was too far away so I don't know, cos it was... I wouldn't have had any means of getting there.

Q Did you have any means to ring him and speak to him?

A There was a phone... where we used to live at the bottom of the street, lodging, there were a phone box there but I can't ever remember ringing him.

Q No, okay, so no contact at all, you think, between you and your mum leaving and the time when you returned, whenever that was?

A Not when I ret... we had contact before I returned and that was on Barnsley market.

Q Okay, and that's the only contact you had?

A That I can remember, yeah.

Q But you can't remember how that was arranged or what led to that meeting in Barnsley?

A It might have been through Donna and Paul.

Q Okay.

A My brother or sister. My brother, Paul, might have helped arrange it. I don't know. I can't remember.

Q I take it you can't help us with a date when it was that you returned back to Denby Dale?

A No.

Q Do you remember a time when your father attempted suicide?

A I remember coming in from school and me mum shouting, "Don't come upstairs" and when I... when... and I did, I ignored her and I got halfway up stairs and me dad were hanging from rafters.

Q You remember that occasion then?

A Yeah.

Q I think it's going to be a matter of evidence one way and... one way or the other, that that event was in June 1983.

A Right.

Q Do we take it from that that by then you were living back in Denby Dale?

A I don't know if that were before me mum had left him then.

Q Right, okay. Well, that was something else I was going to ask you. Do you remember whether your mother was still living with him at that time?

A I don't... I'm not sure...

Q Okay.

A ...whether she was still living with him or they'd tried to make some kind of recon... I don't know.

Q You can't remember?

A No.

Q Fair enough. You mentioned in your interview with the police that your father went on a trip to America?

A Yes.

Q I'm going to suggest that that was right at the very end of the same year, sort of November/December 1983?

A Yeah.

Q That sound about right, does it?

A I don't know. I'm just taking your word for it.

Q Okay, fine, all right. I wasn't sure if you were agreeing with me or just...

A Yeah.

Q ...confirming you'd heard what I said.

A No. Sorry. Could you just give me the date of the...

Q November to December 1983, so it's some time around that period is what I'm suggesting.

A Yeah.

Q And you've said you can't say one way or the other?

A Yeah.

Q And I'm suggesting that therefore you were about 14, 14 and a half when that will have occurred?

A Yeah.

Q And, again, can I check whether you're agreeing with me about that or just confirming you heard what I said?

A I just know it was when he first came back from America on his first hunting trip that that were the first night he raped me.

Q Well, I want to try and see what your recollection of when that was, first of all. That's why I'm putting these things to you.

A Mmm.

Q Are you agreeing that you would have been about 14 at the time of that trip?

A Yeah. I would have said round about 13, 14, yeah.

Q And your dad was away for two or three weeks? Is that correct?

A I don't know if he went for two week. We stayed with me Auntie Hilda, me and me brother.

Q And I think you told the police that, whilst your dad was away, you and your brother held a wild party. That's the phrase you used.

A Yeah.

Q And...

A Well, we held a party and it got wild cos things got damaged.

Q And you'd managed to get a set of keys cut for the house to allow the party... to allow you to get in whilst your father was away, hadn't you?

A Yeah.

Q And when he came back, the house was a mess?

A Yeah. It was a mess and me mum had been and took half the furniture because me dad said he'd always saw it in half if she took it so he wouldn't let her have it, so she'd broke in while he was away as well and got a trailer. She got somebody to bring a car and took half the furniture.

Q Do you know how she broke in?

A No.

Q Were you involved in helping her get into the house with the keys that you or your brother had cut?

A I didn't know she were gonna do it, no.

Q Okay, and when your dad got back, he was furious, wasn't he?

A Yeah.

Q You told the police that you took a knife to your wrist?

A Yeah.

Q Why?

A I told the police when I gave my 15 page statement...

Q No.

A ...17 page statement when I were 15...

Q When you were interviewed, the interview that we watched yesterday afternoon and thismorning...

A Oh yeah, yeah.

Q ...you cut your wrists?

A Yeah. He... when he come back from America he was fuming so... and he said he wanted to know who'd been to the party and he'd gone round to phone Jess, his girlfriend, from Penistone who he was going out with at the time, and he wanted to know by time he got back and I was frightened to death and I took a knife out the kitchen drawer and I tried to cut my wrist and my brother dragged me round to the phone box and me dad brought me back round with Paul and he tied a bandage round my wrist and he says, "You're too ill to... you're too mentally... you're not mentally stable", or something, "to sleep on your own tonight. You've got to sleep with me".

Q I wanted to ask you why it was you cut your wrist?

A Because I was scared of what he was going to do about, you know, the boys coming to the party because he was really jealous.

Q What was he jealous of?

A Like you say, me having friends, going out.

Q So because your dad didn't like you having friends, you took a knife to your wrists?

A Because I was scared what he was going to do to us. I thought he was going to physically beat me cos he said... he'd already threatened, "I want to know by time you come back or else there's gonna be trouble".

Q How far away did your Auntie Hilda live?

A She lived in the next village in Scissett.

Q Right. Could you not have gone there?

A What, after he'd come back from America?

Q Mmm.

A No, it's a long way away and it never entered me head to run away from home.

Q What made you think that cutting your wrists would do anything?

A I didn't think about that at the time. I just was scared of him.

Q Had you ever done it before?

A No.

Q No. And how badly did you do it?

A Well, it felt like it were bad at the time but it were obviously not deep enough for stitches cos he just put a bandage round it.

Q The reality is that the cutting of your wrists never occurred, did it?

A Yes, it did.

Q And the account that you gave the police and that you've just given us of him then bandaging it up for you, that didn't happen, did it?

A Yes, it did, and my brother can witness it cos he took me round to the phone box as well. He dragged me round. He were panicking.

Q And your father never suggested you should sleep in his bed that night, did he?

A Yes, he did.

Q And he didn't have sexual intercourse with you that night?

A Yes, he did.

Q What do you say made you think to ask your dad, "What would grandad say?"

A I don't know. I don't know what made me think to say that. He were still laid on top of me when I said it.

Q Well, I suggest, unsurprisingly, that that was never said.

A Yes, it was.

Q Nor was anything said about "Breaking your daughters in like the Indians do".

A (No audible response)

Q Isn't what really happened here that when he got back he was sufficiently cross with you and your brother, particularly with you, that he told you you should go and live with your mother again?

A No. A social... I don't know where this... what... whether it had happened before he'd gone to America or after America, but a social worker who used to come and give him food parcels and fivers out of his back pocket said to me that I'd been to live with me mum once and if I... and it were obvious that I couldn't make me mind up who I wanted to go and live with and if I... if I changed me mind I'd be... or if I didn't stay where I was, I'd be put in a... if I didn't stay with me dad, that I'd be put in a children's home, and me sister had been in a children's home and she told me she'd been sexually abused in that children's home.

Q Did you contact your mother at any stage around that time?

A No. I don't know. She'd taken... she'd... so... she'd taken the furniture and me dad used to poison me mum. I used to call me mum a slag and that. I were angry with me mum.

Q Did you know where she was living at that time?

A I can't remember if she was still at Mill House or whether she'd got an house with Carl in Thurgoland at that time.

Q That's Carl Higgins? Is that right?

A Yes.

Q And is it right, as I've assumed, that you've taken his surname as yours?

A Yeah. That were a long time... that were quite a while after she married him, yeah.

Q Right, because your mum married him, thank you. You've answered that next question I was going to ask.

A Mmm. No, it wasn't cos me mum married him why I took that name on.

Q Okay.

A I took that name on because his... cos me mum divorced him. I took that name on because he's a nice man.

Q Okay.

A And I didn't want to be an Appleyard anymore. I didn't wanted to be marred with me dad's name. I didn't want to be... I didn't... I was ashamed of being an Appleyard.

Q Do you remember when it was your mum married Carl Higgins?

A It was when she were living at this house, this council house, at Thurgoland.

Q So they were living together before they married? Is that right?

A I think so, yeah.

Q Okay, and did you go to see her or speak to her at any stage when she was living at the house in Thurgoland?

A Yeah, I remember, cos I remember once shouting at her in the middle of street she were a fucking slag and things like that. I was angry with her and I was still living at me dad's. I used to call her a whore and that.

Q When she was living in Thurgoland with Carl Higgins?

A Yeah, and I were living at me dad's and we'd gone to visit her. I can't remember how I got there or how I got back.

Q If that was what you thought of her, why were you going to visit her?

A Cos I... I loved her. She were me mum and I've... that's why, and me sister were there. I wanted to see my sister, Donna.

Q You've already mentioned the fact that your father got custody of you and Paul?

A Yeah.

Q Yeah? And, again, I suspect you won't remember the date that that occurred, will you?

A No.

Q No, but, again, we've been given that information by the prosecution, and it was April 1984?

A Mmm.

Q Okay?

A Mmm.

Q I may have told you that before, I forget, I'm afraid, but it involved a hearing at, I think a magistrates' court? Is that right?

A I don't think I went to it. I don't know where I was but I know when he come out we went to a Chinese restaurant to celebrate but I don't know where I... I can't remember being in a court. I don't know where I was waiting for it.

Q Well, do you remember this? If I... if I suggest something to you that happened, it might jog your memory. Do you remember that you and Paul were asked to speak to the district judge in his room, just the two of you with him and a social worker?

A I don't remember that.

Q No? Did that not take place before the district judge decided that you could both live with your dad?

A I can't remember any meetings with anybody.

Q Were there meetings between you and social workers at around that time?

A Only meeting I've had with a social worker where Mr Sykes told me that if I left me dad's house that I'd be put in a children's home.

Q Did you say to this Mr Sykes or to anybody else what your dad was doing to you?

A No.

Q But at some point...

A Cos me dad were there in that meeting.

Q With Mr Sykes?

A Yeah.

Q That's not something you've mentioned before, is it, I don't think?

A It was in our kitchen at Denby Dale where we lived, a meeting. He come to our house and he said it... we were stood in the kitchen and that's when he said it.

Q And you say you didn't have any other meeting with a social worker any time other than that meeting in your kitchen?

A No. Social workers were regular people who came to our house...

Q Yes.

A ...and I've never been took to an office for a meeting. The only other time I spoke to a social worker were when they came to school before when just the kissing had started before he started having sex with me.

Q At some point after custody was granted by the court to your dad in relation to you and Paul...

A Yeah.

Q ...did you leave and go back to stay with your mother again?

A Could you say that again, please?

Q Was there a time after your dad had been granted custody when you left the house in Denby Dale and went to live with your mother again?

A Was there a time, what?

Q When you left Denby Dale and went to live with your mother again?

A Yeah, when I went to live with my mum again, so after me dad had been raping me for a while, I left when I were about 15 and a half, I'd say, that I ran away.

Q Because I'm suggesting, in fact, that you left within a few months of him getting custody of you, still in 1984.

A I can't remember that because I know that when I moved back to Penistone Grammar School I wasn't there that long.

Q And, in reality, there wasn't, in fact, anything to stop you leaving Denby Dale when you wanted to?

A Yes, there was.

Q And it was, in fact, something you did a number of times?

A What was that?

Q Leave Denby Dale.

A No, no, no. I left once when I ran away when I were 15 and a half about, when I couldn't take anymore.

Q You told the police about a girlfriend your dad had, someone called Jess?

A Yeah.

Q Do you remember when she was around, when she was seeing your dad?

A In that period he were raping me.

Q Which period? Can you be specific?

A No. When he come back from America cos he went to ring her. He come... when he come back that night he went round to the phone box and that were the night that I slit my wrists so he was seeing her then.

Q And do you remember whether she stayed over at the house?

A Yeah, she used to stay over sometimes.

Q Are you sure about that?

A Yeah, I think so. She were over from Penistone.

Q You told the police that you were aware of Paul walking into the kitchen and seeing you and your father snogging?

A Yes, on a Sunday morning he was full on snogging me.

Q What did you say to Paul about it afterwards?

A I didn't speak to Paul, I don't think, about it afterwards. I just remember being in shock and thinking what's... how's he gonna explain this to Paul now and somehow he managed to explain it. I don't know what happened but...

Q Well, were you present when he explained it?

A I can't remember. I don't... we're going... I think I was but not all of it.

Q Okay. Well, what do you remember being present for? What do you remember hearing between your dad and Paul?

A Him saying, "It's not what you think", something to them words.

Q Anything else?

A Saying something about not to worry and... I can't really remember.

Q Did you speak to Paul about it afterwards?

A No.

Q Did he ask you about it?

A No, because I think my... my dad, how he'd explained it to him made him believe that... I don't know. He tried... covered it over for... somehow he covered it over.

Q You told the police that Paul had got really upset and confused?

A Who told the police?

Q You did in the interview that we saw the recording of this morning.

A Well, Paul was stood there. I watched... he was shocked, yeah.

Q Yeah.

A He were like wondering, yeah. I remember his face being shocked.

Q But the upset and confusion didn't lead him to ask you anything about it or for you to discuss it with him?

A No. We didn't... he didn't... we never answered me dad back. Whatever he said went as gospel, always.

Q No, but there must have come a time after that incident when you and Paul were alone together and could have spoken about it when your dad wasn't around?

A No.

Q No? You and Paul never had the chance to be alone together?

A Yeah, we had chance to be alone together but we never discussed it.

Q Okay.

A Paul had seen me in his bed on Saturday mornings while Paul were playing out on his bike and we'd always like... we'd grown up play-fighting in my dad's bed and that and he'd seen me dad being familiar with me. I think we just thought it were normal.

Q Well, again, you told the police in your interview that you used to play-fight with your mum and your dad in bed when you were growing up?

A Not... me mum didn't. She used to just lay there. It were me dad who kept smacking my arse all time and leaving red hand marks on me arse and tickling me till, you know, it hurt and things like that.

Q But playing in your parents' bed was something that you all did as kids, wasn't it?

A I remember me on me own doing it, being there, but sometimes we was all there.

Q Well, I'm simply suggesting that that's something that all three of you would do when your mum and dad were still together.

A When we were a lot younger, but me dad were play-fighting with me and holding me down when Jess were there in the front living room that day when he give me love bites on me neck...

Q And sometimes...

A ...trying to make out as if it were a joke.

Q Sometimes Paul would get into your dad's bed after your mum had left...

A I can't...

Q ...not because anything was happening...

A I can't remember that.

Q Right, but this wasn't something that you and Paul ever discussed, you say?

A No.

Q No? At least not at the time?

A No because I tried to keep it away from Paul what me dad were doing to me.

Q But it's something...

A I tried to keep what little family we'd got left together.

Q It's something that you and Paul have discussed since then, isn't it?

A Yeah.

Q And there was a time, wasn't there, when you and Paul both wanted to have tattoos?

A I don't know. Me dad suggested me having a tattoo.

Q Well, I'm suggesting that it was...

A Then...

Q ...you and Paul who wanted the tattoos and...

A Then Paul wanted one and, when me dad took us, he had a swallow put on his neck that same day as he put that one... had that one put on my neck and Paul had one on his arm but it wasn't our suggestion to have the tattoos. It were me dad who wanted me to have a tattoo on me back.

Q All right. Well, I'm... I've already suggested that it was, in fact, you and Paul who were asking for it and that was why your father took you to have the tattoos put on?

A No.

Q And your dad's tattoo, in fact, said, "Carol and Paul"?
A No, it did not. No, it did not.
Q And it was...
A It said, "Sam and Caz".
Q I'm sorry, Miss Higgins. Your father's tattoo, the tattoo your father had put on his body...
A He didn't have one. He had a... he had a swallow put on his neck.
Q ...said, "Carol and Paul"?
A No, he had a swallow put on his... he never...
Q And it was, in fact, your choice, not his, what the tattoo you had said?
A No, because how would I have known about him being called Sam? He were... it's him who told me he were called Sam. I says, "Your name's Elliott" and he says, "No, they call me Sam when... that were me nickname when I were growing up as a child", and I went, "Well, I've never heard you being called that". It was him.
Q Sam was the dog, wasn't it?
A He had a dog called Sam but it wasn't his name on me back. It wasn't the dog's name. Why would I have a dog's name on me back?
Q You told us, Miss Higgins, that your father would make you masturbate him?
A Yes.
Q How would he make you masturbate him?
A In his bed and he used to sit there, lay... like sat up in his bed and he used to have a magazine and he used to have magazines and I'd be at side of him and he used to make me masturbate him.
Q Well, what did he do to make you masturbate him?
A He lay there naked and told me to masturbate him. Well, he didn't... I don't think he used the word "masturbate", but he told me to wank him off or something or he just put me hand there.
Q And the magazines, you told the police, you would be asked to read out loud to him?
A Yeah.

Q Weren't you meant to be being quiet when you were doing things with your dad?

A Yeah.

Q Because Paul's bedroom was next door? Is that right?

A No. Paul's bedroom, he... was at the other end of the landing and I wouldn't speak loud, that he would ask me to read to him, and Paul's bedroom... and he even swapped us bedrooms cos I had the big bedroom with Donna and then at some stage he made me swap and have Paul's bedroom because it meant he didn't have to walk along the creaky floorboards across the big bedroom to get me. He could just walk to the top of the stairs where the little bedroom was and come in and get me and walk me down the landing to his bedroom.

Q Well, you - I don't know if you remember - you spoke to the police about changing bedrooms when they interviewed you?

A Mmm.

Q Again, we saw that, I think this morning, that bit, and you told the police you thought that, in fact, it was just that Paul had, whilst you were away for that eight, 10 month period, moved from the smaller bedroom to the bigger bedroom because it was the bigger bedroom?

A Well, I know that I was in the big bedroom when he went to America and when... I had the big bedroom at some stage. I know I ended up with the little bedroom. He says, "I want you to swap bedrooms".

Q Might it just be nothing more than Paul, teenage boy, wanting a bigger room that was free?

A I don't think so.

Q Not your dad moving it, or moving you...

A No, I wouldn't have given...

Q ...for his convenience?

A No. I wouldn't have given the bigger bed... Why would I want to go and live in a little bedroom when I had a big bedroom?

Q And, again, I've got to suggest to you, Miss Higgins, that you never read rude magazines, as you put it, to your father and you never masturbated him, did you?
A Yes, I did.
Q Nor did he ever make you perform oral sex on him?
A Yes, he did. He stank.
Q You said he always used a condom?
A Yeah. He used to keep 'em in a little drawer at side of his bed.
Q Do you have any recollection at all of what happened to the condoms afterwards?
A No.
Q Do you have any idea why he might have made a comment about you having an albino baby if you got pregnant then?
A He said that his friends lived happily together as man and wife. He had friends who lived with their daughters. The only thing that wasn't like what we couldn't do as man and wife was have a baby because it would be albino. It would have pink eyes and white hair.
Q But, given that he was using condoms, you say, that wouldn't have happened anyway, would it?
A Not as... no, but I didn't know. I had a pregnancy scare at one time. I thought I were pregnant.
Q And when did that happen?
A During the time that he was sleeping with me.
Q And what happened as a result of that pregnancy scare?
A I went to me mum's and told her that I thought I might be pregnant and she took me to the doctor's for a pregnancy test and she says, "Who do you think..." She says, "Who's the father?" and I says, "It's just this lad I'm seeing", and I wasn't seeing any lad.
Q Why did you not tell your mother that your father was making you do things you didn't want to do?

A Because I didn't want to be put into care and I didn't want to live with me mum. I didn't like her either, how she were treating me.

Q Did you say anything to the doctor?

A I didn't really see the doctor. I think she just got a bottle or something, I can't remember, and I... and I did a wee sample and she took it like that.

Q So you didn't actually go to the doctor at all?

A She took me to the... to a... I think she took me to the reception area in Penistone doctors and she got a... a bottle from behind the counter there and that's how I did it, I think, and I wee'ed and then you hand it over the counter.

Q You weren't pregnant though, were you?

A No.

Q No. If you had been, it wouldn't have been your father's, would it?

A Yes, unless... I don't know if a condom split, but it couldn't have been anybody else's.

Q You told the police about your leg being burned by a fire on one occasion?

A Yeah.

Q How badly burned was it?

A It didn't burn. I could... it were just hot. It was like when he laid me down on the rug in the front living room the fire was roaring and he was on top of me and he was going in and out of me and I wanted it to be over quickly and so I thought I'm not going to tell you so... but I couldn't stand the heat of the fire on me leg anymore, so...

Q So it's not... it's not the - I'm sorry to cut across you - it's not the case that your leg was burned then?

A It was burning. It was red hot. It was red.

Q Right.

A But it didn't burn where I needed to go to hospital or put anything on it because I had to tell him to stop because of the pain.

Q Well, again, unsurprisingly, I suggest that that simply didn't happen at all, did it?

A Yes, it did, because when I said that to him he started getting angry with me and saying, "It's cos you don't really want to do it", and I were going, "Yeah, I do, I do, really".

Q You told the police that on the last occasion it happened you told him, "No"?

A Yeah.

Q What had changed between previous occasions and the last occasion?

A I don't know. I just felt like I couldn't take anymore. We was arguing because he was going out and he was making me stay in as well and I just didn't want to be there and do what he wanted me to keep doing to him anymore.

Q Why were you not able to say, "No" before that last occasion?

A I never said, "No" to my dad.

Q But you...

A I always did as I was told.

Q You did on the last occasion?

A Yeah.

Q Why couldn't you have done it before?

A Cos I weren't brave enough and I kind of accepted that we were like man and wife. I believed him that we could live together as man and wife.

Q You told the police about a tin box?

A Yeah.

Q Can you describe that for us?

A Yeah. It was about that wide and about that big and it was an old army metal tin box and he kept a Polaroid camera in there and he used to take pictures of me in underwear and there was a white-handled brush there. He used to ask me to pose and pretend I was giving it a blow job and stick inside me vagina.

Q Where was that box kept?

A In his bedroom.

Q Whereabouts?

A Not far from the side of his bed and he had a lock on it.

Q Because, again, whilst he might have had an army box in the house, he didn't have one with a Polaroid camera in, did he, in reality?

A Yes, he did.

Q Because there was never a Polaroid camera in the house at all, was there?

A Yes, he did. Yes, he did.

Q And he certainly didn't have you pose for pictures in underwear or with hairbrushes?

A Yes, he did.

Q And he didn't treat you as his wife or his girlfriend?

A Yes, he put me mum's engagement ring on me finger.

Q Well, again, specifically, I suggest that didn't happen either, did it?

A Yes, it did.

Q Which of his friends do you say he was referring to when you say he told you he had friends living as man and wife with their daughters?

A I don't know.

Q Did you ask him?

A No.

Q Did you know who his friends were at the time?

A Not really, no. Sometimes we'd go to Scissett Club. That's where his aunt... his family, me Auntie Hilda and Uncle Peter and Gallaghers would be there and that would be a time as well when he were having sex with me. We used to walk down there holding hands like we were a couple. We used to go to clubs and listen to musicians and that and he once took me to another club. I don't know where it was. It was a drive in his van and we were sat there drinking as if we were a couple.

Q He might have taken you to clubs, Miss Higgins, but not as man and wife?

A Yeah, he did.

Q And he didn't tell you...

A Well, not man and wife, obviously, but it were like engagement ring on me finger, like boyfriend and girlfriend.

Q He didn't really tell you that he had friends who lived with their daughters likc that, did he?

A Yes, he did.

Q You told us that you went to live with your mother?

A Yeah.

Q And that you told her, you say, what was going on?

A Yeah.

Q How and where do you say you told her what was going on?

A On the back of a bus cos, when I left, I got on a bus and I went to Penistone and they'd been out drinking, I think, in Penistone and they was getting a bus from Penistone to Thurgoland and she lived at Thurgoland and I got on a bus and I was surprised to see her there and that's when I told her and she got off the bus and she says, "Where's your dad now?" and I says, "He's at Denby Dale Pie Hall", so she rang the Pie Hall and they brought him to the phone and she says, "Our Carol's here with me now. She's told me everything", and he went, "You can't prove a thing" to her.

Q Because you seem to suggest in your book that you told your mum at her house?

A No. I told her on the bus.

Q So if your book says that you told her at her house, your book would be wrong, would it?

A I don't think I... I didn't say I told her... I told her on the bus.

Q You told the police that there were some of your friends on the bus as well who you told?

A I know at some point, I don't know whether it was that night when I ran away, but I know at some point I told my friends that he'd been having sex with me and I told Diane Croft it as well.

Q And you ran through a list of names of people you said you could remember being on the bus at the time you were telling them about him...

A Yeah, yeah.

Q ...you say raping you?

A I said me dad had been sleeping with me. I didn't say "raping". I didn't know at the time it was rape what he was doing to me.

Q Was there ever a time when your mum said nothing (sic) to you about going to speak to the police about things between you and your dad?

A When I ran away and I told her, she said, "I want you to go to the police" and I didn't go straightaway. I said I didn't want to. I didn't want to get him into trouble and I felt guilty for not saying, "No", and then about a week later I went to the police and gave a 17 page statement and I went to Huddersfield Police Station, had an internal forensic test done and they took pubes, put 'em in test tubes, they took swabs and they had me jump up and down on blotting paper and I was bleeding, and I think they must have thought I were miscarrying but I wasn't.

Q Was it your mother's suggestion to go to the police then?

A I think it was, yes.

Q And did you discuss with her at all what you should say to the police when you got there?

A No, just... she told me to tell them what he'd been doing to me, what had happened.

Q Was your mother present during the conversation you had with the police?

A Not that I know of. I can't... don't think she was, no.

Q Nothing ever happened at that time, did it, in terms of any charge being brought?

A They said to me that because it hadn't... they said to me, if it went to court, they would make me out to be biggest liar, they'd drag me name through the mud and it'd black... blacken me name and I'd be made out to be biggest slag going, could I handle that, and I said, "No", and they said, because it hadn't gone to court, it could be brought back in the future whereas, if it had gone to court and it got thrown out and that me brother would be classed as a juvenile witness, then... and if it got to court and it got thrown out, then I'd never be able to bring it back, but they said, because it hadn't gone to court, I would be able to bring it back in the future, and I've tried five times.

Q I think you met the father of your children, Stephen Marsh, in 1985? Is that right?
A I can't remember what year it was.
Q Okay.
A I was 17.
Q Someone else known as Sam? Is that right?
A Yeah. He's called Stephen Marsh but his nickname's Sam.
Q You never had a conversation with your father in a Barnsley café in which he apologised, did you?
A Yes.
Q Nor did he ever...
A And it wasn't in a café. No, it wasn't in a café. It was at the top near some escalators on some red seats. It wasn't actually in the café, cos his wife had gone in a café and so he... and she wasn't there. It wasn't in a café, no.
Q Nor did he ever say that it was because he loved you like a person, not a daughter?
A Yes, he did.
Q It's right, isn't it, that you had two children of your own?
A Yeah.
Q With Stephen Marsh?
A Yeah. We courted, we got engaged, we got an house, we got married, and I had them when I was 25 and 29.
Q And there were times, weren't there, when you would contact your dad?
A No. There were one time when my son got older and he wouldn't stop going on about his grandad, because everybody else had got grandads, and I'd always said to him that he was a violent man, "You wouldn't want to know him", and...
Q Well...
A And that was after I'd already been to see him, me dad. I've seen him twice in all them years I've been gone and the other time was when my faith told me... I'd been to church and it was Father's Day and I went to his house and

took a Father's Day card because I was trying to learn about forgiveness because I couldn't stand the pain I was in all the time and all the counselling that I'd been having, so Janet answered the door and she went into the front room and I says to him, "I've come to tell you I forgive you for what you've done", and he started talking about what... him and me mum arguing all the time and how me mum wouldn't let him come to Donna's funeral, cos my sister took her own life, and I says, "I know what happened between you and me mum". I says, "I were there", I says, "but you were... but you were both adults. What you did to me, you was an adult and I was a child", I says, "and I thought you'd at least be sorry for what you've done", and he went like that. He went, "Oh, sorry", inaudibly, and I says, "I thought you might at least look me in the eyes and say sorry", and he didn't, and I just said, "I've come to say what I wanted to say", and I left, and then it were after that Jake was going on about seeing his grandad and Jake would not stop, he was so persistent, and I took him and then Jake come away and he were biting his collar all the time like this and he says, "I thought grandads were supposed to be nice", and he never wanted to see his grandad after that. He could see the anger, the vileness in him.

Q You had nothing to forgive your father for, in reality, did you?

A Yes, I did.

Q You contact...

A Well, I didn't... I shouldn't have forgiven him. I didn't forgive him. I don't know why I said it. It just felt like I needed to... to try and help my healing.

Q You contacted him by phone on occasions and he'd respond...

A Never.

Q ...to text messages?

A Never, no.

Q Never inviting him for lunch or telling him you were thinking about him when you were cooking Sunday lunch or anything like that?

A I tried to have a... tried to put this behind me and I couldn't put it behind me, what he'd done to me.

Q I think you and Stephen Marsh divorced in about 2000? Is that right?
A It were about 18 years ago, yeah.
Q That may be right, 2000, 2001, something like that?
A Mmm.
Q And in the... in the mid-2000s I think you - I'm not going to go into it in any detail at all - but you saw the doctor quite a lot, didn't you?
A I've always had to see the doctor and have counselling a lot really.
Q You were, I think, diagnosed as suffering from anxiety and depression? Is that right?
A When I went to Rape Crisis when I was 16 year old and from then onwards I've been... I've... I've been told I've got post-traumatic stress disorder.
JUDGE JAMESON: Sorry, do forgive me. I missed what you said there. You were told that you'd got?
A Post-traumatic stress disorder.
JUDGE JAMESON: Yeah. Thank you.
MR STOREY: But by the mid-2000s I think you were... you were taking medication that was prescribed? Is that right?
A I've been taking...
Q Antidepressants?
A I took Prozac for about 10 year.
Q Okay.
A But I didn't like taking medication cos me mam were on Valium and she were either really passive or really violent and aggressive.
Q Did the counselling that you say you underwent give you ideas about what might have led to your recollections?
A Why would it?
Q Did you get ideas in the counselling about what to say to the police had gone on here?
A I hadn't had any counselling when I went to the police when I was 15 and gave a 17 page statement.
Q You went back to the police in 2005? Is that right?

A Yeah. I rang them.

Q And did they say effectively that they couldn't re-open the investigation?

A Because they couldn't find my statements and they'd got nothing to compare them to.

Q And, moving forward a few years, by 2012 you'd decided to speak to some solicitors about it, hadn't you?

A Jordans Solicitors, yes.

Q And they wrote to West Yorkshire Police on your behalf, didn't they?

A I think three times, two or three times, and said that there was corroborative evidence to open a case.

Q And they told you in a letter they sent to you...

A That the police hadn't...

Q ...that...

A ...responded.

Q They told you in a letter that they sent to you that they were going to investigate whether your father had any assets that were worth pursuing, didn't they?

A Oh well, that were nothing to do with me. I can't help that the solicitors brought that into it.

Q And then they wrote back later to say they hadn't found any so they couldn't do anything more for you?

A I can't help that. That's them not going ahead with the case cos they said, "You can't..." I think they said something, "You can't sue a man and... who lives in a straw house", something like that, but it was never about suing him for money.

Q And they told you you'd have to apply to the Criminal Injuries Compensation Authority? That's right, isn't it?

A It never entered my head until about three year ago, I think I decided to do that. None of... none of that entered me head. I never did none of that back then.

Q	Well, I'm suggesting that in 2012, 2013 Jordans told you they would investigate whether your father had assets. They then told you they had and that he didn't and that you'd have to apply to the Criminal Injuries Compensation Authority?
A	I can't help that they told me that. I didn't ask for that information. It's just what they give.
Q	Okay, so you agree that they did tell you that at around that time?
A	They put it in a letter.
Q	Yeah.
A	They didn't tell me it. They put it in a letter...
Q	All right.
A	...when they said that the police hadn't replied back to them and they couldn't open a case.
Q	And, in fact, you have more recently made an application to the Criminal Injuries Compensation Authority...
A	Yeah, for the...
Q	...haven't you?
A	...years and years of counselling that I've had, the trauma that he's caused and for the work that I've not been able to do for me having to get to counselling, pay for petrol, pay for some of my counselling as well.
Q	And is some sort of financial reward what you're really after here, Miss Higgins?
A	No. I want justice and I want him to go down for what he's done to me, the way he's made me suffer all these years.
Q	You also wanted publicity, didn't you?
A	No. If this had have gone to court when it should have done and... when I went in 2005 and 2012, five times, and 2014, then I wouldn't have had to go public with it at all, and that's the only time I went public with it in 2015.
Q	I think you...

A All them years, 35... well, this case has been... been investigated four year now, so 31 years ago I hadn't done anything about... never entered me head about compensation.

Q I think you appeared on a BBC Radio Leeds programme in about 2012?

A Yeah.

Q About what you say happened to you?

A It was about the climb up Kilimanjaro and battling cancer. It was about conquering mountains.

Q And you've just told us 2014 you again went to the police?

A Yeah, and I was made to sit five hours in a waiting room and then I was told it wasn't exactly a statement and that no case would be opened and I asked for that in writing and I got it back in writing off Sonia Strafford.

Q And you published your book the following year, 2015? That's right, isn't it?

A I did it myself, yeah. I'm... I self-published.

Q And you publicised the book again by... I think you at least tried to get on to Calendar or This Morning or both of them in that time? Is that right?

A No. In 2012 I'd had an operation, an hernia operation, and - I don't watch much telly - and I went downstairs and I put the telly on and it was talking on Newsnight about incest being rife in England and nothing was being done about it and I wrote my story to Good Morning Britain. My friend, Al - he's a school teacher - he came and sat at side of me bed with a laptop and he writ down what I told him to put, and I wrote to Good Morning Britain to say what had happened to me because I didn't... I didn't... I wanted awareness and I wanted justice.

Q Do you know who sent a copy of your book to your father's wife, Janet?

A Me. I posted it to her, as soon as I'd had it... as soon as I published it, because I didn't... I weren't a coward, I weren't going behind his back with what I'd done, and I sent it to her and I sent it to her because, if I'd have put his name on it, he would have ripped it up and not let her see what he'd done to me.

Q What can you tell us about flyers that appeared in the Denby Dale area advertising your book?

A I'd never seen 'em until they pulled me in, the police, for an harassment warning, and they showed me them. I wasn't aware of them.

Harassment Charge

Q Really?

A Yeah.

Q You had no idea that somebody else entirely independent of you was putting flyers up in the area where your father lived, advertising your book?

A No. I live at Ackworth and this was happening in Denby Dale and it's a long way. It's about 18 mile away and I didn't have a clue.

Q Again, around this time, 2015...

JUDGE JAMESON: Could you just go...

MR STOREY: I'm sorry, your Honour.

JUDGE JAMESON: ...a fraction slower? Yes.

MR STOREY: 2015 again, did you start to contact people who you thought could be witnesses for you?

A I did a book launch when I've launched my book, that I was proud of launching, and it was more about my climb up Kilimanjaro, conquering physical mountains and psychological mountains, and the biggest mountain I'd had to climb were my childhood abuse. I decided to have a book launch in Denby Dale where I came from and it was at that book launch people came forward and said that they were sorry to hear what had happened to me and that they remembered me dad saying to me next door neighbour when she were 15, "Has your father broke you in yet?" and also she come camping with us when we were younger to Wales and she was stood in a tent and she was brushing her teeth and she'd got some toothpaste on her top and he says... and she were brushing... and he says to her, "What's up? Did he miss thee gob?" and that's what she said to me at the book launch, and then another lady said to me that she remembers the love bites and she knew me father would be... me father wouldn't let me... allow that to happen by anybody else.

Q Did you specifically choose to have your book launch in Denby Dale?

A I had me first book launch in Ackworth at the Frog and Moose and that's where I had it on me... on me birthday, 23rd of April, and after that I wanted to go back to the village where I'd grown up and have my book launch there.

Q The village where your father still lived?

A Yeah.

Q It was November of that year, 2015, when you were interviewed by the police and that video we... or the video recording of that interview we've seen. I think you tried to further publicise your allegations after that, didn't you?

A What do you mean?

Q Well, you... didn't you apply to go on Big Brother in the early part of 2016 with a view to being able to tell people about your experience?

A Not a view to tell anybody about my experience. I would have liked to go on Big Brother and said, "I'm an author and I've climbed a mountain and..."

Q And did you not publicise that decision on Facebook?

A Yeah, and I think... and I think that awareness should be brought to people's attention that incest is rife and nothing's being done about it.

Q Do you know anything at all about occasions where there have been damage caused to your father's vehicles or to the Pie Hall where he used to drink in Denby Dale?

A Only when they brought me in on an harassment charge against him and... but I didn't know who'd done it or that it had happened.

Q You began, I think, communicating with the police quite extensively, didn't you?

A When?

Q Because you began sending lists of witnesses to the officer investigating? That's right, isn't it?

A Lists?

Q Yes.

A Well, how many's... Lists? You... that...

Q Well, you sent a document that comprised a list of names of people you felt should be seen by the police as witnesses...

A Yeah.

Q ...didn't you?

A Yeah. That was after the police had been out to see him and they said that I had to get witnesses if they were gonna... to give them names of witnesses, and obviously I gave him the name of the lady who he'd said, "Has your father broke you into you yet?" and I gave him names of Ena from the book launch and I gave him... I couldn't understand all these years why they've never taken a statement off me mum or off me brother. They should have done all that. They should have retaken another one off me if they've lost me statement when I were 15 but I've... they've made me wait all these years. They would never let me take one... let me give one.

Q It's the case, isn't it, Mrs Higgins, that you felt the police weren't taking you seriously?

A They wasn't opening a case. They've always said that they believed me but they said that it would be an abuse of process cos he'd been investigated in 1984. Well, I know he hadn't been investigated in 1984.

Q You began to chase the police by contacting the officer, didn't you, the officer in charge of the investigation?

A What do you mean, I began to chase the police?

Q You began to contact him repeatedly or to try and contact him repeatedly?

A The police came out to my... he said he was gonna be there... What year are you talking about?

Q I'm talking about the period after you made your interview with the police that was video recorded at the end of 2015...

A What do you mean? I...

Q ...so 2016.

A He said he was gonna... I gave my video... I gave my video statement and then the police said that they was going to start interviewing Carl Higgins, who was there the night on the bus, and going to see my mum and going to see my brother and things, and they was very slow at it and I couldn't understand and he was saying he couldn't find Carl Higgins and he couldn't find where me Auntie Hilda lived and then he said that, you know, he wouldn't... he'd been to me Auntie Hilda but she was too poorly to come to court so he didn't take a statement and I was getting angry and saying, "So you mean somebody who's witnessed a murder or a rape, if he won't come to court, it stands for jack shit"? That's what I said. I says, "You need to go and get that statement". I was... I was push... yeah, I was persistent in...- in saying that you need to investigate this.

Q And did you think that this was all part of a police cover-up?

A I don't know what it was.

Q Did you start publicising your views about this being a police cover-up...

A It felt like it.

Q ...on Facebook?

A It felt like it to me.

Q Did you start publicising your views about it being a police cover-up...

A I was...

Q ...on Facebook?

A I was recording publicly that, you know, the obstacles that I was facing and that I felt like I was, you know, I was having doors pushed... slammed shut in my face.

Q Did you publicise on Facebook your views were that this was part of a police cover-up, Miss Higgins?

A I didn't know whether it was a police cover-up or not.

Q Did you say that on Facebook?

A It feels like it's been a police cover-up, yes.

Q Did you visit a pub that you knew your father drank in, the Star Inn in Upper Cumberworth in February 2019, sorry, 2017?

A I went there with my girlfriends from Denby Dale. It was... I think it was Boxing Day or something and we had some drinks.

Q And did you leave copies of your book lying around there...

A No.

Q ...with regulars?

A No. There was a gentleman came talking to me and he said that me dad had shopped him for drinking and he asked me if he could buy me book and I said, “Yeah”. He lived at Skelmanthorpe, this man, and I said, yeah, he could buy it, and that’s the only person I sold me book to and he started asking me about it and he were saying like he were, you know, he was... and he were telling me that he were a copper’s nark, he were a snitch, me dad.

Q You were sufficiently unhappy, weren’t you, about the police conduct of the investigation that you wrote to the Chief Constable of West Yorkshire at the beginning of 2017?

A I arranged a meeting with him.

Q You wrote to D. Collins, did you not...

A Yeah.

Q ...in 2017 because you were unhappy about the police investigation?

A And she’s opened an investigation with Police Professional Standards into systematic failures to investigate my case from 1984 to present day.

Q And throughout this time, 2016, 2017, you were publicising your views and what you were doing and what was happening with the investigation on Facebook, weren’t you?

A Yeah. I was frustrated and I felt like that were my only outlet because nobody was listening to me.

Q Well, I’ll ask you a bit more about Facebook in a minute, but there was an incident in August of 2017 at a car boot sale in Fitzwilliam?

A Yes.

Q I don’t need to worry about the details because I suspect there’ll be two sides to a story, but it’s right, isn’t it, that you, amongst other things, took a photograph of your father and his wife?

A I went to the car boot sale. I was set up by one of me dad's friends, Peter O'Kell, to go there and I was lulled under false pretent (sic) because Peter O'Kell says to me, "What would you do if you saw your dad right now?" and I went, "I don't know. I don't want to think about it", and I looked at him and I went, "I feel like you know him more than what you're... what you're letting on", and he went, "No, I don't, no, I don't", so... and then he says, "I just wave to him when I see him and he used to rent land off me dad to keep pigs on", so... and then we carried on looking round.

He wanted to go and get these shorts and I went with him and I saw me dad and Janet and I looked and I... and I nearly walked past with me head down in shame and I thought, "Why should I?" and I... and I says, "How dare you come here next door to where I live when you've got an harassment warning on me... order, trying to get one on me when you live 18 mile away?", and... and he was saying, "Go away", like this, and she were... she were telling me to go away and I started telling 'em and I says to... "Go away, you little girl, you're lie... you're lying", and Janet says, "No, I'm not". I says, "Well, if I'm not... if I'm lying, why did you ask to meet me... when I was 16 I had a telephone call from a lady when I worked at S. R. Gents and they give me this telephone number and I phoned from S. R. Gents from the public phone box", and she says, "I've heard that your... your dad's asked me to marry him and... but I've heard that he's been... you know, he's raped you or he's been having sex with you". She says, "Before I answer him, will you tell me all about it?" and I says, "Only if you're prepared to believe me, otherwise I'm not going to waste me breath", and so she arranged to meet me in Barnsley in Minerva Café and that's when we spoke for about two hours and then she says to me, "Your dad's upstairs. Do you want to see him?" and I didn't know what to say, yes or no, and summat made me say, "Yes", and I went upstairs.

She went in the café. We spoke outside and that's when I looked at him and I said, "Why did you do it?" and he says, "I'm sorry. It's cos I loved you as a person and not as a daughter", and so... and she says to me, "And I shouted that at the car boot sale", and she says, "No, I didn't". I says... and he dragged her away and sat on the van, and then I started on him and saying, "If I'm lying, why when you were still laid on top of me and I said to you, 'What would me grandad say if he knew what you'd just done now?' did you say, 'Don't worry, sweetheart. He believes all fathers should break their daughters in'", and I was saying it loud and I walked away and I thought, "Oh..." and, oh, no, Janet said to me... Janet picked a pair of garden shears up and she come up to me face like that and she went, "I'll fucking have you, I'll fucking have you", like that to me, so he pulled her down and then I started shouting about what he'd done to me so people could hear me.

I were angry because I'd just had a decision to say that in September that they was not going to prosecute him and it was not going to go to court and he'd come to rub my nose in it, the fact that it wasn't, and then he tried to get an harassment warning on me so they could put a lid on it and shut me up once and for all for good, and then he... when I started shouting about what he'd done to me, he come up to my face like that and he went, "I'll fucking have you, I'll fucking have you", like that in the face, and everybody were watching, and there were a lady who saw it and I went to the police and I've said, "He's threatened to have me", and... and they wouldn't do anything about it.

Q My question, Miss Higgins, was whether you took a photo of your dad and Janet?

A And then I walked away and I were gonna... and I thought, "I'm taking a picture of him", and I took a picture of him and I plastered it... and I put it on Facebook, cos I were angry for what he'd done.

Q And you commented, didn't you, about that "Paedophile Appleyard"?

A He is a paedophile.

Q And that was...
A He's not just done it to me.
Q That was, as you've just said, splashed all over Facebook, wasn't it?
A Yeah, I put it up there. Why wouldn't I?
Q And the police came to speak to you afterwards, didn't they?
A Yeah.
Q And you wouldn't speak to them, would you?
A Yes. They didn't speak to me afterwards. I had to go to the police to ask 'em to take a statement for it, and I'm... and I was in a police station three hours. The police didn't come to speak to me at all. I had to go and knock on the police and ask them to take a statement so, no, they didn't.
Q Did you not post on Facebook as well stills from your CCTV system showing police officers at your front door?
A They were coming to try and get... put... serve me with an harassment warning. Three times they came to me house and I wouldn't accept it cos I hadn't been harassing him. They were trying to get me for what people had been doing in Denby Dale and I don't know... I didn't even know what had been happening until they got me in on that harassment warning.
Q Did you know anything about the setting alight of your father's garage door and van shortly after that?
A Not until they got me in on that harassment warning order.
Q But later that same year, 2017, did you then start speaking to people who you hadn't spoken to for many years?
A Who like?
Q Like Diane Croft?
A I went to... I went to Denby Dale to see Diane Croft, cos I was...
Q Trying to gather...
A I was... cos-...because Alex Wilson, who was investigating the case, told me not to go and speak to the witnesses and he said he'd been to see her...
Q Okay.

A ...and that she was too scared, because she still lived in the same village as him, to give a statement to the police and so I went to see her.

Q Despite PC Wilson, or DC Wilson, telling you you shouldn't do that?

A He'd already said there were gonna be no case, they closed it. He sent a letter to me dad saying, in capital letters, "We are not going to prosecute you" in September last year and I did my right to review and that's why I'm here today, cos I appealed the decision.

Q Did you go to her workplace to speak to her?

A I did.

Q And did you phone her up?

A I've... yeah, we spoke... no, she phoned me, I think.

Q Did you record the conversation you had with her?

A I've got an app on me phone and I've had to put it there because of the way I've been treated and lied to by the police, I believe.

Q And did she tell you, "We all need to get together privately without the fucking coppers knowing, we need to talk"?

A I don't know what she said. She'd been having a drink, but she said she could remember me going to her house when I were 15 and telling her that me dad were having sex with me and that I spoke to her... and her mum and dad were there in the kitchen as well and I told them, and she told me about Appleyard coming down the snicket and coming to their house and her dad telling him to fuck off. There was lots of things said in that... in that conversation.

Q At around that time did you take it upon yourself to go onto some land that your father owned...

A Yep.

Q ...and to...

A Because I told Alex Wilson about it.

Q And did you take some items, stealing perhaps, from that land?

A I took a bottle that I thought had got something very poisonous in it and a knife and I handed in to the police because I believe that there's more on that land than meets the eye.

Q And some documents and some ticket stubs?

A Yeah, yeah.

Q And you...

A It was up for sale. He'd... I think it had already been sold and they were sorting it out.

Q And you took photos of that, didn't you?

A Of a container. There was a shipment container that looked like a shrine that had got flowers, plastic flowers on the outside. There was like loads of kids' bikes piled up, all broken, and there was kids' clothes on a bonfire to be burnt, and it... and in his outbuildings there was a wine glass and a pint... and like a man's drinking vessel and there were a latte cup and a man's drinking vessel and to me it just looked like very dodgy.

Q And you put a lot of this on Facebook, didn't you?

A Mmm.

Q The pictures, the visit?

A Yeah.

Q The fact that at some point...

A Yeah, because the police had told me that they wasn't opening a case and I was frustrated and angry.

Q The fact that at some point that land was up for sale?

A Yeah.

Q And do you remember the fact that your father was charged with these offences about a year ago, February 2018?

A Pardon?

Q Do you remember your father being charged with these offences about a year ago in February 2018?

A What offences?

Q The offences he's on trial for now.

A Do I remember what?

Q Do you remember the fact that your father was charged with the offences that he's now on trial for, that explains why we're here now, about a year ago, February 2018?

A Yeah.

Q Because you were made aware, weren't you, that he'd been charged?

A Yeah.

Q And you publicised that, didn't you, on Facebook?

A What, that he was going to court?

Q That he'd been charged by the police with criminal offences and was going to go to court, yes.

A He's never... I didn't think he'd been charged. I thought he'd been summonsed to court, but he went in... I says to him, "Have you... has he given... have you been and arrested him because I wanted you to get his computer", because I believe that if they would have took his computer you would have found, you know, crucial evidence on there, the fact that I believe that, you know, it's not just me who he's done it to, and you've never... you've never... and I couldn't understand why you didn't dawn raid him and go and get his computer, and even to this day you've not got his computer, and he's... and you've never searched his house. All you've ever done is summonsed him to court. He's never been arrested.

Q And you put on Facebook, didn't you, press coverage of his first appearance before the magistrates' court?

A I don't know. I can't remember if I did or not.

Q Really?

A Yeah, I probably would have put he's... he's gonna be appearing, yeah. It's public... it was in the public domain.

Q Mmm, but you felt the need to publicise it more widely, didn't you, Miss Higgins?

A Yeah. I've had a lot of years of anger and not being listened to.

Q And since he first appeared in court you have been back to Denby Dale, haven't you, to the Pie Hall and the Dale Club?

A My friend, Glennis, and her husband run the pub. They're my friends.

Q So you weren't going back to where he lived in an attempt to goad him or anything like that?

A No.

Q No? But you've continued to want to be involved in the gathering of evidence, haven't you?

A Yeah.

Q And you've continued to speak to witnesses, haven't you?

A Yeah.

Q About what...

A Well, they're the people who I know so it's not... they're people who I've grown up with, my relations and the friends who are old friends or neighbours.

Q You've continued to speak to witnesses about their evidence, haven't you?

A No.

Q Really?

A Well, they've told me what they know.

Q Did you not, for example, have a telephone call with Ena Whittle in November last year about her coming to court and about her evidence?

A Yeah. I asked her if she... well, she said she'd give a statement, you know, about what she knew.

Q And you discussed what was in her statement, didn't you?

A I can't remember.

Q Because you recorded the conversation, didn't you?

A I probably would have done cos I keep me app on all the time.

Q And she told you she thought bits were missing from her statement, didn't she?

A Yeah. Somebody's gone out to see her. Joe Taylor's gone out to see her and she felt like she'd... the... three pages weren't there.

Q And that led to you telling the police you thought her statement had been doctored, didn't it?

A Well, I told the police that I thought that, yeah...
Q And you...
A ...it might not all be there.
Q You thought other statements might have been doctored as well, didn't you?
A Well, I've got no faith in the police because of the 35 years I've tried to get justice. I'm not... I'm bound to have these thoughts.
Q And the police have told you repeatedly not to discuss evidence with people, haven't they?
A And I haven't.
Q But you've kept trying, haven't you?
A No.
Q You had a meeting in November with Mr Hampton, prosecution counsel, and with Crown Prosecution Service lawyer?
A Yeah.
Q And you wanted to discuss with them which witnesses were going to be called and what they were going to say?
A No, I didn't want to discuss that with him.
Q And you were told that they couldn't talk to you about the evidence?
A Yeah.
Q And you've still been putting stuff on Facebook as recently as last week, haven't you...
A Nothing about...
Q ...about this case?
A Nothing about the case and evidence that people are bringing forward.
Q You've been publicising the fact that the trial is due to start on the 14th of January...
A It's been in the---
Q ...haven't you?
A It's in the public domain. It's been in the Huddersfield Examiner. Everybody knows about it.

Q Do you think you live your life through Facebook, Miss Higgins?

A No.

Q Because...

A I'm a youth worker. I did Duke of Edinburgh Award. I try and help 'em read maps and things, and I'm a writer.

Q The police have advised you a number of times not to post things on Facebook, haven't they?

A And I haven't done anything to jeopardise my case.

Q The police have advised you a number of times not to post things on Facebook, haven't they?

A I'm allowed to... I've got friends on Facebook. I'm allowed to... it's social media. I'm allowed to speak about my life a little bit.

Q The police have advised you, haven't they, yes or no...

A What about?

Q ...not to put stuff on Facebook that might jeopardise the investigation?

A I haven't put anything on that would jeopardise my investigation.

Q You have plenty of people following you on Facebook, don't you?

A Yeah, the... yeah.

Q And you're quite happy to post stuff on Facebook about your father, about this case?

A It's in the public domain.

Q And some of the responses you get from people who follow you are quite abusive, aren't they?

A A lot of people know him and know what he is.

Q You've been taken off Facebook on occasions, haven't you?

A I think he must have been complaining about me, about... that was a couple of year ago.

Appleyard's Land

Q You have had access restricted on Facebook, haven't you, by whoever?

A No, not for a long, long time.

Q You've said on Facebook things like your father hangs around with the Mayor of Huddersfield and he's rented land from Judge Pickles?

A Mmm.

Q You're nodding? I'm just saying that for the...

A Yeah, yeah.

Q ...purposes of the recording. You said, "He's got away with murder", and that you're afraid you'll be murdered?

A Yeah.

Q You've named the police officers investigate...

A Because I'm afraid of his guns.

Q You've named...

A I'm not... I didn't mean literally he's got away with murder. I'm saying, you know, the things he's got away with over these... with me and other people I feel he's abused. I do feel like he's got away with a lot.

Q You've named police officers investigating this case and said, "They are taking the piss"?

A Yeah, I've been angry.

Q And you have said that people should Google how many unsolved murders there have been within 20 miles of his house?

A Yeah, cos I have, and there's been a lot.

Q And you have said, "The police are protecting him and other influential paedophiles"?

A I didn't say they've been protecting other influential paedophiles. I know it's... I know that my MP, Jon Trickett, his assistant, has said that everybody knew that Judge Pickles was not... was a paedophile and he was part of a paedophile ring.

Q Well, you've asserted on, I think probably quite a few occasions on Facebook, that Judge Pickles was the ring...

A A friend of me dad's.

Q No. Just, just hear me out, please, Miss Higgins. You said, "Pickles was a leading paedophile and ran a paedophile gang in the UK and in America"?

A I didn't know if he run one in America. I know me dad goes out to America a lot and a letter from America from a... from a cult, like a Nazi cult, landed on somebody's doorstep and that... that letter was taken to the police and it was meant to go in Appleyard's... through Appleyard's door.

Q You have asserted that Judge Pickles was a ringleader of a paedophile gang in America and have said he was a friend of your father's?

A I've been told that he was prolific... he were a prolific paedophile and everybody knew that he was and a ringleader by chief inspectors... well, somebody else has... that's... somebody else has mentioned that, and then my MP's right... assistant, Adie, said, and that's been recorded, that he was... everybody knew that he was a paedophile.

Judge Pickles

Q You put on Facebook that your father was part of a huge paedophile ring involving MPs, lord mayors, corrupt solicitors, police officers, celebrities?

A I feel that he is part of something bigger.

Q You've posted on Facebook that he's gonna emigrate to New Zealand where he's police- protected?

A Baragwanath who tried to get the harassment warning on me, he... he wouldn't... he was... he was a sergeant of Inman, who lied to me, PC Inman, and said that if I didn't go to Holmfirth, Holmfirth Police Station, round the back door at six o'clock at night then he would have to come out and arrest me and I says, "Can I bring a solicitor?" He says, "No". He says, "Only if you..." I could only have a solicitor if... What was it he said now? I forgot what he said now. I could only have a solicitor if... Oh, what did he say? He said I couldn't have a solicitor, only if he was gonna arrest me and he wanted to avoid arresting me.

That's what he said, and so I says to him, "You've..." I says to him, "Can I speak to your Sergeant Baragwanath and... so I asked five times to speak to him and cos Inman lied and said that he hadn't said that to me, and I got it on record as well that he did lie to me and said that I could only have a solicitor if he was gonna arrest me and he wanted to avoid arresting me, and I asked if I could speak to Baragwanath and he wouldn't speak to me, his sergeant, and I Googled who Sergeant Baragwanath were and he'd got a relative who was head of Auckland Police in New Zealand and me dad sold his land, that what you're talking about where I took the pictures, he sold it for a hundred and ninety something thousand pound and he told the lady who was buying... who he sold the land to that he was going to emigrate to New Zealand and that's where I got that from, that he was going to New Zealand, and I was scared that he was gonna go before I got justice.

Q Is the reality here, Miss Higgins, that you have convinced yourself that you were abused by your father when you were...

A No.

Q ...a teenager?

A No.

Q It never, in fact, happened at all, did it?

A Yes, it did.

Q Do you think you've spent so long telling yourself what happened that it seems real to you now?

A No.

Q The account is one that you've rehearsed over and over and over again, isn't it?

A No.

Q You've publicised it in detail on Facebook?

A I've... I've lived with this now for 35 years. I would never have gone on Facebook and felt so much anger that nothing's been done for 35 years except for this last four year investigation, so probably 31 years. I've never gone public before with it. I've had so much anger and wondered why it's not... why I've had the door closed in my face every single time I tried to bring it to justice. Every time I've... I've knocked on the police doors and said, "I want to report historical child abuse", they've not let me, for stupid reasons.

Q Is the reality that this is something you've just imagined?

A No.

Q That you're a fantasist?

A No.

Q You told the police in your video-recorded interview that you wanted to remember more details but you couldn't. Was that because there are, in fact, no more details to remember?

A No.

Q Perhaps because things didn't happen as you say they did?

A Yes, it did happen. It happened on a boat in Sweden as well. He knows what he's done but he's always said, "You can't prove a thing".

Q You can't stop publicising details of your allegations...

A When I've got justice...

Q ...or the case, can you?

A ...I will stop publicising it.

Q You can't stop publicising your views about the police or about the existence of this paedophile ring? That's...

A Do you know how much I've been let down and why... anybody would think it were a cover-up if they'd been in my shoes.

Q You believe that paedophile ring allegation to be completely true, don't you?

A He rented land off Chief Inspector Richard Ellis. Richard Ellis was P. W. Johnson's boss, Brian... he was also Brian Fernley's boss. Brian Fernley has seen my statements that went missing and said these... saw a letter with them saying they need to be destroyed cos they're an embarrassment to the family, and they're the original statements that was made in 2000... when I was 15.

Q Just as you believe, Miss Higgins, your allegations against your father to be completely true, don't you?

A Pardon?

Q You believe the allegations about the paedophile ring to be true just as you believe your allegations about your father to be true?

A I believe he is part of something bigger cos I know he's sexually abused his niece and I know other people who've said that, you know, the way he's... he creeps them out and the way he acts round 'em.

Q	But, in fact, the reality is here none of these allegations are true at all, are they?

A	Well, it's what I believe. I'm allowed to have my own belief.

MR STOREY: Thank you very much.

Re-examined by Mr HAMPTON

Q	I've got one or two matters to cover, Miss Higgins. Are you okay to carry on?

A	Yeah. Could I have some more water, please?

UNKNOWN SPEAKER: Yes, of course.

MR HAMPTON: It will take us to about four o'clock…

A	Yeah.

Q	…if not sooner.

A	Thank you.

Q	It's been suggested that you have imagined the sexual abuse you've complained of.

A	Yeah.

Q	When you were telling the police in the video interview about your father pushing his penis into your mouth, were you making that up?

A	No.

Q	Have you come here today to lie about what happened to you as a child?

A	No.

Q	When you masturbated him, you said that he told you to do that?

A	Yes.

Q	Put your hand... put your hand on him?

A	Yeah, get me hand and put it on him.

Q	Sorry to be graphic, but it would help if you tell us exactly what he did with your hand.

A He just... he'd lay there with no clothes on, I wouldn't have any clothes on, and then he'd tell me to read to him and I'd be reading in one hand and I'd be masturbating him with the other hand.

Q So how did your hand end up on his penis?

A Cos he'd tell me to do it to him.

Q And it was asked of you... it was suggested that how could you be reading if you had to be quiet in the house?

A Yeah.

Q Were you shouting any stories out in the bedroom?

A No.

Q In what kind of tone were you reading these pornographic stories to him?

A It would be in a voice like that, just whispering cos... and that was far enough away for Paul not to hear if I spoke like that.

Q Right. You were asked about being in front of the fire and whether you suffered any burn. Did you suffer any burn injury?

A It was burning at the time. It was red raw.

Q Was it an injury or was it just uncomfortable?

A It was burning at the time and I had to tell him to stop.

Q The shooting of the dog, the dog's name was?

A Sam.

Q Right. Were you there when he was shot?

A Yes.

Q Tell us how it happened, please.

A We went for a walk and he brought the dog as normal, he'd have brought the dog and he brought his gun with us this time and we got down to Naylors pipe works where they're all broken. It's like... there's a pipe works up on the top when they make their pipes and then all the broken pipes, it goes down in the bottom, and he... he stood me there and he put the dog over there and he shot the dog and he buried it under the pipes, under the broken pipes.

Q Tell us what you saw him do when he shot the dog?

A I did... I turned away.

Q Did you hear the gun go off?

A Yeah.

Q You told us about the tattoo. Did you have any desire to have a dog's name on your back?

A No.

Q Whose name was it that was put on your back?

A My dad's.

Q Who wanted that name on your back?

A My dad.

Q You've been asked about the book and Facebook posts.

A Yeah.

Q And matters you've put into the public arena. How many times did you say you tried to get the police to look at your allegations?

A Five times in 35 years.

Q Could you understand why nothing was happening?

A It felt like they were covering up for him. I felt like they were covering up for him, and I knew he rented land off Police Inspector Richard Ellis and I just couldn't understand why they wouldn't open an investigation when they always said that I would be able to in the future cos it hadn't gone to court.

Q Did you complain about the police?

A Yes.

Q Why?

A Because they wouldn't investigate my case.

Q Did you understand why they wouldn't?

A No, I couldn't understand why they kept closing the door on me, only that he must be being protected.

Q How did it feel not being listened to?

A Frustrating, angry.

Q You told us about an incident at a car boot sale.

A Yeah.

Q The police wanted to give you a harassment warning. You weren't charged with any offences after that, were you?
A No.
Q You've been asked about recordings of phone calls you've had with witnesses or potential witnesses.
A Yeah.
Q Who made those recordings?
A Me.
Q What did you do with them?
A Give them to the police.
Q Sorry?
A Give them to the police.
Q Why?
A Because I wanted them to open an investigation.
Q You've been asked about CICA, Criminal Injuries Compensation Authority, I think. Have you made all this up in order to get money?
A No.
Q Why are you here?
A To get justice.
Q Were you lying in the mid-1980s when you complained to your mother?
A No.
Q Were you lying when you complained to Diane Croft?
A No.
Q Were you lying to the police when you went to them in the mid-1980s to the late-1980s?
A No.
Q When did you first seek any therapy or counselling?
A When did I first?
Q When?
A When I was 16 I used to go to Rape Crisis in Sheffield.
Q Who were you living with at age...

A And that's not when the first time was actually, cos when I had me own rented house at 16... I ran away from me dad's at 15 and me mam kicked me out at 16 and said she'd done her job as a parent, how the... I was on me... I was on my own now and she also said to me, "When you'd had enough of being treated like an adult you came back to me. What did you expect me to do about it?" and I got me own house, rented house at 16, and a social worker came to my house and she told me to write down exactly what had happened to me, to get, you know, to help me with my feelings, to put all the feelings that I was holding inside me, and I wrote down I think about 15 pages, and you've got the blue folder, and that was the start of my healing journey.

Q I follow, so 16?

A Yeah.

Q And how long have you been receiving therapy and counselling?

A Thirty-five years.

Q How many?

A Thirty-five years.

Q And when you attend these sessions do you just invent what happened?

A No.

Q What do you tell them?

A I tell 'em what he did to me and all the violent things he did to me from being a young child as well, all the beatings, and I feel more than anything grief because I wish somebody on the street had done it to me because then I would at least have had me parents to be able to help me through this time, and they give me homework to do and... and to write my feelings down and write to your inner child, you know, because I blame myself. I feel a lot of shame and guilt for what he did to me for a long time, and that's a lot... the reason why I go to counselling because of the guilt and the shame that I feel.

Q I follow. Just wait there a moment. Why did you want to post matters on Facebook? Why did you want it to be public?

A Because I was so angry and frustrated that nobody would listen to me.

Q Did you think making matters public would help you?

A Yeah. I felt like my voice had been trapped inside me.

MR HAMPTON: Bear with me a moment. There won't be much more from me. Can I ask the court's indulgence just for a 10 minute break before I continue my re-examination? We can be back for five to four, and there won't be very much.

JUDGE JAMESON: Yes, all right.

MR HAMPTON: I'd obviously like to conclude the exercise this afternoon.

JUDGE JAMESON: Yes. I do think that the evidence should be completed today.

MR HAMPTON: We will.

JUDGE JAMESON: All right. Well, as I say, 10 minutes is a bit of a long time for the jury because they're going to have to go back... so I'll say four o'clock, all right, and then you'll be finished by quarter-past?

MR HAMPTON: Yes.

JUDGE JAMESON: Good, all right. Four o'clock, ladies and gentlemen. Thank you very much. Do step down, and if you can be back for four o'clock? Thank you very much.

(In the absence of the jury)

MR HAMPTON: Just before the jury come in, in re-examination I was asking about therapy and counselling.

JUDGE JAMESON: Yes.

MR HAMPTON: That arises out of the assertion, obviously made that her evidence is fabricated. We have the blue folder with accounts in that. It is right to say that any counselling or therapy notes has been unused material to date, as unserved evidence. What I simply want to ask the complainant is, is she able to tell us when material within here was produced, to give an idea as to the decade it was produced.

JUDGE JAMESON: When?

MR HAMPTON: Yes.

JUDGE JAMESON: I think that my learned friend has some concern about me asking about it, which is why I raise it now before I do so.

JUDGE JAMESON: Yes, and this goes?

MR HAMPTON: To credibility.

JUDGE JAMESON: Yes, all right. Well, there may be a factual matrix, may there? I don't know what other evidence there is going to be about when complaints were first made and in what terms.

MR HAMPTON: Yes.

JUDGE JAMESON: Anyway, I mean, I've got the point, I think, yes.

MR STOREY: Yes. There will be no issue about when complaints were made and she has already – effectively given that evidence already. In terms of when the counselling notes were made, she said she sought counselling from the age of 16. She's had counselling for 35 years.

JUDGE JAMESON: Yes.

MR STOREY: I don't know how much of the notes she has made that she has just been describing making are in this blue folder, but certainly some part of them are and the only way I suspect she can answer the question, "When were the notes made?" is by taking out each individual piece of paper...

JUDGE JAMESON: Yes.

MR STOREY: ...and saying, "Well, this comes from then and this comes from then".

JUDGE JAMESON: Well, I can't help wondering whether this isn't best dealt with by way of an agreed fact.

MR STOREY: That is something the Crown have said they are happy to do, but my concern is that up until the current time, these counselling notes have had the status of unused material. They've never been served in evidence. Had they been and had the Crown made clear they wished to elicit the contents of this folder or the counselling notes in evidence, I might have dealt with things differently. And I don't at the moment...

JUDGE JAMESON: I am not sure that they are saying they want to use the contents of it, are you?

MR HAMPTON: No, we want to consider that point more carefully. If we want to use the contents, my learned friend is more than entitled to object to that, but we can argue admissibility before your Honour whether there is any unfairness arising out of it.

JUDGE JAMESON: Well, okay. Isn't the one question dependent upon the other? There is not a lot of point in the jury knowing when the notes were made unless they know at least in rough outline whether the notes are consistent with the account given now or earlier or whatever; in other words, at least have in rough terms obviously what's in the notes?

MR HAMPTON: Well, that's the option, speaking plain, I now want to leave open. I don't want to be criticised for not adducing it.

JUDGE JAMESON: If no decision has been made on that, I think it must be fair to Mr Appleyard to allow Mr Storey appropriate time to know what your approach is going to be.

MR HAMPTON: Yes.

JUDGE JAMESON: And formulate any opposition to it that he feels he should make.

MR HAMPTON: I agree.

JUDGE JAMESON: So, I am not sure there's a lot of point in taking one decision when one decision is dependent upon the whole position now.

MR HAMPTON: Yes.

JUDGE JAMESON: And we are really not going to need this witness, are we, to deal with this, because it's a matter of record, literally.

MR STOREY: I would have thought so. I just didn't want to have any criticism for not speaking to the witness about it, that's all.

JUDGE JAMESON: Yes, well I simply can't see any purpose in this question being put at the moment because in the event that you made an application to adduce part of the counselling records and in the event that I ruled that that could happen, then it would inevitably happen by way of an agreed fact, wouldn't it?

MR HAMPTON: Yes.

MR STOREY: Yes, I...

JUDGE JAMESON: Unless you felt that there was something that you did then need to readdress.

MR STOREY: Yes.

JUDGE JAMESON: But let's cross that bridge when we come to it, shall we?

MR STOREY: Well, I am content that we do that, but my only concern was that the path that I thought my learned friend was wanting to embark upon now with the complainant might lead down a route that caused further difficulties.

JUDGE JAMESON: Well, I think it might because if the position is at the moment unresolved and you both need to think about it, then isn't it best addressed slightly later? What's the worst that can happen? The worst that can happen is that in the event that some of it went in and Mr Storey then felt that there were questions that he would have wished to have put, well, we may have to have the witness back.

MR HAMPTON: Yes.

JUDGE JAMESON: I think that is as bad as it could get, isn't it?

MR HAMPTON: I think so. I'm sure she would be available.

JUDGE JAMESON: Okay, well, let's not trouble with it now then. So, anything else you want to ask?

MR HAMPTON: That probably ends my re-examination.

JUDGE JAMESON: All right. Well, I don't think, then, unless there's any particular – well, I am very conscious of the sensitivities of the case. Would you wish me to have the witness back into court so that she can be thanked for her evidence or are you content – it might be kinder simply to leave it as it is.

MR HAMPTON: Yes. I've given the warning.

JUDGE JAMESON: It also rids me of the difficult problem that every judge always has when a complainant has finished given evidence as to exactly what to say when one wishes not to seem churlish or hard but one doesn't wish to seem partial at all, either way, and it's always a difficult balance and frankly, if we can avoid it, I wouldn't be sorry.

MR HAMPTON: I'm sure there would be no difficulty with me speaking to witness and I can undertake to give the warning about not speaking about her evidence to anybody that would usually follow.

JUDGE JAMESON: Okay. Well, if you're content to do that, then I think we'll simply have the jury back and say there are, in fact, no more questions. I hadn't thought it appropriate or necessary for the witness to be brought back into the witness-box. That concludes proceedings for the day. All right?

MR HAMPTON: Yes.

JUDGE JAMESON: Right, fine. Thank you.

(The jury entered court)

JUDGE JAMESON: Right, welcome back, ladies and gentlemen. Thank you very much for bearing with us. I'm sorry to have kept you outside, but I just wanted to discuss with counsel exactly where we were going and what, if anything, was going to happen now. The short answer is that there are, in fact, no more questions for Ms Higgins and I have not thought it necessary or indeed appropriate to have her brought back into court simply to be told that. So, that concludes her evidence and that concludes our hearing for today.

So, 10.30, everybody, tomorrow morning. Thank you very much indeed. Have a good evening and I'll see you all at half past 10 tomorrow morning.

(The jury left court)

JUDGE JAMESON: Anything else I can help with?

MR HAMPTON: No, thank you very much.

MR STOREY: No, thank you.

(The court adjourned until 10.30 on Wednesday 16 January 2019)

(4.11 p.m.)

Diary: Tuesday 15th January 2019 (continued)

It had been exhausting on the stand, I was happy with the way I had responded to the questioning. I felt the pressure from the defence lawyer in cross examination, however, I stood my ground when he was trying to discredit me. My friends told me they were proud of the way I had stood strong in the witness box and remained composed.

Although I had been asked to look only at the jury, I did glance across at my dad who was seated behind his legal team. He had obtained a GP note before the trial to say he was too ill to stand and had been seen by a friend of mine coming out of the doctor's surgery looking smug. He was still looking smug and arrogant with his arms crossed defiantly in front of him. Several times his movement caught my eye, I saw him reaching his arm out towards his barrister's assistant to get his attention, whistling and making "pssst pssst" sounds on each occasion.

Once again, we did not receive police protection and once again were advised to take a taxi and claim expenses back. Instead, we chose to take the train. On the journey home we avoided talking about the details of the case but generally discussed how the day had gone. I asked Del if he thought the jury would believe me and he said I had done well. I mentioned to him that one of the ladies on the jury had stuck out like a sore thumb to me. I felt like I knew her, her facial features reminded me of my cousin Diana and I wondered if she could be a relative of mine. My dad came from such a large family of fifteen brothers and sisters, most of whom I have never met. I can't put my finger on it, but something did not feel right about the way she was looking at me. Despite this slight feeling of unease, I feel positive with how the day has gone. I hope my mum tells the truth on the stand tomorrow.

Wednesday 16 January 2019

(Transcript prepared without the aid of documentation)

(10.46 a.m.)

MR STOREY: Before the jury come in, I can see the witness has a number of documents in front of her. I think they're statements. I wonder if they could just be turned over or put in her handbag for now.

JUDGE JAMESON: Yes, this is – what material is this?

MR HAMPTON: I think it is memory refreshing material.

JUDGE JAMESON: I see. Yes, all right, yes.

MR HAMPTON: So, you don't want that now?

MR STOREY: No, that's fine, thank you.

JUDGE JAMESON: If you pop that down, that's fine. Lovely, thank you very much indeed, and this lady is...

MR HAMPTON: This lady is Margaret Jean Voss.

JUDGE JAMESON: Yes.

MR HAMPTON: There's a couple of statements but we're starting at I-42.

JUDGE JAMESON: Thank you very much.

(The jury entered court)

JUDGE JAMESON: Good morning, ladies and gentlemen, welcome back. I am sorry to have kept you a few minutes this morning. I'm afraid there were one or two matters that counsel needed to sort out and we've brought in – I've asked to have brought in before you came in – the next witness, who is Jean Voss, about whom we've heard something already. So, that's the lady who is in the witness-box now. Yes?

MR HAMPTON: Thank you. Could the witness be sworn?

JUDGE JAMESON: Yes, of course.

(10.48 a.m.)

Mrs MARGARET JEAN VOSS, Sworn

Examined by Mr HAMPTON

Q Mrs Voss, I ask questions on behalf of the prosecution.
A Right.
Q Could you please tell me, in a nice, loud voice, your full name?
A Margaret Jean Voss.
Q And your date of birth?
A 05/05/1945.
Q And your age as of today, please?
A 73.
Q Now, there was a time when you were married to a man called Elliott Appleyard?
A I was.
Q Do you recall when that marriage took place?
A Where it took place?
Q When.
A When? Oh, God...
Q We do have some documentation. I'm sure there's no objection.
A I can't remember.
Q 27 May 1974?
A Probably, yes.
Q And there came a time that the family were living in Denby Dale?
A Yeah.
Q And there were three children?
A There was, yes.
Q And the father of the three children was?
A Was ...Elliott was the father of two of them. One, I already had.
Q And who was that?
A That was Donna.

Q So, Elliott Appleyard, the father of Carol?
A Mhm.
Q And ...
A Paul.
Q ...Paul?
Q Are you able to help us with dates of birth? Or shall I run through that?
A No. Donna was born 06/03/1968.
Q Thank you.
A Carol was born 23/04/1969. And Paul was born 22/10/70.
Q Thank you. Now, again, we know from other documentation that by the time Carol was born the family were living at an address at No. 8 Gilthwaites Crescent.
A Yes, that's true.
Q You recall that address? You recall living there?
A Sorry?
Q You recall that address? You recall the family living there?
A Yes, I do, yes.
Q And there came a time when the family moved to No. 26 Gilthwaites Crescent?
A 'Cause it was bigger, yes.
Q Because it was?
A Because it was a larger house.
Q Thank you. You're speaking in a good clear voice.
A Aha.
Q Keep doing so and aim for that back wall so everybody can hear you.
A Oh, right. Okay.
Q All right?
A Yes.
Q It's a big room. Now, I want to ask you questions about a number of topics. I'm going to try and deal with it chronologically. All right?
A Mhm.

Q So do the 1980s, 1990s and so on. All right?
A Okay.
Q And I want to start with, please, 26 Gilthwaites Crescent and the nature of your relationship with Mr Appleyard at that time. All right? How would you describe the relationship with your husband at that time?
A Sometimes it could be very volatile. He always turned things round and made it it was your fault, not his fault. And he attacked me many a time - hit me.
Q Are you able to give us any idea how often the physical assaults would occur, when he'd hit you?
A Well, when he'd been out drinking. Most of the time he come home drunk and knocked me about and ... Sometimes just... I don't know, for the hell of it. If I argued back. I had to be very submissive and not answer back.
Q When he was hitting you, what was he hitting you with?
A His fist.
Q Was there any verbal abuse, Mrs Voss?
A From him?
Q Yes, to you.
A Yes, very verbal.
Q Are you able to give us an example?
A He knew my father had abused me and every time we had an argument, it was: "Go let your father fuck you." And just downtrodding me all the time.
Q Downtrodding you?
A Mhm. I don't know if that's a word, but that...
Q We understand what you mean. So at No. ...still at No. 26 Gilthwaites Crescent...
A Yeah. Yeah.
Q ...did any of this violence ever involve anything other than fists?
A A gun - a shotgun, a 12-bore shotgun - and a machete.
Q Could you tell us about the shotgun first of all, then? Well, first of all, where did the shotgun come from?
A Well, he had farmer's land that he could go on, so he owned this shotgun.

Q So he kept guns?

A Yeah.

Q And was it one or two, or do you not know?

A I can only remember one. I don't know if there were any more.

Q You describe it as a 12-bore shotgun?

A Mhm.

Q Where was it kept?

A Do y'know, I've no idea.

Q All right.

A I don't know.

Q If you can't remember something or you don't know, you tell us.

A I can't remember. I don't know.

Q Now, I asked you whether the violence ever involved anything other than fists. You've mentioned a shotgun and a machete. Tell us what you remember about the use of the shotgun first.

A We'd had an argument - I can't remember what it was about - and he held this shotgun to my head. And the children were stood there, and he told them if they went to the phone to do anything, that he would shoot me.

Q Can you remember what prompted that argument?

A No, I can't, no. There was so many arguments, you... No.

Q Can you remember how he held the gun as he put it to your head? How was he holding it? Can you show us?

A I don't know. He was... From the side of me. The children were there, and he was there and he ...he... I was in the kitchen, so he'd just hold it to my head.

Q Where was the barrel of the gun (inaudible)?

A Touch ...pointing at my head.

Q Was he saying anything as he did this?

A I can't remember. All I can remember him saying to the children: "Do not go to the phone," because he would shoot me if they did, and they just stood there.

Q And when he said that, did he say it in a calm tone or an angry tone? Can you remember?

A I can't remember.

Q I don't wish to embarrass, but do you remember having any physical reaction to a gun being pointed at your head?

A No, not a gun, but something else, yes.

Q That something being?

A A machete.

Q And would you mind telling us what that reaction was?

A He came home from the pub... It had started earlier that day and he came home from the pub and he wanted the name of somebody I'd been dreaming of, and I ...I couldn't remember what... And I was in my nightie and he got the machete - I can't remember where he got it from - and he threatened to cut me from my vagina up here, and I wet myself on the floor and went down, and then he'd stopped.

Q Thank you for helping us with that.

A It's okay.

Q Can we go back to the gun, please?

A Yes.

Q Thank you. You said there were children present?

A Yes. All three of them.

Q Carol, Paul and Donna?

A Yeah.

Q Could you see them?

A Yes, they was aside of me.

Q How were they?

A They were frightened. They were frightened to death. I think they were crying. I know they were frightened, very frightened. As I was.

Q Mrs Voss, were any other occasions when you were threatened with a gun, or was it just the once?

A Just the once.

Q Now, you've dealt with most of the incident with the machete, but could I just clarify one or two matters? Did this occur in the house?

A Yes.

Q And you said you'd had a dream. You were being asked questions about it by Mr Appleyard?

A Yeah. I woke up that morning and he said, "You'd had a ...a..." Well, I don't know what sort of dream. Not dreaming of him, obviously, having sex. And he wanted to know who I'd been dreaming about and I couldn't remember, so I probably said him.

Q When did the machete become involved?

A Well, he went to work and said when he came back I ...I had to remember who it was. When he came home from work: "Have you remembered?" I said, "No. It was probably you." He went to the pub and he said, "When I come back from the pub, you'd better give me a name." He came back from the pub. I still couldn't give him a name 'cause I didn't know who it was, and that's when... I can't remember where the machete, where he got it from. It might be the outside toilet. And he came in and he held it here. He didn't actually... But I wet myself with fright, on the floor.

Q So he threatened to cut you from your vagina to your...

A Yeah. Wherever.

Q You...

A Up the front.

Q Up the front. As far as you were aware, on that occasion were any of the children present?

A Not that I was aware of.

Q Where did it take place?

A It took place in the kitchen.

Q At night-time?

A Sorry?

Q Was it... After the pub, was it night-time?

A Yes. Yes.

Q As the abuse went on, Mrs Voss, did you do anything about it?

A Yes, I reported him to the police about the gun and, because he hadn't actually shot me, they couldn't do anything. So, when he went to work that morning, the next day, I hid the gun in the garden. I buried it so he he couldn't use it on me again or threaten me again.

Q Whilst the abuse was going on, could you tell us why you didn't leave?

A I left. He wouldn't leave. I left several times.

Q Several times?

A Yeah.

Q Did you come back?

A I did, with the promises it will never ever happen again, and... You've got three children, what do you do? I got no parents. There's no one to turn to.

Q Who's got no parents?

A I haven't. Both my parents were dead.

Q Did you have any close family in the area?

A No.

Q On the occasions you left, Mrs Voss, where would you go?

A The first time I went, with the gun, I took all my three children and stayed on a farm with my friend, Pauline, and her family.

Q How long did you stay there for?

A I can't remember. Maybe a couple of weeks. Three weeks. I can't remember.

Q Did you go back on that occasion?

A I did, yes. I went back.

Q Why was that, Mrs Voss? Can you explain, please?

A Well, I couldn't stay there all the time. And, again, the promises: "It will never ever happen again."

Q Do you remember ever going anywhere else? You've told us about Pauline and the farm. Were there any other places you stayed?

A I took Carol with me to a refuge once and he found out where we were, and again I went back, with promises. Oh, no, he didn't come back. That's it. He kept out of the house and let me come back to the house.

Q Did he eventually return to the house?
A Well, ne ...it was winter-time, I remember that, and I opened the door. We had a ...a outside toilet.
Q Yes.
A I opened the door and he's sat like this on the toilet, shivering. He said he'd been sat there all night, freezing. The children were there. I had to ask him in.
Q Now, we know there came a time when you left the home for good.
A Yes, I did.
Q Can you help us with when that was?
A All I remember was it was very hot. It was summer and I sat outside on the doorstep, having a cigarette, and Carol came and sat beside me and that's when she told me about her father kissing her.
Q So you remember it being summer?
A Yeah.
Q You remember being on the doorstep and Carol telling you about her father kissing her?
A I'd... Yeah. I asked where, and she said they used to go for scrap, getting scrap, and he used to send Paul way out the way, and then he would put his arm round her and start kissing her. I said, "Where?" She said, "On the mouth."
Q Was there anything that you recall seeing or hearing at that time that helps you date when this was?
A I think I said the Falklands War was on and somebody had been badly injured, and they were changing bandages and he was screaming, and I felt the pain, so I went and sat outside. That's all I can remember. That's why I went outside.
Q So you remember the Falklands War being on?
A Yeah.
Q Just bear with me a moment.

(Counsel conferred)

JUDGE JAMESON: That's television, is it?

A Sorry?

Q That's a television programme?

A It was telling you about how he was burnt badly on the Falklands War.

Q Oh, I'm sorry. Yes. So there was something about something...

A On the television.

Q ...that had happened during the Falklands War?

A Yeah.

Q Yes. Okay.

MR HAMPTON: Something on the television?

A Yeah.

Q So Carol told you that her father had been kissing her on the lips. What was your reaction to this? How did you feel? What did you think?

A I felt sick, and... But she was very upset, and she begged me not to go and confront him, 'cause he was in the front room watching the television. So I didn't confront him straightaway with it. But the next morning, I phoned social services when he'd gone to work.

Q Was there anything Mr Appleyard had ever said or done that had given you cause for concern previously?

A Well, yes. We were very... We watched a lot of cowboy things. John Wayne was ...a lot of films were going on, and Indians, and... It was once mentioned that Indian chiefs broke in their daughters, their oldest daughter and that was what happened, and he agreed that that's what should happen. I just never thought no more about it and... But I remember that being brought up.

Q Who brought it up?

A He did. He said that that's what Indian chiefs... He agreed that Indian chiefs should break their daughters in.

Q The morning after you contacted social services?

A Yes. An elderly gentleman came. I can't remember his name. And I told him what Carol had told me. Carol was there. I kept her off school. And ...

Q Where did this happen?

A In 26 Gilthwaites Crescent.

Q Where was Mr Appleyard?

A He was at work.

Q So there's you there, Carol, and a social worker. Male? Female?

A A elderly gentleman.

Q What do you remember about him?

A Not a lot. When we told him what happened, he said the best thing was ...to do was to take her away from it. Take her out of the situation.

Q Was there any other assistance offered?

A No.

Q What did you do?

A I ...I was on the CB at the time and I was talking to a lady called Angela who lived in Penistone, and she offered her and her husband, David, to take me and Carol in. The same day, they came and picked us up and took us over there.

Q Just to help all of us in the room, CB, CB radio?

A Yeah.

Q This was...

A Citizens' Band radio, yeah.

Q This was something you could...

A You could...

Q ...transmit on and receive...?

A Yeah. And receive ...talk to somebody who was also on one of those CBs.

Q A little bit before my time, I think, but the kind of thing on the films, "10-4 Rubber Duck"?

A Yeah, yeah. All that.

Q Everyone's got a handle?

A Yes. Mine was Whisky Lady and I was talking to Angela. I can't remember what her name was, but...

Q So you left the family home and went to a lady you'd spoken to on the CB radio?

A Several ti... I couldn't take Donna with me 'cause she was in a special school. She had special needs and there wasn't a school where I was going. We were in West Yorkshire, Penistone's South Yorkshire. So she had to stay where she was, but I knew she wasn't in danger.

Q Why do you say that?

A Well, because he used to pick on her a lot. She had fits. She was a severe epileptic and he used to pick on her and... Y'know? I just knew that he wouldn't. And Paul wanted to stay with his dad. He was very much his dad's lad.

Q His dad's lad? So it was you and Carol that went to... Did you give us a name?

A Penistone, to Angela and David's.

Q And how long had you been communicating via CB radio with Angela?

A Oh, for weeks.

Q Weeks?

A Weeks. But not... You know, just chatting.

Q And Carol went with you?

A She did, yes.

Q Before you ...well, before or after you leave him, did you confront Mr Appleyard about what Carol had said?

A I can't remember whether I rung him up or... I didn't go to see him. I can't remember.

Q You can't remember?

A No. (After a pause) Ah, I do remember.

Q It's all right.

A I was told he wanted to see me, and we arranged to meet at the top of the street where there was some garages. And I went there, and he was there, and I told him. And he just said, "It's her word against mine, isn't it?"

Q Was that a garage that's close to Gilthwaites Crescent?

A No. No, this was at Penistone.

Q At Penistone?

A Yeah. He came to see me at Penistone.

Q How was the accommodation at Angela's?

A Well, we slept on the floor on mattresses, but at least we were comfortable enough.

Q Who's we?

A Me and Carol.

Q Did you have a room to yourselves?

A Yes, we had ...we shared a room together, yes.

Q Had you taken anything with you?

A I think I'd taken some clothes and some of Carol's stuff whilst he was at work that day, and...

Q How long were you there for, do you think?

A Maybe about six weeks, two months. Something like that.

Q Six weeks to two months?

A Mhm.

Q Why did you leave?

A We had a falling out, Angela ...with Angela. Her husband didn't really want us there, so...

Q And help me again - I think you may have said but I didn't get a note - where did you go from there?

A We went to Thurlstone, I think it was.

Q Say again...

A I had a friend, Sylvia...

Q Say again, sorry?

A Thurlstone.

Q Thurlstone?

A Yeah, in Penistone.

Q Barn ...is that Barnsley?

A Penistone.

Q Right.

A I knew a girl called Sylvia and she said her mum had got a spare room. We could go there... With two single beds. We could go there and stay there.

Q And who lived there?

A Linda and her daughter - one of her daughters - and David, her son.

Q Do you remember the surname?

A No, I can't remember.

Q How old was David?

A I don't know. He'd be about 16, I would say, 16/17.

Q Were things more comfortable there?

A Yes.

Q Did you have your own room?

A We shared a room, but we'd had our own beds, two single beds.

Q You've told us that whilst at Gilthwaites Crescent you felt downtrodden?

A Mm.

Q How did it feel once you were at the Wadsworths? How did it feel to you?

A Wadsworth. Wadsworth.

Q Yes.

A That was the name of the people we move into.

Q Sorry.

A Yeah.

Q I've got other information.

A Yeah. Relief. And free.

Q And how did you use that newfound freedom?

A I had a boyfriend. I used to go to CB meetings in Stocksbridge in a pub there.

Q Boyfriend's...

A Always came home.

Q Say again?

A Always came back on the last bus from Stocksbridge.

Q Stocksbridge. And boyfriend's name?

A Carl.

Q Carl.

A Carl Higgins.

Q Carl Higgins. Carol was with you?

A No, Carol was with David. They were going out with each other then, and they were gonna come on the half-past nine bus to Stocksbridge and then we'd all come home together. But she didn't turn up, so...

Q Sorry.

A ...me and Carl caught the last bus back.

Q It was bad question. We'll get there in a moment. Just in general terms, Carol was staying with you?

A She was staying with me.

Q Yes. Did you discuss how you were now able to go out and have a boyfriend?

A No.

Q Did she comment at all upon the level of contact she had with you?

A Oh, she once told me that I should sit at home and bake and knit, 'cause that's what mothers do. I think something like that she said.

Q Do you know, whilst you were at the Wadsworths, whether Carol was having contact with Mr Appleyard, her father?

A No, I didn't know. She was going to school as far as I knew.

Q I'm coming to the point I think you were at. Did there come a time that Carol was no longer with you, or she left?

A She left, yeah. I came home and found she'd put a note on the mirror: "Gone back to Dad's."

Q And is that what you were telling us about? Coming back from Stocksbridge on the bus?

A Yeah.

Q How old was she when that happened?

A I'd say about 13, maybe 14.

Q And, that night, you'd been - was it the CB radio meeting in Stocksbridge?

A Mhm.

Q And you came back and she'd gone. Were you with Corl ...Carl that night?

A Yeah.

Q Now, once Carol had left you - she'd left a note saying, "Gone back to Dad's" - during that time period she was at her dad's, did you have any of your children with you?

A Yes. I think... No, I ha... No, I don... I used to meet Paul and Donna in Barnsley at the market upstairs, on a Saturday, but Carol never came then.

Q Did any of the children come to live with you?

A Later on, Donna did. She'd left school by then.

Q Can you remember where you were living when Donna came to live with you?

A We'd moved. We got a council house in Thurgoland.

Q Who's "we"?

A Me and Carl. Well, it was in my name, but then we got married.

Q But Carol didn't come to meet you?

A No.

Q How did you feel towards Carol at the time she left to go back to her father's?

A I was angry. I was upset. I couldn't understand why she would go back after I'd taken her away, and I think that was foremost in my mind: "Why would you go back?"

Q And your best memory, she was 13/14 at the time?

A Mm.

Q Is that right?

A Yes.

Q Did you ever go back to Gilthwaites Crescent whilst Carol was at Mr Appleyard's?

A I went back once but he wasn't there. He'd gone to America.

Q Right. (Inaudible). And what did you do on that occasion, when he was in America?

A I broke in. I got in through the w... I brought somebody with me and we got through the window.

Q So you broke in through the window?

A Yeah. And I had left some things behind. I can't remember what they were. And the person I brought with me mended the window, so there was no damage when we left.

Q Why were you breaking in?

A Because he'd locked the doors. I couldn't get in.

Q What did you want to get in for?

A For some things I'd left behind, but I can't remember what they were now.

Q Did you get what you wanted?

A Probably.

Q Did you see the children?

A I can't remember whether I saw Carol or Paul. I think I did see them. They weren't at school. They'd been having parties. I know they'd told me they'd been having parties. But their Auntie Hilda was supposed to be keeping an eye on them.

Q Was there a visit after that?

A No. Next thing I knew, I was in the doctors at Penistone and a police sergeant came in and called my name, took me outside. He reported ...he'd rung the police and reported me for breaking into the house. The policeman asked me whose name it was in. I said it was in both my name and his, so he said, "Well, you can't break into your own house, and you left no damage," so it was done.

Q So you were spoken to by the police about...

A Yeah.

Q ...going into the house...

A Mm.

Q ...it having been reported?

A Yeah.

Q Right. And just concentrating on this, if we may. Did you ever go back to Gilthwaites Crescent other than that occasion?
A Yes, I did. Once.
Q Right. Could you help us, please, with that?
A Well, I'd put some stuff back ...by for Carol for Christmas. My friend worked... And she bought them from a warehouse. I'd been paying every week. I went there with them wrapped up.
Q Christmas presents?
A Christmas presents. The van wasn't there and...
Q Whose van?
A Elliott's van. So I went next door to Carron - she was my neighbour - and I said ...she said, "I saw them go out."
Q Just stop there.
A Sorry.
Q We've got a rule about hearsay.
A All right. Okay.
Q So I can't adduce, properly, for good reason, evidence that you may have been told by somebody else.
A Right.
Q All right? But you...
A All she did was tell me they'd gone out.
Q All right. You've told us now. Said that they'd gone out. What followed on from there? You'd had a conversation. What happened next?
A I waited in her house for them to come back.
Q Who were you waiting for?
A I was waiting for Carol and him to come back. I had ...I think had Donna with me. I'm sure I had Donna with me, my oldest.
Q Yes. What followed?
A I confronted them both.
Q What did you say?

A I said, "I've brought your Christmas presents," and she told me to stick them up me arse. She didn't want them. And I said, "I've been told that there's something going on between you two."

Q Did you confron... Did you have a view about their relationship?

A Yes, and I confronted them.

Q And without telling us what others said, what was your view of their relationship?

A What I'd been told.

Q Did you have concerns about their relationship?

A Oh, yes.

Q Did you confront them about that?

A Yes.

Q What was the reaction?

A I was nasty ...thinking nasty things. A lot of swearing...

Q What were you think...

A I don't know.

Q What were you thinking?

A I was thinking this is ...this shouldn't be going on. I asked if she'd come back with me and she said, no, she was staying where she was.

Q So you were met with denials?

A Yeah.

Q From both?

A Both.

Q Again, could you help us with Carol's age at this time? Doing your best.

A Probably 14/15.

Q When did you next see Carol after that?

A When did I next see Carol after that? Do y'know, it's just gone out of my mind now. (After a pause) I can't remember.

Q Did there come a time that Carol was back with you?

A Yes, she... Yes, she... Oh, yes. I ...Carl and I had been to Penistone...

Q Yes.

A ...on a night out and we were coming back on the last bus, which was a single decker...

Q Just pause there for now. We'll come back to that, if we may. So was that the next occasion you remember seeing her, on the bus from...

A Yes. Yeah.

Q ...you coming back from Penistone?

A Yeah.

Q Just before we go on to that, do you recall any incidents where Mr Appleyard threatened or made to hurt himself?

A Oh, yes.

Q Can you help us with that?

A I'd gone to the house - I can't remember why I went - and he opened the door and pushed me out and told me he was gonna hang himself. So, I ran round to the phone box, 'cause I couldn't stay in the house, and I phoned the police. And I waited and they came. They...

Q The police came?

A Came. And they kicked down the door 'cause it was locked.

Q We have a record relating to June ...23 June 1983.

A Probably.

Q Sound about right?

A Yeah.

Q Did the police get into the house?

A They did. One stayed with me and one ran up the stairs.

Q And what was going on?

A Well, he'd hung himself, but he'd only ...they said he'd only just done it, and he just had a red mark around... They lifted up and it had a red mark. I didn't go and see that. I was in the kitchen.

Q Did he ever tell you why?

A No.

Q Thank you. Now, just before we go to when you saw Carol on the bus, just a few matters of chronology, please. We know, again from other documentation we have, there was a legal divorce in due course.

A Mhm.

Q Would have any memory as to that date, or shall I assist you?

A No, I don't remember.

MR HAMPTON: We have some documentation provided by the defendant, which will be agreed fact evidence in due course, your Honour.

JUDGE JAMESON: Yes.

MR HAMPTON: 9 April 1984.

A Mhm.

Q Carol would've been 14. Do you have memory of a court order regarding custody of Paul and Carol...

A Yeah.

Q ...into the care of Mr Appleyard?

A Yeah. And I saw a solicitor to try and...

Q There was some legal proceedings?

A Yeah.

Q 11 April 1984. Just bear with me a moment, I just need to find the document. (After a pause) Again from other material we have, there is correspondence between solicitors dated 16 August 1983 referring to an allegation that you'd removed property from the home.

A Mhm.

Q Does that accord with the right timeframe?

A Probably, yes.

Q 16 August 1983.

A I think that was when I broke in.

Q And we have another document between solicitors, 13 October 1983, asserting that on 4 October, Carol was absent from school and had been to see her father. And, again, does that sound like the right timeframe?

A I didn't know about that.

Q	And her "choosing to live with our client". This was from Mr Appleyard's solicitors.

A	Mm.

Q	Finally, there's a statement - an affidavit, or statement. It might assist your Honour, if your Honour's got access to the digital case system...

JUDGE JAMESON: Yes.

MR HAMPTON: ...J110. (To the witness) Following the split, did there come a time that Carol and Donna were living with you?

A	Yes.

Q	Did you want financial support with that?

A	I don't know whether I could get it or not. I was ...I was... I don't know what they called it then.

(<u>Counsel conferred</u>)

MR HAMPTON: I'm just interested in chronology really. This affidavit created during the course of court proceedings, (inaudible) see J111, it's dated 22 January 1980, and the date is missed off at the end. But what we can see is that it was produced by order of the court on 21 September 1984, para.1, and you were married to Carl Higgins on 21 July 1984.

A	Mhm.

Q	Does that sound right?

A	Mhm.

Q	So you've married Carl, I think some three months about, after the divorce from Mr Appleyard?

A	Yes.

Q	It also says that residing with you was Donna, 16, and Carol, 15. Does that sound about right?

A	I think only Donna was living there then.

Q In January 1985, Carol would've been 15, but we'll deal with that by way of agreed fact. Thank you. Right. Can we go back now, please, to the meeting with Carol when you were on the bus, the time you saw Carol on the bus?

A Well, we... I can't remember the exact time but it was the last bus back from Penistone to Thurgoland.

Q Right.

A And...

Q So you're on the bus from Penistone to Thurgoland?

A Yeah.

Q What had you been doing?

A We'd been out with friends for a drink.

Q So you'd taken some drink?

A Mm.

Q Were you falling over, drunk?

A No. No.

Q Who were you with?

A Carl.

Q Now we know that there was a marriage, July 1984, 21 July 1984. Can you remember, was this before or after the marriage?

A After the marriage, I think.

Q After?

A Yeah. Yeah.

Q Right. And tell us what you saw when you were on the bus.

A We were the only ones and then I saw somebody on the back seat, right at the back, huddled over.

Q Right. So yourself and Carl got on the bus. You were the only ones on there?

A Mm.

Q So no other passengers?

A There were no other passengers.

Q You saw someone huddled over and you...

A Yeah.

Q ...put your head down?

A I wasn't sure then who it was until she said, "Mam? Mum?"

Q Just to be clear, had you arranged to meet Carol, or anything like that?

A No.

Q No. This was a chance meeting?

A No, no. (Inaudible).

Q She said, "Mum?" And then? Who approached who?

A I went to the back of the bus and put my arm round her, and she told me that she'd left. She was in tears. She'd left. He'd gone to the pub, and ... She wasn't going back.

Q How did she appear? What was her...?

A She was very, very upset. Very upset.

Q How did you know that?

A Well, because she was crying and she was shaking, and... She was my daughter, I know she was upset.

Q Did she tell you why?

A Yes.

Q What did she say to you on the bus at that time?

A She said that her father had raped her, and she wanted to get away from him.

Q And did you do anything with that piece of information, Mrs Voss?

A Yes, I did. When we got off the bus, I phoned the Pie Hall, Denby Dale Pie Hall, where I...

Q Just before we get into (inaudible) conversation...

A Yeah.

Q ...and who with.

A Yeah.

Q It's a bit unusual - the "Pie Hall", was that?

A That's what it's called, Denby Dale Pie Hall.

Q What is it?

A It's a village hall with a bar.

Q Right. You can get a drink there?

A Yeah.

Q So you phoned the Pie Hall. It's in Denby Dale, is it?

A Yeah.

Q Did Mr Appleyard go there?

A He... Carol told me that's where he'd gone that night.

Q Was he a regular there?

A I think he was quite regular there.

Q Where did you make the phone call from?

A Do y'know, I don't know... I can't remember whether we had a phone, or it was a phone box. I think we had a phone.

Q And by that...

A Not a mobile, 'cause...

Q Yes.

A ...mobiles weren't here then.

Q So when you say "we had a phone", where was that?

A It would be in the house...

Q Right.

A ...if we had one.

Q So from the house or a phone box?

A Yeah.

(Counsel conferred)

MR HAMPTON: I'm told I'm being a little unfair. What are you saying about where the call came from? Where you made the call from.

A From Thur ...Thurgoland. When we lived...

Q Yes.

A ...in Thurgolan... From the house.

Q From the house.

A Mm.

Q Thank you. So, tell us what you said, please.

A I asked for them to bring him to the phone and I ...exact words I said: "Carol's told me everything." And his exact words were: "You fucking prove it."

Q Did he deny it?

A Well, by saying that, "You fucking prove it," that, to me, is denying it. He didn't admit it.

Q Did Carol have anything with her?

A I can't remember. I don't think she did, no. She didn't have any clothes or anything with her.

Q Did you come to speak to Mr Appleyard about that fact that she didn't have anything with her?

A I told him that I wanted all her stuff bringing to my house by half-past eight the next day, 'cause she wasn't going back.

Q When did you tell him that?

A I told him that on the phone, when he said to prove it. I said, "Well she's not coming back, and I want all her stuff over here by half-past eight in the morning."

Q So that was the same phone call?

A Mhm.

Q Did that happen?

A Yes.

Q How did that happen?

A The van drew up and his sister was with him, Hilda.

Q Was this Mr Appleyard's van?

A Elliott's sister. Yeah.

Q Mr Appleyard's van?

A Yeah. I don't know if Peter was there, her husband. I can't remember. But I know Hilda was there, his sister.

Q All right. So, Hilda, the sister, was there. And who's Peter?

A That's her husband, but I'm not sure whether he was there or not. I can't remember.

Q And you mentioned a van. Was that Mr Appleyard's?

A His van, yeah.

Q Did you speak to Mr Appleyard at all on that occasion?

A I just said... What did I say? I picked the things up. I said, "You'll be hearing from the police," and that's it.

Q What do you mean by that, Mrs Voss?

A Well, I wanted Carol to go and make a statement at what ...what had happened.

Q So you wanted Carol to make a statement about what had happened?

A Yes, I did.

Q Do you know if Carol spoke to the police?

A For three or four days, she didn't. She was too upset. She was hysterical one minute and sobbing and... But, in the end, after four days, I persuaded her to go to the police at Penistone and I went with her.

Q Four days of persuading her?

A Mhm.

Q She went to Penistone?

A Yeah, and I was with her.

Q There was a police station there, I think.

A Yes.

Q Were you aware if Carol gave a statement?

A Yes. I was in the room when she made the statement.

Q Was it...

A It was...

Q ...just verbal or was it written down? How did it happen?

A They were writing it down, what she said.

Q "They" being the police?

A The police, yeah.

Q Can you help us with how long that took?

A It was a long statement and I felt sick, and they said that it was no good taking her to the hospital to ...because four days had passed, and they wouldn't be able to prove it.

Q Did you provide a statement?

A Do y'know, I can't remember.

(Counsel conferred)

MR HAMPTON: You provided a number of statements to the police.

A Did I? I know I did when they came to the house.

Q Part of this investigation. We have one dated 27 November 2015. There's no issue as to what's contained here. You're talking about a complaint being made "back in the day" and you talk about being in your home in Thurgoland. Am I pronouncing it right?

A Yeah.

Q "It was then that I provided a written statement about what I knew."

A Yes.

Q Right. So that's what you were saying...

A Yeah.

Q ...27 November 2015.

A Yes. It was two detectives that came and took that statement, from Holmfirth.

Q And, again, what was the process? How was it taken?

A He said if it was taken to court, my son Paul, who was only about 13 at the time, he would be a hostile witness so anything he had to say would be disregarded, so Carol got very upset and she didn't want to do anything else at that time.

Q Was your account written down? Do you remember?

A They wrote it down, yes.

Q Do you recall any action being taken by the police with Mr Appleyard?

A I think they took him to Kirkburton Police Station, and I went there.

Q Yes.

A And I can't remember whether I saw him there or not. I really can't remember. It's 40-odd years ago.

Q All right. Throughout this timeframe, did Carol ever speak to you about pregnancy?

A Yes, she did.

Q Can you tell us about that, please?

A She told me that she thought she might be pregnant. And she had to take a specimen, I think, to the doctors at Penistone, and it was negative. But she said if she was, it woulda been her father's.

Q Can you recall if that was before, at the same time, or after the contact you were having with the police?

A I think it was before.

Q After that complaint to the police, Mrs Voss, did Carol live with you for some time?

A Yes. Carol and Donna.

Q Can you remember how long for? Carol, I'm talking about. How long was Carol there for?

A She was quite a while. But we bought a house in Penistone and we made a bedroom for her in the cellar, a proper bedroom, and Donna was there and me and Carl.

Q And Carol was in the cellar?

A Yeah, but it was a proper bedroom...

Q As a bedroom?

A ...made for her, yeah.

Q Yes. Did there come a time she left?

A Yes, she did.

Q How old was she?

A I think she'd be about 16? Maybe 17. I can't remember.

Q Did your relationship with Carl continue or come to an end?

A No, it continued.

Q Did there come a time it ended?

A Yes, 'cause we became more like brother and sister.

Q And did you start a relationship with somebody else?

A Not straight away, no.

Q No, no. In due course.

A In due course, yeah.

Q And his name?

A Jack.

Q Jack. And where did you live with Jack?

A I ...I ...I got a flat opposite where we had a house together in Penistone, me and Carl, and I'm ...I got a flat opposite, above a hairdressers, and went to college as a ...a stu ...mature student at Sheffield.

Q Thank you. Whilst Carol was with you in Penistone, do you recall her ever speaking to any professionals about what had been alleged?

A No. I wrote to - I can't remember what they're called now - Rape Crisis (inaudible). I wrote them a letter and asked them to help me because I'd been through abuse, and I told them what I was doing, is there anything else I could be doing, and they said I was doing everything that I was supposed to do. So, no, nobody helped.

Q Were you aware if Carol was seeing anybody...

A Was she seeing anybody?

Q ...to do with counselling or anything like that?

A Jack and I... This was after Jack and I moved to Barnsley and I went to the doctors and I asked to ...to get ...if they would get her counselling. She moved with me to Barnsley.

Q Right. I follow. Do you know if she saw anybody or not?

A Yeah, she used to. She... Pretty regular. She worked then at SR Gent's.

Q She worked at SR Gent's?

A Mm.

Q There came a time Carol moved out.

A Yes.

Q Why was that?

A 'Cause we had a row.

Q And she lived on her own?

A She said she lived on her own in a flat, yes.

Q I'm just going to have a bundle of documents put before you. (Same handed) A copy for your Honour. (To the witness) Could I just ask you to look at the first document and just look at it yourself, take it in, and tell me if you recognise it. There's a bundle for your Honour. This is all on (inaudible).

JUDGE JAMESON: Is that supposed to be coming to me, or...?

(Document handed to the learned Judge)

MR HAMPTON: I just want to ask you first of all, do you recognise the first document? It runs to... You see...

A Yeah.

Q ...there's numbers on the top...

A Yeah.

Q ...of the pages. Fifteen pages.

A Yeah. It was a letter I wrote to my daughter, Donna.

Q To Donna. Would you mind me asking this? We know Donna's passed, sadly, but could you help us with when that happened?

A When what happened?

Q Donna's passing.

A We brought her down to Aylesbury. I moved down to Aylesbury.

Q Buckinghamshire?

A Buckinghamshire. And Donna had had a baby then, Millie, and she couldn't look after her properly, she wasn't thriving, so social services got involved and was...

Q I'm just after a timeframe, really, if you can? I'm sorry to interrupt.

A I can't... I can't.

Q All right.

A But the police rung me up and told me to go there 'cause they were going to arrest her husband for abusing... There was abuse going in the family.

Q All right. We'll get the date from...

A Right.

Q ...somewhere else. I want to ask you about a particular passage, if I may, in the letter to Donna. There's two passages actually but the first one is at p.5. You can... Are you... Can you see all right?

A Yeah. Yes.

Q Yes. So p.5.

A Aha.

Q You're talking to Donna about when you left the house...

A Mhm.

Q ...for their schooling.

A Mhm.

Q They're going to a children's home.

A Yes. A weekly one, so she could make friends with teenagers. People would come to the door for Carol and Paul to go out and play, but not Donna 'cause she was epileptic. So she would mix with people her own age and came home at weekends.

Q You also say this, and I just want you to tell us what you mean, if you don't mind, about the children's home. First: "To get you away from some of the tension." And then you talk about the children.

A The tension in the house with me and Elliott.

Q Thank you. And then at p.7, please.

JUDGE JAMESON: I don't think there's... There doesn't appear to be any objection to this but, on the face of it, I can understand you might want to ask about any material that might be thought of as being inconsistent, but material that's on the face of it inconsistent is probably not admissible in these circumstances, is it? It's sort of sometimes referred to rather gnomically as "oath-helping". I mean...

MR HAMPTON: Yes.

JUDGE JAMESON: ...I'm not entirely sure I understand what the purpose of...

MR HAMPTON: Yes. As I'm going through the process...

JUDGE JAMESON: ...a question about anything on para.5 is ...on p.5 is.

MR HAMPTON: Yes. As I'm going through the process of doing this, I'm beginning to think it may be dealt with in a bet ...in another way, in any event.

JUDGE JAMESON: Yes.

MR HAMPTON: And I think that's what I'll do, in fact.

JUDGE JAMESON: I mean, it might become relevant in re-examination...

MR HAMPTON: Yes.

JUDGE JAMESON: ...potentially.

MR HAMPTON: Yes. And it may be that we can produce whatever (inaudible) here that does become relevant...

JUDGE JAMESON: Yes.

MR HAMPTON: ...in a different way. So I take your Honour's point.

JUDGE JAMESON: I don't know what's in here because it's literally just been handed to me, so I don't really know...

MR HAMPTON: No, but I do.

JUDGE JAMESON: ...what the purpose of all of th...

MR HAMPTON: Yes.

JUDGE JAMESON: Yes, course. I'm merely questioning whether, at this stage ...what the purpose of this is.

MR HAMPTON: Yes. There is some of this which I will move on to.

JUDGE JAMESON: Yes.

MR HAMPTON: Shall we discuss it briefly so I can make it clear what the purpose is, just in the absence of the jury? It should be very quick.

JUDGE JAMESON: Sorry, so you want a bit of time?

MR HAMPTON: It'll take two minutes.

JUDGE JAMESON: Yes, all right. Well, let's just think through...

MR HAMPTON: Yes.

JUDGE JAMESON: ...how we're going to go. It's coming up to 10 past 12. I mean, do you need, what... As I say, we can't really have anything between five minutes and 15 minutes, so you're going to have at least 15 minutes. Do you need more time than that?

MR HAMPTON: No.

JUDGE JAMESON: All right. Well, we'll take a 15-minute break, ladies and gentlemen, and see where we get to. Thank you.

(The jury left court at 12.08 p.m.)

(The learned Judge conferred with the witness and counsel)

(Short break)

(12.10 p.m.)

(12.27 p.m.)

MR HAMPTON: I have no further questions at this stage.

JUDGE JAMESON: Right. Okay. You're okay, Mrs Voss...

THE WITNESS: I'm fine, yes.

JUDGE JAMESON: ...to carry on with some questions? Okay. Thank you very much.

(The learned Judge conferred with the Clerk of the Court)

(The jury returned to court at 12.28 p.m.)

JUDGE JAMESON: Right. Thank you very much, ladies and gentlemen.

MR HAMPTON: I've no further questions in...

JUDGE JAMESON: No.

MR HAMPTON: ...examination-in-chief.

JUDGE JAMESON: All right. Thank you very much.

MARGARET JEAN VOSS

Cross-examined by Mr STOREY

Q Mrs Voss, I'm going to ask you a number of questions. There's quite a few. I can't guarantee that I'll be done in the next half an hour, I'm afraid. All right? Some of the things I think I'm going to be suggesting to you, I hope you'll agree with, and some you won't, but I'm sure you'll make it clear either way.

A Yeah. Who ...who are you?

Q I'm the barrister on behalf of Mr Appleyard.

A All right. Okay.

Q Sorry, if that hasn't been made clear to you before.

A Yeah.

Q You agreed, I think, that you and Mr Appleyard married in 1974. That was the date that was put to you.

A Mhm.

Q But you'd been together for a number of years before that, hadn't you?

A Yeah. Yeah.

Q And you told us Donna was your child by somebody else.

A Mhm.

Q Carol and Paul were Mr Appleyard's.

A Yeah.

Q And we can easily tell from the dates of their birth, they were born before your marriage.

A I can't hear. Sorry?

Q They were born before your marriage?

A Yes.

Q Do you remember when it was that you, the family, moved from No. 8 to No. 26 Gilthwaites Crescent?

A No, I don't remember when it was. We did a swap. A young lad moved into what was ours, 'cause his parents had died, and we went into his.

Q Presumably because you were a family and needed more space?

A Yeah.

Q Simple as that?

A (Inaudible)

Q Is it fair to say that the relationship between you and Mr Appleyard was an on-off relationship?
A On-off as... What ...what do you mean?
Q You've described it as volatile but it's a relationship which, at times, was good?
A Oh, yeah. Yeah. Holidays with the ch... Yeah.
Q Times when there weren't arguments?
A Well, yes. There wasn't arguments 24/7 every day, no.
Q And it wasn't the case, lest anyone give this impression, that there was violence in the house all the time, was there?
A No.
Q And I'm going to suggest, in fact, that there wasn't in fact any violence in the house.
A Oh, yes, there was.
Q There were arguments, voices would be raised, but that was as far as things went?
A Mostly in drink he did it.
Q Is it right that you, in fact, left the family home on a number of occasions?
A Yes.
Q For fairly short periods of time?
A Yes. Took the children with me.
Q And then, after a period, you'd return back home?
A Well, yes, because of promises it wouldn't happen again.
Q In the 1970s and 1980s, after you were married, when you were living at 26 Gilthwaites Crescent, Mr Appleyard I think was working, wasn't he?
A He worked on and off.
Q He was...
A He worked for himself, so he... On and off.
Q He was self-employed?
A Yeah.

Q And so that meant he would be contracted out, or contracted himself out, to different construction companies?
A Mmm.
Q And he'd work a full week, wouldn't he? By and large. Sometimes...
A By and large, yes.
Q Sometimes on Saturdays as well?
A I can't remember. Probably.
Q It's the nature of the business.
A Mm.
Q It wasn't the case, was it, that he was always on the sick, or anything like that?
A No.
Q And of the three children, is it also right that he was probably closest to Paul?
A Yes, he was.
Q And he would take the children, but Paul in particular, out with him to walk the dog?
A And shooting.
Q Thank you. Yes, I was going to say that as well - he taught Paul to shoot, didn't he?
A Mhm.
Q And they'd shoot pigeons, I think?
A And ...and rabbits.
Q Rabbits.
A Yeah.
Q And he taught Paul to ride a motorbike and things like that? (Inaudible).
A I don't know where... I didn't even know he had a motorbike.
Q That might've been after you---
A Right. Yeah.
Q ...and he had separated.
A Yeah.
Q But he'd do quite a lot with Paul in particular, wouldn't he?

A Mhm.

Q And sometimes Carol would go out with them as well?

A When they went collecting scrap, yes. Her and Paul.

Q He was strict with the children, wasn't he?

A Very.

Q They had to do what they were told?

A Mhm.

Q They had to do chores in the house?

A Sometimes, yes.

Q But if the picture had been painted that he would regularly, for example, belt them, literally with a belt, what would you say about that?

A No, I didn't. I ...one occasion I used a wooden spoon for a slap (inaudible) but not...

JUDGE JAMESON: I think the witness has misunderstood the question.

MR STOREY: I'll be more direct then. (To the witness) It wasn't the case, was it, that Mr Appleyard would take a belt to the children?

A Yes, he would, yes.

Q It wasn't the case that he would beat the children, having pulled down their underwear?

A I wasn't aware of this till I read this information. But not whilst I was there, he wouldn't have done.

Q Given what you've just said, you were, I think towards the back end of last year, 2018, asked to provide a witness statement by the police, weren't you?

A Mhm.

Q In which you were asked for your comments on certain things that had been written in a book that your daughter, Carol, had herself written?

A That's right, yes.

Q And you've said that witness statement that you gave in late November 2018 that, whilst you didn't remember how many belts Elliott had, he did not use them as a punishment.

A Not on Carol with her knickers down, no.

Q Well, I'm quoting: "I do not remember how many belts Elliott had but he did not use them as punishment."

A No, I can't remember him doing that.

Q No. And immediately after that you said - again, I'm quoting: "He never pulled her knickers down. Certainly not while I was there."

A Yeah.

Q So, if a picture had been painted for the ladies and gentlemen of the jury that that was what life was like in the family home, Elliott Appleyard regularly beating Carol in particular with a belt, that's not what you remember happening at all...

A No.

Q ...is it?

A No.

Q And you went on in this witness statement, didn't you, to say you recalled only one incident when Carol ever wet the bed?

A I think she did, yes. I can't remember.

Q And you, in your witness statement, said that was when she'd been drinking.

A That's when we were at Thurgoland.

Q Right. So not at all at Gilthwaites Crescent?

A No. No.

Q And, again, in relation to the suggestion that he belted Carol and might have had bruises on her legs and things like that, you told the police in this statement from late November 2018: "She never had bruises on her legs."

A No. Not that I ever saw, no.

Q And, similarly, I have to suggest, Mrs Voss, that there was never any physical violence towards you by Mr Appleyard, in fact, was there?

A Oh, yes, there was.

Q Any aggression or violence was verbal only.

A Verbal and fist.

Q And going on from that, there was never an occasion, in fact, when he held a shotgun to your head, was there?

A Yes, there was.

Q Nor did he ever take a machete to you.

A Yes, he did.

Q I just want to ask you about the shotgun.

A Mhm.

Q You've told us that you had no idea where it was kept.

A No, I c... No, I didn't.

Q Was there a gun cabinet, or anything like that, in the house?

A No. No. There was a coal house. I don't know whether he ke... And there was an outside toilet. Whether it was in a wardrobe, upstairs, I don't know.

Q Did you see a shotgun or shotguns - I don't know if there was more than one - lying around in the house...

A No.

Q ...as a matter of generality?

A No. Oh, if he came in from he'd been rabbiting and shoo ...then I would see it.

Q But they weren't just generally kept lying in the corner of the room, or anything...

A No.

Q ...like that?

A No.

Q The machete incident, I think you said, so far as you were aware, the children were not around?

A As far as I was aware, they weren't. Carol said afterwards that she was. She heard it. She was sat on the top step.

Q And when did Carol tell you that? Do you remember?

A I can't remember when she told me that. Not that long ago. She doesn't speak to me now, so it'll be when she was speaking to me.

Q Might it be that that was something you told her about?

A No. I... No. She says she heard it and she saw him with a machete. I didn't realise she had seen. (Inaudible). I was aware that the kitchen door was shut.

Q So that's your recollection, the kitchen door was shut...
A Mm.
Q ...at the time? Was that an incident you reported to the police?
A No.
Q Is there any particular reason why not?
A Well, I felt ...I felt humiliated. I wet myself on the floor. And I just... I just couldn't do it.
Q You told us about an occasion when you were sitting on the front doorstep, having a cigarette.
A Yeah.
Q And you thought you'd been watching something about the Falklands War on television?
A It was that Simon that was disfigured, and he was having his dressings changed and I could hear the screaming and I felt faint, so I went and sat outside and had a cigarette.
Q So it might've been that this was in fact sometime after the...
A Yeah. Yes.
Q ...war had ended?
A Yeah. Yeah.
Q It was just a programme about someone injured in the war?
A Yeah.
Q And do you have any better recollection of when that incident ...that conversation with Carol might have taken place?
A No. It was on that doorstep, there and then.
Q But you told us about that being what led to you phoning social services, who in turn told you to take Carol away?
A Yeah.
Q At that stage, do you remember whether Carol had started hanging around with boyfriends and things like that?

A She had one boyfriend - through the CB, they met - and he used to come over, but there was nothing sexual going on. He'd come and see her, we were there, and then he'd go back home.

Q Right. Okay. And have you got any real idea of how old she would have been at that time?

A She'd be about 13/14.

Q But I think you said nothing said by you to Mr Appleyard at that time?

A Well, he hadn't done anything at that time.

Q As far as you were concerned...

A Yeah.

Q ...nothing at all?

A I didn't find out till after we had left that ...what he was doing.

Q Right. You made reference to watching westerns and one mentioning that Indian chiefs would break in their eldest daughters.

A Mhm.

Q This wasn't something that Mr Appleyard was saying should happen, was it? Or should be done.

A He agreed with it, that that's what should happen.

Q Wasn't he perhaps, as I understand what you've said earlier on, he was simply commenting on the western that you were watching at that particular time?

A I don't know what he was commenting but that was what he said to me: he ...he believed in it.

Q He believed in it?

A He ...he thought that that's what should happen. His exact words was: "That's what should happen."

Q Well, can you remember his exact words now?

A Yes. "That's what should happen."

Q Was it not perhaps an expression of opinion that that was what he understood Indian chiefs to do?

A I don't know what he was thinking in his mind. I can only tell you what he said to me.

Q Did you ask him what he was thinking?

A No.

Q Or what he meant by it?

A No. I just... It was a throwaway thing. I just didn't think anything was gonna become of it.

Q A throwaway remark?

A Mm.

Q And do you remember when that occurred, that throwaway remark when you were watching that western?

A No.

Q Presumably before the conversation with Carol on the steps?

A Yes. Oh, yeah. I think Paul was only about eight or nine then.

MR HAMPTON: (Inaudible) I'm sorry to interrupt. I'm not clear if it's accepted it was said or not, on behalf of the defence.

JUDGE JAMESON: No, well...

MR HAMPTON: I'm just wondering if we could have some help on that?

JUDGE JAMESON: Well, perhaps we'll hear about that in due course.

MR HAMPTON: (Inaudible)

MR STOREY: So, you were saying, Mrs Voss, Paul would've been eight or nine?

A Well, he'd be about that age, yes.

Q Yes. So late 1970s?

A Yeah, I would say so, yes.

Q Moving forwards again in time, the conversation with Carol happened when you thought she was 13 or 14, I think you said, and then you took her away and left the house...

A Yes.

Q ...for a period of time.

A Mhm.

Q And do you remember how long it was that you and she were away then?

A We were in that refuge for about 10 days. But he found out where we were, so we went back home. And he said he would leave, or he said he was sorry. I can't remember.

Q And what do you think he was saying sorry for?

A Because he'd been... I don't know. When I took Carol to the refuge, it wasn't that he was doing anything then. He was beating me then.

Q Right.

A So I took Carol with me. She wanted to come with me.

Q Okay.

A So we went back after he promised me he wouldn't hit me anymore.

Q I've already suggested, and you've disagreed, that he was not beating you.

A He was? Sorry?

Q I've already suggested he wasn't beating you and you've disagreed with that.

A Yes.

Q But I was asking you, really, about the time you left with Carol after the conversation with social services, which in turn was after the conversation on the doorstep.

A Yes. So what are you asking me?

Q I'm just trying to clarify whether we're...

A Right.

Q ...talking about different periods when you were in a refuge or if it's the same time?

A It was after.

Q Which was after?

A Carol telling me about the abuse.

Q Right. Well, the conversation on the doorstep, what did you ...what do you say she told you in that conversation?

A She said, "You know me and Paul go to get scrap with Dad?" I said, "Yes." She says, "Well, when we get there, sometimes he tells Paul to go over a different way and he'll sit and put his arm round me and kiss me." I said, "What do you mean? On your cheek?" She says, "No, on me lips."

Q And it was that led you to speak to social services?
A Yes. Of course, yes.
Q That led you to, I think, go and stay with someone called Angela in Penistone?
A David. Yeah.
Q And do you remember whether you then went from there to stay with someone called Linda?
A At Thurlstone, yes.
Q Thurlstone. How long do you recollect being at Angela and David's?
A A couple of months, I would say. Six weeks to a couple of month.
Q Were you present when social workers spoke to Carol about what she'd told you on the doorstep?
A Yes. I was... The man that came, I was there, and Carol was with me.
Q Okay. And where do you remember that conversation happening?
A In the kitchen, my kitchen, at 26 Gilthwaites.
Q Was anything said about talking to the police about it?
A No, he ...actually he thought maybe she wasn't telling the truth, but I wasn't ...I knew she was, so I... He didn't say he would do anything else about it, he just told me to take her away if I wasn't sure.
Q You've told us two months or so at Angela and David's. How long do you remember thereafter staying with Linda?
A Well, I'd put my name down for a council house, so it would be about six months, maybe.
Q Okay. So maybe eight months in total that you and Carol were away from...
A Mm. Mm.
Q ...Denby Dale? You've mentioned Carol going out with Linda's son, David?
A Mhm.
Q She was how old, do you recollect, at this time?
A She'd be about 13/14.
Q And he was older?
A A think he was a couple of years older, that's all.

Q As old as 19 perhaps?

A Maybe. Eighteen/nineteen, yeah.

Q When you were living in Penistone, was Carol going to school?

A As far as I knew, she was going to school.

Q Yes. So, I take it from that, she'd leave the home in the morning to go to school and come back at an appropriate time, suggesting she'd been there?

A Yeah.

Q But there came a time when she told you she was going back to her father's?

A She didn't tell me; she wrote it on a mirror.

Q Sorry, yes. When she left a note and left?

A On the mirror: "Gone back to Dad's."

Q Had you had any inkling that that was something she was thinking of doing?

A No, no, because she was gonna meet me that ...with her and David at Stocksbridge at ...they call it Eyeball, where you ...CBers mix together and have a disco.

Q Right.

A She was supposed to meet us there and at half-past nine she hadn't got there, so I assumed she wasn't coming.

Q And how do you remember the relationship between you and Carol being before she left to go back to Denby Dale?

A She was all right. Nothing ...nothing wrong, as far as I knew. As far as I was aware.

Q And once she'd gone, did you try to contact her to find out why she'd gone?

A No, not at first, 'cause I was so upset and angry. I'd taken her away from it and she'd gone back. I couldn't understand it.

Q And, again, do you remember whether, at the time she went back to Denby Dale, whether she was still seeing David?

A I don't think so. I don't know.

Q You don't know. But from that point on, what sort of contact did you have with her?

A I used to meet them in Barnsley...

Q Yes.

A ...at the top of the escalator. We'd go and have pie and peas and a cup of coffee, or whatever. Paul, Carol and ...and... Paul, Carol and Donna.

Q So all three of them would meet...

A Yeah.

Q ...you in Barnsley?

A Mm.

Q Okay. And did you ever discuss with Carol how she was?

A Well, I (inaudible). Probably... She never let me believe that anything was happening.

Q No.

A And Carol and Paul were there. They were still in the house. Then Donna came to live with me, so there was just Paul and Carol in the house.

Q Did Carol ever explain to you why she'd gone back to live in Denby Dale with her father? That you can remember.

A I ...I ...I... As far as I knew, he ...she'd meet him in Barnsley, and he'd buy her jeans and bits and pieces. Buy her clothes that I couldn't afford to get.

Q And so did she give you the impression that she quite liked the material goods being bought for her?

A Well, no. I think she was just a teenager that, y'know, when I couldn't afford, I wasn't working, then he was buying her these things.

Q Is it the case that, if she'd asked, you'd have had her back living with you in the Penistone area?

A I don't know. She never did so that never arose.

Q You told us about an occasion when you broke into the house in...

A In...

Q ...Gilthwaites Crescent.

A In Gilthwaites, yes.

Q And do you remember when that was?

A No. I can't remember. It's...

Q If I was...

A ...40-odd years ago.

Q I understand, Mrs Voss. Don't worry about that. If I was to suggest it might have been in the winter one year, November/December-time? Can you comment on...

A No, I don't think it was actually.

Q No?

A No, I don't. No.

Q It was when Mr Appleyard was in America.

A America, yes. And I don't know what date that was.

Q Okay. Well, in that case, there's no point me suggesting anything to you, to be fair. But you told us that you'd seen the children, who had been having parties?

A I... Yes.

Q For the avoidance of doubt, the parties had been at the house. Is that correct?

A The house, yes.

Q And I think you said that their Auntie Hilda was supposed to be keeping an eye on them?

A Yes, she was.

Q Do we take it that you formed that view that she wasn't doing what she was meant to in that respect?

A Probably, yeah.

Q Do you remember seeing evidence of the fact that they'd been having parties at the house?

A No, 'cause I didn't look for any.

Q No.

A It just looked normal.

Q Okay. What do you remember actually taking from the house on that occasion?

A A parasol that I'd bought at a jumble sale. They didn't have car boots then. I bought at a jumble sale. And I can't remember what else, but there was a couple of things anyway.

Q Right. In the period when you were living in Penistone and Carol was living with her father and Paul in Denby Dale, you've told us that you would meet her at the market in Barnsley. How often do you think you would see her? How regularly?

A I don't know. It was mostly Saturdays we'd...

Q Right.

A ...meet up.

Q So was that a regular thing, every Saturday you'd...

A It was pretty regular, I think. I certainly know it was more than once or twice.

Q Did you ever see her with love bites on her neck, or anything like that?

A No.

Q And you told us about a couple of occasions when you went back to Gilthwaites itself. Christmas presents?

A To take Christmas presents.

Q Yes.

A Yeah.

Q That she was not inclined to accept?

A No. She told me... Well, you know what I said.

Q Yes. She was abusive towards you.

A Mhm. And he was.

Q So far as you were concerned, was there any reason for them to be abusive towards you?

A That was just him. No. Well, I hadn't done anything. And I asked her if sh... I told her what I'd heard, and she said it was all lies and... 'Cause I woulda took her. If she'd admitted it, I woulda took her back with me.

Q Can I just make clear that I understand? Is that the same occasion that you have...

A Yeah.

Q ...that conversation? Okay. Sorry, I thought there were two occasions. Right, so she said that there was nothing untoward happening at all?

A	Yeah. She did, yes. And Paul was there as well, so I felt a bit more settled in myself 'cause Paul was living there, my son.

Q	Right. I think the next incident that you've told us about was effectively the meeting on the bus. Just before I ask you about that though, you were asked by Mr Hampton about the occasion when Mr Appleyard was found by the police, hanging, at home.

A	He was what, sorry?

Q	Found by the police, hanging, at home.

A	Yes.

Q	And they had to cut him down.

A	Yeah.

Q	Now, do you remember whether that was before or after you had left the family home in Gilthwaites?

A	After.

Q	So do you remember why it was you were there when that happened?

A	I think the conversation was "Would I come back?" because we often had that conversation. And I said, "No." So he said he was gonna hang himself. But he often said he was gonna shoot himself anyway, and I used to have to pacify the children 'cause they were frightened that he would do it.

Q	Might it have been that that incident occurred after an argument between you, rather than just a request that you come back home?

A	No.

Q	But that's your recollection? It was because he wanted you back and ...

A	Yeah.

Q	...you said no?

A	And I said no, so he slammed the door, locked it, and I ran round to the telephone box... I'm not gonna say what I'm thinking - I wish I'd have walked. But I ran round, and the police came.

Q	Then the incident on the bus?

A	Yes.

JUDGE JAMESON: Now, we're just coming up to one o'clock and I suspect this is going to be a fairly substantial...

MR STOREY: Yes.

JUDGE JAMESON: ...topic. Yes.

MR STOREY: Thank you, your Honour.

(The learned Judge conferred with the witness)

JUDGE JAMESON: Right, ladies and gentlemen, 10 past two. Thank you very much indeed.

(The jury left court at 1.00 p.m.)

(Counsel conferred with the learned Judge)

(Adjourned for a short time)

(1.00 p.m.)

(2.11 p.m.)

(Counsel conferred with the learned Judge)

(The jury returned to court at 2.13 p.m.)

JUDGE JAMESON: Yes?

Mrs MARGARET JEAN VOSS

Cross-examined by Mr STOREY (Cont'd)

Q Mrs Voss, we'd got to the point where I was going to ask you about what I've referred to as "the incident on the bus", the meeting between you and Carol on the bus back (audio jumped to next track) Penistone. First of all, what's your recollection about when that was, as best you can tell us?

A I don't remember a date.

Q No.

A I just know it was... It was probably on a weekend, 'cause Carl worked during the week. So, it coulda been a Friday night, or a Saturday night going into Sunday.

Q And what about Carol's age at the time? How old do you think she was?

A I'd say about 15? Maybe?

Q And you've told us that you'd been out for a drink with friends in Penistone. Is that right?

A We met up with friends in Penistone, yeah.

Q Yes. Do you remember anything about the evening out with those friends before you got the bus home?

A No.

Q No.

A It was just a normal evening. I had a few drinks and then got on the last bus home.

Q And I think you told us there was effectively nobody else on the bus. Is that about right?

A No. I didn't recollect seeing anybody else on the bus. That's why Carol stood out, which I didn't know it was her at the time 'cause she was bent down.

Q Yes. For the record, you're indicating she had her head bowed down.

A Yeah.

Q Certainly no group of half a dozen or so school-aged children?

A Not that I remember, no.

Q No.

A No. It was night-time. The last bus was 11, I think.

Q Right. You've told us that Carol spoke with you?

A Mhm. And Carl.

Q I'm sorry? And Carl?

A And Carl.

Q And that, as a result, when you got off the bus, you rang the Pie Hall in Denby Dale?

A Mhm.

Q And you spoke with Mr Appleyard and told him: "She's told me everything"?

A Mhm. Yes.

Q Do you remember also telling him that Carol was for saying he had abused her?

A No. All I said to him was: "Carol's told me everything." And then his retort straight after that, which I've told you.

Q Well, I suggest that it may in fact be that you had told him as well that Carol was saying he abused her.

A Probably did. I can't remember. All I know was I told him Carol had told me everything.

Q And his response was slightly different to what you told us earlier, I'm suggesting, along the lines of: "I hope you can prove it."

A No. There was...

Q Rather than...

A ...a swear word in it.

Q Okay. Was any...

A And it was "You …", not "I hope …". It was, "You effing prove it."

Q Was there anything else said that you can remember...

A No.

Q ...in that conversation?

A The phone was put down by both of us. Well, I put mine down anyway.

Q And I've got to contradict or suggest that your recollection about his sister bringing Carol's clothes around the following morning isn't quite accurate, with respect.

A His sister was in that van.

Q Certainly that didn't happen the following day.

A It did. In the morning.

Q You told us that you'd said to him - I think? - "You'll be hearing from the police."

A When I picked her clothes up, yes.

Q Although at that stage there'd been no contact with the police at all, had there? By you or Carol.

A No. No.

Q And I think you told us that you spent about four days trying to persuade her to see the police?

A I did. She was so upset. She just wouldn't because... I don't know why. She was just very upset.

Q You've told us that you were aware that Mr Appleyard was taken to a police station?

A Yeah.

Q Can I suggest it was in fact Holmfirth rather than Kirkburton? For what it's worth.

A No, it was Kirkburton. It was Kirkburton Police Station. The two detectives that came and took her thing were from Holmfirth. But it was Kirkburton he went to ...I went to and he was at.

Q What makes you so sure it was Kirkburton that he was taken to?

A 'Cause ...'cause... I don't know whether I saw him there or I just was told he was there. But it was Kirkburton. It was... I've never been to Holmfirth Police Station.

Q You told us also that at some point Carol had told you she'd thought she was pregnant, or might...

A Yeah.

Q ...have been pregnant.

A Mhm.

Q When do you remember that being said?

A Do y'know, I'm not... Before this happened, she came to see me. Her and Paul used to come and see me. And I think, then, she said she might be, but it was only when she moved in that she went for the test, I think, to see if she was pregnant.

Q And did you take her for that test?

A No, she went to ...urine test to the doctors. She took a test, urine.

Q So it wasn't a case of you taking her to the doctors? She went...

A No. She ...she...

Q ...on her own?

A No. She took a urine test.

Q Okay. She said nothing at all at that time, did she, in fact, about who might the father have been?

A Yes, she did. I asked her. And she said, "If I had been pregnant, it was his," her father's.

Q (After a pause) I'm sorry, I'm just checking something in the witness statements. (After a pause) Do you remember, in fact, in relation to the pregnancy, Carol saying to you something about being ...the father, if she was pregnant, would've been "a lad"? Certainly not her father.

A No.

Q All right. You were provided I think, earlier on today, with copies of some letters that you've written.

A Mhm.

Q And Mr Hampton started asking you some questions about them. I don't need to go into them in any detail at all, but do you remember that - and you may have spotted it in the bundle, I don't know - there was a time when your daughter, Carol, asked you to write a letter for her? Do you remember that?

A No.

Q A letter in July 2017?

A She probably did, but I can't remember anyway. 2017?

Q Mhm. Well, let me try this way: do you remember telling the police about the letters you'd written to Carol and, in one case, to Donna?

A I probably did.

Q And do you remember telling the police that the most recent one was a letter written in July 2017 and you knew that because you still had a copy of it on your laptop?

A Probably. I don't... My husband does... I don't...

Q Okay.

A ...bother with computers...

Q Right.

A ...so I don't know.

Q But do you remember telling the police that Carol had asked you to write that letter?

A I can't remember that she'd asked me.

Q No.

A She probably did, but I can't remember.

Q And do you also remember telling the police that you were aware she had put it on Facebook?

A Yeah.

Q That letter, a copy of it? Do you remember seeing your letter on Facebook?

A Did you say I was aware she put it on Facebook?

Q Mhm.

A No, I wasn't aware.

Q Well, I wonder if ...just... Not to be unfair to you, there's a copy of a witness statement that you could be provided with. It's 2 March. I could you hand you mine, but I've got some markings on it, I'm afraid. That's the only reason I'm not going to do that. (Same handed) Unless...

JUDGE JAMESON: Now, where am I going to find this? Is this in the bundle that I was given before lunch, or in the...?

MR STOREY: It is at p.I58 on the digital case system.

JUDGE JAMESON: Thank you very much.

MR STOREY: It's a very short statement.

JUDGE JAMESON: Yes.

MR STOREY: Section I29, if that's easier for your Honour. Do you see that statement, Mrs Voss?

A Yes.

Q Dated 2 March 2018?

A Yes.

Q Yes? Do you see that in the top right-hand corner? Or top right part of the...

A Yeah.

Q ...the heading.

A Mm.

Q And it refers to the letters that you had written to your daughters between 1991 and 1994, doesn't it?

A Yeah. I can remember writing letters to Do ...a letter.

Q Yes.

A I've got the letter here.

Q And it goes on to refer to the most recent one, dated 30 July. Do you see that?

A Yes.

Q 2017?

A I ...I still... It says: "I have a copy on my laptop." I haven't...

Q Yes.

A ...'cause I...

Q No.

A ...haven't got a laptop.

Q Well, you've already explained that. Don't worry about that. The only reason I've given you this is because it says, doesn't it, that you can recall Carol asking you to write this letter?

A I say it here, yes.

Q Yes.

A But I can't remember it now.

Q No. Okay. Thank you for clarifying that. But it also goes on to say, doesn't it: "I do know the letter was put on Facebook by Carol"?

A I didn't see it on Facebook. My husband might've seen it...

Q No.

A ...and told me.

Q But you were aw...

A I don't know.

Q Sorry.

A I never saw it.

Q But you were aware, certainly by the time you made this statement in March of last year, that it had been posted to Facebook by Carol?

A I presume so, yes.

Q Because you've said so in your statement to the police.

A Mhm.

Q Yes. Okay. Thank you. That's all I wanted to clarify with you.

A All right. Okay.

Q Can I just ask you this? Going back to the time when Carol came to live with you after the meeting on the bus and after she'd been to the police station...

A Mhm.

Q ...do you remember now how long she lived with you for after that?

A Oh, it was a bit of a while 'cause Carl and I bought a house in Penistone and we made the cellar into a bedroom for her, so it was a good few months.

Q Yes. And did she, having come back, as it were, to Penistone with you, did she go back to school in Penistone? Or was this to be...

A Yeah, she went back to...

Q Yes.

A ...school at Penistone (inaudible).

Q Again, assuming she went to school when you thought she was going to school?

A Mm.

Q One other matter I just want to ask you about: do you know, or do you remember the fact that Mr Appleyard owned some land in Denby Dale?

A Yeah.

Q Do you know who it was he rented that from?

A I've no idea. No. We used ...he used to grow potatoes and we'd do bonfire night with all the ...the ...y'know, people round us, and fireworks and toffee apples and all that, we used to do there.

Q But it was just used to...

A Yeah.

Q ...grown some vegetables on...

A Yeah.

Q ...and stuff like that?

A Yeah.

Q Okay. Thank you, Mrs Voss. There's nothing else, in fact, that I want to ask you now. Thank you very much.

MR HAMPTON: I just have one area of clarification...

JUDGE JAMESON: Yes.

MR HAMPTON: ...if I may, about the physical chastisement of the children.

Re-examined by Mr HAMPTON

Q You were asked about whether they were belted with belts, I think. Just to clear that up, did you ever hit the children?

A Yes, I did smack them.

Q Did you ever use anything?

A I think I once had a wooden spoon and I ...they were near me and I ...on the top of the leg, but not a belt or anything.

Q And what about the defendant? Did he ever use a belt?

A Do y'know, I can't remember him using a belt.

Q Thank you. Does your Honour have any questions?

JUDGE JAMESON: No. Thank you very much indeed.

Right, thank you very much indeed, Mrs Voss. Now, I don't know exactly what other witnesses are coming and whether or not you would know any of them, but can I ask you, please, not to speak to any other potential witnesses.

THE WITNESS: No. We're going straight home after this.

JUDGE JAMESON: Okay. Good. Thank you...

THE WITNESS: Yeah.

JUDGE JAMESON: ...very much. And, during the course of the trial, make sure that if anybody does speak to you or try to speak to you that you don't speak to them about the evidence that you've given.

THE WITNESS: Yeah. Okay.

JUDGE JAMESON: All right?

THE WITNESS: Yes.

JUDGE JAMESON: Thank you very much indeed.

THE WITNESS: Do you want this back?

MR STOREY: Yes, please.

THE COURT USHER: I'll take it.

(The witness withdrew)

(2.29 p.m.)

Letter from Carol's Mother, Jean Voss

Hi Carol,

I have been trying to see how I can let people Know what a Horrible bully Elliott was.

I was married to Elliott for 15 years, and saw first hand how when he was not bullying me he would be doing it to other people, eg, if we went to the pub and their was someone young at the bar he would put his hand around the back of their necks and squeeze, however he only did it to people he knew were timid to retaliation.

Once while watching a cowboy film on the TV about Indians breaking in their daughters before they got married he said, "it should happen to all daughters". I did not think anything of it then except it being a weird comment.

16th January 2019 – Day 3

When my son was 6 months old, after coming home on a Sunday lunchtime from the pub he punched me in the face and then in the stomach, with my son in my arms. He then ate his lunch and fell asleep on the settee.

I could not take anymore and was scared he might hurt me again and my children were still very young. I put them in the pram and walked up to Cumberworth, where my sister in law lived. They were shocked to see the state I was in, blood all down my clothes. They phoned him and told him I was not coming back unless he promised not to hit me again.

The next day when he went back to work I left my two girls with my mother in law and went to the Doctors to see if there was anything he could do to mend my nose, the result of his beating. The Doctor gave me a prescription for some painkillers. I told him when I got the prescription I was going to take them all and end my life. I was so unhappy I did not want to leave my children but I had had enough of his cruelty.

I was admitted to St Luke's hospital and because my son was only six months old they kept him in with me. The treatment program they put me on was to put me to sleep for three days. Every six hours they would wake me up, two nurses would walk me to the toilet and back then had to drink this stuff and a tablet to send me back to sleep. However, after only two days they had to stop the treatment because my body did not want to wake up. Through all this the staff looked after my son.

I had to see a Psychiatrist and Elliott was not allowed to visit me at the Psychiatrist's say so. The staff started to take me out into the gardens to try to cheer me up with some sunshine. I learnt later he sneaked in to see me and had passed me going outside with the nurses and did not recognise me. The Doctor wanted to speak to him and all I could get from that talk was that he said to me, "A Leopard never changes its spots". Now you must take that as you want. After four weeks he talked me into going back home a few hours in the daytime to start with and then an overnight stay, then a weekend, then back home altogether.

There are two more things that he did. We had an argument, I cannot remember what about and he held a shot gun to my head and threatened to shoot me. My children stood there rooted and terrified and he told them he would shoot me if they tried to get to the phone, which was in the hallway.

When he got to work the next day I phoned the police and told them what happened. They said because he hadn't used the gun there was nothing they could do.

I phoned a friend called Pauline who lived on a farm. She told me to bring myself and the children to her until I decided what I wanted to do. Before I went there I buried the shotgun in the garden because I was so scared he would find out where we were and find his gun. I used to sit on the floor under the window to watch TV at Pauline's because he would see my shadow at night. And yet again after the promises I went back. I had three children and nowhere else to go.

The other time he scared me when I woke up one morning and he said, "Who was you dreaming about last night". I told him I don't know but it was probably him. He went to work and his parting words to me were, "You had better know by the time I get home from work". I thought he would probably forget about what he had said when he got home but before he went to the pub he said, you had better remember before I get home". I got ready for bed, my nightie and dressing gown on and he asked me if I remembered. I told him " I cannot remember, It was probably you". "Not good enough he said". He fetched his machete and pressed it to where my vagina was. I was terrified and I remember wetting my self and passed out. This must have made him come to his senses. My children watched him do this.

There are a lot more of these bullying things and in the end I left him and took my daughter Carol with me as I knew she was in danger. I got in touch with Social Services but they did not want to know. They sent a doddery old fella round.

He would try it on with all my friends, even one of my babysitters who was 15 at the time. Those who know me and knew what I had to put up with know every word I have written is true.

My only regret was on one occasion I would come back. He locked me out of the house and said he was going to hang himself. Fool me, I ran around the estate to the phone box and phoned the Police. They got in by breaking through the back door and ran up stairs. He had put a rope in the attic and hung it round his neck but the Police said he had only just jumped with the rope around his neck when they got into the kitchen and they did not think it was for real. They did take him to hospital but he only had a small mark on his neck. What a pity I ran around to the phone box.

(2.31 p.m.)

CARL HIGGINS, Sworn

Examined by Mr HAMPTON

Q Your full name, please?
A Carl... Carl Higgins.
Q Carl Higgins?
A Yeah.
Q And your age?
A Sixty-one.
Q You, back in the day, Mr Higgins, were in a relationship with a woman called Margaret Jean Appleyard?
A Yes.
Q Can you recall when that was?
A (No audible response)
Q We've got a date from a document that you were married on the 21st of July 1984?

A Yeah, yeah. That'd be about right, yeah.

Q And do you recall how long the relationship had been ongoing prior to your marriage?

A No more than two year.

Q Two years?

A At most, yeah.

Q Before the marriage? How did you meet... I think she called herself Jean, did she?

A Yeah.

Q Jean Appleyard?

A We met through a CB club in Penistone.

Q CB radio?

A Yeah.

Q Did you become aware that Jean had three children?

A Yes.

Q Donna, Carol and Paul?

A Yes.

Q Did you come to know the children?

A Yeah, yeah, I got to know 'em eventually, yeah.

Q Did you meet Carol?

A Yes.

Q And Donna?

A Yes.

Q And Paul?

A Yes.

Q Did there come a time the relationship you had with Jean ended?

A Yes, when we were married.

Q When did the marriage come to an end?

A About 1990, summat like that.

Q About 1990?

A Yeah.

Q Did you divorce?

A Yes.

Q Where did you first live together? What area of the country?

A Thurgoland. It were just outside Penistone.

Q Thurgoland?

A Yeah.

Q And who lived in that house with you?

A Just Donna, just me, Jean and Donna.

Q You, Jean and Donna?

A Yeah.

Q Did you move from Thurgoland?

A Yeah.

Q To where?

A Springvale, Springvale. That's just outside Penistone.

Q Springvale? That's the area, just outside Penistone?

A Well, there's Penistone and Springvale's in between Thurgoland and Penistone.

Q All right, and did anyone else join you there?

A At that time there were just Donna.

Q Did that change?

A Well, it did a bit later on.

Q Right, and who arrived?

A Carol.

Q Carol?

A Then you've got the same as Thurgoland as well. It were just Donna and then Carol... then that changed a bit when Carol stopped with us that time as well.

Q So you remember Carol being at Thurgoland?

A Yes.

Q For a period of time?

A Yeah.

Q And at the house in Penistone...

A Yes.

Q ...for a period of time? Do you know where Carol was living when she wasn't with you and Jean?

A At which time?

Q Whilst you were... whilst you were at Thurgoland and Penistone?

A Well, she were living with her father before she joined us at Thurgoland and she were living with her father before she joined us at Springvale.

Q So with her father?

A Yeah.

Q And could you tell us, please, about events that led to her living with you at Thurgoland, how that came about?

A Well, Jean and I had been in Penistone. We used to go there to CB club and some...

Q Pause there. Just pause there. Jean and yourself had been in Penistone? You used to go to the CB club?

A Yeah.

Q Will you just keep your voice up so everybody can hear?

A Yeah.

Q Aim for that back wall. Thank you.

A And sometimes we'd go up into Penistone for a drink. Then we'd get the last bus from Penistone back to Thurgoland.

Q Yeah.

A So I don't know if we'd been to the CB club on the Monday or it were a night we'd been out up Penistone. We'd got the last bus and Carol was sat on the back... back seat of the bus.

Q Right. Just pause there. Who were you with when you got on the bus?

A Just Jean.

Q So you and Jean get on the bus and Carol's on the back of the bus?

A Yeah.

Q Do you recall if there were any... anybody else was on the bus?

A There might have been odd person cos it were always the last bus back to Sheffield so it were always quiet.
Q Whereabouts was Carol on the bus?
A On... on the back seat.
Q Was she with anybody?
A No.
Q How did she seem?
A She looked upset and what happened, Jean got on... we got on the bus. Jean saw Carol at the back and went, "What are you doing here?" and then Carol started crying.
Q Did she give, or did you hear Carol give any explanation as to why she was there?
A No. I... I... I sat a couple of seats in front and let Jean talk to Carol.
Q Did you hear Carol say anything about why she was there whilst you were on the bus?
A No. It were just a discussion between Jean and Carol.
Q Did you hear an explanation after you got off the bus?
A Later on, yes.
Q What explanation was that?
A That her father had been trying to touch her up and were try... wanting to have sex with her.
Q Her father was trying to touch her up and wanting to have sex with her? And who said that?
A It were Jean... it were Jean what explained it, after they'd made a phone call to Elliott.
Q So is this the same night?
A Yeah.
Q Did you yourself speak to Carol about what was being said?
A No.
Q How many times had you met Carol before this?

A Not all that many times, leading up to the third one, and used to just meet, might have been two or three times.
Q Two or three times?
A You know, summat like that.
Q What's your best recollection of how old Carol was at the time of this incident?
A I... I think she were at school but I'm not quite sure.
Q So just help us with that. What does that mean to you, if you think she was at school? What's your recollection of her age?
A Possibly 15, summat like that.
Q Around 15. You mentioned a phone call?
A Yeah.
Q Could you tell us about that, please?
A Well, after Jean and Carol had been talking on the bus, we got off at Thurgoland and there's a... there's a phone box straight across the road.
Q Straight across the road from where?
A From the bus-stop.
Q From the bus-stop.
A And they both went there.
Q Did you see who made a call?
A I know they... I know Jean went in the... in the phone box cos I waited at the other side of the road.
Q Can we take it from that you didn't hear what was said?
A No.
Q Where did you go after the phone call?
A Back to the house on Fir Tree Avenue.
Q Back to Fir Tree Avenue?
A Yeah. That were at Thurgoland.
Q Where did Carol stay the days after that?
A She stayed at the house at Thurgoland.

Q So would that mean you recollect you, Jean, Donna and Carol at Thurgoland?

A Yeah.

Q What's your best recollection as to what occurred after that, Mr Higgins, in terms of where Carol stayed?

A Well, Carol stopped with us for, I don't know if it were a few months, summat like that.

Q A few months, yeah.

A And then she wanted... all of a sudden she wanted to go back to her father's.

Q And is your recollection that she did so?

A Yeah, yeah.

Q You spoke about a period of time she stayed with you at Penistone, at Springvale?

A Yeah.

Q Is it your recollection that that came afterwards?

A Yes.

Q How did that come about then?

A Well, me and Jean got married and we bought an house, got a mortgage for a house down Springvale.

Q Yeah.

A So we moved from Thurgoland to Springvale and (inaudible) and all of a sudden Carol... Carol came back, said everything had started going off again and asked if he could... if she could stop with us.

Q What was your understanding of "everything had started going off again"?

A Exactly what went off at Thurgoland, why she... why she were on bus.

JUDGE JAMESON: Sorry? Would you just say that again? I didn't quite catch it.

A I was... I was saying that we thought it had started again and I thought exactly the same thing what had started at Thurgoland. That's why she were back with us at Springvale.

MR HAMPTON: Did you ever have any close conversations or long conversations with Carol about what had gone off with her father?

A No.

Q And how was everyone accommodated at Springvale? Where did... where did people stay?

A Well, it were only a two bedroomed house but we'd had a cellar carpeted, wired up and there were shelves in there so Carol stopped down there.

Q So there was you and Jean in one bedroom?

A Yeah.

Q Donna in the other?

A Yeah.

Q And Carol in the cellar that had been refurbished?

A Yes.

Q With shelves and (inaudible). Did Carol come to leave that house? Did she leave?

A Yes. Well, a matter of... well, it left or got... or she got thrown out.

Q She?

A I don't know. You can either put it either left or thrown out because...

Q Can you tell us what you remember?

A Well, what happened, Jean and Carol had a big argument.

Q Jean and Carol had an argument?

A I don't know what it was about but, well, I thought it were, you know, I just thought it were because I were getting on with Carol okay. I don't know if she were a bit jealous or not. I don't know that bit.

Q Yeah.

A So they had an argument and Jean come to me. She went, "It's either Carol goes" or she... or Jean goes.

Q So Carol left?

A So basically, cos I were married to Jean at the time, I gave the marriage a chance.

Q Just one matter: do you recall Carol having contact with the police at all during that timeframe, the 80s?

A No. I don't, no, but Jean might. That's what I'm saying.

Q Well, I'm interested in your recollection.

A I didn't...

Q You don't recall?

A I... No, because I didn't get told everything.

MR HAMPTON: All right. Thank you, Mr Higgins.

JUDGE JAMESON: Yes?

Cross-examined by Mr STOREY

Q Mr Higgins, I've just got a few questions for you. Your recollection is clearly that there were two separate times when Carol came to live with you and Jean?

A Yes.

Q And are you able to remember how far apart those two times were, even if only roughly?

A Possibly 18 month, two year.

Q Okay. The first was after the incident on the bus to Penistone?

A Yes.

Q And I think you'd been out with Jean at a CB club, you said?

A I'm not quite sure...

Q Okay.

A ...if it was the CB club or we'd just been up there, you know, for a drink.

Q All right. Do you remember... so I take it from that you don't remember very much about that evening before getting on the bus?

A All... all it is, it's just if it was on a Monday, it were CB club, basically.

Q Right.

A But if it had been any other night, it had just been a normal night.

Q Night out?

A Yeah.

Q And you paint the picture of there being pretty much nobody on the bus except for you, Jean and...

A Yeah.

Q ...Carol?

A Yeah, because the... that last bus, it used to go from Sheffield but, instead of going to Huddersfield, it used to turn round at Denby Dale, then go back to Sheffield.

Q But you don't seem, with respect, to have been aware of what was being said between Jean and Carol on the bus?

A No.

Q Can you help us with how old Carol was at that time, would you think?

A Well, I'd say... I should say it'd be summat like 14 or 15, summat like that. I've got to try and work it... I've got to try and work it out when we got married and...

Q Yeah. I understand...

A ...you know...

Q ...it's difficult remembering back that time.

A Yeah.

Q And this isn't a memory test for you. Don't worry, Mr Higgins. We know you were married in July 1984.

A Yeah.

Q Okay, so that's the only point of reference we've really got. Was this before or after you got married?

A Which...

Q The meeting...

A The bus... the bus incident?

Q Yeah, the meeting on the bus.

A It were... it were before then.

Q Before the marriage?

A Yeah, cos we were... we were living together at Thurgoland.

Q Mmm.

A We got married and basically more or less straight after marriage we got... we got the mortgage for the house at Penistone.

Q So do you remember how long it was after the incident on the bus that Carol stayed with you in Thurgoland for?

A It might... might have been a couple of months, three month. I'm not right sure.

Q And just looking back to the days after you met Carol on the bus...

A Yeah.

Q ...do you remember what sort of state she was in?

A On the night she were upset.

Q Yeah, but let's say the four or five days after that?

A She seemed to calm down.

Q Right. Was anything else said about why she might have left her dad's house at that time that you can remember, to you?

A The only thing I was told was basically what Jean had told me.

Q And she spent, I think you just said, a couple of months living with you in Thurgoland?

A Summat... could be summat like that.

Q Yes.

A Or it might be a bit longer, you know.

Q Okay, maybe a bit longer? Do you remember what it was that led to her leaving your house in Thurgoland?

A This was at... all I could... well, it were Jean what told me this, by sounds on it. Elliott had been seeing her and trying to entice her back, wanting to buy her this, buy her that, buy her other, promising it'd never happen again and eventually she went.

Q How were things between Carol and her mother in that two or three months that she was living with you in Thurgoland?

A All right.

Q No difficulties?

A No.

Q Were you working at that time?

A Yes.

Q Was Jean? From what you could remember, was she working?

A I don't think so.

Q You told us you don't remember anything about the police being involved?

A No.

Q But then there came a time later when Carol reappeared and came to live with you in Penistone?

A Yeah.

Q What do you remember about first learning that she was coming to live with you in Penistone? How did that come about?

A I were... if... if... I'm not right sure if I were at work or not, but when I got home, she were there.

Q Right.

A And just explained to me that everything had started again and Jean turned round, says, "Can she... can Carol stop with us?" and I just said, "Yes".

Q And I think you told us earlier that that was, to the best of your recollection, about 18 months after...

A Yeah.

Q ...the incident on the bus...

A Yeah.

Q ...that led to her staying in Thurgoland?

A Yeah.

Q And, again, what sort of state was Carol in when she came to stay with you in Penistone?

A She were up... she were upset, just same, but I think Jean had... Jean had been, you know, talking to her so she... Jean had calmed her down...

Q Right.

A ...by time I...

Q Was anything done as a result of why, so far as you were aware, Carol had come to live with you?

A In what way?

Q Well, were the police involved this time round?

A I don't know. This is the bit I don't know about the police bit.

Q Okay. Did you say anything to Jean at any time, "Well, shouldn't we be telling the police about this?"

A (No audible response)

Q No.

A No... well, I think... I think they'd already taken it into their own hands anyway.

Q What do you mean by that? I'm sorry, I don't... don't know what you mean.

A Well, I think... I think the police already were to be involved with her...

Q You told us...

A ...no matter what... no matter what I said.

Q You told us that you weren't aware of the police being involved?

A No.

Q Is that right or not?

A Yeah.

Q So it is right? You had no awareness of any involvement with the police...

A No.

Q ...on either of these occasions?

A No.

Q No, okay. I just want to make sure I understood what you were saying to us, Mr Higgins, about how it came about that Carol left again. There was an argument and I think you said

it... you thought it was perhaps because Jean thought you were getting on too well with Carol?

A Yeah. Well, Jean was a bit jealous type.

Q Right.

A You know, so that's what I thought. She thought I were getting on too well with Carol.

Q Right.

A So that's where the argument with them come up and then come to me.

Q And it was because of that argument that she either left or was...

A Yeah.

Q ...was kicked out?

A Yeah.

Q By her mother? Do you think you were getting on particularly well with Carol at that time?

A Yeah. I'm... I'm easy-going. I got... I could get on with Carol, got on with Donna.

Q Mmm.

A When I saw Paul, I got on with him.

Q Right, and do you know where Carol went after she left the house in Penistone?

A No.

Q And do you remember how long... I think you said that your marriage ended about 1990?

A Yeah.

Q Do you remember how long it was before then that Carol had left or been kicked out by Jean? Again, see if we can get some dates.

A It might have been two year.

Q Okay.

A Summat like that.

MR STOREY: All right. Thank you very much, Mr Higgins.

MR HAMPTON: I don't have any re-examination. Does your Honour have any questions?

JUDGE JAMESON: No, thank you very much indeed, no, I don't. Right, thank you very much indeed for coming and helping us with your evidence, Mr Higgins. That's it...

A You're welcome.

JUDGE JAMESON: ...finished. Thank you.

(The witness withdrew)

(2.59 p.m.)

(3.00 p.m.)

Mr PAUL APPLEYARD, Sworn

Examined by Mr HAMPTON

Q Can you tell us your name, please?
A Paul Appleyard.
Q How old are you?
A Forty-eight.
Q Date of birth?
A 22/10/1970. (Handed water) Thank you.
Q Twenty-two?
A 22/10/1970.
Q I'm going to ask you a number in a moment, Mr Appleyard, and then this gentleman to my right, for the defendant, will ask further questions.
A Okay.
Q If you need a break at all at any time, let us know.
A Okay.
Q All right? This situation's rather unique. It's not a typical conversation. So, would you mind facing towards the members of the jury, so you're face on...
A Okay.
Q ...looking towards them. I won't take offence. This is how it works. And it'll help with the judge and jury hearing what you've got to say.
A Okay.
Q All right? You're the middle child of three?
A Yes, I am.
Q Donna's your older sister?
A Yes, she ...she was.
Q She was, sorry. She was your older sister. And Carol, younger?
A Yes.

Q I want to ask you questions about a period of time you lived at 26 Gilthwaites Crescent, Mr Appleyard, if I may?

A Yeah.

Q In your own words, please, tell me how you would describe growing up at 26 Gilthwaites Crescent.

A Tough. Tough. We didn't have much as we were ...when we were kids. Grew up basically on hand-me-downs and things from jumble sales. Me dad was tough on us. Me mum was tough. If we didn't get the leather belt off me dad, we'd get the wooden spoon off me mum, just from menial things. Yeah, life was hard.

Q Who'd give you the belt?

A My dad give us a belt, leather belt.

Q How did that happen?

A Could be for anything. If we were giggling, playing as kids, being too noisy, not eating us tea, being out too late... Anything, just as normal children do. If ...if anything got on his nerves or... I remember one night we ...we was ...we were left alone and we were screaming out the back window for us mum and dad, 'cause we didn't know where they were. They'd just gone out. And when they came back, we all got the leather belt for that. Pulled us pants down, belted us until we were red raw and screaming.

Q Was this... The belt, would it be over the clothing, the underwear? Or would the underwear be pulled down?

A Oh, no. He'd pull his ...pull his belt off his pants and ...and he'd strip us ...bend us over his knee, strep ...strip us down. Usually, they'd send us to get ready for bed first, or if we was in us pyjamas, we thought it was just easier for him. But if we had clothes on, just pull us pants down over us knees and whack us with a belt until we were screaming.

Q You've just gestured being over ...a child being over his knee and the belt being brought down, with your arm.

A Yes.

Q How was the belt? How was it held?

A It was held... So, you had the buckle and the end in your hand, so the belt was doubled over.

Q Doubled over?

A Doubled over. And ...and he'd just keep whacking until he'd had enough, not until you'd had enough.

Q Who received that type of punishment?

A All three of us.

Q Was it common or uncommon?

A Very common.

Q And you mentioned a spoon.

A Yeah. If ...it'll be me dad was out, and we'd done summat. Me mum was just as bad really in the way that ...handed out punishments. She ...y'know, she used to say that she weren't but she ...she did. And if me dad wasn't there, you used to get the wooden spoon off me mum. Same thing: pants pulled down, wooden spoon across bare ...bare bottom.

Q Were there happier times?

A There were ha ...some happy times, what we thought was happy times, so... When we went on holiday we was pretty much left alone to go playing out. So we very rarely got into trouble on holiday, but then they left us alone, really. Street parties. We... The happy times were really when we was out playing with us friends or s... I mean, I was happy when I was going shooting with me dad. I were going collecting scrap. But, no, not many of them.

Q You've mentioned going shooting with your dad.

A Yes.

Q He had his own gun?

A He had several.

Q Several?

A Several guns.

Q Could you help us with a type?

A His favourite was a duck gun that he had the barrel cut down on, cut it down himself, and that was his. It was a single barrel 12-bore. And he used to be good at shooting through the trees for the wood pigeons with that gun. We had a double barrel 12-gauge side by side which, after a while, became my gun. He had a over and under.

Q I'm not sure what that means.

A Over and under - the barrels are over and under. A side by side is two barrels at the side of each other.

Q I follow that, yes.

A An over and under is where the two barrels are over ...one over the top of each other.

Q I follow. So that's three you've mentioned.

A Yes. At least three.

Q And were these all over the same time or different times?

A No, at the same time. There was also a 20-gauge in the house which was supposedly my gun. A 20-gauge shotgun. A single barrel.

Q Where were they kept?

A Behind the bar.

Q I'm sorry?

A We had a ...we had a bar in our living room, made of stone.

Q A drinks' bar?

A A drinks' bar. We had a stone fireplace and a stone bar and he used to keep the ...the guns behind the bar.

Q Putting yourself back when you were a lad, how would you describe your relationship with your dad at that time? If I asked you about him, how would you describe him?

A Growing up, he was my hero. I though... Y'know, he was ...he was an hard man. Everybody knew him around the villages. He was my hero. He took out me shooting, showed me how to catch fish with me hands. But it was still tough. It was all still tough going through childhood, y'know? I... It was funny, really, because you expected the good ...the bad to come with the good. Whenever you had a good time with your father, you knew something else was going to happen afterwards. You knew you'd get, the next day, a leather belt or something. But I used to enjoy being with me dad. I used to go working in the fields with him, working on the farms. I used to earn money from it, working for the farmers, going shooting on their land, so... I really thought he was my hero and never thought he could be anything else than that.

Q Thank you. How would you describe your parents' relationship whilst you were at 26 Gilthwaites?

A Stormy.

Q Stormy?

A Very stormy.

Q In what way?

A Oh, they were arguing all the time. I used to put me head under the pillow so I couldn't hear them shouting at each other. And if we ever tried to interfere, we got ...we got it worse back. So we...

Q You got?

A Got it worse back. Got it ...got shouted at or screamed at, or the belt, for interfering. So, we used to just go and hide in us room, get in bed and put your head under the pillow.

Q Was the ...were the arguments always verbal or was there physical incidents between your parents?

A You heard... It was really really verbal, but you heard things - squeals, screams - now and again and you didn't know what to do. You didn't know whether you could... Well, you wouldn't dare. You wouldn't dare go out. You never knew. You never saw your mum the next day with marks or anything like that, but you knew something but you didn't know what, and you didn't dare ask about it.

Q Did you ever see anything yourself?

A No.

Q You have mentioned going for walks to collect scrap metal.

A Yes.

Q Who would go on those walks?

A It used to be always with me and me dad until we was... Until I was probably 12/13, it used to be always me. I was the strongest. I was ...I was a really strong lad because I used to work on the farms. From being ...from being as ...being able to lift up a shovel, I used to mix ...mix for him on ...when he was building. I used to, y'know...

Q Mixing concrete?

A Mixing concrete, sand cement, so I was ...I was quite a strong lad, so it was always me going collecting scrap.

Q Did that change?

A And that changed.

Q When did it change?

A When he come back...

Q Doing your best.

A When he come back from America, I think. Just before that maybe, but certainly when he come back from America, as far as I remember.

Q Do you know when that was?

A I think... I was 13, I think. Either...

Q So you think around when you were 13?

A About when I was 13. Twelve/thirteen.

Q And who was going on the walks after that?

A Carol.

Q Carol?

A Carol. I think, if I remember right, he ...she ...it started... Before then, he started taking her on walks but not ...not many that I can remember.

Q "Before then", before what?

A Before America. Before he come back from America.

Q How did you feel at the time about Carol coming on the walks?

A She didn't come on the walks with me. I wasn't on the walks. She ...he ...he just ...he just stopped taking me and he started taking me sister, Carol.

Q Okay. Right, I follow. Let me put it another way. How did you feel about Carol going with him rather than you?

A Devastated.

Q Did you ask about it?

A You daren't. I dare not. I think ...I think maybe a few times I used to say, "How come I'm not going with you?" "Oh, it's ...Carol's coming with me this time." So if... I did ask. But you daren't say, "Well I want to go instead," or... I wouldn't have dared said that to him.

Q There came a time when your mum and dad split up. Do you recall how old you were then?

A See, it all seems to be to me around about the same time.

Q That's how it feels?

A Yeah. It feels to me like it was all around the same time. I remember the ...I remember the exact day when it happened. I come downstairs; I was to go to school. And there was ...me mam was sat there with a suitcase at the side of the table. The table was in front of the kitchen window and there was a suitcase there at the side of her and now... I'd heard screaming and shouting the night before, arguing, and it had gone on probably for a few days up until that point. And I knew. I just ...I just knew in me mind. I come downstairs and I seen the (inaudible). And I says, "You're going aren't you?" And she says, "Yeah. I can't take you with me." And she left me a packet of cigarettes, a packet of Benson & Hedges, and a gold ring on the table and went.

Q She said she couldn't take you with her?

A That's correct.

Q And she left a packet of cigarettes and what, sorry?

A And a gold ring.

Q What...

A I think she said it belonged to her father, but...

Q Were they for you?

A They were for me.

Q Did she take anybody with her?

A Yes, she took Carol with her and... I think that was it. I think our Donna was in care at the time.

Q Were you told why your mother had left?

A No. We wasn't told anything. I just knew ...knew it was... To be honest, it was on the cards for all the arguing what was going on. Me mum was talking to men on ...in my bedroom. She was... I used to wake up in a morning and she'd be sat at the side of me bed on the CB radio, talking to truckers, and just... Basically, I wake up with her talking to men, so... All the arguments fitted into place that it wasn't going to last. You never want that, as a child. You never expect it to happen, but, looking back, that's what I can see.

Q So did it come to be that yourself and your dad were living alone for some time?

A Yeah, we was for a ...for a few months and everything was good. Me dad'd take me to the pub, go for a game of pool, go for some lunch. I'd go working with me dad. It got to the point where he didn't even want me going in school 'cause he wanted me working with him.

Q Did you sometimes miss school?

A Yes. Regular. To work with me dad.

Q Did there come a time that somebody else was living at the house?

A Yes. He met somebody called Janet Thom.

Q Janet Thom?

A Janet Thom. I think I was 14, maybe. Maybe 15. Mm, 15 maybe when ...when he ...when he met Janet. Fourteen.

Q Did Carol or Donna come back?

A Carol came back. Carol came back after six ...maybe six or eight months.

Q Around six to eight months?

A Yeah, maybe. Maybe less.

Q When Carol came back... She's a year older than you?

A That's correct.

Q Yes. How was she towards you? What was your relationship like when she came back?

A It was great. It was great. I love me sister. But we had problems, as every brother and sister do. But the other ...other people didn't help. We had social services in ...in and out of us lives. I remember them quite saying ...saying to her if she leaves again, they'll split us up, they'll put us both in care. Our Donna had been in and out of care. Our Carol went off with me mum, then she come back. And I don't know why the social services said that, but they did: if ...if anything happened again, then they'd ...they'd split us up and put us both in care, and it's something that you don't want with your sister.

Q Did Carol have any kind of role in the house, in your eyes?

A At the t ...at the... When she first come back, no, I didn't see it, and then she sort of like grew into a role of being like a ...a mother figure, sort of bossing me around. I couldn't get in the house when I wanted to do. I couldn't get everything I wanted to do. But she was still me sister, and I just ...just accepted her, just accepted that she was the older sister, if you like, and that she's gonna tell me to do things. And then I just started going ...playing out more with me friends.

Q I want to ask you about this period of time now, when there's yourself and Carol and your father in the house...

A Okay.

Q ...and what you saw as the interactions between your dad and your sister, Carol.

A Okay.

Q Are there any particular incidents that you remember that now stick out in your mind?

A Oh, yes. Lots of them. I remember hearing bedroom doors on a night-time, the creaking of the hallway as me sister was taken along to his bedroom. I used to go to football training, or if I went out playing sometimes, I couldn't back in the house.

Q Just pause there a minute. So you went to football training.

A Yeah. I used to play Sunday league football. I was quite good at football when I was a kid.

Q So is there anything in particular about the football that you recall?

A Yeah. I come back from training one time... Oh, we went to a football match, it was one Sunday morning. I went to play football and the match had been called off. I found out before we even got there, to the football match, and so I headed back home to go and get changed and go out and play, and I couldn't get in the house.

Q You couldn't get in the house?

A I couldn't get in the house.

Q So you couldn't get in. What did you do?

A Well, I was knocking at the door, banging at the door, wondering why I couldn't get in. I knew that they were in. I'd just not long since left there. So...

Q So who was in the house when you left?

A Me dad and me sister.

Q Carol?

A Carol.

Q How long had you been gone?

A Twenty minutes/half an hour. I'd only walked up the village and it ...it'd been cancelled. So, yeah, 20 minutes/half an hour.

Q What happened next, Mr Appleyard, please?

A Me sister opened the bedroom window in ...with little or nothing on.

Q What was she wearing?

A Knickers and bra, as far I could see. There was nothing... I could see her from the waist up and it was just a bra, so I presumed knickers and bra.

Q What bedroom was that?

A The front top bedroom. Me dad's bedroom.

Q Did anybody say anything?

A No.

Q You or Carol?

A No.

Q Were you let in?

A Not at that time, no.

Q How...

A I disa ...I went ...I went... I don't know. I can't remember too much. I know I wasn't let in and I ...I think I went out ...to play out with me friends, me up with me friends or ...for another hour or so. I know I wasn't let in at the time. I woulda probably just seen that, probably dumped me bag down at the house and ...and run off with me friends.

Q Is there any other incident that you recall that sticks out?

A Well that happened on a few occasions. On a few occasions, I come home, and I couldn't get in the house and I knew that they were in the house. I never really said anything about it to them. But I remember, on a fair few occasions, that I could not get in the house. And I just... I don't know why I didn't have me own key. They wouldn't give me my key. Our Carol had one. I didn't have me own key, so when they wasn't... They know they just... I mean, the door was locked. You could see the key on the inside of the door, through the door lock, but I couldn't ...I weren't allowed in, so I just used to turn round and go out again.

Q Was there anything that you saw directly that occurred in the house?

A Oh, seen me dad touching me sister many times. I seen her walk downstairs one time, one morning - I think it was a weekend 'cause we weren't at school - and he was there, and he had me sister, grabbed her, and he was kissing her full tongues, holding her, kissing her full tongues.

Q So you're gesturing. You've got your arms held out in...

A He ...he had her...

Q ...in an embrace?

A He had her in an embrace, kissing her, full tongues, head to the side, which was... I've seen him touching her as she goes past him and in the kitchen.

Q Was it a... As you saw it there, was it a fatherly kiss?

A No.

Q Did you ask your dad about it?

A No.

Q Did he say anything about it?

A He said that's just... Well, he turned round and let go sharpish and said, "Ooh, just giving ...giving me daughter a good morning kiss." At the time, I remember feeling it's not right, but... I just didn't want to believe it. You just don't want to believe something like that about your father. And I sort of like, if any ...if anything, I dismissed it.

Q How old were you?

A About 13. Twelve/thirteen. Thirteen.

Q Did you ever share a bed with your father?

A Yes, when me mum and dad split up. And when me ...when I was there on me own with me father, before our Carol come back, I would often go sleep with me dad in his bed, because I hated it. I hated me mum and dad splitting up. It hurt. And I was close to me dad, so I'd go and get in his bed and... It was a comfort to know that your dad was there and you had somebody, 'cause me mum had left me. So, yeah, I used to go get in me dad's bed. And then when Carol come back, it started off she would also get in bed with us, and then it'd end up me, sort of like, not getting in the bed with them. I remember one time I was in bed and our Carol was in bed with me, and I used to sleep at one side of me dad and our Carol would sleep at the other side, with me dad in the middle.

Q So you're telling us about an occasion where all three of you were in the same bed?

A Yes.

Q You on one side of your dad and your sister on the other?

A Yes.

Q Thank you. Which bed?

A Me dad's bed. And the next morning I remember him asking me, he said, "I'm sorry if I touched you last night." He said, "I didn't mean to. I leant over and touched you. Did you feel anything?" And ...and I said, "No." Looking back now, I know what he was meant to be doing, or in his mind he was meant to be doing.

MR HAMPTON: I'm just moving to the statement at p.I65, your Honour. (To the witness) Have you ever had tattoos?

A Yes.

Q When was your first tattoo?

A About the same time, when I was 13/14. Thirteen. No, I was... Yeah, definitely 13. And we went to... Well, to start off with, I heard that me sister was getting a tattoo. Our Carol said she's getting a tattoo. I said...

Q Carol said that?

A Carol said that she's getting a tattoo. I said, "What? You're getting a tattoo?" And me dad said, "I'm taking her to Barnsley, getting her a tattoo." And I sort of like: "Well, I want one. If she's having one, I want one. Can't have a tattoo without me. She's underage and I'm underage." "So what?" So he took us to Barnsley. And I remember where it was, it was right next to the train station in Barnsley, a building that said "Tattooing" on a white building. And he took us upstairs. You had to go up some stairs to it.

Q Did you go together?

A Yes, all three of us.

Q The three of you?

A All three of us.

Q Yes. Sorry, I interrupted.

A And we goes into the tattoo and look and things and ...and she said, "I'm having that." And she ...and me dad says, "Right, okay." So I said, "What you having, sis?" "Well, she's having this rose with 'Sam' underneath it." "Well I want the same." Being a kid, 13, I want the same. So I got the same. I said, "What's ...what ... what's 'Sam'?" "Well that's my nickname when I was a child," he said.

Q Who said that?

A My father. Elliott.

Q So what did your tattoo show, Mr Appleyard?

A It was on my right arm. It was a rose with "Sam" underneath it. Exactly the same as Carol's but Carol's was on her shoulder.

Q Was there another name on yours or was it just the... Did you say a rose?

A It was rose.

Q With "Sam" in it?

A A red rose with "Sam". Three letters, S-A-M, underneath it.

Q And whose name was that, as far as you were concerned?

A Me dad's nickname. He explained to me that he grew up in Skelmanthorpe and that's what his nickname was growing up through Skelmanthorpe as a kid. He ...he was... They were a bit feral, really. There were 15 of them.

Q So that was his nickname?

A And his nickname was Sam.

Q Do you still have the tattoo?

A No.

Q Why not?

A I al... As soon as I could afford to get it covered up... I joined the Army when I was 19. As soon I was old enough and joined the Army, I got it covered up.

Q When was the last time you had contact with your dad?

A I've not looked him in the eye since I was 18, I don't think.

Q Thank you. Would you wait there, there'll be some more questions, I think.

A Okay.

JUDGE JAMESON: Yes?

Cross-examined by Mr STOREY

Q Some happy memories and some not, you say, Mr Appleyard...

A Correct.

Q ...from when you were a child. You were close to your dad?

A Yes, I was.

Q You liked being taken by him to go and shoot pigeons and rabbits and the like?

A Correct.

Q And I think, when you were a bit older, he'd taught you to ride a motorbike and things of that sort as well?

A Yes, he did.

Q He wasn't always able to take you out with him, was he, because he worked?

A Not very much.

Q He was a self-employed building contractor?

A No he wasn't. He was on the social, working on the side, and he only had days here and there.

Q And how much of that do you think is you looking back with hindsight now, 35/40 years later?

A Oh no, I ...I remember. Most of the time, he was at ...he was ...a lot of the time, he was at home. He very rarely had a ...very rare had a full-time job. I can't remember... I can remember him having one full-time job and he used to go ...and he used to call us on a CB when he'd be coming back from work. That's the only full-time job I remember him having.

Q You'd presumably have been going to school...

A Yes.

Q ...at the time?

A Yes.

Q And so you'd have been out of the house for a large chunk of Monday to Friday?

A From maybe nine... School was only up the road. From maybe eight till...

Q Yes.

A ...three. Half-past three/four o'clock.

Q And so you obviously can't say what your dad was doing when you were at school?

A Well I know what me dad was doing because he'd be out the field. He'd be either at the field, tending ...tending the crops what we had. We grew us own stuff. Most of the time he'd be at the field, 'cause he weren't working.

Q Well I suggest, in fact, he did work, self-employed.

A Well that's fine, if you want to suggest that.

Q I think you said you were about 13, is it, when your mother left?
A Yes, about that.
Q Yes. And you had been aware that that was likely because of the arguing that you had heard before, building up to it?
A Yes.
Q You never saw any violence between them?
A I never saw any violence between them, no.
Q I've got to suggest to you, Mr Appleyard, that your recollection of being on the receiving end of violence from both your parents isn't an accurate recollection?
A You're suggesting that?
Q I'm suggesting that.
A You're wrong.
Q Okay. We know that there were guns in the house. You've told us they were kept behind the bar?
A Yes, there was.
Q Was that pretty open and obvious to anyone in the family that that was where they were kept?
A Everybody knew where they... Everybody knew in the house where the guns were.
Q Were they in a cabinet or...
A No. They was just...
Q ...case, or anything?
A No, they was just thrown in a corner, behind the bar.
Q And you said there came a time when your mother left with the girls, I think you said?
A No, I said with one girl, as far as I can remember. Me other sister, I think she was in care at the time.
Q You're quite right, you did say that. That's my error. The ring that she left you, that she told you was her father's, what happened to that?

A Oh... I wore it. I wore it for years and it just went thin and snapped. I might still have it somewhere actually, but it went too thin and snapped, so... Yeah.

Q Once your mum had left, how much contact did you have with her in the following months or years?

A Oh ...oh, we used to ...used to go and try and see her every week. We used to get the bus from up ...up Denby Dale, where the Salvation Army used to be. There was a bus there that went to Penistone. It was the only bus that went through our village that went to Penistone. And we used to get on that and go see me mum once a week. I mean, to start off with, for the first six months, I hardly saw me mum. I don't think I seen her when she left.

Q Right.

A It was only when our Carol come back. (Inaudible). I used to go see her with me sister, so it must have been when Carol come back that we used to go see me mum in...

Q So... I'm sorry to interrupt you. You used to go and see her with your sister. Is this Carol we're talking about?

A Yes.

Q Yes. And where do you remember going to see your mum?

A I remember me mum staying in Millhouse Green in Penistone. She was there for a little while. And then she moved to Thurgoland, if I remember right. And then, from there, she moved back into Penistone.

Q And when you went to see her, would you see her at the places she was staying or living?

A Yes.

Q Did you used to go and meet her at the Barnsley market on Saturdays? Was that something you can remember?

A No.

Q You went with at least one if not both of your sisters on a regular basis?

A I can't remember that.

Q No.

A I'm not saying it didn't happen, I'm just saying I can't remember it.

Q All right. And I think you said it was about six months after that that Carol returned, six to eight months later?
A Like I say, it's me memory back then. Yeah, as far as I can remember, but it might not be totally correct, the timelines.
Q And by then, you said that your father had met someone. Janet Tongue, was it? I didn't quite catch...
A No, not by then.
Q All right. Okay.
A Not by then.
Q What was...
A No, he didn't ...he didn't meet Janet for a while ...for a while after that.
Q Right.
A I think I was 15 when he met Janet.
Q All right.
A Or close to 15 when he met Janet. I know I was ...I was... Yeah. Definitely. Definitely 15.
Q All right. You said that Carol came back and grew into the role of being a mother figure?
A Yes.
Q Bossing you about...
A Yes.
Q ...and the like. Do you think at that time you and she were close?
A Yes.
Q Did you talk to each other about what you were up to, either at school or not at school?
A No.
Q The "mother" role that she took on for herself, was it just a case of her doing the jobs that your mother had used to do when she was around the house?
A No.
Q Right.

A No, it wasn't cleaning-up work. She never ...very rarely... We ...I mean, we both had to keep the house clean, but it was ...wasn't cleaning-up and cooking that she did.

Q Right. What was it then?

A It was just bossing me around.

Q Bossing you around. Right.

A Bossing me around. But not: "You can't come in," y'know, "you've gotta do this, you've gotta do that." She just ...just got really bossy.

Q Right. You mentioned earlier on that your dad had gone to America.

A Yes.

Q Do you have any recollection of when that trip took place?

A No.

Q No.

A I remember him going but I can't tell you exactly when it was, what month it was ...what ...what ...when it was, no.

Q Right. Do you remember that you and your sister were meant to stay with your Auntie Hilda?

A That's correct.

Q And do you remember that you and she perhaps decided to have a party or parties in the house whilst he was away?

A That's correct.

Q And did you get yourselves a set of keys cut so that you could go back into the house and let yourselves in when he was out...

A Yes.

Q ...or away?

A Well I didn't, our Carol did.

Q Right. And was the house left in a bit of a state after the party?

A Yes, it was. But then, when you move to an house and you find a full, empty house - there was nothing in there - you'd think, well, we can leave this house a mess. Because me mam had already been in and taken everything from the house.

Q She took everything?

A Well, lots and lots of stuff. So there was hardly anything there.

Q What do you mean by everything, or...

A Well, she...

Q ...lots of stuff?

A Big cabinets. She had... There were a massive cabinet. She come in, she took absolutely loads of stuff - cabinets, tables, chairs, whatever - and it was all put next door, which we didn't know at the time she was hiding it next door.

Q Next door at the neighbour's house, you mean?

A Because ...because she took the chance while me dad had gone away to come and get some stuff that she was owed.

Q Right. What, just emptied the house of furniture and left it next door for...?

A To go and collect it...

Q Right.

A ...another time. We only found out that it'd been next door afterwards ...sometime afterwards. So, when you go into an house what's been robbed, they're probably just kids...

Q Right.

A ...partying. They di... I mean, they went too far, without a doubt. We all did.

MR STOREY: Your Honour, I'm conscious of the time and I'm conscious of your Honour's need to rise a little earlier than (sic) today.

JUDGE JAMESON: Yes. Unfortunately...

MR STOREY: I can't...

JUDGE JAMESON: ...we're going to have to, yes.

MR STOREY: I can't guarantee I'll finish my cross-examination in the next five minutes, I'm afraid.

JUDGE JAMESON: No.

MR STOREY: Maybe 15, but I appreciate that might cause difficulties.

JUDGE JAMESON: Yes, well... Let's just see. Mr Appleyard, would it be very inconvenient for you to come back tomorrow morning?

THE WITNESS: Tomorrow? I thought tomorrow morning wasn't on. I thought Thursday wasn't on, it was Friday, for some reason.

JUDGE JAMESON: Oh, I'm so sorry. Yes, you're quite right. Not tomorrow morning. Yes, Thursday.

MR STOREY: Friday.

THE WITNESS: Friday.

MR HAMPTON: Friday.

JUDGE JAMESON: Friday even.

THE WITNESS: Friday, your Honour.

JUDGE JAMESON: Yes, thank you.

THE WITNESS: Yes, I can be here Friday, your Honour.

JUDGE JAMESON: Somebody's on top of it.

THE WITNESS: Yes.

JUDGE JAMESON: Yes, you can. That's all right, is it?

THE WITNESS: Yes. No problem.

JUDGE JAMESON: All right. Well, thank you very much indeed.

THE WITNESS: Okay.

JUDGE JAMESON: Yes. All right. Well, in that case, we'll call it a day for the moment then. Now, I really don't know what your domestic circumstances are, and I don't want to know, but can I just ask you not to speak about the evidence that you're giving with anybody until you're back on Friday.

THE WITNESS: No problem, your Honour.

JUDGE JAMESON: All right. Thank you very much indeed.

THE WITNESS: Okay.

JUDGE JAMESON: Right. Okay. Don't ...please don't stay in the witness box unless you wish to.

THE WITNESS: No. Okay. Thank you.

JUDGE JAMESON: You can step down now. Thank you.

(The learned Judge addressed the jury)

(The jury left court at 3.43 p.m.)

(Adjourned until Friday, 18 January 2019)

(3.44 p.m.)

Diary: Wednesday 16th January 2019

After hearing mum's evidence I was really worried that she had jeopardised the trial. She had lied several times. Five things really stuck out in my mind, firstly she denied that my dad had ever beat us with his two thick black leather belts; she said she had only hit us once with a wooden spoon; she also claimed that my dad had always worked, when actually he hadn't and fourthly she gave the impression that I was continually moving back and forth between living with her and living with my dad. Fifth was she told the court that I had left a note for her on a mirror saying I had gone back to my dad's, when in fact she was there in the bedroom with me when I told her I was leaving. She was holding a bottle of tablets and shaking it, threatening to take an overdose if I left. For me this was the point that she knew what my dad had in store for me and could have prevented it all if only she had told me.

Before the trial my sister's daughter, Millie, had come to stay with me for the weekend. I asked her if she would be coming to court and she replied that she would not. I was disappointed and asked her why. She said that her Nana had told her that I had "asked for it" by keep going back to my dad's house and it was my fault he'd raped me. She also told me that my mum had said I was going to get annihilated in court and she did not want Millie to see that happen. I felt like I had to defend myself with Millie and she became angry with me. We both ended up crying.

I noticed that when my mum took the stand she was nervous, her hands were shaking like a leaf as she lifted her glass of water to take a drink. I had not seen her for months before the trail and she had given me no support whatsoever. Our relationship had always been difficult, one minute we were talking, the next we were not. Unless I was agreeing with her and doing as I was told, she always fell out with me. My mum did not have any support from her husband or anyone else in court. I believe that she did not want him to know the truth about how bad our childhood had been, just like my dad did not want his wife to know.

As my mum left the stand she blew me a kiss and mouthed "I love you," as she passed the public gallery where I was seated. I was dumbfounded, and thought that she sure did not act like she loved me after the lies she had just told. This was the last time I saw my mum, she did not join me or my children and went straight home. The feelings of confusion about what real love is flooded back. I remembered another time when she had tried to poison my own daughter's mind against me. She had told her that I was a liar and always made out that my life had been really bad when it hadn't been. This left me feeling that I had to defend myself with my daughter once again.

Whilst I thought my mum may have put the trial in jeopardy my brother Paul gave a really good recollection of what life was like for us children, the violence, the living in fear. I wondered who the jury would believe.

Friday, 18th January, 2019

(Transcript prepared without the aid of documentation)

(10.42 a.m.)

JUDGE JAMESON: Right. Now, Mr Appleyard, obviously the oath that you took still binds you...

THE WITNESS: Yes, your Honour.

JUDGE JAMESON: ...on your evidence now. Thank you. Yes?

Mr PAUL APPLEYARD continued

Cross-examined by Mr STOREY

Q Thank you, Mr Appleyard. I'm sorry we weren't able to finish my questioning of you the day before yesterday.

A Okay.

Q I don't think I'll have very much more for you, in fact. Can I just ask you this: we know that in 2000 ...sorry, 1984, your father was granted custody of you and your sister, Carol, by a court. Do you remember being present at a court hearing when that custody was granted?

A No, I don't.

Q Are you even aware of that happening? Or do you remember it happening now?

A No, I don't.

Q Was there not a hearing at the magistrates' court in Huddersfield at which you and Carol and your father, and possibly your mother as well, attended?

A I cannot remember that. I have no recollection of that.

Q Okay. Do you remember speaking to a judge in his room with your sister about what you and she wanted to do and where you wanted to live?

A I have no recollection of that.

Q Okay.

A I'm not saying it didn't happen.

Q Okay.
A But I can’t remember it.
Q No. I understand. That’s quite clear. You told us on Wednesday that there were, I think you said, lots of incidents that stuck out in your mind from your childhood, your teens.
A Yes.
Q And you referred to a particular occasion when you came back from football training and you found...
A No, I went to a ...I were going to a football game.
Q Sorry.
A I was going to play football on a Sunday morning.
Q All right. And the match was called off?
A And the match was called off.
Q So you went back home?
A So I went back home.
Q And you told us that, having knocked on the front door, you then saw your sister at the bedroom window?
A That’s correct.
Q Now, can I just ask you about the layout of the house, to begin with, and what sort of building we’re talking about. Was it a semi-detached?
A It was a semi-detached, yes.
Q A council house?
A Council house.
Q Small garden at the front?
A Yes.
Q A front door that gave onto a path, leading...
A No.
Q ...through the front garden?
A No. There was a front door there, but we never used that door. We used the...
Q No.

A ...the side door, so you walked through the porch. And we always used the side door.

Q Right. And the side door went into the kitchen. Is that right?

A Went into the kitchen, yes.

Q And so when you said you went to the door and found it locked, do we take it you're referring to that side door, or back door as...?

A Well the doors were locked.

Q Did you try both doors?

A Yes.

Q Okay. And how was it that you came to see your sister in the front - I think front upstairs window?

A Because the window opened, and she told me... I wish I could remember what she told me. It was something like, "Go away." I can't remember what was said. I remember her opening the window. I have... I can't remember what was said but it was ...it was something along the lines: "Go away." And I just went away. I never thought nothing about it. I wouldn't think nothing about it because me sister was bossy at the time. If she told me to do something, I just did it.

Q Are you sure she said nothing to you at all?

A No, I didn't say she said nothing at all. I said, like, she said something, but I can't remember what she did say.

Q My question was: are you sure she said anything at all?

A Yes.

Q Because my note of what you told us on Wednesday was that no one said anything at that time.

A No, I didn't say that.

Q Okay.

A She ...I said she was at the ...she was at the window. But this happened on a few occasions. This wasn't just the once. This was a few occasions. So it coulda been any one of the few occasions that I did see them. Knocked at the door, knocked at the window, and I couldn't get in. And I (inaudible).

There's was only one time when she opened the window and said something. I wish I could remember what she said. But on several occasions, I went back and I couldn't get in, and I saw movement in the bedroom, me sister there, or me dad there, through the window. It was ...it was quite a low window in the bedroom of his house, maybe waist height, so you could see that there was people in the bedroom. But it was only on one occasion that I recall her saying something, but I can't remember what it was. She opened the window. Maybe "Get lost." I don't know.

Q Do you remember on that one occasion when she, you say, opened the window, where you were when she said whatever to you? Whereabouts...

A I were in the front garden.

Q ...you were standing? You were in the front garden?

A (Inaudible) I would've been in the front garden or just at the end of the front garden.

Q Because to see someone through an upstairs window, you presumably have to be some way back from the house just to get a line of sight?

A No. I mean, you said before that the front garden was small. Relatively, yes. I would say that the front garden was from here to that wall, so you could... The ...the bedroom height would normally be at this ceiling height, so you could see somebody there no problem. You could see them from there upwards.

Q You, I think, said nothing at all about this at the time?

A No.

Q And you say it happened on several occasions, essentially?

A Several occasions.

Q I don't know if we've got copies of your witness statements that... Two sets it seems. I wonder if you could just be provided with the witness statements that you made to the police, to have a look at, please, Mr Appleyard? (Same handed)

A I've read through these.

Q I was going to say, I assume you read those...

A I have.

Q ...on Wednesday?

A Yes.

Q And just so that people are aware, there are two statements. One of them's dated 26 November 2015. Is that right?

A (After a pause) That's correct.

Q And the other's dated 5 October 2018?

A That's correct.

Q The longer of the two statements is the one that will perhaps be of most assistance to you in answering this (sic) next few questions. But it's right, isn't it - and by all means have a look in your statement to check this Mr Appleyard - that you made no mention in either of them, in fact, of there being multiple occasions when you couldn't get into the house but being aware of your sister and/or father in the front upstairs bedroom?

A Oh, you really want me to answer that? Yes. Even over the last few days things have been coming to me. Now, as a child it was hard, and you block a lot of things out, and I have blocked a lot of things out - a lot of things that me mother did, a lot of things that me father did. The pain growing up, you... I went and joined the Army so I could get away from all this, change my life around. So I ...I do... And I keep... The more I talk about it, the more comes back. There is more that's come back in these last few days, but I can't tell my barrister about it because I'm a witness. But there is more things that have come to li ...come into my memory in these last few days. And as this case has been going on, there's been more and more things that come to light. I've been sat up till one o'clock, two o'clock in the morning remembering things, and writing them down and jotting them down. So I don't remember everything. And in this ...this is only a patch of what I really need to say.

Q It's right, isn't it, that you knew full well why the police were taking a statement from you in 2015?

A That's correct.

Q	And again in 2018?

A	But the police... At the time, when they was conducting these interviews, they weren't very thorough. They didn't ask me enough questions wh... The more questions I'm getting asked, the more that's coming to light. The more I'm remembering, the more things are coming to light. So, no, they didn't ...the police didn't ask me enough questions at the time, and I didn't have chance to get through everything.

Q	Presumably, the police asked you questions like: "Tell us everything you can remember about your dad and your sister"?

A	And, like I've just said, there's stuff that I could remember at the time.

Q	And as you went through things and told them things, did that not jog your memory...

A	No.

Q	...about other things?

A	Not at the time, no.

Q	It's right, isn't it, that you and your sister are in fairly close contact these days?

A	Oh, yeah. We're in close contact because we have nobody else. My mother gave up on me. She gave up on five ...five of her children. That was my... Me, I was the one ...last in a long line of five children that she gave up. She gave up Stephen, she gave up Gary, she gave up Donna, she gave up our Carol to a monster - she let him (sic) be there with a monster, she gave up me for the packet of fags and a ring. Yes. So me and me sister... Me other sister's dead, God rest her soul, so me and me sister are all we've got.

Q	And you have obviously been well aware of your sister's allegations about your father for some time, haven't you, Mr Appleyard?

A	Yes, I have.

Q	And is it perhaps the case that you and she have discussed those allegations on occasions?

A	Of course we've discussed them. Of course. Of course we've discussed them. We've discussed them when I... The first time it ever came to light with me was when I was 13 and I didn't accept it. I didn't really believe it, but I... I remember dragging my sister round to a phone box, having ...after she slit her wrist. I could hear ...I could hear a noise, like a ...downstairs on a night-time. I was upstairs and it was like an angry ...angry crying of somebody that couldn't do something but wanted to do something. I walked downstairs and seen my sister with a knife, slitting her wrist ...trying to slit her wrist. I had to tie a bootlace round her wrist and drag her round to the phone. And when she was doing that, she says, "I can't do this anymore." "What, Carol? What, Carol?" "You won't understand. You won't understand." She even tried protecting me from it then.

Q So you obviously assume, Mr Appleyard, that that was an act that she committed on herself because of what was going on between her and your father?

A At the time I didn't. At the time I didn't.

Q But you do now?

A I do now. Now I know why ...what mess ...what it's done to my sister. How it's impacted on all of us.

Q Is it, do you think, possible that hindsight has affected your recollection of events back in the eighties?

A What's affected my recollection of things back in the eighties is I blocked them out. I blocked them out. I didn't... I've kept out of most of it. I've always been the one in the middle. I want ...I loved me mum even when they split up. I loved me mum, but I loved me dad just as much. I was always the child that was in the middle. I never got pulled from pillar to post, I just got left. I got left to do whatever I got left to do. Nobody seemed to be bothered about me.

Q It's right, isn't it, that in your witness statement from 2015 - and if it helps you, I'm looking at the third page - that you told the police - and this is three lines down from the top of the third page - "Throughout that whole time I never for one minute thought that anything was going on between Carol and

Dad. It's only now that I look back and actually believe what Carol has said happened." That's what you told the police in 2015, isn't it?

A Correct, because back in 20... In 2015... And when I was 13, you would never think that your dad could do something like that. Why would you think your dad could do something like that? You love your dad. You would never... I would never think that my dad was a paedophile. Never in a million years. And if somebody had o' said that to me, I'd o' gone mad. I'd o' gone mad. I believed me dad. I loved him. He was my hero. Why would I believe it? But then... When I realised it happened is when... He chased me down the field with a pitchfork one time. He wanted to kill me. He chased me down the pitch ...at the field with a pitchfork. Now, I'd already seen our Carol, I'd seen this, that and the other, but I sort o' like kept out of it. And I went to see me sister and she was a mess. She was a mess. She'd not long ...she'd not long put her hand through a glass window at Stanhope Street and tried slitting her wrists again. And we sat down and we had a right good chat, and I realised what a monster we'd been living with. And ...and it was only then that everything just fitted into place. Everything that I'd seen. Even though, in my mind, I didn't think I'd seen much, over the years, more and more's come back to me. But, no, at the time, that's correct.

Q And it's only because of talking to your sister and you believing what she's said to you that these events have acquired significance. Isn't that the reality?

A No. No. No. (Inaudible). There was always something, but you just never want to believe it. There was always something. The signs were always there. It was just me that was ignorant to it because of the love for me father.

Q You told us about an occasion when you say you saw your father snogging your sister.

A That's correct.

Q Was that something that upset you or shocked you...

A Yes.

Q ...at the time?

A Yes.

Q Did you say anything about it at the time?
A No, I was too embarrassed. I was too embarrassed. If I'd o' said something me dad mighta smacked me.
Q Did he say anything at the time?
A Yes, he did, and I think I've already said that. He said that, "I'm just giving your ...giving your daughter a good mor ...me daughter a good morning kiss." Or, "… your sister a good morning kiss." And it wasn't a good morning kiss. He never give us a kiss good morning.
Q Did you discuss it at all with your sister at the time?
A No. My sister was bossy.
Q The reality is, Mr Appleyard, I've got to suggest, that that is an event that simply never happened.
A You can suggest what you want but it did happen. I saw it with me own eyes.
Q And it's something that you've perhaps remembered because of conversations you've had with your sister in more recent years.
A No. It's something... I ...I remember there was a silver box at the side of his bed. It had photos of me sister in it.
Q And have you seen the...
A I saw the photos.
Q ...contents of the box?
A I saw the photos. I seen everything that was in that silver box. I know what went on and I seen it. It's just, at the time, I was just too young and too blind with love for me father to see it. I saw inside that box. I can tell you exactly what was inside that silver box at the side of his bed. I could tell you there was porn magazines at the other side of his bed. I could tell you everything about that.
Q Well, again, I've got to suggest no porn magazines by the side of his bed at all, no photographs of your sister in a tin box by his bed.
A You can suggest what you want. You're wrong.
Q Are these things that your sister has put has in your mind by telling you things more recently?

A You can still suggest as much as you want. You are wrong.

Q You told us about the tattoo, or tattoos more accurately.

A (Inaudible)

Q One each for you and Carol.

A That's correct.

Q It's clear, I think from what you said to us on Wednesday, that Carol wanted a tattoo?

A No. Me dad suggested (inaudible). It must have been a conversation that's gone on between Carol and me dad on their own, and I didn't know nothing about it until I got up one day, or one day she said she was having a tattoo, me dad was taking her for a tattoo. Right? So, I jumped on the bandwagon, "Well, if she's having one, I want one."

Q And so help us, please, with what part of that conversation makes you say that it must have been at your dad's suggestion or behest?

A If I look back on it now, there's no way that a 13-year-old girl would want a tattoo, or a 13-year-old boy would want a tattoo like that. Never in a million years. And why ...why ...why was she ...why would me dad go with her? "Okay, then, I'll come with you to the tattoo artist, and get 'Sam' put on your back." Why? I mean, at the time, to me, it's "I wanted a tattoo", but it just doesn't make any sense whatsoever.

Q You wanted a tattoo as well, didn't you?

A Yes, I did.

Q And that's why you went along.

A That's correct.

Q And did your dad also get a tattoo with your and Carol's names?

A I think he did (inaudible). This is a good ...good thing because now you are bringing back memories. I think he got a swallow done at the time, if I recollect. I might be wrong. I might be wrong. But something in me mind tells me that I think he got a swallow done at the time. Maybe he had us names put on that. But I can't swear on oath that that is true.

Q You told us on Wednesday that you had had nothing to do with your father for, I think, pretty much the entire time since you turned 18 and left to join the Army?

A That's correct. No, I le ...I joined the Army in (sic) 19 but I left home.

Q Sorry. But I think it's right, isn't it, that amongst other things you did contact your father to send him details of your passing out? A copy of your parade ...passing out parade leaflet...

A No.

Q ...telling him that you'd won an award for best shot.

A I have no recollection of that. I think maybe my mother did that. I didn't.

Q And did you make attempts more recently, in about 2014, to contact him through your, I suppose stepbrother, Simon?

A I wanted to speak to Simon.

Q Did you not contact Simon to ask for your father's details?

A I asked him something about me father. Why ...why would I want his details when I know where he lives? But I asked him something about it. I can't remember when I asked him about it ...asked them about it. I was reaching out to (inaudible) to be honest. I grew up... When I was there, Simon, he arrived ...he arrived ...he was probably about eight or nine, maybe a little ...maybe ...maybe six or seven. He was only young, Simon, when he ...he come to our house with Janet Thom. And when I left, I felt for him. I know that he had to do all the carrying, all the hard work that I used to have to do. I had to do everything. All the scrap metal carrying and that, everything. And my dad treated me like dirt, when I look back. So I know that he would've had to o' gone through the same. So I'd love to talk to him. I still love to talk to him now.

Q It's right, isn't it, that your sister has waged something of a Facebook campaign in relation to her allegations against your father?

A That's correct.

Q And you've been perfectly aware of that, haven't you?

A That's correct.

Q And, on occasions, you have posted comments on Facebook in support of her?

A Correct.

Q And you are, I think it's probably fair to say, one hundred per cent behind your sister, aren't you?

A Without a doubt. The truth has to come out. It has to come out. It has to be told. This story cannot stay hidden. We've got to help others. We can't just... I'm not here to just help me sister, I'm here to help others that haven't got a voice. Everybody needs to know what's happened here. And the Facebook ...the Facebook, if you're going on about the Facebook, the reason why she's done this (inaudible) for writing her book and done all this "Conquering the Impossible", is because she wants to help people. She needs ...she needs the truth to come out. The truth has to come out. The police did nothing for 35 years. We have tried five times. Five times we've tried to get him to face justice and the police have done nothing apart from hide ...hide him because he has got something on the police. He has got something... Whatever. They ...he run me off the road one time. Run me off the road in a car. The police took him for a drive round and got him sober at an all-night café until he'd ...and then breathalysed him. But he's... If the police aren't gonna do anything... How ...how are you supposed to do something? How are you supposed to get heard? That is one good thing about social media. That is one good thing. Because the truth will come out.

Q And, finally, I suggest one last time, Mr Appleyard, that what you've told us about has come directly from your sister and not from events that you actually witnessed.

A You can suggest what you want. You're wrong.

Q Thank you very much. Nothing else from me.

JUDGE JAMESON: (After a pause) Yes, Mr Hampton?

MR HAMPTON: Sorry, your Honour, I was just checking my note.

Re-examined by Mr HAMPTON

Q You've been asked about remembering more than is in your statement, Mr Appleyard. Just remind me again of your age, please?

A Forty-eight.

Q And how long were you in the Army?

A Six years.

Q Do you find it easy to talk about your childhood?

A No.

Q Why not?

A Who... I'm embarrassed about it. I am seriously embarrassed about my parents. How can ...how can I be proud of them? I can't take my children to see their grandfather ...their grandfather after what he's done. I can't take them to see (inaudible). Me mother gave up... How... What kind of a mother gives up five children? Five children! Unbelievable! What kind of a father does that to his daughter, treats his children like he has? I'm embarrassed about me father and me mother.

Q You spoke about blocking things out.

A Yes.

Q Could you tell us about that?

A I ...I ...I d... How to explain it, I don't know. Do ...do ...do you block things out on purpose? I don't think so. I think that it just ...just happens that you ...you don't want to see the truth. You do see it. You see things and it's not right to you, but I ...I'd loved me dad. I was going out shooting with him. I learnt so much off him. But there is some things you cannot do. You cross that line ...you cross that line and that's it. I mean, he crossed the line many times with his punishment on me and ...when I look back, but not ...not like he was. You block things out because it was ...it's too painful of a memory, I think. You don't want to see it. I hadn't... Some of ...some of this stuff I haven't even spoke to me sister about.

Q Have you slept much the last two nights?

A Not much. I've slept... I ...I did all right. I think I got to six hours last night, six hours the night before.

Q You spoke about seeing your sister at Stanhope Street.

A Yes.

Q Where was that address?

A That's in Barnsley. Just down from the hospital, down from Barnsley Hospital. Six ...No. 6, I think it was, 6 Stanhope Street.

Q Who did she live with there? If anybody.

A She lived there with Sam. Now, Sam was ...Sam Marsh was our Carol's husband. But she wasn't ...she wasn't married at the time.

Q Ah.

A She was ...they were partners at the time. Future husband at the time.

Q You spoke about an incident with a pitchfork. How did that come to pass?

A I used to work at BGM Plastics in Shepley, near Huddersfield, and it was continental shifts and I was working a night shift. And me dad, like I said, he never really had a proper full-time job. He used to work doing bits for farmers, for builders, bits on the side. And he was ...he was doing something for a farmer. I can't remember which farmer it was. He used to work for many farmers. I don't think it was Derek Pickford. And he had a field to pick potatoes, so it must be going ...it must be September/October-time, or late October, and the potatoes were ready for picking and ...and he asked me to help. I told him I was working. I was only 17 and I was ...I was... I'd got a job, like I say, at BGM Plastics and I don't even think I was supposed to be working night shift 'cause you were supposed to be 18, but I was doing it anyway, and I come off shift at eight o'clock in the morning and he'd asked me to help and I thought, okay, I'll ...I'll ...I'll help him. I'd just done a 12-hour shift. And I went across the road - it was only round the corner - and I helped them potato pick, and he was there with Janet and a few other people that he'd got together. And I was doing some driving on the tractor, I was picking the potatoes. And I ...and I worked hard till about two/three o'clock and I'd had enough. I needed to get home, get some sleep for the next shift on the next night. And I said something to Janet that I was ...“Right, I’m going. I’ve had enough.” And sh... “You can’t leave now. You can’t ...can’t...” “(Inaudible).” And she went to say summat to me dad (inaudible). I just said ...and ...I just ...I’d had enough. I snapped at Janet for being so horrible and wanting me to do it. “Just be grateful I’ve come and helped you.” They weren’t even grateful. And then he says something to me, I said something back. I can’t recollect what it was. And he just... “I’ll fucking kill you.” And he come running down the field with a pitchfork, hay bailing fork, running down after me. I set off running and got in me car and went.

Q How old were you then?

A Seventeen.

Q And was that... Did you say that was the moment contact pretty much ended?

A Yes.

Q I asked you questions about the name “Sam” on your tattoo the other day.

A Yes.

Q If anybody were to suggest that were the name of a dog, what would you say about that?

A That’s laughable. It’s laughable. But we did have a dog called Sam. We had brother and sister, both of them. Sam and Zimba. I think me dad shot Sam. He ...he was epileptic, an epileptic dog. Both of them were epileptic. But to start off with, they wasn’t ...they wasn’t so bad. They were good gun dogs and they used to go out shooting. We only had one of them. I can’t remember which one we got first, Sam or Zimba. I think it was Sam. We got off them off John Emelia(?). John Emelia was a guy we used to shooting with.

Q I’m going to stop you there, if I may.

A Sorry.

Q Not a dog? The tattoo, not a dog?

A No. Never in a million years.

Q Thank you, Mr Appleyard.

A Okay.

MR HAMPTON: Does your Honour have any questions?

JUDGE JAMESON: I'm just wondering if it would be helpful just to look at one matter that was referred to in the statement. Let me just look at that. (After a pause) It was put to Mr Appleyard that he hadn't mentioned any other incident of...

MR HAMPTON: (Inaudible)

JUDGE JAMESON: ...Carol looking out of the window...

MR HAMPTON: Yes.

JUDGE JAMESON: ...in a state of undress in a statement, but I don't actually think, looking at it, that that's quite accurate.

MR HAMPTON: I see the point your making.

JUDGE JAMESON: On continuation sheet 2...

MR HAMPTON: It's the paragraph underneath. The central paragraph. Yes. I'm just referring to your statement, Mr Appleyard, of 26 November 2015, on p.2. The sixth paragraph down, you describe an incident where Carol came to the window.

A Yes.

Q But there's a two-line paragraph just under that. Could you just read that to yourself for a moment, please? Begins, "It was not the on..."

A Yes.

Q Could you tell us what's recorded there, please?

A She was wa ...always walking round the house in knickers and bra.

Q It's here: "It was not the only time that I saw Carol walking round the house in skimpy underwear and, looking back, she was always walking round the house like that."

A That's correct.

JUDGE JAMESON: But it's also the next paragraph, I thought. "Can recall another occasion which would've been around the same time as she leant..." Oh, I'm sorry.

MR HAMPTON: Yes.

JUDGE JAMESON: "… as she leant out of the window." Sorry, I've misread that.

MR HAMPTON: (Inaudible).

JUDGE JAMESON: Yes. All right. Thank you.

MR HAMPTON: I think that deals with it. Is there anything else, your Honour?

JUDGE JAMESON: No. Thank you very much.

MR HAMPTON: Could this witness be released, please?

JUDGE JAMESON: Right. Thank you very much indeed, Mr Appleyard.

THE WITNESS: Thank you.

JUDGE JAMESON: That's it.

(The witness withdrew)

(11.14 a.m.)

(12.01 p.m.)

Mrs HILDA MAY GRAHAM, Sworn

(via link to Huddersfield Magistrates' Court)

JUDGE JAMESON: Okay. Onto you, Mr Hampton, then, please.

MR HAMPTON: Thank you. Mrs Graham, can you see and hear me okay?

THE WITNESS: I can't see you. I can hear you.

MR HAMPTON: All right. Oh, right. Just some problems with your eyesight?

THE WITNESS: No, it's a thing that's on screen. A login thing that's on...

MR HAMPTON: Oh.

THE WITNESS: ...screen.

MR HAMPTON: Right.

(Link problem discussed)

MR HAMPTON: I don't think there's any real need, Mrs Graham, that you have to see me, but can you see at least an outline and the courtroom?

THE WITNESS: I can see that a bit, yes.

JUDGE JAMESON: That'll do.

MR HAMPTON: All right.

THE WITNESS: I can see the top of your head.

MR HAMPTON: That's probably enough.

Examined by Mr HAMPTON

Q Mrs Graham, could you tell us your full name, please?

A Hilda May Graham.

Q And, may I ask you, please, how old you are?

A I'm 76 next month.

Q And what was your date of birth, Mrs Graham?

A 22/02/1943.

Q Thank you. What was your maiden name?

A Appleyard.

Q Do you know a man called Elliott Appleyard?

A He's me (inaudible).

Q You just dropped out. He's your what, sorry?

A Brother.

Q Thank you. And who's the eldest of the two of you?

A Me.

Q By how much?

A About four years, I think. Something like that.

Q Thank you. Mrs Graham, I'd like to ask you some questions, please, about your brother, Elliott, regarding a period of time in the 1980s.

A Yeah.

Q Did you become aware at that time that he was living in Denby Dale at an address of Gilthwaites Crescent?

A Yes.

Q Did you know he was married?

A He was married and then he got separated from his wife.

Q Thank you. And she was called?

A	Jean.
Q	Jean?
A	Yes.
Q	Did you know if they had children together?
A	Yes. They had three.
Q	Do you remember their names?
A	There was... I can't remember the oldest now, and Carol and then Paul. Donna. Donna ...Donna were t' oldest.
Q	Yes.
A	And then Carol.
Q	Yes.
A	And then Paul.
Q	Thank you. So, during the 1980s - I'm concentrating on that period, Mrs Graham, all right?
A	Yes.
Q	Did you see much of Elliott and his family?
A	Not a great deal.
Q	But you did become aware that there came a time that Elliott and Jean were no longer living together?
A	Yes.
Q	Did you know where Jean had gone following the split?
A	I didn't know for a start but then I found out afterwards.
Q	Tell us what you found out about where Jean was.
A	When he (inaudible) see her.
Q	Thank you. And where was it that you ended up going?
A	To Penistone.
Q	Do you remember how it came to be that Elliott was asking you to take him to Penistone to see Jean?
A	He hadn't got a car at the time.
Q	Did you?
A	Pardon?

Q Did you have a car?

A Me husband did.

Q What was your husband 's name, please?

A Peter. Peter Graham.

Q Thank you. Can you remember what the purpose of the trip was? Why you were going?

A Because he told us that he'd got to go and see Jean because Carol had been on to t' police about something.

Q Did you go to Penistone?

A We took him, yes.

Q And did you go by car?

A Yes.

Q Who was in the car?

A Me husband were driving, I were int' passenger seat, an Elliott were int' back.

Q Do you remember anything about the time of day or the time of year?

A I know it were int' summer 'cause it were a hot day, but I can't remember what time it was.

Q Thank you. Could you please tell us what happened when you got there?

A Well he ...he had to show us where to go 'cause we didn't know.

Q Yes.

A And then when we got there, we stayed int' car and he got out and went to Jean's house.

Q Was that Elliott?

A And then... Yes.

Q Yes.

A And then ...and then he came straight back down t' path and she come following him and they were arguing. We couldn't hear what they said then. And then they come right at side of t' car and she shouted at him.

Q What did she shout, please?

A She shouted, words to this effect: she took the pregnancy test to the chemist as though it was hers, but he knew full well it wasn't, it was Carol's.

Q Do you recall if Elliott responded to that? Did he say anything?

A I don't know.

Q Did you...

A I didn't hear anything more. We'd put the windows up on the car.

Q And why did you do that?

A I was shocked.

Q How did you get back? How did you return?

A In the car.

Q What were the seating arrangements? Can you remember?

A There were two front seats, driver and t' passenger, and then t' back seat.

Q It was a really bad question.

A (Inaudible)

Q I think what I meant to say was: who sat where on the way back?

A As ...as we came.

Q Same as before?

A I was in the passenger seat. Yes.

Q Did you say anything about what you'd heard?

A No.

Q Did Elliott say anything about what you heard?

A No.

Q How was he during the journey back?

A Quiet.

Q Thank you, Mrs Graham. The barrister acting on behalf of the defendant will now ask you some questions.

A Okay.

MR STOREY: Your Honour, I'm told I have to move forward.

JUDGE JAMESON: Yes.

MR STOREY: The camera is fixed in one position.

Cross-examined by Mr STOREY

Q Mrs Graham, can you at least hear me?
A Yes.
Q I don't know if you can see me or not, but so long as you can hear me that's probably...
A No.
Q ...the main thing. All right. I don't have very many questions...
A Yes.
Q ...for you but I do need to ask you some things.
A Okay.
Q I think it's right, isn't it, that you and your brother have not had very much to do with each other for quite a long time?
A No.
Q Does that mean, no, it's not right? Or, no, you haven't had much to do with each other?
A Oh, no. No, we haven't, no.
Q I think you fell out with him some time ago, didn't you?
A Yes.
Q About some family matter that I don't need to ask you about.
A Yes.
Q And I think you may also have fallen out with other members of your family. I don't know. Is that right?
A Not specifically, no.
Q We know that you obviously made a statement to the police because that's why you're here, or why you're in Huddersfield now giving evidence.
A Yeah.
Q And I assume you've been given a copy of your witness statement to read at some point this morning?
A Yes.
Q And your witness statement was made in 2016.

A	I don't know when it was.
Q	Don't worry. I've got a copy of it in front of me, so I ...I...
A	All right.
Q	...know the date. All right?
A	Right.
Q	I want to ask you, please, Mrs Graham, how you came to make that statement to the police? Did they come to visit you and ask you?
A	Yes, they came to visit me.
Q	And was that the first time you knew anything at all about the police wanting a statement from you about your brother?
A	Yes.
Q	Had anybody rung you up before to say, "The police want a statement from you"?
A	Oh, no. So ...sorry, Carol had said earlier would I be a witness.
Q	Right. So that's Carol Higgins, is it?
A	Yes.
Q	Or Carol Appleyard, as you may have known her?
A	Yes.
Q	And had she phoned you, or did you see her in person when she...
A	No, she...
Q	...asked you to be a witness?
A	She ...she came to our house.
Q	And did she say to you, when she came to your house, what she wanted you to be a witness about?
A	She ...she just told me her version, what had happened, and I said I didn't know anything about it.
Q	And so what did she want you to be a witness about then? Did she say that when she spoke...
A	Well...
Q	...to you at your house?

A Sorry. She came to see me before I gave a statement, before we went to Penistone.

Q But did she know that you'd been to Penistone in the 1980s, as you've told us happened?

A I don't know whether she knew or not.

Q Did she ask you anything at all about it?

A No. Not that I can remember. I don't know.

Q Did she say anything to you about what she might like you to say when you spoke to the police?

A No. No.

Q When you made your statement, Mrs Graham, how good was your recollection of this event you've told us about in the 1980s?

A Well, me memory were good then. I hadn't had me stroke then.

Q How good's your memory of it now?

A Well, like I said, (inaudible). I've had two strokes since, so it's not as good as it were ...it were. I can even forget me name sometimes.

Q All right. Well, please do tell us...

A That's not literally.

Q Please tell us if you don't remember something I'm asking you about. All right?

A All right.

Q The conversation you say you heard, or the comment you say you heard Jean make, that must've been quite shocking...

A Yeah.

Q ...to hear.

A It was.

Q Did you not think to ask your brother what it was about, or what she was talking about?

A No.

Q Is there any reason why you didn't ask him?

A I was shocked.

Q In the mid-1980s, were you still talking to your brother then, or had you fallen out with him by that time?
A You mean when I gave a statement?
Q No. When... You've told us about this trip to Penistone. Were you and your brother still talking to each other then?
A Well, yeah.
Q But did you never think to ask him what that comment you say Jean made was all about?
A No. We weren't that close.
Q I've got to suggest to you, Mrs Graham, that there was in fact never an occasion when you and your husband drove your brother to Penistone to see Jean.
A You're saying?
Q I'm s...
A Sorry, what did you say?
Q I'm suggesting that what you've told us isn't correct. You and your husband never drove your brother to Penistone to see Jean, in fact, in the 1980s, did you?
A Oh, we did. Yeah, we did. I wasn't driving at the time.
Q And in the 1980s, your brother had his own car or van the whole time, didn't he? He wouldn't have needed a lift anywhere.
A No, he didn't.
Q And there wasn't, in fact, any conversation or any comment made by Jean about a pregnancy test that he...
A Yes, there was.
Q ...knew was Carol's.
A It wasn't a comment. She shouted it ...it at him.
Q Why do you say that you wound the windows up, or put the windows up, after you heard that comment, that shout?
A I didn't want to hear any more. I was in shock.
Q But you didn't want to ask your brother about it either at any stage?

A No. I were gobsmacked. I couldn't get over it.

Q And you're sure this isn't something that someone might have suggested you say or put the idea in your mind about?

A No.

Q All right. Thank you, Mrs Graham. There's nothing else I want to ask you. Thank you for your attendance.

MR HAMPTON: Just give me one moment.

THE WITNESS: (Inaudible)

MR HAMPTON: (After a pause) I have no further questions.

JUDGE JAMESON: All right. Thank you very much indeed. Back to me with the camera, please. There we are. You may or may not be able to see all or any part of me, Mrs Graham, but it's the judge again, so ...just to say thank you very much indeed for coming and helping us with your evidence. It's finished now so as soon as the screen goes blank, you're very ...you're entirely free to go. So thank you very much for coming and helping us.

THE WITNESS: Thank you.

(The witness withdrew)

(12.22 p.m.)

(12.24 p.m.)

Mrs JULIE CLARKE, Sworn

Examined by Mr HAMPTON

Q Afternoon.

A Hiya.

Q Could you tell us your full name, please?

A Julie Clarke.

Q Thank you. Would you mind giving us your age, please?

A Forty-nine.

Q And your date of birth?

A 31/03/1969.

Q As is normal when somebody's talking to you, you politely turn to face me. This is a slightly unusual exchange we're going to have. It's not typical of a conversation. Would you turn to the jury, please...

A Yeah.

Q ...so you're facing them? Thank you very much. Only because they need to hear what you have to say, and if you're facing the right direction, the judge and the jury have more chance of that.

A Yeah.

Q All right? I won't take it as being impolite to me that you're not looking at me. Do you know Carol Higgins?

A Do I look that way?

Q Look that way.

A Yeah, I do, yeah.

Q How?

A We've been best friends for 33 year-ish.

Q So, 33 years. Could you help us with what kind of timeframe we're talking about when you met?

A Yeah. We were both 16, went to work at a sewing factory SR Gent in Barnsley.

Q You've got a memory of both being 16. How did you end up at SR Gents?

A We started on a YTS government scheme where they learnt you how to sew.

Q So you would have been about 16 around 1985?

A Yeah.

Q Do you have any memory, going back to that timeframe now, 85, where Carol was living when you met her?

A She lived with her mum at...I can't remember what road, but it was either at Penistone or then she lived in Barnsley off Summer Lane with her mum and her sister, Donna.

Q So, living with mum either at Penistone or Barnsley?

A Yeah, when we first met. I think it was Penistone first off.

Q Did you say Summer Lane? Or did they...

A That were in Barnsley, that.
Q Barnsley, yes.
A They moved to a terraced house on the corner of Summer Lane.
Q With her mum, Jean?
A Yeah.
Q And sister, Donna?
A Yeah.
Q You've been friends for a long time. Going back to this timeframe again, were you able to observe Carole's relationship with her mother, Jean?
A Yes.
Q From those observations, how would you describe it to us?
A Rubbish. Not nice. Not like a proper mum and daughter.
Q Now, did there come a time when Carol's living arrangements changed?
A There did, yeah. Her and her mum were always arguing, falling out, and her mum weren't, in my opinion, a very nice lady, not like my mam, and they were always falling out, and one day, Carol...her mum kicked her out and we ended up... She got nowhere to go so she went to stay...she went out with a boy called Kerry at time.
Q A boy called Kerry?
A Kerry.
Q Right.
A And I were going out with a boy called Ricky, and then she had got nowhere to live and...
Q Yes.
A …she ended up - We all worked at a factory where there were like quite a lot of women and there were a lady called Sharon Westermann. She were our boss at the time, and we all did, like, a whip round because Carol got a... She went to stay with Kerry's mum and dad for a spell.
Q So, she went to stay with Kerry's mum and dad?
A For a bit, and then she managed to get a little terraced house on...I want to say Stanhope.

Q Stanhope?

A Road. It were in Barnsley. It were a terraced house and everybody like mucked in and give her curtains and bedding and...

Q From the factory?

A Yeah. Everybody just donated stuff, cutlery. She got nowt, nothing.

Q Just give me a moment. Is it Miss Clarke or Mrs Clarke?

A Mrs.

Q Mrs Clarke. Sorry. When she was at Stanhope Street, did you remain friends?

A Yeah, we did.

Q And were you still spending time together?

A Yeah.

Q Were you were aware from your friendship with Carol that she had any tattoos?

A She had a big one on her shoulder, a big rose, and then underneath it there were two scrolls with names in, Sam and Kaz. Were horrible.

Q It what?

A Horrible.

Q Sam and Kaz?

A Yeah.

Q Did she tell you anything about the names?

A Obviously she's Kaz for Carol. She said her dad had put it on when she was around 13, which horrified me, and Sam was her dad's nickname when he used to work on the fair, but Carol didn't know that was his nickname because he were called Elliott.

Q When she was telling you this, how was she?

A There were times when she were okay; there were times when she were absolutely in a mess, panicky. She always had a scary feeling in the bottom of her stomach. She always used to do this with her hair when she were thinking. She used to twirl her hair around and put it in her mouth like that. That were when she was thinking, I always thought.

Q When you say she was "in a mess," what do you mean?

A She used to cry a lot.
Q Did she say anything about her father to you?
A Yes, she did actually. When... It was around the time of the tattoo business and she said that her dad was a bad man, nobody liked him in Denby Dale.
Q Did she say anything about what had passed between him and her? That's what I'm interested in.
A Yes, she said that he used to rape her and abuse her, smack her, beat her and her brother and Donna.
Q Are you aware of Carol having anything done about the tattoo?
A Yeah, yeah. Well, first we went to try and cover it up. We used to buy makeup and go into Boots and have like trial covers with this camouflage makeup.
Q So, "we went to try and cover it up," "we" is?
A Me and Carol.
Q Makeup from Boots, was it?
A Yeah.
Q To try and cover it up?
A Yes, like, camouflage makeup. They always come off.
Q Yes.
A So, then we ended up going to a tattoo shop to ask if they could help, which they did.
Q Did you both go together?
A We did, yes. Not all the time, but I went with her for it removing but not every session because it took a while.
Q Was there more than one session?
A Yeah, there were quite a few sessions.
Q How old were you about this time? I won't hold you to the exact age, but just give us an idea.
A I would say probably about 19.
Q Thank you. What happened at the tattooists?

A All I can remember is it was very, very painful for her and they stuck little needles in the acid and it like all bubbled up and formed like a scab, and then when the scab came off, it were going to remove the ink, but the first time she had it done she...well, actually, she stuck to Kerry's mum and dad...Shirley, they called his mam...she actually slept in little brother's bed and she stuck to bed sheets. I can right remember that because they'd got to physically soak the pillowcases off to pull it off her back.

Q To get it off her back?

A Yeah because it was stuck on the tattoo. It were like a big scab.

Q Do you recall her saying anything else about what had passed between her and her father, any further detail?

A Oh, lots of details. I went counselling with her.

Q I'm not so much concerned about that...

A Yeah.

Q ...but conversations you were having around this time...around the time of the tattooing or earlier?

A Like what? Sorry.

Q Did you ever talk about photography?

A Yes, we did. She were always adamant...I don't know if this is what you mean. She were always adamant there were a metal box...sorry...a metal box and it were like – this is what I can remember – a metal army box, she used to describe it, a small one, and inside that there were photographs of Carol, an hairbrush that she used to say that were used on Carol...

Q And when was she telling you this, Mrs Clarke, again, rough timeframe?

A Well, 16/17.

Q So mid-eighties?

A Mid... Yeah. We'd became close quick.

Q Thank you. A slightly different topic now.

A Yeah.

Q Did you ever meet her father?

A I saw her father on two occasions.

Q Tell us about the first please.

A The first one: her dad had asked to marry his partner, then, called Janet, and Janet had been in touch with Carol to see whether they could meet up so Carol could tell her what had gone off between her and her dad.

Q Just pause there. Do you know who asked for the meeting?

A Janet phoned Carol as far as I can remember.

Q Do you know if there was a meeting?

A There was a meeting.

Q How do you know that?

A Because I were there, in Barnsley.

Q Whereabouts in Barnsley?

A In Barnsley...it's not there now but there used to be, like, an upstairs market, and there were a big escalator, and at top of escalator there were all pie and pea stalls.

Q Yes.

A And Carol went into the pie and pea stall, and I walked on landing if you like and there was a shop called Dancerama and don't even think it's there now.

Q Dancerama?

A Yeah, were like a dancing shop, clothes thing.

Q Yes, I don't know it.

A And I sat outside a bench there and waited.

Q Why were you there?

A To support her like I'm here now today.

Q So, you were stood somewhat away from the pie and peas store?

A Sorry?

Q You were stood a bit away from the pie and peas store?

A I were, yeah, quite a...well, not quite away, but...

Q A little?

A Yeah, (inaudible).

Q Tell us what happened, please, Mrs Clarke.

A All I can remember is I never actually saw Janet but, where escalator were, Carol was stood up and... I can't even describe him. It were just a man in a checked shirt stood talking with Carol and then she came back to me. She weren't there very long, perhaps minutes. It weren't long at all and she...

Q The conversation with the man?

A Yeah.

Q Yes. She came back?

A She came back to me. She come walking up. So, I was sat over there and she come walking up and she was in a terrible, terrible state.

Q Describe it for us, please.

A Panicky, hyperventilating. She couldn't breathe. Her legs were like jelly. She was just in a terrible, terrible mess and I says, "What's wrong?" and she says, "It were me father." I can right remember that, and she said he were a...

Q Go on.

A Can you swear?

Q Yes.

A She said he were a "bastard."

Q Carol said that?

A What?

Q Carol said that?

A Carol said that, yeah, and she also told me – and that was the day she told me this – that he said he was sorry he loved her like a wife, not as a child, not as a daughter, and she was in an absolute right mess. She was crying. She couldn't breathe, and I was only a young girl myself. I didn't know what to do with her, so we got a taxi from town centre and I took her back to me mum and dad's because my mum and dad were adults...

Q Yes.

A ...and me mum saw to Carol.

Q Then you mentioned a second occasion?

A Yeah. A few weeks later, we finished work at one o'clock on a Friday at work and we walked down from our factory into town centre, and we were walking up...there were Littlewoods on us right-hand side.

Q Littlewoods?

A Yeah, and a man were coming up to us. I'd not even noticed him, and I don't know whether he spoke to Carol or not, but then we carried on walking together. We were a gang of us, and she just said, "That's me dad," and I went, "Never." She went, "yeah," and she got herself in a right old tizz again, panicking, crying, felt sick, shaky, and she was convinced he were going to come and get her because it weren't long after that we'd seen him prior to that, and I've never seen him again until...

Q Yes. You've mentioned counselling.

A Yes.

Q Were you aware if Carol was having counselling?

A Yes. I begged her to go to the doctors when we first met after a few months because I was really concerned that...I worked in a factory with 300 girls, and there were only Carol in the state she were in, and I were really worried about her, and I begged her to go to the doctors, and they gave her some antidepressants to lift her mood, and we were advised to go to rape counselling. She were advised to go to rape counselling, which we did. We went to Sheffield. We finished work at one o'clock on a Friday, walking to the bus station and we always got a steak bake or a sausage roll from Hagenbachs, got on the train and went to Sheffield to this rape counselling.

Q Did you go with her?

A Yeah, for months. I think it were every other Friday. It weren't every single week, perhaps once a fortnight on a Friday afternoon, and I couldn't tell you to where it was, but all I can remember is it were like two shopfronts and then a doorway. You went up the...to open the door and it were just immediate set of steps and there were three doors at the top, and we always went in left and there were always two ladies waiting for us.

Q And, again, timeframe roughly?

A Probably about 19.

Q Late eighties, early nineties?

A I can't say for definite. It's a long time ago, isn't it?

Q It is. Thank you, Mrs Clarke. Would you wait there, please. There'll be some more questioning from my learned friend who defends.

A Yeah, that's fine.

Cross-examined by Mr STOREY

Q Not in fact very many, Mrs Clarke, so won't keep you long.

A Yeah.

Q It's pretty clear from what you've said that much of what you've told us about is what Carol Higgins herself, as she calls herself now, had told you?

A It is, yeah.

Q And until, you say, you saw her meet a man in Barnsley, you had never set eyes on her father?

A No.

Q And so you rely entirely on what she told you for this information?

A Yes.

Q Just so we've got it right, you, for example, didn't see her having to have pillowcases soaked off her or anything like that? Presumably, again, that's part of what she told you?

A It is, yeah.

Q Yes, okay.

A But I can remember it because it was very real, and the scabs on her back were awful.

Q Right, but it's not something that you were present to see?

A I didn't see it, no.

Q No? Okay.

A I did see the scabs when...

Q Yes, I meant soaking the pillowcases.

A I didn't see the soaking, no.

Q No, don't worry about that. You're obviously a close friend of Carol's.

A Yeah.

Q And I assume, therefore, you're still in close contact with one another?

A Yeah, not like we were because obviously we've both got married.

Q Sure.

A We've both had children, work, life, but yeah.

Q And presumably you're aware of her use of Facebook, social media and the like to publicise her allegations?

A Yeah.

Q And is it the case that you and she have discussed things about what she says happened to her when she was a child?

A Yeah.

Q Recently, I mean, not back in the eighties or the nineties.

A When I came to gave me statement – how long ago is that? – we were talking about it then.

Q June 2017?

A Yeah, last year.

Q If that helps you. Year before last?

A Yeah, yeah and, obviously, when she wrote her book, she asked me opinion about naming her dad because, obviously, it's massive naming somebody for something like that and she said that...she says, "Well, I might get my day in court because he'll come and get me."

Q Presumably she asked you if you'd speak to the police to give that statement in June '17?

A Yeah, she did.

Q You told us about them meeting in Barnsley, which I'm not sure if you were able to say when that happened. Can you help with that?

A Not really. I mean, you might be able to piece dates together a bit better than me. Elliott had asked Janet, his partner then, probably still is, if he could marry her, so around that time. You might have them dates.

Q But you said that as far as you could remember, this meeting had been set up because Janet phoned Carol?
A Yeah.
Q Again...
A Again...
Q ...that is the information you got from Carol?
A Yeah.
Q Are you quite sure you were there?
A Yeah, quite sure. My mum and dad will verify that afternoon because I took Carol... I didn't know what to do with her.
Q Do you remember Carol going and speaking to someone in a cafe or anything like that?
A Well, she was supposed to be meeting Janet in the cafe in...because that's where we was going Friday for us lunch.
Q I don't need the name, don't worry if you do not remember.
A No.
Q But do I take it from what you've just said that she didn't in fact meet Janet at all?
A Carol met Janet. I didn't meet Janet.
Q Right, okay. So, you saw Carol go into the cafe, did you?
A No, I saw Carol. All I can remember is she were meeting Carol in the cafe, but then I can remember this escalator at top of the market and that's where I saw her dad.
Q Well, you saw a man in a checked shirt...
A A man.
Q ...yes, to be fair?
A In a checked shirt, yes.
Q But do you remember anything at all about Carol going into this cafe and speaking to Janet?
A I don't know.

Q Presumably you've been there if you went to Barnsley with her, came out of work with her?

A We came out and worked together, but I can't remember. I'm sorry.

Q No, don't worry and, again, Carol's response was what she was saying to you. You didn't hear anything that passed between her...

A I didn't, no. I didn't even see the man as such, only from a distance.

Q And, again, a few weeks later, all you can tell us about is her commenting, "That's me dad"?

A Yeah.

Q Okay. Thank you. There isn't anything else, Mrs Clarke. Thank you for coming to answer my questions.

A No problem.

MR HAMPTON: Does your Honour have anything?

JUDGE JAMESON: No, I don't. Thank you very much indeed. Right. Well, Mrs Clarke, thank you very much indeed for coming and helping us with your evidence. That's it, you're free to go. Thank you.

(The witness withdrew)

(12.48 p.m.)

(Break for lunch)

(2.14 p.m.)

CARRON WARD, Sworn

Examined by Mr HAMPTON

Q Could you tell us your name, please?

A It's Mrs Carron Ward.

Q Would you mind telling us your age?

A Fifty-nine.

Q And your date of birth?

A 20 of August 1959.

Q Thank you. I'm going to ask you a number of questions, principally about one incident, Mrs Ward. Would you, in giving your answers, would you just turn towards the members of the jury and the judge so they can hear what you're saying? Keep your voice nice and loud, all right? It's a big room and, if you're heard, a note can be taken. All right? Where did you do your growing up?

A Denby Dale.

Q And did there come a time you lived on Gilthwaites Crescent?

A Yes.

Q Can you help us with the time period you were there?

A From about seven years till about 1999, till I were about 37.

Q Until you were 37, from?

A About 37, from seven... seven years old.

Q Right, so until... from you being seven till you being about 37?

A Yes.

Q You lived at Gilthwaites Crescent?

A Yes.

Q So with your date of birth, we're looking at the mid to late-60s onwards?

A Yes.

Q Now then, did you know the Appleyard family?

A Yes.

Q Did you know Elliott Appleyard?

A Yes.

Q Did you know the rest of the family who lived there?

A Yes.

Q And who was that?

A Elliott, Jean, Donna, Carol and Paul.

Q And how did you know them? In what form?

A As neighbours.

Q What was the age difference between you and Carol, doing the best you can?

A About 15 years.

Q	About 15 years between you?

A	Be about four... about 14 years, 14, 15.

Q	Was Carol older or younger?

A	Younger.

Q	My memory is telling me that Carol was born in 1969 - well, we know that - so if I were to suggest about a 10 year difference, would you disagree with me?

A	No.

Q	Did you have much to do with Carol when you lived there?

A	No, not as a... not as a friend because of the age gap.

Q	Were you able to form a view as to how Carol seemed as a child?

A	Yes.

Q	What was your view?

A	Very frightened and timid.

Q	Now, with Gilthwaites Crescent in mind, do you have any memories about Elliott Appleyard that stick in your memory when you were growing up?

A	Yes.

Q	Can you help us with that?

A	I was about 15.

Q	You were about 15?

A	Yes.

Q	So the mid-1970s?

A	Yes.

Q	1974, 1975? Yeah?

A	Yeah.

Q	And tell us what you recall, please.

A	I recall him saying to me, "Has your dad broke you in yet?" I said, "What?"

JUDGE JAMESON: Sorry, just forgive me. Would you say that again?

A	"Has your dad broke you in yet?" He says, "All dads do it to their daughters".

MR HAMPTON: "Has your dad broke you in yet? All dads do it to their daughters"?

A Yes.

Q So you were around 15? It's the mid-1970s?

A Yes.

Q Did you say anything back?

A I can't recall.

Q Did you know what he meant, at the time?

A Well, yes and no, yes and no. I wasn't... more yes to... I was... slightly, slightly.

Q Did you ask anything of him?

A No.

Q Did he say anything more about it at that time?

A I can't remember.

Q Who were you living with?

A My family - parents, siblings.

Q At that time did you mention it to anybody?

A I can't remember.

Q When did you first recall this happening?

A Truthfully, it came back to me after I'd read Carol's, Carol Higgins's book.

Q Can you help us with when that was, roughly?

A Roughly about three years ago.

Q We're in... we're just into 2019.

A 2019? About 2016.

MR HAMPTON: Around 2016. Thank you. Would you wait there, please? There'll be some more questions from this gentleman who acts on behalf of the defendant.

<u>Cross-examined by Mr STOREY</u>

Q Mrs Ward, I think you spoke to the police twice about Carol Higgins and Elliott Appleyard? Is that right?

A Yes.

Q You gave two witness statements?

A Yes.

Q Which I assume you've been shown copies of today at some point?

A Yes.

Q Okay. You won't, I'm sure, remember the dates on the top of them but we've got them here, so, if I tell you the dates, you can take it that they're accurate. Okay?

A Yes.

Q The first statement you gave on the 15th of September 2014? Okay?

A Yes.

Q And the second was on the 9th of October 2015, just a little over a year later?

A Yes.

Q Do you remember now how it was you came to give the first of those witness statements back in 2014?

A I said... I told Carol I'd be a witness; I'd give a statement for her.

Q Right, so you spoke to Carol around that time?

A Yes.

Q And, presumably, the next thing you heard was the police contacting you or something like that?

A Yes.

Q So you were obviously in contact with Carol Higgins in 2014 for that conversation to take place between you and her?

A At the book meet... at the book signing.

Q Well, I think the book signing may have been the following year, 2015?

A I can't remember.

Q Okay. Well, again, I'm working from your witness statement that gives us a date for that, so...

A I can't remember.

Q Don't worry, because I was going to suggest it was, in fact, after the book launch meeting that you made your second statement. All right?

A I can't remember.

Q No? Okay, but I'll just ask you to think again about the question I asked you a moment ago. Your first statement from 2014, do you remember what might have led to you giving that first statement to the police or can you still not remember any more than you told us?

A No.

Q Okay. Well, the date you've included in your witness statement for a meeting effectively at a pub in Denby Dale, was the 16th of August 2015. Okay? Now, do you think that date might be about right for the date of the book launch?

A I can't remember.

Q Okay. Did it take place in the Dalesman Inn in Denby Dale?

A It did.

Q And had it been fairly widely publicised in the Denby Dale area?

A I don't know.

Q How do you remember hearing about the book launch taking place?

A A friend.

Q Do you remember who the friend was?

A Yes.

Q It sounds like you don't want to tell us?

A Is it appropriate to tell you?

Q Well, there's nothing wrong with telling us who the friend was that told you...

A Right.

Q ...about the book launch.

A It was a friend, just call her Ena.

Q Okay. Is that Ena Whittles?

A Yes.

Q So she told you about the book launch?

A Yes.

Q And I take it you went along?

A Yes.

Q And did you speak there with Carol Higgins?

A Yes.

Q Had you already read the book by that time?

A Yes, I had.

Q Okay, so you'd bought it somewhere before the event at the Dalesman Inn?

A Yeah, it was lent to me.

Q Okay, and is it the case that you spoke with Carol at that event at the Dalesman?

A Yes, because I hadn't seen her for over 30 years.

Q You hadn't seen her for over 30 years?

A Yes.

Q Okay.

A And it was lovely to see her.

Q All right, and is that the occasion when she asked if you'd be a witness for her, or was it shortly after that meeting?

A I can't remember.

Q Okay. Was it around that time?

A I can't remember.

Q Okay, because, again, going on the dates you gave to the police, that meeting was in August 2015. You'd provided a statement 11 months earlier, September 2014, and I'll ask you again if you can think back and see if you can remember how you came to provide that first statement.

A I can't remember.

Q Might it have been that Carol contacted you a year earlier about giving a statement on her behalf?

A No.

Q No? But you've no idea how the police might have had your details to contact you in September 2014?

A No.

Q The second statement, October 2015, can we assume that that came about after you'd spoken to Carol at the book launch in August of 2015?

A I can't remember. Could you re-word it?

Q Sorry?

A Could you re-word it?

Q Of course, yes, my fault, not yours. If... we know the date of your second statement was October 2015 and in that statement you said the meeting, or the book launch at the Dalesman Inn was in August 2015 and you've told us you spoke to Carol at that book launch at the pub.

A Yes.

Q Might it be that it was after speaking to Carol that the police contacted you to say, "Can we have a statement from you"?

A I'm not sure.

Q All right. Now, the conversation that you've told us about in the mid-1970s between you and Elliott Appleyard, can you tell us where that took place?

A At the end of my garden path.

Q Okay, and how did that conversation come about?

A He used to walk up and down a lot.

Q Do you mean walk up...

A He just stopped...

Q ...and down the road?

A Yeah.

Q Had you ever spoken to him before?

A Yes.

Q Did you live... well, you obviously lived nearby? Is that right?

A Yes.

Q I think you lived with your family at number 20? Is that right?

A Yes.

Q And the Appleyards lived at that time at 26?

A Yes.

Q So three doors down?

A Yes.

Q Are you sure you remember that event accurately, Mrs Ward?

A Yes.

Q Or might it be that that meeting, that conversation, is something that popped into your head as a result of reading Carol Higgins's book?

A No.

Q Or as a result of something she may have said to you...

A No.

Q ...when you spoke to her at the pub?

A No.

Q Why... why are you so sure about that?

A I remember.

Q But you don't remember the events in 2014 that led to you giving your first statement or how you gave your second statement in 2015? Is that... is that fair?

A That's fair, because the dates, you just... things happen so quick, you get mixed up with the dates. I'm sorry.

Q Don't worry. Did there come a time when you actually moved to number 24, I think it was?

A Yes, I bought the house.

Q And do you remember when you bought number 24?

A I think it was 1982, 1983.

Q Okay. Was there ever an occasion when Jean Appleyard brought a load of furniture round to your house?

A I can't remember.

Q It's the sort of thing you would remember, isn't it?

A Yes.

Q Yeah.

A Yeah.

Q You can't remember that happening?

A No.

MR STOREY: Okay. All right, thank you very much, Mrs Ward. That's all I wanted to ask you.

MR HAMPTON: No, thank you. Does your Honour have any questions?

JUDGE JAMESON: No, thank you very much.

MR HAMPTON: May the witness be released, please?

JUDGE JAMESON: Certainly. Thank you for coming and helping us, give evidence.

A Thank you.

JUDGE JAMESON: That's it. You're free to go.

(The witness withdrew)

(2.31 p.m.)

(2.34 p.m.)

Mrs ENA WHITTLE, Read

MR HAMPTON: This, then, members of the jury, is the statement of Mrs Ena Whittle, and the statement, as to all statements in this case, has a declaration at the top of the statement which reads as follows:

> "This statement consisting of three pages, each of them signed by me, is true to the best of my knowledge and belief and I make it knowing that, if it is tendered in evidence, I shall be liable to prosecution if I have wilfully stated in it anything which I know to be false or do not believe to be true."

And there's a signature under the declaration, and it's dated 1 October 2015. And Mrs Whittle states as follows:

> "I'm originally from Scotland and moved to the Huddersfield area when I was 14 years old, initially living in Scissett. I moved to 20 Gilthwaites Crescent, Denby Dale, when I was about 30..."

JUDGE JAMESON: Just in case it's relevant, I think you said 20, the statement actually says 22.

MR HAMPTON: I'm sorry, I meant 22.

JUDGE JAMESON: I think it may be relevant because 20 is...

MR HAMPTON: Yes.

JUDGE JAMESON: ...the address...

MR HAMPTON: I'm grateful.

JUDGE JAMESON: ...at least at some stage of Carron Ward, she told us.

MR HAMPTON: I'm grateful.

JUDGE JAMESON: Yeah. Okay.

MR HAMPTON: I'll start again.

> "I moved to 22 Gilthwaites Crescent, Denby Dale, when I was about 30 - three-zero - years old, so that would've been about 1975 approximately.
>
> "When I first moved to Gilthwaites, I lived alone with my five children. I soon became aware of a family called the Appleyards who lived at 26 Gilthwaites. I can recall that Elliott Appleyard, his wife, Jean, and three children lived at the address, one of whom I knew was called Carol. My children played with Elliott's children, Carol, Paul and Donna.
>
> "I can recall one day seeing Carol with a number of love bites all over her neck. I would say she would've only been about 10 to 12 years old. I can still remember to this day thinking: how had she got those love bites? I assumed at the time they would've been from a boy, but she was still very young. I suppose I didn't think too much else of it at the time. Other than that, I didn't really have anything to do with Carol as she was a child to me."

That's the statement of Mrs Whittle.

(The learned Judge addressed the jury)

(The jury left court at 2.37 p.m.)

(The learned Judge conferred with counsel)

(Adjourned until Monday, 21st January, 2019)

(2.38 p.m.)

Monday 21 January 2019)

(Transcript prepared without the aid of documentation)

(11.22 a.m.)

JUDGE JAMESON: Good morning, ladies and gentlemen, and welcome back. There are a number of parish notices, I suppose. The first of them is to say sorry we are in our third court. I'm not quite sure why we're playing musical chairs in this way, but anyway, there we are. I hope it won't be too much of a problem for you and that you've all got your appropriate papers in front of you.

Secondly, I'm sorry that we've having a rather delayed start. There have been a number of technical issues. I think that may be why we're here, I don't know, but you will get the idea, I am sure, that this court was built quite a while ago now. It was designed in the 1970s, opened in about 1980 and of course at that time we didn't have any of this technology and it's all been retrofitted at different times and one bit doesn't talk to another as well as you would wish. The thing to do of course is to clear it all out and start again but there's no money for that so we do the best we can with what we've got. So, I'm afraid sometimes there are delays and this is such a time.

Now, the next witness that we are going to see is, again, on a video-link, I think simply for reasons of convenience.

MR HAMPTON: Geography.

JUDGE JAMESON: Yes, something of the sort. At least that's the theory. I hope it's convenient for the witness. It's not wildly convenient for us, but there we are. We crack on. Now, I think that the cameras are not panning around. They are supposed to be pre-set so it will take the camera specifically to where counsel are sitting, and I. They are not working. I don't know why not, so my clerk is going to have to do some manual moving of stuff about. It's going to work but just bear with us because it's not going to be perfect. Right. We'll crack on. And this witness is?

MR HAMPTON: Diana Thorpe.

JUDGE JAMESON: Diana Thorpe.

MR HAMPTON: At I-13.

JUDGE JAMESON: Thank you.

(11.28 a.m.)

DIANA JUDITH THORPE, Sworn

Examined by Mr HAMPTON

(Via video-link)

Q Could you tell us your full name, please, Mrs Thorpe?

A Diana Judith Thorpe.

Q And could you tell us your age, please?

A I'm 65.

Q Sixty-five, did you say?

A Yes.

Q And your date of birth, please?

A 15/3/1953.

Q Thank you. Could you tell us, please? Do you know Elliott Appleyard?

A Yes. He's me uncle.

Q And which of his siblings was your parent?

A Rose Appleyard, Margaret Rose Appleyard, his sister.

Q Was that your mum?

A Yes.

Q Thank you. I'm going to ask you a number of questions now, Mrs Thorpe, concentrating on a period some time ago now in the mid to late-1980s, so that's the timeframe I want you to think about. Okay?

A Yes.

Q Were you aware back then that Mr Appleyard had a family?

A Yes.

Q	Did you know he had children?
A	Yes.
Q	Do you remember their names?
A	Yes.
Q	Could you...
A	Donna, Carol and Paul.
Q	Thank you. Did you see the children very often back then?
A	Occasionally.
Q	Were you living in the Scissett area of Huddersfield?
A	Yes.
Q	Do you recall a time around the mid to late-1980s that Carol came to see you?
A	Yes, I do.
Q	Did she speak of her father?
A	Yes.
Q	I want to ask you, please, Mrs Thorpe, what Carol said about her father when she came to visit you.
A	Carol told me that her father had been sexually abusing her, he'd been having sex with her and making her do oral sex on him, and things like that.
Q	Can you remember where you were when you were told this?
A	I was at home in Scissett.
Q	Whereabouts in your home? Can you recall?
A	In me front room, sat on the sofa.
Q	Can you help as best you can with how old Carol was when she told you this?
A	She was in a great distressed state, sobbing and crying and trying to tell me and stumbling because she couldn't speak because she was crying so much.
Q	Thank you, so that's how she appeared? Can you, doing your best, recall how old she was, roughly?
A	I think she was about 19. I'm not sure though.
Q	Thank you. Do you recall if she said when this abuse had occurred?

A She said after her mum had left, it started.

MR STOREY: Sorry. I missed the first part of that.

MR HAMPTON: "After her mum had left, it started."

MR STOREY: "After her mum had left, it started."

MR HAMPTON: Did you give her any advice about what she should do?

A I said she should go and tell her mum.

Q Did you advise her to tell anybody else?

A When she told me that she'd already told her mum, I said then she should go to the police and tell the police.

Q After that, did you see Carol again?

A I saw her a couple of weeks later. She came to visit me with Paul.

Q Paul Appleyard, her brother?

A Yeah.

Q Were you aware of where she was living at this time?

A I thought she was still living at her dad's and she was making arrangements to get a flat.

Q That's what you understood?

A Yeah.

Q Now, just going back a bit from there, from Carol coming to speak to you and telling you about the abuse, can you tell me if, prior to that, you'd ever visited the family home in Denby Dale?

A Yes. I visited occasionally if I was in the area. I visited on one occasion when no-one answered the door when I knocked so I stood there for a few minutes knocking and, because no-one answered, I tried the door handle and it was unlocked...

Q Right. Let me just...

A ...so I went in...

Q Let me just stop you there, so this is... can you remember the address?

A No, I can't.

Q Right, so whose house was it?

A Elliott's house at Denby Dale.

Q So you'd been knocking but no-one answered so you went in?
A Yes.
Q In what room did you go into?
A I walked in the kitchen and I shouted, "Hello, hello" a few times.
Q Was there any response?
A Not... not straightaway. It took a few minutes before there was a response and then Elliott came down the stairs and Carol followed him down the stairs.
Q How did Elliott look?
A Very dishevelled, like he'd just got up out of bed.
Q How did Carol look?
A The same, very dishevelled and very unhappy.
Q Can you help us with how old Carol may have been at the time of this incident?
A I think she... she looked... it's a long time ago. I think she was about 12 or 13.

MR HAMPTON: Thank you, Mrs Thorpe. If you wait there, there'll be some more questions from the gentleman defending Mr Appleyard.

Cross-examined by Mr STOREY

Q Can you see and hear me all right, Mrs Thorpe?
A Yes, I can.
Q Good, all right. If that changes, please tell us.
A Okay.
Q You told us initially about a time when Carol came to see you at your house in Scissett?
A Yes.
Q Do you have any idea when that was?
A Well, what do you mean? The date?
Q Yes, the year, anything like that?
A No, no. It's over 30 years ago so, no, I don't remember.

Q You've told us you thought that she was about 19?

A Yes.

Q What is it that makes you think that that was... that was her age when she visited you?

A Because she was on about leaving home and, as far as I know, you don't leave home till after you're 18.

Q You said that you thought she was still living at her dad's in Denby Dale? Is that right?

A Yes, to the best of my memory, yeah.

Q Had she come to see you for a specific reason or was it just a chance, casual visit?

A She'd come for a specific reason because I had revealed that Elliott's sister, my mother, had sexually...

Q Well...

A ...abused me. I'd been to the police and she came to tell me that the same had happened to her. I think she came to give me a bit of support.

Q You say that she told you that her father had been abusing her?

A Yes.

Q That she'd told her mum? How did she react when you told her that she should go to see the police and tell them?

A She was very distressed at the time. She... I think she was taking it in, what I was saying, trying to take in what I was saying, the advice I was giving her, but she was very distressed at the time.

Q And did she give you any impression as to how long before the visit she'd told her mum about this?

A No.

Q You said you saw her a couple of weeks later with Paul?

A Yes.

Q That second visit, did you gather whether she was still living at the family home or whether she'd left by then?

A I think, because at the time I was also very distressed and getting... making arrangements to move house, so it's all a bit of a jumble what was happening with Carol and me at the same time.

Q So do you mean you didn't really get an idea when you saw her two weeks later with Paul?

A Idea about what?

Q About whether she was still at the family home.

A No, I'd no...

Q Yeah. At around that time was... how often would Carol visit you?

A Not very often.

Q And we know that you don't live in the Scissett area anymore. That's right, isn't it?

A No. Yeah.

Q Once you left Scissett, did you have much contact with Carol after that?

A I didn't have any contact with Carol after that.

Q You obviously made a statement to the police about what you've told us?

A Yes.

Q And I'm sure you'll have been shown a copy of that this morning whilst you're in court where you are?

A Yes, yes.

Q You won't remember the date that statement was made but I've got a copy of it in front of me, so I can tell you that was February 2016 when you made your statement to the police. All right?

A Okay, yeah.

Q Do you remember how it was you came to make your statement to the police?

A I made a statement because Carol got in touch with me daughter on the internet and asked if I would be prepared to make a statement.

Q And did you tell her you would?

A Yes, of course I would, yes.

Q Is that why the... did the police then contact you?

A Yes.

Q Did you speak to Carol yourself about giving a statement?

A I think me daughter gave her me phone number and she rung me up and asked, yes.

Q And did she tell you that she wanted you to give a statement?

A Yes.

Q Yeah, and did she tell you what she wanted you to give the statement about?

A About when she came to visit me those two times and what had been said and things and she also asked me if I remember anything about, you know, her childhood and if anything... if I'd seen anything.

Q And you told us that there was a time when you visited Denby Dale?

A Yes.

Q And you went to Elliott Appleyard's house and knocked on the door to no answer?

A Yeah.

Q Do you remember when that was?

A No, I don't. I don't remember the date. It's like over 30 years ago.

Q And how often would you visit Elliott Appleyard's house at around that time, Mrs Thorpe? Do you remember that?

A If I was in the area, I would pop in. I had reason to be in Denby Dale at the time so I thought I would pop in while I was in Denby Dale.

Q And you say you walked in and put the kettle on in the kitchen?

A Yes, I did.

Q Sorry? We didn't really hear what you said then. The sound broke up a bit.

A Yes, I did. I walked in and shouted, "Hello" a few times and put the kettle on. I thought, "Well, they won't be long because they've left the door unlocked".

Q Is that something you would do often in those days, walk into a relative's house and put the kettle on in the kitchen?

A If the door was unlocked, then I would assume that they weren't going to be long so, yes, I would.

Q You say that Elliott and Carol came downstairs looking dishevelled. Can you help us with what you mean by that?
A Well, they looked like when you first get up in a morning with your hair all over and your clothes all over, they looked like that.
Q Were they dressed?
A Yes.
Q Do you remember what they were wearing?
A No.
Q What was it about their clothes that you say looked dishevelled?
A Like they'd just got up, like their clothes was all creased and dishevelled and pulled out from their trousers and things, you know, the shirt, things like that.
Q You told the police when you made your witness statement that you didn't think anything of it at the time?
A I didn't, no.
Q So at the time it didn't look like anything had been going on, nothing to cause you any concern?
A It never entered me head to think anything. I was just saying, "Hello". I put the kettle on.
Q Is it the case that you've only thought something of it as a result of speaking to Carol?
A No. Carol hasn't influenced my... my memories.
Q I'm sorry. I... we couldn't hear that again, Mrs Thorpe.
A What Carol has said has not influenced my memories.
Q Do you remember what time of day it was that you'd arrived at Elliott Appleyard's house?
A It was afternoon.
Q Are you quite sure this has happened at all?
A Yeah, a hundred per cent certain, positive, yes.
Q How old were you, do you think, when this happened?
A About 33, 34.

Q Because I have to suggest, Mrs Thorpe, that there was never an occasion when you walked in uninvited and put the kettle on at Elliott Appleyard's house, in fact, was there?

A Is that a question? Sorry?

Q Well, I'm suggesting to you that that never actually happened.

A You can suggest all you want but it did happen.

Q And you certainly didn't see anything like Elliott Appleyard coming downstairs dishevelled followed by his daughter, Carol, in the same state, did you?

A Are you telling me or asking me?

Q I'm suggesting again. I'm asking you.

A I certainly did see that.

MR STOREY: Thank very much, Mrs Thorpe.

MR HAMPTON: I've nothing more, in fact.

JUDGE JAMESON: No? All right. Thank you very much indeed.

(The video-link was terminated)

(11.49 a.m.)

MR HAMPTON: Your Honour, I am sorry to have to ask, but before the next witness I am going to have to ask for around 20 to 30 minutes.

JUDGE JAMESON: Yes, all right. Well, shall we try and aim for quarter past 12?

MR HAMPTON: Yes.

JUDGE JAMESON: All right. Sorry about this, ladies and gentlemen. There is a reason for this. I need not trouble you with it. Counsel are doing the best they can to keep things going as fast as they reasonably can but about quarter past, we think. Thank you very much.

(The jury left court)

JUDGE JAMESON: Right. You need to be doing other things now?

MR HAMPTON: I do, really, yes.

JUDGE JAMESON: Yes, all right. Well, we'll deal with the matters that you raised over the weekend at some point but not necessarily, I think, at this stage.

MR HAMPTON: No, I don't think so, thank you.

JUDGE JAMESON: Okay, thank you.

(Short break)

(12.21 p.m.)

Miss DIANE LOUISE CROFT, Sworn

Examined by Mr HAMPTON

Q Good afternoon. Could you tell us your full name, please?
A Diane Louise Croft.
Q And your age?
A 49.
Q And your date of birth?
A 05/06/1969.
Q I'm going to ask you a number of questions. Should I call you Mrs Croft?
A Miss.
Q Miss Croft. Miss Croft, about your childhood. When giving your answers, would you keep your voice nice and loud, please?
A Yeah.
Q And, rather unusually, would you mind facing towards the jury...
A Yes.
Q ...straight on, so that they can see and hear you. You face straight on to them.
A Okay.
Q Don't worry about looking at me. I won't take any offence. All right?
A Yeah.
Q Okay. Ready to go?

A Yeah.

Q Good. Where did you attend primary school, Miss Croft?

A Gilthwaites First School.

Q And where's that?

A Denby Dale.

Q And secondary school?

A Scissett Middle School, and that's in Scissett.

Q Do you know a lady called Carol Higgins?

A I do.

Q Did you once know her as Carol Appleyard?

A Yes.

Q How did you know her?

A We were friends.

Q How did you come to be friends?

A Through school.

Q You're similar ages?

A We are, yes.

Q Did you both attend Gilthwaites First?

A Yes.

Q And Scissett Middle?

A Yes.

Q Did you know her father?

A Yes.

Q I want to ask you questions about when you were a child and you were ...and you knew Carol.

A Yeah.

Q Did she ever tell you anything about her father that sticks in your memory?

A She told me that her father was messing around with her.

Q What did you think she meant?

A I just thought "joking" around with her.

Q Did you ask her anything?

A Yes.

Q What did you ask?

A I asked her what she meant by “messing around”.

Q What did Carol say?

A Touching, kissing.

Q Did she give any other detail?

A No.

Q How old were you?

A Thirteen/fourteen.

Q Can you recall where you were when she said this?

A We were on a public bridleway, going for a walk.

Q Whereabouts was it?

A In Denby Dale, down near the river. The River Dearne.

Q Aged 13 or 14, what did you suggest you should do with that information?

A To tell an adult, preferably my parents.

Q Your parents?

A Yes.

Q What did you do?

A I to... Well, I took her back to my house and I told my parents.

Q Who was there when you told them?

A My mum and my dad.

Q Yourself?

A Yes.

Q Anyone else?

A Carol.

Q Can you help us with your mum and dad’s reaction?

A Shocked.

Q Was any action taken as a result of what you told your parents, that you’re aware of?

A I can’t remember.

Q Did you ...did the two of you remain together that day or did you split?

A We split. Her father came looking for her.

Q Where did she go?

A I guess back home.

Q So she left you...

A Yeah.

Q ...going somewhere?

A Yeah.

Q Did she leave on her own or with somebody else?

A I believe with her father.

Q Did you say anything to Mr Appleyard?

A No.

Q Do you know if your parents did?

A I don't know.

Q Where did Carol live?

A Gilthwaites Crescent.

Q Did that change?

A Yes.

Q How did it change?

A She went to live with her mum.

Q Did you know where?

A Cubley, Penistone.

Q Cubley in Penistone?

A Yeah.

JUDGE JAMESON: So, in relation to the incident you've told us about, Miss Croft, Carol going to live in Penistone, is that before or after that?

A It was after.

MR HAMPTON: So Carol going to Penistone was after the conversation?

A Yes.

Q Thank you. (After a pause) Thank you. Would you wait there, Mrs (sic) Croft?

A Yes.

Cross-examined by Mr STOREY

Q I want to just ask you a few questions, Mrs (sic) Croft, about your recollection of the conversation you've told us about.
A Yes.
Q Do you have any idea when it was that you had this conversation with Carol Appleyard?
A The year?
Q Any memory at all of when it might have been.
A Roughly, '83, '84. Eighty-three. Nineteen eighty-three.
Q You've told us you were on a public bridleway near the River Dearne?
A Yes.
Q What was it that led to her telling you this?
A I don't know.
Q Do you remember what you and she had been talking about before that might have prompted her to come out with this?
A No.
Q I don't need to know where you were living at the time, but was it far from where she was living?
A Not that far, no.
Q In the Denby Dale area?
A Yes.
Q And presumably close enough to walk between the two addresses?
A Yes.
Q When you told her that she should tell an adult, how did she respond to that?
A I'm sorry, I don't understand.
Q Well did she say anything?
A She was upset.
Q But when you said to her, "You should tell a grown-up," or...
A Yes.

Q ...words to that effect, did she say, "I know I should," or "I already have," or anything at all like that that you can remember?

A Oh, she agreed that it would be a good idea for us to tell my parents.

Q Do you remember discussing with her whether she should tell anybody else?

A The police.

Q That was discussed, was it?

A Mm.

Q Did she give you any idea of whether that had happened already, or not?

A No.

Q Or whether she would?

A No.

Q You say you told your parents and that Carol was present when you did that.

A Yes.

Q I take it it was you that actually said...

A Yes.

Q ...to your mum and dad what she'd told you?

A Yeah.

Q And that they were shocked. Do you remember what they said?

A I can't remember.

Q You said you couldn't remember if any action was taken. Is that something you've discussed with your parents since the time it happened in the early eighties?

A Yeah, but my family were currently grieving the loss of my brother.

Q This isn't in any way critical of anything that might or might not have been done, I'm just asking you whether you remember discussing with your parents what they had done or thought to do at the time.

A No.

Q And you said, essentially, that she then went home at some point later that night?

A Yes.

Q And did you continue to see her at school after that conversation and visit to your house?
A Not really, no. Just on and off. I was off school for quite a long period of time.
Q Presumably given what you've just told us?
A Yes.
Q And did you and Carol resume any contact in the eighties?
A We did later on, yes.
Q And is that how you came to learn that she'd gone to live in Cubley?
A Yes.
Q Did she say anything to you after that visit to your parents' house about what she'd said on the riverbank? Or the bridleway, I'm sorry.
A No.
Q Nothing at all?
A No.
Q You obviously came to speak to the police about your recollection.
A Yeah.
Q And you gave them a witness statement...
A Yes.
Q ...which you've presumably been shown today?
A Yes.
Q And you probably won't remember the date at the top of it?
A I don't, no.
Q Well I can tell you. It was 19 January 2018, so almost exactly a year ago.
A Okay.
Q I think it's right, isn't it, that Carol contacted you three months or so before you gave that statement?
A Yes.
Q October 2017, or thereabouts?
A Somewhere round there, yes.
Q And that was the first contact you'd had with her since you were teenagers?

A Yes.

Q And you certainly told the police that she'd come to your place of work.

A Yes.

Q And did she also contact you by phone around that time as well?

A Yes.

Q And when she spoke with you, did you and she talk about your memories of times when you were teenagers?

A Yes.

Q And did she tell you why she was coming to visit you?

A Yes.

Q And might it be, Miss Croft, that you've picked up your recollection of that conversation in the eighties from what Carol said to you in October 2017?

A Yes.

Q And that what you've remembered is in fact something that might've been planted in your mind by that conversation, or those conversations?

A No.

Q You've told us you remember the phone call. Was there just the one or were there a number of phone calls from Carol Higgins, as she then was ...now is?

A Just the one.

Q Just the one. Were you aware that that call was recorded?

A No.

Q Do you remember the sort of things you discussed in that phone call?

A No.

Q Do you remember telling Carol that: "We all need to get together privately without the fucking coppers knowing"?

A No.

Q Or telling her: "We need to speak to a lawyer to see if we can do it without him knowing"?

A No.

Q And that: "We need to nail the bugger"?

A No.

Q Are you saying you don't remember or that those things weren't said?
A I don't remember saying them things.
Q Okay. Might it be that you and Carol were getting your heads together precisely "to nail the bugger"?
A No.
Q Thank you, Miss Croft. There's nothing else.

Re-examined by Mr HAMPTON

Q You don't recall that conversation?
A No.
Q Just one matter. Do I understand it correctly - I don't wish to cause upset - but you lost your brother...
A Yes.
Q ...around the time Carol said this to you?
A Yes.
Q Thank you. Does your Honour have any questions?

JUDGE JAMESON: No. Thank you very much indeed.

MR HAMPTON: Could I ask that the witness remain in the witness waiting room?

THE WITNESS: Yes.

MR HAMPTON: Thank you.

THE WITNESS: Thank you.

JUDGE JAMESON: All right. Thank you very much indeed. If you'd...

THE WITNESS: Thank you.

JUDGE JAMESON: ...just like to go with the usher now, please. Thank you.

(The witness withdrew)

(12.37 p.m.)

21st January 2019 – Day 5

Police Sergeant ALEX WILSON, sworn

Examined by Mr HAMPTON

Q Name, rank and number, please, officer.
A It's Alex Wilson. I'm a police sergeant and my collar number is 6496.
Q Which police station are you based at?
A Based at Heckmondwike Police Station.
Q Heckmondwike?
A Yes.
Q You are the officer in the case in relation to this investigation?
A I am, that's correct.
Q The investigation that has led to these proceedings?
A Yes, that's correct.
Q That means, that title, "officer in the case", that you have overall responsibility for the investigation of the case?
A Yes.
Q So, you follow lines of inquiry?
A Yes.
Q Wherever they may lead you?
A Yes.
Q You are involved in gathering evidence?
A Yes.
Q And you are involved in obtaining accounts from witnesses?
A Yes.
Q And I think you were involved on one occasion in interviewing the defendant about the allegations?
A Yes.
Q I think you became involved in this inquiry around September 2015?
A That's correct.
Q You were aware, of course, that this was a historic matter dating back to the mid-1980s?

A Yes.

Q I think you made a number of inquiries relating to documentation that may have existed at the time. Is that correct?

A Yes.

Q I think you made inquiries with the relevant departments of West Yorkshire Police regarding whether any papers that may be in – whether there were any papers that may be in existence relating to the original complaint by Carol Higgins, then Appleyard?

A Yes.

Q And you were told there was nothing in the archives?

A No, that's correct.

Q I think there's a force policy about allegations such as this.

A There is, yes.

Q And what is that?

A I think there was a rule change, I think, that cases relating to this, the records were destroyed after 10 years, legally, back at that time.

Q Back in the day?

A Yes.

Q So, 10 years after the allegation...

A They were destroyed.

Q ...the records destroyed by way of force policy?

A Yes.

Q I think you also physically searched various archives of various police stations?

A That's correct.

Q And did you find anything?

A I didn't. Initially we searched, obviously, under the name, "Appleyard", because that's what – and Carol Higgins, obviously, because that's what the victim had reported.

Q You searched under all relevant surnames?

A Yes.

Q And I think you made similar inquiries with the Crown Prosecution Service archives?
A Yes.
Q But I think they also had a similar policy at the time?
A That's correct.
Q I think you were also aware that Carol Higgins had reported some physical examination at the police station in the mid-1980s?
A Yes.
Q And you made inquiries with the scientific support service?
A Yes, that's correct.
Q But again, no records?
A And no records, no.
Q You, I think, did obtain with the assistance of Carol Higgins, some historic medical and counselling records?
A That's correct.
Q You also, as I understand it, made inquiries with Kirklees Social Care Department?
A Yes, that's correct.
Q So, the Social Services Department. It would have been the relevant department at the time?
A Yes.
Q And you asked if they had retained any records pertaining to the family for the relevant time period?
A That's correct.
Q And again none were held?
A None were held.
Q And as I understand it, you made similar inquiries with the Schools Educational Department?
A Yes.
Q For the relevant timeframe?
A Yes.

Q And was anything...

A And some of those inquiries were conducted after by DS Bellhouse but yes, nothing was located.

Q That is all I have for you for now, PC Wilson.

A Okay.

Q The next stage, your Honour, would be to deal with the interviews with the defendant.

JUDGE JAMESON: Yes.

MR HAMPTON: I know that they were agreed between myself and Mr Storey and I think they're probably being printed, but I wonder if we could – in the process of printing...

JUDGE JAMESON: Yes.

MR HAMPTON: ...start that at two o'clock?

JUDGE JAMESON: Yes, all right. Can we do anything useful at this stage?

MR HAMPTON: Yes, I think we could in the time we have.

JUDGE JAMESON: Yes, all right. Thank you very much. Right, ladies and gentlemen. I am sorry, this is rather a bitty day for you but there it is. Two o'clock, thank you.

(The jury left court)

JUDGE JAMESON: Right, thank you very much, officer. We'll see you again at two o'clock. Thank you very much.

(The witness withdrew)

MR HAMPTON: I am in your Honour's hands, really. There are two matters.

JUDGE JAMESON: Yes.

MR HAMPTON: There is the bad character matter, which won't take very long at all.

JUDGE JAMESON: Yes. Well, I would have thought that is perhaps best. Subject to anything Mr Storey may say, Mr Storey would probably want to know what the ruling is before a decision is made about Mr Appleyard giving evidence, or Mr Appleyard giving evidence.

MR STOREY: That would assist.

JUDGE JAMESON: Yes, well can I just ask you this, Mr Hampton. Are there any details about these convictions?

MR HAMPTON: No.

JUDGE JAMESON: Nothing, no. Well, I think in those circumstances at least at present there is simply not enough to make it sufficiently relevant.

MR HAMPTON: I follow.

JUDGE JAMESON: It is still a matter that can potentially be explored evidentially and of course circumstances could change, but as they presently are, I wouldn't let that in.

MR HAMPTON: We understand, thank you, and the defence understand our position if things were to develop.

JUDGE JAMESON: Yes, right so that's that. Now, the indictment.

MR HAMPTON: Yes.

JUDGE JAMESON: I don't know what Mr Storey's position about this is, so perhaps unwisely I'll just say what I think at the moment. I agree, I think in theory, it's probably a very good idea to take out concerns about which particular year it was, unless there is some specific purpose for them being in, which could either arise out of a time, a relevant time limit in relation to the count itself – I don't think that applies to any of the ones you are speaking of...

MR HAMPTON: No.

JUDGE JAMESON: ...or, for that matter in the event of any conviction an alteration in the approach that one might take to sentencing, but again I don't think that arises, does it?

MR HAMPTON: That's how we understood it, yes.

JUDGE JAMESON: Yes, all right. So, on the face of it, the general approach seems to me likely to be helpful to the jury. I didn't totally understand from your note exactly what it was you – well, I did understand but I wasn't sure I quite followed the logic behind the suggestion of altering the dates from counts two to six and then having not guilty verdicts. I don't think that's a good idea.

MR HAMPTON: All right. I was struggling, to be honest, which is probably why the logic isn't there.

JUDGE JAMESON: Yes.

MR HAMPTON: It seemed to me that there was a risk of those later counts then being duplicitous or a repetition of what the jury would be deciding once I've amended the earlier counts to reflect the 13 to 14...

JUDGE JAMESON: Well, let's just have a look at...

MR HAMPTON: That was my concern.

JUDGE JAMESON: ...the indictment itself. I've got the existing indictment. I've got a hard copy here.

MR HAMPTON: Yes. So, it's really trying to cure that.

JUDGE JAMESON: Shall we just look through it together? So, count one...

MR HAMPTON: Yes.

JUDGE JAMESON: ...it is probably helpful that there is some indication of date there but again, is that actually relevant?

MR HAMPTON: I don't think the dates are a problem for count one.

JUDGE JAMESON: Unless, of course, I mean it could be relevant whether it's above or under 13 but before or after 13, not from the point of view, I think of – I'd have to remind myself, to be honest, whether it actually matters from the point of view of the charge, but it potentially could matter to the approach to sentencing in the event of conviction.

MR HAMPTON: It could. Well, I'll check that.

JUDGE JAMESON: So, I do see that if you want that to be under 13, then it has to remain as it is.

MR HAMPTON: Yes.

JUDGE JAMESON: So, the idea then is counts two to six you simply extend that to be two years.

MR HAMPTON: Yes.

JUDGE JAMESON: Yes.

MR HAMPTON: And then I have to say I was struggling with how to approach seven to 10.

JUDGE JAMESON: Well, I think two issues arise here. Firstly, on the face of it, is there any reason why they shouldn't simply have their dates amended in the same way subject to the question of whether that is overloading the indictment. The second question is given that it's all very well describing a count as a specimen count, and it's helpful to the jury to understand what's meant by that, but this is said to be on any occasion that they see a specimen account, a specimen of a kind of behaviour having happened on more than one occasion. But, of course, one has to bear in mind that in the event of convictions, they are convictions only for what's on the indictment; not for anything else.

MR HAMPTON: Yes, we had considered that.

JUDGE JAMESON: We can't then say, "Well, I'm going to sentence you on the basis that you did this dozens of times, or hundreds of times", because that's not omitted and it hasn't been proved---

MR HAMPTON: We follow that.

JUDGE JAMESON: ...by the indictment so I think you want to – you will want to consider whether or not counts two to six are a sufficient representation of what you are alleging or whether really counts two to 10, is it...

MR HAMPTON: We'd be losing if we were to follow this course, seven to 10 – counts, seven to 10.

JUDGE JAMESON: Yes, exactly.

MR HAMPTON: So, still we'd have...

JUDGE JAMESON: But counts seven to 10 could simply have their dates altered to exactly the same dates as counts two to six, so it would have to be a slight change to the way in which the particulars were...

MR HAMPTON: I think that's what I'm struggling with, because I'm struggling as to how we could differentiate those counts from two to six once we'd extended the age on two to six without making it quite confusing.

JUDGE JAMESON: Well...

MR HAMPTON: But balancing that against, your Honour rightly made there...

JUDGE JAMESON: Well, let's have a look. Counts two to three are two allegations of rape which would become, if your amendment is permitted, and of course, this is all subject to hearing, of course, from Mr Storey, so that would be simply two instances...

MR HAMPTON: Yes.

JUDGE JAMESON: ...at ages 13 to 14.

MR HAMPTON: Yes.

JUDGE JAMESON: And count seven – it's a matter entirely for you but count seven, if the dates were changed to the same date, that simply makes it three occasions instead of two. I'm not entirely clear I understand what the difficulty is that you were wrestling with. I may have missed something.

MR HAMPTON: I think it's because they were both specimen counts designed to cover a multiplicity, the same behaviour again and again.

JUDGE JAMESON: Yes.

MR HAMPTON: So, I was concerned it wouldn't...-

JUDGE JAMESON: Well, the direction would have to be along the lines, wouldn't it, if it was once – if it was no times at all, of course, not guilty on all counts.

MR HAMPTON: Yes.

JUDGE JAMESON: If they were sure that it had happened and that all the constituent ingredients of rape were proved but they weren't sure it had happened more than once when she was 13 or 14 then it's guilty count two, not guilty counts three and seven. If they were satisfied it was at least twice, two and three – but not more than that, two and three but not seven. If they're sure it's three or more, two, three and seven. I don't actually see a difficulty with that, so it's really a question of how many counts representing each individual kind of allegation should be on the indictment and whether you would be satisfied, in the event of adverse findings, that there were only two.

MR HAMPTON: Well, your Honour elucidates how we get round the problem very clearly and very logically, if I may say, that I anticipated we would have. So, subject to my now change of position reflecting the fairness of matters...

JUDGE JAMESON: But can we just look, before we move on and before I ask Mr Storey for his position about this, let me just check exactly how this fits in with, for example, while we're just looking at rape, allegations of rape...

MR HAMPTON: Yes.

JUDGE JAMESON: ...count 11. Count 15 is straightforward enough because that's a specific allegation.

MR HAMPTON: Yes.

JUDGE JAMESON: And the jury either will accept that that happened or they won't.

MR HAMPTON: Yes.

JUDGE JAMESON: And in those circumstances, in relation to that, there's probably no relevance to the date at all.

MR HAMPTON: For count – the last count?

JUDGE JAMESON: Fifteen.

MR HAMPTON: I agree.

JUDGE JAMESON: But just help me with count 11, which speaks of it being a specimen, but at a time when – between 1984 and 1985.

MR HAMPTON: Mm hm.

JUDGE JAMESON: If that remains as it is, then there is an issue about Carol Higgins' age.

MR HAMPTON: Yes.

JUDGE JAMESON: And all counts, two, five and seven, the jury would need to be sure they were not later than the amended later date, which I think would become – would that become 15 then?

MR HAMPTON: No, that would be 14.

JUDGE JAMESON: It's...

MR HAMPTON: It's still 14, yes.

JUDGE JAMESON: 2014, I'm talking about. Sorry, would that become 1985? Forgive me, I don't just have your proposal up on screen at the moment. I can get it easily enough. I mean, is there going to be a difference, I suppose is what I'm really saying...

MR HAMPTON: There will be.

JUDGE JAMESON: ...between the dates in counts – other things being equal, which they may not be, but we'll see. I said two, five and seven. I meant two, three and seven, of course. Would there be any distinction in date between two, three and seven and count 11?

MR HAMPTON: Your Honour is quite right, there would. There would. The same problem would still exist.

JUDGE JAMESON: I don't think it would be helpful to have one...

MR HAMPTON: No.

JUDGE JAMESON: ...because then you are getting yourself back into the problem...

MR HAMPTON: Where we were earlier on.

JUDGE JAMESON: --that you are trying to avoid by changing the dates in counts two, three and seven.

MR HAMPTON: Yes.

JUDGE JAMESON: So, is there really any need for there to be any distinction? You just need to decide, I think, how many counts alleging each particular type of behaviour you actually want and then have them all with the same dates, and I'm not even sure that it would be sensible to have different dates for count 15, would it?

MR HAMPTON: No. I think, following your Honour's logic, the proper course would perhaps be to change two to 15, counts two to 15, from ages 13 to 15.

JUDGE JAMESON: Yes, and if they are between 13 and 15, you wouldn't even necessarily have to have it starting at 13 provided it was clearly understood, and it would have to be that if there was an indeterminate earlier start date it could not be said that it had been proven because it clearly wouldn't be, that anything had happened under 13 if the jury was sure anything had happened at all.

MR HAMPTON: Yes.

JUDGE JAMESON: But I don't think it's actually necessary to have a start date like that provided that it's absolutely clear that there could never be a sentence based on it having been earlier than 13.

MR HAMPTON: Mm hm.

JUDGE JAMESON: With the exception of course, of count one, I'm talking about allegations of rape.

MR HAMPTON: Yes, two to 15 would read something along the lines of, "at an age before 15 years", and with a date.

JUDGE JAMESON: Yes, something like that but of course it would have to finish at 15 otherwise – well, I say it would have to finish. Of course, in the allegations of rape, consent is a relevant issue but for all the allegations of indecent assault, it isn't, provided, of course, that there's no allegation that it happened after 16. So, there would have to be the cut-off date on the day before her 16th birthday.

MR HAMPTON: Yes. Yes.

JUDGE JAMESON: Right. So, that's a possible way forward for all of those matters. Now, the other issue – again I still have to come back to Mr Storey, but just before I do, the other issue, of course, is whether or not the indecent assault counts are well founded in relation to the allegation of masturbation.

MR HAMPTON: Yes.

JUDGE JAMESON: Again, ultimately, it seems to me that that is really not a matter that I should be intervening in. You are entitled to put the case any way you choose and Mr Storey's remedy, if he has one, is to make a submission if he thinks that that will succeed in relation to those counts.

MR HAMPTON: Yes.

JUDGE JAMESON: So, I don't think I really propose to say anything more about that.

MR HAMPTON: Not at this stage, no. I simply flag that because Mr Storey was kind enough to flag it with me.

JUDGE JAMESON: All right, okay. So, Mr Storey, what I think it really comes down to is whether there's any injustice in amending the dates, essentially, so that they are no longer really relevant.

MR STOREY: No. As a general proposition I agree that that must be right. It doesn't affect the allegations, therefore more substance, and it doesn't prejudice the defendant in any way. Can I reserve my position though...

JUDGE JAMESON: Of course.

MR STOREY: ...until I've seen the final form the prosecution wish to put forward as an amended indictment...

JUDGE JAMESON: Yes.

MR STOREY: ...before I decide whether I need to comment further?

JUDGE JAMESON: Yes, quite. Okay, well that's fine. No, I entirely understand that position. Let's see what Mr Hampton comes up with.

MR STOREY: Certainly.

JUDGE JAMESON: All right, but I do think that there really must be a fixed and nailed down indictment before – not necessarily even before you have closed your case, actually, but certainly before the prosecution start theirs.

MR HAMPTON: Yes, I'll start work on it over lunch and it shouldn't take too long.

JUDGE JAMESON: Okay.

MR HAMPTON: Thank you.

JUDGE JAMESON: Two o'clock then.

(Adjourned for a short time)

JUDGE JAMESON: Could I just ask, Mr Storey – you mustn't, of course, tell me anything you prefer not to, but just because it may be that the jury will be in at a time when I need to talk about timetabling, assuming that we finish the prosecution case today, which I trust we will achieve...

MR HAMPTON: Well, other than the technical matters to do with the dates and one or two agreed facts.

JUDGE JAMESON: Yes, so we're not therefore going to be starting your case until tomorrow at the earliest. How long do you think it might last? I understand the difficulties of saying that.

MR STOREY: Yes. I obviously have no way of knowing how long my learned friend is going to be in cross-examination.

JUDGE JAMESON: No.

MR STOREY: There is no secret, there's no mystery. The defendant, as I understand it, is going to be giving evidence.

JUDGE JAMESON: Yes, I would imagine that he would, although it must, of course, be his choice.

MR STOREY: Yes, I would have thought...

JUDGE JAMESON: And then other evidence?

MR STOREY: Potentially one other witness...

JUDGE JAMESON: Yes.

MR STOREY: ...who will not be long. He, however, I could see taking the lion's share of the day tomorrow.

JUDGE JAMESON: Yes, so it's likely that the evidence will be finished if not tomorrow, at least not late on Wednesday?

MR STOREY: Yes.

JUDGE JAMESON: Well, early on Wednesday, I would think, reasonably?

MR STOREY: Yes.

JUDGE JAMESON: So, we should get in speeches and at least a start on the summing-up with luck on Wednesday, so...

MR STOREY: I would have thought at least a start, yes.

JUDGE JAMESON: Yes.

MR STOREY: It may be that we finish the evidence tomorrow...

JUDGE JAMESON: Yes, okay. Yes, that's fine, good. So, we're still on target?

MR STOREY: Yes.

JUDGE JAMESON: Good. Thank you very much. Yes, the jury, please, thank you.

(The jury entered court)

JUDGE JAMESON: Yes?

MR HAMPTON: We were just about to turn to, your Honour and members of the jury, interviews with the defendant and before I hand out transcripts of the relevant parts of those interviews, I just want you, officer, to help us with a few general matters. It's right, isn't it, that Mr Appleyard attended Dewsbury Police Station for interview on two occasions?

A That's correct.

Q And when a person attends the police station for interview, he's assessed by a custody officer independent of the investigation to ensure that he's fit and well?

A He was invited in for voluntary attendance so...

Q So, perhaps they didn't occur?

A Yes.

Q There were no concerns as to his fitness or understand of the matters?

A No, in fact he did attend before – I think there was actually a third occasion he initially attended but was ill and obviously he couldn't come...

Q So, it was re-arranged?

A So, it was re-arranged, yes.

Q And he would be given advice as to his legal rights?

A That's correct.

Q Regarding his right to free and independent legal representation?

A Yes.

Q His right to private consultation with his lawyers at any time?

A Yes.

Q Including during the interview if he required a break?

A That's correct.

Q And was there any disclosure in this case of what he was to be asked about?

A Yes.

Q So, that would be provided to his legal representative in shorthand format?

A Yes, yes.

Q And the interviews are recorded?

A They are.

Q Could you tell us about the recording procedure, please?

A It's a digital recording device. What do you mean, sorry?

Q It used to be tape...

A It used to be tape, yes.

Q And then it used to be DVDs.

A It's just digitally recorded. It's a case that we set it up on a computer in another office and it generates the interview which has a unique digital reference code, which then gets sent down to the machine. It's a simple case of starting, pressing the button, start the machine and stopping at the conclusion of the interview.

Q And then if anybody wants to have a copy, a copy can be made?

A That's correct.

Q And written documents can be produced from the digital recording?

A Yes.

Q Thank you very much. If we turn to the first interview, then, which will be 21 December, I think...

JUDGE JAMESON: Now, ladies and gentlemen, you are going to get copies of these. These are obviously your documents, so if you want to mark them or note them in any way, please feel free to do so. (Same handed to the jury)

MR HAMPTON: We will set about reading these into the record then, officer.

A Okay.

Q The person interviewed was Elliott Appleyard. The place of interview was Dewsbury Police Station, the date 21 December 2015. The interview lasted two hours between 1139 a.m. and 13:13, 1.39 p.m. The interviewing officers were PC Wilson. Is that you?

A That's correct.

Q And DC Brear, and Mr Appleyard was represented by Mr Danny Maloney, his solicitor.

I will deal with, officer, all the summarised parts and the questions by the officers. Could you deal with the defendant's actual replies?

A Yes.

Q So, formal introductions were made by people present. It was explained that there was an investigation into an offence of rape of a child, which occurred between January 1981 and January 1985, the victim being his daughter, Carol Higgins. The defendant was reminded of his legal entitlements and we've discussed those.

A Yes.

Q The caution was administered and explained fully. Could you help us with that, please?

A Yes, if you're cautioned, so the caution is, "You do not have to say anything, but it may harm your defence if you do not mention when questioned something which you later rely on in court. Anything you do say may be given in evidence". I generally break it down into three stages, the first part being, "Your right is you do not have to say anything", but I always ask them to reply "no" – say, "no comment" or "no reply", and then at least I know that they've understood the...

Q So, you break down the caution?

A Yes, I break it down.

Q Explain it?

A Yes.

Q And ensure that the defendant understood?

A Yes.

Q "Did you rape Carol Higgins?"

A "No, I did not".

Q "Have you ever engaged in any sort of sexual activity with Carol Higgins?"

A "No, I have not".

Q "What can you tell me about why you are sat here today about this allegation?"

A “I’ve no idea. I can only – the only thing that I can think of is peer pressure from her mother. Her mother and me – I kicked her mother out and that was in ’82 and, so you stated that the allegations were from ‘81 to ‘85 and that’s impossible because I was with her mother until ’82, late ’82, and in ’84 I was living with my present wife, and Carol was not with me. If there’s any allegations to be made of rape, it’s got to be between ’82 when the mother left and ’84.”

Q “So, as I understand it rightly, the allegations – there was an allegation previously made. What can you tell me about that sort of time and what happened?”

A “I can’t remember anything what happened in ’84 at that interview. I can’t remember any questions that was asked of me.”

Q “So, let’s go back to the beginning then. So, that time, tell me about your family at that time. So, what did your family comprise of when you were with Carol and Carol’s mum? Who was in the family?”

A “Up to ’82 there was myself, her mother, Carol, Paul and Donna Marie, who is now deceased.”

Q The defendant confirmed that Donna Marie was the eldest, then Carol, and Paul was the youngest. It was clarified Carol’s mum is called Margaret Jean, and the defendant stated that he did not have any contact with Margaret Jean now. “So, generally, at that time, how was family life when you were all living together?”

A “I got on well with the kids. I didn’t get on too much too well with their mother. As I say, she was having affairs behind my back and then one Friday I was going to work on a Friday, one Friday morning, and I told her it was payday, but she wasn’t having none. When I got home I said, ‘I want to see you gone’. I says, ‘You can take what you want and if the kids want to go with you, they can go with you. If they want to stay with me, they can stay with me’, and when I got home, she’d gone.”

Q “What sort of year would that have been when she’d left?”

A “That was ‘82”.

Q “1982. So, when she left on that occasion, then, had she – was that the end of the relationship? Did she come back?”

A “No, no, no, no, no. It ended the relationship as far as I was concerned, but not as far as she was concerned. She was – she’s an evil bitch.”

Q The defendant stated they were married for approximately seven years getting married in 1975. “So, when she’s left the house, who did that leave in the house with you? Who was living with you at the house?”

A “Donna Marie went with her, for a start, and Carol and Paul stayed with me, and then after a few weeks, Donna went to her mum’s and Carol came back to me.”

Q “Sorry, did you say that all the children went with her originally?”

A “No, Donna Marie – Donna Marie stayed with, went back with her and Carol, and Paul stayed with me and then Donna Marie came back to me for a few weeks and Carol went to her mother. I ended up with the two of them.”

Q “So, Carol left?”

A “Yes.”

Q “And so when Carol left, how did she – was that permanent? Did Carol leave permanently?”

A “No, no, no. She went to her mum’s for a few weeks, a month or so, and then she came back to me and Donna went with her mum”.

Q “So, why did Carol leave?”

A “They had the choice. They could go where they wanted. They could go with their mum and they could stop with me”.

Q “And Carol – there wasn’t any reason why she left then? Did she ever give you an explanation?”

A “Not as far as I’m concerned, no, no, no, no. Got no explanation whatsoever. They had their choice to go where they wanted with who they wanted.”

Q “She returned sometime after that?”

A “Yes”.

Q “And what was her reasons for returning? Can you remember?”

A “No, didn’t give any reasons. Sometimes she didn’t get on with her mum or she didn’t agree with her mum, that her mum wouldn't buy her this, that or the other, so she came back to me. If she had a fall out with me for whatever reason, and I put my foot down or something, she’d go back to her mum”.

Q “And then how would you describe, obviously, your relationship with your children, when obviously you’ve been separated?”

A “Paul, he was like a shadow to me, he was. I took him shooting, went camping, did everything, learnt to drive. Got him a motorbike and that, a scramble bike. He was like a shadow. He stayed with me until he was 18 year old.”

Q “And Carol, how was your relationship with Carol?”

A “Carol, as I say, she was coming backwards and forward all the time”.

Q “At that age – how old would she have been at that age when she came back?”

A “Thirteen, 14 year old”.

Q “So, when you say she was 13 and she was coming and going as she pleased, how did that come about, because obviously she was only a child at that age.”

A “Well, as I say, if she was getting her own way with her mother and that, she’d come back to me. If she didn’t get her own way with me, she went back to her mum”.

Q “And where were you living at this time? What address were you living at?”

A “26 Gilthwaites Crescent, Denby Dale.”

Q “And do you still live there now?”

A “Yes”.

Q The defendant described the house as a three-bedroomed, semi-detached. “In terms of when you were living at that time, where did you sleep in that house? Which was your bedroom at the time?”

A “Front bedroom.”

Q “Where did Carol – did Carol have her own bedroom?”

A “Carol had her own bedroom and Paul had his own bedroom.”

Q “And did they always sleep in their own bedroom?”

A “Yes.”

Q “Sleep in their own beds? What about Donna? Did Donna have a bedroom?”

A “Donna slept with Carol when they were together, but it wasn’t often they was together because Donna went to mother’s and stayed with her mother.”

Q “Did any of the children ever sleep in the same bed as you?”

A “No.”

Q Would there be any occasion or any reason why any of them would go into your room to sleep?”

A “They didn’t come into my room to sleep. What they did, as I was working all week and because I was working all week and many a time on a Saturday morning, Sunday was the only day that I didn’t work, so sometimes when I was laid in bed, they’d come in. Both Carol and Paul would come in and jump in bed at the side of me and we’d discuss what we were going to do, what we were going to do today. ‘What do you fancy doing today?’ – talk about whether we were going off or whether we’d go somewhere for a meal or what we’d have, what we wanted to do. It was just something we did. Didn’t do it every week. It was just on occasions when they came, both came and jumped into bed to discuss what we were doing with dad.”

Q “Would there be any occasion – I know you’ve just said that Paul and Carol would both come and jump in bed with you and talk about what you were going to do and what plans you’ve got – can you remember any occasion when it was just Carol?”

A “No.”

Q “So, moving on to Carol, tell me about Carol. What was she like when she was growing up? What was she like as a child? Start off when she was a child. What was she like?”

A “As a child, fine. Her mother used to say she could wrap me round her little finger and she often said that and – because if she couldn’t get her own way with her mum, she’d come to me, daddy’s little girl, sort of thing, and then as she got older it was a case of because she’d been that way, she’d be – it’d be

– it were, 'notice me', and she always wanted to be centre of attention and one thing and another."

Q "In about 1984, Carol would have been about 15 years old."

A "Yes."

Q "What was she like at that time?"

A "Typical 15-year-old girl. She wanted to be seen and she was wanting the best clothes and wanting the sort of things that teenagers wanted".

Q "And were you aware if she had any boyfriends or…"

A "In 1983 I went on a hunting trip to America, once in a lifetime job with a friend of mine. Carol and Paul was with me at the time. They were supposed to stay with my sister who lived a mile-and-a-half down the road and they were staying there until I came back after a couple of week. Apparently, they all went to school together. She'd thrown a party and an orgy in the house. They drunk all the beer that I'd got in there, the whiskies and that, that I'd got in there. They'd put cold tea in some bottles, put water in other bottles that were gin and things. I went to and found out who these lads and these people were and went and knocked on every one of them's doors and told their parents what had been going off and I says, 'You owe me a tenner for all the booze that you've supped', and 99 of the parents, and that, they were shocked and they actually paid up. I went back, I had a fall out and told Carol if there was any more of it she'd be on her bike, same as her mother and that was it, and just after that she did go."

Q "What year did you say that was? That was about?"

A "That was '83".

Q "So, at that time she was living at the house with you and Paul?"

A "Yes".

Q "So, immediately after that you said she left and went to live with her mum"?

A "She did."

Q "What was the reason behind her going to live with her mum at that time?"

A "Well, basically, because I'd given her a rollicking and I wasn't having that carry-on in my house, she'd lied, she'd deceived me. She lied to my sister.

She told my sister she was going to stay with friends and she hadn't. She'd gone to the house that weekend and had a party in the house."

Q "So when you spent any time with Carol – so you said she was a difficult teenager, so up until when she was about 13, how would you describe your relationship with her? What sort of things would you do as father and daughter?"

A "Not a lot, really. She claims that I used to take her shooting and one thing and another, hunting and that, and I didn't. She might have gone with me one time, but that was – that was only, it was Paul that was with me. Paul, as I say – Paul was like a shadow. I took him shooting and showed him a lot of field craft and one thing and another, but Carol certainly didn't."

Q "So, you didn't take Carol regularly?"

A "No".

Q "Would there be any occasion where you ever took Carol with you alone, just you two, for instance? Was there any reason why you'd take her on her own?"

A "If, when I was going shooting, if she wanted to come with me, tag along and that, yeah, the odd occasion but it was very, very, rare occasions".

Q "I understand that Carol then moved, didn't she? She moved to live temporarily with her mother in Penistone. Is that right?"

A "That's right."

Q "What was the impact on you and the rest of the family when she left?"

A "It didn't bother me. I just wasn't having that sort of thing going off in my house, so it didn't bother me. She'd gone. Paul decided if he wanted to stay with his dad."

Q "When there was you, Carol and Paul all living together as far as housekeeping and things like that, who took on that role?"

A "Nobody took on the role. I did in a way but there was many a time Carol, when she was there, she'd try to make a meal or something. Sometimes we went out for meals, went to the pub for a meal. Sometimes she'd start making a meal and that."

Q “What about cleaning and washing and stuff like that?”

A “She wanted to clean up and that there” – sorry. “They were supposed to clean up and they were supposed to make – keep their own bedrooms tidy. If she wanted to clean up and that there, I used to ask her to clean up. She was home. She was supposed to come home from school.”

Q The complainant’s allegation that the defendant struck her with a belt was put. Question: “Did you have any belts you’d ever use?”

A “I did have belts, yes. I’ve got a belt on now.”

Q “And did you ever use them?”

A “When they were children, if they’d done wrong, I did it. It was a way that I was brought up and that to me, you know it instilled discipline. What you could do 30 years or so, 40 years ago, you couldn’t possibly do now.”

Q “You said that when she was growing up that you’d take her for walks and she would help break into skips for scrap metal, that she would then in turn take to Barnsley flea market to sell.”

A “Rubbish.”

Q “She said at one point you stopped taking her brother Paul on the walks so it was just her and you.”

A “No, I did not.”

Q The complainant’s allegation that the defendant had kissed her like an adult whilst on walks, aged 12, 11 to 12, was put. “Did you start kissing her?”

A “The only time that I kissed Carol or Paul was in an affectionate way as a father would kiss any child.”

Q “She told her mum Jean, who in turn told you, and she says that this was the reason why she’s ended up leaving home with her mum. Does that ring any – does that jog any memories?”

A “No, I don’t ever, ever recall that conversation or anything like that”.

Q “Do you ever remember meeting Carol at Barnsley Market with her boyfriend, David?”

A “No.”

Q “She says that she returned back to Denby Dale to live with you after about six to eight months of leaving and she says that you bought her a bikini and a pair of jeans. Do you ever recall that?”

A “I bought most of her clothes anyway, so whatever it was, whether it was swimming costume or whether it was a pair of jeans or whether it was a top, I bought most of her clothes. I was working. Her mother wasn’t.”

Q “And she recalls that when she moved back at that time, you were going out with a female called Jess at the time”.

A “I don’t recall of anybody – any girl called Jess”.

Q “You’ve never gone out with anybody by that name or...

A “No. What year was that?”

Q “She doesn’t say what year because she can’t exactly say.”

A “Right.”

Q “She says that you would playfight with her and that you started to give her love bites on her neck.”

A “No, I did not.”

Q “And she recalls that you went to America. Is that the same hunting trip that you made reference to?”

A “Yes.”

Q The defendant stated they went in November until December 1983 to America. “She said that whilst you were in America, they had a party at your house and her mum returned back home and took some furniture from the house, and that when you returned back home, you were furious.”

A “I did what I’ve told you.”

Q “She says there was an incident – she can’t remember the full details – that she took a knife from the drawer and she slit her wrists and at that time you told her that she was mentally disturbed and that she had to sleep in bed with you.”

A “Definitely not.”

Q The allegation of the first occasion was then put. “She states that she’d asked you at the time what her grandad would say.”

A “I think it’s disgusting, the fact that she’s brought her grandad into this because her grandad died in 1977 and when he died in ’77, he’d been living at Shelley for about 18 month prior to that so she’d only be five or six years old when he died. She wouldn't recall anything about her grandad whatsoever.”

Q “Was there an occasion – did you ever – did that happen?”

A “No.”

Q “Did you get a condom out of a drawer and did you have sex with her?”

A “No.”

Q “She says the sexual abuse continued from there and she states that her brother, Paul, saw you both kissing in the morning, what she describes as snogging in the kitchen. Did you ever kiss or snog Carol in the kitchen?”

A “I did not snog Carol in the kitchen. I may have kissed her before I went to work or when I come home and did the same, put my arm round Paul. That doesn’t make me gay. They were my children.”

Q “In the video she says that she’d be made to – you’d make her masturbate yourself and that you’d make her read dirty magazines. She said that you’d make her wear her mum’s engagement ring on her finger and tell her that it was normal.”

A “Well, that’s disgusting for a start, and her mother’s engagement ring she took with – with her, so you couldn’t wear her mother’s engagement ring when she took it, and she’d still got her rings on her fingers when she left. In fact, her mother sold them.”

Q The allegation that the defendant made the complainant masturbate him and then have sex with her in front of the fire was put to her. The defendant denied it. “She says that she’d previously reported the matter to the police where she provided a statement at the time. She says that you wanted both yourself and her to live as man and wife and that you both did so for approximately two years.”

A “She’s got a vivid imagination. I met my present wife in 1983.”

Q "You mentioned, obviously, Jess earlier in the interview. Can you recall anyone by that name?"

A "No."

Q The allegation that the defendant regularly had sex with his daughter was put.

A "Rubbish."

Q The allegation that the defendant had sex with his daughter in a cabin on a boat whilst on a trip to Sweden was put. "Did that happen? Did you ever take a trip to Sweden?"

A "After the breakdown of my marriage and, as I say, she left and went with her mum, she came back for a few months and I took them on a cruise round Norway and into Sweden around the area of the Norwegian Fjords and into Sweden. I took both her and Paul on that cruise. They had to get over the breakdown, what I thought was the breakdown of my marriage and their mother being in separation, with the separation, so I took them both on a holiday, but at no time did I have sex with her on that boat."

Q The allegation that the defendant had groomed the complainant and then forced her to perform oral sex was put.

A "No, I did not and I think that's disgusting."

Q The replies continued.

A "I find – I find a lot of what she's saying there disgusting. I was in a relationship with someone else at the time."

Q "You had a partner. Did we get the name of the partner at the time? Is that your current partner now?"

A "The partner that I was seeing at the time..."

Q "Yes."

A " ... is my wife now and I started seeing my wife. I met my wife in 1983. I'd go and stop at her house sometimes and even take Paul with me in '84 and we got married and she came to live with me, and she had a son, Simon. Simon was a young lad and he started school in '85."

Q "So, when Carol did go back to the house, you mentioned the chores, the cooking side of it – are you saying that you were responsible from time to...

A "If I was at work, which I was at work, so I didn't see where she says that I could do all this during the week because I was at work – I was working for a company called Taylor Woodrow Construction. I was working after I left Taylor Woodrow Construction. I went to work for a company called Triple B construction and I was a concrete finisher for Taylor Woodrow. We laid concrete and I finished it and then I went to work for Triple B Construction working on a dam over the River Aire at Garforth and I was working there, and I was working five-and-a-half days a week. When I worked for Taylor Woodrow Construction I was often having to go back to work at 10 and 11 o'clock at night to finish the concrete off."

Q "Were you aware that Carol was still going to school at that time?"

A "I didn't know whether Carol and Paul were going to school. I admit that they were latchkey kids and I was going to work and 7 and half past in the morning because I had to be at work for eight and sometimes it was half past five, six o'clock when I got home at night. If they came home from school, I expected them to do – keep the house tidy or I expected them, you know, at least to start making a bit of tea or whatever."

Q "You said you were obviously close to Paul."

A "Yes, Paul often – yeah, when he was a kiddie, he'd go to work. I'd take him to work because I was self-employed at the time and we used to do a lot of subcontract work. I'd take him to work with me and that – there, and he'd play about because we did a lot of work on farms putting big corn silo bases down, and if they had children and that there, I'd take Paul with me and he could spend the day there with them. When he was young there, I'd take him out and he'd go with me and when I was going shooting and one thing and another, I showed him now to shoot" – sorry, "I showed him how to shoot. I learnt him how to drive a car, got him a motorbike."

Q "You said Paul lived with you up until 18?"

A "He was 18, he was. I got married to my present wife in September 2 1988 at the Denby Dale Pie Celebration and that there was in the following day of September 3 '88 and Paul was with me then and I've got photos with us all at the Pie and that there, and he's with his present girlfriend then, so he was 18 year old."

Q "And do you still have a relationship with him now?"

A "I haven't seen Paul for years."

Q "For years, so when was the last time you think you saw him?"

A "About '89 when I kicked him out for he'd not been paying. He was supposed to pay. He was unemployed at the time. He'd been doing little jobs and he was supposed to pay my present wife and that, £20 a week towards his keep, and after we got married she said, 'You know, Paul hasn't been paying me anything, given me anything for his keep', and I said, 'Since when?' and I think he owed about five or six weeks, and I told him at the time. I got on to him about it, why he hadn't been giving Janet some money and I says, 'I'm not a fucking bus driver.' I says, 'I don't carry passengers. You either pay your way or get off the bus'."

Q "That's quite a long time not to see him, isn't it? Is there any other reasons why?"

A "It's his choice, not mine."

Q "Did it have anything to do with the allegation that Carol has made?"

A "Nothing whatsoever as far as I'm concerned."

Q The defendant denied taking Carol out on her own to collect scrap. "Paul's saying that you took Carol out on your own and stopped taking him."

A "I didn't take him because mostly I was working."

Q "Paul recalls Jean left because his mum had been having an affair with another man".

A "Which is what I told you, she'd been having affairs."

Q "Paul says he cannot recall how long exactly, 'but I lived at home, then with my dad for approximately six months before Carol returned back home.' Does that probably ring about true?"

A "It's about right."

Q The defendant was asked if he recalled an occasion when Carol was in his bedroom in her bra and knickers whilst Paul knocked on the door. Can you recall that?

A "No, I cannot."

Q "Would there be any reason why Carol would be in your bedroom in just her knickers and underwear as a teenager?"

A "No, I cannot, and I'd like to ask the question, is how would he know if, looking up there, when you couldn't see. You can't see the bedroom because it's up there, the wall there. How could he possibly see that she was in knickers and bra?"

Q "Did Carol walk round the house in just her underwear?"

A "I wasn't there. I was at work most of the time."

Q The defendant was asked if he had ever snogged his daughter in the kitchen using tongues. "Can you recall that incident?"

A "No, I cannot."

Q "Have you ever passionately kissed Carol at any point?"

A "No, I have not."

Q "Since she was a child?"

A "The only time I've kissed Carol, same as what I've told you before, is as a father and a daughter."

Q The defendant was asked if he recalled an incident where he'd been in bed with Carol and Paul and asked Paul in the morning if he had touched her. "Can you ever recall anything like that?"

A "No, I do not, but I've told you that they used to come and jump in bed with me and he's just admitted that."

Q The allegation that the defendant had put a shotgun to Jean's head was put. The defendant said the allegation was not true. The defendant was asked about telling Jean that he believed it was right that fathers broke their daughters in like the Indians do.

A "I have no idea where they've got that from because I didn't know nothing about American Indians at all apart from what you've seen on TV."

Q “Did you have a belief, though, about breaking the eldest daughter?”

A “No, I did not. That is disgusting.”

Q “Did you ever share those views and beliefs with anybody?”

A “No, I did not.”

Q The defendant was asked if he recalled his wife contacting social services. “So, she’s saying that she’s left you because Carol told her that you kissed her.

A “That occasion, what you’re talking about there, when she went to a home, the refuge, she’d gone to the social services. She’d gone to the council and said that I was abusing her and that was far – and that was for battered women and that there – and that refuge, what they put her in, they found out in that refuge that she was lying, so they kicked her out and she came back to me from that refuge.”

Q “So, yes, she goes on to say that she came back home for a couple of weeks. ‘I can remember, I explained to Elliott about the kissing with Carol but he denied it. He just said it was a kiss on the cheek.’ Did Jean ever confront you or ask you about what Carol had said?”

A “No, she did not.”

Q The defendant was asked if he recalled an occasion where Jean had attended 26 Gilthwaites Crescent and confronted Carol and him about her relationship. “Can you remember the occasion where Jean’s turned up at the house?”

A “She turned up at the house after, long after, I’d started divorce proceedings and the children were not there. She came one morning and for some unknown reason that day I wasn’t working. She came to the house. It would be about nine or half past. It was after the school had gone in. She came up there and she said she wanted to talk about the kids. I said, ‘They’re not here. Can we talk about them?’ She came in, she sat down at the kitchen table and she says, ‘I suppose you’re going to tell people now that me and you’s gone to bed and had sex?’ I says, ‘What the hell for?’ She says, ‘To stop divorce.’ I said, ‘I aren’t stopping the divorce’. I said, ‘If that’s what you’ve come for, there’s the door, piss off’ and I kicked her out again and there was none of that there is true. It's rubbish. I mean, Carol even admits – how can you think that of her own daughter? She came back to me, did Carol, as what I've told you. Carol had come to me for a few months, stopped with me for a few months when she'd had a fall out or whatever, she couldn't get her own way with her mother, and then she'd go back. When she couldn't get her own way with me, she'd go back to her mother."

Q The defendant was asked if he had received a phone call from Jean whilst at the Pie Hall regarding allegations made by Carol to her to which he had replied, "You fucking prove it".

A "I remember her ringing the Pie Hall up on one occasion when I was in, but it wasn't over that. She rung me up to say that she – she'd – she'd accused her own father of sexual abuse when she was younger and that, and she hadn't spoke to him for over 20 years. Her father, well, she didn't know where he was but she was trying to trace – she had had a couple of brothers and she rung me up at the Pie Hall one night and she said, 'I've found my family'."

Q "So, what she's saying there, can – you can't recall any..."

A "No. The only conversation – the only conversation that I recall having with her at the Pie Hall was that time when she'd said that she found her brother, her family up in Richmond."

Q The defendant was asked whether he had ever spoken to the police about Carol's allegations.

A "It was a Sunday morning and there was an officer. I can't remember what they called him – Charlesworth or Kenworthy, or something. He came knocking. He was a detective in plain clothes. He was in an unmarked car and he knocked on the door one Sunday morning. I was in bed. Paul was in bed. I opened the door, the bedroom window, to find out who was knocking at the door. It was this guy that was there and he showed me his badge. He says, 'Detective so-and-so'. He says, 'Could I have a word with you, please?' So, I went downstairs, opened the door. He came in and then that's when he told me about it and we went to Holmfirth Police Station. We didn't go to Kirkburton. He told me he'd to question me and I said, 'What about my son there?', who was sat on the steps was Paul and he was crying, and I said, 'What about my son?' and he says, 'Can you get somebody to look after him?' and I just asked Paul. I said, 'My sister's down.' I said to Paul, I says, 'Do you know where your Auntie Hilda lives?" and he says, 'Yes'. I says, 'Can you manage to get down there?' and he says, 'Yes', and he walked all the way from Denby Dale down to Scissett while I was taken to Holmfirth."

Q The defendant said he was interviewed at the time.

A "Do you know" – oh, sorry.

Q "Do you know if at the time they spoke to Paul?"

A "No."

Q "Did anything happen between you and Carol at the time, other than the arguments, obviously and you state that she left?"

A "Carol spent most of her childhood in those years between '82 and '85 with her mother. She didn't spend it with me. She just spent odd times with me. She came to me odd times."

Q The defendant was asked about the evidence provided by Jean of Carol's complaints to her of sexual abuse."

A "She's lying and the only reason I can understand and I can think of why she's saying she think was – that she did is because I kicked her. She did not leave, she was kicked out of the house. She was told one Friday morning when I was going to work, 'It's payday, but when I get home, you're not having none.' I got fed up of every Friday coming home with my wage and I'd be sat down for my tea, it'd be the clothing man, it'd be the insurance man', it'd be some other guy thing, money, money, money, 'you owe me' thing. I'm not going and working all bloody week to be giving money away to every tom, Dick and Harry what you get in debt with, so I said, 'It's Friday, it's payday but you're not having none. When I get home, I want to see you gone. Take what you want. If the kids want to go with you, they can go with you. If they want to stay, they can stay'."

Q The defendant was asked about Paul's evidence.

A “The only reason I can think of Paul making a statement like that at this time is peer pressure.”

Q “Did you have any contact with school when they were at school?”

A “Yes, I had contact with them.”

Q “What about their attendance, then, Paul and Carol’s attendance at school?”

A “They were skipping school.”

Q “What about Carol’s attendance at school?”

A “Carol wasn’t with me. Carol wasn’t with me”.

Q “But you said she was with you and then she’d go back to her mum’s and then come back.”

A “Yeah, she’d come back and things, and that there. I didn’t have any contact with the school at all as regarding Carol and that.”

Q That is a continued reply.

A “Donna stayed with me for a short while after school, after we bust up.”

Q The defendant then provided a letter dated 16 August 1983 from Eaton Smith and Downey, Solicitors, a second letter dated 12 October 1983 from Eaton Smith and Downey, Solicitors, and an affidavit from Margaret Jean Higgins dated 22 January 1980-something. “But she did live with you there for a period of time, though, didn’t she?”

A “Short months which is what I explained to you.”

Q The defendant then produced a court order dated 2 April 1984 detailing a custody order relating to Paul and Carol Appleyard, and then it’s a reply, officer.

A “This is at the time when she’s still claiming that I was having sex with her daughter. Now what happened was this was a custody order. We went to magistrates’ court in Huddersfield to go through the custody battle. The magistrate at the time and the social worker – we had to take the children and she took Donna. I took Paul and Carol and that there to the court there. The judge took them in a room and at the back, I think, which I’m assuming was chambers and that, there were her chambers with the social worker to discuss with the children who they wanted to be with and one thing and another.”

Q “Yeah.”

A “Well, that’s not me pushing her because he’s taken her back in my chambers, in the chambers. They’re talking to them in private. That’s not under my influence.”

Q “So, you’re saying that when she came back to you, she may stay for a couple of months and then go. If things working out she’d go back to her mum”.

A “Yes.”

Q “Would that be the sort of the longest she would stay with you, a couple of months?”

A “The longest she stayed with me was two, three months, something like that, and then she’d go back.”

Q “And what would the shortest period be that she’d stay with you?”

A “I couldn’t tell you. I didn’t keep a diary of it. I didn’t keep a check. They were free to go. Every one of them was free to go where they wanted. I didn’t put no restrictions on them.”

Q “How did you feel about Carol flitting from one to the other?”

A “It didn’t bother me. If that’s what they want to do, that’s what they want to do.”

Q “And after the party, when she’s had the party, how old would she have been when the party happened?”

A “That was November ’83 when they had the party, when I went to America on a hunting trip. She was born in ’69 so she will be 14-year-old.”

Q “My question was going to be, ‘Has she been back since the party’ but I should obviously state that she was back after that point.”

A “She was. She came back and then went again and she came back again. Now, since Carol has left, she rung me up after I’d been married this second time with Janet. She rang up and she wanted to meet us to make things right, put things right, and we arranged to meet in a café in Barnsley. We went, me and my thing. I wouldn't arrange to meet her without Janet, my wife being present. We went to the café in Barnsley, we had a coffee, we had a natter there and then we left and we went home. She rang up after that and she's got a son called Jake, I believe his name is. She wanted Jake. She said Jake had been asking about his grandad. She says, 'Can he come? Can I come through and bring him?' I says, 'Yeah, if you want'. So, she came back to the house again, at 26 Gilthwaites Crescent with her son."

Q The defendant was asked if he'd seen Carol with love bites when she was young.

A "If Carol had love bites on the neck at that age, it wouldn't just be that would be aware – it would be her mother because at 10 year old, that would be 1979 and I was still married to her mother. I was still living with her mother and even if she was 12 year old, that would make it 81 and I was still married and I was still with her mother, and that there – so it isn't a case of me noticing love bites. Her mother would have noticed love bites. They came from some other person. They certainly didn't come from me."

Q "Do you remember seeing Carol with those love bites?"

A "No, I do not."

Q The statement of Carron Ward read out and Mr Appleyard confirmed Carron used to live next door. The defendant was asked if he recalled any occasion where he had asked Carol Ward, "Has your dad broke you in yet?"

A "No."

Q "You making reference to breaking in your daughter and back to the Indians – at any point in your lifetime have you said that?"

A "I've never, ever, at any time in my life spoke to any of them about North American Indians because I wouldn't know about North American Indians and that other than watching them on TV and that. How would you know? They certainly don't do that on TV."

Q "And in terms, what about the belief though of breaking in your eldest daughter?"

A "I've never heard of it until you've told me in the statements."

Q The defendant was asked about the complainant's allegations. "Why do you think she's continuing?"

A “I think – I think personally, myself, I think that a lot of this has kept on going and kept on going and kept on going because of the mother. I can only think of that. A lot of it is peer pressure from her mother because it had gone on and on with the bitterness that’s gone on and that’s the only thing.”

Q “And how has that left you feeling?”

A “Bitter that they can carry on and carry on like this and they can do this year after year as long as I’ve been making mine and my new wife and my new family’s life a bloody turmoil. It makes me bitter that they can carry on doing this. They have the right to do this for infinity. I do not. I haven’t got the money but they can carry on making allegations, allegations, getting friends to make statements and that, yeah, for infinity and that puts my – I’ve had my windows smashed. I’ve had graffiti dobbed on walls in Denby Dale. I’ve had flyers put on cars in Denby Dale for people that doesn’t know it, like Carol and her friends and that. It’s making mine and my wife – my new wife’s life and kids there a bloody misery and I don’t know – it’s about time it stopped because it goes on and on and on, and all this is, is pure harassment, and it is harassment.”

Q “Carol’s obviously made this allegation when she’s been 15 years old. Why would she make that allegation when she’s 15 years old?”

A “I’ve no idea. She was with her mother at the time when she made it and I’ve already kicked her mother out then. I’ve no idea why she should make that other than getting her head together with her mother and why it continues, that I’ve no idea other than the bitterness of her mother, me and her mother.

Q “You speak about your ex-wife Jean and you’ve called her an evil bitch during interview.”

A “She is.”

Q “So why when she phoned you when you were at Denby Dale at the Pie Hall asking to take her to see her brother if she’d got in touch with..."

A “I was with her then.”

Q “So, you were with her at that point?”

A “I was with her at that point. We were living together at that point when she rung me at the Pie Hall. That’s the only conversation I ever recall having her ringing up at the Pie Hall and that’s what I told you. She’s made a statement in there and what you said and there is – she rung me sometime when she was living with Carol and when were split up, and I said I didn’t recall it.”

Q “You’re saying that the only time she’s phoned you at the Pie Hall is..."

A “No, that’s the only time that I can recall her ever phoning me at the Pie Hall was when she was with me. I was in one night and she rang up to say that she’d traced her family.”

Q “But you don’t recall the conversation where she’s disclosed to you what Carol’s told her?”

A “No, I do not. That’s the only conversation that I recall.”

Q “Carol talks about you taking her to collect – go collect scrap metal and you said that you’d never done that, take her to collect scrap metal.”

A “I didn’t take her out to go. It’s implying that I took her out and we went around collecting scrap as what, gypsies and one thing and another did. That is not the case. I didn’t go out then. She implies that we went to skips and one thing and another, and that there – if I drove past skips when I was going down the road, if I drove past skips and I saw a set of bloody drawers, a wardrobe or whatever it was, or there was a bloody old washer at the top of the skip, yes, I’d stop and I’d pick it up”.

Q “So, are you saying that you didn’t go out with Carol on your own just to get scrap metal?”

A “Just to collect scrap, no. If I took Carol out on her own in the car, we was going somewhere, if I took Paul out in the vehicle on us own, we were going somewhere. I didn’t take them specifically to collect scrap.”

Q “Did Carol and Paul ever sleep in your bed?”

A “No. They come and got in my bed on a Sunday. More often than not, on a Sunday morning, they’d jump in. Now, if we fell asleep, we fell asleep but they specifically got in my bed, come and jumped in on a Sunday morning and we’d often talk about what we were going to do for that day.”

Q “Paul speaks about him getting out and going to football on more than one occasion, so was that a regular occurrence on a Sunday morning, the jump in bed?

A “No, Paul didn’t. Paul wasn’t a regular football player such like that. I’ve got photos. I’ve got umpteen photos right up until the time that he left home, an 18-year-old, my Paul, from being a little kid where he went out with me shooting and where he was with me in the car on his motorbike, and God knows what, sat there playing. Paul wasn’t a football fan as such there. He was a kid that played out and he went shooting. He went – he loved to go shooting with his dad and go ride in the car with his dad.”

Q “Do you remember any occasions on a Sunday morning then where he would get up and get out of bed leaving you and Carol alone?”

A “No, I do not.”

Q “Do you remember any occasions where Carol would be in bed with you in just her bra and knickers?”

A “No, I do not, not unless she came out on a Sunday morning and climbed in bed with me then.”

Q “Yeah, but that’s what I’m asking you. Do you remember her on a Sunday morning getting in your bed in just her bra and knickers?”

A “No, I do not. No, I do not.”

Q “Do you remember what Carol used to wear for bed when she was a child?”

A “No, I do not. She’d probably have a nightie on.”

Q “Do you remember Carol walking around the house in her bra and knickers?”

A “No, I do not, but even if she did, she was in her own home.”

Q “Yeah, I appreciate that, but I’m just asking, do you remember seeing her walking around in just her bra and knickers?”

A “No, I was at work most of the time and things, Monday to Friday, sometimes Saturday morning. I was at work. I’ve told you, they were latchkey kids. I’ve admitted to the fact that they were latchkey kids. When I was off at seven o’clock on a morning, I didn’t get home until half five, six o’clock at night time.”

Q “Just going back to your relationship with Paul, you describe him as your little shadow when he was a kid.”

A “That’s right.”

Q “And you did a lot together?”

A “Yes.”

Q “In terms of the allegation of rape by Carol, you deny that?”

A “Totally.”

Q The interview concluded. That was December 2015, officer, and the investigation continued. You were making various inquiries, I think?

A Yes.

Q And then the defendant came back for a further interview on 8 December 2016.

A Yes.

Q That’s almost a year after.

A Yes, that’s correct.

MR HAMPTON: There are copies again for the judge, witness, defendant and the jury. One between two, please. (Copies of documents distributed) So, if everybody can see a copy, we are now back at the Dewsbury Police Station. It’s December 16th, 2.54 to 3.55, an hour and one minute. Because these transcripts are summaries, there will only be relevant matters discussed. This time yourself again, with PC Ringrose.

A Yes.

Q Mr Arif representing Mr Appleyard.

A Yes.

Q Formal introductions, explanation as to the investigation into historical offence of rape, the amount of legal entitlement, cautioned. “The defendant stated that..."

A “I’ve never said sorry or shown any remorse to Carol because I’ve never had any reason to.”

Q “So, you’ve never admitted to Carol, you’ve never apologised for..."

A “No.”

Q The defendant was asked about the statement of Karl Higgins.

A "I wasn't there so I don't know. As far as Carol is being on a bus and upset and running away from me, that is quite possible, not running away from me for a sexual thing. She could have been running away from me because we had a fall out at home and that's it."

Q And the defendant asked...

A "What date was that, please? Have you got a date for that?

Q It was clarified that Karl Higgins stated that this would have been possibly 1984 to 1985.

A "I was with my present wife in 84/85. Carol wasn't even with me. She was nowhere near the house in 84/85. She's making out that the offences happened, right, up to her being 15 years of age, from being 12 years of age and I'm telling you, she wasn't with me. She's making it out that it happened on a daily basis, a weekly basis and that – there for three or four years and it couldn't possibly be because she wasn't with me."

Q "Do you recall anybody by the name of Diane Croft?"

A "Carol used to knock about with Diane Croft when they were at school and that's as far as I know. I know Diane Croft's mother and father."

Q "What are your thoughts about Carol, then, telling all these different people that you know at the times in 1984 and still now about this sexual abuse and the allegations against you?"

A "I can't understand why Carol should make statements of that nature and yet tell a judge in '84 that she wants to come and live with her father when she could have a judge and – when she could have told a judge and the social worker that, 'My father's abusing me', and I could have been arrested then and taken to court then for doing it. I fail to understand why she'd want to come and live with a person who's abusing her."

Q The statement of Hilda Graham was discussed and Mr Appleyard confirmed this is his sister. "Question: What are your thoughts about that?"

A "I have no thoughts. I don't even know when she heard the argument or where we was when we..."

Q The defendant was asked if he recalled his sister, Hilda Graham, giving him a lift to Jean's address in Penistone. "Can you recall that?"

A "No, I do not recall that at all."

Q "Can you recall this incident where Peter and Jean might have driven?"

A "No, I don't. I don't even recall ever going to her house when she lived in Penistone."

Q "So, you can't remember going to Penistone at any point to see Jean?"

A "No, I remember on one occasion there where she rung me up and she wanted to speak to me and we got the kids and I went and picked them up. I met them in Penistone and picked them up, but as far as going to a house was concerned, I don't even recall."

Q "Where did you meet in Penistone?"

A "I can't remember, to tell the truth, but I picked her up. There was her and there was Paul there. There was Carol there and that and we went – we went for a drive and we went over towards the reservoir."

Q The defendant was asked if he recalled an occasion where his sister Hilda Graham was present and Jean mentioned a pregnancy test of Carol's.

A "No, I do not recall that. I don't recall, in all honesty, ever going to her house where she lived."

Q "So, in the aftermath of, you know, there's obviously the initial investigation when it first came to police attention in 1980s, so it would have been around that time, I would imagine. Can you remember? You can't remember that at all?"

A "No, I don't even remember who the officer was in charge. It began with E, or something. I don't even recall who the officer was who interviewed me at the time."

Q In terms of the pregnancy test, can you remember anything about a pregnancy test being discussed?"

A "No, no. I don't remember discussing anything with her in that sense."

Q The statement of Diana Thorpe, previously known as "Romano" outlined. Mr Appleyard confirmed this is the daughter of his niece, the daughter of his sister, Margaret. The defendant was asked about one occasion where Diana Thorpe had been present in the kitchen with the defendant, Carol. "So, what are your thoughts about that?"

A "For a start she would – she would never come walking straight into my house and put kettle on if there was nobody around. If I was upstairs and that – there, how would she know that there was anybody around?"

Q The defendant discussed the phone call he recalled from Jean when he was in the Pie Hall.

A "I was in the Pie Hall having a drink, which is the village hall in Denby Dale. I was in there one Friday night when the phone rang. We'd no mobile phones at the time. It was in the eighties, around about 1980, something like that, '79, '80. The phone rang there. The steward gave me the phone. He says, 'It's for you, some woman, I think.' He gave it me and she said, 'I've phoned my brothers', and I says, 'Oh, yeah?' because she hadn't spoke to her brothers or her father or anybody for years, and I says, 'Oh, yeah. Oh, yeah?" – sorry. "She says, 'Yeah, and they were last heard of up in Richmond in North Yorkshire.' She said, 'I rang direct inquiries' and she says, 'They had a number so I've rung it and my brother answered the phone and my father lives across the road', and she hadn't spoken to her father for over 20-odd years. She wanted running up there. I run her up there to her brother's house. We stayed at her brother's house for a few hours and she went across. She wanted to go and talk to her father on her own. She wouldn't take me with her. She wouldn't take her brother with her, and she went across to talk to her father on her own and she came back about an hour later and said, 'It's fine', and that – and that was basically it."

Q "Did Diana ever pop in and have a cup of tea with you?"

A "No, no."

Q "So, is she lying there?"

A "She's lying there because I'm not saying that they didn't come to the house, but in the context as what she's saying."

Q "Did she ever just pop round and have a cup of tea with you..."

A “No.

Q “ ... unannounced?”

A “No.”

Q “Did any of your family members ever do that?”

A “No. They don’t just walk in a house and put a kettle on, and that, if there’s nobody there. You just don’t do it.”

Q Mr Appleyard confirmed he knew Carron Ward. She recalled an incident approximately from 1974 when she was living with her family at 20 Gilthwaites and she can remember that you approached her and said to her, ‘Has your dad broke you in yet?’”

A “She’s a liar.”

Q “She asked what Elliott meant and you said it went back to the Indians and all dads should break their daughters in.”

A “That’s what Carron, Carron Garside has said.”

Q “Yeah.”

A “Right, well isn’t that funny because doesn’t Carol Higgins say exactly the self-same paragraph in her statement, that I’m supposed to have said to Carol Higgins the thing?”

Q “Yeah.”

A “It’s ironic they both say the same thing in both their statements.”

Q “So, you’re saying she’s lying?”

A “Yes, definitely.”

Q The defendant was asked about physical abuse of the children.

A “Physically abusing her – if they started making a noise and one thing and another, I was strict with them, I’ll admit that, and I gave them a crack, a clip round the lughole. I gave them a crack on the backside. What was – what you’ve got to understand was in the fifties, the sixties and seventies and that, what was more acceptable then is not acceptable today and people’s being tried today on what was acceptable then. You corrected your kids – I can’t go to Kirklees Education Authority and say, ‘I’m suing you for physical abuse because I used to get the cane at school’. Where do you stop? What wasn’t the norm and what was accepted then as discipline – I mean the local police officer used to give you a clip round the lughole rather than take you to court."

Q The defendant was asked about Carol having a tattoo. "Can you recall that?"

A "I recall taking her and Paul. They wanted a mod – they wanted a tattoo when they were at school. It was Scissett Secondary Modern School or Shelley High School, whatever. They would be about 12, 13 year old. They wanted a tattoo and that, and you had to have some parents' consent to have it on. They had tattooed on – they could have a small tattoo on and they could have on exactly what they wanted."

Q "Can you remember what Carol had?"

A "No."

Q "She said that she had the name Sam."

A "Well, she may well have."

Q "What does that mean to you, the name Sam?"

A "Well, Sam was my nickname for a start and it was also the name of the dog that we had at the time."

Q "Okay."

A "We had a springer spaniel dog, a liver and white dog, and that dog was called Sam, and it was called Sam. I didn't call it Sam. It was called Sam by the previous owner."

Q "Why do you think Carol would have the name Sam put on if it's your nickname?"

A "I've no idea – or the dog's name. I've no idea. They were entitled to have one small tattoo on, which I agreed to, one each, and what they had on was what they wanted, not what I made them have on."

Q "One last question in terms of obviously the allegation that Carol's made: what are your thoughts about the allegation that Carol's made and why she's persistently pursuing that allegation?"

A "The only way that I can see it, it's money, payback time for kicking them out, I don't know. The fact that she'd written a book there and she's mentioned names, she is liable. She is liable. If nothing's done about this, she is liable. If something's done then she can say, 'I've got away with it', in which case she's getting money."

Q And that second interview concluded, and that is all I have for you at this stage, officer. Would you wait there for cross-examination?

Cross-examined by Mr STOREY

Q I think you told us, officer, that you were appointed officer in the case as far as this investigation is concerned in about September 2015?
A Yes, that's correct.
Q And that you made initial inquiries to locate the paperwork. Nothing was found.
A That's correct.
Q And it's right, isn't it, you can't say for sure why not, but at the time it seems there was a force policy...
A Yes.
Q ...which involved not keeping documents for more than 10 years?
A Yes.
Q You also, I think, made inquiries of social services about whether they had records?
A That's correct.
Q And again nothing found. Do you know whether they had a similar policy?
A I'm not aware.
Q No.
A I think some inquiries have been made since but I don't know the exact answer. I think nothing's been located.
Q Right, so it could either be that there was a policy and records have been destroyed or perhaps on the other hand nothing was ever recorded at the time?
A No, that's correct.

Q I think you made reference to the Crown Prosecution Service archives?
A Yes.
Q It's right, isn't it, that in 2005 the Crown Prosecution Service had been involved in making a decision about the case?
A Yes.
Q Nothing held from even that date?
A No, no. There's no paperwork, obviously, throughout the investigation. Whilst that was being reviewed we did – we submitted an IT request to try and retain any documentation from the officer at the time who had investigated the case in 2005, but there was nothing located in terms of CPS paperwork.
Q No, because there was a different police officer tasked with looking into it back in 2005?
A That's correct, yes.
Q That's right, isn't it?
A (no reply)
Q You obviously spoke with Carol Higgins at some length.
A Yes.
Q Both initially in 2015 when you were given the role of officer in the case and subsequently. Is that right?
A Yes.
Q You were made aware of the book she had written?
A Yes.
Q I think she gave you a list of names of people she felt should be spoken to?
A Yes.
Q New areas of evidence that she felt...
A Yes, when I first...
Q ...you should be exploring?
A When I was first allocated the matter, I visited her at her home address and she obviously showed me her book and obviously I was tasked with – you know, finding out what this new information was.

Q And you set about trying to contact people who she'd named for you?
A Yes.
Q You didn't always have contact details. Is that fair?
A No, that's correct.
Q And so there were some people you could contact reasonably easily, others you couldn't?
A Yes.
Q You took some statements?
A Yes.
Q Including from people well outside the West Yorkshire area?
A Yes, that's correct.
Q And is it right that Ms Higgins rather chased you repeatedly wanting updates?
A Yes, that's fair to say.
Q And did she express dissatisfaction that you had been unable to contact people?
A Yes, that's correct from – we had a difficult relationship but I think a lot of that was due to her mistrust of the police and how she felt she'd been treated previously.
Q And did she make it pretty clear that she felt you weren't investigating the case properly?
A Yes, yes.
Q She, I think, on a number of occasions provided documents to you?
A Yes.
Q We know that you interviewed her in November 2015?
A Yes.
Q The video recorded interview that was played last week...
A Yes.
Q And I think that she had some documents with her then but...
A Yeah, I...
Q ...you suggested she should bring them all together at one and the same time?

A It was trying to manage Carol, and you know, there would be conflicts at times when Carol would want things doing her way but I sort of had to, you know, manage her as I wanted to manage her as the officer in the case, so she did come with documentation. I took a copy of a letter but I'd agreed with her that I'd come back at a later date and recover copies of those documents.

Q And we know that the defendant, Mr Appleyard, was interviewed for the first time in December 2015...

A That's correct.

Q ...having attended, you told us, voluntarily at the police station.

A Yes.

Q The investigation continued through the following year.

A Yes.

Q And again Ms Higgins continued to tell you of people that she wanted you to speak to or inquire about?

A Yes.

Q Retired police officers were named...

A Yes, that's correct.

Q ... who she was for saying had seen paperwork sometime in the past?

A Yes, yeah, that's correct.

Q At some point I think you visited Mr Appleyard's home address to speak to his wife.

A That's correct, yes.

Q And whilst – which may have been after his first interview?

A I can't remember ...

Q Okay.

A ... the exact date but I did attend at his home address.

Q I think in fact in your witness statement you make it clear that it was in October 2016 at Wadsworth?

A Yes.

Q Do you remember during the course of that visit that Mr Appleyard spoke to you about the line of sight one could have to the front upstairs bedroom window?

A I do not.

Q Do you remember having a look, effectively, with him and commenting on how far back one would have to be to see into that window?

A I don't recall that, no.

Q A second interview with Mr Appleyard took place in December 2016. We know that. But is it also right that during 2016, and I think into 2017 as well, Ms Higgins would provide you with various items at various times?

A Yes, that's correct.

Q Not just documentation?

A Not just documentation but other names of, like, potential lines of inquiry.

Q And did she provide you with a number of items that she'd told you she'd taken from the land that her father rented?

A I think this is not – I think these were recovered by another officer so...

Q That would be my mistake then.

A Yeah, so – yeah.

Q All right.

A Okay.

Q Let me put it this way. It's right, isn't it, that she provided it to the police rather than perhaps you specifically?

A Yes, I believe so, yes.

Q And a number of items which she made clear had taken – she'd taken from land that her father rented?

A Yes.

Q And were you aware – and you may not be, given what you just said – were you aware why it was that she was of the view that these items might be significant?

A I think it probably would have been about April 2017 that I'd been promoted, so it went through a stage where I was being assisted on the investigation, but

Carol believed that this – she believed that he was going to flee the country and there was this piece of land which was up for auction and she'd mentioned things about there might be dead bodies there on the land and such.

Q Yes.

A And there was items up there which she thought was of significance for us.

Q And did she not make the police aware that her view was that her father had murdered children?

A She did mention that, yes.

Q And that she thought the police should be digging up this land?

A Yes.

Q She provided, I think, you or colleagues with recordings of conversations she'd had with people?

A Yes.

Q Both people who you knew to be witnesses...

A That's correct.

Q ... and people you had not spoken to, I think, as well?

A Yeah, that's correct.

Q And she provided you with the recordings of radio broadcasts that she'd been involved in?

A Yes.

Q And is it right that on a number of occasions you either personally or the police generally had to speak to her about her involvement in the investigation?

A Yes.

Q And to warn her that it might not actually be helping?

A That's correct.

Q I think she nevertheless continued to provide you with documents, lists of questions that she felt should be asked ...

A Yes.

Q ...of the Crown Prosecution Service and things like that?

A Yes. She'd complained about me so it was – you know, there was an ongoing complaint with our professional standards department, so...

Q And you were presumably well aware of her use of Facebook?

A Yes, that sort of – the matter was being reviewed at the time by Sarah Nelson from the CPS and sort of – the prominence, if you like, of the website sort of came to the attention of the prosecution at that time.

Q And you said a website. Was that a website that Ms Higgins had set up to promote the book?

A It was a Facebook page.

Q A Facebook page?

A Yes.

Q All right, and again she was publicising allegations about various people, some named, some not named, being involved in a paedophile ring?

A Yes.

Q Making clear her displeasure with the police generally?

A Yes.

Q And her views about her father and the like?

A Yes.

Q And I think you said you moved departments in April 2017. Is that right?

A It was April 2017, so I think – yeah, April 2017. So, I moved roles out of child safeguarding and the matter, the initial decision in the case was in July.

Q Mm hm.

A And then the victim – following the victim's right to review, James Bellhouse, DS Bellhouse, sort of oversaw many of the actions and responsibilities up until this point.

Q Right. Just something you mentioned there a moment ago, the victim's right to review. It's right, isn't it, that in July 2017, the date you've just mentioned, a decision was made by the Crown Prosecution Service that the case should go no further?

A That's correct.

Q	And it's right also that victims now have a right to have decisions like that reviewed?
A	That's correct.
Q	And that's what happened here...
A	Yes.
Q	... before court proceedings ultimately began in early 2018?
A	Yes.
MR STOREY: Thank you very much, officer. I just wanted to go through that history with you.
A	Okay.
JUDGE JAMESON: Yes?

<u>Re-examined by Mr HAMPTON</u>

Q	So, the investigation ongoing from the end of 2015 through 2017?
A	Yes.
Q	Did the complainant sometimes display displeasure as to how long that things were taking?
A	Yes, she did. It was trying to manage her expectations but I understood, you know. She was obviously very upset about what had happened and how she felt she'd been treated by the police previously, so, yeah.
Q	You have spoken about her having contact with witnesses or other people.
A	Yes.
Q	Did you ever ask for assistance in finding certain witnesses?
A	Yes, you know. The onus largely was on Carol to provide us with the information. There were times where we'd have disagreements on the phone because she wanted us to go out and do all the inquiries but, you know, the offences – the allegations were from the 1980s, so obviously we – I wasn't around at that time. I wasn't in my role, so...
Q	There were occasions when you asked for assistance in locating them?
A	Yes.

Q And we have heard about recordings being made between the complainant and others and these were provided to you by Carol?

A That's correct.

Q The items regarding the land, as I understand your evidence, were provided at a time where, I think you said she thought he was going to flee the jurisdiction?

A Yes, she feared that we were coming to, obviously a charging decision and she feared that because the land was up for auction, she'd heard that he was possibly going to be emigrating or leaving the country and obviously she wanted justice to be served.

MR HAMPTON: Thank you. Does your Honour have any questions?

JUDGE JAMESON: No, thank you very much. Thank you, officer. Thank you for coming and helping us.

A Thank you.

(The witness withdrew)

MR HAMPTON: The last leg of the prosecution case, agreed facts.

JUDGE JAMESON: Yes. Are they ready?

MR HAMPTON: They are ready. We might not be able to finish them today but we can certainly make a start.

JUDGE JAMESON: Yes, all right. Thanks very much. Right, well, ladies and gentlemen, what you are about to get next is a document – it will probably be headed, "Agreed Facts", or "Admissions", one or the other, I would imagine. They are exactly what they say. It's just a very convenient way of marshalling together evidence that everybody agrees is factually accurate and placing it before you. Sometimes it's much more convenient to do it that way than reading out bits of undisputed statements for example, and getting you to put everything together. It's much better just to marshal it in a document but it is agreed as factually accurate, all the representations you are going to get now. So, you can use them for drawing whatever conclusions you think appropriate from them.

MR HAMPTON: Thank you. The same format, please, members of the jury. One between two. (Documents distributed)

"R v Elliott Appleyard, agreed facts pursuant to s.10 of the Criminal Justice Act 1967. It is agreed between the prosecution and the defence that",

And then we deal first of all with some key dates. So:

"In chronology taken from documentation gathered as part of the police investigation, 5 May 1945, Margaret Voss born. 27 June 1947, Elliott Appleyard..."

JUDGE JAMESON: We had better just put in "Jean" there because I think the jury will probably know Margaret Voss more as Jean.

MR HAMPTON: Quite right.

JUDGE JAMESON: That's obviously Mr Appleyard's first wife.

MR HAMPTON: It is, so Margaret Jean Voss or Appleyard. Thank you.

"Elliott Appleyard, born 27 June 1947. Donna Appleyard born 6 March 1968. Carol Denise Higgins born 23 April 1969. Paul Appleyard born, 22 October 1970. 27 May 1974, Elliott Appleyard and Jean Voss married. 1978, Elliott Appleyard granted a shotgun certificate. April 1979, Carol turned 10 on the 23rd. In April 1980, she turned 11. In April 1981 she turned 12. 2 April 1982, the Falklands War begins. 23 April 1982, Carol Higgins turned 13. 14 June 1982, the Falklands war ends. 23 April 1983, Carol Higgins turns 14 years of age.

"23 June 1983, police log of Elliott Appleyard's suicide attempts. On 23 June 1983, police officers were called to his house by his wife and family doctor following a domestic dispute. Mr Appleyard had locked his wife out of the premises and threatened to commit suicide. Police officers forced an entry into the house and found Mr Appleyard hanging by a rope from the roof joists. He was near to death and had left a suicide note, that record taken from a police minute sheet dated 26 March 2001.

"16 August 1983, a letter from Eaton Smith & Downey to Bruce & Co in the matter of Appleyard v Appleyard. The letter indicates that Carol was living with her mother at Penistone at this time and suggested Donna resides with her father during the weekdays and mother's at weekends.

"30 October 1983, a letter from Bruce & Co to Eaton Smith & Downey in the matter of Appleyard v Appleyard. The letter indicates that Carol missed school and came to see Elliott Appleyard on Tuesday 4 October 1983. 'Such has been your behaviour towards the client'" – 'towards the child, we understand that she has now chosen to live with our client'."

JUDGE JAMESON: That may be a little bit difficult to follow.

MR HAMPTON: Yes.

JUDGE JAMESON: Which solicitor is writing to which?

MR HAMPTON: That is Elliott Appleyard's solicitors to – this is Bruce & Co to Eaton Smith & Downey.

JUDGE JAMESON: Yes, I've got that but who is for who?

MR HAMPTON: Bruce & Co for Mr Appleyard.

JUDGE JAMESON: Mr Appleyard, right, okay.

MR HAMPTON: It's him saying to his lawyers, "Such has been your client's behaviour, the mother, towards the child, we understand that she's now chosen to live with our client, the father".

JUDGE JAMESON: Thank you.

MR HAMPTON: Thank you.

"2 April 1984, Huddersfield County Court orders that Carol and Paul Appleyard remain in the custody of Elliott Appleyard with order amended on

11 April to correct Paul Appleyard's date of birth. The order also provided for the petitioner, Elliott Appleyard, to allow the respondent, Margaret Jean Appleyard, access to the children, Carol and Paul, in his custody between the hours of 11.45 a.m. and 3.45 p.m. every Saturday, such access to take place at the respondent's home.

"23 April 1984, Carol Higgins turns 15 years of age. 9 April 1984" – they should be the other way round, of course – decree absolute in the marriage of Elliott and Jean Appleyard.

"21 July 1984 Jean Voss marries Karl Higgins. 22 January 1985"...

You will notice the question mark in the footnote. This is reference to an affidavit produced as a result of a court order dated 21 September 84, and post the marriage to Karl Higgins, 21 July 1984, the suggestion being that that's why it's January 1985.

"Affidavit of Margaret Jean Higgins" – Margaret Jean Higgins, yes, it would be – "regarding maintenance payments and confirms Donna and Carol are living with her as of this date and indicates Carol was attending Penistone Grammar School and Donna is attending Barnsley College of Technology.

"April 1985, Carol Higgins turns 16. April 1986, Carol Higgins turns 17. April 1987, Carol Higgins turns 18.

"May 1987, doctors' notes record Carol Higgins referred to the Rape Crisis Centre.

"8 July 1987, doctors' notes record Carol Higgins referred to plastic surgeon re tattoo. July 1987, doctor's letter referring to tattoo removal. 'I have explained to her that this might mean a scar but she feels that this would be preferable to the tattoo'."

"23 April 1988, Carol Higgins turns 19. 22 November 1988, hospital records demonstrate that between 22 November 1988 and July 1995, Carol Higgins attended regular counselling sessions run by Barnsley Community and Priority Service NHS Trust. A note within the records dated 22 November 1988 reads: 'Raped by father when 14-and-a-half until aged 15'. An undated document from within hospital records from this time period records that, 'Carol was last under your care in January 1990 for counselling. She's planning to get married in August of this year and finds that many of the fears and anxieties are now coming to the surface again at a time when she feels she ought to be putting her past life behind her. She is also undergoing painful tattoo removal surgery at the moment. She associates the tattoo strongly with her history of abuse.

"Correspondence dated 15 May 1995. She has been troubled by a tattoo over her right scapula, shoulder. For many years", and "in the past", it should say – "past, has had some 10 treatments by a tattoo artist in Rotherham to try and remove this with acid. Records show that she was seen again on 27 June 1996 when it was decided that her prescription for Prozac should be continued. Counselling records from Rape Crisis in Sheffield could not be recovered, due to the passage of time from any counselling to the current investigation.

"April 1989, Carol Higgins turns 20. April 1999, Carol Higgins turns 30 years of age.

"9 March 2000. At 2.40 p.m. at 26 Gilthwaites Crescent, Denby Dale, a machete in a green cover was found on top of the gun cabinet in the rear bedroom. At 2.45 p.m. a curved sword was found by the right side of the fireplace in the lounge.

“5 March 2001, Elliott Appleyard was the holder of a shotgun certificate recording his possession of one 12-bore Cooey shotgun and one 12-bore Falcon shotgun.

“12 April 2001, the defendant’s firearms licence was revoked. Simon’s Appleyard, who at the time lived at the same address as the defendant, subsequent application for a firearms licence was refused.

“2 April 2002, Donna Appleyard’s death.

“May 2008, Carol Higgins recorded as suffering with anxiety and depression. September 2008, Carol Higgins undergoing weekly counselling. 23 April 2009, Carol Higgins turns 40 years of age.

“24 January 2014, the date of the letter written from Jordan Solicitors to Carol Higgins which contained the following paragraph:

“I initially saw you in March 2012 when we discussed various concerns that you have had. It was agreed that I would write to West Yorkshire Police to ask that they investigate your case further and that they make direct contact with you. This letter was done on 2 March 2012 and a copy was sent to you for your attention. They also agreed to look at a potential case against Appleyard direct in case he had assets which would mean he would be worth pursuing. Unfortunately, I’ve not been able to find any evidence regarding whether Mr Appleyard had sufficient assets in his own name that mean he would be worth pursuing. Because I have not been able to trace any assets in relation to Mr Appleyard, then unfortunately there is no further action I can take in relation to this matter. As such, I will have to take steps to close your file of papers."

"February/March 2013, Carol Higgins still attending counselling. 15 April 2013, GP notes, Carol Higgins history. 'Emotional at the moment as daughter E is the same age she was when her dad was abusing her. Working with her counsellor to work through it.

"31 July 2015, GP notes, Carol Higgins. Request referral for counselling".

On 2 November 2015, the video-recorded interview that you have seen took place. Carol Higgins is 46 years of age.

"21 December 2015, Elliott Appleyard attends voluntary interview. 23 June 2016, date of submission of application for compensation by Carol Higgins to the Criminal Injuries Compensation Authority.

"27 July 2016, GP notes, 'Carol Higgins going through counselling'.

"8 December 2016, Elliott Appleyard attends second voluntary interview." We have just read it.

"13 June 2017 GP notes. 'Carol Higgins ongoing counselling'.

"27 August 2017. These records show PC Carter issued Carol Higgins with a harassment warning. A harassment warning can be given by police following an allegation which is true and repeated, would amount to an offence under the Protection from Harassment Act. The prosecution do not need to prove the commission of a criminal offence before providing a warning and a warning does not mean the person who received it has committed a criminal offence. Carol Higgins was not charged with any offence arising out of any allegations of harassment.

"November 2017. Charges authorised by the CPS in the case of R v Appleyard.

"25 April 2018, GP notes: 'Carol Higgins seeing counsellors in Bradford'.

"December 2018. In December 2018 Carol Higgins called Ena Whittle on the phone. She recorded the conversation and then provided a copy of the call to the police. In the conversation Ena Whittle told Carol Higgins that half the stuff she had told Alex Wilson was not in the statement, that her statement had been three pages long but a document she was shown by the police was only one-and-a-bit pages long and that there was a signature of E Ward halfway up the statement, which was not her signature. Ena Whittle's original statement has been checked. The original handwritten statement was three pages long and the typed version, produced for the court proceedings, was one page and one line long. However, the contents were identical. There was no signature of E Ward on the original statement. The only signatures on the statement were that of the witness and officer, Alex Wilson, who had taken the statement. There were three initials of EW on the document where corrections had been made to the text in accordance with normal practice."

JUDGE JAMESON: Could you just pause for a moment? E Ward?

MR HAMPTON: There isn't an E Ward. It's simply a misreading. It's the letters EW.

JUDGE JAMESON: Oh, yes, I've got it.

MR HAMPTON: Ena Whittle.

JUDGE JAMESON: Yes, I see.

MR HAMPTON: Yes, it's next to the word, "and".

JUDGE JAMESON: So, that's what Ena Whittle had thought she'd seen but it wasn't.

MR HAMPTON: Exactly.

JUDGE JAMESON: Yes, okay, got it.

MR HAMPTON: Number two deals with the defendant's arrest.

"Having voluntarily attended a police station, Elliott Appleyard was interviewed under caution", on the dates and times that we read out into the transcript already. "The caution is, 'You do not have to say anything but it may harm your defence if you do not mention when questioned something which you later rely on in court. Anything you do say may be given in evidence.'

"The defendant's interviews are produced into evidence in the case, the documents provided by the defendant who was being interviewed were retained by the police at that time or produced into evidence.

"The book. The epilogue to her self-published book, 'Conquering the Impossible' contains the following paragraph: 'After two years of sexual abuse and being called pathetic, I couldn't take any more. I finally plucked up the courage to leave. I went to my mum's house and told her about the abuse I'd suffered, the rapes and the sexual abuse my dad had put me through. Immediately, my mum contacted my dad'."

"Exhibit number five. On 2 January 2018, Carol Appleyard provided the photograph of Donna, Carol and Paul Appleyard to PC Pont."

Other than one or two minor matters that may form a couple of further agreed facts, that is as far as I can go today.

JUDGE JAMESON: Yes, very well. Anything else tomorrow morning will be dealt with very swiftly.

MR HAMPTON: Briefly.

JUDGE JAMESON: All right. Thank you very much indeed. Right, well, ladies and gentlemen, then that is as far as we can go today. I have, however, spoken to both counsel just to make sure that we are still on track timewise and the answer is that we are. Obviously at the conclusion of the prosecution case, which won't be a long delay tomorrow morning, we will then turn to the defence case and that, of course, must take us as long as it needs to take. There must be no rush about it but nevertheless, Mr Storey has indicated that he believes the evidence will finish, if not tomorrow then certainly not long into Wednesday. So, on that basis, I anticipate that you will be beginning your deliberations some time probably on Thursday. So, we are on track. Good. Thank you all very much indeed and have a good evening.

(The jury left court)

MR HAMPTON: We are in your Honour's hands.

JUDGE JAMESON: Well, I was wondering if it would be helpful if – I don't know whether it's possible to make any further progress on the indictment front. I think that's really in your hands now but anything else that you are...

MR HAMPTON: I have emailed a proposed version of the indictment to my learned friend.

JUDGE JAMESON: Oh, have you?

MR HAMPTON: Your Honour won't have a chance yet...

JUDGE JAMESON: Well, I haven't seen it yet, no.

MR HAMPTON: It's just whether or not we can make any progress with the submission point regarding the assault on the masturbation, count five?

JUDGE JAMESON: Ah, yes. Well, certainly we can do that because that nature – that type of count will be on the indictment, I assume.

MR HAMPTON: Yes.

JUDGE JAMESON: I mean, I haven't seen the new proposed indictment.

MR HAMPTON: It is.

JUDGE JAMESON: Whatever the ruling on that is, I mean, whether it's agreed that it should go forward in the new form or in any other form, there will be such a count on it, presumably. So, yes, I don't see any reason why I shouldn't, at least in principle, deal with any submission that Mr Storey wants to make about that.

MR STOREY: Certainly. Well, I am content to do it now, your Honour, thank you.

JUDGE JAMESON: Yes.

MR STOREY: Your Honour will have seen, obviously, my learned friend's skeleton argument document.

JUDGE JAMESON: I have, yes.

MR STOREY: I am afraid I haven't responded in writing. It was, as you know, uploaded to the digital case system last night. The position, though, is that the defence would say in relation to the counts which I think on the new indictment retain the same numbering that they are, for the record, certainly on the original indictment, counts five...

JUDGE JAMESON: Well, I can probably turn up the new indictment. First, is there in fact going to be any dispute about the new indictment do you think or...

MR STOREY: I think it's unlikely other than this point about the indecent assault allegation.

JUDGE JAMESON: Yes, okay. Well, let me just get that then. Where will I find that?

MR HAMPTON: I am sorry, I haven't uploaded it. I did email it.

JUDGE JAMESON: Oh, you've emailed it?

MR HAMPTON: Yes. Shall I upload it as well? Mr Smith has a paper copy. Would your Honour mind having that?

JUDGE JAMESON: Well, if you've got one. I've just found it, in fact. Right, yes, so let's have a look. So, count one is presumably exactly the same?

MR HAMPTON: The same, yes.

JUDGE JAMESON: I mean, probably, ideally, I suppose, it would have been easier to have all the different types of different examples of types of conduct alleged in consecutive counts, but it doesn't really matter.

MR HAMPTON: Yes.

JUDGE JAMESON: All right. Anyway, so we've got now count two, an allegation of rape just under the age of 16.

MR HAMPTON: Correct.

JUDGE JAMESON: Yes, and that is the first occasion, so specific. Count three, other than count one.

MR HAMPTON: Yes.

JUDGE JAMESON: Yes. Count seven, other than counts two and three. Wait a minute. It should be count three – it should be other than in count two, shouldn't it, just for – count three, specimen, repeat offending of the same kind other than –

MR HAMPTON: Count two, thank you.

JUDGE JAMESON: It should be count two.

MR HAMPTON: Yes, I will change that.

JUDGE JAMESON: So, that can just be changed. All right. Then going forward, count seven, other than two and three, yes. And count 11, other than two, three and seven, yes.

MR HAMPTON: Yes.

JUDGE JAMESON: And then count 15 is the final matter.

MR HAMPTON: Yes.

JUDGE JAMESON: The final allegation. Ah, well, you have simply put it, "other than two, three, seven and 11", but was that not said to be the last occasion?

MR HAMPTON: Yes.

JUDGE JAMESON: Ah, sorry, it says here, yes.

MR HAMPTON: Yes.

JUDGE JAMESON: Right, the final occasion. It probably doesn't need the bit about, "on an occasion other than two, three, seven"

MR HAMPTON: No.

JUDGE JAMESON: Well, perhaps – yes, it does, actually, thinking about it, otherwise...

MR HAMPTON: Yes, it does.

JUDGE JAMESON: ...technically there could be an overlap.

MR HAMPTON: It could be the same, yes.

JUDGE JAMESON: Okay, that's fine. Yes, good all right. And then – so we've got count four is indecent assault.

MR HAMPTON: Yes, that's the oral sex.

JUDGE JAMESON: Yes. Well, now, that's not repeat offending of the same kind, is it, because it's a first reference to that. The first indecent assault is the allegation of the kissing after the shooting of the dog.

MR HAMPTON: Yes, so I'll delete those words. It will just read, "requiring the complainant to perform oral sex upon him."

JUDGE JAMESON: Yes, so you just take out the words, "repeat offending of the same kind", I think.

MR HAMPTON: Yes.

JUDGE JAMESON: So, it then is, "requiring complainant to perform oral sex upon him, aged 13 to 15". We'll just finish this process first and then come back to the submissions. So, count five is again – wouldn't be repeated offending, would it?

MR HAMPTON: No, I'll delete that.

JUDGE JAMESON: So, that comes out.

MR HAMPTON: Six has the same problem.

JUDGE JAMESON: And six, ditto. That comes out. So, we've got – those are the three kinds of indecent assault asserted.

MR HAMPTON: Yes.

JUDGE JAMESON: Oral sex, masturbation and digital penetration, right. So, count seven – oh no, that we've already looked at. So, count eight is oral sex. So, that is a repeat offending other than in count four. Yes, that's correct. Count nine, the same – masturbation other than count five, yes. And count 10, yes, other than count six. Count 11 we've looked at. Count 12 is oral sex other than four and eight. I think that's correct, yes. Thirteen, masturbation other than five and nine, and count 14, digital penetration other than six and 10. Yes, okay. That all seems fine. Right, so, the ones that we're looking at, then, that Mr Storey, you would like to address me on relate to counts five...

MR STOREY: Nine and 13, your Honour.

JUDGE JAMESON: And 13?

MR STOREY: Five, nine and 13.

JUDGE JAMESON: Five, nine and 13.

MR STOREY: The three counts which allege specifically that...

JUDGE JAMESON: Yes, right.

MR STOREY: ...the defendant required the complainant to masturbate him.

JUDGE JAMESON: Yes.

MR STOREY: And your Honour, as you have already indicated, has seen the document that my learned friend Mr Hampton disseminated last night.

JUDGE JAMESON: I have. I haven't, I have to confess, seen them terribly recently. Are they actually on the DCS? I think they are.

MR STOREY: Yes, they are.

MR HAMPTON: Yes, they are section...

JUDGE JAMESON: Yes, can we just get that up, and I'll have them immediately to hand.

MR STOREY: Section Q. It's at item Q7.

JUDGE JAMESON: Yes, I've got it. Right, so we're on Q20, essentially?

MR STOREY: Yes. The authorities that were attached, *Fairclough v Whipp...*

JUDGE JAMESON: Yes.

MR STOREY: *DCP v Rogers* and *R v Christopher Dunn* are at sections Q9, 10 and 11, for what it's worth. Your Honour will, I am sure, have gleaned, if you have been able to read that document, that skeleton argument, that the law in relation to indecent assault makes clear that there has to obviously be a touching in circumstances of indecency.

JUDGE JAMESON: Yes.

MR STOREY: And the first of those three authorities, *Fairclough v Whipp* is authority for the proposition that essentially where there is an invitation to, as in that particular case, a child to touch the penis of the inviter without anything further taking place, which the child then goes on to do...

JUDGE JAMESON: Yes, these are quite old authorities. Things have developed a bit since then.

MR STOREY: They are and it has.

JUDGE JAMESON: Yes.

MR STOREY: But, of course, we are dealing with an old offence.

JUDGE JAMESON: Yes.

MR STOREY: But what that case essentially established was that where, as I say, an invitation was made to somebody else to touch the penis of the inviter without anything else being done and the child in that case exceeded to that request, there was not in fact deemed to be an assault upon the child. And that very simply is the issue which we say is or at the very least may be relevant to the court's consideration of counts five, nine and 13.

JUDGE JAMESON: Yes, well there are two aspects to this. I have given this matter a bit of thought. Sorry, I tended to jump in...

MR STOREY: Don't worry. It helps me, your Honour, thank you.

JUDGE JAMESON: The first, I suppose, is whether there is an evidential basis for the count and secondly, if there is, how I should sum it up.

MR STOREY: Yes.

JUDGE JAMESON: I think the answer to the first is that there plainly is an evidential basis, isn't there?

MR STOREY: Well, what I was going to say about that, with respect, is this. the evidence as to whether there was a physical touching beyond a request or whatever...

JUDGE JAMESON: Yes, well, it's the placing of the hand.

MR STOREY: As I read the evidence, if I can put it that way, the evidence is equivocal because whilst the notes of the Bar in relation to what she said in cross-examination suggest that there may have been a taking of her hand by the defendant...

JUDGE JAMESON: Yes.

MR STOREY: ... and a placing of her hand on his penis, which I concede readily would amount to an indecent assault, when my learned friend was asking her about that very issue in re-examination, the answer – I think the Bar is generally agreed – was to the effect that, "He would tell me to do it to him". She didn't seem to reiterate or affirm that which she may have said in cross-examination. And so there's a question mark, I would submit, as to whether there is in fact an evidential basis for saying that...

JUDGE JAMESON: That's in re-examination, is it?

MR STOREY: It was.

JUDGE JAMESON: I have to say I don't have that note but...

MR HAMPTON: I agree that.

JUDGE JAMESON: ... I was doing the best I could to keep up and also to try and anticipate what was going to be relevant and what wasn't and I haven't, I must confess, thought of that. So, what is it agreed that she said in re-examination?

MR STOREY: "He would tell me to do it to him".

JUDGE JAMESON: Yes, all right.

MR STOREY: As opposed to what she'd said in cross-examination.

JUDGE JAMESON: Yes.

MR STOREY: So, a question mark over whether or not that undoubted evidential sufficiency is met. Your Honour knows that the prosecution go further and say that she committed these acts – if it's the case that her hand was not placed on his, she committed these acts through fear of assault or violence but again I would say that there is some equivocal aspect of that as well. It may be that, as Mr Hamilton's document says, she was conditioned to do whatever was asked of her, but that is not necessarily the same thing as being in fear of being the victim of immediate assault or even assault in the not too distant future if she were to have refused. Whilst the prosecution draw your Honour's attention in their document to a couple of passages within the ABE interview transcript, it's right also to, with respect, draw your Honour's attention to other passages in the same areas where she said the following. Perhaps I can take your Honour directly to it by reference to the transcript.

JUDGE JAMESON: Yes, I have the transcript.

MR STOREY: Page 60, first of all.

JUDGE JAMESON: Sixty?

MR STOREY: Sixty, yes. I think we are working from the same transcript with the editing marked on it...

JUDGE JAMESON: I hope so, yes.

MR STOREY: ...of 71?

JUDGE JAMESON: Seventy-one? Yes, I don't think there actually is a page 71. It appears to end on 70 of 71, but – my version, anyway.

MR STOREY: Right. It's the version on which the highlighted passages were included which your Honour was asked to consider at the very outset of the trial.

JUDGE JAMESON: Yes.

MR STOREY: And certainly...

JUDGE JAMESON: That's the only one I've ever had.

MR STOREY: That's what I thought.

JUDGE JAMESON: Yes.

MR STOREY: If your Honour was to look at page 60 of 71...

JUDGE JAMESON: Got it.

MR STOREY: ... and the first time, towards the top of the page, is 1407.15.

JUDGE JAMESON: Yes.

MR STOREY: A large passage of narrative, commentary by the complainant. A little over halfway down the page, your Honour may see a line that reads, "You know, he didn't strangle me to do it, he didn't", before – I don't know---

JUDGE JAMESON: Yes.

MR STOREY: ... before she then says, and it's this line that I am drawing to your Honour's attention, "I just were compliant with everything he wanted me to do." And she goes over two pages further on in the transcript at page 62 of 71 – the section that's highlighted about five lines, four lines down from the top of the middle section on that page, which begins, "So, he – he knew, he knew".

JUDGE JAMESON: Yes.

MR STOREY: Four lines down, she said, "You know, he never – he never had to beat me during it to make me do anything. He'd already groomed me and done all that to me when I were a child". And again she makes the same observation in the last highlighted section, some six or seven lines up from the bottom of the page: "So, no, he didn't beat me, you know, when I were doing it."

So, those passages, I would say, with respect, point to an absence of anything within the evidence to indicate that at the time she was being asked to masturbate the defendant, that she feared immediate violence if she refused, or even the possibility of immediate violence if she refused. And it's for that reason the equivocal nature of those two strands of the evidence that I would submit that the allegations at counts five, nine and 13 of indecent assault are not made out here, notwithstanding the subsequent developments in the cases that my learned friend refers to.

They, of course, are authorities relating to cases of assault and the way in which assaults can be committed. They make clear that assaults can be committed where somebody is put in fear of or apprehension of violence being directed towards them either in the immediate or, it would appear, in the further future. But here the evidence is equivocal as to whether there was even that fear at the time of the request to masturbate. And so it's for that reason, as I say, that I would submit that there is not an evidential basis for the Crown to leave here to the jury – I am sorry, there is no evidential basis for the court to leave here to the jury the three counts of indecent assault that specifically relate to the allegation of masturbation, and that is as simply as I can put my submissions.

JUDGE JAMESON: Yes. I am just wondering if this is – an interesting argument, and of course it may have a practical consequence but I am just wondering whether it's an argument that's actually necessary and even if I were to rule, Mr Hampton, against – in your favour and against Mr Storey, I am going to have to give the jury some fairly complicated directions about what they would have to find in relation to those three counts. Gross indecency? What's the matter with that?

MR STOREY: Well, that was the discussion that we had at the start of the trial, if my memory serves me right.

MR HAMPTON: The answer's in the footnote of my document.

JUDGE JAMESON: Yes.

MR HAMPTON: It's not indictable. We can't charge him because of her age. She wasn't a child. Yes, she wasn't a child.

JUDGE JAMESON: Does it have to be charged within...

MR HAMPTON: No, no, she wasn't a child – because of her age.

MR STOREY: Prior to 1997, the offence had to be committed upon someone under the age of 14.

JUDGE JAMESON: Oh, right.

MR STOREY: And so here where we're considering...

JUDGE JAMESON: Yes, I've got it.

MR STOREY: ...a period where she at least may have been 14 or 15.

JUDGE JAMESON: So, it's indecent assault or nothing?

MR STOREY: Yes.

JUDGE JAMESON: Yes, okay. In that case we do have to have a debate.

MR STOREY: I'm afraid so.

JUDGE JAMESON: Yes, okay, assuming, Mr Hampton, that you do actually want to have the counts on the indictment – I mean, the evidence remains.

MR HAMPTON: The evidence remains whatever the decision, yes.

JUDGE JAMESON: Yes. My provisional view, and I will listen to further argument about this – I see that there is – she said various different things at various different times, but of course it's all a question, really, of the precise issue that she's seeking to address at any given moment. What I think is a more helpful way of really looking at it is, is there evidence at any point that indicates that there was a fear of potential violence and that appears pretty clear from page 60. So, I think it would be – I think I probably could and would leave these counts to the jury but I am going to have to give them fairly complicated direction about they would have to be satisfied either that her hand was placed upon his penis or that she was in fear of violence. I can do that, of course. I mean...

MR HAMPTON: I see why you...

JUDGE JAMESON: ...they are not particularly complicated directions, but it just means that instead of the issue being did it happen or didn't it...

MR HAMPTON: It becomes more complex.

JUDGE JAMESON: ... it gets a bit more complicated. It's a matter for you. I mean, I can't – I'm perfectly happy to. I can't prevent you from having what you want on the indictment. I'm entirely – provided that it complies with the indictment rules, but I just wonder whether one possible way forward would simply be to remove those counts but the evidence is still there. I mean, let's put it this way. I haven't yet discussed this with you, but one of the things I will need to discuss with you at the end of Mr Appleyard's – or at the end of defence evidence is whether I should be saying anything to the jury along the lines, "This is really all or nothing". It may be that that is a realistic way to put it to them. If that is how it eventually is, then if they're going to acquit, they will acquit regardless of whether those counts are on the indictment, and if they're going to convict, they would convict regardless of whether the counts were on the indictment and whether they were on the indictment would make no difference whatsoever to the ultimate sentence.

MR HAMPTON: Your Honour's course has its attractions.

JUDGE JAMESON: It would need explaining to the jury of course.

MR HAMPTON: Your Honour would explain fully why we were not requiring a verdict on those counts or entering not guilty verdicts, whichever way it has to go.

JUDGE JAMESON: Do you want to think about it overnight? We can always – we can sit at 10 tomorrow and you can decide what you want to do.

MR HAMPTON: Yes, I think that's probably best.

JUDGE JAMESON: Also, I'd like – I mean, if there is anything else that either of you would like to say, if I am going to have to make a ruling, I'll have to make a ruling. I'm merely indicating at the moment that I think that's how – likely how I would find.

MR HAMPTON: Yes.

JUDGE JAMESON: But I haven't formally made such a ruling because I wouldn't want Mr Storey or for that matter Mr Appleyard to think that Mr Storey hadn't had every opportunity to make the submissions that he wants. But if I have to make a ruling, I'll make it. I'll make it tomorrow morning if required to, but you might just want to think whether or not there is really a practical benefit in having them as counts on the indictment.

MR HAMPTON: I appreciate it could become a side issue. One of the difficulties I will have is in many people's worlds it's not a difficulty, but in some people's worlds, it is. These counts have been on the indictment from the beginning so to remove them, there would have to be some rationale for that. It would a have to be explained to others, so it would take some time.

JUDGE JAMESON: Yes.

MR HAMPTON: I'm fairly neutral about it, I have to say but if your Honour gives me time to consult...

JUDGE JAMESON: Well, yes I understand the dynamics and the difficulties of the case, so I am not directing the approach here.

MR HAMPTON: No, I know that.

JUDGE JAMESON: I'm merely setting out what the options are and...

MR HAMPTON: Yes.

JUDGE JAMESON: ...ideally I would like to keep this as simple for the jury as it possibly can be.

MR HAMPTON: Yes. Well, could I undertake to email all parties this evening with a decision?

JUDGE JAMESON: Yes, whenever is convenient and what I suggest is that we'll sit at 10...

MR HAMPTON: Yes, please.

JUDGE JAMESON: ...just in case there's anything else that needs to be discussed because I would like, if possible, to crack on promptly at 10.30 with our jury who are just starting, I think, to get a little concerned about the type of stop/start nature of things.

MR HAMPTON: I don't think there could be any other disposal of those counts other than not guilty verdicts given the jury are charged...

JUDGE JAMESON: Well, what would have to happen if they were – I think they probably – they could simply stay physically on the – well, they could be taken off the indictment that the jury are actually going to have to consider.

MR HAMPTON: Yes.

JUDGE JAMESON: But they have been put in charge of Mr Appleyard in relation to them and so something will have to happen to them. In the first instance, I will tell the jury that they would not be required, whether they were on the indictment or whether they weren't, that they weren't required to return verdicts in those counts and then in due course, we'd have to decide what we were going to do with them at the end of the trial.

MR HAMPTON: Yes.

JUDGE JAMESON: But, I mean in reality if there were acquittals, then I would anticipate that you would offer no evidence on them.

MR HAMPTON: Yes.

JUDGE JAMESON: I think it would be abusive to do anything else.

MR HAMPTON: No, of course.

JUDGE JAMESON: If there were convictions then they could simply be left on the file.

MR HAMPTON: Yes, and there would be no objection – I can't see there would be any objection to your Honour explaining why that course of action was being taken.

JUDGE JAMESON: I don't think there would be any difficulty at all. I'd just say, "There is a technical point as to whether or not these amount to assaults and, in the circumstances, it's not thought necessary for you to have to make that decision and the evidence remains and you can make such decisions as you think about the evidence and that will impact one way or the other upon your decisions for the counts that remain."

MR STOREY: Mm hm.

MR HAMPTON: With some explanation as to the issue of the assault, I think, that being the legal issue.

JUDGE JAMESON: Yes, I could tell them that it's – yes, I'll think of a way of doing it but certainly there can be some explanation of it, yes.

MR HAMPTON: Thank you.

JUDGE JAMESON: Okay. (Brief discussion with associate)

(Adjourned until 10 a.m. on Tuesday 22 January 2019)

(3.55 p.m.)

Diary: Monday 21st January 2019

I found it very frustrating listening to Alex Wilson recount his thoughts and opinions about the investigation he had conducted, half-heartedly in my view. I still felt extremely angry that the blue folder had not been included in evidence, neither would my medical records have been if I had not been persistent. He described me as argumentative and of pestering him, when, in fact I had been anxious that all avenues were not being thoroughly investigated and all witnesses were not being contacted I had had years of being failed by the police and of evidence going missing, being lost or burnt, statements not being taken. I had been forced to be assertive. He and other officers should have been aware what the effect of this has on a victim. Instead, they had been dismissive and condescending throughout, and my thought s and feelings had continually been ignored. When I suggested who statements should be taken from, he said "Don't argue with me Carol, it's up to me and my supervisor who we do and don't take statements from." When I told him about my babysitter contacting me concerning witnessing my dad punching me as a baby, I suggested he talk to her. He told me "I am not investigating physical abuse, Carol, I am investigating rape." Yet when I told DI Thornes of this, he had said that it was evidence which would have built up a picture of my dad's character. So many contradictions! Similarly, when I told Alex Wilson of the black Nazi cult paedophile ring which I know my father to be part of, he said "I am not investigating a paedophile ring, I am investigating your father for rape."

Tuesday 22 January, 2019

(Transcript prepared without the aid of documentation)

(In the absence of the jury at 10.11 a.m.)

(10.11 a.m.)

JUDGE JAMESON: Good morning, gentlemen. I don't know if Mr Appleyard's actually here, is he?

MR HAMPTON: He is, yes.

MR STOREY: Yes.

JUDGE JAMESON: Yes, well, he'd probably like to be in court then to hear...

MR STOREY: I expect so, yes.

JUDGE JAMESON: ...what happens. (After a pause) Do sit down, Mr Appleyard. Right. Well now, Mr Storey, you'll have received the email last night (inaudible)

MR STOREY: I did, thank you very much indeed.

JUDGE JAMESON: Good, not from me but from Mr Hampton.

MR STOREY: I received both his and your emails, thank you.

JUDGE JAMESON: Well, yes and mine also considering whether or not there will need to be a *Brown* direction. I don't think we need to think about now but we will need to before you address the jury.

MR STOREY: Potentially, yes. In relation to the submission, I made yesterday, just for the avoidance of doubt, I'm conscious that I didn't specifically make reference to the case of *Galbraith*. I know your Honour...

JUDGE JAMESON: Yes.

MR STOREY: ...will have that in your mind and that this submission was based on the second limb...

JUDGE JAMESON: Yes.

MR STOREY: ...given the way that I've put it. There's nothing that I need to say further in relation to the submission. Your Honour made your ruling fairly clear, although you didn't give a formal ruling...

JUDGE JAMESON: Yes.

MR STOREY: ...I don't necessarily seek one and I'm content to accept what you said yesterday about that.

JUDGE JAMESON: Well, I'm grateful. If there isn't anything else, essentially what I have in mind is that there is evidence there that would support those counts in one or both, potentially, ways. I can see...conceive and understand that, at different times, there have been different ways of expressing those concepts. I don't think it goes quite far enough to, essentially, reduce the evidential basis to one that's insufficient to support the case. It's certainly grist to defence submissions, absolutely, I see that but the situation really where one can withdraw it is where something has been said and then, perhaps, in cross-examination or some time later, it's been completely negated by what's being said and I really don't think we've got to that situation here. So, although it makes life a little more difficult, both for me and for the jury, perhaps also for counsel, I don't think I can, unfortunately intervene.

MR STOREY: No, well I understand that and I don't take any issue...

JUDGE JAMESON: Yeah.

MR STOREY: ...with that, thank you very much. In terms of the prosecution stance relating to those specific counts, the indictment and its form and content, is, obviously, a matter for them and I can say nothing about the decision that they have indicated...

JUDGE JAMESON: Yeah.

MR STOREY: ...to the Court and to the defence. It's a matter for them entirely.

JUDGE JAMESON: Yeah.

MR STOREY: ...and I think that's as far as we can take that aspect of it.

JUDGE JAMESON: Yes. All right. So, all that's left then, from the Crown's point of view, I think you indicated no more evidence, Mr Hampton.

MR HAMPTON: There's one agreed fact that my learned friend seeks which we're happy to make...

JUDGE JAMESON: Yes, of course.

MR HAMPTON: ...it can be done at any point.

JUDGE JAMESON: All right. So, that's going to come as part of your case, is it?

MR HAMPTON: We can do it as part of my learned friend's.

JUDGE JAMESON: All right.

MR STOREY: I don't mind when it goes before the jury so long as they've got it at some point.

JUDGE JAMESON: ...(inaudible) if it's for your purposes probably better if it goes in as part of your case. Right so, it's simply just...how are you going to do that, an amendment of the indictment, I think that would probably be better, wouldn't it, cos it's all the...it's still the same 15 counts?

MR HAMPTON: It is, that's what I've anticipated, it's simply now...

JUDGE JAMESON: All right.

MR HAMPTON: ...and then just a date and specifics.

JUDGE JAMESON: Okay. Well, would you indicate, perhaps in front of the jury, that that's what you propose to do.

MR HAMPTON: Yes.

JUDGE JAMESON: Give it to them and I'll indicate that we've obviously discussed it. I'll tell them briefly what the purpose of the alterations are and tell them that they'll get full directions about it in due course.

MR HAMPTON: Thank you very much.

JUDGE JAMESON: Okay. Right.

MR HAMPTON: Should I hand out now to your Honour and my learned friend the amended indictment?

JUDGE JAMESON: Yeah, certainly. I've probably got it actually but...

MR HAMPTON: It's the last one I emailed.

JUDGE JAMESON: No, I think you gave me this yesterday, a hard copy but it may be that it's changed, I doubt it.

MR HAMPTON: It may have, yeah.

JUDGE JAMESON: But give me one of those so, that there's absolutely no doubt that I'm getting precisely what...

MR HAMPTON: Yes.

JUDGE JAMESON: ...the jury will be getting.

MR HAMPTON: Can I alert your Honour to one matter...

JUDGE JAMESON: Yes.

MR HAMPTON: ...that I've just noticed, Count 4...

JUDGE JAMESON: Yes.

MR HAMPTON: ...is missing the words "Prior to" before the date.

JUDGE JAMESON: Ah, yes.

MR HAMPTON: It was my typo. I've only just noticed it.

JUDGE JAMESON: Well, we don't need to. We'll just get the jury to put that in there.

MR HAMPTON: Thank you.

JUDGE JAMESON: Yes, all right. Thank you very much. Anything else then at the moment?

MR STOREY: No, thank you for my part.

MR HAMPTON: No, thank you.

JUDGE JAMESON: Okay.

MR HAMPTON: I'll close my case subject to the agreed fact.

JUDGE JAMESON: Well, I don't think the jury will be down until half past 10 so, thank you both very much for being here and I'll come back in at half past 10.

MR HAMPTON: Thank you, your Honour.

(10.17 a.m.)

(Short break)

(10.29 a.m.)

MR STOREY: Just before the jury come in, your Honour. I did email your Honour this morning and my learned friend and I have also uploaded to the digital case system a very brief letter from the defendant's general practitioner. I don't know if you've seen that.

JUDGE JAMESON: I'm sorry, I haven't, no. Has that been emailed this morning?

MR STOREY: It was emailed this morning and I thought I had uploaded it to the digital case system as well.

JUDGE JAMESON: Right, I'll just get that up.

MR STOREY: And it is at section 08 or p.017 on the digital system.

JUDGE JAMESON: Right. Sorry, has it been emailed to me or has it gone onto the DCS?

MR STOREY: Both.

JUDGE JAMESON: Right. It hasn't arrived as an email curiously.

MR STOREY: Okay, I'm sorry about that.

JUDGE JAMESON: Let me go onto the DCS. Where would I find it there?

MR STOREY: At 08.

JUDGE JAMESON: 08.

MR STOREY: That's item 08, rather than page number.

JUDGE JAMESON: I'll just have to refresh that. Yes, here it is.

MR STOREY: There are, in fact, three...three pages. It's only the first page that's relevant for present purposes.

JUDGE JAMESON: Right.

MR STOREY: And it simply makes a request on his behalf that for the reasons that are set out in that letter he'd be allowed to sit down...

JUDGE JAMESON: Yes, certainly, of course.

MR STOREY: ...whilst giving his evidence. Simple as that.

JUDGE JAMESON: Yes, thank you very much indeed. Yeah.

MR STOREY: Thank you.

JUDGE JAMESON: Yeah, of course Mr Appleyard can sit throughout his evidence.

MR STOREY: Thank you.

JUDGE JAMESON: Good, yes. Thank you very much. (After a pause)

(The jury return to court at 10.31 a.m.)

JUDGE JAMESON: Good morning, ladies and gentlemen, welcome back.

MR HAMPTON: Before the prosecution closes its case, your Honour, there is an application to amend the indictment.

JUDGE JAMESON: Yes.

MR HAMPTON: It's an application of which your Honour and my learned friend is aware and it regards the issue of dates. Could I hand out a copy of the indictment to the jury in the amended form, please?

JUDGE JAMESON: Yes. Ladies and gentlemen, what you're going to get now is an amended version of the indictment you've already got. When you've got it, I'll just take you through it and explain what the differences are and why they're there. This was an application that the Crown actually made yesterday so, I've heard submissions about it and this is the result of those submissions. This is what you're going to get. You will, at the moment, have got the original indictment. I don't know if anybody has made any notes on that. You may want to keep them. If you do, if you have, then could you just mark it "Original indictment", perhaps, so, you know which one it is. If you haven't then we'll simply take it away and replace it. So, just have a quick look and see if you have made any notes and if anybody has and wants to keep it, it's absolutely fine but we do just need to make sure that you've got it all marked up so, that there's no possibility of a mistake later. But you don't, you really don't need to keep it if you haven't made any notes on it. Okay. So, our usher will come round now, collect up those who don't need to keep and give everybody the new version. Right, can I just check then, so, has anybody kept theirs, the old one, nobody? Good. All right. So, you'll just have the new one, that's fine.

Now, I'm not going to take you through this in detail now, ladies and gentlemen, I'll do that at the end of the case. But, really, the only significant difference is that in relation to many, not all of the counts, but many of them, originally, they were divided up as between ages of Carol Higgins 13 and 14 and it's been taken...the view's been taken, I think generally, that that just gives you a completely unnecessary and irrelevant decision to make, whether it falls one side or another of a birthday and it really has no legal significance at all. So, those dates have, essentially, been taken out and the dates have just been expressed in a different way. So, essentially, if one looks, for example, at Count 2 as an example. Count 1 is different, that's a specific count but if we look at Count 2, which is the first allegation of rape, it's now simply being put in as a girl under the age of 16 years. So, it just means that an irrelevant issue that you really don't need to deal with, has been taken away in that way and that's really what it's all about. Okay? So, we'll go through all of that in due course when I sum the case up to you and there may be submissions about it before we get there, we shall see. But that's the purpose of it. Yes.

MR HAMPTON: Thank you your Honour. Well, subject to one further agreed fact that will be put before the jury in due course, that is the close of the Crown's case.

JUDGE JAMESON: All right. Thank you very much indeed. Yes.

MR STOREY: Can I please call Elliott Appleyard to give evidence, your Honour?

JUDGE JAMESON: Yes, of course. Now, ladies and gentlemen, Mr Appleyard is going to sit throughout his evidence. There's a perfectly proper medical reason for that so, he'll be sitting down. I'll ask him to keep his voice up nice and loud but he will be sitting.

ELLIOTT APPLEYARD, Sworn

Examined by MR STOREY

Q Can you just begin, please, by giving us your full name?

A It's Elliott Appleyard.

Q Thank you, Mr Appleyard. You've heard what his Honour has just said. He's explained that he's allowed you to give evidence seated but it's important that you keep your voice up because the ladies and gentlemen of the jury opposite need to hear what you're saying and that microphone might not actually make much difference, all right?

A Okay.

Q So, can I suggest that you look at the ladies and gentlemen of the jury across from you and if it looks to you as though they're struggling to hear what you're saying you know you're not speaking loud enough. All right?

A Okay.

Q Can I begin, please, by asking you this? Are you responsible for sexually abusing your daughter, Carol Higgins?

A No, I am not.

Q We know from the agreed facts that you were born in 1947.

A Correct.

Q I think you now are 71, is that right?

A Correct.

Q Can you tell us, please, when it was you first met your former wife, Jean Voss?

A It was end of July, beginning of August 1967 at a place called Balby. It's on the outskirts of Doncaster.

Q And did you start living together from that point onwards or did you...

A No. I was travelling with a fairground at the time. I'd been travelling with them in 1966 and '67 and that were my second year with 'em. We...she kept coming onto the machine where I worked and we started seeing one another from there. We saw one another for a few months in...I were moving round and in October of '67 I was...we were based in Hull, a fairground there. We were there for three weeks and it was coming to end of season. I left and I went back home to me parents' house and I never saw her ever again until March of 1968.

Q Right. Did there come a time when you and she started living together?

A She...I were working on a construction site in Huddersfield with me brother at the time and I got home one day and me sister was there, in me parents' house, and when I walked through the door she says, "You kept that quiet didn't you, daddy?" I said, 'What are you talking about?' She says, "A little girl." I says, 'What are you talking about? I don't know what you're talking about.' And she held up a piece of paper and it was a telegram that had come from Jean Voss or Thorpe she were called at the time. It were from her and it said, "A little girl born 6th March." And that were basically it.

Q I'm going to interrupt you there, Mr Appleyard, because I asked you, 'Did there come a time when you and Jean Voss started living together?'

A No, she turned up at my house a week after I'd received the telegram. Well, she turned up at me parents' house a week after I'd got...I received the telegram and I got home from work that night and she were sat on me parents' settee there with a baby in her arms.

Q And was that baby Donna?

A That was Donna.

Q Was Donna yours?

A No.

Q And did you and Jean Voss start living together?

A It was March, beginning of March and it was...it was...it was cold and wet. It was like a winter's day, like it is today. Me parents...me father took me to one side and he says, "Is it yours?" I says, 'No, it's not.' And he says, "Get rid of her." And I says, "You can't turn a baby out in winter time." And I couldn't turn it out. So, I persuaded me parents to let her stop and she stopped there at me parents' house and me father didn't want it and me parents didn't want it. So, being in a village and they had village councillors in them days, he went to see the village council and it was me father who got us a council house and we moved down there in...I think it were July-time, something like that, in 1968. We moved into a two-bedroom council house in Denby Dale and we stayed there...we lived there until I think it were about '74, '75 when we got married.

Q Right. We know from the admissions, the agreed facts, that Carol was born in April 1969 and Paul in October 1970.

A Correct.

Q You married in 1974. Where were you...what was the address you were living at when you married?

A No.8, Gilthwaites Crescent.

Q There came a time, we know, that you moved to 26, Gilthwaites Crescent.

A The same year. There was a...there was a lad and his father living on their own in a three-bedroom house (inaudible) they were on a three-bedroomed house, ours were two-bedroom house and by that time Carol and Paul was on the scene so, I went and talked to them about it and the council said that we could have an exchange if both parties were agreed. So, we exchanged houses. We moved into the three-bedroomed house at No.26 and they moved into No.8.

Q How would you describe the relationship between you and Jean at first in, let us say, around 1974 when you married.

A It wasn't too bad. Kept having arguments like every normal couple did but it wasn't too bad.

Q What about over the following decade or so, into the early 1980s?

A After we got married in the late seventies and that there, there was rumours every time I were coming home from work and I were...I'd go for a pint on a night-time, a couple of pints, and that there and you were hearing rumours about her having affairs and that's when the arguments started. She kept denying it. One occasion I came home from work, I were walking past and one of me neighbours just stopped me and she says, "Elliott, who's them two little blonde-haired kids that keeps going into your garden and that there, there's a gentleman brings them?" I said, 'I don't know what you're talking about.' I said, 'It would probably be Carol and Paul.' And she says, "No, no there's Carol and Paul and he comes during the day with them and they're playing in your garden." I says, 'I don't know.' So, when I confronted her, she said the woman were lying. She said, "She's imagining it." And it started basically...it started from there about...the rumours got worse.

Q You said that there was arguments.

A Yes.

Q It's been said there was also violence. What do you say to that?

A I never ever hit her. We were...we had...we had bad arguments and there was times and that there when, through the heat of the moment and the arguments, and that there, I may have threatened her. But I never ever hit her.

Q Were there ever occasions when she left the family home?

A She left, yeah, after bad arguments she left. On one occasion she went to live with someone at a farm, one of her friends that she'd met on CB and that there. She went...she went to her house, she stayed with her for a couple of weeks and then came back home. She rung me up. I couldn't ring them because I didn't know the number where she was. But she rung me up and she wanted to talk so, I'd go and talk to 'em and then we'd talk it over and she came back.

Q And you...

A Another occasion I got home from work, the door was all locked up and the house was all locked up. I rung the police up to find out what had happened and they gave me a number for social services. I rung them and they said that they'd put her in a battered wife's home. They wouldn't tell me where it was and they said they'd put her in there. I said, 'Why?' She says, "Well, she'd been and made a complaint that you've been beating her up." I said, 'That's a lie, I never touched her.' We've had bad rows. We've had some real stinking rows over that and I said, 'I never touched her.'

Q I was going to ask you Mr Appleyard, can you give us an idea of how many times she might have left before she left you for the last time?

A Twice, just them twice, that twice.

Q Just twice.

A The once when she went to her friend's house and once when she went to...she persuaded social services to put her in that battered house...that battered home.

Q We know, again from the agreed facts, that in 1978 you were granted a shotgun certificate.

A I'd had one before then. I'd had one...prior to 1978 you used to get 'em from the post office and that there. I'd had a shotgun since I were 15-year-old.

Q Paul, when he gave his evidence, described a number of firearms that he recalled you owning. Do you agree with his description of the firearms that you owned?

A Definitely not.

Q How many firearms do you say you owned in the, let's say late 1970s, early 1980s?

A There was three firearms. There was a single-barrel shotgun 12 bore. There was a double-barrel shotgun which was a side by side and there was a gun that I'd been given from a friend of mine in America for Paul and that there because the friend of mine in America, his father had bought it him for his 15th birthday. He had no children to pass it onto and when Paul were 15 years of age, he asked me if I could give it to Paul if I thing(sic) so, it was...they was...they was...they was the only three guns that was in the house.

Q Where were they kept?

A They was kept in my wardrobe.

Q You know it's said that, during the course of an argument, you held a shotgun to the side of Jean's head. What do you say to that?

A If I did and I don't recall it but if I did it was in the heat of the moment in an argument with her when I'd been out shooting or I were going out shooting and that there. There was nothing. There was...there was no...the gun was certainly...were never loaded in the house. None of them was ever loaded in the house and that there and it'd have been done in the heat of the argument.

Q It's also said that on an occasion you held a machete and threatened to slit her from her vagina to her neck effectively.

A No, I didn't.

Q What do you say...what do you say about that allegation?

A No, I did not. I kept...when I was going out shooting, I did have a machete with me. What I did is, I had a little rucksack and the machete had a sleeve at side...that hooks onto the side of the rucksack and the machete was in there and I used to use that machete for cutting branches and that and making hides for shooting pigeons and one thing and another and that was...that was what they're there for. As I say, if there were at any time and that there there was never ever, I never ever hit her once.

Q I want to ask you about how you treated the children, please. How would you describe the way in which you behaved towards them?

A There was...when they were little they was...they were fine. Paul, I couldn't ask for a better son. He was fine when he was with me and that there, I took him out and showed him out to shoot. I showed him how to do fieldcraft, I showed him how to drive. I bought him a motorbike, I learnt him how to drive that. When he was with me, he were fine. I had no problems with him. But when he was away from me it were like a Jekyll and Hyde. He was...he was getting in trouble in school. He was...got expelled from school. He was...

Q But what I asked you, Mr Appleyard, I'm sorry to interrupt you, is how you treated the children. How you behaved...

A If they'd...

Q ...towards them.

A ...if they'd done wrong, I used to give them a clip round lug-hole, I'd (inaudible) crack 'em one and that there. But the mother she did...she did most of it. She used to whack 'em with a wooden spoon and that there across the backside and across the legs.

Q You know that it's said that you would regularly remove your belt and beat them with the belt across the bare backsides.

A No, I never did. Even their mother said that I didn't do that.

Q It's also been said that there were occasions when you would pretend to land a blow on Carol's head in particular and she'd flinch almost as you walked past her doing that.

A No, no, no, no.

Q Do you remember ever doing that?

A No, no, no.

Q How did you spend your time on weekdays in the late 1970s, early 1980s?

A I was working on construction sites, working for different builders. I registered self-employed in 1972 and I was registered from then on there and

I produced a certificate to that effect and that there. I was self-employed. Paul said that I wasn't working and he wouldn't know when I got that certificate cos he were only two years old at time.

Q And how much of the week would you spend working?

A I was out every day working, often on a Saturday morning.

Q You know that it's been said that you would also work on local farms. Is that right?

A If they wanted me to do work for 'em there, tractor driving or building, doing some building work and repair works and that there, I used to go and do it.

Q And when would you do that work?

A Whenever they wanted. I was self-employed.

Q What about collecting scrap, is that something that you would do?

A I collected scrap many, many times when...it wasn't every day and it wasn't every week. Every...every year...every year I made sure that them kids had a holiday. I took all...the whole family went on holiday. We'd go camping in Wales; we'd go camping up Loch Lomond in Scotland; I took 'em to Butlins, Paul and that, they to Butlins for a break. I took 'em on a cruise round the Norwegian Fjords and into Sweden, that cost money. The average wage then was £60/£80 pound a week. I couldn't afford that with bringing up a family. So, I used to collect scrap and that. They had 'em when I weighed that scrap in and took it in and that the money was saved to pay for them holidays. But they wouldn't understand that.

Q When you went collecting scrap did you ever take the children with you?

A Sometimes I'd take Paul with me. On the odd occasion, if we were out and about and that there and I saw scrap and that there and Carol were with me we'd pick it up but I didn't tell...I never ever took Carol just going out specifically for scrap or collecting stuff like that, never.

Q What, so far as you were aware, was their attendance at school like?

A It were terrible. They were always skipping school. I had lots of letters, especially for Paul and Carol, I didn't get many letters for Carol because her mother, she saw to 'em. But she were often off school, skipping school and that there from where they was.

Q Was that something that they did at your instigation, your request?

A No, definitely not.

Q How did you react to finding out that they were off school...

A I were bad.

Q ...when they should've been there.

A I were cross, anybody would do. You've got high hopes for your kids.

Q And what did you do when you were cross with them for missing school?

A I'd give 'em a clout round lug-hole. I'd have an argument with their mother, their mother'd belt 'em and that there. They were...they were running away from school and not...they were just, you know, we thought they were at school and they were running off. We hadn't a clue where they were. I were getting letters from headmaster, especially at Paul's school, telling me that he was concerned of other people that he was knocking about with at school, knocking around with older boys.

Q We've heard that the family had at least one dog.

A Yes.

Q Who was responsible, by and large, for walking the dog or the dogs?

A I was.

Q And when you did that would you do it alone or would anyone accompany you?

A No, no. If they wanted to come with me, they could come with me for walks. I never ever stopped 'em.

Q And which of the children came with you on walks?

A More often than not, Paul. Carol came with me on occasions but she were more around house with her mother or with her friends.

Q We heard about one dog in particular that was shot it's said.

A Yes.

Q Is that right?

A Correct.

Q Was the dog shot?

A Yes.

Q And who shot it?

A I did.

Q And why did you shoot it?

A The dog...the dog was...the person that I went to America with, it was his dog and he'd bought it from a farm down in...from a gamekeeper down in Wales which would train, part train. It was a gun dog and when he got it it had a lot of fits. I don't know for why but it started having a lot of fits and he was gonna get rid of it. He were gonna shoot it. He gave it me and when I had it, for a start it never had any fits and then it started out, it started having the odd one and I was out shooting one day and I'd got the dog with me and I were out shooting one day and we were walking through this field and there was a lot of sheep in the field and the dog started taking off. I don't know whether it were having a fit or what, it just took off and it started running. The sheep were scattering all over the place and the farmer was leaned...he was there at the time, he was the other side of the field, then he was looking over the gate, leaned over the gate looking and he started shouting and bellowing at me to get the dog under control. The dog wouldn't come back. I couldn't get it back out there. As I said, the sheep were running all over so, I shot it. It was either me shoot it or he could have shot it. You don't have to have a dog killing animals. It only has to be frightening them to be classed as worrying and the farmer has a right to shoot that dog. I didn't want him to shoot the dog.

Q Was Carol present with you at the time?

A No, she was not.

Q How did she learn about the shooting?

A When I got home, I told 'em. I told 'em where I'd been...been shooting and I told 'em what had happened and I told 'em that I'd buried it over there.

Q What was the dog called?

A Sam.

Q And how did Carol react to the news that the dog had been shot?

A Well, they were upset.

Q It's been said, Mr Appleyard, that having shot Sam, the dog, in front of her you then began to kiss Carol inappropriately.

A Definitely not true. She wasn't even with me when I shot that dog.

Q Was there ever a time, when out on a walk, you kissed Carol inappropriately?

A No, I did not. The only time that I gave Carol a kiss was as a father and a daughter and that there, where you give 'em a kiss when I were going to work on a morning or they were going to bed or whatever it is and they were going out somewhere, you kissed her as a thing, you often put your arms round her, sometimes you kiss her at top of head or foreheads. Sometimes you give them a kiss on lips and that but it was only as a father, daughter. I never ever kissed her in that manner.

Q We've heard that you would sometimes use the phrase, "Who loves you, baby?" Is that a phrase you ever used in the late seventies, early eighties?

A Possibly, might well have done.

Q What was the significance...what was the significance of it so far as you were concerned?

A In the seventies and eighties there was a programme on TV called Kojak with Telly Savalas and he was a detective in America, cop programme. His brother was also a detective in the same office and when he solved problems, cases and one thing and another, he used to go up and he used to pat his cheek, the cheeks of his brother and that there and he used to say, "Who loves you, baby." And it was only a phrase that was taken off the television, that's all.

Q There came a time when Jean left, Jean left for the last time, that's right, isn't it?

A Correct.

Q When do you remember that being?

A It was a Friday morning; I was going to work. I was working at a company called Triple B Construction at the time. I'd been working for a company called Taylor Woodrow and I'd gone to move to this other company and every Friday night, when I got home from work, I'd sit down having my tea and there'd be (defendant makes knocking sound) on door and it'd be either the rent man, or it'd be the insurance man, it'd be a clothing company as she got...stuff that she got from...they'd always knock and he was just taking money out of your pocket and you're shelling it out.

Q I'm going to interrupt you, I'm afraid, Mr Appleyard, because I asked you when was it that Jean left?

A It was a Friday and I told her that morning, when I was going to work, I got fed up of this coming home with money and shelling it out and I says, 'It's Friday, it's pay day but you're not having none. I wanna see you gone when I get home.' I says, 'You can take what you want, you can take what furniture you want. If the kids wanna go with you they can go with you. If they wanna stay they can stay.' And I got home that Friday tea-time from work. I got home, pulled up...pulled into the drive with me car and Paul came out and his exact words were, "Stop there, dad" and I opened...he opened the door and he said, "Stop there, dad." I said, 'Why what's up?' I said, 'Has your mam gone?' He says, "Yeah." I said, 'There's nowt to stop here for then, is there?' And I went into the house and I said, 'Whose here?' And Donna was with...had stayed with him, Carol had gone with her mother.

Q When was this, Mr Appleyard? What year was this that?

A This was 1982.

Q Right.

A It was back end of 1982.

Q So, you found that Carol had gone with Jean. Paul and Donna stayed in Denby Dale...

A Yes.

Q ...in the house in Gilthwaites Crescent.

A Yes.

Q Right. And what did Jean take with her when she left?

A Not a lot, mostly clothes and one thing and another. She didn't take...I didn't...I don't think she took any furniture at all with her at the time. She took some clothes with her and, basically, what they needed and that were it, gone.

Q One of the things Carol says is that you would make her wear her mother's wedding ring. What happened, so far as you were aware, to Jean's wedding ring when Jean left?

A She had 'em with her. She took 'em with her. She didn't leave any rings at all. She had 'em with her.

Q Did you know where Jean and Carol had gone to?

A Not originally, no. Not first off.

Q Did you find out where they'd gone?

A I learnt it after there, she rung me up for some money or whatever it was and she told me that they'd gone to Penistone. She was stopping with friends in Penistone but I didn't know what part of Penistone they wor(sic) or where they wor.

Q There came a time, didn't there, when Carol returned to live with you in Gilthwaites Crescent?

A Yes, it was possibly beginning of '83 but she stayed with me for a few...she'd been with her mother for a while, a few months, two or three months whatever it was and then she came back with me, to stop with me.

Q Between her leaving with her mother and returning to you, you said in 1983, what contact had you had with Carol?

A None, none. I didn't even see her that Christmas.

Q What do you remember being said about why she'd come back to live with you in '83?

A There really wasn't an excuse. There was thing...she just...used to come back and said, "I've come back" and then she started telling me that...about her mother going out and leaving her on her own and one thing and another.

Q Does that mean that from the point when Carol returned, you had all three children living at the house?

A No, Donna went, I don't know for why but Donna went then...then went to her mother's.

Q So, Donna went to live with her mother.

A Yes.

Q You had Carol and Paul.

A Yes.

Q And who was responsible at that time for taking care of things inside the house by which I mean washing, cleaning, cooking and the like?

A My washing...every week I took my washing and I dropped it off on a Monday morning on me way to work there at Deanna Thorpe who gave evidence yesterday. I dropped it off at her house. She lived at Scissett. Originally, I dropped it off at me sister's, Hilda Graham's house, and Hilda Graham and that she even...she did it for a few...two or three months and that there and then Deanna says, "I'll do it for you" so...cos Hilda were working part-time at the...at thing so, Deanna Tindall said, "I'll do it." So, I dropped me washing off on a Monday morning, picked it up on a Monday night on me way home and as far as the house was concerned and that there what I didn't do I expected them because they were 13, 14 years of age at time. I expected them to do bits, make their own beds, go round with Vac and get some veg and summat ready for when I got home at night-time.

Q And in that period, 1983, where were you working?

A 1983, I were working for a company called Triple B Construction.

Q And, again, what sort of hours were you working?

A We were working on a dam that was built over River Aire at Garforth...near Garforth. That dam and that, there was a concrete dam and sometimes we were pouring up to 200 tonnes of concrete a day and I were working five days a week. I were off at seven o'clock in the morning. I were coming home, sometimes it were six o'clock at night-time when I were getting home and I was definitely working on a Saturday morning. We had to go back to prepare...take...strip the shuttering off the concrete and get it ready for Monday morning.

Q We know, again from the agreed facts, that in June 1983 there was what is described as an attempt to commit suicide by you.

A Correct.

Q When the police, essentially, had to break into the house and they found you hanging by a rope.

A Correct.

Q What led to you taking that step, Mr Appleyard?

A I were burnt out. I was...I was on the verge of a breakdown. I was suffering from depression. I was taking tablets for depression and that. I was burnt out. Their mother kept ringing me up and wanting money. I kept...my solicitor kept getting letters from her solicitor wanting money and wanting this, that and the other and I ju...I were just...I'd had enough. I just didn't want no more. She could have taken kids and gone there and I just...I just...I were burnt out.

Q In case it is asked or wondered, did that have anything at all to do with Carol?

A Nothing whatsoever, nothing whatsoever.

Q You mentioned, a couple of minutes ago, taking children, I think Carol and Paul, on a cruise around Scandinavia.

A That's correct, that was the beginning of '83.

Q Right.

A Just after Carol had come back to live with me.

Q And there's been mention made of you going to the United States on a hunting trip.

A That was at back end of 1983. That was...we went in November...John and meself went in November and we came back...I think we were there for just short of three weeks. We came back in December.

Q You said John and yourself went. Who's John?

A John Omelia(?) a lad that I'd gone to school with, grown up with and we used to go hunting a lot together, shooting a lot together.

Q In this period, when Carol and Paul were living at the family home with you in Denby Dale, did you ever sexually abuse Carol?

A No, I did not.

Q Specifically, did you ever have sexual intercourse with her?
A No, I did not.
Q Did you ever kiss her inappropriately as adults would kiss?
A The only times I ever kissed Carol was as a father that kisses daughter. No other way whatsoever.
Q Did you ever require her to masturbate you and to read pornography to you?
A No, I did not. I didn't have any mucky magazines despite what they say. I didn't have none.
Q Did you ever require her to perform oral sex upon you?
A No, I did not.
Q And did you ever digitally penetrate her vagina?
A No, I did not.
Q It's been said that Carol would walk around the house wearing just her underwear, is that right or not?
A I never saw her walking round the house in her underwear. Never saw her once walking round the house in her underwear.
Q Did she and Paul sometimes get into your bed...
A Yes, often.
Q ...when you were there?
A Yes, more or less on a Sunday morning. It wasn't Saturday, as they said, because most Saturdays I were working. But a Sunday morning was day off and I'd be laid in bed with no hurry to get up. Because they were kids they used to come in and jump in. One would jump in one side of me and one on the other and we just used to lay there. We'd talk and whatever it is and what we were gonna do, what we weren't gonna do and what we were having for dinner, whether we were going for a pub meal or whatever.
Q Was there ever a time when they would spend the night in your bed with you?
A Never spent a night in my bed with me, not...not once.
Q Was there ever a time when Paul was locked out of the house after going to play football or anything like that?

A He never ever got locked out of the house at all. If he couldn't get in the house, it were because he dropped the latch or whatever it was hiself(sic) He never ever got locked out intentionally, in any shape or form.

Q And do you recall Carol ever leaning out of your bedroom window to talk to him when she was wearing just her underwear?

A No, I do not. He couldn't...he...there's...there's no way he could see her looking out of that bedroom window, there's no way. The building regulations state that a window height has to be three feet. It's now 900 which...900mm which is three feet and the window height has to be three feet to give you privacy. The walls are a foot thick. So, at the time she wouldn't be no more than five foot tall. If she leaned out of that window, he could only see her from shoulders up at the most stick her head out. But there's no way he could see her in her knickers and bra.

Q Was there ever an occasion when Paul walked in on you and Carol, as he put it, snogging in the kitchen?

A No. If Paul came in...if Paul came anywhere and saw me kissing Carol it was a father kisses daughter and I were going somewhere or she were going somewhere or whatever. There was no way did I ever snog, as he puts it, Carol in that manner.

Q And when you were on the Scandinavian cruise, was there an occasion when Paul was trying to get into the cabin but couldn't because you were having sex with Carol inside?

A No, Paul...on occasions Paul'd go for a walk round. It were a big ship which it was, a big ship and if Paul went for a walk round, he'd want to go for a walk round hiself, sometimes they'd walk round together but he'd walk...he'd walk round and if he come back, he couldn't possibly get in the door because you have...they have little swipe cards. They're only like little cardboard things, you swipe them like you get in a hotel. You don't have a normal key, so, he couldn't have took a normal key with him, there's only little cardboard things and if you lose them, you can't get in and out. If you bend 'em you can't get in, they won't work. So, he wasn't given a swipe card (inaudible) I kept the swipe cards for to get in and out the door. He went out so, he had to knock on the door when he came back.

Q It's been said that you gave Carol love bites on her neck. Did you ever do that?

A No, I did not.

Q Did you ever see her with love bites?

A After her mother had gone, she came home from school several times and that, there were love bites on her and I'd go mad about what she (inaudible) and she told me it were lads at school, they were mucking about, they were mucking about at school and that (inaudible) lads that (inaudible) it for fun. I never ever, and her mother...well, all the time that her mother was living with me and that there she never ever saw her with love bites on her neck. Carol didn't have love bites on her neck until after she'd come back in '83 when she...as I say she were playing...mucking about with lads at school.

Q The trip to the United States in late 1983, where were Paul and Carol to stay when you were away in America?

A They were supposed to be staying at me sister's, Hilda Graham's, at Scissett, about a mile and a half down road.

Q And what happened when you came back from that trip?

A When I got...when I got back from that trip, they was at the house waiting on me. I walked in the house. Some of the furniture, not all of it, had gone. Some...a few bits of furniture had gone missing which their mother had...she'd broke in while I was on...in America. She took some furniture out. There were switches, light switches broke. There were...they'd had a party and they'd even been sleeping...she'd been sleeping with boys in my bed and that there and they'd drunk...I had a corner...a corner bar in the corner of the living room and I had optics on there and they'd drunk all me wines and spirits and that there, the beer what I'd had there. In some of the bottles they'd put cold tea. In others, same as the gin and the vodka, they'd put just water in 'em and they'd filled them back up and they were just to make it look as though they hadn't done anything.

Q I'm going to interrupt you just because a note's being made of what you're saying, Mr Appleyard. A number of times you've given very long answers.

A Sorry.

Q I don't want people to feel they can't take a note of what you're saying. What did you do when you got back to the house and found it as you've described?

A Same as any parent'd do, I went mad. I went mad. It wasn't just the abuse of trust that they'd done. It were the fact that they'd been sleeping and they'd been having sex in my bed and the things what they'd done. I went mad.

Q What do you mean by you went mad? What did you actually...

A Oh, I...

Q ...what did you do?

A ...(inaudible) playing hell with 'em, shouting and blurting at 'em, carrying on with them. I were mad.

Q Were the children at the house when you got home?

A Yes, they was. I asked them what the hell had gone off and then it were Paul that told me...it were...it were him that were telling me what lads had been there and that. I didn't know who'd been in the house. I knew that there'd been a party going off but I didn't know who'd been in the house. It were Paul that told me who the lads names was and that what had been there and the fact that they'd been sleeping over with Carol.

Q How did Carol react to you going mad with them?

A She started...she started crying and they were upset and they (inaudible) I wasn't bothered. It were just what...the fact what they'd done. I went round then when the furniture was gone and there was what had happened with the things and that. I went round to the phone but it wasn't to ring Jess up, as Carol said, I went round to ring the police up.

Q And, again, it's been said that Carol cut her wrists that night.

A Not that I recall. I know Donna had done it when she were with her mother but I don't recall.

Q Did you bandage Carol's wrists that night?

A No, I did not.

Q Where do you remember Carol sleeping that night?

A In her bed. She stayed in her bed and Paul stayed in his.

Q Did she sleep in your bed...

A No, she did not.

Q ...at your invitation?

A No, she didn't. There was no way was I going to comfort her in any shape or form after what they'd done. As far as I were concerned and I told them so, they might as well just bugger off back and live with their mother. I were...I were mad. I was annoyed about it so, there were no way was she sleeping in my bed or anybody.

Q You know it's said that that was the first occasion on which you had sexual intercourse with Carol. What do you say to that?

A That's a lie. Just after that incident and that, they were there, Carol went back to her mother. Carol never spent Christmas with me in 1982, '83 or '84 or any Christmas after that. She wasn't with me. Just after that there, when I came back and that there and I was still mad about it there, she went back to live with her mother.

Q At that time did you know exactly where her mother was living?

A No, I did not. I've never known which house her mother lived in.

Q Carol has also described an Army tin in which she says you kept a Polaroid camera and photographs of her. Did you have an Army tin in the house?

A No, what it...it wasn't an Army tin. What it was, I had a tin box in the corner of the bedroom and it was like a little sailor's chest-type thing, it was a half round top on it and in that was kept family papers. There was me mother's and father's birth certificates, death certificates, their wedding certificate. There was a couple of family Bibles in there. There was family...a lot of family photos and that in there. They were, basically, all family heirlooms and things like that kept in that box because I had no safe and had no filing cabinet or anything that was kept in there.

Q Did you have a Polaroid camera?

A No, I didn't. I've never had a Polaroid camera in my life.

Q Did you take pictures of Carol posing for you?

A No, I have not, at any time.

Q What do you say to her suggestion that there was a hairbrush in that tin that you would require her to pose with?

A I find it disgusting that she could even think of that.

Q Were you aware, around this time or, for that matter, any other, of Carol thinking that she might be pregnant?

A No, I never heard of that until I saw it in the papers the police gave me.

Q Was there ever a conversation or discussion between you and Jean about a pregnancy test?

A No, I never saw...I never heard anything and I never saw anything until, as I say, I saw it in the papers when the police questioned me about it.

Q You know that it's said you would make comments about breaking daughters in like the Indians did. Is that something you remember saying at any stage?

A I never recall saying that at any time but their mother said, when she was sat in this dock bay, she said that if it was said it was said in passing while me and her were watching a cowboy film on telly and if Carol took that in the wrong context and that there, I can't help that but I don't recall ever saying it.

Q Do you remember watching a cowboy film on television...

A We watched...

Q ...in which that sort of suggestion was made?

A No, we watched several cowboy films on TV, me and when I was with her mother (inaudible)

Q Did you ever say anything like that to Carron Garside or Carron Ward?

A No, I did not. At any time, I've never ever, in fact, I'd never got on with them. Never spoke to 'em at all in that manner.

Q The agreed facts tells us that in April 1984 you were granted custody by the county court in Huddersfield of Carol and Paul.

A Correct.

Q Were you at the hearing when that custody was granted?

A I certainly was. There was...I was there, Carol and Paul was there. I don't know where Donna was. She were probably at school or in a home. I was there, Carol and Paul was there and the mother was there and it was at Huddersfield Magistrates' Court.

Q And what do you remember of the hearing?

A We went to that hearing, her mother...her mother kept sending solicitor's letters and wanting money off...off me for maintenance for when Carol was there and when Donna was there and that and then she kept wanting money, maintenance money off (inaudible) and I refused and so, she wanted...basically she wanted custody of 'em. If she got custody of 'em then she could have...she'd get maintenance money off me. So, we went to court for that and, at the time, Carol she'd come back and she stopped with me for a couple of month and we went to court and when we got to the magistrates' court in Huddersfield, they read out basically the basic names and addresses and one thing and another and then the magistrate, because they were teenagers, the magistrate and a social worker took 'em in a back room, I'm assuming that he went into his chambers. He was in there for about half an hour talking to Carol and Paul and then they came back out. They both come walking up to me and stood by me and the magistrate read out that he was granting custody to me of 'em both.

Q And how long did you say that Carol had been living with you at that point?

A For maybes a couple of months at most.

Q What...

A I think it was April when...when we went to court for custody.

Q Yes.

A And, as I say, she was never with me at Christmas. She never spent any one Christmas with me. So, it'd be after Christmas. So, a couple of months or so.

Q Can I ask you, what, so far as you were aware, had led to her coming back to you a couple of months before that custody hearing?

A She was never getting what she wanted from her mother. Her mother was leaving her in on her own all the time or so she said. She wasn't buying her any clothes. She wasn't...she wasn't giving her any love and attention and what she wanted and that there so, she came back and she came back home to me and if she did anything wrong with me, I'd go...get mad with her and say, 'You can piss off back to live with your mother.' So, she'd go and live back with her mother and tell her mother stories just like she used to tell me stories when she came to live with me.

Q You said, a little while ago, that Carol didn't spend Christmas '82, Christmas '83 or Christmas '84 with you.

A Definitely not. No, she didn't.

Q When do you remember her leaving after custody had been granted and before Christmas '84?

A It wasn't long. It wasn't long. It was maybe a month, a couple of month but after that she was only with me that period of time about three or four months.

Q And what led to her leaving then?

A I've no idea. I can't remember. We'd probably have had a fallout over something but, by that time, I was going out with me present wife. I was seeing me present wife and Carol went and I never saw her back again. She never ever came back home to stop again. She was, by that time, we got...I got custody of 'em and that was only maybes a couple of weeks, three week at most before her birthday. It'd only be a couple of weeks before her birthday, 15th birthday and...

Q Do you...I'm sorry to interrupt you, Mr Appleyard, do you remember when it was that you married your current wife?

A Yes.

Q What's the date?

A It was September 2nd, 1988.

Q When did you start seeing her, do you remember?

A I first started seeing her end of September beginning of October 1983 about...maybes about four or five weeks before I were going to America. I told her...we had a couple of dates, two or three dates. I told her I was going to America on a hunting trip and she says, "Well, I'll still be here when you get back. Give us a bell." So, when I got back from America in December and that and we'd had a fallout over this and Carol had gone back I spent that Christmas...Christmas Day Paul and I went to Janet's house, she lived at Huddersfield and we went there and we was there Christmas Day and then we started seeing one another. After Christmas we started seeing one another and then after Carol had gone back Janet had come and stop at my house sometimes at weekend cos I were working during week and then, sometimes, I'd go and stop at her house.

Q Right. In the period around the time when custody was granted, so, April '84 and the months either side of that, was Janet living with you at Gilthwaites Crescent?

A Before custody?

Q Around the time custody was granted.

A No. She came...she came to live with me. As I said we were living...we were...we wasn't living full-time with one another. She got...her kids were at school and that there. Janet had gone through a divorce at the same time as I was going through and I didn't know it...we didn't know it at the time when we met and we...she got her house with her children at school and that there and I'd go and stop at her house at weekends and sometimes she'd come and stop at mine. But, at no time, was Carol ever at my house when Janet was coming to stay with me.

Q You know, Mr Appleyard, it's said that there was a time when Jean rang you at what's called the Pie Hall in Denby Dale to tell you that Carol had told her something. Do you remember that ever occurring?

A I didn't remember it at the time until the police started talking. When I first...the police started asking me...

Q Can I...can I interrupt you, please...

A ...I didn't, no.

Q ...just ask you this, do you remember it now?

A I remember it now.

Q Do you have any idea when it occurred?

A I don't remember what date it occurred on. I think it would probably...

Q What...

A ...be a Friday night.

Q What year?

A It'd be 1984 sometime.

Q And what do you remember of that conversation?

A She just...she rung me up...she rung the Pie Hall up because we'd no mobile phones and the steward picked the...picked the phone up and he says to me, he says, "There's some woman here on phone for you." So, as a joke I just says, 'I don't know no women' and passed me phone and he says, "I think it's your lass." So, anyway, I just said, 'Hello' and she says, "Carol's told me everything." I said, 'What are you on about?' And she says, "She's told me everything and that there and we're going to the police about it." And I says, 'I hope you can fucking prove that' cos, to me, it were a hell of an accusation.

Q Right. What was she saying Carol had told her?

A She didn't. She just says she tell...Carol had told her that I'd been having sex with her or something. I wasn't listening to the rest. I didn't want to know. I put the phone down.

Q Now, we heard yesterday that in 2015 the police asked you questions in interview, on an occasion in 2015 and, again, in 2016.

A Yes.

Q All right and we heard summaries of those interviews read out. When the police asked you about that call being made by Jean to the Pie Hall and the conversation you've just told us about, you said you didn't know anything about it.

A I couldn't remember it. The only...at the time the only conversation when she rung up was when she rung up the Pie Hall when I was in one night and she said that she'd found her brother's family.

Q After that conversation in the phone call to the Pie Hall were you spoken to by the police?

A Sometime after...a few weeks after...I don't know whether it were two or three weeks, I can't remember what it wor. But one Sunday morning there was just me and Paul in the house and the knock came to the door and I got up and I looked through the bedroom window and there was a car parked on thing, it wasn't a police car it was an unmarked car parked by the gate and I leaned out of the window and I shouted down and I says, 'What can we do for you?' And he said, "Mr Appleyard?" I says, 'Yes.' And he just hold his warrant up...his card up, his badge up and said his name, I can't remember if it was Charlesworth or Kenworthy or whatever it were. He mentioned his name. He said, "Can I...you come down and talk to you?" So, I put me trousers on and went downstairs and opened the door and let him in.

Q Did he make you aware of why he was there?

A He did while he was in the house, yes.

Q And what did he tell you was the reason for him attending?

A He told me that me ex-wife and me daughter had made an allegation of me sexually abusing her.

Q So, did you go to the police station with him?

A I did.

Q Which station did you go to?

A Holmfirth.

Q And did the police interview you then?

A They kept me there over two-day period.

Q Did they interview you?

A Yes, they did.

Q And do you remember now what you said in that interview?

A I told 'em I'd never done it. He just kept asking me and that there and...about that I'd done this, that and other that there. I says, 'It's never ever happened. It's never ever happened.' And then I was in the...they put me back...they brought you out, they'd question you for half an hour or so there and then put you back in cell and then they leave you in for a couple of hours, fetch you out and then he came into the cell this particular time and he says, “Get your boots on.” I says, ‘Why, where am I going?’ And he says, “I’m taking you home.” So...

Q And were you told anything about what was going to happen from that point on?

A Nothing.

Q You were told nothing?

A Nothing. He says, “You’re free. You can go.” When I asked him what...what decision were on that and he says, "Because whenever they tried to interview Carol on her own her mother kept...

Q Just...

A ...butting in...

Q ...just...just...

A ...and telling her.”

Q ...just pause there, Mr Appleyard, please. I was simply asking you what you learned about what was to happen and you told us the answer was...

A ...nothing.

Q Nothing.

A Nothing. “You are free to go.” He took me home (inaudible)...

Q Sorry to keep interrupting you, Mr Appleyard. I want to move on, if I may please, to ask you about something else that Carol has told us about. She’s described a time when she met you in Barnsley Market and had a conversation with you. Now, can I just ask you this, do you remember ever meeting with Carol in Barnsley Market?

A Not by meself.

Q Do you remember ever meeting Carol in Barnsley Market?

A With Janet, yes.

Q How did that meeting come about?

A I think she rung up which I think she rung the house. I can't honestly remember how it came about. I think she rung the house up and wanted to talk.

Q Do you remember whether you spoke to her in that phone call or not?

A No. I just...when I got there and that there I said, 'What's up?'

Q Do you remember when this meeting was?

A It was a Saturday.

Q Do you remember when it was in relation to the interview, the time you spent at the police station in 1984?

A It could well have been. Janet and I got together to live together, full stop, at Christmas 1984 to '85 Christmas period and Janet was living with me at the time so, it'd have to be at least 12/18 months or more after that.

Q And when you met Carol at Barnsley Market, whereabouts in the market did you meet her?

A It was upstairs. The cafes and that was upstairs. There was...there were some shops upstairs but mostly the cafes were upstairs on the market and we went to meet her up there at the market and I can't remember whose café it was or anything.

Q Did you speak to Carol on her own?

A No, I did not.

Q What do you remember the meeting being about?

A I can't honestly remember. It didn't...it didn't honestly have any meaning to me or any effect on me. I went up...when we went there Janet and I went there and met her and I says, 'What's up?' And then she...she started, she did most of the talking of things.

Q You know she says that in that meeting you apologised to her?

A Certainly not. I've never apologised to her and I've no intention of apologising for something I haven't done.

Q Did you tell her that you loved her like a person, not a daughter?

A No, I did not. I've always loved her and Paul as my kids and that there and nothing more.

Q Carol told us that she, on an occasion some years later, took you a Father's Day card, is that right?

A She came to the house with a...she'd sent me text messages on me phone.

Q Well, just...just deal with the Father's Day card...

A That she...she came...

Q ...first of all...

A ...she came...

Q ...please, Mr Appleyard.

A ...to the house, she came to the house with a Father's Day card, yes.

Q And did she come into the house?

A I don't honestly remember.

Q Do you remember speaking to her?

A No, I don't honestly remember.

Q Did you apologise to her then?

A Certainly not.

Q Now, you told us that you had text messages from her.

A Correct.

Q Do you remember, roughly, when that was?

A Yes, 2007 I had the one on me phone, in 2007. There was three or four on me phone in 2008 and there was another one in 2009 and that was after I think the...how the Father's Day card came about is she came to my house, she wanted to see us. She asked if she could...cos she rung up and wanted to know if she could come to the house to talk to us. She came to the house and when she came to the house she started on about her son, Jake. She said Jake had been threatening her and pushing her up against the wall...

Q Right, we don't...can I interrupt you there, Mr Appleyard, because I don't think we need to know about this particularly? You've mentioned or you've agreed that you met Carol in Barnsley Market.

A Yes.

Q That she came to your house with a Father's Day card.

A Yes.

Q You said that there were a number of text messages. I think you said 2007, 2008 time.

A Yes.

Q Did you have any other contact with Carol from the point when you were interviewed by the police in 1984 or thereabouts?

A Other them occasions and that, no.

Q We know that in 2015 she published a book.

A Correct.

Q When did you become aware of that?

A We didn't even know it was hers, it were just something that... This little parcel came through the letter box and addressed to me wife, Janet, and when we...when we opened it up and that there, Janet opened it up and there were this book in, "Conquering the Impossible" by Carol Higgins. Well, we hadn't a clue who it were. There were no note in it. There was nothing in it. We hadn't a clue who it were.

Q At that time did you know what surname your daughter, Carol, was using?

A No, I did not. We actually looked on the computer. Me...Janet looked on the computer to see who Carol Higgins was and it was an American...it's an American authoress.

Q Were you aware of any publicity at the time you received that book, publicity about the book itself?

A None whatsoever...be...prior to receiving that book, none.

Q What about after you got it?

A After we got it there was...at the time I was chairman at Pie Hall, I'd only been chairman there three or four months. I was chairman at Pie Hall and we had one pushed through letter box at Pie Hall which were picked up by the steward and stewardess and then there was others. We were...I were told that there was others that had been pushed through letter box at the post office and certain pubs in the village and then when I was going out, cos I used to do a lot of quizzes and that there, we were in a quiz team and we used to go to different pubs and came out of pub and there'd be fliers. There was A5-

sized fliers stuck on windscreens in car advertising book by Carol Higgins and it had got...all the fliers had got my name on 'em, every one of 'em and I handed them over to the police.

Q You were made aware, in November 2015, that Carol had gone to the police because, again, they contacted you and that's when they interviewed you.

A They did, yes. Just...they rung me out of blue and just told me that they'd received another sexual harassment com...sexual abuse complaint from Carol Higgins and that there and would I go to the Dewsbury Police Station which I contacted the solicitors and we went down.

Q And we know you were interviewed again, a year later, in December 2016.

A Correct.

Q And we heard, yesterday, that, initially, you were told, in 2017, you were not going to be prosecuted and at the beginning of last year you were told, in fact, you were.

A Yes. They sent me a letter. The police sent me a letter and...

Q We don't need to hear about this letter, thank you, Mr Appleyard. If you can just confirm...

A Yes.

Q ...what I've just put to you, please?

A Yes (inaudible)

Q I just want to ask you this, finally, are you responsible for any of the allegations that Carol Higgins has made against you?

A Definitely not.

MR STOREY: Thank you. If you wait there, please, there will be some more questions for you.

JUDGE JAMESON: Right. Now, Mr Appleyard, you've been giving evidence for just over an hour now. Would you like a break before cross-examination?

A No, I'm fine, sir. I'm fine, thank you.

Q You're okay. All right. If you do need a break at any stage, just let me know.

A Thank you.

JUDGE JAMESON: All right. Thank you. Yes.

Cross-examined by MR HAMPTON

Q These are pretty shocking allegations, Mr Appleyard.
A Well, they're shocking for me.
Q You find them to be disgusting.
A I certainly do.
Q And the first time you heard about the allegations you were taken by surprise, at the Pie Hall, by the phone call from Jean.
A Yes.
Q How did you feel?
A Cross. Somebody could just ring you up on that day you were out having a drink with friends and that and somebody just rings you up and springs that on you.
Q Shocking.
A Yeah.
Q You're 71.
A Yes.
Q You have a pretty good memory.
A It's not as good as what it wor.
Q But you can recall being with the fairground in '66 to '67.
A Yes.
Q You can recall being in Balby in Doncaster in '67.
A That's where I met their mother.
Q October '67, three weeks in Hull, remember that?
A Yes. It were second time I've been there.
Q You recall the telegram from Jean about the little girl.
A Yes.
Q She turned up a week later.
A Yes, couldn't get away from it.
Q You were good enough to take on the bairn even though it wasn't yours.

A I couldn't see a bairn out. I couldn't see somebody out that had just had a...had the baby a week ago. You just can't throw 'em out. I just couldn't do it. I couldn't see a week-old baby thrown on the street.

Q No. You recall getting the house in Denby Dale in 1968.

A Yes. I don't remember the date, June, July, August-time but I don't remember the date.

Q You recall the move from 8, Gilthwaites Crescent to No.26.

A I couldn't tell you the date and I couldn't even tell you the year, '74, '70...it'd be roundabout '74.

Q '74, the same as the marriage I think you said.

A Sorry?

Q Same as the marriage I think you said.

A Yes, yeah.

Q You recall your hours of work during the relevant period.

A I don't recall me hours but I know I worked every day and many times on a Saturday morning.

Q When the police put to you in your interview, December 2015, if you'd received a phone call from Jean, whilst at the Pie Hall, regarding allegations made by Carol to her to which you'd replied, "You fucking prove it."

A No, I did not.

Q What did you say?

A As far as I recall...I couldn't recall for a start.

Q We'll come to that in a minute, what did you say?

A If I said anything at all I said, 'I hope you can fucking prove it' which is not the same as saying, "Fucking prove it."

Q So, it's your evidence, when interviewed in December '15 about this phone call, you had no memory of it.

A I couldn't remember it at the time until they started telling me about it.

Q You had no memory of the first time you were told that your natural daughter was alleging that you'd raped her?

A No.

Q You had no memory of that.

A I couldn't remember the conversation on the phone.

Q That's a lie, isn't it?

A No.

Q That's a lie.

A That's not a lie.

Q Because, Mr Appleyard, it would have triggered that memory of that significant event and it triggered another memory, didn't it, Hilda Graham?

A I don't see what Hilda Graham had got to do with that conversation.

Q It was after that phone call, Mr Appleyard, you went with Hilda Graham, didn't you, to see Jean in Penistone? Remember this trip?

A No.

Q It was a hot day.

A No.

Q Summer.

A No.

Q No memory of this.

A Not with...not with Hilda Graham and her husband.

Q And there was an argument with Jean at Penistone and Hilda heard what was said, something along the lines that Jean had taken the pregnancy test to the chemist as hers but you knew it was Carol's.

A No.

Q And you didn't want the police going to speak to Hilda Graham, did you?

A How could I stop the police going to see...speak to Hilda Graham?

Q And you were remembering all of this at the time in December 2015...

A No.

Q ...weren't you?

A Hilda Graham says that I went with her and her husband in the car to that house where the mother lived. Her mother said that I went in my van and Hilda Graham was in my van with me.

Q Is Hilda lying about this?

A They're lying about some things. I didn't go with her in her car to Penistone to house. I've never known where they lived in an house in Penistone. She's never given me the address and she's never given me her telephone number to contact 'em.

Q Is this an invention of Hilda's?

A If there was any contact with them at all they rung me. I did not and she'd arranged to meet me somewhere.

Q So, rather than telling the police about this significant phone call in your life, from Jean about Carol, you told them a story about a phone call by Jean to do with abuse of her and a trip to Richmond. Invented, wasn't it?

A No. She rung me up one Friday night, when I was in the Pie Hall, and she said that she'd found her family.

Q So, there were two calls, were there, whilst you were at the Pie Hall, both about sexual abuse?

A There had to be two calls. There was nothing...not two calls about sexual abuse. There was one call about her...her receiving...her meeting her family or wanting to meet her family. She'd found 'em through Directory Enquiries, her family, and she rung me up at the Pie Hall and told me about she'd traced her family in Richmond in North Yorkshire.

Q Page 12...

A That was a totally different phone call.

Q Page 12 of your interview, Mr Appleyard. The police have just put or asked you...

JUDGE JAMESON: Well, I think it would be helpful, wouldn't it, if Mr Appleyard actually had the document so that he can check and, of course, the ladies and gentlemen can follow it as well?

MR HAMPTON: Certainly. It's p.12, Mr Appleyard.

JUDGE JAMESON: This is the thicker of the two...-

MR HAMPTON: It is...

JUDGE JAMESON: ...exhibits you've got.

MR HAMPTON: ...it's the first interview.

JUDGE JAMESON: The one dated the 21st December, 2015.

THE WITNESS: Page 12?

MR HAMPTON: Yes, please.

A Right, where am I looking?

Q Can you see the time 55.50 on the lefthand column?

A Yes.

Q The defendant was asked if he'd received a phone call from Jean, whilst at the Pie Hall, regarding allegations made by Carol to her to which he replied, "You fucking prove it." Response; "I remember her ringing the Pie Hall up on one occasion when I was in but it wasn't over that, she rung me up to say that she'd accused her own father of sexual abuse when she was younger." So, as I say, your evidence is now that you received two phone calls about sexual abuse whilst at the Pie Hall.

A She rung me up to say that she'd found her family and that...which was up in Richmond in North Yorkshire and her father lived across the road from her brother. Her father was still alive and he lived there and she told me that her father had sexually abused her when she was younger.

Q Yeah and what did she want to speak to her father about?

A I don't know; she went on her own.

Q Did you go with her?

A I took her up to her brother's house and she went to the...she went to see her father on her own.

Q The same evening?

A Same afternoon. We arrived there roundabout dinner time.

Q Friday night according to your second...

A No, no, I didn't...

Q ...interview at p.3.

A No, no, no, no, I did not...when she rung me up at the Pie Hall, on the Friday night, I didn't go straight home and say that I'd take her up there. From where we lived up to Richmond and that there is a good hour and a half, an hour and three-quarters drive.

Q That's what I'm asking you.

A Right. Well, I didn't take her up there and then at the time.

Q Right.

A She wanted to go see her family and that there and I took her to see her family but it wasn't that particular night or that day.

Q So, what was the urgency of the phone call?

A She was just glad that she'd found her family.

Q She couldn't wait until you got home to tell you.

A I can't help that.

Q Because you were still together, weren't you?

A Yes, we were...at the time when that was, we were together. We wasn't together when we...I got the second phone call.

Q An invention, Mr Appleyard.

A Definitely not.

Q The phone call was from Jean and it was about Carol, wasn't it?

A No, the phone call that she made to me to say that she'd found her family there was never ever a mention of Carol at that...in that phone call. Not one mention of her. She phoned me up to tell me that she'd found her family and she traced them. She knew that her family, her brothers and that, they had lived in Richmond, North Yorkshire and she'd rung Directory Enquiries up and she'd found them there and she got a number for it and it was her brother that answered the phone and he told her that her father lived across the road from him and it were a council estate and that was all what we talked about there and when I got home that night she told me about it and, "Can we go see 'em?" And I says, 'Yeah, we'll go see 'em. I'll take you up and see 'em.' And when I took her up to see 'em, I don't know whether it was the following week or the same weekend, I can't remember when I took her up there. I took her up there. I went up there and, at the time, I had a Transit pick-up, twin-wheel Transit pickup for all work that I were doing. I took her up there. I went to...we went straight to her brother's house and I stayed at her brother's house while she went across road to talk to her father.

Q That phone call from Jean about Carol must have been one of the most significant moments in your life, mustn't it?

A No.

Q No.

A No.

Q Your own daughter accusing you of sexual abuse?

A It wasn't nice but it wasn't the most significant thing in me life.

Q So, December '15 you had no recollection of that?

A No.

Q No.

A Not until they reminded me of it and what was said and that there.

Q When did it come back to you?

A Possibly the same day, the following day, I don't know when it came back to me.

Q Well, it didn't because you were interviewed a year later in December of 2016, p.3 and, again, you can see your interview.

A Page what, sorry?

Q Page...it's the second one, Mr Appleyard, it's coming to you now, all right? December '16.

A Yeah.

Q Top right-hand corner, there's page numbers, p.3. "The defendant discussed the phone call he recalled from Jean when he was in the Pie Hall." And just previous to this the evidence of Hilda Graham which had been obtained was put to you and you give the account that you're pretty much giving now about a trip to Richmond. But, again, there's no mention, Mr Appleyard, of a phone call from Jean about Carol. So, when did this come back into your memory?

A I don't recall when it came back into my memory.

Q Some time after December 2016.

A Possibly.

Q What triggered it?

A The ongoing...the ongoing conversations with the police and my solicitor.

Q Or was it there all the time?

A No, it was not there all the time.

Q But you didn't want to discuss it.

A No, I didn't want to discuss it. But it wasn't there all the time in that sense.

Q Because after that call you went on a trip with Hilda to see Jean.

A No, I did not go with Hilda Graham to see Jean at all.

Q And your sister heard what Jean was saying.

A No, I did not.

Q A different topic if I may, please, you have some interest in America and hunting, I think.

A You what, sorry?

Q You've got some interest in America and in hunting.

A I had a friend in America.

Q Because you went there.

A Pardon?

Q You went there.

A Yes, I've been there a couple of times.

Q Yeah, you went hunting with a friend.

A A friend that I grew up with, yes.

Q Whereabouts?

A We went into Appalachian Mountains. We flew into Canada and then we went over to...into Ohio, West Virginia and came through the Appalachian Mountains and we were up there all the time.

Q When you were...were you camping?

A Yes.

Q When you were in the Appalachian Mountains by the fire did you discuss how it should be that fathers should break their daughters in like the Indians do?

A Definitely not.

Q No?

A Never even...never even mentioned anything of that nature.

Q Because when you came back from that trip, Mr Appleyard, you saw your daughter in a sexual way, didn't you?

A No, I did not.

Q Well, why were you presuming she'd had an orgy in your house?

A The state of the bed.

Q What.

A And what Paul had telled(sic) me about lads stopping there.

Q So, Paul was saying stuff about lads staying over.

A Uh, uh.

Q Anything else?

A No. He just said they'd been sleeping in my bed and that there...

Q How...

A ...and the state of bed.

Q How did that make you feel, Carol in your bed with someone else?

A Carol and the boys and that being in my bed full stop and in the house while I was on holiday, I was mad and Paul.

Q How did it make you feel, Mr Appleyard?

A I was cross.

Q Should've been you breaking her in, should it?

A Don't talk silly.

Q There was nothing upon which you'd conclude that Carol was having sex in your bed, was there? Paul said that she'd have boys' round, that was it. Anything else?

A Paul telled me that they'd had boys' round and they'd been stopping in my bed sleeping--well, I could see they'd been sleeping in my bed.

Q What do you mean by that?

A Well, the bed was all ruffled up and all a mess.

Q What, the bed was ruffled up?

A Yeah, it was all a mess.

Q And that meant your daughter was having sex in your bed.

A Or someone had had.

Q That's how it worked in your mind, isn't it?

A Boys and girls don't climb in beds (inaudible) there to play Tiddlywinks, do they?

Q And you thought it should be you.

A No, I didn't think it were me at all.

Q And there was an argument. You were furious, weren't you?

A I was furious of the state of the house when I got back.

Q And she slit her wrists, cut her wrists I should say.

A No recollection whatsoever. I know Donna did but I don't recall her ever slitting her wrists. If she'd have slit her wrists there, I'd have taken her to hospital and doctors there.

Q And that night you bandaged her...

A No.

Q ...took her into your bed and you had sex with her, didn't you?

A No, I did not. I didn't even want either her or Paul in the house at that time after what...what...what had gone on in the house. I didn't even want 'em in the house let alone in me bed.

Q And they were there well after that, Carol and Paul, because you were fighting for custody of them in April 1984.

A She went and after that...after that...that incident and that there that, when I come back from there she went and she came back in the new year.

Q We may re-visit chronology. Can we move to a different topic, please? Can I ask you something which we haven't covered yet? Can you tell me about the tattoo, please?

A Which tattoo?

Q Carol's.

A Carol's tattoo. Carol wanted a tattoo on her...well, she just wanted a tattoo and her friends--some of her friends at school had got some, I'd got some and I says, 'You can have one but you can only have...you can have a little 'un' about there and, at the time I had to take 'em because you've got to be 16-

year-old and what to have one. I says, 'I'll take you and you can have a little one.' And she told Paul about it. So, Paul said, "Well, if you're having one, 'm having one." I says, 'If you're having one, you'll have a little 'un. You can have a little one a piece on and I'll have yours on'. And I took 'em. They chose what they wanted putting on and I had their names put on me arm.

Q Did you ask her what she wanted tattooing on her?

A Did I ask her what, sorry?

Q What she wanted tattooing upon her?

A She hadn't decided until she got there and she were looking at some pictures in the tattooist.

Q Whose name is it?

A Whose name is what? The tattoo?

Q Yeah.

A The tattoo she had I think it were Caz that she had put on and she had Sam put on.

Q Right. Who's Sam?

A Well, Sam was my nickname, Sam was her boyfriend's nickname and Sam was the dog's nickname.

Q We're talking about when she's 13, 14. So, we can rule out the boyfriend, can't we?

A Well, Sam was...Sam was my nickname and Sam was the dog's name.

Q Right. So, who was it, you or the dog?

A No idea. She wanted Sam putting on so, she put Sam on.

Q Did you say, "Who's Sam?" Did you say, "Carol, who's Sam? Why are you having Sam put on your body?"

A Why didn't she have Dad put on? If she was having my name put on, you'd have thought she'd have had Dad put on and Caz.

Q Mr Appleyard, listen to the question and answer it. Did you ask, "Who is Sam?"

A No, I did not. I didn't ask either of 'em.

Q So, it's your case that you don't know who Sam is and you didn't ask at the time.
A I didn't ask at the time when she were having it put on. She could have...they could have what they wanted put on their things so long as it was a small tattoo. They could have whatever they wanted put on so long as it was a small one.
Q Did you ever see Sam, the dog, do anything to cause Carol upset?
A The dog do anything?
Q Yeah.
A Like what?
Q I don't know, anything. Nothing.
A I don't recall that.
Q She's spent years trying to remove it from her body, Mr Appleyard.
A It was their choice to have a tattoo on, not mine.
Q Sam is you, isn't it?
A Sam was my nickname.
Q And it's Sam that's tattooed upon her. Your nickname. It's not the dog, is it?
A That was her choice not mine.
Q You had some influence on that though, didn't you?
A No, none whatsoever. They was told they could have what they wanted on so long as it was a small tattoo and I paid for it.
Q You had no interest in what she had.
A She wasn't going to have the hare and hounds put on her back. She wasn't going to have anything else put on her back. She wanted a small tattoo on. Her friends had got some on, got tattoos on. I got some on. She wanted one on. So, she was allowed to have a small tattoo on whatever she wanted. I didn't pick the tattoo. She chose it and so did Paul.
Q Were you there when it was put on?
A I had to be.
Q Yeah.
A They was under age.

Q Yeah and as Sam was being inked onto her body did you say, "Who's that Carol?"

A I might have said it at the time at thing but I don't recall ever having any conversation about names or anything.

Q Were you happy to have her body marked with your name?

A I've got my parents on my arms.

Q So, were you happy about that? You've got your parents on your arms. Were you happy about that?

A Of course I'm happy. I wouldn't have put 'em on if I wasn't.

Q Right. Were you happy about Carol having your nickname on her body?

A That's what she wanted. My parents didn't make me have their names put on my...my arms. I didn't make her put my name on her arm.

Q If you had thought it was the dog would you have said, "Carol, are you sure you want the epileptic sheep-worrying dog who I shot in the head on your body?"

A The dog wasn't dead then.

Q Not dead then.

A No.

Q Okay. The epileptic sheep-worrying dog, did you say, "Are you sure you want that?"

A Why would it be a sheep-worrying dog, if the dog wasn't dead then? The dog were only dead when I shot it, it were worrying sheep. When she had the tattoo on the dog wasn't dead so, therefore, it wasn't worrying sheep then.

Q You knew it was epileptic from when you bought it.

A It never had...it was epileptic when...I didn't buy it. He gave it me because he was gonna to shoot it.

Q There was a single red rose between the names.

A I don't remember what it was and I don't remember what it was.

Q Sign of affection from one person to another.

A I don't recall what tattoo either she had on or Paul put on. After they'd had it put it on...had it put on 'em it meant nothing to me.

Q When you had them tattooed were you marking your territory?

A No.

Q Like you did when you put love bites on her neck.

A I didn't even put any love bites on her neck.

Q You treated Carol like she was your property and she was there for your sexual gratification, wasn't she?

A She wasn't there all the time. She stayed with me for a few months, then go back to her mother's and then come back to me for a few months. She was free to come and go as she chose. So, how could she be my property?

Q Let's talk about that then, please. Move to a different topic, we'll leave the tattoo, all right? We're going to discuss now what went on in the family home. As I understand your case you, pretty much, subject to the rows, a good dad and a good husband, is that fair?

A I thought so.

Q You were hard-working, bringing in the money. Yeah?

A Yes.

Q You were tough but fair as a dad.

A Pretty much.

Q Yeah. They'd get the odd clip round the lug-hole in the good old-fashioned sense but nothing really beyond that from you, the kids.

A No.

Q And you got on well with them.

A To a degree.

Q Yeah. What was it then that caused Jean to flee the house?

A Us rows, us arguments, us fights, whatever you want to call them and that, they're over me hearing stories of her having extra-marital affairs, for better words.

Q She didn't go to a lover's home, did she?

A I don't know where she went.

Q You do, she went to somewhere called a refuge.

A No, no, no, no, no.

Q Do you remember that?

A I remember that very well.

Q A refuge, a place of safety.

A She lied to 'em and she was kicked out after 10 days.

Q She came back after 10 days because you persuaded her to.

A No, I didn't. I didn't even know where she was.

Q And she said, "I won't do it again", Jean.

A She...I didn't even know where she was. I didn't even know where she was so, I had no contact with her whatsoever. The phone calls and the conversations that we had is what she'd made to me from the pub or the club or wherever it was that she was on a night-time with the other women that was in the refuge.

Q What was preferable to being in a refuge for battered women rather than being in her own home...

A She wasn't a battered woman, that's why they kicked her out. She'd lied to 'em. She just wanted to teach me a lesson.

Q ...other than getting a break from your violence?

A If she wanted to get a break from my violence she wouldn't have come back. She'd have gone full stop.

Q You'd beat her, Mr Appleyard...

A No, I did not.

Q ...when you came home from the pub...

A I never ever beat her.

Q Sorry. You never ever beat her.

A No.

Q When you came home from the pub in drink.

A No. I never got drunk during the week. I was working. I had to get up for work the following morning.

Q Do you recall her urinating on the kitchen floor through fear?

A No, I do not.

Q You owned shotguns and machetes, didn't you?

A I owned a machete and I owned three shotguns.

Q And they were in the home.

A They was.

Q And we know they were in the home many years later in 2000 as well. Just on the shotgun; you were asked a question by my learned friend, in examination-in-chief, whether or not you put a shotgun to Jean's head. I don't recall it. "If I did it was in the heat of the moment" was your answer.

A Yes.

Q Yeah. Is, in your view, putting a shotgun to your wife's head, whether loaded or not, a memorable incident?

A I didn't put a shotgun to her head. If I had the shotgun in my hand and we were arguing, as I've told him (inaudible) if I was going out or I'd just come back in and I'd heard rumours and we got on arguing again if I've got the shotgun in my hand. I never picked that shotgun up and pointed it directly at her head and said I were gonna blow her fucking head off...

Q I'll stand...

A ...that never ever happened.

Q ...I stand to be corrected, that you were being asked about a shotgun to Jean's head is my note.

A Right.

Q You said, "I don't recall it. If I did, it was in the heat of the moment."

A Yes.

Q So, what was in the heat of the moment?

A Arguments.

Q Putting a gun to her head.

A Arguments. I didn't put a gun to her head.

Q So, it didn't happen.

A I'm not saying I didn't have the gun in me hand but I didn't point it directly at her head.

Q Jean would flee because of the violence, wouldn't she, from you?

A No. She left many a time because she was...well, she left two occasions prior to actually leaving me full stop, one was to the refuge and one was to her friend's house who she was talking to on CB and she was talking to men on the CB at the same time.

Q Your relationship with the children; we discussed you were tough but fair. The kids had their own bedrooms, didn't they, Carol and Paul?

A They did.

Q They had nice holidays.

A Every year I took 'em on holiday.

Q You were relaxed about them being with you or your(sic) mother, you didn't really have any strong views.

A No. They were free to go...come and go as they chose. All I asked of them that they were right when they were in the house and they did their job, they got...had to do their chores.

Q So, other than the odd rollicking they had nothing to worry about really.

A Nothing.

Q Did you see Carol in the months and immediate years after the phone call from Jean about Carol's allegations when you're in the Pie Hall?

A I don't understand the question.

Q When did you next see Carol after the phone call you got from Jean in the Pie Hall about the abuse?

A I don't recall. It was...it were well after I'd been interviewed.

Q After the police.

A Oh, yes.

Q Barnsley Market?

A No.

Q When then?

A I don't know.

Q Can you tell us.

A The Barnsley Market wasn't until years after that, long after that.

Q When did you see her in between?

A She'd come back home. She were with her mother...she were with her mother for about 10 months or so.

Q She came back home after you'd been interviewed by the police.

A Yes.

Q Do you want to think about that.

A She came home, she stayed for a while and that there, I didn't want...I wasn't...I didn't want to know. If she'd nowhere to go this...this were her home. If she'd fallen out with her mother and that there, which she often fell out with her mother, and that there, I wasn't gonna put her...turn her away.

Q Right. Do you know what it was that caused Carol to flee on that occasion from the house when you got the call from Jean?

A No.

Q No.

A No. I was (inaudible) she told her mother that I were in the Pie Hall, in the pub.

Q So, you don't know what caused her to leave the house?

A No. They were free to come and go as they chose. If she wanted to go back to her mother's she could go back to her mother's. I wasn't even there when she left.

Q She didn't like being at her mother's though, did she?

A She says not.

Q No. So, why would she...

A Her mother said not.

Q ...why would she leave her own bedroom, your relaxed attitude to parenting, why was she leaving that behind to go to her mother's?

A If she'd done anything wrong if she...anything wrong and she'd argued, fallen out with me, I'd say, 'I didn't want it. You can go. I just don't want it. I'm working every day. I'm working all week and that, there to come home and get grief and that from your kids and that and from school, get letters from school and God knows what else, I didn't want it. I just don't want it.'

Q Had you had sex with her, beaten her and kicked her while she was on the kitchen floor...

A Definitely not.

Q ...in the stomach and back?

A Definitely not.

Q Telling her to get up, that she was pathetic.

A Definitely not.

Q And she was saying, "I want it to stop, I can't take any more."

A Definitely not.

Q And that was the incident of the last rape, wasn't it?

A That was what, sorry?

Q The last time you raped her.

A No, never raped her, never touched her.

Q And she got on the bus and bumped into her mum.

A No.

Q And that's when you got the call from the Pie...to the Pie Hall, isn't it?

A I don't know when I got the call from the Pie Hall. I don't know whether it was the night, the same night. I don't think it was the same night. I don't know whether it was the same night or when it was after.

Q I'm just searching for a passage that I want your help with, please, Mr Appleyard, as to clarification. (After a pause) Just bear with me a moment. Ah, here we go. Do you still have your interview, please, interview 1? (After a pause) We're going to p.6 please, Mr Appleyard and can you see the counter time on p.6, please, that says 18.20?

A No, all these pages are mixed up.

Q Are they? Do you want some assistance?

A Six, yeah.

Q Have you got it?

A Yeah.

Q Counter time 18.20, can you see that, left hand column?

A Yes.

Q Thank you. "The complainant's allegation that the defendant struck her with a belt were put. Did you have any belts you'd ever use?" Answer, "I did have belts. Yes, I've got a belt on now." "And did you ever use them to" and then the question trails off you see and you say, "When they were children if they'd done wrong, they did it, it was a way that I was brought up and that and to me, you know, it instilled discipline. What you could do 30 years or so, 40 years ago, you couldn't possibly do now."

A Correct.

Q Could you help us, please, just clarify this, are you saying there you did belt them...

A No, I didn't belt 'em.

Q ...or you did?

A You give 'em a belt round the lug-hole, you give 'em a belt across the bottom and that there with your hand.

Q So, you're referring to...

A This is giving 'em belters in that...

Q Beltings and hitting rather than belters...

A Exactly.

Q ...and hitting with a belt.

A Correct.

Q Paul described the belt being doubled over and the buckle being in your hand as you struck his bare bottom with it. True or false?

A False. His mother even turned round and said that she never ever saw me hitting him with a belt, it was her that did it.

Q You tell us that Jean struck them with a spoon.

A That's correct. She admitted that.

Q You were violent to both children, Mr Appleyard, weren't you?

A No, I corrected 'em when they was doing something, when they were either skipping...coming home skipping school they were swear...they were doing whatever it was. Not doing what they should be doing.

Q You ruled through fear.

A No, no, no, no.

Q That's why Carol was cutting her wrists when you were angry about the party, wasn't it?

A No.

Q Why did Paul flee the house years later?

A Paul fled the house years later, it was...it was after (inaudible) he was with me right up until the end of September of '88. It would be beginning of '89 and Janet and I...what he were supposed to be doing, he wasn't working, he was doing odd jobs and that there at the time and when he was working at a plastic factory which is said that'd be '86, '87.

Q You remember that, do you?

A Him working at a plastics factory.

Q In '86, '87.

A '86/7. He didn't stay there long.

Q No.

A But in 80...it'd be '89, late '88, '89 and that there and Janet and I we'd gone out one Saturday night for a drink and he was supposed to pay Janet £20 a week or whatever it was for his board and for his thing, out of his wages, and we went out for a drink one Saturday night and as we were talking, she said, "Did you know Paul hasn't paid his board?" I said, 'Well, get it off him, you deal with finances. You do housekeeping and that and they(sic) get it off him.' She said, "He hasn't paid for the last five or six weeks." I said, 'Why the hell didn't you say summat?' So, when we got in that night he was there and I got onto him about it. I said, 'I'm not a fucking bus driver, I don't carry passengers. You pay your way or get off the bus.' So, he decided to get off the bus. I didn't kick him out. Paul could have been...still been there now if he'd have paid his way and done right. He...it were his choice to go, not mine.

Q You were violent to him, Mr Appleyard.

A No, violent in what way? He were 18, 19-year-old. Violent in what way?

Q You chased him with a pitchfork.

A I didn't. No.
Q And when he was old enough, he was off, wasn't he?
A No. He was old enough at 18, 19-year-old. He were old enough at 16-year-old to go.
Q Paul's told us that he loved you.
A I loved him as a son. I couldn't ask for a better son when he was younger.
Q You enjoyed hunting together...
A Correct.
Q ...shooting...
A Yes.
Q ...fishing...
A Yeah.
Q ...bike riding.
A I didn't take him fishing.
Q Sorry, bike riding...
A Yeah.
Q ...camping.
A Yes.
Q He was your shadow.
A He was.
Q As you tell us again, his life was comfortable at your house when he was a child.
A He was happy with it. If he'd done something wrong, he were corrected...
Q He had his own...
A ...that's...that's punishment.
Q ...bedroom and a good relationship with you.
A Yes.
Q But you tell us you've not spoken to him since, what is it 1989?
A Yes.
Q Some 30 years.
A Yes.

Q Over £120 keep.

A That were his choice. I had no mobile phone for him. We didn't have mobile phones then. I had no way of contacting him. I didn't even know where he was. As far as I were concerned, he'd gone to stay with his mother and then in 19—sometime, late in 1989, Carol came to the house and she said she wanted his birth certificates. I said, 'What do you want that for?' She said, "He wants to join Army." So, I gave it him...I gave it her and she took it.

Q You wouldn't dismiss your son for as little as £120 who you loved, Mr Appleyard, would you?

A I've never dismissed him. I've never dismissed him. He contacted...in 2014 he contacted my other son, Simon, on Facebook and he said that he wanted to...he said, "It's about time I made it right with old man" meaning me and Simon said, "Yeah, it is. It's been too long." And he...

Q There's contact between Simon and...

A Paul.

Q ...Paul, yeah.

A And he gave...

Q Have you seen the contacts?

A ...he gave Simon his phone number.

Q Mr Appleyard, did you see the contact?

A Did I see what sorry?

Q Or were you...were you told about it or did you see it?

A I saw it, he printed it off.

Q All right.

A Simon printed it off for me. He also sent hiself...he also sent a photo of hiself.

Q He left because you were violent and he'd begin to understand, as an 18-year-old, what you did to his sister, didn't he?

A No.

Q Because he saw you snogging...

A I hadn't...I hadn't seen his sister for...when he left, I hadn't seen his sister for God knows how long.

Q He saw you snogging Carol in the kitchen.
A No, no.
Q He saw Carol in your bedroom in her underwear when he was locked out after football.
A He couldn't possibly see anybody in my bedroom. He couldn't possibly have seen me in me underwear and I'm taller than her so, he...he certainly couldn't.
Q Was there ever a time when you and Carol and Paul were in bed and you asked if you'd touched him in the night by accident?
A I don't recall that.
Q Don't you recall it?
A No.
Q Could it have happened?
A I don't recall it at all. The only time that they were in bed with me was on a Sunday morning when they'd come in and jump in that there. That's the only time. They never ever slept all night with me...in my bed with me.
Q Is he lying about you snogging Carol in the kitchen?
A He's certainly lying about something cos that never ever happened. I've told you I never ever kissed her other than a father kissing his daughter.
Q Do you know what could have passed between you and Paul that would cause him to tell such lies about you?
A No idea, sticking up for his sister. He didn't speak to his sister for long enough.
Q The tin box you agree existed.
A Not an Army box.
Q A tin box.
A A tin chest, it was in the corner of the bedroom.
Q And you had explicit photos of Carol in it.
A No, definitely not. There was no photos of Carol in it at all.
Q A hairbrush?
A No.

Q Dirty magazines by your bed.

A Definitely not.

Q And when alone with Carol, on occasions, you put her on her knees, put your hand on her shoulder, unzip your trousers and push her down and she'd have to give you oral sex.

A That's disgusting.

Q And when you did that you'd say, "Who loves you, baby."

A No, I certainly did not.

Q That is something you said, isn't it?

A No, I did not.

Q Not in the context...you say not in that context but you say you did say it, as I understood your evidence earlier.

A I didn't say and I've never said that I said that, 'Who loves you, baby' at the time when she was doing anything like that.

Q No, I understand. I follow. I think we're at cross purposes. Put aside the context of the oral sex, is that a phrase you used in any situation?

A It was in fun, we'd be in the living room, we'd be in the kitchen, we'd be...I don't know. It was just...

Q Something you'd say in fun.

A It was just something you say. You put your arms round her...around your daughter and say, 'Who loves you, baby.'

Q So, you...

A This thing was taken off the television.

Q ...you said it to Carol.

A Well, of course I said it to Carol. I said it to Paul.

Q Did you say to her if she ever got pregnant it would be an Albino baby.

A No, I do not recall ever having a conversation of that nature at all with her.

Q Cos a baby would be a disaster, wouldn't it?

A Never had that conversation with her at all.

Q Because it would be the product of incest, wouldn't it?

A Never had that conversation with her at all.

Q Is that what led you to travelling with Hilda to see Jean when you heard about the pregnancy test?

A I've no idea what you're talking about. I've never had that conversation with her at all.

Q Deanna Thorpe used to do your washing.

A She did for a...for a while, yeah.

Q She popped round one day for a cup of tea and let herself in.

A Deanna Thorpe has never ever, at any time, been to my house on her own, never.

Q And you came downstairs and they looked...you looked a bit dishevelled.

A No.

Q Putting your clothes in order.

A Deanna Thorpe has never ever been to my house at any time on her own.

Q Can you help us if there's anything that's passed between you and her that would cause her to lie about that?

A I've no idea, she accused her own mother. She accused her own mother. She accused her own mother of things; she's accused her own mother not just of abusing her when she were a baby. I don't know how the hell she remembered it but she didn't just accuse her, she accused her mother of abusing her brother's baby.

Q Was her mother your sister?

A Yes.

Q You weren't at work all day, were you? You were at home a lot of the time with Carol...

A No.

Q ...and the sex would occur then.

A No.

Q Because you spent your time working and being on the sick...

A Never drawn...

Q ...claiming Benefits.

A No, I had not. I left school two weeks after me 15th birthday and went straight into work and I've worked since. I was self-employed...registered self-employed in 1972.

Q And you worked sometimes.

A I worked...I worked all the time.

Q Sometimes you were out collecting scrap.

A Not every day and not every week.

Q Sometimes you'd work the land.

A Yes.

Q But you weren't out of the house all day every day, were you?

A Well, where was I then?

Q At home with Carol, having sex with her.

A So, where did I get the money from to take 'em on holiday every year and buy the clothes and pay the rent and pay the bills? Where did that come from?

Q Work, Benefits, scrap.

A Give up.

Q I think you said, in evidence, that Carol was back with you at the beginning of 2000--1983, is that right?

A Could have been, yeah.

Q Yeah. She was with you in June '83 when you had burnt yourself out through working too hard.

A It wasn't just burning meself out through working too hard, it was everything that was going off around me.

Q Did it have anything to do with what you were doing to your daughter or the thoughts you were having about her?

A Beginning of 1983 had nothing, whatsoever, to do with Carol. Carol states...in her statement she states that the first time I touched her was when I came back from America. That was December 1983. She states that that was supposed to be the first time that I touched her in December 1983, not the beginning of 1983, at the end of 1983.

Q You'd been kissing her since she was 11 or 12, Mr Appleyard.
A I hadn't kissed her. Her mother was there.
Q Was it anything to do with the thoughts you were having about Carol?
A No, no, no, no. Her mother left when she was 13 years of age and she went with the mother.
Q The...I'm moving topics, the Barnsley Market meeting, when did this happen?
A I don't recall it, don't remember.
Q '88, '89 sound about right, maybe a bit earlier?
A Possibly.
Q Had you asked your partner, Janet, to speak to Carol and ask to meet with her?
A I asked Janet to do that?
Q Yeah.
A No.
Q And then you surprised her at the market.
A No.
Q Apologised.
A I never apologised to her and I have no intention of apologising for something I've never done.
Q You wanted it to go away.
A No.
Q When had you...when did you marry Janet?
A September 2nd...
Q Of?
A ...1988.
Q You wanted to...
A Sorry?
Q ...you wanted to close down Carol's allegations at that time, didn't you...
A I've never wanted...
Q ...because you were marrying Janet.

A ...I've never wanted...I've never wanted them full stop.

Q And you said you loved her like a wife or a person and not a daughter.

A No, no, no, no, no.

Q Carol...

A You love...you love your kids and you love 'em as kids and that's what it'd do, when you show 'em affection. You show 'em affection by giving 'em a cuddle and you give them a kiss and there is nothing more than that in it.

Q Carol left upset, didn't she?

A I don't know what Carol did.

Q Why not?

A I wasn't taking any notice of what she did. She got up and she went, she walked...she walked off.

Q What was discussed then?

A I don't know what was discussed. I can't honestly remember what was discussed. I went up there, we went there for a start, I said, 'What's up' and that's it? (Inaudible) I'm not...I can't honestly remember what...anything was said after that.

Q You said, "What's up?" Did she tell you what was up?

A She wanted to meet her whatever. I can't remember what was said after that. I wasn't over-interested.

Q Did you see her walk off and meet her friend, Julie Clark?

A I didn't see her meet anybody.

Q No.

A No. She walked away, we walked away. She went one way. We went another way and we went shopping and didn't see no more after that. I didn't see who she were with that is, who she met nor nothing.

Q Carol's lying about all this then?

A I'm not saying she's lied about the meeting.

Q About the sexual abuse.

A Definitely.

Q Can you help us with why?

A I don't think Carol's worked since she were at YTS on that YTS scheme at S.R. Gents as such, there, she's always wanting money for one thing and another and she's admitted that this is about money...

Q All about money.

A ...she tried...she tried...she tried a few years ago to put in...have a solicitor, whatever it was, searching into my private affairs. She's applied for Criminal Injuries Compensation Board, it's all about money.

Q She's here for money.

A She's...she poses nude for magazine and for books...

Q Thank you, thank you.

A ...she does all sorts.

Q Thank you, Mr Appleyard, thank you.

A That's what it's all about. Sorry.

Q Thank you, that's enough.

A That's all it's about.

Q Carron Ward says that when she was 14 to 15 you approached her and asked if her father had broken her in yet. True or false?

A False. I never approached her. She didn't...

Q Anything...

A ...she didn't even...she didn't even say that I'd approached her. She said that I was walking up the road and she was stood at the end of the thing.

Q I'm sorry. Anything pass between you and Carron that you could help us with as to why she'd lie about that?

A They were neighbours of ours. Never really got on with them as such and that there. She got sons...she got two sons, one of 'em used to light bonfires in his back garden and God knows what else and that. You're always playing hell with them to put 'em out if you've got washing out or whatever. Never really got on with them as such.

Q So, a bit of a neighbour dispute going on.

A No, there were no dispute about it. There were no dispute. You just tell somebody off for lighting a bonfire or whatever it is. It's not a dispute.

Q But you didn't get on.

A Didn't bother me. Just somebody you talk to some people and you don't talk to others, it's as simple as that. Some people you can get on with and some you don't. There was no fallout, no arguments, no nothing about it.

Q And Hilda Graham, just in case I haven't covered this, anything pass between you and Hilda that would help us understand why she'd lie about what happened?

A Meself and Hilda we had an argument, a fallout, it was personal and that and then that was roundabout 1986, '85, 80...it'd be '85, '86 and we had a fallout over that because it was a New Year's Eve and there was meself and Janet and there was her and her husband, Peter, which I used to get on very well with and we were having a drink. We were in a pub in Scissett having a drink, all four of us, and while the women were nattering at bar and the pubs were full and while they were nattering at bar me and Peter bobbed next door for another drink and we left them there and that there when we came back, she blew her stack. She said that shouldn't have done and that there was...we...we just went for a drink and that and then she started saying I were trying to bust her and her husband up which weren't true. I had no reason to bust her and her husband up and then it got into a personal thing like that and after that she didn't even...even have...there were certain members of the family. There wasn't just me, there were certain members of the family that Hilda Graham didn't get on with.

Q So, Hilda's had a grudge since around 1985 regarding...

A '86, summat like that.

Q ...'85, '86 regarding...

A She tried talking to me in 2011. She did come talking to me in 2011.

Q Regarding her unhappiness about you and her chap going off for an extra pint.

A That's what it started off as and then in 2011 it were at me brother's funeral.

Q But you were friends with Hilda in '83, weren't you?

A We were friends with her in '83, '84, '85.

Q Yeah, because...

A She used to do...she used to do me washing before Deanna Thorpe did.

Q ...she was keeping an eye on the house, yeah. But the grudge began in 1985.

A ’85, ’86 whenever.

Q Finally, Mr Appleyard, can I suggest this to you, it is you who is telling untruths about what happened between you and your daughter. You sexually abused Carol, didn’t you?

A No, I did not.

MR HAMPTON: Just bear with me a moment. Thank you very much.

MR STOREY: Nothing by way of re-examination for me, thank you, your Honour. Unless your Honour has any questions for Mr Appleyard.

JUDGE JAMESON: There are two matters I just wanted to check with you, just to make sure, Mr Appleyard, that I’ve got it right, one is this; you said, I think twice or maybe three times, that when your first wife, Jean, had left and gone to a refuge that she’d lied to them and was kicked out after 10 days. I just wanted to check what...what the source of that information was.

A Social worker used to come to our house on occasions...

Q So, this is something a social worker has said, is it?

A And it was social worker that told me and that there.

Q All right, okay. And the other thing is...is...really is to try and make sure I’ve understood it because I think my note, perhaps, may be inaccurate and I want to make sure that it’s right. But you spoke about seeing Carol after you’d been interviewed by the police and I think, at that stage, that the interviews you were talking about was the interview back in 1984.

A Yes, sir.

Q Yeah and you spoke about, as I understood it, her coming home, she’d fallen out with her mother and you weren’t going to turn her away.

A That’s correct, sir.

Q So, that is right, is it, that your account is that Carol comes back home after you’d been interviewed and told that she’s made...

A She came back several times.

Q ...sexual allegations against you.

A She came back several times.

Q Okay. Right okay, that was all I wanted to check with you. Thank you very much indeed...

A You're welcome, sir.

Q ...for helping us with your evidence. If you go back to the dock now, please.

(The witness withdrew)

MR STOREY: Your Honour, I wonder if I could, please, have a little time before we take things any further?

JUDGE JAMESON: Yes, certainly. Well, we'll take a slightly earlier lunch then.

MR STOREY: Your Honour, thank you.

JUDGE JAMESON: Ladies and gentlemen, if we can be back at two o'clock is that all right for everybody? Yeah. Thank you very much.

(The jury leave court at 12.37 p.m.)

MR STOREY: Your Honour, this may be my error in underestimating the time that Mr Appleyard would be giving his evidence for.

JUDGE JAMESON: No, it's admirably concise so, no need to apologise for that.

MR STOREY: Well, I think I mentioned yesterday that there was the possibility of a witness being called on his behalf...

JUDGE JAMESON: Yes.

MR STOREY: ...and the prosecution have been alerted to this. When I spoke to my instructing solicitor last night, it was left on the basis that she would be asked to attend tomorrow morning, in fact.

JUDGE JAMESON: Right.

MR STOREY: My learned junior, Mr Yates, has tried to contact or has, in fact, contacted the solicitor to see if efforts can be made to see if she can come this afternoon and we don't know what the up-to-date position is...

JUDGE JAMESON: Right.

MR STOREY: ...so, I'll certainly find that out over lunch. If it remains or if it is the case that, for whatever reasons, she's unable to attend this afternoon I'm afraid we won't be able to deal with her evidence until tomorrow morning...

JUDGE JAMESON: Yeah.

MR STOREY: ...and I'm very sorry about the delay. But, that said, I don't think that we need to wait until the conclusion of her evidence, for example, to discuss the law or anything like that.

JUDGE JAMESON: No, well, that was what I was thinking. I'll do a bit of think...well, I've done a certain amount of thinking but one or two things have changed...

MR STOREY: Yes.

JUDGE JAMESON: ...and my original draft of some directions has been overtaken by events. So, I'll...between now and two o'clock I'll try and get that up-to-date so that you can see it and we can discuss matters if we have the time.

MR STOREY: Thank you.

JUDGE JAMESON: Well, I'm sure we will at some point this afternoon, whether...

MR STOREY: Yes.

JUDGE JAMESON: ...it's at two or if you can get the witness after that I'm sure we can do it at some point.

MR STOREY: Thank you very much.

JUDGE JAMESON: Yeah. Okay. Thank you.

(12.39 p.m.)

(Adjourned for a short time)

(2.03 p.m.)

MR STOREY: Your Honour, I'm afraid that the witness who it's intended to call has not...is not able to re-arrange her work as...

JUDGE JAMESON: Yeah.

MR STOREY: ...such that she can be here this afternoon.

JUDGE JAMESON: Okay.

MR STOREY: She lives a good couple of hours drive away, I'm told.

JUDGE JAMESON: Yes, all right.

MR STOREY: (Inaudible)

JUDGE JAMESON: So, tomorrow morning.

MR STOREY: I'm afraid so.

JUDGE JAMESON: Yeah.

MR STOREY: There is one other admission that is to be read which I can do this afternoon or I can hold that over 'til tomorrow morning as well.

JUDGE JAMESON: No, let's do that all of a piece I think...

MR STOREY: It makes sense I agree.

JUDGE JAMESON: I think it makes better sense. Yeah, well there it is. Now, the...again with, obviously the difficulties that are involved in predicting anything accurately but you'll know what the issues are that your witness will go to.

MR STOREY: I don't think she'll be terribly long, half an hour maybe.

JUDGE JAMESON: Yeah, okay. Right, fine. Well, what I'll do then, we'll get the jury in. I'll tell them that's the position but that we don't anticipate evidence will take more than perhaps up to an hour tomorrow morning but probably not as much as that.

MR STOREY: I think much less, yes.

JUDGE JAMESON: And that, with luck, and I'll tell them that we're going to use the rest of today, which we will, in sorting out directions so that we'll crack straight on with speeches...

MR STOREY: Yes.

JUDGE JAMESON: ...and I would hope to be summing up by tomorrow afternoon probably...

MR STOREY: Yes, I think that's...

JUDGE JAMESON: ...or thereabouts.

MR STOREY: ...that's...I think we think that if the witness is, as I estimate, half an hour then we will, in all likelihood, finish our speeches at around lunchtime.

JUDGE JAMESON: Yeah.

MR STOREY: Which will, obviously, leave the afternoon for your Honour's summing-up.

JUDGE JAMESON: Okay, good, excellent. Well, I'll tell them that so, just really keeping them all content that...

MR STOREY: Of course.

JUDGE JAMESON: ...we're on track. Yeah. Good. Yeah. Thank you. Mr Storey, can I say that you will or may...

MR STOREY: Will.

JUDGE JAMESON: Will, yeah.

MR STOREY: Unless something changes that I'm not aware of.

JUDGE JAMESON: Yes, yes.

(The jury returned to court at 2.05 p.m.)

JUDGE JAMESON: Right, ladies and gentlemen, welcome back. Now then, Mr Storey is anticipating calling one witness, defence witness. Unfortunately, or potentially fortunately, depending on how we look at these things I suppose, because the evidence of Mr Appleyard was dealt with particularly efficiently, both in chief and in cross-examination, and, therefore, took half a day, it was thought that it might well take considerably longer than that but it hasn't. That's absolutely no criticism, on the contrary, examination both in chief and in cross-examination focussed on the relevant issues. So, it's a matter for congratulation not condemnation of any kind. But because it has gone rather quickly unhappily the decision had been made for the witness, who's coming from some distance, to be here tomorrow morning. There'd been attempts made over lunchtime and, indeed, before lunchtime when it became apparent that things were going quite quickly to see whether or not the witness could be brought forward and be here this afternoon but, unhappily, that simply isn't possible. So, that means that so far as you're concerned that's as far as we can go today.

Don't, please, be concerned about timing of matters because I've been asking counsel about this and tomorrow morning which, of course, is only Wednesday it's thought that the remainder of the evidence will probably not be more than half an hour or thereabouts. So, the evidence should finish quite quickly.

Now, I don't know, would it be possible, ladies and gentlemen, for you to be here at 10 o'clock tomorrow morning? Can I...I think I got nods from everybody but can I simply put that the other way round, is there anybody for whom that would be a problem? Nobody. Okay, good. Excellent. Well, can I...I'm just going to check with my clerk. (the learnered Judge confers with the court clerk) Assuming...they have this habit, when you're in the middle of doing trials, of putting in sentences that have been hung over from before at 10 o'clock or earlier sometimes. (Judge Jameson confers with the court clerk) Anyway right, thank you very much. Right, sorry. Forget that, then 10.30. Sorry. Just as well I asked. Okay, so 10.30. I don't think it matters to be honest because if we start at 10.30, evidence finished. Let's suppose it's a bit longer, even half past 11 something like that. That probably wouldn't mean that counsel would finish their addresses to you by lunchtime and they must take as long as they reasonably need. But it will certainly mean that I'll, at least, start the summing-up tomorrow and probably finish it fairly early on Thursday and I'll see whether I can have a word with listing now and tell them not to list anything on Thursday and see if we can make a 10 o'clock start on Thursday if we can. But I'll let you know about that. Anyway, that's where we are. So, we are well on track, in fact. And what we're going to do now, in your absence, and we would have had to have done this at some point anyway so, this is, in fact, a convenient moment is that I want to discuss with counsel the legal directions and, particularly, the written document that I'm going to give you with them so, that I've got their input now. We always do this in any case and it has to be done at some point and the evidence that the witness may give tomorrow isn't going to have any bearing on that counsel tell me so, we can do it now and it may take a little while, not because the ultimate directions are going to be very complicated but I can tell you the idea is to make them as simple as possible but making them simple isn't actually that simple itself as a process. So, that's what we're going to do now to get everything ready so that we can get straight on with it tomorrow. Good.

So, you get the afternoon off, enjoy, we don't and so, there we go. See you tomorrow morning, half past 10.

(The jury leave court at 2.10 p.m.)

JUDGE JAMESON: Right, I've got drafts. I'm afraid I've only done two, apologies to your juniors. I could have run...

MR HAMPTON: Thank you.

JUDGE JAMESON: ...more off, I suppose, but by no means finished as you will see, particularly as they go to the end. Well, I say, they're not a million miles off actually. But have a look and see...take as much time...don't...don't, please, stand. Do sit down. Just take as long as you need to read through them.

MR STOREY: Thank you. (After a pause)

JUDGE JAMESON: I see I've missed some rather important missing word in para.7...

MR HAMPTON: Paragraph 7.

JUDGE JAMESON: ...third line. (After a pause) Don't, of course, think this is the only opportunity you have for a comment on this. If anything occurs to you at any time overnight, or at any other time, you've only, of course, to let me know. Now what I have changed, just as I read it through with you, I've put in the word "Sure" in line 3 of para.7...

MR STOREY: Yes.

JUDGE JAMESON: ...which wasn't there.

MR STOREY: No.

JUDGE JAMESON: I...because I changed things around, the first reference to what a specimen count is wasn't very happily put. So, I've just changed that now under the heading "Counts 4, 8 and 12, oral sex." The top of the following page I have changed that simply to this; these three counts are described on the indictment as being specimen counts, that is to say they are specimens of that alleged course of conduct. It's just a happier way of describing it, I think. Yeah, okay. So, this is my or most of my initial proposal. I obviously haven't finished and would like to discuss with you what to put in the rape direction and, of course, I'm going to draft a para.13 which isn't there yet.

MR STOREY: Yes.

JUDGE JAMESON: The specific defence points that arise out of the passage of time.

MR STOREY: Yes. For my part, in relation to para. 9, your Honour knows that the defence case here is that this simply never happened.

JUDGE JAMESON: Yeah.

MR STOREY: To that extent it may not be necessary to deal with the question of consent at all, other than by saying, effectively, because this is what the defence is, that issue doesn't arise. But I don't know what my learned friend's view is about that specific issue. Similarly, I think it's perhaps for the Crown initially to address your Honour on the question of whether there should be alternative verdicts left to the jury.

JUDGE JAMESON: Sorry, any?

MR STOREY: Whether there should be alternative verdicts of indecent assault left to the jury...

JUDGE JAMESON: Yes.

MR STOREY: ...as was highlighted as a possibility.

JUDGE JAMESON: Yeah. Well, that only applies, of course, if it's thought necessary to leave the issue of consent.

MR STOREY: Yes, well...

JUDGE JAMESON: I'm not sure that it really arises but unless you...

MR STOREY: I don't think, for my part, it's necessary with respect.

JUDGE JAMESON: In those circumstances, I mean it really comes, very simple, did it happen or didn't it?

MR STOREY: Yes.

JUDGE JAMESON: And, I mean, that's really what the case is all about, of course...

MR STOREY: Yes.

JUDGE JAMESON: ...for all counts really but, unfortunately, it gets a bit more complicated than that with specimen counts...

MR STOREY: Yes.

JUDGE JAMESON: ...and the issue on the masturbation counts.

MR STOREY: Yes.

JUDGE JAMESON: There it is. But, yeah, if you're content with that then I will simply say, in relation to Count 9...well, unless, Mr Hampton, you want an alternative.

MR HAMPTON: No. No, I don't.

JUDGE JAMESON: All or nothing.

MR HAMPTON: No.

JUDGE JAMESON: Yeah, fine. I think I have said I think that's sensible. I mean it doesn't really arise on the evidence.

MR HAMPTON: No.

JUDGE JAMESON: Okay, good. Well, in those circumstances then I'll simply say, "The only issue is, did these happen and, if so, once, twice, three times or more?"

MR HAMPTON: Yes.

JUDGE JAMESON: Okay. Good, that's that. Now, you'll note in...I suppose it's really, I think, ultimately for me whether or not I think, but I would be interested in your views, whether you think there really ought to be any route to verdict. I'm not sure it's really necessary.

MR HAMPTON: If your Honour is going to be saying this is down...this is in rough terms I'm speaking, it happened or it didn't and consent's not an issue. I don't think there has to be a route to verdict.

JUDGE JAMESON: Yeah, I'm not specifically thinking there about...about the rape allegations. I was thinking more really about Counts 5, 9 and 13, whether there's any possibility of the jury becoming a bit confused as to exactly what it is they've got to decide.

MR HAMPTON: We had reached the conclusion, that's the prosecution, that it didn't have to be an either/or scenario though your Honour's put it there. We think it could be put in a different way.

JUDGE JAMESON: Right.

MR HAMPTON: We don't think a *Brown* direction is necessary for the same reasons.

JUDGE JAMESON: No, well I was coming to that conclusion myself but I'm grateful for any submissions about it.

MR HAMPTON: See what your Honour feels about this; it could be that in relation to the large paragraph beginning "CH masturbated EA."

JUDGE JAMESON: Yeah.

MR HAMPTON: Could we not just put at the end of that something along the lines of, "This would include occasions whereby the defendant placed the complainant's hand on his penis and occasions where he may not have" because the underlying issue is that apprehension of violence, not so much the placing of her hand on his penis, it's the apprehension of violence that is the underlying ingredient proving assault whether or not they're satisfied that the hand was placed on the penis.

JUDGE JAMESON: Yes, I have to say I think the way I've put it more accurately reflects the law...

MR HAMPTON: Yeah.

JUDGE JAMESON: ...but, perhaps, your concern can properly be addressed by simply saying, "Or both."

MR HAMPTON: Yeah.

JUDGE JAMESON: It doesn't have to be one or the other it can, of course, be both.

MR HAMPTON: Yes.

JUDGE JAMESON: If I put that in, I think that would...

MR HAMPTON: Yes.

JUDGE JAMESON: Well, or put "Either and/or." That's all it requires, isn't it? "Either that EA placed CH's hand on his penis and/or."

MR HAMPTON: I agree.

JUDGE JAMESON: And I'll explain to them what that means, it can be both.

MR HAMPTON: Yes.

JUDGE JAMESON: But if it's...if it was only one then it's got to be one or the other.

MR HAMPTON: Yes.

JUDGE JAMESON: Okay...

MR HAMPTON: Yeah. I don't think...

JUDGE JAMESON: ...and no *Brown* direction, I agree, I don't...I thought about it fairly carefully. I don't think it is a *Brown* direction situation.

MR HAMPTON: No.

JUDGE JAMESON: Okay. Good.

MR HAMPTON: So, and as to your Honour's question, in those circumstances, "No, we don't think a route to verdict...

JUDGE JAMESON: Yeah.

MR HAMPTON: ...is necessary or helpful."

JUDGE JAMESON: Yeah. So, no alternative verdicts on Counts 2, 3, 7, 11 and 15.

MR HAMPTON: No.

JUDGE JAMESON: No, fine, okay.

MR HAMPTON: I obviously mentioned, in opening, an interpretation of consent when I opened the case...

JUDGE JAMESON: Yes.

MR HAMPTON: ...if your Honour's making clear in this document that it's not an issue...

JUDGE JAMESON: Yeah.

MR HAMPTON: ...then I don't think we need to delve into that.

JUDGE JAMESON: Yeah. Okay. Yeah, I'll do that. Coming back, then, to the specific issue as to whether or not you think there's any chance of the jury getting confused, in particular in relation to Counts 5, 9 and 13 where the direction's a bit more complicated. Not really complicated, a little less simple is, perhaps, a better way of putting it. I mean what...I'm obviously going to not just read this out parrot-fashion, I'm going to explain to them what it all means.

MR HAMPTON: Yeah.

JUDGE JAMESON: I'm hoping that that will be sufficient really.

MR HAMPTON: I think so. As your Honour says, it's not as simple as the other counts but it's not particularly complex...

JUDGE JAMESON: No, it isn't...

MR HAMPTON: ...now, no.

JUDGE JAMESON: ...particularly complicated. I'll just explain to them, "Issue 1; did these things happen? Issue 2; was it either and/or."

MR HAMPTON: Yeah.

JUDGE JAMESON: "Issue 3; if you're satisfied with all of that then was it just the once and you're sure...and you're sure of it could you only be sure of once or twice." I don't know whether I'm going to say anything about twice seems a bit illogical but it is, in reality, isn't it? But, anyway, I think I have to say that or three times or more.

MR HAMPTON: Yeah.

JUDGE JAMESON: Anyway.

MR HAMPTON: Yeah, yeah.

JUDGE JAMESON: Right good. Okay so far so good, so, let's go on then to "Approach to particular areas of the evidence" so, para.10 on. I don't know whether I'm going...I don't think I'm going to put any...you'll see I put a note to myself after the second sub-paragraph, whether I need to say anything more specific about what their assessment of that issue may affect. I might say something but I don't think I'm going to put in writing because it rather gives it a...

MR HAMPTON: Slant.

JUDGE JAMESON: ...status that it isn't really for me to give it.

MR HAMPTON: No.

JUDGE JAMESON: And just...I might say something to help them a bit about the sort of thing that it could be relevant to...

MR HAMPTON: Yes.

JUDGE JAMESON: ...and, you know, it could go both ways. I mean there are potential arguments on both sides that could arise out of that.

MR HAMPTON: I'd agree that any rehearsal of what it might be relevant to in a written document is not helpful.

JUDGE JAMESON: Yeah, okay. I have put in and I will take out, Mr Storey, if you would wish me to, what is, essentially, a *Lucas* direction...

MR STOREY: Yes.

JUDGE JAMESON: ...in relation to potential lies...

MR STOREY: Yes.

JUDGE JAMESON: ...if they have a conclusion...reach an adverse conclusion to Mr Appleyard about what I've described as physical and/or emotional abuse.

MR STOREY: Yes.

JUDGE JAMESON: It seemed to me it probably would be helpful.

MR STOREY: Well, my initial discussions with my learned friend, Mr Hampton, upstairs over lunch were to the effect that I was not minded to seek a *Lucas* direction because, not least, there are not admitted lies here. But having read the way your Honour's worded it in that paragraph I think I've changed my mind...

JUDGE JAMESON: Yeah.

MR STOREY: ...and I'm inclined to agree with your Honour's observation that, in fact, it may help...

JUDGE JAMESON: I tend to be very much guided by defence counsel. Sometimes defence counsel will say, "Well, I really don't want it and, you know, tactically I just don't want a direction like that." But I don't...what I want to guard against is what does seem to me to be the obvious reason that they could if they...obviously depending on their conclusion but if they say, "Yes, well we believe the evidence about physical abuse and, indeed, about..."

MR STOREY: Yes.

JUDGE JAMESON: "...emotional or emotional abuse or both we believe that and he's denied it so, he's a liar so, we'll convict him."

MR STOREY: Yes, well I think this does just that very thing, guarding against the risk of that conclusion."

JUDGE JAMESON: Yeah, and it's not quite as simple as that.

MR STOREY: No. I'm content with that.

JUDGE JAMESON: So, I...well, let me put it this way, I think if I was defending, I'd want it in but I will always be guided by defence counsel in these circumstances. So, if you're happy with it, I'll leave it.

MR STOREY: I am, thank you very much.

JUDGE JAMESON: Okay.

MR STOREY: Your Honour's s.11 gone on to deal with complaints...

JUDGE JAMESON: Yes.

MR STOREY: ...made. One of the directions that are contained within the compendium or Bench Book of course relates to the myths and stereo-type issue in a very general sense but one of the...one of the suggested directions relates to consistency which, of course, has some relevance to the complaints direction...

JUDGE JAMESON: Yeah.

MR STOREY: ...and it is sometimes, I know, the case that courts are prepared to give a direction to the effect that consistency is not necessarily evidence of truthfulness and I wonder whether you would be prepared to work into that, perhaps, that part of these directions something to that effect. I don't know whether you were going to go on to deal with myths and stereotypes in a later part of this document in isolation or not.

JUDGE JAMESON: Yes, those...those sort of directions I was rather going to wait and see whether anything was said. I mean, potentially, you might want to say something, I don't know, it's entirely a matter for you...

MR STOREY: Yes.

JUDGE JAMESON: ...I'm not suggesting what arguments you should deploy. But if you were to address the jury along the lines, well, if this was happening then it seems to have been going on for quite a long time with nothing being said and Carol Higgins remaining in the home. I might need to say something about that.

MR STOREY: Yes.

JUDGE JAMESON: But you know exactly what that would be...

MR STOREY: Yeah.

JUDGE JAMESON: ...so, it wouldn't come as any surprise.

MR STOREY: No.

JUDGE JAMESON: But I think, really, it's rather going to have to be reactive to the submissions that are made in the hope...

MR STOREY: Very well.

JUDGE JAMESON: ...that whatever I say is fair. But I do think your specific point about consistency not necessarily being to be equiparated with truth is a perfectly good one and if you'd like me to put something in about that I will. Although I think it would have to be along the lines of consistency...the trouble is, if you give the conventional direction that neither consistency nor inconsistency necessarily means one thing or the other...

MR STOREY: No.

JUDGE JAMESON: ...then inviting them to look to the evidence and see whether she's been consistent is arguably irrelevant and I don't think it really can be. I'll try and think of a proper way of doing it and I'll put something in.

MR STOREY: Thank you.

JUDGE JAMESON: But, as I say, you will want to mull over these things and if other thoughts occur to you any time up to and including the moment, they get handed to the jury is fine.

MR STOREY: Well, thank you.

MR HAMPTON: Could I just make a comment on myths and stereotypes? I think we're probably already there in terms of directions being needed generally, in any event because...

JUDGE JAMESON: Yeah, I tend not to put stereo-type directions into written directions.

MR HAMPTON: Right.

JUDGE JAMESON: I mean I can do but the problem isn't...you just don't know exactly what is going to be said in speeches and I'm not asking for drafts or anything like that...

MR HAMPTON: No.

JUDGE JAMESON: ...that would be ridiculous. Apart from anything else, you know, these things are a question of feel really and I'm just going to be very aware of trying to make sure that whatever I say is helpful to the jury in the light of the submissions that have been made and is fair to everybody involved in the trial, that's what I'm aiming for.

MR HAMPTON: Of course, what I'm thinking of it's not only speeches it's cross-examination as well and my recollection of cross-examination, quite proper, quite fair was, there was...there were elements of "Why did you stay?" There were elements of, "Why didn't you go to your mum's? Why didn't you complain at the custody hearing?"

JUDGE JAMESON: Yeah.

MR HAMPTON: So, when I say, 'I think we're already there' that's what I'm referring to.

JUDGE JAMESON: Well, let me just...hang on, I'll just make...the notes then that I'll make is...I'll just put a note to myself, "Stereo-types", I may well have to say something about that and I'll just, also, make a note about consistency. Yeah, okay.

MR HAMPTON: I've got no strong view about whether that's written or oral.

JUDGE JAMESON: Yeah. Okay. Well, as I say, if you have any further thoughts let me know. But anything else?

MR STOREY: Just one small point if I may...

JUDGE JAMESON: Yes, of course.

MR STOREY: ...in relation to, effectively, the last paragraph in s.12, "Difficulties that any witness may have in recalling detail" would your Honour be so kind as to make it clear that any witness, of course, includes the defendant?

JUDGE JAMESON: Oh, yes, of course.

MR STOREY: I'm sure you'll do that in any event...

JUDGE JAMESON: Yeah...

MR STOREY: ...and I don't mind...

JUDGE JAMESON: Well, I will, of course, have said that...

MR STOREY: Yes.

JUDGE JAMESON: ...when about treating all evidence in the...

MR STOREY: Quite.

JUDGE JAMESON: ...same fair-minded way but I will put that in. "Any witness including the defendant."

MR STOREY: Thank you. Just...just so that they don't lose sight of that fact.

JUDGE JAMESON: "Including EA" and (inaudible) "And his witness?"

MR STOREY: Yes, if it becomes necessary although I'm not sure whether it will.

JUDGE JAMESON: Well, look I'll say that if it's obvious...

MR STOREY: Thank you.

JUDGE JAMESON: ...that it's to be said, I'll say it.

MR STOREY: Yes.

JUDGE JAMESON: But I'll just put at the moment, put in "Any witness including EA..."

MR STOREY: Thank you very much.

JUDGE JAMESON: "...may have in recalling detail." Yeah. Good. All right. Fine. I'll try and finish this off...

MR STOREY: Thank you.

JUDGE JAMESON: ...and let you have it tonight if I can but we'll see how we go.

MR STOREY: Thank you very much and we'll...if we need to raise anything tomorrow morning then we can...

JUDGE JAMESON: Of course, yeah.

MR STOREY: ...I'm sure.

JUDGE JAMESON: It'll probably be headed "Draft 2" until it actually gets...goes to press.

MR STOREY: Thank you.

JUDGE JAMESON: Right. Good. All right. Well, we'd better get on with the box work then. Sorry, while I'm here, I did have one further thought. Because it's rather been overtaken by events, I've really completely forgotten all about it but now that it's come...just came back to mind as I was walking out, one of the things I'm going to have to remind the jury about, I'm sure you will have done so, anyway, but I will be reminding them about is some of the things that Carol Higgins clearly now believes and I may have to invite them to consider that there may be a difference, and that's for them, between believing, potentially irrationally, things that she's been told and actually recollecting what has or hasn't happened. But the point that I just wanted to raise was this, one of the spectres that was raised was the position of, I'm not sure if he's the late but certainly the retired Judge James Pickles. Now, of course I have absolutely no intention of saying anything whatsoever, evidentially, about James Pickles. I just wondered whether I should say anything at all about the difficulties of one judge commenting or not commenting on another, I think probably nothing at all, I think, simply...just say nothing.

MR STOREY: No.

JUDGE JAMESON: Say, "That's what she believes" and...

MR STOREY: I think my recollection is...

JUDGE JAMESON: ...there it is.

MR STOREY: ...that that is as much as your Honour needs to say.

JUDGE JAMESON: Yeah, I just...I wouldn't want the jury to feel that I was adopting any view, one way or another, in...

MR STOREY: No.

JUDGE JAMESON: ...relation to what she said about James Pickles. I think, basically, what I'm probably going to say because I don't really think the Crown would disprove this, although...disapprove of this, although I understand your difficulties in exactly what you can say is that if they can conclude that these are irrational beliefs you, nevertheless, need to go on to consider what, if any, significance that has on the real issues in the case. I think that's...I'm going to say something along those lines.

MR STOREY: I agree and I agree with your Honour's suggestion of saying nothing about a judge commenting on another judge.

JUDGE JAMESON: Yeah.

MR STOREY: There's no need.

JUDGE JAMESON: Good, all right. Thanks.

MR STOREY: Thank you.

(Adjourned until the following day)

(2.40 p.m.)

Diary: Tuesday 22nd January 2019

Once again, his wife Janet was not in court to support him as he took the stand.

I had to listen to my dad telling his lies today and going round the houses with his long answers and avoidance tac-tics. The judge directed him frequently to just answer the question, yes or no. I felt how he tried to talk his way out of things was dropping him deeper in it and making him look guilty. His answers reminded me of the "Little Britain" comedy character Vicky Pollard , with his "Ye but, no but, ye but, no but."

My father's defence was that he would not have raped me because he claimed I had had an orgy in his bed whilst he was on his hunting holiday in America. This was not only a lie, it did not make sense. He had said in his evidence that he had knocked on the doors of all the parents of the boys who had been present at the party to get money back for the damages they had caused. But he did not report them for having sex with his fifteen year old daughter. I could not believe that the police had denied me justice all these years because they believed his crummy defence.

I was extremely impressed with how Mr Hampton conducted his examination of my father. Everyone was listening intently and you could hear a pin drop. At the point where he referred to the "epileptic sheep worrying dog" the whole public gallery cracked out laughing.

Wednesday 23 January, 2019

(Transcript prepared without the aid of documentation)

(10.47 a.m.)

JUDGE JAMESON: Yes.

MR STOREY: Your Honour, thank you. We received the second version of your Honour's...

JUDGE JAMESON: Yes, yeah

MR STOREY: ...legal directions to the jury.

MR STOREY: There's nothing...

JUDGE JAMESON: ...then took out the word "Either" I thought that probably worked.

MR STOREY: Yes. There's nothing that I wish to raise...

JUDGE JAMESON: No...

MR STOREY: ...as a result of what you sent to us last night. Thank you very much.

JUDGE JAMESON: ...all right. Thank you very much indeed. Good and you're ready to...

MR STOREY: We're ready to proceed, yes.

JUDGE JAMESON: Excellent. Thank you very much. Yes, jury please.

(The jury return to court at 10.48 a.m.)

JUDGE JAMESON: Welcome back, ladies and gentlemen. I'm sorry to have kept you a few minutes. I got through what I had to do as quick as I could but there it is. Yes.

MR STOREY: Thank you, your Honour. Can I please call Sarah Thomas?

SARAH THOMAS, Sworn

Examined by MR STOREY

Q Can you just start, please, by giving us your full name?

A	Yes, it's Sarah Thomas.

Q	Thank you and is it Miss Thomas or Mrs Thomas?

A	Mrs.

Q	Mrs Thomas, thank you very much. Obviously, I'm asking you questions to begin with and the gentleman to my right will ask you some questions in due course.

A	Okay.

Q	It's very important that the ladies and gentlemen of the jury opposite you hear what you have to say and, so that you're aware, his Honour is also going to be making a note of your evidence as well. So, we may have to take it a little steadily at times. All right?

A	Right, okay.

Q	Do you mind me asking you what your date of birth is, first of all?

A	Yes, it's 16 June, 1970.

Q	And I think it's right, isn't it, that you're related to the defendant in this case, Elliott Appleyard?

A	I am, yes.

Q	And can you tell us how you are related to him, please?

A	Yes, I'm his niece.

Q	You...forgive me, for the avoidance of doubt, is it that you're related to him through your father?

A	My dad and Elliott were brothers.

Q	Thank you very much. I don't need to know, at all, where you live at the moment but can you tell us whereabouts you grew up?

A	I grew up in Huddersfield area...

Q	And...

A	...attending Scissett Middle School and Shelley High School.

Q	Okay. Obviously, there's a familial connection with Mr Appleyard and his family. When you were growing up how much did you see of them?

A	Not a great deal to be honest. We weren't what I would consider a close family. My dad had got his own family and so, he focussed on them. We did see each other, from time to time, at my grandma and grandad's house is Skelmanthorpe.

Q Right. And were you aware of the extent of Mr Appleyard's immediate family?

A Yes.

Q Did he have any children that you knew of?

A Yes, he had a daughter that wasn't biologically his and then he had another daughter, Carol, and a younger son, Paul.

Q Did you ever visit their family home?

A Not that I can recall of as a young girl. It was more at grandma and grandads.

Q You told us, I think, that you were at school in Scissett and Shelley.

A That's right.

Q Did you see anything of Mr Appleyard's children when you were at school?

A I met Paul there. He was in the year below me. Carol may have been there but I wasn't aware of her presence because I was...because it had been such a long time since I'd seen them. I was actually introduced to Paul. I walked past him and he walked past me and a friend of mine, that lived in Denby Dale, said, "Don't you speak to your cousins?" To which I said, 'Well, I do when I see them' and she said, "Well, you've just walked past one now."

Q So, you said you met Paul there. Can we be clear where you're talking about?

A At Scissett Middle School.

Q Okay and what sort of age do you think you were, as best you can remember, when you met Paul in the way you've just described?

A Well, I started in 1980 so, he wouldn't have been there that year so, it would have been '81, '82.

Q So, do we take it you would have been 10...

A I would've been 11, 12.

Q ...11, 12.

A Yes.

Q And Paul, you said, was the school year below you.

A Yes.

Q You said you weren't aware of Carol being at that school when you were there.

A No, I wasn't.

Q Did there come a time when you did become aware of Carol?

A Not until Shelley High School.

Q Okay and do you remember when it was, roughly, that you became aware of Carol?

A It wasn't the first year that I was at Shelley High School, which would have been 1983. So, it would have been '84, '85.

Q So, again, you'd have been 14, 15.

A Fourteen, 15, yes.

Q And was Carol someone who was in the year above you, the same year as you, two years above you?

A She was in the year above me.

Q Okay and how did you become aware of Carol? How did you first realise that you and she were at the same school?

A I don't know if Paul had mentioned me to her but, all of a sudden, she approached me one day and put her arm around me and said, "Hiya, Sarah, I'm Carol." And there were other people around. I think some of her friends were there and she said, "We're really close. We're a close family."

Q What did you think about that?

A I was a bit taken aback because we hadn't been a close family. That was my first meeting of her and I was shy at the time and so, I didn't want to contradict. But, yes, it didn't feel natural. It didn't feel genuine.

Q You say it...

JUDGE JAMESON: I think I must then have slightly missed something. "I got the arm round me shoulder and "Hi, Sarah, I'm Carol." There must then have been something more or is that it?

MR STOREY: Well, I think the witness went on to say...

JUDGE JAMESON: Did I miss something?

MR STOREY: ...that Carol said that they were really close as family. I don't know if your Honour got that part of her evidence.

JUDGE JAMESON: Oh, that was it, was it, yes?

A Yes.

Q There was something, yes, all right. And so, what do you recall her as having said, that?

A She put her arm around me and said, "We were a close family."

Q "We were a close family", yeah.

A Yes.

MR STOREY: And who was she saying that to, to you or to others in the area?

A No, it was other people.

Q Right.

A And she did approach me again, at other times, and it became we were close, me and her.

Q Right.

A Sorry.

Q Just pause whilst his Honour makes a note, please, Mrs Thomas. You said that this first approach by Carol at Shelley High School was, I think, you said the first time you'd seen her. Do you mean it was the first time you'd ever seen her or the first time you'd seen her for a period of time?

A The first time I'd seen her for a period of time.

Q And can you give us an idea of how long that time had been?

A Oh gosh, it must have been...we used to see other members of the family when grandma and grandad were living. Me grandad died in 1977 so, after that, I didn't see her.

Q Right. So, nothing from 1977, or thereabouts, until this...

A '84, '80, yeah.

Q ...1984, '84, '85. Yeah. You told us just now that you...I don't want to put words in your mouth but you clearly didn't agree with the assertion that you were close as a family.

A No, I didn't.

Q And how much did you have to do with Carol or, indeed, with Paul once you'd reacquainted yourselves with your cousins?

A Well, Paul I spoke to probably once a week, maybe twice at the most, at Scissett Middle School. He was friendly, he was polite. We...we laughed and chatted about family. You know, I got the impression that he thought the world of his dad. If I'm honest, he had his dad on a pedestal and he used to compare, you know, and ask questions like, "Did your dad go shooting and things like that?"

Q What about once you re-acquainted yourself with your cousin, Carol, at high school?

A I thought I would have the same relationship as with Paul to be honest, that, you know, she certainly seemed friendly, she seemed bubbly, she seemed confident. But it was the fact that she was putting her arm around me and squeezing me and she was saying that we were close and it was a blatant lie. It was...it...we weren't close at all.

Q Okay. What, if anything, was said by her or, if Paul was at the same high school as you, by him, about family life, by the time you're talking about meeting Carol again in '84, '85?

A Well, from my perception they loved their dad. They thought the world of him and he took them on holidays and I know he took Paul shooting, whether he did with Carol or not I don't know.

Q Do you remember being aware of where they were living in '84 or '85?

A Yes, they were living at Gilthwaites in Denby Dale.

Q And how much did you have to do with your cousins at high school?

A Well, with Paul I always said, 'Hi' whenever I saw him and, 'How are you doing?' And 'How is your dad?' Or he'd ask, you know, how's my family. How I was doing. With Carol she was...I felt uncomfortable with her, to be honest, because of the blatant lies that she was telling. It was almost as if she didn't want to engage with me. There was no eye contact with me. She was...it was a performance. That's how I felt. That she was talking to her friends and other people that were observing us and it didn't feel genuine.

Q You are, obviously, aware of the allegations that have been made in relation to Elliott Appleyard, which is why we're here.
A Um.
Q Can I ask you when the very first time was that you became aware of those allegations from what you heard from family members or elsewhere?
A Not 'til a couple of years ago. Certainly nothing at school.
Q Was anything said that might have given you cause to wonder about the family relationship between Mr Appleyard and his children whilst you were at school with them?
A No, not at all. She seemed confident; she seemed bubbly; easy-going. I knew she had a reputation at school.
Q I'm not interested in that, I'm sorry.
A Okay.
Q I'm asking specifically about her family life if that's all right, Mrs Thomas. But you said nothing until a couple of years ago, that you were aware of, in relation to these specific allegations?
A Yeah, that's right.
Q All right. Thank you very much, Mrs Thomas. There's nothing else I want to ask you but can you wait there, please, because I suspect there'll be some questions for you?
A Okay.

Cross-examined by MR HAMPTON

Q Just one or two please, Mrs Thomas. Carol said that you and she were close...
A That's what she said.
Q ...whilst friends were round, yes.
A Yeah.
Q And you weren't.
A No, we weren't.
Q You called it a blatant lie and a performance.

A Yeah.

Q Do you think she might have been trying to make friends with you, as a family member?

A Then why would you tell a lie like you're supposed to...

Q Trying to say you're close.

A No.

Q You didn't get that impression?

A No.

Q No. Paul; you described him as...I'll just find it, friendly, polite and you'd speak to him on occasions.

A Yeah. He was always polite and friendly to me.

Q And, finally, you mention that before you were at the school, Shelley, I think, and you saw Carol, you had seen her in the past.

A As a young child, yes.

Q As a young child and I got the impression that that was at grandfather's, was it?

A At grandma and grandads.

Q So, you'd seen Carol there.

A Yes.

MR HAMPTON: Nothing else, thank you.

JUDGE JAMESON: Thank you.

MR STOREY: Thank you. There's...

JUDGE JAMESON: Thank you very much for coming and helping us with your evidence,

Mrs Thomas, that's it.

THE WITNESS: Thank you.

JUDGE JAMESON: You're free to go.

(The witness withdrew)

MR STOREY: Your Honour, the last part of the evidence in the trial and on behalf of Mr Appleyard is one further admission.

JUDGE JAMESON: Yes, certainly.

MR STOREY: Ladies and gentlemen, I think you were told yesterday or the day before, by Mr Hampton, that there would be one more admission coming your way which I can now hand out to you and then once you've got copies of this last agreed fact then I'll read it out into the record. There's a copy for your Honour as well.

JUDGE JAMESON: Yes, would you just wait for a moment until I've read it? Thank you. Yeah, okay, thank you.

MR STOREY: Ladies and gentlemen, this is numbered to follow on from the other agreed facts in the document that you've already had and that you were taken through by Mr Hampton earlier on in the trial and, as you can read, this says;

> "On 29th October, 2017 a telephone call took place between Carol Higgins and Diane Croft. This call was recorded. During the conversation Diane Croft said, quote; "We need to all get together privately without the fucking coppers knowing. We need to speak to a lawyer to see if we can do it without him knowing. We're going to nail the bugger and we all just need to talk to each other. During the conversation Diane Croft also said, "If we could have done this 20 years ago, love, if we could have got together a lot sooner but, anyway, that's whatever, isn't it? Let's get something sorted but we need to do this the right way. Do you know what I mean?"

And that concludes that last agreed fact and with it that concludes the case on behalf of the defendant, your Honour.

JUDGE JAMESON: Yes, thank you very much indeed, Mr Storey. Right. Well, now, ladies and gentlemen, that then is the conclusion of the evidence. So, the next part of the trial is addresses from counsel. I'm just going to check with Mr Hampton whether he's ready to begin that.

MR HAMPTON: I am, thank you.

JUDGE JAMESON: All right. Everybody...I don't know how long addresses will be but they make take a little while. Is everybody happy to get on with it? Nobody needing a break? No. Okay. Thank you very much indeed. Yes, Mr Hampton.

MR HAMPTON: Sometimes there is a voice and sometimes there is a voice that cuts through the mists of time with such clarity that it serves as a shining beacon of truth. It serves as a guide that lights the path through choppy waters, past jagged rocks towards anchor in the calm waters of a just and equitable harbour. One such voice is that of Carol Higgins. A beacon of truth safely bolstered up high on a clifftop of an abundance of supporting evidence, secure, steady, safe and certain.

Many sexual offences come before this Court, many of them occurring decades ago. Many sexual offences, because of their very nature, involve, in the main, one person's word against another. When you are considering who is telling the truth in this case the starting point is Carol Higgins' account in her video-recorded interview. Is the detail of that account invention, is it fantasy or is it utterly compelling, candid and truthful? Evidence that drives you to the conclusion that Carol Higgins is telling the truth about what happened to her some 35 years ago at the hands of the defendant, her father. We do not under-estimate the size of your task. We know it's not easy. You are charged with a responsibility of listening to the grim detail of this case, looking back through the mists of time, sifting the evidence, identifying who's truthful and who is not. Sexual offences are, by their very nature, private acts. They're not for public consumption usually, therefore there's not hundreds of witnesses to tell you about it. There's no CCTV of it. Sometimes it's simply one person's word against another. But where that person's word is compelling, where it is truthful, that is enough, that can be enough to make you sure, particularly when it is supported by other witnesses who talk about what they saw at the time and what Carol told them at the time, importantly. Sure, of course, the necessary standard in this case in relation to each count. You can be sure if somebody's truthful and compelling as a witness. Look at the detail, the devil is in that detail. The truth is to be found there even when you are examining matters decades ago. A voice heard now, for the first time in a courtroom, since a first complaint by Carol in the mid-1980s. A voice ignored until now. A voice that, for 35 years, has shouted out to be heard and has not been listened to, desperate to give her account about the sexual abuse that has undermined the whole of her adult life. At crucial points in her life the trauma of what happened to her coming back to haunt her causing her pain and anguish.

You don't need to turn it up but from the agreed facts, 22nd November, 1988, a document from hospital records. So, three or four years after the offending;

> "Carol was last under your care in January 1990 for counselling. She's planning to get married in August of this year and finds that many of the fears and anxieties are now coming to the surface."

Sorry, that's a document between 1988 and 1995. But coming to marriage;

> "Fears and anxieties coming to the surface again at a time when she feels she ought to be putting her past life behind her."

Fifteenth April, 2013, GP notes, Carol Higgins;

> "History; emotional at the moment as daughter, E, is the same age as she was when her dad was abusing her, working with her counsellor to work through it."

Invention, fantasy, lies or examples of how her life is dominated by the trauma suffered by her by the sexual abuse of this defendant when she was a child? It may be that the defence ask you to consider Carol Higgins' conduct, I think from around 2014 onwards, in particular, in attempting her own evidence gathering; publicising her allegations; contacting witnesses; her mistrust of police officers; contacting the officer in the case repeatedly; suggesting her father must, in some way, be protected by local high-profile figures; suggesting that certain items on his land pointed to further criminality or evidence that he wished to flee the jurisdiction. Well, you consider those matters carefully, it's your job. If you reach the view that her credibility, on the allegations she makes about her father abusing her in the 1980s, is fatally undermined then you cannot, therefore, be sure of the allegations she makes you will, of course, acquit the defendant. However, first of all, we suggest that there is a very big difference between Carol's beliefs in 2014 about unrelated matters and her ability to accurately remember her father abusing her in the 1980s, a very big difference indeed. Please also examine carefully, when you consider those points, firstly what she actually did; secondly, why it maybe she did it. You will conclude, we suggest, that Miss Higgins' evidence is far from undermined at all.

Well, firstly, what did she do? Well, she did publicise matters on Facebook and she explained why. It felt like a police cover-up; it felt like her father was escaping justice; put it bluntly, getting away with it. She published a book, she told you why. She wanted justice. She wanted her day in court. She did contact witnesses but on this you'll recall the evidence of DC Wilson who, in fact, did ask her to obtain their details, the onus being on her to help find the evidence. She sometimes recorded conversations. But importantly, you may think, she provided that material to the police. If acting dishonestly in some way, why would she record conversations? Why would she give that material to the police? In recording a conversation may, at first, seem odd unless you've walked in the shoes of the person making that recording. She was told, Carol Higgins, in the mid-1980s that she could bring a complaint later perhaps and then they lost everything, her statement, other items. You'd be recordings things too, perhaps.

Why is she mistrusting of the officer in the case, DC Wilson, it's not his fault? But, firstly, as a child, back in the 1980s, she was told by the officers that if she went through with this complaint, she would be called a slag, her reputation would be brought into it. It seems, from this morning, that some people still hold those views. That her name would be blackened but she said she was told, "The material will be stored." But when she came, in 2005, to make the first complaint, gone, destroyed and then not listened to by the police, the state. No wonder she records things. No wonder she has difficulty trusting the police and other officers of the state. So, walk a few yards in her shoes. It's understandable in the circumstances, don't you think?

You may have some comprehension, I don't know, of how it feels not to have a complaint taken seriously, not to be listened to. For most of us it's minor matters, your wing mirror being knocked off, your shed been broken into. When you form the view the police aren't really listening, they've got better things to do, don't really care, it's frustrating, isn't it? Now, imagine how that would feel if that view was taken of matters that had destroyed the whole of your adult life, imagine how that would feel. Can you begin to wonder why Carol began to think why it was or wonder why it was that the defendant was not being brought to book. Was he protected? Was he well-connected? Was this something bigger? Is he about to flee before his trial? So, do we come to understand why it is that Carol Higgins, in later years, acted in the way she did? Because it comes to this, we say, the sad reality is that Carol's behaviour from 2014 onwards, in terms of these matters, is the product of the abuse of her by her father coupled with the subsequent failure of the police and prosecution to listen to her allegation in the decades that followed. It is not indicative of her recollections about her father being, in any way, untruthful.

On occasions Carol Higgins more recent beliefs have been fuelled by other, perhaps, entirely innocent and understandable matters but, when taken together and given what's passed, she may have taken it in a different way. The investigation took a very long time, we know that. We have the agreed fact about Ina Whittles telling Carol that half the stuff she told Alex Wilson was not in the statement and it had been three pages but it was now only one page and there's someone else's signature on it. None of that's right. It was a handwritten statement. It was turned into a typed statement that's why it decreased in size and there was only her signature on it. Miscommunication, misunderstanding fuelling Mrs Higgins' belief. And, in any event, all of the matters the defence rely on come very late in the day. The reality is that Carol Higgins has been complaining of the abuse from the very evening of the final rape, 1984/1985, the point being, her first complaints pre-date all of this by decades. There is also evidence from other witnesses who witnessed the defendant's behaviour back in the day, Carron Ward, Deanna Thorpe and Hilda Graham.

So, in a moment we're going to turn to, please, a little of the detail Carol Higgins provides about what happened to her, then we'll look at the evidence that comes from other witnesses who recall what occurred back in 1985. Please, as we do this, would you bear in mind really the single, central issue, did this happen? No legal niceties, no legal complications, did this happen?

There is no doubt, is there, that there was something rotten in the house of Appleyard? At its core, say the prosecution, was the patriarch, Elliott Appleyard. Of the four surviving members of the family, three of them fled the home. You may want to ask yourselves why Jean fled; why Carol fled; why Paul fled, because the defendant portrays himself as really a put-upon husband and father who may have been a bit tough but was fair. Well, if that was the case why did the other three flee? Three of the four surviving members of the family recall a house filled with violence or the threat of violence. Carol; "I know he's been violent to me as a child, if I wet bed, if I was naughty he had...he had two belts, a thin belt and a thinner black belt, it wasn't thin and a thick black belt and he used to, depending on the severity of my punishment he used to hit me, hit me with that and I know that we were always flinching because he'd hit me round the head and he'd joke and sometimes he'd walk past me and he'd scratch his head and I think he were gonna hit me but he'd laugh, do you know what I mean, that kind of thing but I didn't know that was all part of him gaining power over me, you know?" Jean, of course, the memorable incidents, the terrible acts of violence perpetrated against her; the machete held to her vagina, the threat to slit her to her throat. I think it was put at one point, "Well, did you tell anybody about this?" She said, "No, I was embarrassed. Because I was so scared, I wet myself." Well, we know the defendant, he tells us, had a machete, he had guns. He's told us that and we know that in 2000, from the agreed facts, he had shotguns.

The defendant himself accepts that Jean moved to a refuge for battered women or at least a refuge, I think I put to him "Battered women." Why? For fun? Because it was more comfortable in a refuge than at home? Or because she'd be beaten when Elliott Appleyard came back from the pub. There's a tension between Jean's evidence and that of the children. Paul and Carol both say their parents would beat them. Jean says she rarely did and does not recall the defendant using a belt. The defendant says, in fact, it was Jean who would hit them with a wooden spoon. Well, those are matters for you to assess. But contrast how Paul recollects his parents' actions because he remembers the violence very clearly, doesn't he? Do you remember how he immediately demonstrated, in evidence, how the belt would be delivered to him using his hands, the belt would be doubled up and the buckle would be in his father's hand? Was that a lie? Was that an invention? Do you remember him telling you about the wooden spoon from his mother who later abandoned him? Do you remember him telling you about putting his head under the pillow as he listened to the noises of a violent father acting towards his mother? By the way, did you form the view that Mr Appleyard enjoyed giving evidence somehow? He, the former soldier, having to speak in public about the childhood which he said embarrassed him, trying to speak of memories he'd tried to block out for years, that were now coming back to him as he went through the process of having to speak about it. Was he here to lie, to enjoy his moment in the limelight? Was he just telling you, as we suggest he was, how it was?

There was, undoubtedly violence in the home. This defendant ruled through fear. He denies any violence. You have to assess that point. You may find it rather odd that he had some trouble, in examination-in-chief, recalling whether or not he may have put a gun to Jean's head something you may think is fairly memorable, putting a gun to your spouse's head. In cross-examination later he said he had not done that but he may have been holding a gun during the argument in the heat of the moment. You would know, absolutely, wouldn't you, if you'd ever pointed a gun at your spouse's head? So, that's the violence.

Of the four surviving members of the family, two recall sexual abuse, Paul and Carol, and one recalls having it reported to her, Jean. The defendant is the only one who says he saw, heard nothing of the sort.

The first kiss, Carol's account; "What happened was, I was then growing up. He used to take me for walks. We used to go collecting scrap metal and breaking into skips, council skips then" and I'm paraphrasing, "Then the walks got where he didn't used to ask my brother anymore to come, he was asking me as though like, as I were like 11, 12-year-old and he just asked me, you know, I used to wonder why he'd just ask me but I think my mum never said owt because she wanted to keep the peace, I'm not sure. Then one time he took me, this...we took the dog and he shot the dog in front of me and he sat me down on broken pipes, these pipes, had (inaudible) like a scrapyard for broken pipes and stuff and he sat me down on there and I think I were about 11, I think 12, and he started kissing me. He used to talk to me all the time about him and my mum falling out. He used to make me feel quite adult (inaudible) and important cos he was telling me things and my mum would be telling me stuff on her side and then he'd be telling me stuff when we went on these walks all the time. This one time he started kissing me properly, proper kissing me and I didn't know what to do about it. So, just after a few times, I don't know, it happened a few times I told my mum. It were like a boyfriend girlfriend kiss."

There is no doubt, we ask you to conclude, having heard all of the evidence, that as Carol approached puberty the defendant began to see her as a sexual being because we know in October/November '83, when she was 14, you have this rather odd turn, you may think, about the orgy at the party, that's the defendant's term. This was a teenage party at a house, wasn't it, that she didn't tell her mum and dad about? But the defendant tells you in evidence he was happy to conclude his daughter was having sex in his bed on the basis of what he was told by Paul and the state of the bedsheets. And it was clear, wasn't it, that this made him furious, not through any paternal instinct we say, but due to the fact that he was jealous? He, having returned home from the Appalachian Mountains, confirmed in his view that it should be he, the father, in his bed with his daughter. It's the father who should break the daughter in. And the first rape happened shortly after that, didn't it? "And then he brought me back round, my dad got off the phone box and brought me back round home and he started bandaging it." She'd cut herself cos she was scared. He told her she didn't have to go to hospital "But you're too mentally disturbed for you to sleep by yourself tonight. You'll have to sleep with me in my bed." "Never thought anything about it. Just thought, 'He's not angry with me anymore. I'm going to be okay.' So, I went to bed that night and I went to sleep, him cuddled up to me and then I woke up and I felt this tickling here" and she pointed towards her lower stomach. "You know where your belly goes in like that. So, I didn't know what he were doing and then he started touching me places. Then he turned me over and got a condom out of his side of the drawer and he had sex with me and then when he finished having sex with me, I just said to him...I weren't even close to my grandad, his dad, I didn't know my grandparents on my mum's side. So, I said to him, I don't know why I said this and I went, 'What would my grandad say if he knew you'd just done?' And he says, "Don't worry, sweetheart, he wouldn't say anything. He believes the same as me that fathers should break their daughters in like the Indians do"." Made up? Invented? Fantasy? (inaudible) the detail of what happened to her?

And then she talked about the ongoing rapes, "I remember him coming upstairs. I remember the room being black. I must've had my nightie or pyjamas on. I'm sure I would have slept in my underwear because I always knew that when I was in that room and I'd be turning I'd always sleep with my back. It'd be pitch black because I'd wanted to shut everything out. I always remember that room being back and I'd have worn my underwear because I wanted--I'd want to feel as much protected as I could to try and protect myself. I remember that feeling and I didn't. I used to...I used to want to block everything out and go to sleep but then it wouldn't. It never happened because I'd hear his footsteps. I'd hear him coming in from the pub and coming upstairs but it would be in the black and then I'd...sometimes I'd just think, 'Please, please' cos sometimes he'd just go straight past my door and go to bed and like I'd be there hoping that that would happen but then...but...but most of the time he didn't. He just come in and I'd be asleep or pretend to be asleep. He'd get my shoulder like this and pull me round and I'd pretend I was asleep and he'd grab my arm there and then and take me. Paul would be in that room there so the both rooms were close together. I wanted it to be over quick. I just kept quiet and sometimes I used to pretend I was enjoying it and make some noises just so that it would be over quicker." Invention? Lie? Fantasy? Or truthful detail? Matter for you. "He told me that if I ever got pregnant it would be an Albino baby?" Invention or is that what the defendant was telling her, they had to be very careful because if there was a baby, for obvious reasons, it would be a disaster for him?

The oral sex; he used to make me have oral sex with him and, you know, he stank, he were vile, he were dirty. He used to say, "Who loves you, baby and you better." I used to have to say to him, 'You do' and he used to say, "You better believe it." If I didn't say, 'You do' he used to repeat it. I really were just complying to everything that he would ask." Well, we learnt yesterday that, apparently, it's Kojak, "Who loves you, baby." The defendant would say that, he said, in the context of him playing and hugging Carol but it was much more than that, wasn't it, something said to her when oral sex occurred? Officer, "Discussing it like this it brings it all back to...to the front of your mind, doesn't it?" Carol Higgins, "It does, it's vile. I can feel his knob in my gob, do you know what I mean? Everything I can feel, I can taste, every smell I can. None of it ever goes away. Times he tried to make me feel it were normal because his friends did it with their daughters and they lived happily as man and wife. I didn't know what to do and it's not I fucking treated like an adult. It were nothing to fucking do with that, it was survival at the time. I didn't know what else to do. I would've been put in a children's home. I couldn't go back to live with my mum. All these things are the things I've never been able to relax and move on and be totally happy with my life because they think that about me like I'm a little slag. I'm not a fucking slag, I were a child." And she was a child. And she spoke about having to masturbate him and him digitally penetrating her. How he would play with her breasts and her nipples. Is all of this invention, as the defence ask you to conclude, or the recollections of an abused girl?

Paul Appleyard witnessed the abuse or some of it. He saw the snog in the kitchen. He saw Carol in the defendant's bedroom in her underwear when he returned home early from football. So, it's not just Carol Higgins' account. There are recollections from others who recall her complaining contemporaneously to when the abuse occurred. So, when the defendant says, "Well, this is all about money" and, by the way, if this did happen, she's perfectly entitled to compensation, isn't she? But when he says that she was complaining when she was 14, 15, it wasn't about money then, was it? It's not about money now.

Jean; "She told me about her father kissing her. She begged me not to confront him." There was a report to social services. Can I suggest this, it seems they were like the police back in the day, not much cop? Their advice, move out, so, they did. I think we'd call it sofa-surfing now. But they were going to the homes, weren't they, of people they hardly knew that Jean had met on the CB radio, sleeping on floors, in cellars? Why, unless escaping something, escaping somebody?

Diane Croft; a complaint to her, as children, by Carol that dad was touching and messing with her. It seems her parents didn't really know what to do with it, it seems they had rather a lot on. No assistance for Carol there. You had the agreed fact about the later phone call. But what is in there? Is Diane saying, "I wish we could have done this 20 years ago. We've got to do it the right way?"

Deanna Thorpe; the incident in the kitchen, seeing both Carol and Elliott coming down, dressing themselves, tucking themselves in. This is evidence from Mr Appleyard's first cousin. And there's some documentation, isn't there, to show that Carol's pretty much got the timeframe right, '83, '84, we don't know precisely but somewhere around that period? We know it's two months after Carol turned 14 that the defendant was attempting suicide. What was that? Was he putting too many hours in? Or had he begun the sexual abuse of his own daughter? We know, don't we, he'd previously exhibited such proclivities to, or thoughts at least, to Carron Ward in 1974, a 14- or 15-year-old girl, at a time when Carol was four or five, "Has your dad broke you in yet? All dads do it to their daughters?" So, by June '83 he was actioning those beliefs.

Why would Carron Ward come to lie to you about something like that decades later, something to do with a neighbour dispute that's not a neighbour dispute but people lighting fires in their back gardens? Is she lying? Or is she just telling you what she remembered?

Jean recalls the defendant commenting that Indian chiefs broke in their daughters and that he agreed that that should happen and that's precisely what he would say to Carol when he raped her on the first occasion. He'd said this to Jean, apparently, whilst watching a western film. You may be asked to consider why it was that Carol, having left with her mother, returned back to the defendant. We know there were gifts from him to her. It seems there was a breakdown in the relationship with her mum who, you may conclude, was off now seeing other people, having gained a bit of freedom, at the CB club. She wasn't home, as she put it, baking, cooking, washing. Did she have anywhere else to go, Carol, when that relationship began to break down? Does it matter? She was a child with a child's thought processes? Her return to his house did not invite what happened to her, nor did she consent to it. He raped and assaulted her and once she was back where could she go? Told, apparently, she'd end up in a children's home if she jumped between her mum and dad and we know that Donna had told Carol of her experiences there. So, it was that Carol remained in that house with her brother and father, a child scared until she could take no more.

And there did come a time she fled and you may want to ask why it was, if the defendant's evidence is correct, she was cared for, she had her own bedroom, holidays, he was a hard-worker, provider, tough but fair. Why run? There's no doubt she did because Jean and Carl Higgins found her on a bus to Penistone crying, distressed. She only had what she was stood up in. She'd had enough, she'd asked him to stop and he'd beaten her and she complained immediately to her mum that he had raped her. Why flee? The defendant, in evidence, said she returned after he'd been interviewed by the police. Well, in most areas, the defendant is a fairly good historian but this, clearly, cannot be right you might think because there's no way on this planet, is there, that the defendant would have her back after those allegations, given he would throw out the son he loves for £120. He doesn't carry passengers on his bus. There's no way he had her back after those allegations. He hasn't spoken to Paul for 30 years over £120 he says. There's no real explanation from the defendant as to why all three fled but there is from those three witnesses.

And then we reach...I'm not too far from finishing, so, I hope you bear with me, we reach an important juncture of the evidence, very important, because Jean told you that she then rang the defendant at Pie Hall, sounds like an odd place, and confronted him as soon as he got off...as she got off the bus. The defendant's response, she says, "You fucking prove it." He says different. And the defendant in evidence, for the first time, yesterday, as far as we're aware, recalled that phone call happening and we're only aware of that yesterday because he said the opposite in his interview. Apparently, he tells you he had no recollection of the call in his interviews in 2015 and 2016 and this aspect of the defendant's evidence is entirely unconvincing. This is a man who can recall, to the year, when he worked on a fair, when in Hull, in the sixties; when his son worked at a plastic factory in the eighties, he did not want to mention that call, did he? He wanted to keep it quiet. He tried to conceal his knowledge from the police. It is unbelievable to suggest he could not recall the call from his wife who revealed to him, for the first time, that his daughter was saying he'd sexually abused her. There's no explanation as to how or when he came to recall it. The truth is, he always knew about that call, he always remembered it. He tried to say he remembered after the 2015 interview, not true because he didn't mention it in 2016 either.

You are best qualified to resolve issues like this, members of the jury, drawing upon your collective common sense and experience of life. Use those skills together and they'll drive you to the correct conclusions as to issues such as this. You know when someone's being truthful. You know when someone's lying. That was a lie. For a reason, he knows its importance. Not only was it the first time he was told of Carol's complaint but it's more importance than that, I'll come to that in a moment, but he knew of it because he made up this tale about Richmond. Why would Jean have to tell him that over the phone, they were together at that time? He could have come home and she could have told him about this personal matter at home, sensitive matter. Of course, none of this put to Jean Voss when she was here to give evidence so, her only comment, upon phone calls to Pie Hall, was the one about Carol. And the importance of it is expressed in two ways; (1) timing of complaint, Karl Higgins, you may conclude, is not a great historian in terms of sequence of events but his evidence on one point is particularly important because as soon as Jean got off that bus she went to the phone box across from the bus stop in Thurgoland and she confronted the defendant using that phone call. Well, if that's correct, members of the jury, this 36-year conspiracy, as the defence wish you to believe it is, to lie about the defendant was concocted on the back seat of the night bus to Penistone. Nonsense, it was a mother's reaction, even a mother such as Jean, to an immediate complaint by her daughter in a manner you would expect. It was immediate.

And it has a second telling factor, this phone call, because what follows on from it immediately is an important witness, Hilda Graham, the defendant's own sister, who recalls a visit to Jean in Penistone, evidence which the defendant could not admit because it damns him. What of her? Very compelling, you may think, on the video link, clear in recollection. "Elliott asked us to take him to Penistone. He told us he had to go and see Jean because Carol had been onto the police about something. My husband was driving. I was passenger. Elliott was in the back. I know it was summer. It was a hot day." She remembers the day. "He had to show us where to go. He got out and went to Jean's house, come back, they were arguing. She shouted words to the effect, she, Jean, took the pregnancy test to the chemist as though it was hers. He knew full well it wasn't hers, it was Carol's. There was silence on the journey home. So, the defendant's own sister inventing that, fabricating it? Why? Why are all these people here to lie about this defendant, what's in it for them? The best Mr Appleyard can say is that Hilda seems to have borne a grudge for him for some 30 years as he'd snuck off for an extra pint with her husband. Is it the case that these people are just telling you the truth?

So, back in the day Carol complained to the police and also to Deanna Thorpe and, shortly afterwards, Julie Clark. Let's talk about Julie Clark now cos we'll deal with the aftermath. Age 16, Carol's mother kicked her out and she was on her own. She had a good friend, though, Julie Clark. You'll remember her, the witness with the strong, proud Barnsley accent. She spoke of Carol's difficult relationship with her mother and we know what she means when she said, "She's not a mum like my mum."

Carol was pretty lonely, you might think. She'd tried to keep her family together. Mrs Thomas, who gave evidence earlier, thought it was a performance. Was it Carol just trying to make friends with family? Anyway, Julie became her friend and Carol told her about the tin box. There is a tin box that exists apparently and the photos and the hairbrush, all back in the mid to late 1980s. Carol recalls the meeting in Barnsley Market. Carol told her, Julie, that Janet had asked for it but the defendant appeared, that was sprung upon her, wasn't it? And Carol came to Julie and said, "That's me dad, the bastard." Is Carol inventing that back in the day, in the mid-80s, to Julie, her reaction, faking it? And Carol says the defendant apologised to her, "I loved you as a wife not a daughter." Again, reported at the time and she was so upset, so upset Julie Clark remembers getting a taxi, probably less common than it is now back in the 80s, to her parents' home to try and calm her. The defendant recalls the meeting. He recalls nothing other than, "What's up?" Can't recall anything else that was said. Because there was an apology, wasn't there, because he was about to marry Janet or had just married Janet and he wanted to move on and why is there now another significant memory failure on a telling point in the case from him, consider that, please?

Julie was present when Carol went for counselling. You've got the flavour of how long that's been going on for. What's she discussing at those counselling sessions, something she's made up, a lie for the last 30 years that takes its toll when she's about to get married, when she sees herself and her daughter when her daughter turns 13, 14? All made up? Discussing it over and over again.

And so, we're left with one final point, the tattoo. It's not Sam the dog, is it, even though the defendant attempted to suggest so in interview and in cross-examination, even though he took the children, still doesn't know if it's him or the dog? Why would Carol want the epileptic sheep-worrying dog tattooed on her? What would be wrong with having her dad's name on her unless, in the years to come because of what he did, she spent years trying to remove that mark from her body, trying to erase it from her body through acid, treatments as witnessed by Julie Clark, trying to rid herself of that physical mark put upon her by her father, and it was his idea we ask you to conclude, he did mark her as he did with the love bites, trying to rid herself, using acid, a scar being more preferable, of his name, her abuser, for what? For a lie on behalf of a mother she hasn't spoken to in years or through necessity to rid herself of her abuser's name?

On all of the evidence, members of the jury, the correct verdicts in this case are guilty. Thank you very much for listening to me for about an hour, I think.

JUDGE JAMESON: Thank you. Right, ladies and gentlemen. Well, it is quite hard work listening to speeches. So, I think we'll take a 15-minute break and I'll ask Mr Storey to begin then and, of course, he must take as long as he wishes. Good. Thank you very much indeed. See you in about 15 minutes.

(12.00 p.m.)

(Short break)

(12.20 p.m.)

JUDGE JAMESON: Yes, thank you, Mr Storey.

MR STOREY: Ladies and gentlemen, can I invite you to start, please, by thinking back to the very beginning of this trial, to the thoughts and feelings you experienced when you heard, for the first time, the charges you were to try this defendant upon? Now, I have no idea what they were, for obvious reasons, but I suspect that most, if not all of you, will have immediately wracked with some sort of emotion and, being brutally honest about it, human nature being what it is, I imagine that one of the emotions you are most likely to have felt is something along the lines of disgust or revulsion directed towards the defendant in this case or, perhaps, at a less extreme level, sympathy for the complainant about whom, of course, you knew nothing at that point of time. Those reactions based purely and simply on the words comprising the names of the charges you were to try him upon. Emotions of that sort, perhaps, perfectly understandable for people learning that they were going to have to consider a case involving this type of allegation and it may even have been that some of your number will have sat there wondering how it is that somebody like me could possibly sit or stand and represent somebody like him, based purely and simply on the names that are given to the allegations that you are to try him upon. Now, if that sort of emotional response is one that you recognise or can relate to having felt at the start of this trial, or at any time since, then, please, can I ask you to take a step back because in our criminal justice system we do not try people on the basis of emotional responses to charges that they face.

We try people on a calm, clinical assessment of the evidence that is put before a jury like yourselves and on nothing else. And if you take a moment just to think about it, I hope you will see and understand why it is that that is how we ask jurors to operate in this country. Because however daft it may sound, I'm afraid that experience shows that people are, in fact, sometimes wrongly accused of having committed criminal offences of all types and people sometimes are on the wrong end of a decision that somebody makes about their involvement in a criminal offence. Let us just suppose for a moment, please, that you were one of those people on the wrong end of a decision of that sort. How would you want any case that you might have been unlucky enough to be on the receiving end of to be considered, on the basis of emotion or prejudice or on the basis of a calm rational evaluation of the evidence.

Now, you may all, and I understand why this might be, you may all be sitting there thinking, "What on earth is he on about? There's no way in the world we could ever be wrongly accused of a criminal offence. That could never happen, could it?" But I'd like to just give you a couple of examples and these are real examples, just to show that it's, perhaps, not as fanciful as you might at first think. Let's say you're out for a night with a few friends in Leeds City Centre having drinks in pubs or bars. Through no fault of yours somebody else, who's, perhaps, had rather too much to drink decides to pick an argument with you and let's say that argument suddenly becomes physical and the other person begins pushing you and then starts to swing their fists in your direction. You react defensively and you briefly swing your fist back at them and connect with them. But, however, perhaps because you're bigger or you're more sober, your single defensive blow knocks them off their balance and they fall backwards cracking their head on the corner of a table in the process and that impact causes a fracture to their skull and a consequent bleed on the surface of their brain and they are taken to hospital, three days later they die. The police investigate and speak to everybody who's present, including friends of the person who was causing you some grief, and they say it was you who'd started it and not their friend. And so, as a result, you're arrested and, in due course, you find yourself, after the Crown Prosecution Service have been asked to consider things, on the receiving end of a charge of manslaughter and you find yourself sitting where Mr Appleyard is now in the dock of a court here in Leeds Crown Court. So, that's one example of how things can happen that you might, at first blush, think wouldn't happen to you in a month of Sundays.

Another; let's say you're driving home from work one day, rush hour, stop/start traffic. It's this sort of time year, it gets dark early; everyone's got their headlights on; you're crawling in traffic uphill to a set of traffic lights at a junction, a crossroads, as you near them they begin to change from green to amber and then, obviously, to red. You're driving at a sensible speed within the limit and, to your mind, it's a perfectly legitimate manoeuvre for you to make to carry on across the junction as the lights go from green to amber. However, coming in the opposite direction and, in the process, turning across your path is another driver who's going faster than you, who takes a chance and goes through the lights thinking, wrongly, that you're going to stop. That other driver collides with the front end of your vehicle, which is still moving, but it forces your vehicle to the side, off direction and the layout of the junction means that your momentum carries you onto a small island where pedestrians wait to cross at the lights and standing there is a lady in her seventies, struck by your car which has been knocked off course by the other vehicle. The impact is such that she's fatally injured and, again, dies in hospital a day or so later. The police investigate. Other drivers in the area at the time say they thought you jumped the lights. So, that leads to the police arresting you and, again, the Crown Prosecution Service being asked to consider whether you should be charged with any offence and they decide to do just that and you're on the receiving end of a charge of causing someone's death by dangerous driving and so, once again, you find yourself sitting in the dock of a courtroom in this country.

As I say, those are real examples and the point of them is just to show to you, I hope, that things like that can and do happen and it happens to people like you and me. I very much hope that you can see, therefore, why it is I say to you that when you are considering this case that you should put emotions, like sympathy or disgust, completely out of your minds because I'm pretty confident that if you were ever unfortunate enough to be sat somewhere like Mr Appleyard is sitting you would want whoever was considering your guilt or innocence to do so in a calm, rational way without any trace of emotion in their minds. And just keep that thought in your minds for the moment please, how it would feel to be sat where Mr Appleyard is sat.

I know his Honour is going to tell you in due course and I know and you may remember that Mr Hampton mentioned, at the very start of this case, that the prosecution, as with every case in our country, are responsible for bringing this case to court and the consequence of that is that the prosecution are the ones who have to prove their allegations to you. I'm pretty sure you'll all have heard the phrase, at some point in time, "Innocent until proven guilty." That is the law which we operate in this country. Essentially it means that any defendant, any defendant charged with a criminal offence, be it Elliott Appleyard in this court or be it one of you on the receiving end of an example like I just cited to you, any defendant has to prove nothing at all.

The prosecution are the accusers and I hope you will see that it is only fair that they, as the accusers, have to prove their accusations to you, the jury, considering this case.

And, again, returning to those examples and the situation that they might present someone with, how would you want a case you were on the receiving end of to be handled if you had been unfortunate enough to be wrongly accused of a criminal offence that you did not commit? Would you want to have to prove your innocence or would you want some safeguards, safeguards that include a requirement that the prosecution have to prove their allegations against you? It is something you should remember, at all times, when considering the evidence in this case, Elliott Appleyard has to prove nothing. And following on from that as, again, Mr Hampton mentioned at the very outset of the case and, again, as his Honour's going to mention in due course, before you can convict Mr Appleyard of any offence at all you have to be sure, on the evidence that you've heard, that he is guilty of those offences you're trying him upon. Again, a safeguard designed to protect people who've been wrongly accused of criminal offences that they did not, in fact, commit. Once again ask yourselves how you would want your case to be considered if you were sitting somewhere like him.

So, bearing all that in mind, where to start, well, the obvious place, as Mr Hampton did, was to start by considering the evidence of Carol Higgins. But just before I do that can I make a couple of other points, please? You know there have been a number of other witnesses called on behalf of the prosecution, giving evidence about various aspects of matters. Mr Hampton says that that all supports Carol Higgins' account and supports the allegations she makes against her father. But I'm going to suggest to you that, in fact, none of that evidence is, in reality, independent of Carol Higgins and that the vast majority of it derives from her herself and that's important because it can lead to the conclusion, a matter for you, that it doesn't, in fact, therefore, add any support at all to what she says happened 35-odd years ago. And in that situation, ladies and gentlemen, what you would be left with, ultimately, is the evidence of one person's word against another's.

And, secondly, of course and it may be perfectly obvious, but it's a point perhaps worth making, you've just heard from Mr Hampton, and he's given you a lot to think about, but you should remember that his oratory and his declamatory assertions that Carol Higgins is a compelling and truthful witness do not, of themselves, mean that she is. That, ultimately, is the issue for you and you alone to consider. You will, I suspect, be glad to know that I don't propose to rehearse all the details of Mrs Higgins' account for you again. I don't want to insult your intelligence by doing so, not least because Mr Hampton has already taken you through much of it, his Honour is going to remind you of it in due course as well. But there are some points of detail in what she has said that I would like you to specifically consider. You know well enough what the generality of her account is. Mr Hampton has invited you to consider the detail as well and has used the expression, "The devil is in the detail." I'd invite you to do exactly the same thing, not just in relation to Carol Higgins but in relation to all of the evidence you've heard and I would adopt and repeat that phrase because what you might think it essentially means is that whilst things may appear quite clear cut, when looked at in general, in the round, once you've drilled down to some of those details things may not, in fact, be quite as clear cut as you first thought.

You know, don't you, that Carol Higgins has pursued a campaign, as she would have it, to bring her father to justice? She's made a number of complaints, repeated over the years, to the police about what she says the defendant, her father, did to her. You must be very careful about that. You must not fall into the trap of thinking that that, necessarily, gives any more weight to what she says. Simply because someone repeats something and does so again and again does not mean that whatever is being said is any more likely to be true. It's easy enough, you may think, to repeat a lie over and over again but you don't give it anymore force by doing so.

You've heard about the book that she wrote in which she refers, in part, to the abuse she says she was the victim of and she's publicised the writing of that book not least in the area where she knows her father still lives. Do you accept that she did that, as she would have it, simply because she still knows people in the area? Or was it something she did rather more deliberately, rather more calculatedly so as to cause difficulties for her father. You've heard about fliers being put up in the area advertising her book, fliers that she claimed to know nothing about. How credible, how believable is that? Remember this isn't a book that was published by Penguin or anybody like that, any well-known publisher, this was a book published by Carol Higgins herself. Do you really think it's likely that somebody else would advertise it in that way, in that area, without her knowing anything about it at all despite the book launches that you've heard she held in local halls and pubs?

And you know, don't you, that Carol Higgins has used Facebook extensively to publicise her book herself, her allegations against the defendant, these proceedings? And the prosecution say to you, "Well, effectively, so what? What of it?" But, again, look at the detail. You know, don't you, fundamentally she's expressed some fairly extreme views, you may think, on Facebook? She told you she conceded that she believed paedophiles should be hanged and, frankly, it's hard to think of a more emotive state of belief. She publicised the fact that her father had some land which he was trying to sell. So, what, you might think about that? She posted photographs of shipping containers on that land. Told people on Facebook that there piles of kids' bikes there. Suggested that people should Google how many unsolved murders there had been within 20 miles of her father's house. Clearly, you may think, a suggestion that she felt he was responsible for those murders. She said, expressly, her father had got away with murder although she tried to backtrack from that assertion a little later. She told you she was afraid she would, herself, be murdered, clearly that hasn't happened. And any suggestion that she made that he might be a danger because he had shotguns, that suggestion made fairly recently. You know his shotgun licence was revoked in 2001. She made public assertions that that particular land was rented from the late Judge Pickles and that he, Judge Pickles, was a leading paedophile. She was publicising allegations that that was a paedophile ring involving her father, Judge Pickles, local councillors, MPs, solicitors, police officers. She made reference, didn't she, to a letter from a Nazi cult which she said was meant for her father? And she said that he was going to emigrate to New Zealand well, that clearly hasn't happened either, has it?

You need to consider, ladies and gentlemen, what you make of allegations of assertions like that and the publicization of them. You might come to the conclusion that they show that, at the very least, Carol Higgins has some fairly extreme ideas or, perhaps, might be a little paranoid or even hysterical. But, taking things further, you might be justified in coming to the conclusion that they show that she is, indeed, something of a fantasist and that's important. It's important when you consider the allegations she has made against her father. Because if she is, indeed, something of a fantasist, prone to some fairly extreme views of the sort that she's clearly been quite happy to disseminate on Facebook for whoever wants to look at them, who is to say that she hasn't also concocted these allegations against her father and over time, for whatever reason, to have become as convinced about the correctness of her views about her father as she clearly is about her views relating to the late Judge Pickles.

She also told you, at one point, in her evidence that she believed her father was part of something bigger, whatever she meant by that and that he'd gone on to abuse his niece, someone else in the family and you, of course, have heard precisely no evidence whatsoever to back up that assertion whatsoever.

Given the nature of the allegations which this case concerns, you can guarantee that if there were any evidence to confirm that sort of assertion by Carol Higgins, you'd have heard about it. So, again, is that something she's convinced herself of the truth of without any basis, in fact?

So, I'll turn now, if I may, to the detail or some of the detail of her account. You know that she said violence was a feature of life in the family, specifically violence directed towards her and her sister...I'm sorry, her brother and she's supported in that by her brother, Paul's, evidence. But significantly, you may think, a matter for you, perhaps tellingly she's not supported in that by the evidence of her own mother, Jean Voss. Now, she's someone who you might have formed the pretty reasonable view that she felt no love whatsoever for her ex-husband so, why on earth, would Jean Voss lie or conceal that sort of behaviour to protect him if it was, in fact, already taking place? Why would she say to you, "No, he never belted the kids with his belt on their bare bottoms as they described? Yes, I might take a spoon to them but not him, not a belt." A matter for you, ladies and gentlemen, to consider whether the reality is here that the alleged violence meted out to his children, as they've told you happened, never, in fact, happened at all.

There's also the issue for you to consider, that Mr Hampton's made quite clear reference to, as to whether the defendant was violent towards Jean Voss herself when they were married and living together in Gilthwaites Crescent. Carol Higgins tells you she can recall seeing that, two incidences she referred to, the shotgun to the head, the machete to her mother's vagina, threatening to slit her open. And mother said those two occasions happened and, also, that he'd use his fists upon her. Contrast what brother, Paul, said, fierce arguments, shouting, he hid his head under the pillow to stop himself having to listen to it. But he never saw violence directed towards his mother. He never saw her bearing the marks of a beating that she might have been on the receiving end of. Carol Higgins said the police were always round at the house because of her father's violence towards her mother. But her mother and her brother made no mention of those regular attendances by the police because of alleged domestic violence. So, you have to weigh all those competing pieces of evidence up, ladies and gentlemen and decide, if you think you need to, where you think the truth lies in relation to allegations of violence in that family home.

You've also heard it said, haven't you, that at around the time you're considering, Elliott Appleyard was never at work; he was always going collecting scrap metal? On the fiddle was the effect of what Carol Higgins said to you. But, again, compare that with what her mother told you. Yes, Elliott Appleyard worked. Yes, he was a self-employed building contractor. Yes, he worked five...five to six days a week. You know, as he told you himself, it doesn't seem to be in dispute, he took his children on holidays, some of them reasonably significant, a cruise around Scandinavia and the like. Is that the sort of thing you can afford to do when you're living on Benefits and scraping a living by flogging a bit of scrap metal that you pick up here and there?

Mr Hampton has asked you, repeatedly, to consider whether Carol Higgins' account is made up, invented, fantasy. And a question which follows that most obviously, you might think, ladies and gentlemen, is why would it be that she has invented or made these allegations up? But going back to what I said at the outset, it is not for Elliott Appleyard to say, nor, on his behalf, is it for me to say why she might have done so. The prosecution has to prove the allegations to you. A defendant never has to prove anything in our criminal justice system.

And, as I said earlier, experience, I'm afraid, shows that people do invent allegations and not just allegations of this sort and their reasons for so doing are never known. Sometimes it is, indeed, the case that people are motivated by money. Mr Appleyard has voiced the suggestion that that might be what's behind all this remembering, at all times, that he doesn't have to voice an opinion about what's behind it at all. But you know, don't you, that there were solicitors' letters written back in the 2012/2013 period because one of them is referred to within your agreed facts, a letter from January 2013 from a firm of solicitors called Jordans to Carol Higgins in which the writer says; "I also agreed to look at a potential case against Appleyard direct in case he had assets which would mean he would be worth pursuing? Unfortunately, I've not been able to find any evidence whether Mr Appleyard had sufficient assets in his own name that might mean he would be worth pursuing and because I've not been able to trace any assets in relation to Mr Appleyard unfortunately there's no further action I can take in relation to this matter and, as such, I will have to close your file of papers." Carol Higgins told you she knew nothing about that but you might think it doesn't take a genius to work out that that does not exactly sound like something the solicitor was doing on a frolic of his or her own, "I'm going to close your file of papers because I've not been able to trace any assets held by the defendant, Mr Appleyard." So, what had the file been opened for if not to pursue some sort of potential claim against him? And you know that much more recently Miss Higgins has made an application for compensation from the Criminal Injuries Compensation Authority. So, might that be, at least partly, what's behind things?

As I say, Mr Appleyard doesn't have to prove a motive at all. The human mind does, indeed, work in mysterious ways as those of us who work in the courts see, perhaps, more often than some people do. It's not for us to say why the allegations might have been fabricated nor even is it for you to say why they might have been fabricated. All you have to do is to decide whether you're sure or not about the truth of them.

Just whilst we're looking at and thinking about the admissions, ladies and gentlemen, Mr Hampton pointed, of course, to the admissions that tell you about the counselling Carol Higgins underwent for many years and he pointed to that which she had said to counsellors and medics, as quoted in the agreed facts, making again the point that that all supports what she says was happening to her back in the 1980s. Once again, that's a trap you can fall into and I'll invite you not to. Do not conclude that those records necessarily prove the veracity, the truthfulness of what Carol Higgins is saying because, once again, the ultimate source of the information that's contained in them is Carol Higgins herself. They do not add weight to what she is saying, they simply repeat it. You have to be sure that what she said had happened to her in the 1980s was correct before you could go on to place any reliance at all on the fact that she'd told people about it in the years after she left the family home.

You know it's said that Mr Appleyard's behaviour towards his daughter was something witnessed by his son, Paul, at the time who told you he walked in on his father as he was snogging his sister in the kitchen; who said he would see her wandering around the house in her underwear, who said that, on occasion, he'd be locked out of the house one time having come back, unexpectedly early, from a football match that was cancelled to find the house locked, he saw his sister leaning out of their father's bedroom window in her underwear. Do not forget, please, when you're considering any of Paul Appleyard's evidence, that he was quite frank in telling you he was a supporter of his sister, clearly believing everything that she has told him and they both agreed that, yes, they've discussed these things many times since they left their home. So, again, ask yourselves, in those circumstances, whether he, Paul Appleyard, really is that independent of his sister. And if he's not all that independent of her then you need to consider how much extra weight can you place on his evidence over and above that of Carol Higgins herself. Because it's very easy to plant in someone's mind the seed of an idea, particularly if you're convincing enough or if you've convinced yourself of the correctness of your point of view. And remember this, please, as well, he conceded, didn't he, that at the time, in his teens, he didn't think anything of what it was he says he saw taking place? Can that be right or might it just be that what he, in fact, witnessed was, indeed, innocuous, inter-familial behaviour, father behaving in a perfectly legitimate ordinary way with his daughter? That this is something that has become tainted, over the years, by ideas or views planted in his mind by discussions with his sister.

You know, don't you, that Carol Higgins left the family home at some point, she says, when she was about 12 or 13, with her mother, and the reasons for doing so are, obviously, for you to consider? But notwithstanding what Mr Hampton said about this being a child making child's decisions, you're quite entitled to consider why it was that, even on her own account, she chose to go back to her father a few months later. This was the father about whom she had allegedly complained to her mother, to social workers, was the reason she and her mother left home, she knew what she said. Because you may think, ladies and gentlemen, that the picture that she's painted for you is that the household at Gilthwaites Crescent was one which she really didn't want to be a part of at all.

So, as I say, why go back? You've heard, amongst other things, allegations relating to love bites. Carol Higgins said they were inflicted on her by the defendant and he denies it. As with the allegations in this case more generally, it's a very easy allegation to make, isn't it, one person says the other did something to them? And allegations like these are very difficult to disprove which is, at least, partly why defendants don't have to disprove allegations in our system. But just on the love bites point, you will, no doubt, recall the statement of Ina Whittle which was read to you, telling you she'd seen, at some unspecified point in time, she'd seen Carol Higgins with love bites and she assumed, understandably enough, that they would have been from a boy. Now, how unrealistic is that? You may think, ladies and gentlemen, that that's something which could quite possibly be the truth of the matter. You know, don't you, Carol Higgins had at least one boyfriend during the time you're considering, the son of thc lady with whom she and her mother stayed, several years older than the 13- or 14-year-old that Carol Higgins was at the time, for what it's worth? So, a matter for you whether someone seeing love bites on Carol Higgins' neck really helps you very much at all. But, again, is it significant that neither her brother nor her mother seemed to have seen these love bites? Is that some indication of the relative infrequency with which she had them? The relevant inconsequential nature of such things?

You know, don't you, that Miss Higgins allegations are that after her return to Gilthwaites Crescent her father's abuse of her started in earnest? And much of this part of her evidence comes down to what you may think is a straight conflict between her account on the one hand and that of her father on the other.

Mr Appleyard's evidence, as his Honour will tell you in due course, has just as much weight as evidence coming from prosecution witnesses. You have to evaluate it just as much as you have to evaluate and weigh up the evidence you've heard from prosecution witnesses.

Remember what I've already said about the way in which Carol Higgins has approached the protracted history of these proceedings, these allegations and some of the more outlandish ideas that she's disseminated.

You know there came a time when she left the family home, seemingly for the last time, and how she bumped into, clearly by chance, her mother and Carl Higgins, mother's new partner, on the bus from Penistone. And you were told, of course, that that was when Carol Higgins first told her mother about what had been going on.. You're invited, by the prosecution, to recall Carl Higgins and his evidence and I would endorse that because there's a little point of detail, a matter for you, the devil is sometimes in the detail, that you might think is a point of detail with some significance because Carl Higgins didn't recall Carol Higgins saying that she'd been raped by her father. What he remembered was her saying that her dad had tried to touch her. Is that a significant difference? Does it, perhaps, show that someone rather more independent than some of the other witnesses might be recalls things a little differently for a reason? And is it also significant that in her interview with the police Carol Higgins claims to have told a number of her friends, apparently on the same bus, that her father had raped her and she named them. One of the people she named as having been there at the time, these friends, was Diane Croft from whom, of course, you have heard evidence. But no mention, by Diane Croft, of having been told anything of this sort by Carol Higgins on a bus, whether from Penistone or from any other place. And you've not heard, of course, from any of the others named in that interview by Carol Higgins. You can be reasonably confident again that if they had heard anything like this they'd have been called as prosecution witnesses. It's a matter for you but you can draw what conclusions you see fit from that.

Your Honour, I'm pausing because I'm conscious of the time. If your Honour's content for me to carry on.

JUDGE JAMESON: Yes, you pick a moment, whenever's convenient, Mr Storey.

MR STOREY: The prosecution criticised the defendant in relation to his failure to recall, in interview, in November 2015, the phone call made by Jean Voss to the Pie Hall. They say, essentially, "How would you forget something like that?" But just think about it for a moment please, is that a fair criticism? Don't forget that a number of the prosecution's own witnesses were unable to recollect certain things. At least Paul Appleyard told you there were things he couldn't remember or was still remembering. Carron Ward couldn't remember certain key events so, why should it be any different for the defendant? Why should prosecution witnesses by allowed to forget things and it's not a problem. Mr Appleyard doesn't remember something, it's a huge problem. Quite a long time, isn't it, from 1984 to 2015? Whatever was happening in Carol Higgins' world, whatever she was doing, so far as the defendant was concerned, nothing at all was happening in relation to these allegations because he wasn't spoken to by the police about them between 1984 and 2015, was he? Is it so fanciful to suggest that he might have forgotten some points of detail in the intervening 30-odd years?

The next event which is said to have happened chronologically, of course, was the visit by Hilda Graham together with her brother, the defendant, to Penistone, a visit that Mr Hampton places great reliance on because of the comment that Hilda Graham says she overheard being made by Jean Voss. You know, don't you, that Mr Appleyard, for what it's worth, doesn't accept that this occasion, this event, happened at all? So, look at the evidence of Carol Higgins and her mother on this issue. Carol Higgins said she'd told her mother about the pregnancy scare, as she called it, and that she told her mother the pregnancy, if there was, indeed, a pregnancy, was down to a lad she was seeing. She did not name her father. So, on that basis, if Carol Higgins is right about that, there would be no reason at all for Jean Voss, her mother, to think this was anything to do with the defendant and, therefore, no reason at all for her to make any sort of comment along the lines that Hilda Graham recalled. And Jean Voss didn't remember making a comment like that either because the only visit she recalled was one to drop off some clothes or belongings. That trip made by Hilda Graham, she said, and the defendant. So, can you really be sure, on the basis of the evidence, that the prosecution witnesses have provided you with, that that comment, that conversation really took place as Hilda Graham recalls? Don't forget she told you she'd only come to be asked by the police to give a witness statement after Carol Higgins had visited her at her home address and had told her her own version of what had gone on. So, again, you can ask yourselves, how much does that affect the weight to be attached to what Hilda Graham told you?

Another aspect of the evidence you've heard, of course, ladies and gentlemen relates...

JUDGE JAMESON: Is that a convenient time?

MR STOREY: I'm sorry, if your Honour wishes me to break, I wasn't sure if you were happy for me to continue into the usual lunchtime or not?

JUDGE JAMESON: Well, I mean I think we'll probably take a break...

MR STOREY: Very well.

JUDGE JAMESON: ...at the conventional time. I just wanted you to pick a moment, that's all and that might be, as you're moving onto another topic...

MR STOREY: Yes.

JUDGE JAMESON: ...that moment.

MR STOREY: It would.

JUDGE JAMESON: All right. Okay. Thank you very much. Right, ladies and gentlemen, quarter past two, thank you.

(The jury left court at 1.02 p.m.)

JUDGE JAMESON: Right, any rough idea just so, I know where I'm...

MR STOREY: Yes, I've probably got about 15 to 20 minutes at most.

JUDGE JAMESON: Right, okay. We'll say half an hour. Yeah, I think probably what we'll do is take a short break. Then I think I'll do the law today and move onto facts tomorrow because they've had a lot of...

MR STOREY: Yes.

JUDGE JAMESON: ...a lot of addresses entirely properly, absolutely, of course. But I think that's probably what I'll do.

MR STOREY: Certainly.

JUDGE JAMESON: Yeah, okay. Thank you.

(1.03 p.m.)

(Adjourned for a short time)

(2.16 p.m.)

(In the absence of the jury at 2.17 p.m.)

JUDGE JAMESON: I think I'm rather minded, Mr Storey, to give the jury quarter of an hour after you're finished because, it seems to me, they had a break during which they will have thought about what Mr Hampton said, it's probably fair that they should have the same...

MR STOREY: Very well. Thank you very much.

JUDGE JAMESON: ...after your address. So, I think that definitely means I won't get beyond the law today.

MR STOREY: No, I follow. Thank you.

JUDGE JAMESON: Thank you.

(The jury returned to court at 2.18 p.m.)

MR STOREY: It's always hard to resume after a break like that, part-way through one's speech and it's probably just as hard for you as it is for me. So, I think I've probably got about another 15 to 20 minutes remaining. I was drawing your attention to various aspects of the detail that's contained within the evidence of Carol Higgins and other witnesses from whom you've heard and I was about to turn to the evidence relating to the comment that Mr Appleyard is said to have made about breaking children in like the Indians used to do. You will remember, I am sure, that his former wife, Jean Voss as she now is, told you that this was something that she and he had seen in a western film they were watching on television, goodness knows when, and that he made some throwaway comment about it, a comment that she clearly, she told you, thought nothing of at the time. So, you might want to ask yourselves whether, if he really had been making assertions like that to his daughter, Carol, to other girls in the neighbourhood or, at least, had been adopting and making them a pronouncement of his own beliefs don't you think it would have been the sort of thing that would have caused his wife some little concern? And, again, you need to decide the extent to which you think Carol Higgins' own evidence on this point might be tainted as well. Because is it just possible that she was aware of this throwaway comment one way or the other, has remembered it, has given it more significance over time, placing it in and amongst other aspects of the allegations she's making, dwelling, perhaps, extensively on those allegations as you can imagine she has clearly done over the intervening years.

Carron Ward was the other person who gave evidence to the effect that this was something of the sort that Elliott Appleyard had said to her. But just examine, for a moment, please, how her involvement in this case came about. She'd had nothing to do with Carol Higgins for many, many years and then, in August 2015, she took herself along to the Dales Man Inn in Denby Dale, to one of the book launches that you heard about. She spoke, at length, with Carol Higgins who told her about her childhood. In short, she came out with the allegations that you know are the subject of this case. And it was only after that, in October 2015, that Carron Ward made the second of her two witness statements and it was only in that second witness statement that she remembered the defendant having asked her if her father had broken her in yet. So, you might want to ask yourselves just how independent is Carron Ward? Just how much was that recollection she told you about hers or how much might it have been planted in her mind, no doubt entirely inadvertently as a result of the conversation she had at that book launch with Carol Higgins. You know, don't you, how determined she was by 2015 to have her father charged with the offences that you're now trying him upon? Who was to say she didn't deliberately or inadvertently plant in Carron Ward's mind the memory of that exchange?

Following on from that, the evidence relating to that and what Carol(sic) Ward told you...sorry, what Carol Higgins told you about the defendant's use of that expression. She told the police, in her video-recorded interview, that the defendant had gone on to claim that his friends did it with their daughters. Well which friends is she referring to then, none that she could name when asked that direct question? None that you heard about from any other source. So, again, is that an allegation based on fact or might it just be another wild assertion that you've heard about?

And you will remember Mr Hampton, not least because Mr Hampton referred to it, the expression, "Who loves you, baby?" Mr Hampton seemed to rather dismiss the suggestion as nonsense but I suspect there are some of you old enough to remember having watched Kojak on the television in the late 1970s, early 1980s and I suspect those of you who can will have recognised that phrase as soon as you heard it. Might it just be that that was a catchphrase from a television programme around that time which people would, no doubt, repeat finding it, I suspect, amusing so to do. Again, is that something else that she's heard her father say when she was a child or a young teenager and which, given the passage of time, given her fixation with these allegations, something that she has given a significance to which it doesn't, in fact, warrant?

You know you heard from Julie Clark, Carol Higgins' friend since they were about 16 when they started working together in Barnsley, someone who's obviously stood by her ever since and, again, to that extent, someone about whom you might want to ask yourselves just how independent is she? She told you about the tattoo on Carol Higgins' shoulder which the prosecution say was, effectively, the defendant branding his daughter as his own, putting his mark on her, I think, was the phrase used when the case was opened to you. There's no dispute, of course, that Carol Higgins had a tattoo but so, too, did her brother, Paul. Don't forget his take on it. His sister was getting a tattoo so, he wanted one too. Not a suggestion from Paul, was there, that this was anything other than his sister's idea. She wanted one. She was being allowed to have one so, he wanted one as well. The prosecution say, "Well, there's the name, Sam, how significant is that?" Well, a matter for you. It's her father's nickname. What tattoo did Paul have on his body? Sam. The prosecution aren't saying that this was the defendant branding his son as well, are they? Why is it branding his daughter but not his son? Think about that.

Mr Hampton also pointed to the fact that Carol Higgins made efforts to have the tattoo removed once she left home and they say, "Well, that supports what she has told you about the abuse." Does it? Who knows why it was that she had that tattoo removed as she did? Maybe because there was a fallout of some sort. Maybe because the defendant was, indeed, violent towards her. It doesn't automatically follow that because she had that tattoo removed, he abused her sexually as she alleges. Paul had his tattoo removed as well, didn't he? It's not said that he was sexually abused by his father, is he?

And, again, still on Julie Clark, she told you what Carol Higgins had told her about the abuse she was the victim of. So, again, it comes back to the point I was making earlier, Julie Clark's information and where it came from. Carol Higgins was the ultimate source of that information. As I said before, the fact that Carol Higgins has told people this, before telling the police and you, doesn't necessarily prove what she was saying to anybody was the truth. It doesn't necessarily add weight to her allegations. Because repeating things doesn't give them an extra layer of truth each time you say them.

There was the trip to Barnsley Market which you know took place at some point. We don't seem to know when that was but Julie Clark was for telling you that she was present. Although she wasn't present at the meeting she was hanging around in the general area where Carol Higgins met her father. But there's a little point of difference between the two ladies, isn't there, that might affect the weight you can attach to their recollection of this meeting? Because the fact that Julie Clark was with her, when she went to see her father, is something that Carol Higgins didn't make a single mention of. No suggestion that she'd gone there with a friend from work or anything of that sort.

Diane Croft, another witness the prosecution called, someone else who gave evidence about something Carol Higgins had told her again at the time when they were about 13 or 14 so, on the face of it, a complaint made by Carol Higgins at roughly the same time Carol Higgins says she told the police that she was being abused by her father. Again, when you drill down into the detail it might not be quite what it seems at first glance. Because at the time Diane Croft told you about what Carol Higgins said was going on was that her father was messing about with her, touching and kissing her was what she meant when pressed by her friend. Carol Higgins, on the other hand, says that Diane Croft was one of the people she was telling at this time that she'd been raped by her father, that he was having sex with her. So, is that a difference that's significant? Diane Croft said she told Carol Higgins, "You should tell an adult." And she told you that Carol Higgins response was, "I have, I've told my mum." But can that be right because Diane Croft's recollection was at this time Carol Higgins was still living in Denby Dale. She didn't leave there until some time later to move to Penistone. You know Carol Higgins says that as soon as she told her mother, social services were involved and she was out of that house like a flash.

Diane Croft says she told her parents what Carol Higgins had told her and, for whatever reason, they seemed to have been unable to do anything to help. Make of that what you will. But, once again, look at the circumstances that led to Diane Croft's involvement in these proceedings. Carol Higgins went to see her, at her workplace, in about October 2017, first contact they'd had since they were teenagers. Three months later, January 2018, Diane Croft's statement is made to the police and you know, because it was admitted, that they spoke on the phone at around the same time, October 2017 or thereabouts. So, again, the question arises as to the extent to which Diane Croft's recollection of the events in the 1980s were genuine or influenced by or based, in fact, on what she and Carol Higgins had spoken about.

And don't forget the contents of that agreed fact that I read out to you this morning because a recording was made of that conversation between Carol Higgins and Diane Croft and you have a few choice excerpts from the conversation. "We need to all get together privately without the fucking coppers knowing. We need to speak to a lawyer to see if we can do it without him knowing. We're gonna nail the bugger" and so on and so forth. What does that tell you that that conversation was all about, a cosy catchup after 30 years, friends who haven't seen each other or something more significant? As always, ladies and gentlemen, this is a matter for you.

Deanna Thorpe, the relative who said she'd visited 26, Gilthwaites Crescent at some point unannounced, walked into the kitchen, put the kettle on only to see the defendant and Carol Higgins coming downstairs looking dishevelled. Her evidence was she thought nothing of that at the time. So, what is it that has made her think since then there was some significance to that event? Once again you know, don't you, she moved away from the Scissett area, no further contact with Carol Higgins for many years, until late 2015, when Carol Higgins got in touch with her through her daughter on Facebook, of course what else? They spoke on the phone. Carol Higgins told her she wanted to take her father to court and that she wanted Deanna Thorpe to provide a statement. So, again, you must ask yourselves the extent to which what Deanna Thorpe has told you was driven by, prompted by, planted subconsciously in her mind by the conversations she had with Carol Higgins and, again, ask yourselves just how independent was she.

As I said to you at the outset, ladies and gentlemen, witness after witness called on behalf of the prosecution, they say to provide evidence that supports Carol Higgins' assertions. When you drill down into the detail and the circumstances in which they, ultimately, began the process of appearing before you as witnesses, the giving of statements, what happened before they did that, you might wonder just how independent are these supposedly independent witnesses. And if you come to the conclusion that they are not, in fact, independent and, as I said earlier on, you might feel that what you're left with is one person's word against another's and that's when it starts to get quite difficult for you to say, "We are sure, on the basis of one person's word against another's, what happened 35 years ago."

Now, again, I don't propose to insult your intelligence by rehearsing all of Mr Appleyard's evidence, you only heard it yesterday and you know, very basically, that his case is these allegations are simply not true, for whatever reason. This alleged abuse didn't happen for reasons best known to Carol Higgins or whoever about which he can only guess. Do not forget, he does not have to prove his innocence. He does not have to provide you with some explanation to explain why it is the allegations might have been fabricated.

The prosecution invited you to consider whether the suicide attempt by the defendant might have been connected to what he was doing to his daughter. How reasoned is that as a suggestion, ladies and gentlemen? You know when it occurred, June 1983. According to Carol Higgins the abuse didn't start until after her father's trip to the United States of America. When was that, November/December 1983, five or six months later? So, why on earth, do the prosecution choose to make that suggestion you might wonder? Is it because they, too, are a little fixated on the idea that everything Elliott Appleyard did in the 1980s, everything which happened was to do with or was as a result of the abuse which he is alleged to have committed?

Lastly, of course, evidentially, you heard from Sarah Thomas and you may wonder what the impact of her evidence was. She hardly knew Carol Higgins, she told you. But the significance, you might think, lies in the fact that here was a cousin, someone who, on the face of it, Carol Higgins was trying to befriend or trying to demonstrate or, perhaps, even show off to others that she was close to, yet was utterly unaware of there being any problems at all in Carol Higgins' domestic life. So far as she was aware, Carol and Paul still lived happily at home at Gilthwaites Crescent in Denby Dale and this was in the period 1984 to 1985, precisely when, according to Carol Higgins, her world was falling apart.

In conclusion, ladies and gentlemen, as I've said already, before you can convict Elliott Appleyard of any one of these offences, you have to be sure of his guilt. Essentially what that means is, that if there is any doubt in your mind at all about the truth of what Carol Higgins has said, that doubt has to be weighed in Elliott Appleyard's favour. In other words, you've got to give him the benefit of that doubt. Obviously, if you are quite quite sure and in no doubt whatsoever about what Carol Higgins has told you, then the correct verdicts here are verdicts of guilty. But, given the various points I've raised, drawn to your attention, I hope you will see that, perhaps contrary to the initial view you may have formed in this case, particularly the initial feelings and emotions that I ask you to put to one side that you undoubtedly felt when you heard the charges you were trying him upon there is, in fact, here room for real doubt about the veracity of what Carol Higgins has said and if that is so, as I've just said, doubts of that sort have to be weighed in Elliott Appleyard's favour and, in that case, the only verdicts you can return are verdicts of not guilty. Thank you for your time.

JUDGE JAMESON: Thank you, Mr Storey. Right, now, ladies and gentlemen, let me tell you how the case is going to progress from now on. The time has now come for me to sum the case up to you. What I'm going to do is just give you a short break now before I start doing that. You had a break after the conclusion of the prosecution's address to you although, in fact, you've had lunch to contemplate probably the bulk of what Mr Storey had to say. I think it's probably fair that, at this stage, he, having concluded his remarks, you have a short break at this stage and then what will happen is that I'll begin my summing-up. Don't...you're not going to be beginning your deliberations today as I'm sure you must have realised already. All I'm going to do today, but it will take a little while, is just deal with the law. I'll give the document I told you I was going to give you, take you through it, explain it all so, that you'll have all of that. With a bit of luck, we'll finish a bit early this afternoon. But I'll start the review of the evidence, which I'll do as quickly as I reasonably can, but it is my duty to make sure that you do have all the evidence well in mind when you begin your deliberations. I'll start that and I have spoken to listing, is 10 o'clock all right for everybody? Yeah. Excellent. Ten o'clock tomorrow morning and you'll be beginning your deliberations sometime tomorrow morning. Okay so, that's how it's going to go. So, we'll take...I think 10 minutes is probably sufficient. So, we'll just take 10 minutes now and then I'll deal with the law and that'll be it for the day.

(Short break)

(2.41 p.m.)

(2.54 p.m.)

JUDGE JAMESON: Well, ladies and gentlemen, it's not always easy to be precise about dates in this case but from some time in probably the early 1980s, it would seem, until late in 2017 Carol Higgins, as she now is, has been complaining about sexual abuse by her father. If you accept her evidence and that of her mother, Jean Voss, the initial complaint, which was only about kissing, because at that stage nothing more is said to have happened, would have been some time certainly no later than November 1983. November 1983, you may remember, is the date upon which Mr Appleyard went to the United States. He came back, he told us, in December 1983 and no allegation of rape or any of the other forms of indecent assault is said to have happened prior to that date but the kissing is said to have happened prior to that date, so, if you accept the evidence of Carol Higgins and her mother, there will have been a complaint some time perhaps in the middle of 1983.

On any view, there was a complaint about much more serious matters within a period of some months - difficult to say how many - I use the word to include the possibility that it may have been many months or more than a year, but it would be very much for you to assess the timescale of these things, but there did come a time after Jean Voss had finally left her husband - she had left him, of course, on a number of times before and come back - having been joined by Carol, who then left in circumstances that I'll remind you of in due course and went back to her father. It's accepted that there was a meeting. It seems to have been accepted that it was in the bus, as described, and Mr Appleyard accepts that there was a telephone call to him at the Pie Hall in which he was told that Carol was making allegations that he had had sex with her, so, from whatever time that was, some time in the early to mid-1980s, Carol Higgins has been making those complaints.

We know that there was some form of contact with social services early on, or at least that is her evidence - a matter for you to determine it. It is, I think, accepted that there was some form of complaint and police investigation in 2005, all trace of which had disappeared by the time that Sergeant Wilson, the officer in this case, came to be involved in matters in September 2015, and from September 2015, over a period of getting on for a couple of years, Sergeant Wilson investigated what he was being told by Carol Higgins.

It's pretty clear that that wasn't an easy experience either for him or for her. Their relationship seems to have been somewhat fractious. He may very possibly have regarded her, if I may borrow the phrase used by Kenneth Clarke about our present Prime Minister as "a bloody difficult woman", but eventually the time came when the Crown Prosecution Service did decide to bring this case. The fact that they brought it, the fact that they didn't bring it earlier, neither is remotely relevant to the rights and wrongs of the case. It's just background information, but the fact is that they did decide to bring the case and here we are. Now, I suppose at the heart of all of this is whether this is, therefore, a quest of 30 years or more by Carol Higgins to have her account taken seriously and heard or whether she is or may be somebody who is either fantasising or lying about matters and has been over that period of time.

As I told you at the outset, you and I try the case together but we have very different roles. Just as a reminder - you'll remember it anyway - the law is my area of responsibility and the facts, the assessment of the evidence, what evidence you accept and what you don't and what you make of the evidence that you do accept, that is for you and only for you. Nobody else's views matter, not mine, not counsel's, not even those of the witnesses. Ultimately, it's for you to make those decisions, so it's probably helpful just to have a quick recap of how each of us is going to play our role at this stage, you and I. For me, it's really very straightforward, it's just the case summing the case up to you, and, as you know, there are two aspects to that: giving you the legal directions and summarising the evidence for you.

Now, because the law is my responsibility, you must, please, when - I'll give you this document in a minute or two - when I give you the legal directions, you must, please, accept them and apply them faithfully. That's because it's my responsibility to get it right, but, when I turn to my summary of the evidence, I am in, I suppose, quite a significant way trespassing on your role really because, obviously, when I summarise the evidence for you, I'm not going to read out every word that you've heard. I can't really remind you of every single piece of evidence or we'd be here for another week while I did it, so what I'm going to do is to summarise it, much as counsel have done. I have to do it, I'm afraid, rather more fully because I'm not here to argue the case; I'm just here to make sure that you've got all the evidence before you, but that I will do, but, as you'll appreciate, any summary is, by definition, selective, so it won't be word for word, everything that you've heard, and it's important that you bear these principles in mind.

If you remember a piece of evidence and you think, "Well, that's important" but I don't mention it, please don't think, "Oh, well the judge hasn't mentioned it, it can't be that important after all". I may simply have overlooked it. If you remember a piece of evidence and you think it's important, it is important because that is precisely why you are here, to make those judgments.

Other side of the same coin is this: if you think that in my analysis - not analysis - in my summation of the evidence, I'm stressing a piece of evidence that you consider less important or even entirely unimportant, fine. If that's your view, that's all that matters. What I'm really saying in two different ways is I'm not here to tell you what you should think. What I am here to do is to try and help by just making sure that you have a full grasp of all of the evidence, you're reminded of it fully. If I make comments - I probably will make some comment, I'll try not to make too much - the purpose of it will be not to steer you one way or another but simply to make sure that you have all of the relevant material before you, all of, perhaps, some assistance with the approach that you may need to take to some of that evidence. That's as far as it goes.

So, as I say, it's for you and only for you to make decisions about what evidence you accept, what evidence you don't and what you make of the evidence that you do accept. When you do that, will you please treat all of the evidence in exactly the same, fair-minded way, wherever it comes from. That may seem no more than a statement of the obvious but I suppose in this case what it really means is that Mr Appleyard, although he is the defendant in the case, is a witness in the case like any other and, for that matter, so is the lady whom he called this morning. The fact that Mr Appleyard is the defendant and therefore sits in the dock, because that's where defendants sit in our courts, is neither here nor there to how you should approach his evidence. He doesn't start one step further back because he's the defendant, obviously not. All witnesses, of whom he is one, start level.

Now, of course, the trial process is designed to assist you in determining whether all witnesses finish level and in a case such as this where there is a diametric opposition of evidence, it may be that you will conclude that inevitably some witnesses will not remain at the same level as others in your deliberations, but that is entirely a matter for you, so the trial process is essentially designed to assist you to determine where witnesses finish in your estimation. What is critical is that they all start level.

You are considering events that took place a long time ago and over quite a substantial period of time and, of course, you've had to consider not only the events that took place in the 1980s but also, and importantly, the events that took place in the last couple of years while the matter was being finally investigated, because Mr Storey has just addressed you about matters that he would wish you to have well in mind when you are determining whether witnesses are independent or have been influenced in any way. He has adduced evidence and asks you to consider the circumstances in which many of the witnesses made their statements, and so it follows that we're looking not only, or you're looking not only at the events in the 1980s but the events, as I say, in the last two or three years, so it's quite a lot to look at, and, of course, we're looking really at the dynamics of family relations within a family of whom there were not a huge number but a number of different people.

You will, I imagine, be relieved to hear that you do not have to decide every disputed issue of fact in the case. There will, of course, be some issues that are central to your decision-making process and those, of course, you will need to decide but there are others that may be peripheral or even entirely irrelevant. You choose which is which. I'm not here to tell you, "This is important and this isn't". You decide that.

All I am here to say is that what you need to do is concentrate on whether the evidence, taken as a whole, does or does not prove each or all of the counts, the charges laid against Mr Appleyard, so, if you concentrate on that, it will become apparent, I am sure, that there are some key issues that you will feel that you have to decide and others that will be progressively less important and, once you've made important decisions and reached conclusions about whether or not Mr Appleyard is guilty or whether he is not, you don't have to keep on deciding every last issue. Once you've reached that point, that's fine. Okay?

You may, of course, draw sensible conclusions from evidence that you do accept. What I mean by that is the sort of process that we all do in our everyday lives. "I'm sure of this and I'm sure of that and, if I'm sure of those two things, then the obvious conclusion is that this must be the case". That's what we all do subconsciously, sometimes consciously, in our everyday lives when we're deciding anything. It's no different for you except that it's an important matter, of course, important decision for you to make, but it's absolutely a part of a jury's task to draw sensible conclusions from the evidence that you do accept.

All I want to do is just to make sure that you have very clearly in mind that, although that is part of your task, just please contrast that with guessing or speculating about anything where there hasn't been evidence. If there are areas...even if there are areas where you think, "Well, I wonder what happened then?" or "I wonder what X might have said about this", well, if there's been no evidence about it, there just is no evidence about it. That's all there is to it, so don't, please, be tempted to supplement the evidence that you do have by guesswork or speculation. Just work on the evidence that you do have but, as I say, it is absolutely a part of your task to analyse it, decide what it means and what conclusions you draw from the evidence that you do accept.

Now, I said I'd give you a document. Here it comes, one between two, like all documents, and I'll take you through it. Don't please be concerned about the apparent length of it. Sometimes it takes quite a lot of words to set out that which is, in fact, very simple.

Right, well, the first thing that you'll see is that I've headed it, "Summary of Directions", and the reason that I always call a document of this nature a "Summary" rather than simply calling it "Directions" appears in the first paragraph, so let me just read that to you. I will expand on some of these directions as I explain them. "Please apply the full directions as given orally". What I mean by that is that some of these directions, in fact, I'll simply read through to you. They really won't need, I think, any expansion, but some undoubtedly will. I think it will be helpful if I just explain some of them to you rather more fully and, when I do, please just apply the full directions that I give you when I am explaining them to you.

A good example of where this document is essentially only an aide memoire - it's not the full direction - is in paragraphs 2 and 3 and, if you just look at those paragraphs, para.2 is headed, "Roles: law for me, facts, assessment of the evidence for you", and then para. 3, I hope you'll recognise because that's what I've just been saying to you. I said it rather more fully and that's a direction to follow. This is an aide memoire, just to remind you of what

I've said. Right, so paragraphs 2 and 3 I have already dealt with, no need to go over those again.

Let me move on then. Paragraph 4, probably not necessary really to remind you of this but, just to make absolutely certain that matters are scrupulously fair, I've put it in. I remind you by way of direction that the fact that Carol Higgins - and hereafter she's CH in this document - the fact that Carol Higgins's evidence-in-chief was video-recorded is entirely normal and not to be held in any way against Mr Appleyard, who is EA after this in this document.

Now, next, para.5: there are 15 counts on the indictment. Although the background evidence is common to them all, the specific evidence in relation to each count is different. You must consider each count separately and you will be asked to return separate verdicts in relation to each count, so 15 verdicts altogether. It follows that your verdicts do not have to be the same in respect of each count, although, of course, they may be.

Paragraphs 6 and 7 - 6 on this page, 7 the top of the next page, or the back of this page - are important principles that apply in all criminal trials in our courts and they are matters that both counsel have already addressed you about but nevertheless it is important that you have a full direction about them. They are known as the burden and standard of proof. Paragraph 6 is the burden of proof. The prosecution must prove guilt in respect of each count. No defendant is required to prove innocence or, for that matter, anything else, and the fact that Mr Appleyard has given evidence does, and called a witness, does not alter this decision.

Over the page, para.7 is the standard of proof, what we mean by proof. The prosecution will have proved guilt in relation to whichever count you are deciding if they make you sure of it. If, having considered all the evidence against and for Mr Appleyard, you are sure that he is guilty of the count you are deciding, your verdict on that count must be guilty. If you are not sure, your verdict must be not guilty.

The next few paragraphs deal with the legal ingredients and the issues that arise for your consideration in relation to all the various counts, and I start in para.8 with the allegations of indecent assault, and you'll see I've set out the numbers of the counts on the indictment which are indecent assaults, so, in respect of each of these counts, all of the counts that charge Mr Appleyard with indecent assault, the prosecution must prove that Mr Appleyard deliberately touched Carol Higgins and the touching was indecent. Now, quite a lot of that isn't in dispute, and so what I need to do is just set out with you what is and what isn't and therefore what the issue really is for most of these counts. Unfortunately, the issues aren't quite the same for all of the indecent assault counts, but I'll go through it and explain exactly what does apply.

So, let's go back to para.8. It is not disputed that the touching specified in each count, if it occurred, would have been both deliberate and indecent. Count 1, of course, is the sexualised, if you like, kissing, kissing as an adult, not as a parent. The other counts, there are three individual examples of three different kinds of conduct. One is the allegation of oral sex, one is the allegation of digital penetration of Carol's vagina and the final one is Carol masturbating...the allegation of Carol masturbating her father, so, fairly obviously, you may think, and it's not disputed, that the touching specified in all of those counts, each of the indecent assault counts, if it occurred, must necessarily have been both deliberate and indecent.

Next, no issue of consent arises in any count of indecent assault because in law a child under the age of 16 cannot consent to indecent touching. As you know, the defence of Mr Appleyard in relation to each count of indecent assault is that the incident or incidents described did not happen, so these are the issues that arise count by count for your consideration. If you find it helpful, by all means get the indictment out so that you've actually got it. You might find that helpful, I think, while I just go through it with you.

Right, so Count 1, the first of the indecent assault counts, and the matter that it relates to is set out in italics at the bottom of the particulars of offence, so this is the occasion when Mr Appleyard is alleged to have kissed Carol as though she was a sexual partner. Her age is given as being about 11 or 12 and there are a range of dates from April 1980 to April 1982 during which this incident is said to have occurred. In fact, dates are not material in this case. They may be evidentially important but they are not legally material. All that must be proved is that any count that you're looking at must have happened before Carol was 16. Well, there's no dispute about that, if they happened, that they were before she was 16.

The issue really is: did they happen, so, although dates may be important evidentially for you to consider when you're deciding, "Well, what did happen? Did this happen? Do we accept that or don't we?", legally you may find that...well, you will find that they actually have no relevance at all in this case, so don't worry if you don't know exact dates; of course, you don't. A lot of these counts are what are known as specimen counts, and I'll give you a direction about that in just a moment. Don't concern yourself too much, therefore, legally with dates.

So, going back then to the direction document, para.8, Count 1, kissing, if the incident occurred as described by Carol Higgins - I may, I think, from here on simply call her Carol - I hope you won't mind if I do that, it's not to show partiality, it's just easier, I think, so Carol - if the incident occurred as described by Carol, then Mr Appleyard would be guilty of Count 1. As you know, Mr Appleyard has denied that he ever kissed Carol sexually. He accepts, of course, that he did kiss her as a father would a daughter. Well, any kissing of that nature would not, of course, be a criminal offence. It follows that, before you could convict Mr Appleyard of Count 1, you would have to be sure that there was an incident in which he kissed Carol in the way that she has described, what I perhaps loosely could describe as sexualised kissing.

Next, Counts 4, 8 and 12 - these are the allegations of oral sex - now, the indictment has developed, as you know - and it might be more helpful if these were actually consecutively numbered, but they're not, so there it is, we'll deal with them as they are - so these are Counts 4, 8 and 12, and my direction is this. If Mr Appleyard made Carol perform oral sex upon him, he would be guilty of indecent assault. Well, that may not come as any great surprise to you. Carol says that this happened on very many occasions. Mr Appleyard says that it never happened.

Now, these three counts, and if you look perhaps first then at Count 4, are described, as most of the counts on the indictment are, as specimen counts, that is to say that they are specimens of that alleged course of conduct. Specimen counts are routinely used in criminal trials where it is either impossible to specify individual incidents or where there are too many allegations of the same conduct to include them all in an indictment, and, arguably, both things apply here.

If you are not sure that oral sex took place at all, then your verdicts on each of these counts would be not guilty, so that would be not guilty on all the three counts, 4, 8 and 12. If you are sure that oral sex did take place but were not sure that it took place more than once, your verdicts would be guilty of Count 4 and not guilty of Counts 8 and 12. If you are sure that oral sex took place twice but not sure that it took place three times - it's not easy, I think, to see how you could reach that conclusion but all conclusions are open to you - if you reach that conclusion, your verdicts would be guilty of Counts 4 and 8 and not guilty of Count 12. If you are sure that oral sex took place on three or more occasions, your verdicts would be guilty on each of Counts 4, 8 and 12.

Now, I hope that's clear. Everybody follow? Okay, excellent! There is just one thing before we move on. I don't know whether you've actually put a couple of words in. I don't think you've been asked to. In Count 4, in the particulars of offence of the document you've got it reads, "Elliott Appleyard, on a date, the 23rd April--" What it should say is, "Elliott Appleyard, on a date prior to the 23rd day of April 1985--" The significance, of course, of the date of the 23rd April 1985 is because that is the date of Carol's 16th birthday. Right, so that is all the direction that you require in relation to the allegations of oral sex.

Next, Counts 6, 10 and 14, the allegations of digital penetration: if Mr Appleyard put his finger or fingers into Carol's vagina, he would be guilty of indecent assault. Again, Carol says that this happened on very many occasions; Mr Appleyard says that this never happened. These three counts are also therefore specimen counts and you should reach your verdicts in exactly the same way as described in relation to the oral sex counts above, in other words, not sure it happened at all, not guilty all three counts; sure it happened but not sure it happened more than once, guilty of the first of those counts, which would be Count 6 and not guilty of Counts 10 and 14; the logically difficult but still technically possible position of being satisfied it happened twice but not three times, guilty, Counts 6 and 10, not guilty Count 14; if you're satisfied it happened at least three times, guilty on all three counts. Okay, so exactly the same way. I haven't set it out again but I hope that it's sufficiently clear you can refer back to the direction for the oral sex. It just makes the document a little shorter.

Now, I wish I could give you exactly the same direction in relation to the final three specimen counts of indecent assault, which are the allegations that Carol was required to masturbate her father. Unhappily, I can't because there is one slight complication in these counts, and I'll come to it now. Again, Carol says that she masturbated her father on very many occasions, Mr Appleyard again says that this never happened, so, again, specimen counts and in these three counts, as in the previous two sets of three counts, the oral sex and the digital penetration allegations, in these three counts the principal issues are whether you are sure that such conduct occurred and, if so, whether you are sure it occurred on one, two or three or more occasions, so, in other words, your approach thus far is exactly the same as it is for the other indecent assault counts.

However, in relation to these three counts there is a further issue for you to decide because in law - and I'm not going to give you a law lecture, I'm simply going to tell you what the law is and therefore the decision that you have to make - in law, masturbation of Mr Appleyard by Carol would only amount to the offence of indecent assault if you were also sure, and I don't know whether your copy still has the word "either" on. It probably...if it does, it really doesn't need it and you can cross it out, but it may not have. I tried to do copies that had got them taken off, but there we are, but you would also need to be sure that Mr Appleyard placed Carol's hand on his penis and/or - so it can be either but it may, of course, be both - that Carol masturbated Mr Appleyard because his conduct at any time up to the moment of masturbation was such that Carol was in fear that she would be forced to masturbate him if she did not do so of her own accord or was in fear of violence of any kind, and whether immediately or in the future, from Mr Appleyard if she did not masturbate him.

I don't really think there's any need to explain that any further. That is the law, and so there is that additional element that you would need to be sure of before you could convict of indecent assault in relation to the masturbation allegations.

Paragraph 9, the allegations of rape: there are five of these, Counts 2, 3, 7, 11 and 15. In respect of each of these counts, the prosecution must prove that Mr Appleyard deliberately penetrated with his penis the vagina of Carol and Carol did not consent to the penetration. The defence of Mr Appleyard to each count of rape is that the incident or incidents described did not happen.

Now, in this case, the issue really is a very simple one because it is accepted that all of the matters that the prosecution must prove in each of these counts would be proved, including lack of consent, if you are sure that Mr Appleyard had vaginal sexual intercourse with Carol. It follows that the principal issue in each count of rape is whether such intercourse occurred. If you are sure that it did, the offence of rape would be proved.

Now, if you will forgive me - again, I am really not going to give you law lectures about consent and what is true consent and what isn't - as you can imagine, counsel and I have discussed these matters and Mr Storey is not asking me to give you any direction about consent. The only issue here is: did it happen? If it did in each of the counts, and we'll look at them in just a moment because some are specimens and some are not, then you would convict, if you're not sure of it, then you will acquit, so that is the simple issue in all of the rape counts, but there are differences between them because - just going back to my written direction - Counts 2 and 15 are specific counts and they relate respectively to the first and last times that Carol says that Mr Appleyard raped her, and, if you just look at Count 2, you'll see the word "specific" here in brackets as opposed to a specimen for most of the other counts, the same for Count 15.

Counts 3, 7 and 11 are specimen counts of the other occasions on which Carol says that her father raped her, and you should reach your verdicts in respect of these specimen counts in exactly the same way as is set out in relation to the oral sex counts. Please note, of course, that you would have to be sure of at least either one or two or three or more acts of intercourse on occasions other than those specified in Counts 2 and 15.

Right, well, you can probably see why it did take a little while to actually write all of that down. In fact, it's all very simple but, in order to make it so and to make it absolutely clear, does require quite a lot of words.

Now, the remainder of my directions, which I will go through now, I've headed, "Your Approach to Particular Areas of the Evidence". As I go through them and by the time I conclude them, you may well think, "Well, that's really no more than common sense". I rather hope that you do think that because, after all, legal directions should be based on fairness and common sense. Nevertheless, it is, I think, helpful and necessary just to set out particular areas of evidence that the courts have found juries sometimes may have difficulty with, just to make sure that you think about them logically and fairly, so that's what these directions are all about.

Right, para.10: although each count on the indictment is an allegation of sexual abuse, you have also heard evidence of physical and emotional abuse of Carol and her siblings and of their mother by the defendant, Mr Appleyard. These allegations are, as you know, largely denied by Mr Appleyard, and what you make of them, what you accept and what you don't, is absolutely a matter for you, but why have you heard about them, given that that's not what's on the indictment?

Well, the answer is this. You've heard about these matters because they may be relevant to your understanding of the dynamics within the Appleyard household. Your conclusion about them may be relevant to your assessment of a number of issues that may affect your conclusions about the allegations of sexual abuse that are on the indictment, and, as I review the evidence with you tomorrow morning, I may refer back to this proposition so that you just have in mind, well, it may be relevant to this issue, but, ultimately, of course, it's for you to say what it is relevant to and what it isn't.

However - back to the direction - however, if you accept that Mr Appleyard did either physically or emotionally, or both, abuse his family in any or all of the ways described by the witnesses, this does not mean that he must necessarily also have abused Carol sexually. You must not convict Mr Appleyard of any count on the indictment simply because you disapprove of how he behaved in other ways, if you do, only if you are sure that the count you are considering is proved. Of course, if you do conclude that Mr Appleyard either physically or emotionally abused his family, I say this would mean...perhaps it would be better to say this might very possibly mean that you would also conclude that he had lied to you in denying such abuse.

If that is your conclusion - it's entirely a matter for you whether it is - but, if that is your conclusion, it is a factor that you are entitled to consider when deciding whether you accept his evidence that he did not commit the sexual offences that he faces on the indictment. However, you should be careful before concluding that a lie or lies about physical or emotional abuse necessarily supports the prosecution case in relation to the counts on the indictment. It may do so, but bear in mind that a person facing criminal charges may well be reluctant to admit other disgraceful conduct, whether or not he is guilty of the matters charged.

Paragraph 11, things, essentially, that Carol told others before she was video-interviewed - which you've seen, of course - before she was video-interviewed on the 2nd November 2015, and I'll just read through the direction. You've heard about complaints made by Carol before she was video-interviewed on that date. What Carol said to others before her video interview is not independent evidence of the truth of her evidence to the police and to you because, of course, on each occasion it was what she herself was saying. You have heard the evidence because it may help you to decide whether her position has been consistent and whether her evidence is true. When considering the evidence of witnesses as to what Carol told them and when she did so, you will need to decide, first, whether you are sure that such things were said and, if you are, what conclusions you draw from that finding.

Paragraph 12, although there is evidence that Carol complained of sexual abuse by her father from about 1983 onwards, you know that no prosecution was begun until 2017. That fact is irrelevant to the issue of whether her complaints are true or false - fairly obvious, if you think about it. The fact that it wasn't thought fit to prosecute previously is no more evidence that the allegations aren't true than the fact that there is a decision to prosecute now means that they necessarily are. Neither is a logical conclusion so it's irrelevant, it's just background. It may, however, be relevant to your assessment of the relevance, if any, of the lengths she has gone to in recent years to publicise her account and to insist on a prosecution being brought. Nevertheless, it remains the case that many years have passed since the events you are considering in the early 1980s. That is bound to have affected the memories of all witnesses, including Mr Appleyard. Make appropriate allowances in respect of all witnesses for the difficulty of recalling the detail and perhaps particularly the dates of particular events.

Over the page, para.14, you should also bear the following factors in mind: first, it is agreed by many of the prosecution witnesses that they have spoken together about the past and about the prospect of giving evidence. Mr Appleyard asserts that they, or many of them, are simply lying, but you should also consider whether the evidence that each has given has or may have been affected by their discussions, in other words have witnesses or may they have given evidence that either deliberately or subconsciously has been coloured by what they have heard rather than being an accurate account of what they truly observed? Please remember I'm not, in giving these directions, pushing you one way or another. I just want you to think about these things.

Second, the passage of time may have put Mr Appleyard at a serious disadvantage. He may no longer be able to recall details that might have helped him. In particular, because it is impossible to put a specific date on any incident that is the basis of a count in the indictment, it is impossible for Mr Appleyard to do more than deny the allegations in general terms. It would not be realistic to expect him to give more detailed denials. Bear in mind both of those factors when deciding whether the prosecution have made you sure of each count on the indictment.

Finally, para.15: in relation to Counts 2 to 14, it is accepted that Carol did not complain immediately about what she says happened to her. Can we just pause? I am sure you've got it all in mind, but para.1 is the kissing which she said she told her mother about immediately, Count 15 is the final allegation of rape, after which she says she got on the bus, met with her mother and immediately complained about what had been happening, so there are...there is evidence - a matter for you what you make of it - there is evidence of immediate complaint after Counts 1 and 15 but, obviously, Counts 2 to 14 are said to be matters that went on over a period of months and were not reported, at least to the authorities - you'll look at all of the evidence in due course - immediately after each incident had happened.

Exactly when - back to para.15 - exactly when and the circumstances in which she did complain are disputed. Carol says that it was when she met her mother on the bus as she was leaving the family home for the last time, and obviously the question that you will need to consider is whether the fact that Carol remained in the family home with her brother...with her father and with her brother, Paul, for some time during which she has said that she was being repeatedly sexually abused without revealing what was happening, does that cast doubt on her account?

That's the question or one of the questions for you to consider but, in considering this, you should take into account all the circumstances as you find them to be in the family home at the time, and so this, for example, is one area where your assessment of whether there was physical and emotional abuse may be important, and you should also consider Carol's own explanation for remaining in the home and for staying silent. Your conclusions as to whether physical or emotional abuse was going on may be, as I've said, relevant to that issue. I'm sorry, I'd forgotten that I'd put that in the written directions, so I've said it twice. Forgive me.

Well, what do we know? This isn't a long summary - I'm going to remind you of all of the evidence - but, just briefly, Carol was 13 or 14 at the time you are considering. Her mother had left home and, although Carol had initially gone with her - this is said to be after the kissing but before any other count - she had returned home to her father. She told you in her evidence that she had forgotten or perhaps put to the back of her mind the events alleged in Count 1, the kissing, and that her mother had neglected her, they'd fallen out, she told you that her father told her that what was happening was normal and she believed him, although she did not like it.

She was guilty - I'm sorry - she was ashamed and felt guilty. She tried to protect her brother by not telling him. She wanted to maintain what was left of the family. She was told by a social worker that, if she left her father, she will be put into her home ...a home. Her sister, Donna, had been sexually abused in such a home. There came a time when she could not put up with the abuse any longer and did leave. She met her mother on the bus and immediately told her of the abuse. Now, that is, in summary, Carol's account. I'm not putting that forward as a statement of fact, just of her evidence, which you must assess.

So, finally this when you're considering these matters, not everyone who is abused complains immediately and the circumstances in which somebody, particularly perhaps a child is, domestic circumstances may be very important to your assessment of this issue. The fact that a complaint indecent assault delayed is no more proof that it is false than the fact that a complaint is made immediately is proof that it is true. I mention these points so that you think about them. I am not expressing any opinion in doing so. It is for you and will remain for you to decide whether or not Carol's evidence is true.

Well, there we are, ladies and gentlemen. With the exception of final matters of law that I will come to right at the end of my summary of the facts, and those directions will only take a minute - they're very, very short - that's all I need to tell you about the law.

Now, you've had a long day, listening hard, and thank you for your attention to me. I'm really not going to start on my assessment...my summary of the evidence now because it's too much for you and, frankly, if I have overnight to refine it, it will probably be a bit more focused, so I'll see you all at 10 o'clock tomorrow morning. Okay? Thank you all very much indeed. Have a good evening and I'll see you in the morning.

(3.48 p.m.)

(Adjourned until the following day)

Thursday, 24 January 2019

(Transcript prepared without the aid of documentation)

(10.04 a.m.)

MR STOREY: Your Honour, can I just mention one matter before the jury come in?

JUDGE JAMESON: Yes, certainly.

MR STOREY: The defendant has brought to my attention that he has been made aware by –

JUDGE JAMESON: I am sorry, the?

MR STOREY: The defendant has brought to my attention that he has been made aware of further use of social media to publicise...

JUDGE JAMESON: Further?

MR STOREY: Use of social media...

JUDGE JAMESON: Yes.

MR STOREY: ...to publicise these proceedings.

JUDGE JAMESON: What, during this case?

MR STOREY: Overnight last night or yesterday.

JUDGE JAMESON: Yes.

MR STOREY: The publicization amounts to the posting to Facebook of a copy of a press report from I think the Barnsley Chronicle, which appears to have been written last week...

JUDGE JAMESON: Yes.

MR STOREY: ...because it refers to the trial likely ending next week, in other words this week. There is nothing reported in it which hasn't already been ventilated in court.

JUDGE JAMESON: Yes.

MR STOREY: And I suspect that isn't going to be contained within your Honour's summing-up beyond the fact that the complainant purports to have waived her anonymity and is named within the article. Given that there is nothing beyond that which has been said in court, I think I need say no more than ask your Honour just to remind the jury at this stage in the proceedings that it is even more important now than it was before that they should pay no attention to social media. They should not make any online research into the case or anything of that sort.

JUDGE JAMESON: Yes, okay.

MR STOREY: Thank you very much.

JUDGE JAMESON: I'll do that. Yes, jury please.

(10.06 a.m.)

JUDGE JAMESON: Good morning, ladies and gentlemen. Thank you all very much indeed for making the effort to get in early. I hope nobody was too much delayed trying to come in on the York road, which they chose to dig up this morning, but, anyway. Right, now, I'm going to just conduct a review of the evidence with you.

Just before I do that, can I just say one thing? I understand there has been a certain amount of reporting of the case and some of the reporting has been posted on social media. You already know, of course, that you are not to look at social media or try and make any sort of researches into the case. Well, that's as important now, probably even more important now than it's been throughout the whole of the case, so let me just remind you of that direction, and, if you did happen to see any particular reporting of the case in the press or in any other way and you've read it, well, you've heard the case. The reporting isn't going to help you. It's what you hear in the case that matters.

All right, let me turn then to a review of the facts. Can we start that by just looking briefly, please, at our agreed facts, if you'd be kind enough just to get those out, and the reason I want to do that is because a large part of it, all of section 1, which is the first four...five pages really, so really all of it, almost all of it, is a chronology and it's probably helpful for you to just to...for us all just to look together at it. It anchors us, as best we can be anchored, with some dates at least. I'm not, of course, going to read all the way through it but it gives us some dates.

Now, of course, the dates that it doesn't contain are the dates of any of the allegations on the indictment. The reason for that, of course, is, as you know, the prosecution aren't able to put a date on any of them and, of course, Mr Appleyard denies that any such things happened in any event, but there are some dates that may help in pinning things down a bit. One date that isn't on it, if you look at p.2 - and the reason it isn't on it is because it's a date that isn't agreed, it comes only from Mr Appleyard's evidence - but, if we look at some of the other material in the agreed facts, it may be that you'll conclude that his evidence about this is likely to be correct and it may be a potentially important date is November/December 1983 when Mr Appleyard says that he went to the United States on his hunting trip for about three weeks.

Now, I've just put it in there on my own copy. It's entirely a matter for you whether you do. If you do - as I say, it's not an agreed fact because the only source of the information is Mr Appleyard - but, that having been said, if you look at some of the other matters that are on this document, you'll see that correspondence between solicitors, and at the top of p.2 you'll see on the 16th August 1983 there's a letter from Eaton Smith & Downey. They, we were told, were acting for Jean Appleyard as she then was, Jean Voss as we know her now, to Bruce & Company, who were acting for Mr Appleyard in the matter of Appleyard and Appleyard so, obviously, they are contemplating a divorce at that point, so you may be satisfied that by the 16th August 1983 it's perfectly plain from that that the separation has occurred, the final separation essentially has occurred, and that letter indicates that Carol is at that stage living with her mother at Penistone, and I assume what it means and suggest that "Donna reside with her father during weekdays and mother at weekends" isn't a suggestion that that's what's happening; it's a suggestion that that's what should happen.

Am I right about that, gentlemen? It's a little unclear as to exactly what that means but I don't think anybody suggests that that is, in fact, whatever did happen so, presumably, that was just a potential suggestion for the future.

At all events, coming back to dates, it's clear then from that letter that by the 16th August 1983 Carol and her mother have left and are living in Penistone. It's also clear, if you look at another letter, the next letter, in fact, on the 13th October 1983, that Mr Appleyard's solicitors are writing to Jean Appleyard's solicitors and saying, "Such has been your client's behaviour towards the child" - so this is accusing mum - "we understand that she has now chosen to live with our client", so it may be that you'll be able to be clear from that that the time when Carol first, not first actually, because there had been times when she'd left home with her mother before when they went, for example, to the refuge and probably one earlier occasion that she can't remember but Jean Voss did tell us about - in fact, I think Mr Appleyard told the police about when they went to a farm for a while - but those are, essentially, in the past and aren't going to help us very much.

But, looking at the separations during the period that we are looking at, you may think it's clear that that first separation when they go, essentially, and are - the way the Crown describe it - sofa surfing in Penistone for a while clearly must have happened by some time prior to the 16th August 1983 and it's clear from the letters that Carol is back with her father by the 13th October 1983, so that may be quite a helpful anchor at which to look at all other dates, so it may well be, you may think, that when Mr Appleyard tells us that he went to the United States in November/ December 1983, he is very probably right about that. It would seem to fit in with all the other dates.

Of course, he did also tell you that Carol never spent a Christmas with him after separations began at any stage. Well, she's back with him by October

1983 and we know, if we carry on down the chronology, that by April 1984 Huddersfield County Court is dealing with the custody issue and, as we know, gave custody of Paul and Carol to their father.

On the face of it, it's not easy to see why Carol wouldn't have been with her father at Christmas in 1983 but Mr Appleyard's evidence is that she wasn't, but there it is. That's the sort of logical consideration that you can undertake. I say no more about it other than to remind you of what he said about it, but the real purpose of this, just as a start, is to try and anchor you as best we can in dates. I'm not going to say any more about them. There they all are, but it does rather look as though three dates that you can probably tie things to is, mid-August 1983, Carol has left and is sofa surfing with mum in Penistone, by October she's back with dad, in November/December he goes off to America, and in April she's with him - whether still with him or with him again is for you to decide, if you think it's important to decide it - and custody is awarded.

By January 1985 it seems that Carol is now at Penistone Grammar School, so the final leaving must, it seems, have happened by then, so that probably gives us a maximum time over which Carol is back with her father after she's first left and then returned. It can't be longer, it would seem, than between August 1983 and January 1985, so that gives us a reasonable timescale, I think, to work on but, of course, all these matters are ultimately for you, but I hope that's just helpful. Now, there are masses of other dates. I'm not going to take you through any of those at the moment but we will come back to other matters in the agreed facts in due course.

Right, so, with that in mind, let me turn to the evidence, and I'm simply going to remind you of it in the order in which you heard it. I think that's probably the easiest thing to do, so that began, of course, with Carol Higgins, and you'll remember that we watched together the video-recorded interview that took place with her and with the police in 2015 and, briefly summarised, this is what she said: that her father was violent to her. If she wet the bed, she would be beaten with a belt. She described a thick and a thin belt. She described how her father would sometimes put his hand to his head and make her flinch, thinking that she was going to be struck and he would then scratch his head, so in other words, essentially, well, there we are.

She described going out with her father collecting scrap. She said that after a while he didn't ask Paul to come anymore and when she was, she believed, about 11 or 12 years old she was out with her father and he shot the dog, Sam. "Then", she said, "he sat me down on some pipes and he kissed me. It was proper kissing as a boyfriend and girlfriend would kiss. I told mum but I begged her not to tell him but she must have done because some social workers came to school and I did tell them and then another social worker, a man called Mr Sykes, came to the house and, a few days later, mum left dad and she took me to Penistone. We had left before".

She told us about going to the refuge but, coming back to Penistone, she said that, "There we slept on a mattress on the floor and after a few months we were kicked out and we went to another address where some people called the Wadsworths lived", and you'll remember we were to hear a bit more about this, that the first address that they went to was owned by some people that her mother had met over the CB radio and they had a bit of a falling out - one can perhaps imagine that it won't have been an entirely happy situation to have a mother and daughter living on your sofa for more than a very short period of time, so, at all events, whatever happened or whatever the reason was, that came to an end and they moved to the Wadsworths, still in the Penistone area, you'll remember.

The Wadsworths had a son, David, age various but certainly a few years older than Carol, and he and Carol had a sexual relationship. It wasn't...it was entirely consensual. Carol was later to say...one of the things that she was later to say, one of the reasons that she was very concerned about telling the police, even after the rape allegations had happened and she'd gone back to her mother's and her mother told us that she was trying to persuade her to go to the police but she was reluctant, one of the things that Carol was to tell us as a cause for her reluctance was that she was told, "Well, that will come out and you'll be called a slag", and she didn't want that boy, David, to get into trouble because she said, "He didn't rape me. I was fine with what happened and I didn't want him to get into trouble", and, of course, he could have done because sex at that age, however old she was - it would seem 13 or 14 - is, of course, unlawful and, if he was over the age of 18, if he was an adult, and he may have been, he probably did commit what we would now regard as a not insignificant criminal offence, but there it is. Those are just some of the background matters that you need to just have in mind.

"After a while", she said, "I couldn't take living with mum anymore. I guess that I'd forgotten about the way that my father had kissed me. I met up with him on occasions. He bought me clothes and I went back to live at No. 26. When I was there, dad gave me love bites". You'll remember that a statement was read to you from Ena Whittle, indicating that at some point she had seen love bites. She thought actually that Carol was about 10 or 12, which would be significantly younger than she would have been at this stage, but, of course, she has no idea who put them there, so Ena Whittle's evidence is perhaps not going to take matters very much further.

At all events, back to Carol Higgins's evidence to the police, she said then her dad went to America, so that, again, seems, doesn't it, to fit in with it being about November/December, the account that Mr Appleyard gave, because Carol put that as being fairly shortly after she'd come back. We've looked at that date and that's obviously sometime between October...between August and October 1983.

"He went to America. Whilst he was in America, mum came and took some furniture", and Jean Voss told us that she'd broken in, although she got somebody to mend the window afterwards, she tells us, and took some of the furniture. There it is. It probably doesn't add a great deal to the real issues in the case but it gives us something of a background, and Carol told us, or told the police that, "Paul and I had a party". We heard rather more about the party from Mr Appleyard later, but I'll remind you about what he said in due course.

Carol said, "When my father returned, he was fuming. He went to the phone, phone box" - this must have been a time when they didn't have a phone in the house and probably pre-mobile phones or certainly a lot of people having mobile phones, and really all of the phone calls that we've heard about are made from phone boxes - so, in order to make a phone call to his new girlfriend, Jess, with whom he had apparently just begun some sort of a relationship, Mr Appleyard went off to a phone box and Carol said that, so frightened was she by his anger that she...the way she described it was that she cut into her wrist. When her father returned, he said it wasn't bad enough to go to hospital. She was bandaged up, but then he said, "You're too mentally disturbed to be in your own bed. You'll have to sleep with me", and then she described what is Count 2 on our indictment. The kissing, of course, is Count 1 that I've already described for you.

Now, what I'm doing, as you will appreciate, is summarising but, when it comes to certain points, because a summary runs the risk of editorialisation, of putting a gloss on things that shouldn't be there, when it comes to some matters, I think it's probably better if I actually read out the exact words that she used, just to remind you of that, so this is what she said about Count 2, the specific allegation of the first allegation of rape.

She describes her father coming back and then said this. “He started to bandage it up, saying, ‘It’s okay, it’s not too bad for you to get stitches or for you to go to hospital, but you’re too mentally disturbed for you to sleep by yourself tonight’ so he says, ‘You’ll have to sleep with me in my bed’, still never thought anything about it, just thought, ‘He’s not angry with me anymore’ and, you know, ‘I’m going to be okay’ and then I went to bed that night and I went to sleep, him cuddled up to me, and then I woke up and I felt this tickling here” - and she indicated with her hand - “you know, where your belly goes in like that, so I didn’t know what he were doing and then he started touching me places and then he turned me over and got a condom out of his side of the drawer and he had sex with me and, when he finished having sex with me, I just said to him - I weren’t even close to my grandad, his dad, and I didn’t know my grandparents from my mum’s side - and so I said to him, and I don’t know why I said this, and I went, ‘What would my grandad say if he knew what you’d just done?’ and he said, ‘Don’t worry, sweetheart, he wouldn’t say anything. He believes the same as me, that fathers should break their daughters in like the Indians do’, so I thought, ‘Right’, didn’t think nothing about it. I can’t remember if I got back in my own bed or just stayed there all night, got up next morning. I can’t remember getting up the next morning. I just got on as normal, doing things as normal, I think”, and then she went on to describe, “I just know it became an everyday occurrence”.

Now, back to - so those were the exact words that she used - now, back to a summary: she described Mr Sykes, a social worker, telling her that, because she was clearly torn as to where to be living, or she said that - that’s her evidence - that she would go into a children’s home if she could not choose between her parents. She told you that she was very frightened at that prospect because Donna had been in a children’s home and Donna had been sexually assaulted in the children’s home, so she was very frightened of that prospect.

“Then” she said, “dad got custody”, and we’ve just looked at the sequence of dates, so, again, that does appear to fit in with the dates as we see them in the agreed facts. “The sexual abuse carried on. By this time, dad was going out with Jess”. Jess was a new girlfriend. She obviously wasn’t on the scene for terribly long because, of course, there was then Janet, who became the second Mrs Appleyard, but at some point there was this lady, Jess.

She spoke about one particular matter where Paul had been involved. She said this. “Paul caught us snogging. Dad said that it was nothing”. She came back to that a little later on and, again, I think it’s probably helpful just to remind you of her exact words about it. She said this. The officer who was interviewing her said, “You spoke about two incidents that you can remember where you think that Paul, your brother, saw your dad kissing you”, and she said, “Full on kissing me, yeah”. “In the kitchen”, says the officer, “and then once in bed”. She described an incident when they’d been in bed and Paul had seen them, and she said this. “I don’t know if he saw me kissing him...kissing me in bed but I know he used to see us on a Saturday morning when Paul were playing out. He’d see us in bed but, you see, we used to have play-fighting with our mum and dad, you know, in bed and things like that, growing up, so I don’t know if he” - that’s Paul - “just saw it as that”.

Question, “Did he ever say anything to you when he saw your dad kiss you in the kitchen?” Answer, “I remember Paul being really upset and confused and I remember being...I were upset and confused that he’d seen it cos I tried to keep everything from Paul and I remember my dad getting flustered and panicking and how he were trying to explain, you know, that kind of thing what had happened, so I can’t remember how it got resulted. You know, I just remember it being, ‘God, how’s this gonna...you know, how you gonna hide this one?’” So that’s how she described that act.

She described being taken to her father's room, sorry, from her own room to her father's room in order for sexual activity to take place. This is how she described that. No, that's another section. It's probably not necessary, I think, to give you the exact words. That is how she described matters happening.

She described various forms of sexual activity. She said that, "He made me masturbate him". She said that, "He put my mother's engagement ring on my finger. He told me that lots of his friends had sex with their daughters". You'll remember that Mr Storey said, "Well, there is a total lack of any evidence that that is the case", but the issue perhaps isn't really whether it was the case but whether it was said and, if it was said, whether she believed it. That's perhaps really the issue there, but it's a matter for you.

She described having sex in front of the fire on one occasion and the fire being hot, and this is the way she described that, that, "He made me go upstairs and get a condom out of his drawer and masturbate him while I put the condom on to get him hard to put the condom on and then laid me down in front of the fire and the log fire were burning my leg but I knew it would be over quick if I just kept quiet", and she said this. "I sometimes used to pretend I was enjoying it and make some noises so that it would be over quicker and this one time I couldn't stand, you know, the fire were burning me too much so I said, 'My leg's hurting' and he got really angry, saying, 'You're only fucking saying it cos you don't want to have sex', you know, 'cos you don't want to do it' and I was saying, 'No, no, no, I do, I do, I do', and so there was never any screaming or shouting, saying, 'Get off me'. I just accepted this as my role. It's just something I had to do", so that's how she described that particular incident.

She spoke about photographs in a tin box and a hairbrush with which she had to pose doing either actual or pretended sex acts with the hairbrush. She said that her father told her to call him Sam, and then she spoke about the tattoo. She said that she and Paul had both had tattoos. She said a little more about it later. I'll come back to that later.

She said, "I think I lived like this for about two years". Well, it can't have been as long as that if one looks at the dates, but that was her belief, and, of course, when one looks back at childhood, sometimes, perhaps times, dates over a long period of time may not be quite as easy to assess, but that's entirely a matter for you.

She spoke about the incident in which she said her father threatened her mother with a machete. This is how she described it. Again, I'll use her actual words for this because they may be important for you to have them exactly. She described her mother as having had a sexy dream. Now, plainly, she can only have got that from her mother. She can't, of course, have known that from her own observation, so this is an example, and it's only one, of times when, plainly, she has been told things, and one of the things that Mr Storey particularly wants you to bear in mind, and it is an important issue, is whether, when people are telling you things, they are telling you what they have seen or what they've been told about, so this is an example, where, obviously, Carol is telling you, must be telling you at least something that she has, in fact, been told about, but it's fairly obvious in this case, but you do always need to look at that possible issue.

This is how she described it. "She" - that's mum - "once had a sexy dream and something and he dragged her downstairs and ripped her nightie off and he had this big machete and he held it to her vagina and he says, 'If you don't tell me who it is, who you're talking about, I'm going to slit you from your vagina straight up to your neck' and she was screaming and crying and just pee'ed herself. She'd got no clothes on. She just pee'ed like a cow peeing in a field. I remember this pee gushing out of her and him saying...she shouting,

'Phone the police, phone the police'", and - the word she used was "They" but she must have meant "He" - "said, 'You'd better get upstairs, else I'm gonna do the same to you'".

Just pausing there, Mr Appleyard, of course, denies that such a thing happened at all; Jean Voss says that it did, but I remind you, and I will remind you again, I hope, when we get to Jean Voss's evidence, that she did say that she was not aware that either of the children were present when it happened although she did say that Carol later told her that she had seen it through the bannisters from the top of the stairs, so that's the evidence on that point.

She said, "I haven't had contact with my father since the day I finally left. On that day he was beating me, calling me pathetic. He had been sexually abusing me for about two years".

This is how she describes the final matter, and this is, essentially, Count 15. She said, "The night I left I was crying and asking him to stop. I was on the floor, I was shaking and he was saying, 'Get up, you're pathetic. Get up' and he were kicking me in the stomach and I just thought, 'That's the last time', even though I'd been threatened that I would go in a children's home if I did say something. I was 15 and I just couldn't take anymore, so he went to the pub that night to the Denby Dale. I got on the bus from Denby Dale Salvation Army steps and I got on the bus to Penistone and, when I got on the bus, my mum was on the bus with Carl, her boyfriend at the time" - that's Carl Higgins from whom we heard - "and she got...she'd gone to" - sorry, there's sort of a bit of, confused bit there - then she said, "When I got on the bus she says, 'What are you doing here?' and I told her everything that my dad had been doing to me about the abuse and she said, 'Where's your dad now?' and I said, 'He's at Denby Dale'", something inaudible, probably Pie Hall, not altogether surprising if a transcriber didn't catch the word, Pie Hall, because it's not perhaps the most obvious phrase, but we know, in fact, and Mr Appleyard agrees that there was a phone call to the Pie Hall so that's probably the word that she was using which the transcriber did not catch.

"So she" - that's mum - "she phoned him and they brought him to the phone and he says, 'Our Carol, she's here with me now and she's told me everything' and his first words to my mum, 'You can't prove a thing' and then my mum wanted me to go to the police then and make a statement but I didn't. I felt partly to blame for what been happening. A week went...but I went a week later and they took a 17 page statement off me and then they took me to Huddersfield Police Station and I had forensic tests, internals and things like that, (inaudible) and I were bleeding internally and I'd be jumping up and down on blotting paper. I think they thought I were...was miscarrying, I don't know, even though I've told them that he had always used a condom, so then, then they told me that my brother would be classed as a juvenile witness and that, if it went to court, that my name would be made mud and blackened and that I'd be made out to be the biggest liar going and that I'd be made out to be the biggest slag going.

"The police officer said that, if it went to court, this is how he" - that must be a reference to father - "would blacken my name and they said he would, because I'd had sex before, I felt guilty and ashamed and I didn't want that lad to get done, you know, David, because he didn't rape me. He was older. I think he was about 17 or summat like that, maybe 19, I don't know, that I was reaching out for attention and affection at that time and it just didn't feel like it, but I think that's what my dad thought. That's why now, looking back, that's why he were angry when David were in Barnsley shopping with me because he didn't like him being that familiar". You may remember in cross-examination she described that, this, "I must, I must improve my bust" business that David had apparently said as a joke and her father had realised from that that they were perhaps more intimate than, whether for good reason or bad, any father perhaps wouldn't want, so there we are.

"Because", Carol went on, "he obviously knew he wanted that role, to break me in, and so I'm sure I think I told him as well, I think I told him at Barnsley bus station that I had sex with him so he knew that he wouldn't be actually breaking me in, I think he did", and then she went on to describe oral sex. She said, "He used to make me have oral sex with him, you know, and he stank. Even though he were vile, he were dirty, but he used to say, 'Who loves you, baby' and I used to have to say to him, 'You do', and he used to say, 'You'd better believe it', and, if I didn't say, 'You do', he used to repeat it and really I were just complying to everything that, you know, he would ask of me", so that was one...there were other references in her interview to regular acts of oral sex.

You probably, probably, some of you, may remember Kojak, and the point that Mr Storey makes clearly "Who loves you, baby?" is, was, a catchphrase from a television series. That's perhaps where it came from, but that's not really quite the issue. The issue is whether it was said, whether it was said in this way, whether it was coercive - matters entirely for you to consider. That was Carol's evidence about that matter.

"Dad", she said, "poisoned me against my mother to the extent that I used to call her a slag and I was angry with her. I didn't want to live with her although I now realise it would have been better if I had.

"When I was...later, after I'd left and when I was working for S. R. Gents", who were the tie manufacturers in Barnsley, "I got a telephone call from Janet, who was then engaged to my father", and became, as we know, the second Mrs Appleyard. "We met in a café in Barnsley. I saw my father there.

I asked him why he did what he did and he said, 'I'm sorry but I loved you as a person' or, 'I love you as a person and not as a daughter'".

She was asked, "How often did these incidents happen?" and she said, "About three or four times a week", and she gave some further descriptions that I will just remind you of. She said that...describing who slept where, she described Paul having the little bedroom, although later, apparently, he'd moved into the larger bedroom, but at one point she described him as having the smaller bedroom, and she said, "I was in...if I was in that room, I remember him, that's dad, coming upstairs and I remember the room being black.

"I must have had my nightie or pyjamas on and I think I would have slept in my underwear because I always knew that when I was in that room I'd be turning...I'd be sleeping on my back. It'd be pitch black cos I wanted to shut everything out. I always remember that room being black. I would have worn my underwear because I wanted to feel as much protected as I could to try and protect myself from that feeling. I used to want to block everything out and go to sleep.

"I'd hear his footsteps. I'd hear him coming in from the pub and coming upstairs and then I'd sometimes I'd just think, 'Please, please', cos sometimes he just goes straight past my door and go to bed, and I'd be hoping that that would happen, but most of the time he didn't. He'd just come in and I'd be asleep or pretend to be asleep and he'd get my shoulder and pull me around and I'd pretend I'd be...I was asleep but he'd grab my arm and take me to his room which was at the other end of the landing so I know that when I used to get out of the bed and he used to do that, it was all very silent. He was silently coming in and silently I'd walk, not trying to make any noise on the landing, into his room and he'd take me into my (sic) bed.

"Sometimes the light would be on because he'd have porn magazines at the side of his bed and there always used to be pink pages and blue pages in these magazines and he used to like me to read stories to him out of them and masturbate him at the same time as I was reading and then he'd put the books down and he'd get the condoms, which he always kept in a drawer at the side of his bed, and I remember him lifting my nightie up, so I was wearing a nightie, and taking my pants off and he would sometimes have me straddle him and sit on top of him and, you know, move up and down on top of him. Most of the time he would get on top of me and he would open my legs and get on top of me most of the time and it would probably last for about 10 minutes, something like that, so the whole process would probably last about 10 minutes and I would moan and make noises and I would like wriggle underneath him because I worked out that, if I did and he thought I were enjoying myself, it would make him come quicker so it would be over and done with. I'm trying to think now. I can't remember what he did with the condom afterwards. Sometimes he'd get to that point halfway through, he would put a condom on. I'd have to put a condom on. He'd get the condom, reach for it. Sometimes he did it; sometimes I did it.

"I'm trying to describe what it were like. It were just normal for me to be quiet and for me to go in there. He didn't have to talk to me to give me instructions. I just followed whatever he said. I knew what to do. If he walked in his bedroom and he were fully clothed, say it was in the afternoon or teatime, he'd like bend me down on my knees, he'd put my hand on my shoulder and put me down and that were...he wouldn't have to say, 'Give me a blow-job'. It were just his actions. He just did things to make me know I just had to comply. He'd take me in his bedroom in the afternoon, unzip his trousers and his jeans, if he was wearing jeans, he'd unzip them, and he would often have a lumberjack shirt on. He'd do that and then he'd just push me down and so I knew I had to give him a blow-job".

She said she thought she was about 13 when she was first raped. The love bites and the sexualised kissing had taken place earlier.

She said that she told Diane Croft and her parents, Diane Croft's parents, just before she left. I think that must be leaving for the final time. She was asked who else she had told and she described going to counselling throughout her life, going to the Rape Crisis Centre in Sheffield. She would take the train on a Friday afternoon after work at S. R. Gents and go to the Rape Crisis Centre.

She did then speak about telling people on the bus, and this is an incident, or a matter, that Mr Storey asks you to consider. She described it, in fact, I think on two occasions, probably most fully in cross-examination, so I'll come to that in just a moment, but she did talk about telling friends on the bus in her video interview.

She spoke about the trip to Sweden, or to Scandinavia, and that her father had sex with her in the cabin. Paul had returned but he hadn't been able to get into the cabin. She said this. "He made me feel like it were normal, you know, that his friends did it with their daughters and they lived happily as man and wife. I was confused. I didn't know what to think. I didn't know if to fight it or if to agree with it, to go along with it. I didn't know what to do, and it's not...I was fucking tret like an adult. It were nothing fucking to do with that. It was survival at that time. I didn't know what else to do. I would have been put in a children's home. I couldn't go back to live with my mum, I'd been told, and it weren't right. I didn't like it anyway. I just didn't know what to do, not the fact, you know, all these things were things. I've never been able to relax and move on and be totally happy with my life because they think that about me, that I'm a little slag. I'm not a fucking slag. I were a child."

She spoke about telling her mother that she was pregnant. Jean Voss told us about that and there is also, of course, the evidence of Hilda, Mr Appleyard's sister, that bears on that. We'll come to that in due course, but let me just remind you that there is a point here that Mr Storey asks you to consider, and that is this, that Carol told you that, when she told her mother that she thought she might be pregnant, she had told her mother that it was a boy. She hadn't told her mother that it was her father. Jean Voss's evidence is that she was told that it was Mr Appleyard and that, if she was pregnant, the child would be his, so there is that difference in the evidence between mother and daughter there.

I've described in part the final matter - that is Count 15 - but she did come back to this. I'm not going to read it all out because much of it is exactly what she had previously said, but she did say this, when she'd described an incident when she was curled up and her father was kicking her, she said, "He had sex with me that teatime. He'd had sex with me. I can't remember if it was in his bedroom or if it was downstairs. The times just come back to me as...I think it was on the front room on the rug and he'd had sex with me.

"Paul must have been out, or I don't know if he'd been that day, and we'd had an argument about something. I think there'd been an argument about summat. I can't remember. I can just remember me getting really angry and upset and crying and throwing myself to the floor, shaking, bringing my knees up and shaking and everything, saying, 'Leave me alone, leave me alone, I just want you to leave me alone', and, like I say, he was sticking the boot in, saying, 'Get up, you're pathetic', and I remember thinking, 'This is it. I've got to go. I'm gonna wait while he goes to the pub'.

"He went to the pub and then I went", but this is where she said it. "But I saw my friends on the bus. I'm sure I saw my friends on the bus and I told them what had happened but then, when I did get to my mum's and during that week, I hadn't got any clothes and I remember thinking, 'Should I take clothes with me?' I never took any clothes with me so my mum went back and he filled a dustbin bag liner full of clothes and I got my Bible from being young, my kids' Bible, I got an armadillo and I got certain toys that I wanted to bring back with me that I wanted to take from my childhood and he wouldn't let me have them. All he'd let me have were this bag. That's all I got".

So, there she is describing sexual intercourse, which is accepted would amount to rape, on that final day but she is talking about having met friends on the bus, and we heard evidence from Jean Voss and from her at that time partner, Carl Higgins, the discussion, it was just them on the bus, there were no friends there, so there is something of a dislocation here as to recollection. Whether this is significant is for you to say, but there it is. I remind you of what the position is.

Now, Carol Higgins was cross-examined and I'll remind you briefly of what she had to say. She said, "I have worked towards my day in court but I have not been looking forward to it. I publicised these matters". She'd been asked, of course, all about the Facebook posts and the book and flyers that had been posted in Denby Dale and so forth. "I publicised it because nobody would listen. I went on social media. The book was mostly about climbing Mount Kilimanjaro after I had had bowel cancer but there was something about this in it".

She was asked what she thought should happen to paedophiles and she expressed, as has perfectly properly been argued to you, some fairly extreme views with which probably most of us would not agree. She indicated that she thought paedophiles should be hanged. She was asked, "Well, do you want money from your father?" "No", she said, "I do not want money from him".

She was asked about work patterns. "Dad", she said, "was always on the sick. We got food parcels for backhanders. He did the odd job for people for backhand cash but he didn't have a full-time job. He never had a 9.00 to 5.00 job. We would hide food upstairs when the social services came so that they'd think we didn't have any. I did tell my dad about sex with David Wadsworth", and she described the meeting at which, at Barnsley market, when David Wadsworth had been there and it became apparent that their relationship was intimate.

"I'd been back to No. 26 a couple of months before the custody hearing". It looks as though it must have been quite a bit longer than that, but that's a matter for you. I took the name, Higgins, because Carl Higgins was a nice man. I didn't want to be an Appleyard anymore. I was ashamed. My father's then girlfriend, Jess, was about during the abuse period and she must have stayed over sometimes".

About the tattoo, she said, "Dad suggested my tattoo. Then Paul wanted one. It wasn't a question of me asking for it; he suggested it. It wasn't... Sam, the name on it, wasn't the dog. Why would I want a dog's name?"

About the masturbation, and you'll remember the direction that I gave you about this, legal direction, she said this. "He would tell me to do it or put my hand there. He did tell--" Sorry. "I did tell mum that I might be pregnant by a lad rather than by my father. By the end, when I finally left, I felt I couldn't take it anymore but I wasn't brave enough to say, 'No' before. I did tell mum on the bus and not at her home.

You will remember there is an agreed fact at number 4. It's on the final page. Don't turn it up. It's the only extract that we've been - we've heard about from her book, "Conquering the Impossible", which does indicate that she actually told her mum at her mum's house, so, again, that is an alteration in her recollection of matters.

"I said at one point that I did go to see my dad. I'd been to church. I was into the idea of forgiveness and I said I'd forgiven him but I hadn't really. I was trying to heal myself. I tried to put it behind me but I couldn't. I had not started counselling when I went to the police when I was 15, the first time", and we got some dates then. She'd been to the police in 2005, and there seems to be no dispute that that did happen, but all the documents have been lost so by...the next time anything happened was 2012 when she got a firm of solicitors called Jordans involved but by 2015, when she went back to the police, the documentation had all been lost.

She said, "I didn't want publicity about this. If it had gone to court earlier, I wouldn't have done it. I only started publicising it on social media and in other ways in 2015. In 2014 I'd been to the police and were told that it was too late and they wouldn't pros...they wouldn't--" The word she used was "prosecute". She must, I think, really mean "investigate it".

"I did send my book to Janet, the second Mrs Appleyard. I was not, in fact, aware that flyers had been posted in Denby Dale. I live 18 miles away from Denby Dale but I did do a book launch". In fact, she said, I think, that she did two book launches, one of which was in Denby Dale in 2015, and in November 2015, as we know, she was interviewed by the police.

She was then asked about some of her beliefs. She said, "I do think that incest is rife and that it should be dealt with. I did give the police the names of witnesses. They said that I needed witnesses", and Sergeant Wilson does appear to confirm that that is correct, that they did say, "Well, if there are witnesses, you'd better tell us who they are", essentially. "The police were very slow. I was pushing. I was persistent. It did feel like a police cover-up to me. I arranged a meeting with the Chief Constable".

She described a meeting with Janet and her father at a car boot sale, and it was quite a dramatic moment in her evidence. What you made of it is a matter for you, but she describes being shouted at from very close-up, "I'll fucking have you". You will remember how that was done, quite a dramatic moment. Whether...where it takes you is entirely a matter for you. I simply remind you of it. "I do think that my father is a paedophile and not just with me.

"I went to Denby Dale to see Diane Croft. I had been told she was too scared to give a statement. She told me what she could remember", which is the evidence that she ultimately gave. "I did tell Sergeant Wilson, the officer in the case, about my father selling some land. I took a bottle and a knife" - that had somehow been recovered from there - "and showed them to the police. I think there is more to be found there. There are loads of kids' bikes, clothes, and there is a shrine with flowers. It all looked very dodgy.

"I probably did put a notice about my father's first court appearance on Facebook. I've had a lot of years of anger and not being listened to. I have" - sorry, I can't read my own note - "I have been involved in gathering evidence. I have spoken to the people I've grown up with and they've told me what they know. I did record phone calls, including one with Ena Whittle, and she told me she thought her statement had been altered". Well, I don't think, ultimately, anything turns on that. It's just an example, perhaps, of people misunderstanding things sometimes.

"My father told me that everyone knew that Judge Pickles was a paedophile". This is...I think we know that this is a judge who is now dead. "He led a paedophile ring. I've been told this and that everybody knew it".

She was asked a few questions in re-examination. "I felt the police were covering up for my father. He rented land from a detective inspector. They wouldn't investigate my case. I couldn't understand why not. I recorded my conversations with witnesses but I gave these to the police".

Well, it's entirely a matter for you what you make about this. It may be that you will conclude that some of Carol Higgins's beliefs are irrational, but you will... It's a matter for you. There's no evidence really one way or another about it, but they may perhaps be thought of as, well, at least extreme, but you are going to need to consider what, if any, impact that has on matters because, if you're told something and you know that you've been reporting matters since the 1980s and nobody's done anything, and there's no doubt that she had done, nothing's ever happened, and then, when you go back to the police, they say, "Well, sorry, but we've lost all the material", then is it that surprising that you start to think, "Well, it's all a conspiracy"? A matter entirely for you, but the real point perhaps is whether irrationally believing something that you've been told in those circumstances has an effect upon her credibility or veracity, truthfulness, in relation to what she says actually happened to her. That's the question. It's for you to say what your conclusions about that are. I make absolutely no further comment at all.

Right, let me take you really, I think quite quickly, through the remainder of the prosecution evidence and then a little more steadily through Mr Appleyard's own evidence. Is everybody all right to carry on? We'll take a break if you like but... Everybody okay? All right.

Next witness, Jean Voss, Carol's mother, Mr Appleyard's first wife: they married - we've got the date - in 1974. You've got it in our agreed facts. They lived together firstly at No. 8 and then at No. 26 Gilthwaites Crescent in Denby Dale. She described her relationship with Mr Appleyard as volatile, or at least it could be volatile. "He'd always turn things round so that it was my fault. He attacked and hit me many times, usually after he'd been drinking. He had a 12 bore shotgun - I only remember one - and a machete". She described the incident where she said he'd put the 12 bore shotgun to her head. She said, "The children were there on that occasion and he said that, if they went to the phone to phone the police, he would shoot me".

She described the incident with a machete. "I'd had a dream and he asked me repeatedly on different occasions who it was about", and she said, "He threatened to cut me from my vagina to my throat and I was so frightened that I wet myself. It was in the kitchen. I was not aware that Carol was there although Carol later said she had been on the stairs and had seen it.

"I've left him several times but I would return. I had three children. I had no close family nearby". She described the occasions that she'd left. She said that she had taken all three children to a farm on one occasion for two or three weeks. It doesn't seem that either Carol or Paul have any recollection of that. We don't know how old they were. She described going with Carol to a refuge.

And then she said, "Finally, I left for good. It was a hot summer". She was sitting on a step outside the kitchen because she was rather upset having seen a programme about the Falklands war. That's why there's some evidence about the Falklands war in our agreed facts. Of course, the difficulty with that is we've no idea whether it's contemporaneous with the Falklands war or something later, so it may not really help us very much, but what she does say is that she'd been watching a programme obviously about, you'll remember, the soldier, Simon Weston, who was very badly burnt. She found it upsetting and she'd gone to sit outside on the steps outside the kitchen. She said, "Carol came and told me about being kissed on the mouth when she was out collecting scrap with her father. She was very upset and begged me not to confront him, but the next day I phoned the social services and an elderly chap came" - that may be Mr Sykes - "but no action was taken. He simply said, 'Well, if you think there's a problem, take her out of the situation'".

She said that at that stage she thought back to a comment that he had made earlier whilst watching television, which she had described as thinking at the time was a throwaway comment, about fathers breaking in their daughters.

They went to Penistone, that's her and Carol. Initially they went to a friend called Angela. She met up with... She said that she met up with Mr Appleyard and he had simply said, "Well, it's her word against mine", that's, "Carol's word against me".

They slept on a mattress with the first lady, Angela. It was okay. They were there for about two months but then they fell out, she and Angela fell out, and she and Carol went to live with the Wadsworths, who had a son, David. She thought he was about 16 or 17 and he did have a relationship with Carol.

"I began a relationship with Carl Higgins. I was out a lot with Carl". She talked about going to a CB club and so forth. "Carol was very unhappy. One day when I got back there was a note on the mirror saying, 'Gone back to dad'. At that time Carol would have been about 13 or 14. I got a council house and I married Carl".

In relation to Mr Appleyard's trip to the United States, she said that, "Whilst he was there, I went back to No. 26 and I broke in. I saw both Carol and Paul and they told me that they had been having parties. At Christmas", and, again, of course, this is contradicted by Mr Appleyard later - "at Christmas I went" - that would be, presumably, then Christmas 1983 - "I went to the house taking presents for everybody but I was rebuffed and I had a row with both Carol and her father". You will remember her describing Carol saying, "You can stick your Christmas presents up your arse".

She then moved on to a date that we do know about because it's in the agreed facts, the 26th June 1983, so, in fact, she's gone back in time. That's the date upon which the police were called because Mr Appleyard had tried to commit suicide by hanging himself. She said, "I'd been to the house, we had a row, Mr Appleyard pushed me out, he locked the door and he hanged himself. I ran to the telephone box, called the police, they came and he was rescued".

Now, whether or not there is any real significance in this is entirely a matter for you, as all matters of fact are, but it is, of course, the case that 23rd June 1983 is before substantial sexual abuse is said to have begun, maybe after some kissing. Whether the attempt to commit suicide really takes matters much further is a matter for you. Mr Appleyard gave his explanation as to why he had done it when he gave evidence. I'll remind you about that in due course.

In April 1984 she and Mr Appleyard were divorced. In July she married Carl Higgins, and there are the letters that we've looked at in April and October between the solicitors.

Now, her account of the incident on the bus, she said, "I'd been out with Carl. We were on the last bus back to Thurgoland", by which time was where they were living. "I saw somebody on the back seat. It turned out to be Carol. I think this was after I had married Carl", so that would put it after July 1984, 21st July 1984. "The figure said, 'Mum, and it was Carol. She was crying and shaking. She was very upset. She said that she had left her father and she was not going back, that her father had raped her and that she wanted to get away from him. I phoned the Pie Hall and said, 'Carol's told me everything' and he said, 'You fucking prove it'. Carol had nothing with her. She was just in the clothes she stood up in. I told Mr Appleyard to bring her things and the following day he came round with his sister, Hilda.

"I wanted Carol to make a statement but for three or four days she wouldn't. She was too upset. She was hysterical and sobbing but I persuaded her to. We went to Penistone Police Station and she made a long statement. When I heard all the things that she was saying, I felt sick. Two officers, police officers, came to the house. They said that, if Paul was involved, he would be hostile and his evidence would be disregarded. Carol was very upset and didn't want to do anything else".

About the pregnancy, she said this. "Carol told me that she might be pregnant. A urine sample was taken to a doctor in Penistone. It was negative but it would have been, the baby, if there had been one, would have been Mr Appleyard's.

"Carol and Donna were then living with me and Carl in a house in Penistone and we made a room in the cellar" - you'll remember Carl Higgins told us about this as well - "for Carol. I wrote to Rape Crisis and they said that I was doing everything right in the way I was trying to address the matter with Carol. Then", she said, "I parted company from Carl. He'd become more like a brother", and she obviously wanted more out of a relationship than that, "and I moved to Barnsley with another man called Jack. I got...I arranged counselling for Carol, which she went to when she was working at S.R. Gents and Carol eventually moved out on her own".

She was challenged in cross-examination about her account of violence. She said that it had happened as she had described. She was asked about Mr Appleyard's work patterns. She said, "He worked on and off for himself but by and large it would be full weeks. He was not always on the sick. He was very strict. He did take a belt to the children but he didn't take their clothes down, at least not when I was there".

Her statement, which she had made in November of last year, sorry, yes, last year, was put to her in which she had said that Mr Appleyard had not used a belt on them. She said, "I was not aware of any bed wetting and I have not seen bruises on Carol. I did not report the machete incident to the police. I was too humiliated". She was asked about the breaking--fathers breaking in daughters comment and she said that, at least at the time, she had regarded it as a throwaway remark.

In re-examination, she said that she would smack the children with a spoon to the top of the leg but she could not remember her then husband using a belt.

Carl Higgins, briefly her second husband, his account of the bus incident was this. He described again, essentially, coming back on the last bus. "I stayed in the front and I let Carol talk to Jean. Later I was told that her father was trying to touch her up and trying to have sex with her. Jean explained this after she had phoned Mr Appleyard", and he confirmed that the telephone call had been made. "I did not speak to Carol about it". Describing the phone call, he said, "We got off the bus in Thurgoland. Jean and Carol went to a phone box. I waited over the other side of the road. Then we all went back to our house. Carol was there for a few months. Then she wanted to go back to her father and did".

Now, pausing there, of course, Mr Appleyard also says that there was a time when Carol came back to live with him after she had made her substantive complaint of sexual abuse. Carol does not accept that, and it is potentially a significant issue. It's for you to say. The prosecution say that simply cannot have happened, that Mr Appleyard is not the sort of man who would dream of allowing his daughter to come back to live with him after she had accused him of sexual abuse, whether the accusations were true or false, but Mr Appleyard said that she did and maintained that because I asked him specifically about it and Carl Higgins does say that that is his recollection. Whether he's right about that is entirely for you to judge, but that is what he said.

We move to Springvale. "Carol came back and returned and said that it had all started up again with her dad and at that point we fixed up a bedroom". Well, how it fits together is a matter for you.

He was asked, "Well, do you remember any contact with the police?" He said, "I don't recall contact with the police", and then he said this, which may have been telling - a matter for you - "I don't get told everything".

He was cross-examined. He said, "Carol was with us twice". Mr Storey, obviously, was investigating the possibility that Carol had returned to Mr Appleyard after her substantive allegations of abuse and he did say, "Carol was with us twice. There were about 12 to 18 months between her visits. The first was after the incident on the bus and the second was when we were living at Penistone when Carol came and asked to stay and told us that everything had started again".

Paul Appleyard, Carol's brother, of course, and Mr Appleyard's son: "My childhood was tough. We didn't have much. We would get a belt off my dad and a spoon off my mum. He would strip us down. We'd be bent over his knee. He'd buckle...he would hold his belt", and you'll remember he described it, "buckle in one hand and doubled over, and he'd whack us until we were screaming, all three of us, that's including Donna. It was very common. Mum was just as bad. She said that she wasn't but she was. She would hit us on the bare bottom with a spoon.

"There were happy times, on holidays when we were with friends, when I was out scrapping or shooting with my dad. Dad had several guns. He was my hero. He was a hard man. He took me shooting. He taught me how to fish and catch fish with my bare hands". I think Mr Appleyard - it may be an irrelevant detail but, as it happens - says that didn't happen. "We would work together for local farmers. My parents' relationship was stormy. I would hear screams and put a pillow over my head to try and block them out. I got the belt if I interfered or asked what had happened.

"It was always me and my dad until I was about 12 or 13 and then it changed. Before the US trip, dad started taking Carol for walks and stopped taking me. I was devastated".

He then described his mother leaving. He said, "I came downstairs one morning. I'd heard screams in the night. I saw a suitcase on the floor. I knew what was happening. I said, 'You're going, aren't you?' She'd been talking to truckers on the CB radio. She left me cigarettes and a gold ring and left. Me and my dad were alone for a few months". Obviously, Carol had gone with Jean, and Donna probably was in a child's home at this point. "So me and dad were alone for a few months and things were good. Then Carol came back after about six or eight months. The social services would come. They told us that they would split us up or put us both into care".

Then Carol became what he described as a mother figure. "She became very bossy. I can remember that I heard bedroom doors on a nighttime creaking as Carol was taken to his bedroom. There was a time when I couldn't get in after I'd gone to football training and it was cancelled and I came back after only about 20 or 30 minutes. I knocked on the door. Carol opened dad's bedroom windows. She was in her knickers and bra, or at least I could see that she was in a bra because I could see her top so I assumed she was in knickers. I wasn't let in. I was told to go away and I did. On a few occasions I couldn't get into the house when I knew that they were there. One morning - I think it was a weekend - my father had Carol in a full embrace. They were kissing with tongues, it wasn't fatherly, and, when he saw that I was there, he let go sharpish and said, 'Just giving my daughter a morning kiss'.

"I would often sleep in my father's bed after the split-up. It was for comfort. When Carol returned, she would come into his bed too but then it was just her. One time my father said to me in the morning, 'I'm sorry if I touched you last night. I didn't mean to'".

In relation to the tattoos, he said that he asked what Sam was. You'll remember he also got a tattoo with Sam on. "Dad said it was his nickname. I got mine covered up when I joined the army at 19. I have not looked my father in the eye since I was 18".

He was asked questions in cross-examination. He said, "Dad did not work much. He was on the social security, working on the side. A lot of the time he was at home. I only remember one full-time job but he did work a lot of the time on farms. I don't remember the custody hearing". He was asked whether he had expressed a desire to stay with his father. You may think, in all probability, he would have done but he said he did not remember that.

He said, "Well, more things come back to me the more I'm asked. My statement is only a patch on what I really need to say". He was asked, "Well, you've discussed this with Carol, haven't you?" He said, "Of course I've discussed this with Carol. I saw her cut her wrist, tied a lace around it, and she was saying, 'You wouldn't understand'. She was trying to protect me even then", and he described ultimately being chased by his father with a pitchfork.

Later, he said, he went to see Carol. "She was a mess. It all fitted in. I realised what a monster we had lived with. There was always something but I didn't want to believe it because of my love for my dad. I did see photographs in a silver box by the bed. There was pornography on the other side of the bed. It's right that Carol has waged a Facebook campaign and I have supported her. I am 100 per cent behind her. The truth must come out. I am here to help her and others. The police have done nothing".

The next witness was Hilda Graham, by video link, you'll remember. Hilda Graham is, of course, Mr Appleyard's sister, four years older than him. She said, "I didn't see a lot of my brother and his family at the time. I found out that he and Jean had separated when he asked us - that's me and my husband, Peter - to take him to see her, and so Peter and I took him to Penistone. He said that Carol had been to the police about something.

"Peter drove, I was in the passenger seat and my brother was in the rear. It was summer. It was a hot day. When we got to where Carol was living in Penistone we stayed in the car. My brother got out. He went to the house. After a short while he came back down the path. He was followed by Jean. They were arguing and I heard Jean shout, 'She took the pregnancy test to the chemist as if it was her own but you know full well it wasn't hers, it was Carol's'. I was shocked. I put the windows up. We drove back. My brother was quiet. I said nothing about what I had heard".

Well now, this, as you know, is denied by Mr Appleyard and it's for you to decide what evidence you accept and what you don't. She was cross-examined. She said, "I did fall out with my brother about family matters. I've not had a lot to do with him for some time. The police came for a statement in 2016. Carol had asked me if I would be a witness and come to our house. She told me what had happened to her. I said that I hadn't known anything about it. I don't know if she knew about my trip to Penistone. She did not tell me what to say. My memory was very good then. I have had two strokes since".

Well, it was put to her that this had simply never happened and she said it had, and you may remember that she was asked, "Well, what do you say--" Mr Storey referred to what Jean had said as a comment, and you may remember her specific answer to that, "It wasn't a comment. She shouted it at him. I didn't want to hear anymore. I was gobsmacked. I couldn't get over it". Well, that was her evidence.

Julie Clarke: Julie Clarke was the lady who had been best friends with Carol for many, many years. They'd met when they worked together at S. R. Gents as teenagers. She said, "We've been best friends for about 33 years. We met in about 1985 when we were both working at S. R. Gents in Barnsley. At the time Carol was living with her mum", and she thought also with Donna, either at Penistone or Barnsley.

Carol's relationship with her mum she described as rubbish. She said that it wasn't nice, not like a proper mother/daughter relationship. She described Jean Voss as not a very nice lady. She said that she kicked Carol out and Carol came to her, and live with her then boyfriend's parents for a while and then she got a council house and the workers at S. R. Gents had a whip-round to buy her some things for the house.

She was asked about the tattoo. She said, "It was horrible. It was a rose and a scroll with the names, Sam and Caz, on". Carol told her that dad had had it put on when she was about 13 and that Sam had been his nickname when he worked on the fairgrounds.

She described Carol as being sometimes okay and sometimes in a mess. "She cried a lot". You'll remember she gave this description of her putting her hair in her mouth when she was thinking. "She told me at the time...that at the time that she'd had the tattoo put on that her father had raped her, that he was a bad man who'd smacked her and her siblings. We tried to cover up the tattoos with make-up but it didn't work, it always came off, and I would go with Carol to the tattoo shop for removal. It was very painful. I was about 19 when that happened, and we went to rape counselling together in Sheffield after finishing work at S. R. Gents on the Friday. Carol did speak to me in those days about a metal box which contained photographs and a hairbrush. She was about 16 or 17 when she told me that.

"I believe that I have seen Mr Appleyard twice. The first time was in Barnsley. I had gone there with Carol to meet Janet, who was at that time engaged to Mr Appleyard". You'll remember the point that Mr Storey has made that in her account to the police, Carol didn't mention anybody else being there. I don't think Carol was ever actually asked about that in cross-examination, so I don't think it was ever clarified and, anyway, there it is.

She said that she had kept somewhat in the background. She really didn't want, obviously, to be part of this. She said, "I waited outside a shop called Dancerama and Carol went off to a pie and pea stall", and she never actually saw Janet but she did see a man in a checked shirt and, "When Carol returned, she was in a terrible state. She was hyperventilating, her legs were like jelly and she said, 'It's my father'. She told me that he had said that he was sorry but that he loved her as a wife and not as a child. I was so concerned about her that we got a taxi and went to my parents.

"The second time I think I saw him was when we were in Barnsley town centre and we saw a man and Carol said, 'That's my dad'. She was panicky. She was convinced that he had come to get her. I became really worried about her and I begged her to go to a doctor's, which she did, and she received some antidepressants and we went together to the rape counsellors on a number of occasions. She was about 19 then".

In cross-examination, she said, "Well, as to what really happened, I am reliant on what Carol told me", although, of course, her observations are her own. For example, she was asked...well, she'd described the scabbing from the tattoo artist's attempts to remove the tattoos sticking to the sheets. She said, "Well, I didn't see that. I was told about that but I did see the scabs", so there is an example, I suppose, of things that she saw and things that she was told. That's always something that you need to bear in mind.

"I am still in contact with Carol but not as much as previously. We've got our own lives to live. I made my statement in July", sorry, "June 2017. We did talk about it then. She asked my opinion about naming her father again. It was massive for her. She did ask if I would give a statement".

Just pausing there, of course, it's important for you to know how the statements were taken and how witnesses were contacted and it's undoubtedly the case that it's largely been as a result of what Carol Higgins has done, but you also know that she was told to do it by the police and you have to consider whether or not the way that it has happened, which I think is not really the subject of criticism of itself, could nevertheless have led people to say things...or been led to say things by Carol or whether they are really their own recollections. They've all been asked about it and they have all said, "She did speak to me, she did tell me things and she did ask me to make a statement but what I am telling you is what I remember". They've all said that, and it's a matter... That's an issue and quite an important one for you to look at. I make no further comment about it, just to make sure you've got the two sides of the argument well in mind.

Carron Ward, she was a neighbour of the Appleyards back in the 1980s but she was quite significantly older than Carol, about 10 years older. She described Carol at the time as a very frightened and timid child. When she was about 15, so at that time Carol would have been only five, she saw Mr Appleyard in the street and she said that, "He said to me, 'Has your dad broke you in yet? All dads do it to their daughters'". She said, "It came back to me after I read Carol's book about three years ago in about 2016".

She was asked, in cross-examination, about two statements that she'd made. She'd made one in September 2014 and one in October 2015. Between the two and nearer to the second, in August 2015, the book launch - I think it seems to be the second book launch but the one that took place in Denby Dale - had taken place and she had attended at that book launch and had a conversation with Carol.

There was no mention of this conversation in the first statement and so what was put to her is, "Well, you've had this idea put in your head at the book launch, or possibly at some other time, and that is where it has all come from". "No", she said. "I remember the circumstances. It wasn't something that I thought about for years but I remember the circumstances. It was a conversation with Mr Appleyard. I was at the end of my garden path and he was walking by in the street. I am sure that I remember this accurately. It is not a result of what Carol said to me. I remember it".

The statement of Ena Whittle was read to you. That was about love bites. I don't want to say anything more about that to you.

Next, Deanna Thorpe, a niece of Mr Appleyard, her mother was his sister, Rose: they lived in Scissett in the mid to late-eighties, and she said, "In that time, in the mid to late-eighties, Carol came to see me. She told me that her father had been sexually abusing her, having sex with her, making her do oral sex, things like that. She was very distressed. She was struggling to get it out, she was crying so much". She thought Carol would have been about 19 then. "She said that it started after her mum had left. I think she said that she had told her mother and that her mother had said that she should tell the police".

She then described an incident when she had previously visited No. 26. She said she'd gone there. She'd knocked on the door. There was no answer. The door was unlocked so she'd gone in. She'd gone into the kitchen. She'd shouted, "Hello" a few times. Because she had assumed that, with the door unlocked, they couldn't be far away, she put the kettle on and after a few minutes Mr Appleyard and Carol came downstairs. They both looked dishevelled, as though they had just got out of bed. Carol", she said, "looked very unhappy". She thought that Carol would have been about 12 or 13 at the time.

She was cross-examined. She said, "Carol came to see me because I had revealed that I had been abused by my mother and she came to support me. We were both very upset. I've had no contact with Carol after this", although there had been apparently a visit when Carol came with Paul about a fortnight later but after that they had not met again or had any contact.

"How", she was asked, "did you come to make your statement in February 2016?" She said, "Carol got in touch over the internet and asked if I would make a statement and, of course, I would. Carol wanted me to tell the police about visits or what had been said or if I remembered or had seen anything", and she was specifically asked about the visit to No. 26, which, as you know, is challenged by Mr Appleyard.

She said, "I was in the area. I popped in. I thought they'd be back soon as the door was unlocked so I put the kettle on". She was asked, "Well, what do you mean by dishevelled or looking as though they've just got out of bed?"

She said, "Well, hair all over the place, clothes as though they'd just been put on and not fully tucked in. They were dressed", and, again, she was asked, "Well, is this the result of what Carol has said to you?" She said, "This is not a result of what Carol has said". She said, "I can remember it. It was in the afternoon. I'm 100 per cent certain". Put to her, "I suggest that this never happened", her answer was, "You can suggest all you want but it did happen".

Diane Croft, similar age to Carol and knew her through school, she said, "She told me that her father was messing about with her. She described touching and I asked her what she meant. I thought, 'Well, that just might be play-fighting', but she said, 'No', and she described touching and kissing. She was about 13 or 14. It was on a public bridleway. We were going for a walk in Denby Dale. It was near the river. I took her home to tell my parents. They were shocked but I can't remember if any action was taken", and later she said that at the time her family had just suffered the loss of her...the death of her brother and they had other things on their minds. "This", she said, *"was before she went to live...Carol went to live with her mother in Penistone".

She was cross-examined. She said, "I think this was in 1983, 1984, 1983. Carol agreed that she should tell an adult. It wasn't clear to me if she had told her mother at that stage. At the time my family was grieving the loss of my brother. I only saw Carol once after this because I was off school myself for quite a while. We did resume contact later but we didn't discuss what she had told me. I made my statement in January 2018. Carol contacted me in October 2017. She did make it clear why she was contacting me and we did speak about our memories. I wasn't aware that that phone call was recorded but we were not getting our heads together to give a false account".

Well, as you know, the additional page of unused...of agreed facts relates to Diane Croft and it's a matter for you to determine what all of this means and whether it casts doubt on her evidence. It is a fact that these things were said. It is also a fact that, having recorded this telephone conversation and, obviously, the defence have got it so there's nothing in the contents of what she's saying that they proposed to cross-examine her about so there obviously is no material there that is inconsistent with her account. It's a question of tone really, and you've got it. You make what you will, but remember that this material is in the hands of the defence because Carol Higgins gave it to the police, and the prosecution therefore, of course, have disclosed it to the defence to allow them to make what use of it they wish. "Were you getting your heads together?" she was asked. "No" she said, "we were not".

That was it for civilian witnesses, and Sergeant Wilson, the officer in the case, gave evidence. He told you that he'd been involved since September 2015 and he described the difficulties of the relationship and that one of the things we'll see in the main part of the agreed facts is that they gave Carol Higgins what is known as a harassment warning although, as you see from the agreed facts, that doesn't mean she'd actually done anything wrong but things had been said and maybe she had, maybe she hadn't, but there it is. You know something about that. I'm really not going to go into that any further, but she was given a harassment warning. No doubt, Sergeant Wilson thought that some of the things she was doing weren't terribly wise. At all events - I've already described - one of the first things I said to you yesterday was about the difficulties of their relationship and how you should consider that. I'll say no more about it.

He did his best to try and discover what material was still available. He'd looked for the documents in police files and Crown Prosecution files. They'd all been destroyed. The policy was to destroy these things after 10 years. He was able to find counselling notes. We haven't seen any of the counselling notes, so obviously nothing arises out of them that anybody wishes to put to Carol Higgins is potentially inconsistent and neither Kirklees Social Services nor any of the schools that he was able to visit have kept any records, so they've done their best to try and check all these things. There is really, essentially, no material except for the counselling notes.

He told us about the interviews. You've got those interviews. I'm not going to take you through them, not because they are not significant - of course, they are - they are Mr Appleyard's first, well, actually probably not his first account because, of course, we know that he was interviewed in earlier parts of the investigation, but the first account in this investigation at least and it is undoubtedly the case that he denied all matters throughout those interviews, as he has done in his evidence.

The only matter that I do remind you about is that in neither of these interviews - one is in 2015 and one a year later in 2016 - does he give an account of the telephone call from Jean to the Pie Hall being about accusing him of sexually abusing Carol. He does talk about a telephone call which was about something totally different, about Carol having found her brothers and father living up somewhere further north, and the prosecution make the point that, when considering phone calls to the Pie Hall, it would be difficult to imagine anybody forgetting the first time that he was told that his daughter had accused him of sexual abuse, entirely a matter for you what you make of that. That is the Crown's argument, so they say that in these interviews, even though he is denying matters, you can be sure, they say, that he was covering up that phone call. A matter for you what you make of it. Mr Appleyard accepts now that that phone call was made and that he was told that Carol was accusing him of sexual abuse at that stage.

Of course, he was asked questions in cross-examination and this is what he said. "Carol gave me a list of names and areas for investigation. She gave me a copy of her book. Some people were easy to contact, some weren't. It was a difficult relationship. She made it clear that she didn't think I was investigating properly. She did say that bodies might be buried on the land that was up for auction. She believed that her father was part of a paedophile ring.

"She did record" - I'm sorry - "provide recordings of the conversations with witnesses and we did have to talk to her about her involvement and gave her this harassment warning. The problems were really about the Facebook. She'd set up a page. The file was passed to the Crown Prosecution Service in July 2017. They were not proposing to take it any further but that decision was appealed and reviewed and changed". He agreed, when asked in re-examination, that the onus was on Carol Higgins to provide the information.

Mr Appleyard... Is everybody still okay? Sure? Yeah, okay. Mr Appleyard himself gave evidence. He said, "I am not responsible for these offences". He described meeting Jean in about 1967 while he was working on a fairground, that in March 1968 he received a telegram that she'd given birth to a daughter. That was Donna. A little later she turned up at his home and, although he understood that Donna was not his, he persuaded his parents to let her and Donna stay. They were married - and we know this is the case - it's in the agreed facts - in 1974 and they had lived firstly at No. 8 and then at No. 26 Gilthwaites Crescent, as we know.

He said, "Our relationship was not too bad. We had arguments like any couple but then there were rumours about Jean having affairs. I have never hit her. I may have threatened her during arguments. She would leave home. She went to a farm; she went to a refuge", although he says that he was told that she'd told lies about why she was there and they threw her out - there is no direct evidence about that at all - but she would come back. “I did have guns and a machete. If I held a gun to Jean’s head, it would be in the heat of the moment.

“The children were fine when they were little. They’d get a clip to the ear if they were naughty but I did not use my belt on them, but school attendance was always a problem”.

So far as work were concerned, he said he registered as self-employed in 1972 but he worked all the time, in construction mostly. He also collected scrap to fund the holidays that they took but he never did that, he said, with Carol.

About the dog, Sam, he said, “Yes, I did shoot him”. He gave a description as to the circumstances and as to why he had done that but, he said, “Carol was not there. I’ve never said this, ‘Who loves you, baby?’ That is something from Kojak.

“Jean left for the last time on a Friday”, and he described the circumstances. He said that he’d said to her in the morning, “It’s pay day but there’s no money for you. When I get back, I want you gone. The kids can go or stay. It’s up to them”. That, he said, was the circumstances in which Jean first came to leave him and took Carol with her. It was, he said, at the back end of 1982. “I didn’t even know where they had gone. Jean did ring up for some money. She said they were in Penistone and after about three months Carol returned. She told me that mum was always out and that she was left on her own.

“In 1983”, he said, “I was working five and a half days a week in Garforth, building a dam. I was burnt out. Jean was asking for money. The suicide attempt had nothing to do with Carol.

"The trip to Scandinavia took place in 1983". He did not, he said, have sex with Carol on the boat or indeed anywhere else. The trip to the United States, which he took with a friend, he said took place in November/December 1983. It had lasted for three weeks.

He was asked specifically, "Well, what do you say about all of these matters?" He denied each matter in turn. He said, "I had no mucky mags. I never saw Carol walking around the house in her underwear. The children would only get into bed with me on a Sunday morning and we would simply be there planning our day. Paul has never been locked out of the house, at least never deliberately. The snogging never happened. The most I have done is give Carol a fatherly kiss. On the cruise there was no incident when I was having sex with Carol. If Paul couldn't get back into the cabin it was because he did not have a card, a cardboard key card, in order to get back in. Carol did have some love bites at one point. She had got them at school, kids messing about".

He came back then to the trip that he had taken to the United States. He said, "The children were supposed to be at Hilda's but they had a party. They had drunk my wine and my beer. Carol had had sex in my bed. I went mad. Paul told me that lads were sleeping over with Carol. I do not recall Carol cutting her wrists. The children slept alone that night. I wasn't going to comfort them. I told them they could bugger off with their mother. Before Christmas 1983 Carol did just that and went to her mother's". This would be then for the second time. "I have never known precisely where that was.

"I do have a metal chest, I did have at the time, but there are no photographs in it. I have never taken photographs of Carol. I have never had a Polaroid camera. There was no hairbrush there. I am not aware that Carol ever believed that she was pregnant. The visit to Penistone with Hilda and Peter did not occur. I don't recall making the comment about fathers breaking in their daughters to Jean. I did not say it to Carron. I never got on with that family at all.

"In April 1984" - and we know that this is correct from our agreed facts - "I got custody of Carol and Paul. They spoke to the magistrate. It was actually in the county court so it would have been a county court judge, but that is probably an entirely forgivable mistake. "Carol was with me for about three or four months. She told me that she wasn't getting any love or attention or clothes from her mother. If we rowed, which we sometimes did, I would tell her to piss off back to her mother. I can't recall why she left again. By then I was in a relationship" - in my notes I've put Janet but I think probably he will have said Jess, yeah, Jess. "Carol was never at No. 26" - and, again, my note says - "when Janet came to live with me". I may be wrong about that. That may be Jess.

UNKNOWN COUNSEL: I think it was Janet, in fact, your Honour, there.

JUDGE JAMESON: Yeah. Thank you. "I do now remember Jean calling the Pie Hall. She said, 'Carol's told me everything. We're going to the police. She says that she's had sex with you'. I said, 'I hope you can fucking prove it' and put the phone down. I did not remember this when I was interviewed in 1984". It can't be 1984. Sorry, that must be my error, the first of the interviews, 2014.

He spoke about his recollection of an incident on the Barnsley market when he'd gone there with Janet. This is now definitely Janet when she was engaged to be married to him, and she said...he said, "This was about 12 to 18 months after I had been first interviewed, which was in 1984", he said. "Carol had rung to talk and I met her with Janet. I did not apologise to her. The whole incident had no effect on me whatsoever". The Crown ask you to contrast that with the evidence of Julie Clarke about how Carol reacted to it, but a matter for you. "I did not apologise to her. She did come round to my house for Father's Day and she texted me on a number of occasions in 2007 and 2009.

"In 2015 her book was put through my letter box. It meant nothing to me. I had no idea who Carol Higgins was. A book was sent to the Pie Hall, of which I was by that time chairman, and flyers were put on windscreens of cars round about Denby Dale with my name on. I was interviewed again in 2016. I was told that I would not be prosecuted and then later I was told that I would be".

He was asked a number of questions in cross-examination. I'll deal with it as swiftly as I can. He said, "Yes, these allegations are appalling but I cannot remember Jean's, or I could not remember Jean's call to the Pie Hall to tell me for the first time what Carol had said when I was interviewed in 2015. I don't know when it came back to me, perhaps the same day or maybe the following day". He was then asked to look at his second interview, which again you've got, December 2016, and, as we know, there's no reference to it in that interview either. When that was pointed out, he said...

(The Clerk of the Court conferred with Judge Jameson)

JUDGE JAMESON: I'm very sorry, ladies and gentlemen. For some reason, I need to rise - I don't know why - but could I just ask? Is it all right if the jury just wait outside?

THE CLERK OF THE COURT: Yes.

JUDGE JAMESON: If you'd be kind enough just to wait in your room outside, I'll get back to you as quickly as I can.

(The jury left court at 12.02 p.m.)

JUDGE JAMESON: Sorry, I've got to just rise for a moment. I've no idea what this is about.

(12.03 p.m.)

(12.04 p.m.)

JUDGE JAMESON: Right, we've got a slight difficulty. I hope we'll be able to manage it appropriately, but you need to know about it and certainly Mr Appleyard needs to be aware of it. The reasons for the urgency is because the court staff have just received a telephone call from somebody who works at the LGI who is very concerned because the person who made the phone call – I don't actually know if it's a man or a woman; I think it's a woman, but it doesn't matter – has indicated that one of our jurors works with her on, I think, the Brotherton Wing and has at some point during the course of the trial been at work. No reason why that shouldn't happen, of course.

MR STOREY: No.

JUDGE JAMESON: But the person's concern is that she had been talking in the staff room about the case and mentioning – the only two words I've got written down are "rape" and "knickers". I'm not quite sure where the knickers come from, although I suppose there's been some talk about pants being taken down for beatings. That's it. That's as much as I know.

Now, it's unfortunate. I suspect that it's not going to be more than that but the question is how best to deal with it. I think probably there should be – I haven't had much more time than you have to think about it, but I think there probably should be some sort of investigation into it, if only to ensure that there has been – dissemination of information is unfortunate and contrary to my directions but not actually that important to the process. It's potentially the receiving of information or the discussions and expressions of opinion and that sort of thing that would matter.

Now, there are a number of ways, I suppose, we can deal with this. I mean, one way is simply to discharge that juror, full stop. Another is to make some investigations first and discuss together whether we think that that is a necessary step or – it ultimately has to be my decision but I would welcome, of course, your help with it. I think those are really the two ways.

MR STOREY: Yes.

JUDGE JAMESON: We either just take the dramatic step now and say, "Right, that's it. This witness – this juror goes" and that brings us down to 11, of course. Sometimes defence counsel are concerned about this. I confess I'm never entirely sure why because from the defence point of view, 11 seems to be rather a good idea, or I always used to think so, but, you know, there it is and you would have to speak with Mr Appleyard, of course, and you will have to before you make any response at all.

MR STOREY: Thank you.

JUDGE JAMESON: But those on the face of it seem to be the obvious things to do. Either we discharge that juror full stop or I make some enquiries and we decide where we go.

MR STOREY: Yes. Can we assume that the information that the court has does not include a means of contacting the source?

JUDGE JAMESON: Sorry, do not include?

MR STOREY: Any means to recontact the person who called the court.

JUDGE JAMESON: Oh, no. It does.

MR STOREY: It does?

JUDGE JAMESON: Yes, we can.

MR STOREY: Thank you.

JUDGE JAMESON: Or there's a phone number.

MR STOREY: Can I...

JUDGE JAMESON: At least, I think actually the phone number is that witness's manager rather than – sorry, I say, "witness".

THE CLERK OF THE COURT: She wouldn't give her name.

MR STOREY: No.

JUDGE JAMESON: But yes, the person is...

MR STOREY: I was thinking merely in terms of the nature of any inquiry that the court or inquiries that the court could conduct because of course if we didn't...

JUDGE JAMESON: Well, I suppose we could try and get that person back on the phone.

MR STOREY: The reality is, of course, that whoever he or she is...

JUDGE JAMESON: I think it's a she.

MR STOREY: ...felt sufficiently strongly about that which had taken place to feel it was incumbent upon them to contact the court.

JUDGE JAMESON: Yes, yes.

MR STOREY: Whether or not they know the trial is still ongoing. I wonder if I could speak with Mr Appleyard before I make any further submissions to your Honour?

JUDGE JAMESON: I think you should. Yes, absolutely. Right. I think what we'll do, Jo, is give apologies to the jury, say that we will probably be about 15 minutes or something like that, so if they'd like to go back to their retiring – they can stay where they are, of course, but if they want to go back and relax or do anything, they're welcome to do so. I'll try and get back to them at, say, half past 12. That gives them a bit of an idea. We are not tied to that, of course, gentlemen.

MR STOREY: No, thank you.

JUDGE JAMESON: If we need more time, we'll take as long as we need, but I just want to manage the jury at the moment. I would like them to think that this isn't going to take terribly long, at least for the moment. If it does, well, we'll have to change things. Okay? Right, thank you very much. I'll rise then. Unless you just want to have a word with Mr Appleyard – I don't want you to rush this.

MR STOREY: No.

JUDGE JAMESON: Mr Appleyard needs to know you're dealing with it fully.

MR STOREY: Thank you. I think I'd prefer it if your Honour did rise.

JUDGE JAMESON: Yes. Let me know when you are ready.

(12.11 p.m.)

(12.27 p.m.)

(In the absence of the jury)

MR STOREY: Your Honour, thank you for the time you allowed me to speak with Mr Appleyard.

JUDGE JAMESON: Not at all. Just before you say anything at all, Mr Storey, I haven't at the moment thought it necessary to separate this juror off. I don't think...

MR STOREY: No.

JUDGE JAMESON: ...this is the sort of case where there seems to be, on the face of it, any necessity for that at the moment.

MR STOREY: No, at the moment. Having discussed it with Mr Appleyard...

JUDGE JAMESON: Yeah.

MR STOREY: ...my submission is, essentially in brief, that the juror should be discharged.

JUDGE JAMESON: Yes.

MR STOREY: I think that is a submission with which the prosecution agree.

JUDGE JAMESON: Well, that's certainly the simplest way forward.

MR STOREY: Yes. I understand your Honour's comments about numbers when defending. I don't have concerns that others do about that sort of thing.

JUDGE JAMESON: No.

MR STOREY: The next step, or there are several consequent steps, if your Honour is in agreement that the juror should be discharged, first and foremost how that is done, whether the juror is brought into court on his or her own and told, "You're being discharged". I suspect there may be some prospect of belongings still being in court so he or she may have to come back into court anyway, whether the juror is told by your Honour in our presence why it is he or she is being discharged, and then, so far as the remaining 11 are concerned, it might be, and I would, with respect, invite your Honour to strongly consider doing this, it might be that they should be reminded again of your direction not to discuss the details of the case outside their number...

JUDGE JAMESON: Yes.

MR STOREY: ...not to undertake any online research into the case whatsoever because there remains, given the nature of what we know about this case, an underlying concern that there may have been some attempt to contact the complainant or, at the very least, to look at her Facebook posts, which are, of course, in the public domain.

JUDGE JAMESON: Yes.

MR STOREY: And also a reminder that they should not allow themselves to be influenced by anything they have heard or seen outside their number, and that, of course, would include anything they might have been told by the juror who, by the time your Honour addresses the 11 of them, will have been discharged, because we don't know...

JUDGE JAMESON: Yeah. Well, I just need to ask Mr Hampton first. Mr Hampton, you agree that the best course is to discharge the juror, without more?

MR HAMPTON: Yes, we agree with...discharge is the...

JUDGE JAMESON: Yeah.

MR HAMPTON: ...most pragmatic way forward.

JUDGE JAMESON: Yeah, well, I think it is, frankly, otherwise we're going to spend a lot of time...

MR HAMPTON: Agreed.

JUDGE JAMESON: ...debating and we'll probably wind up...

MR HAMPTON: In the same place.

JUDGE JAMESON: ...in the position where she says, "Oh, it's all been misinterpreted and I didn't say this", but I think it's the safer course, frankly.

MR STOREY: Yes.

MR HAMPTON: Our fear is, pragmatically, whatever the result of an enquiry, she'd be distracted from trying this case dispassionately...

JUDGE JAMESON: Well, quite.

MR HAMPTON: ...and clinically. Could I just...

JUDGE JAMESON: Well quite.

MR HAMPTON: Sorry.

JUDGE JAMESON: Right, so I think really that juror needs to come in on her own first.

UNKNOWN COUNSEL: Yeah.

JUDGE JAMESON: I think it's probably only courteous to indicate that we have received some information, that I am not asking her to comment on it, that I am not making any findings about it but that, on a practical basis, I've made the decision that she will be discharged. She will also be discharged, of course, from further attendance at this court, full stop, reminded that she is no longer now part of the jury and she must not therefore have any further communication with those who are and, as far as she's concerned, that's it. I am...

UNKNOWN COUNSEL: Yes.

JUDGE JAMESON: ...not proposing to invite the Attorney General to investigate this matter. I don't think it's got remotely near that stage, and that's it, finish. Then we'll have the remaining jurors back in. I'll make... They will obviously realise that something is happening and I'll tell them that they are now 11, that we've discharged one of their number. I think it would be unrealistic not to, if I give the directions, and I agree that I should, or remind them, I should say, of the...

UNKNOWN COUNSEL: Yes.

JUDGE JAMESON: ...directions, and I agree that I should, as Mr Storey has said, it would be unrealistic if they don't realise, put two and two together that that's something to do with the discharge of the other juror...

UNKNOWN COUNSEL: Yes.

JUDGE JAMESON: ...so I think I will just say something very neutral about the fact that information has been received which has meant that I've had to discharge that juror and, in the light of that, I just want to make it absolutely plain to them that these directions apply and are extremely important.

MR HAMPTON: This is to do with discussing matters outside the jury room, not to social media. I wouldn't want the jury to be left with any impression by mistake that this is anything to do, for example, with the complainant's Facebooking activities.

JUDGE JAMESON: Yeah.

MR HAMPTON: It's not, so I don't know if your Honour would make it clear that it's got nothing to do with any party in the case, and I don't think it's necessary to give the reminder about social media. There's no basis for that about this issue. Your Honour can remind them not to discuss it with people not involved in the case. That's the issue.

JUDGE JAMESON: Well, I think what I will do, I...I agree, it's probably sensible if I do indicate that that's the...discussing the case with others outside the jury panel is the matter that has caused concern...

MR HAMPTON: Yes.

JUDGE JAMESON: ...but, to make sure it's doubly sure, I think I will go through all of the directions again just to ensure that they've got them all in mind whilst making plain that it's actually only that narrow issue that has arisen.

MR HAMPTON: Thank you, yes, and nothing to do with the...

JUDGE JAMESON: Yeah, I'm quite happy to do that.

MR HAMPTON: Thank you.

JUDGE JAMESON: All right? Okay, well, thank you both very much indeed for your help with that. Then, in those circumstances, we'll have that single juror brought down to court first and discharged, and I'm just wondering whether we ought to allow a few moments for her...I don't quite know...what will happen to her then? You see, I don't want her, as it were, going back...

MR STOREY: I suspect once...

JUDGE JAMESON: Could I just ask you? Just before you go, can I just check exactly physically what's going to happen because, obviously, the juror will leave court through that door. What will then happen to her, because I don't want her going...I don't want any more contact between her and the remaining 11.

THE CLERK OF THE COURT: No. I was thinking that I can just bring her on her own...

JUDGE JAMESON: Can that be achieved? Do you need somebody else with you to help with that?

THE CLERK OF THE COURT: I will get somebody to help me, yes.

JUDGE JAMESON: Right. I think we could do with getting another, at least temporarily, please, another usher in, Joe, so that one can take away our discharged juror and the other can bring in our remaining 11, keeping them apart, and by the time we get to...

UNKNOWN COUNSEL: Yes.

JUDGE JAMESON: ...one o'clock, then I would hope that the discharged juror will have left the building.

(<u>The Clerk of the Court conferred with Judge Jameson</u>)

JUDGE JAMESON: All right, so you probably need just to sort that out, do you, first? All right, well, I'll rise while you do that. Okay. Fine, thank you.

(<u>12.34 p.m.</u>)

(<u>Short break</u>)

(<u>12.43 p.m.</u>)

JUDGE JAMESON: Right, we've now got two ladies in who'll help. Just before I carry on, Mr Storey, the Criminal Procedure Rules do indicate that all of this is supposed to happen in what is described as open court. I rather take the view that this is open court. I have asked for the public gallery not to be present because these are sensitive matters...

MR STOREY: Thank you.

JUDGE JAMESON: ...and I just don't want anybody reacting inappropriately.

MR STOREY: No. Once your Honour...

JUDGE JAMESON: So...

MR STOREY: Sorry.

JUDGE JAMESON: If you feel that anybody should have been in court while all this was done, please say so now. I just take the view that, essentially, this is open court but with the public not in.

MR STOREY: Yes. I think, given the sensitivities and...

JUDGE JAMESON: It's recorded.

MR STOREY: ...the undercurrents...

JUDGE JAMESON: Mr Appleyard is here.

MR STOREY: ...in the case, your Honour's view is right that it was better that the public gallery be cleared. Obviously at a point when your Honour has sent the jury out - whether we achieve that before lunch or not, I don't know now - but, once that position has been reached, then the prosecution will, of course, be entitled and they may well be asked by Miss Higgins and those who are with her for an explanation...

JUDGE JAMESON: Actually, that is a very good point. What are we going to do about them? They'll want to hear the end of the summing-up.

MR STOREY: We can't stop them being in...

JUDGE JAMESON: But I don't particularly want them to hear and/or react to what I say to our 11 jurors. I suppose it won't matter that much.

MR HAMPTON: If I were to be allowed a quick word to say that there be an explanation as to what's happening to the jury with the public gallery in attendance and there shouldn't be any reaction.

JUDGE JAMESON: Yes.

MR HAMPTON: That would...

JUDGE JAMESON: All right. Well, I don't want them in when I have the single juror here.

MR HAMPTON: No.

MR STOREY: I agree.

JUDGE JAMESON: When that's happened, bring them in then, have a word with them...

MR HAMPTON: Give me a word for a moment (sic)...a moment for a word.

JUDGE JAMESON: Yeah, if you just have a word with them and say that they're going to hear something about...the trial will continue but...

MR HAMPTON: Yeah.

JUDGE JAMESON: ...it will continue with 11 jurors, they'll hear something, they must not react to what they hear.

MR HAMPTON: Yes.

JUDGE JAMESON: Okay? Yeah, all right, thank you. Yeah, so we'll get the single juror in first, please. Thank you.

(Juror entered court)

JUDGE JAMESON: Hello. Do come on in and sit down. I'm sorry to have to bring you back in on your own. You're probably wondering what's happening.

JUROR: Yeah.

JUDGE JAMESON: The court has received some information which gives ground to be concerned that you may have been discussing the case at work. Now, can I just say that I'm not asking you to react to this. I'm not going to make any sort of an enquiry about it.

JUROR: Mmm.

JUDGE JAMESON: But it has left us in a position where, having discussed matters with counsel, I take the view that the safest and simplest and quickest, I have to say, thing to do is to discharge you from being a part of the jury. I'm sorry if that's a disappointment to you, having heard all of the evidence, but it's something that I need to do, given the information that we've received. As I say, I'm not judging the rights and wrongs of it, but I have to make a pragmatic decision and that's what it is.

JUROR: All right.

JUDGE JAMESON: So I am going to discharge you from further attendance on this jury or, indeed, further attendance at jury service at all.

JUROR: Yeah.

JUDGE JAMESON: So what's going to happen to you now is that you will simply leave with one of our ladies, I think, is it - yeah, this lady here - through that door actually because I don't want you going past the other jurors. Now, I don't think that you'll be seeing them again because I'll be bringing them in and your jury attendance has finished but, in the event that you were to do so, please remember that you are now no longer part of the jury, so...

JUROR: Okay.

JUDGE JAMESON: ...you mustn't talk to them about the case or indeed at all...

JUROR: All right.

JUDGE JAMESON: ...if you were to see them before you actually leave the building. Okay? All right? Thank you very much for your service. That's it.

(Juror left court)

JUDGE JAMESON: Right. If you'd be kind enough just to pop outside, Mr Hampton? (After a pause)

MR HAMPTON: Thank you, your Honour.

JUDGE JAMESON: All right?

MR HAMPTON: Yeah.

JUDGE JAMESON: Well, they can come on in now then, yeah.

MR HAMPTON: The usher is just removing the sign.

(The public gallery was reopened)

JUDGE JAMESON: Yeah. Right, thank you very much for bearing with us, ladies and gentlemen. You're going to hear a little bit. I'm going to have to give an explanation to our jurors as to what's been happening but, in brief, I've, on a pragmatic basis, had to discharge one juror. The trial will continue with the remaining 11. I just need to say something to them about what's happening so you will hear that. Please don't react to it at all. We're just going to carry on. Okay? Thank you.

(The jury returned to court at 12.50 p.m.)

JUDGE JAMESON: Welcome back, ladies and gentlemen. I'm sorry to have kept you out for a little longer than we had hoped. Right, you're now 11, as you will see. You need to know, at least in rough terms, why that is so that you're not left speculating.

What has happened is that the court has received information that the juror who is no longer with us, who I have discharged from being part of your jury, may have been speaking at work with others about the trial. If that has happened, that would be in breach, obviously, of the directions that I gave you all at the start of the trial and, of course, it gives rise to the possibility that, in discussion, she might have heard things that might influence her.

Now, I don't know the rights and wrongs of that and, rather than launching a lengthy investigation into it, which would delay the trial, I have taken the view on a pragmatic basis that the safest thing to do is to discharge that juror from being part of the jury anymore, so that's what's happened. Don't, please, worry about it, concern yourselves about it or even think or talk about it anymore. It's happened; it's in the past. You now are 11 jurors and we carry on exactly as before.

What I do want to do before I finish my summing-up, and I'm going to do that before the adjournment so that you can make a start on your important work, what I do just want to do is just to remind you, and I'm sure - this is only out of an abundance of caution - just to remind you what the directions were, which were, number 1, don't, please, discuss the case with anybody outside your own number, now the 11 of you, and when you're all together and when you're in private, and the reasons are exactly as we've just seen because, if you do or it's thought that you have done, then I may have to take action, as I've done for this other juror, so that's why it's so important, because everybody in court needs to know that you are making your decisions on the evidence and on nothing else, uninfluenced by what anybody else may say.

The second direction, as you know - this isn't what's said to have happened here but just to remind you out of an abundance of caution, because it's so important in this case because there is so much material, we know, on the internet and on social media about the case - critical that you don't search or anything of that nature for that material or make any investigations of any kind into the facts of the case. You just judge the evidence you've heard in the courtroom, so I just remind you of that - not suggested that that's happened here, but I do just remind you of that direction as well.

Right, thank you very much. Will you now put all of that, remembering the directions, but put the reason for me reminding you of them, the discharge of the juror, out of your minds. Let's go back and concentrate for probably no more now than, I hope, 10 or 15 minutes at most, I trust, just to complete my review of the evidence.

I was reminding you of Mr Appleyard's evidence and about matters that were put to him in cross-examination and I had reminded you that he was being asked about, essentially, in brief, what the Crown were saying, "Well, these...if you accept that these allegations are appalling and you accept that you were told about them, then you did not say that to the police. You were covering it up". Whether you accept that analysis is entirely a matter for you, but that was what was being put to Mr Appleyard.

He accepted that it wasn't in either of the two interviews, the one in 2015 or 2016, and, ultimately, he said this. "I don't know what triggered it. It may have...my memory of it. It may have been discussions with my solicitor, but what I did say to the police in my interviews about the call to the Pie Hall about Jean finding her family was true. That did happen as well. Hilda, my sister's account of a visit with me and her husband, Peter, to Penistone, to see Jean is a lie. That did not happen. I did not know Jean's address".

He was asked about the tattoo. He said, "Well, the children got what they wanted. I did not ask who Sam was when Sam was put on the tattoos".

He was asked, essentially, questions going to the issue about, "Well, why might Carol be saying this if it isn't true?" Bear in mind, of course, the direction that I've given you that Mr Appleyard, no defendant, is required to prove innocence and it's not for Mr Appleyard to prove a reason why this might be untrue but it, of course, remains an important question for you to consider and so it was entirely legitimate for him to be asked questions designed to reveal if there was any obvious reason for it, and he said, "Well, I thought I was a good husband and father. I was bringing in money. I may have been firm with the children but no more than that. The children had nothing to worry about. I've never beaten any of them with a belt and I've never beaten my wife. I have no recollection of her urinating in the kitchen. I have never pointed a gun at her head. I'm not saying, however, that I might not have had a gun in my hand when we were arguing.

"Carol did come home to live with me after I had been interviewed by the police in the 1980s. She'd been thrown out by her mother and I wasn't going to turn her away. She came back several times. I don't know why she left again. I was saying that I didn't want letters from school and arguments and I'd had enough.

"Paul's account of the evidence of violence within the household is false. He stayed with me until September 1988. At that time he was supposed to be paying £20 a week for his keep but Janet told me that he had not done that for some five or six weeks and I told him, 'I'm not a fucking bus driver. We don't have passengers', and he left. I did not chase him with a pitchfork. I have not spoken to him since 1989. His evidence is lies because he is sticking up for his sister.

"Deanna Thorpe" - who spoke about the incident of him coming downstairs with Carol - "has never been to my house so that account is untrue. Carol's account is simply lies. I think that this is about the money. The solicitors looked into my affairs". You will remember there's an agreed fact that they wrote a letter indicating that they had done that and that he had no assets and she has applied...Carol has applied for compensation. We know that she has. Again, that's in the agreed facts. It's entirely a matter for you to consider whether that is what all this is about but, of course, in doing that, you will remember that these allegations were first made in the 1980s, decades before the solicitors were instructed and Carol made any application for compensation.

"Carron Ward, about me saying, 'Has your dad broken you in yet?' that did not happen. We were neighbours but we never got on. There wasn't a dispute as such. There was some argument about lighting a bonfire in the garden but I simply never said that".

Hilda: he was asked about his sister. "Why would your sister lie about you?" "Well, we had arguments in 1985 or 1986. One New Year's Eve I went for a drink with her husband and she accused me of trying to break us up, but we'd been friends until then".

Sarah Thomas gave evidence, the final live witness in the case. She is Mr Appleyard's niece. His brother is her father. She told you that she was at Shelley High School in 1984 and 1985 and that Carol, who was a year above her, came and put an arm around her and claimed to be very close. She said she wasn't. She described that as being a blatant lie - a matter for you to determine whether that aspect of her evidence takes matters much further, whether Carol claiming to be or wanting to be closer to other members of the family may tell you one thing or it may tell you another - a matter entirely for you. However, she did go on to say that Carol seemed bubbly and confident and that she, Sarah Thomas, was not aware of any allegations whilst they were at school together.

Well, there it is, ladies and gentlemen. That is - I'm sorry it's taken a wee while - but that is a review of the evidence that you have heard, so what I am going to ask you to do in just a moment, when we've sworn in our jury bailiff, is to begin your deliberations. I'm just going to ask, gentlemen, is there anything that you would wish me specifically to remind the jury of that I haven't?

MR HAMPTON: No, thank you.

MR STOREY: No, thank you.

JUDGE JAMESON: Or any egregious errors?

MR HAMPTON: No, thank you very much.

MR STOREY: No.

JUDGE JAMESON: No? All right, thank you very much. Right, so when we've sworn in our jury bailiff, I'm going to ask you to begin your task. Now, just a number of things: firstly, if you need any help to be reminded of a specific piece of evidence or any further explanation of directions, don't hesitate to ask. It's very straightforward, as I told you at the beginning of the trial. Send a note, we'll have you back. I'm here; counsel will be here. We'll help you in any way that we can, so don't feel you're on your own. If you need help, ask for it, but, if you don't, I'll simply leave you alone to get on with your work.

Next thing, if you haven't already done so, it's probably a good idea if you do select one of your number to chair your discussions. It's up to you how you proceed but it's usually helpful to do that because, if you've got somebody at least nominally in charge, that way the proceedings will go smoothly, everybody will get their chance to contribute fully to the discussion, so you'll probably find that helpful. If you do do that and in any event at some time, that person will probably return your verdicts, so don't volunteer for the role or allow yourself to be volunteered for the role unless you're content to do that.

Finally, I said there would be one last direction that wasn't in the directions that I've given you thus far and here it comes. It's this. It'll only take a minute. As things presently stand, the only verdicts that I can accept in relation to each of the 15 counts on the indictment are unanimous verdicts, that is to say verdicts upon which all 11 of you are agreed. You will, I think, have heard of the concept of majority verdicts, because I think there's something in one of the documents you get, or a briefing, that says something about that.

The time, obviously, has not yet come at which we could contemplate majority verdicts and it may, of course, never come. If you return unanimous verdicts, then it never will, but, if the time ever were to come at which I could consider majority verdicts, I would, in any event, have to have you all back into court, give you a direction about what...a further direction about what a majority verdict is and how you should proceed and then ask you to go out again and continue with your deliberations, so, unless and until all of that happens, forget about majority verdicts, 11 nil, please, one way or the other, all counts, if you can.

Right, will you take with you all the material that you've got and, when we've sworn in our jury bailiffs, begin your work.

(The jury retired to consider their verdicts at 1.05 p.m.)

(The jury returned into court at 2.56 p.m.)

THE CLERK OF THE COURT: Would the foreman please stand? Madam foreman, please answer my first question simply "yes or no". Have the jury reached verdicts upon which you are all agreed?

THE FOREMAN OF THE JURY: Yes.

THE CLERK OF THE COURT: On count one charging indecent assault, do you find the defendant guilty or not guilty?

THE FOREMAN OF THE JURY: Guilty.

THE CLERK OF THE COURT: You find the defendant guilty and that is the verdict of you all?

THE FOREMAN OF THE JURY: Yes.

THE CLERK OF THE COURT: On count two charging rape do you find the defendant guilty or not guilty?

THE FOREMAN OF THE JURY: Guilty.

THE CLERK OF THE COURT: You find the defendant guilty and that is the verdict of you all?

THE FOREMAN OF THE JURY: Yes.

THE CLERK OF THE COURT: On count three, charging rape, do you find the defendant guilty or not guilty?

THE FOREMAN OF THE JURY: Guilty.

THE CLERK OF THE COURT: You find the defendant guilty and that is the verdict of you all?

THE FOREMAN OF THE JURY: Yes.

THE CLERK OF THE COURT: On count four charging indecent assault, do you find the defendant guilty or not guilty?

THE FOREMAN OF THE JURY: Guilty.

THE CLERK OF THE COURT: You find the defendant guilty and that is the verdict of you all?

THE FOREMAN OF THE JURY: Yes.

THE CLERK OF THE COURT: On count five charging indecent assault, do you find the defendant guilty or not guilty?

THE FOREMAN OF THE JURY: Guilty.

THE CLERK OF THE COURT: You find the defendant guilty and that is the verdict of you all?

THE FOREMAN OF THE JURY: Yes.

THE CLERK OF THE COURT: On count six charging indecent assault, do you find the defendant guilty or not guilty?

THE FOREMAN OF THE JURY: Guilty.

THE CLERK OF THE COURT: You find the defendant guilty and that is the verdict of you all?

THE FOREMAN OF THE JURY: Yes.

THE CLERK OF THE COURT: On count seven charging rape, do you find the defendant guilty or not guilty?

THE FOREMAN OF THE JURY: Guilty.

THE CLERK OF THE COURT: You find the defendant guilty and that is the verdict of you all?

THE FOREMAN OF THE JURY: Yes.

THE CLERK OF THE COURT: On count eight, charging indecent assault, do you find the defendant guilty or not guilty?

THE FOREMAN OF THE JURY: Guilty.

THE CLERK OF THE COURT: You find the defendant guilty and that is the verdict of you all?

THE FOREMAN OF THE JURY: Yes.

THE CLERK OF THE COURT: On count nine, charging indecent assault, do you find the defendant guilty or not guilty?

THE FOREMAN OF THE JURY: Guilty.

THE CLERK OF THE COURT: You find the defendant guilty and that is the verdict of you all?

THE FOREMAN OF THE JURY: Yes.

THE CLERK OF THE COURT: On count 10 charging indecent assault, do you find the defendant guilty or not guilty?

THE FOREMAN OF THE JURY: Guilty.

THE CLERK OF THE COURT: You find the defendant guilty and that is the verdict of you all?

THE FOREMAN OF THE JURY: Yes.

THE CLERK OF THE COURT: On count 11 charging rape, do you find the defendant guilty or not guilty?

THE FOREMAN OF THE JURY: Guilty.

THE CLERK OF THE COURT: You find the defendant guilty and that is the verdict of you all?

THE FOREMAN OF THE JURY: Yes.

THE CLERK OF THE COURT: On count 12 charging indecent assault, do you find the defendant guilty or not guilty?

THE FOREMAN OF THE JURY: Guilty.

THE CLERK OF THE COURT: You find the defendant guilty and that is the verdict of you all?

THE FOREMAN OF THE JURY: Yes.

THE CLERK OF THE COURT: On count 13 charging indecent assault, do you find the defendant guilty or not guilty?

THE FOREMAN OF THE JURY: Guilty.

THE CLERK OF THE COURT: You find the defendant guilty and that is the verdict of you all?

THE FOREMAN OF THE JURY: Yes.

THE CLERK OF THE COURT: On count 14 charging indecent assault, you find the defendant guilty or not guilty?

THE FOREMAN OF THE JURY: Guilty.

THE CLERK OF THE COURT: You find the defendant guilty and that is the verdict of you all?

THE FOREMAN OF THE JURY: Yes.

THE CLERK OF THE COURT: And finally on count 15 charging rape, do you find the defendant guilty or not guilty?

THE FOREMAN OF THE JURY: Guilty.

THE CLERK OF THE COURT: You find the defendant guilty and that is the verdict of you all?

THE FOREMAN OF THE JURY: Yes.

THE CLERK OF THE COURT: Thank you. Sit down.

JUDGE JAMESON: Thank you very much indeed, madam foreman. Thank you, ladies and gentlemen. Now, Mr Hampton do the Crown need to put any more material in front of me?

MR HAMPTON: We had drafted although not completed, for obvious reasons, a sentence note which we'd like to upload, principally.

JUDGE JAMESON: Yes, I'm just thinking about the practicalities of the matter. I don't, obviously want to delay this matter longer than is strictly necessary but it may be that tomorrow would be a better day than...

MR HAMPTON: A short period of reflection, hours, would be convenient and appropriate, I would submit.

JUDGE JAMESON: Yes, all right. Could I deal with the matter tomorrow morning?

MR HAMPTON: As far as we are concerned, yes.

JUDGE JAMESON: Yes. Mr Storey, also for you?

MR STOREY: Yes.

JUDGE JAMESON: All right. Thank you very much. Well, I will sentence tomorrow morning. Mr Appleyard, I'm afraid you will be remanded in custody now. I will sentence tomorrow morning. All right?

Right, ladies and gentlemen. Well, thank you very much indeed. I'm sorry that I am not going to go straight on now but you can understand there's quite a lot of material that I am going to need to look at. If you want to know what happens, of course, you've only to make arrangements to find out. I think you will probably be here tomorrow in any event, I imagine, so I will leave that matter entirely with you but thank you very much indeed for your assistance in the case. If you would go with Penny, our usher now, we will find out what the future holds but that may be it for the fortnight. I don't know, but if it is, thank you very much. If it isn't then I may see you tomorrow. That will be my pleasure; it might not be yours, but thank you very much for your help in this case. Thank you.

(The jury left court)

JUDGE JAMESON: Yes, right. Thank you very much. Yes, Mr Storey?

MR STOREY: Just this. I wanted to check with your Honour, if I may, please, what time do you think the case will be listed, whether it be at 10 o'clock or in the 10.30 list?

JUDGE JAMESON: I don't know what else is supposed to be happening tomorrow. When I last looked it was only this part-heard, but 10.30.

MR STOREY: Very well. Thank you very much.

JUDGE JAMESON: Right.

MR STOREY: Just so that your Honour is aware, the only document that I anticipate putting before your Honour on behalf of the defendant is a letter that's in fact already been uploaded to the digital case system. It was attached to the short letter that related to him giving evidence seated.

JUDGE JAMESON: Yes.

MR STOREY: And for your Honour's assistance, it's at pages O-18 to O19.

JUDGE JAMESON: Thank you.

MR STOREY: It sets out his medical background and difficulties in a little more detail, but I don't think there's anything else that's likely to be coming beyond that.

JUDGE JAMESON: All right. Thank you very much indeed. Right, well I am going to rise because I think it's better to allow people to disperse and then, Mr Hampton, unfortunately, I'm told that (inaudible) is not available today. (Brief discussion re the next case)

MR HAMPTON: No.

(3.02 p.m.)

(The court adjourned until 10.30 on 25 January 2019)

Diary: Thursday 24th January 2019

During the session this morning, two male officials ran into the court and approached the Judge. Whatever they said to him must have been very urgent because he stopped proceedings immediately. The court was adjourned, and everyone was ordered to leave. We waited in the assembly room for an hour and half and my heart would not stop pounding, I was wondering what was wrong and whether the trial was going to be stopped. Mr Hampton called me into a consultation room, as he had done many times throughout the trial to discuss proceedings. He told me about the juror breaching the rules. The two choices were to either stop the trial or to continue with just eleven jurors. My fears that the trial would be sabotaged surfaced again. Mr Hampton told me he and Mr Storey had spoken with the Judge and they had decided on the latter. I mentioned to Mr Hampton that I had been suspicious about one woman juror all along, the one who had stood out like a sore thumb when I was giving evidence. I wondered if it was the same juror who had disrupted proceedings on the first day by notifying the Judge at the last minute about a doctor's appointment. Mr Hampton said it was not a discussion to have now. I was just relieved that the trail was going to continue now that we had got so near the end.

When we returned to court, my suspicions were justified, the juror who was dismissed was indeed the woman who had stuck out like a sore thumb and looked like a relative!

When the jury retired to consider their verdict, we had lunch and returned to wait in the assembly room. Only an hour and fifty minutes passed before we were called back into court. The jury had already made their decision, I was expecting it to take much longer. Once again my heart was pounding while I sat in the public gallery holding hands with my children as the verdict was given. To my left I could see my dad standing in the dock with a lady security guard. Behind them stood a third person with a chain of keys attached to his trousers, who reminded me of the grim reaper. My dad tapped the lady on the shoulder and asked "Who is that?" She shrugged her shoulders. I took my eyes off my dad and focussed on the first member of the jury as they delivered their verdict. "Guilty." I couldn't believe it, this was music to my ears. But every one of them needed to say guilty, it was all or nothing. The next member said "Guilty." The tension was unbearable. Finally, everyone said "Guilty." We all shouted "Yes." I heard my brother shout "Send the paedophile down," or words to that effect. I felt elated that justice was finally being served. I couldn't help thinking though, that if the member of the jury had not been dismissed and my suspicions had been right, she might have been the one juror to say "Not Guilty."

The judge gave his closing address and I was relieved to hear that my father was being remanded in custody overnight before sentencing. I still feared that he would kill me, given the chance.

Friday, 25 January 2019

(Transcript prepared without the aid of documentation)

(11.39 a.m.)

MR STOREY: Your Honour, before the prosecution address you, I just want to check your Honour is aware of the reason why the defendant and the hearing, therefore, is late. He was not produced by the Prison Service.

JUDGE JAMESON: Yes, so I've understood, yes. Thank you very much indeed.

MR HAMPTON: Your Honour, may I begin by reading into the record relevant passages of Ms Higgins' victim impact statement?

JUDGE JAMESON: Yes. Has that actually been uploaded?

MR HAMPTON: Yes. It's contained at I-45. It's been there a while.

JUDGE JAMESON: Right, I'm sorry. I didn't...

MR HAMPTON: Not at all. It could easily be mistaken for an evidential statement.

JUDGE JAMESON: Yes, I'm afraid it had been by me, so let's have a look.

MR HAMPTON: Some of it is in fact, so with Ms Higgins' agreement I've prepared those parts that are relevant to this part of the exercise.

JUDGE JAMESON: Yes, I've got it now, thank you.

MR HAMPTON: It is I-45.

JUDGE JAMESON: Yes, I've got it.

MR HAMPTON: So, this is passages from Carol Higgins' victim impact statement from 18 May 2018.

Carol's Personal Impact Statement

"When I was an innocent little girl, I loved and trusted you and hung on to your every word because you were my dad, even though you often beat me, but gradually you stole my innocence and took advantage of my trust in you. I just wanted you to love me like a normal dad should love his daughter.

"Social services and my school did nothing when mum reported the kissing, so when I came back to live with you months later because mum wasn't looking after me properly. I just thought everything was going to be okay.

"I'd been told that if I tried to leave again, I would be put in a children's home. Then you went and got legal custody of us. Little did I know at that time that I had been trapped. You stopped me from living the life of a normal teenage girl because of your jealousy and even marked me by giving me love bites so that lads would think I had a boyfriend and leave me alone. I felt confused and embarrassed to tell anybody that it was you."

She describes the ongoing abuse that your Honour has heard about.

"Part of me felt good about being treated like an adult but I wasn't an adult. I was a child. You took my childhood away from me and treated me like a slave. I couldn't go back to live with my mum and was afraid of being put in a children's home. Donna had already been put in a children's home and I felt like it was my responsibility to try and keep what bit of family we had together. I was so lonely. Even on the rare occasions I went to school or saw my friends, I couldn't concentrate or be my true self and I had to cover up my pain with cockiness and rudeness showing no respect to others or to myself. Because you kept me off school, I was always behind everyone else and put in the bottom classes, which added to my embarrassment and shame but I had to act like everything was normal. I couldn't confide in anyone. I felt different. I felt ashamed of my attitude and had no one to turn to, and I daren't tell anyone what you were doing to me. I was confused about what was normal."

Then on to continuation sheet three.

"I was powerless to say 'no' to you. It was just not an option, but me not daring to say 'no' does not mean I was saying, 'yes'. You tried to justify raping me by saying that I wanted it, but it would never have entered my head to come up to you and kiss you or initiate sex with you. I often wonder what would have happened if I'd have said, 'no'. I now feel guilt and shame for not saying, 'stop' but at that time I did not feel this guilt or shame. I knew it did not feel right but I did not know for sure that what you were doing to me was wrong. I did not realise that it was child abuse. I was just not strong enough to stand up to you or go against anything you said, so it feels like I allowed you to play your filthy game and that somehow I am to blame for being part of it, but I was just a child and you were the adult, the dad who I trusted and thought knew what was best for me. You betrayed my trust."

Towards the bottom of the page:

"Mum told me that I should tell the police. I didn't want to because I thought I was in some way to blame for what you had done to me. I thought I could just forget about it, but I could not. My emotions were all over the place and I was starting to realise that what you had done to me was seriously wrong. I did go to the police a week later, even though I was very scared, and I made a 17-page statement and had to undergo internal forensic tests which themselves made me feel violated. I was told by the police that if it went to court, my name would be dragged through the mud, my reputation would be blackened, I wouldn't be believed and I would be made out to be the biggest slag going. This was just the start of a horrendous 35-year battle for justice, which your actions had forced me into because you say I am lying. You know very well that I am telling the truth."

And on to page four.

"For 35 years you have made me suffer the loss of a father and my family. I used to think, 'why me?' and wish that someone on the street had raped me because then I would at least have had my family to love and support me. Instead of being surrounded by my family at the age of 16, I had to sleep in a strange town in a cold, rented terraced house on my own feeling terrified, abandoned and worthless. I was too ashamed to tell people what had happened to me and people would say to me that I must have done something bad for my parents not to like me and kick me out. The loneliness and the grieving for my family was excruciating. My heart was broken and I didn't know how to mend it. Through no fault of my own, I'd been forced to live on my own and I hated it. The first night in my rented house I slept in a big, dark, brown wooden bed with a mattress that had been slept in by God knows how many people before me. I had to sleep with my arms wrapped tightly round myself for comfort. I felt like that worthless piece of shit you made me believe I was. I was suicidal and living with panic attacks and shame.

"My new friend from work told me I needed to ask for help from the doctor. I wanted to reach deep into the pit of my stomach to tear out the vileness you have planted inside me, but I could not make it go away or understand why you had put it there. My anger and hurt was overwhelming. Eventually I was referred to the Rape Crisis Team by another doctor. For about a year I had to go every Friday after work on a train to Sheffield to access the counselling. This was just the start of many years of therapy up to present day.

"This is the first opportunity I have had to tell you how you made me feel when I was a young girl. However, your actions, you have had a massive impact on my health both physical and psychological throughout my adult life. Sadness and anger are part of my everyday life. The stress and tension that I carry around in my body is constantly wearing and tiring, making it impossible for me to relax. I struggle to hold back my tears because what you did to me still breaks my heart. You will never understand or know the physical pain and sickness that I suffer as a result of all the vile things you did to me and made me do to you. As an adult looking back, I cannot describe the utter disgust and shame I feel.

"I purge nearly every day trying to get the vileness you put inside me out. I physically gag, choke, vomit, sweat, hyperventilate and cry. I can't control it.

Sights, sounds and smells are all there ready to trigger me off. It took me six years to remove the tattoo with your name on it which made me feel branded. I'm still left with a scar from the painful acid and needle treatment.

"As a result of your abuse and keeping me off school, I left the education system without any qualifications and limited job opportunities. Combined with this, I had a huge lack of confidence and no belief in my ability or potential to succeed. You've made me believe I was stupid and incapable of learning, and I felt vulnerable, naïve and out of my depth.

"Depression is always with me. I always have to fight it and push myself to get up every morning so that I do not fall into a deep, dark hole where I cannot get myself back out. I suffer from sleeplessness, nightmares and have flashbacks. It is exhausting.

"Maintaining any sort of routine is impossible for me. I have to fight back the suicidal thoughts of slitting my wrists or cutting my chest wide open to get rid of my pain. The guilt I feel for having these thoughts makes me feel worse and I have to fight even harder to pull myself out of bed and overcome them. I struggle with addictions to alcohol and nicotine.

"The feelings of isolation and loneliness I felt as a teenager continue now, even though I have my own family. Relationships have always been difficult for me because of my inability to trust people and to get close to them. When the people you love and trust more than anybody in the world take away that love and trust, you find it so difficult to ever trust anybody again. This has saddened me greatly all my life and even made me afraid to have children of my own. I worried that this feeling of detachment and the void you had created would prevent me from forming a bond with them and I had to work really hard to make sure this did not happen. I went on parenting courses and volunteered in schools so that I could learn what normal family life was all about. I spend days on my own hiding in my bed because I don't want people or my children to see me when I'm feeling at my weakest and when I can't stop crying from the pain and anger.

"The reality of having to take my own dad to court is devastating, even though you did all those vile things to me. It has taken me years and years to bring my case to court to get justice and along the way I feel I have been let down and badly treated by my parents and the establishment.

"The process has been violating, humiliating and abusive in itself and every day of my life I have had to relive what you did to me. Fighting for justice has nearly killed me. The system has put obstacles in my way and put me through hell."

The bottom of page five:

"To the outside world I wear a smile and am strong but underneath I am trying to hide my low self-esteem and feelings of worthlessness and negativity which you created inside me. I carry them around with me all the time. They never leave me. It takes all my energy and willpower to create positive things in my life. I will never know what it is like to feel completely normal and happy and part of a loving family. I feel like I'll never be able to break free from the chains you bound me in. You tried to trick me into believing your truth and that what you were doing to me was right, and now you deny it. I cling on to the hope that my truth will finally be heard and this will help me to break free from your evil lies. I long for the day when I feel peace in my life."

That is the statement of Carol Higgins, your Honour.

JUDGE JAMESON: Yes.

MR HAMPTON: May I read, please, two short passages again from the victim impact statement from Ella Marsh at I-74?

JUDGE JAMESON: Yes.

MR HAMPTON: Ella Marsh is Ms Higgins' daughter and speaks of the impact upon the family generally.

Ella's Personal Impact Statement

"As I grew older, I became aware of the different types of abuse that Elliott made her go through with her mother. I would sit with her and still be most days trying to talk her out of being stuck in the hole that her father put her in. She purges and screams as if no one is listening to her, and questioning why he did what he did. I can't put into words how heart-breaking it is to see the mum that has been strong for me all these years break down like a helpless child. I've always felt like there is nothing I could do but be there for her which is why I was so relieved when the police decided to take on her case after all these years of feeling like she should get over being raped as a young teenager.

"Each time I find her purging and crying, all I can do is assure her that she has a loving family which will love and protect her as much as possible and that her dad can't control her any more. I hope that this case will be taken as seriously as it is because I fear that my mum will feel this pain for the rest of her life if Elliott isn't brought to justice.

"I'm finding it difficult to write this letter because there are really no words to describe what it's like to see my mother relive and repeat the disturbing thoughts and words to me and how helpless I feel. I'm not 20 years old and fully understand that what Elliott Appleyard did was a disgusting and life-ruining crime that no individual or child should be put through. Although I've had some amazing memories as a child and a teenager, my mum's depression has still been a huge part of my life and now that I've grown up, I believe that it's my responsibility to try and fight these feelings with her, which I can honestly say is exhausting. I don't think that my mum will ever forget all the revolting things that her so-called parent did to her, as I don't believe anyone could knowing what she has been through. But I do believe that she won't feel the same burdens as she does and has done for years because she will know that she has finally been heard and that her dad will be brought to justice. What he did was wrong and I pray that for all our families' sake that she gets the justice she deserves and believe me, she deserves this."

Those are the victim impact statements.

JUDGE JAMESON: Yes.

MR HAMPTON: We have uploaded, your Honour, two documents to the case system dealing with guidelines and...

JUDGE JAMESON: Yes, thank you. I've read those.

MR HAMPTON: I am grateful. Are there any particular points I can assist with in terms of the guidelines?

JUDGE JAMESON: No, I don't think so. I would just say this, that in relation to count one, where you've suggested there's a five-year maximum, in fact, I don't propose to adopt that principle because you'll remember in order to make directions to the jury as simple as I reasonably could...

MR HAMPTON: Yes.

JUDGE JAMESON: ...I directed them only that they would need to be satisfied that Carol was under 15 – I'm sorry, under 16.

MR HAMPTON: Yes.

JUDGE JAMESON: And that otherwise, dates were irrelevant. I did not direct them, and I deliberately did not direct them, that they would have to find that she was under 13 for that count, so I'm not prepared to sentence on the basis that the maximum for that count is five years. I have to say, it makes no difference.

MR HAMPTON: No. We follow your Honour's reasoning. Thank you. Unless there are any principle points I can assist with, your Honour has our submissions in writing.

JUDGE JAMESON: Yes, I do.

MR HAMPTON: I would invite the court to consider the rubric at the top of the guideline...

JUDGE JAMESON: Yes.

MR HAMPTON: ...the case of *R v JH.* The defendant is 71. He has some convictions for dishonesty and violence, none for sexual offences and those convictions ending 1982.

JUDGE JAMESON: Yes.

MR HAMPTON: There is application for a restraining order.

JUDGE JAMESON: Yes, again, is there a copy of that uploaded or...

MR HAMPTON: I don't think we have. It would be done in the usual terms, non-contact, directly or indirectly...

JUDGE JAMESON: Yes, I think before I will – I will obviously make such an order but I think before I do I should see it.

MR HAMPTON: We'll draft the terms. Certainly.

JUDGE JAMESON: Please, yes.

MR HAMPTON: Very well. We will do that while the exercise is ongoing.

JUDGE JAMESON: All right, thank you.

MR HAMPTON: May I assist with anything else?

JUDGE JAMESON: Yes, thank you very much indeed. Yes, Mr Storey?

MR STOREY: Just on that last point first, if I may, there will be no opposition to a restraining order in the terms we anticipate that we'll see in due course.

There is, with one exception, nothing that can be said in relation to the offending of which the defendant has now been convicted.

JUDGE JAMESON: Yes.

MR STOREY: But that exception is this. Given the date span that now attaches to the offences on the indictment, and the evidence that was adduced at trial, whilst the prosecution opened the case essentially on the basis that this abuse lasted for at least two years if not three, your Honour observed with respect in summing-up to the jury that the earliest it could have been on Carol Higgins' account that the abuse proper – if I can put it that way...

JUDGE JAMESON: Yes.

MR STOREY: ... began, was around November/December 1983.

JUDGE JAMESON: Yes.

MR STOREY: When she was...

JUDGE JAMESON: Well, I conclude it's a year.

MR STOREY: Thank you. That was the only point I sought to make. So far as the defendant is concerned, your Honour knows that he is now 71 years of age.

JUDGE JAMESON: Yes.

MR STOREY: And if your Honour has been able to see the entirety of the medical documentation that's on the digital case system, you will note from a letter dated 27 November last year he suffers from a number of difficulties. His age...

JUDGE JAMESON: Right, well, you had better take me to that. I went back to Dr Kaye's letter of 18 December...

MR STOREY: Yes.

JUDGE JAMESON: ...because that was quite brief.

MR STOREY: It was.

JUDGE JAMESON: Is there more?

MR STOREY: There are two pages attached to the same item on the digital case system, behind that.

JUDGE JAMESON: Right.

MR STOREY: It's at pages O-18 and O-19.

JUDGE JAMESON: Right. Thank you very much. Ah, yes, right.

MR STOREY: And what your Honour should see there is a letter from a Dr A Pollack to Dr Kaye...

JUDGE JAMESON: Yes.

MR STOREY: ... setting out the relatively recent position relating to the defendant's overall health problems. Your Honour should see a list of those problems at the top of that letter: angina, previous coronary artery stenting seven years ago. In fact, the defendant has undergone two different heart operations and has been fitted over time with three separate stents. Postural hypotension, which seems to derive from, to some extent, those heart problems. I am told that in addition and not named on this – not listed on this document, he also suffers, having been diagnosed many years ago, with an enlarged heart. I suspect the problems all relate one to the other. Previous spinal fracture operated on. He suffered a fracture to his upper vertebrae in 1997 as a result of which he has a number of pins permanently in his neck, which produces a very restricted range of movement of his head. He is consequently registered disabled. The various ailments, if I can put it that way, referred to in this letter, as well as the body of the letter itself, make clear that he is someone who has to take medication on a very regular basis: a constant need to take painkillers; medication to control his heart difficulties has to be taken several times a day, and he has already experienced the hard way the difficulties that those who are incarcerated within our prison system with health problems experience because the reason that he was not brought to court on time was because arrangements had not been made last night for him to receive any medication at all.

JUDGE JAMESON: Yes.

MR STOREY: He has to take medication at 8 a.m. The Prison Service finally provided it to him after half past nine, he having been kept at the prison to await the opening of the pharmacy and then when he was given medication, he was only given some of the medication that he is prescribed currently. And obviously that increases the difficulty for someone of his age and his health in coping with the environment of a custodial institution in our country in this day and age.

So far as his antecedent history is concerned, the Crown have simply observed that he has no previous convictions for anything relevant to these matters.

JUDGE JAMESON: Yes.

MR STOREY: And that is indeed the case. He was last before the courts in 1982, his offending of a very different type, and when he was considerably younger to the 71 years that he bears today.

Your Honour knows that he remains married to Janet and has a close relationship, I understand, with her stepson. Prior to his retirement, relatively recently he has worked notwithstanding the evidence that you heard. My instructions are that he has worked all his life. As I say, prison is clearly going to be difficult for him, more difficult than it might be for some younger and fitter but he acknowledges, as do I, that a lengthy prison sentence is inevitable.

JUDGE JAMESON: Yes.

MR STOREY: And given his age, given the health difficulties that he suffers from, he is alive to the reality of the consequences of the type of sentence that your Honour is likely to impose today. In short, he acknowledges he is highly unlikely to leave prison.

I am sorry, the prosecution have drawn your Honour's attention to the guidelines and to the case of *R v JH.*

JUDGE JAMESON: Yes.

MR STOREY: There are some points of detail within the prosecution's observations about the guidelines with which I could take issue but, frankly, it would be academic and it is perhaps academic whether we try to categorise this offending as falling within category one or category two because either way, your Honour is going to sentence him for a protracted course of offending of a particular type and the various aggravating factors that are listed in the guidelines identified in my learned friend's document are clearly relevant.

Perhaps the only point of distinction that I would seek to draw between this case and that of *JH,* which, on the face of it has a number of similarities – however, the points of distinction are two. First of all, the period over which the offending appears to have been committed...

JUDGE JAMESON: Yes.

MR STOREY: ...is much shorter – well, it is shorter in this case than in the case of *JH* and in addition, in the case of *JH* there was some previous sexual offending on his record.

JUDGE JAMESON: Yes.

MR STOREY: There is none on the defendant's record. Those, your Honour, are the submissions that I feel able to make on Mr Appleyard's behalf at the present time, unless there is anything else that you wish me to address?

JUDGE JAMESON: No, I am grateful, Mr Storey. That is extremely helpful, as always.

MR STOREY: Thank you.

JUDGE JAMESON: Thank you.

(12.04 p.m.)

JUDGE JAMESON: Elliott Appleyard, I don't require you to stand during the sentencing process. It will take some time because I do need to set out some detail of the offences for which I have to sentence you and the approach that I'm taking to the guidelines. There will come a time, and it will be as early as I reasonably can within these sentencing comments, when I will tell you the overall length of the sentence. At that point I will by then have made supplementary orders and explained one or two things to you. If you wish to leave the dock and go down at that point, you have my leave to do so because inevitably when you receive a lengthy sentence it is a difficult moment because there will necessarily have to be some parts of the sentencing remarks that go on after that because there are a number of explanations I am required to make and they are matters that will not be of immediate interest to you and, as I say, if you wish to leave at that point, I will make clear when that point comes.

You are 71 years of age. You have a number of previous convictions for dishonesty and violence but they ended in 1982. You have no convictions since. However, the jury has convicted you of 15 sexual offences committed against your natural daughter, Carol, from approximately 1983 or in the years approximately 1983, 1984 and 1985. These comprise five offences of rape, three offences of what necessarily were charged because of the dates on which the offences were committed – three offences of indecent assault by making her give you oral sex – they would now be charged as rape; three offences of indecent assault by digital penetration of her vagina, and these would now be charged as assault by penetration; three offences of indecent assault by making her masturbate you and one offence of indecent assault by kissing her in an indecent fashion.

There is a background of serious domestic violence against all three of your children, two naturally your children and one your stepdaughter, Donna, and against your then wife, Jean. The first offence, count one, is the indecent kissing. Although it is specified on the indictment as being when Carol was 11 or 12, I directed the jury only that they had to be satisfied that Carol was under the age of 16 and that dates were otherwise irrelevant. Accordingly, I cannot and do not sentence you on the basis that Carol was under 13 when that kissing took place. It makes no difference.

Count one is simply sexualised kissing – I say “simply” – count one is sexualised kissing. It took place in curious circumstances when you had been out with her and shot the family dog. You sat her down on some scrap metal tubing and kissed her as a boyfriend would kiss a girlfriend. That matter was complained of by Carol to her mother and a few days later Carol was taken from the family home by her mother. That was in 1983. Unhappily, her mother either did not or could not care for her as she should have done and after some months Carol returned to you. You had had the opportunity to recognise that the feelings for your daughter were wrong and to behave differently. I say you have had that opportunity because you had been confronted by your then wife, Jean, with what you had done, although you had denied it. You did not take that opportunity. Instead, on a date that seems clearly to have been some time in December 1983, you raped her for the first time, that is count two.

It is clear that by January 1985, Carol was no longer with you and was back with her mother, so it follows that the offences that are counts two to 15 on the indictment were committed over a period of approximately 12 months at times when Carol was 14 and 15. I do not accept your evidence that Carol was never with you at Christmas. I am satisfied that she was living with you throughout that period of time.

She was a vulnerable child, partly because of your violence towards her and, indeed, her mother's violence towards her when she was still living there, partly because of the violence that she had witnessed and no doubt been terrified by from you to her mother involving on occasion the use of a shotgun and a machete or at least threats with those items.

She was vulnerable also because she was or felt unable to return to her mother. Her mother was unable to care for her properly and Carol feared that she would be taken into care or into a care – be sent to a care home where her sister, Donna, had herself been sexually assaulted. It is an appalling thought that you seemed to her to be her best option.

At some point you took her to have a tattoo. It was a tattoo of a rose and with your name or nickname and hers. Over those 12 months you abused her sexually repeatedly as is set out on the indictment. Essentially for a 12-month period you treated Carol as your wife. You used her for sex and you abused her physically and emotionally as you had done to your real wife, Jean. You raped her vaginally, you penetrated her vagina with your fingers, you made her give you oral sex, you ejaculated into her mouth, you made her masturbate you. It is not on the indictment but you also made her pose for photographs on occasions simulating sexual acts with a hairbrush and you made her read pornography to you on occasions as she masturbated you. You told her that all this was normal and to her it became so. It is not surprising, as is revealed in her victim impact statement, that she felt then and feels now confusion, embarrassment, shame and even guilt.

At the end of that period of time, Carol could take no more. After you had raped and then kicked and insulted her in the incident that is count 15 on the indictment, she left the house with nothing but the clothes on her back. She went back to her mother. That was, perhaps, not surprisingly, not a happy experience and as soon as she was 16, she obtained a job and council accommodation.

From shortly after that time, she attended at a rape crisis centre. It required her to take the bus from Barnsley to Sheffield after work on a Friday evening for years, it seems. She was still attending, counselling notes indicate, in 2013 and as I understand it may still be, 30 years later. The tattoo with your name on it she tried to have removed by the tattoo artist who originally put it on her body. There were, it seems, 10 treatments in which acid was injected under her skin in an attempt to remove the tattoo. It was painful. In 1987 she was referred to a plastic surgeon. It is not clear what, if anything, followed in that regard.

Medical records reveal anxiety, depression, fears for herself and for others, particularly when she wanted to get married, and prescriptions for anti-depressants. I have just and we have all just heard parts of her victim impact statement read out. It is clear that the effect of these offences is profound and lifelong.

Social services were notified of inappropriate kissing in, it would seem, 1983. No action was taken. Your wife confronted you. Your response was, "It's her word against mine". As I've indicated, you had the opportunity to reflect on matters. You chose not to take that opportunity.

The first complaint to the police was made, it seems, in 1985. In 2005 the matter was investigated at least to some extent, and on that occasion, you were, as I understand it, interviewed. You denied the offences, there was no prosecution. In 2012, your daughter, Carol, went to solicitors. They were little, if any, help. In 2015 she initiated a further police investigation. That took some two years and not far short of four years to trial.

I turn now to the guidelines. I will sentence in accordance with the sentencing regime as is applicable now bearing in mind, of course, that no individual sentence can exceed the maximum sentence for the offence that applied at the time that the offences were committed. For all the offences of indecent assault, therefore, there is a maximum of two years' imprisonment and that includes count one for the reasons that I have set out.

However, the offences of rape, of which there are five, even in 1983, carried life imprisonment and I will impose concurrent sentences for each offence of rape which reflect the totality of your offending. There will also be concurrent sentences for all offences of indecent assault. I should indicate that in reflecting the totality of your offending, and having indicated that there are five offences of rape, there are, of course, a further three offences that would now be regarded as rape, and I take that matter very much into account when considering the total sentences that I will impose for the offences that actually were charged as rape.

I have been asked to make a restraining order. The terms of that have not yet been made plain, but in essence they will prevent you from contacting either directly or indirectly either Carol or you son, Paul. I will make such an order and that order will be indefinite. I tell you now that the sentence that I am about to impose will mean that the matters on the document that you will need to sign before you leave this court building, that is to say the sex offenders register – that document will set out your obligations to notify the police of certain matters if you are and when you are released. Your obligation to notify the police by virtue of the sentence I am about to impose will also be indefinite. That is to say, it will remain for the length of your life.

The sentence that I do impose is a determinate sentence, that is to say a fixed number of years. You will serve approximately one-half of it. When you are released, you will be released on licence. You must understand that if you were to breach the terms of the licence or if you were to reoffend, the chances are that you would be recalled to serve some or all of the balance of the sentence.

I tell you now that the total sentence in your case is one of 20 years' imprisonment. At this point, if you wish, Mr Appleyard, you may leave the dock. You do not have to if you wish to be here for the remainder of what is a rather technical approach to the sentencing. You may, but you do not have to do so. You may go down now if you wish.

In fixing that total term, I've considered the following matters. Firstly, the prosecution submissions that I should regard each of the offences of rape as falling within category 1A. I am satisfied that culpability is clearly in category A. These offences involved a gross breach of trust. There was previous violence towards Carol. There was a number of matters of additional humiliation. Photographing her sexually is perhaps the principal one.

So far as harm is concerned, there are a number of category two factors. There is obviously no doubt that these offences caused serious psychological harm. There was additional degradation and humiliation. Carol was particularly vulnerable and I turn now to the third person because at my invitation, Mr Appleyard has left the dock. It is plain that Mr Appleyard was aware of her particular vulnerabilities. The guidelines indicate that the extreme nature of one or more category two factors or the extreme impact caused by a combination of category two factors may elevate the sentence to a category 1A and that is the submission that the Crown make.

The starting point for a single offence under a category 1A is 15 years with a range of 13 to 19 years. The starting point for a single offence under category 2A is eight years but there is a very wide range of sentencing from five to 13 years. That is deliberate because, of course, it requires the judge to make a careful assessment of the factors and allows a court to reflect the factors specifically in a very wide range of sentencing.

Aggravating features are, of course, that these offences were committed by Mr Appleyard against his own daughter. There was ejaculation on many occasions, including oral sex, and the location of the offences were in Carol, then a child's own home, which she had to leave on more than one occasion.

Mitigating features are essentially no previous convictions for sexual offences and Mr Appleyard's ill health. On any view, I would be of the view that a single offence of rape would be in excess of 13 years, in other words probably above the borderline between category 1A and category 2A, but the prosecution have also invited my attention helpfully to the case of *R v JH* [2015] EWCA Crim. 54 in which comparable offences were met with a total sentence of 22 years. I have also considered the case of *R v G* [2013] EWCA Crim. 1821 in which sentences for comparable offences were met with a sentence of 17 years after a plea with 25 per cent credit, which would indicate a starting point of 22 years and eight months.

In the case of *JH*, Bean, LJ, amongst other pithy comments, said this, that in the particular circumstances of that case, which were not dissimilar to these, one has to focus on the statement in the Sexual Offences Guidelines 2014 that offences may be of such severity, for example involving a campaign of rape, that sentences of 20 years and above may be appropriate. Because of this, it is unnecessary to consider whether this is a category one case, and he held that the factors in that case, which as I've indicated – many of which were very similar to this – fell within the description of offences of such severity that sentences of 20 years or more might be required.

Now, it would be uncomfortable – it might, frankly, be thought insulting by Carol Higgins – to compare her ordeal and the trauma that it occasioned to her to that of others and I do not therefore propose to compare cases further. In any event, all cases, of course, are uniquely fact specific. Suffice it to say that I have considered the facts of those two cases and this case. In considering the guidelines I have concluded that the overall sentence must fall into the 20-year plus category but at a marginally lower level than in the cases of *R v G* and *R v JH,* because, as Mr Storey has correctly pointed out, the offences in this case were for a less protracted period. Mr Appleyard has no previous convictions for sexual offences and I have also taken into account to the extent I feel able to do his ill health.

Taking that matter into account, I have as I have indicated, fixed an overall sentence of 20 years. Unhappily this was a trial. There was, therefore, no credit for a guilty plea and it is entirely clear that Mr Appleyard feels no remorse of any kind whatsoever. I am, of course, aware, that an overall sentence of 20 years is a long sentence for a man of 71 and a man who is not in the best of health, but I am satisfied that the depravity of the conduct and the destructive effect it has had on the life of the defendant's own daughter, Carol Higgins, requires an overall sentence of that length.

The sentence will be made up as follows. On count one, 12 months' imprisonment; on count two, 21 – I am sorry, 20 years' imprisonment; on count three, 20 years' imprisonment; count four, two years' imprisonment; count five, two years' imprisonment; count six, two years' imprisonment; count seven, 20 years' imprisonment; count eight, two years' imprisonment; count nine, two years' imprisonment; count 10, two years' imprisonment; count 11, 20 years' imprisonment; count 12, two years' imprisonment; count 13, two years' imprisonment; count 14, two years' imprisonment; and count 15, 20 years' imprisonment. All of those sentences are concurrent, one with another.

I have already indicated that I will make a restraining order. The precise terms of that will be notified to the court in due course. If it requires further attention by me, it will receive it. I have explained to Mr Appleyard the necessity of signing the sexual offenders register before leaving the court building and the notification period that follows, and unless there is anything else that either counsel would wish me to address, that is the sentence imposed in this case.

May I thank both counsel – in fact, all counsel involved in the case – very much indeed for their help and for the skill with which they conducted the case. Thank you very much indeed.

(12.30 p.m.)

Diary: Friday 25th January 2019

As Janet had not been in court throughout the trial, I was surprised to finally see her today. She laughed out loud when the Judge said that my dad had taken pictures of me in sexy underwear.

Sentencing started later than expected because my dad was complaining that he did not have his medication. It was a shock to see him in the dock in his grey prison sweatshirt and joggers, he had been reduced to having his choice of clothing and freedom taken away. After being informed that he was being sentenced to twenty years, his final act of defiance was to leave court before the remainder of sentencing was completed. As he was led away by the "grim reaper" I turned and waved to him and said "See ya."

Interview Outside Court

Look North Interview

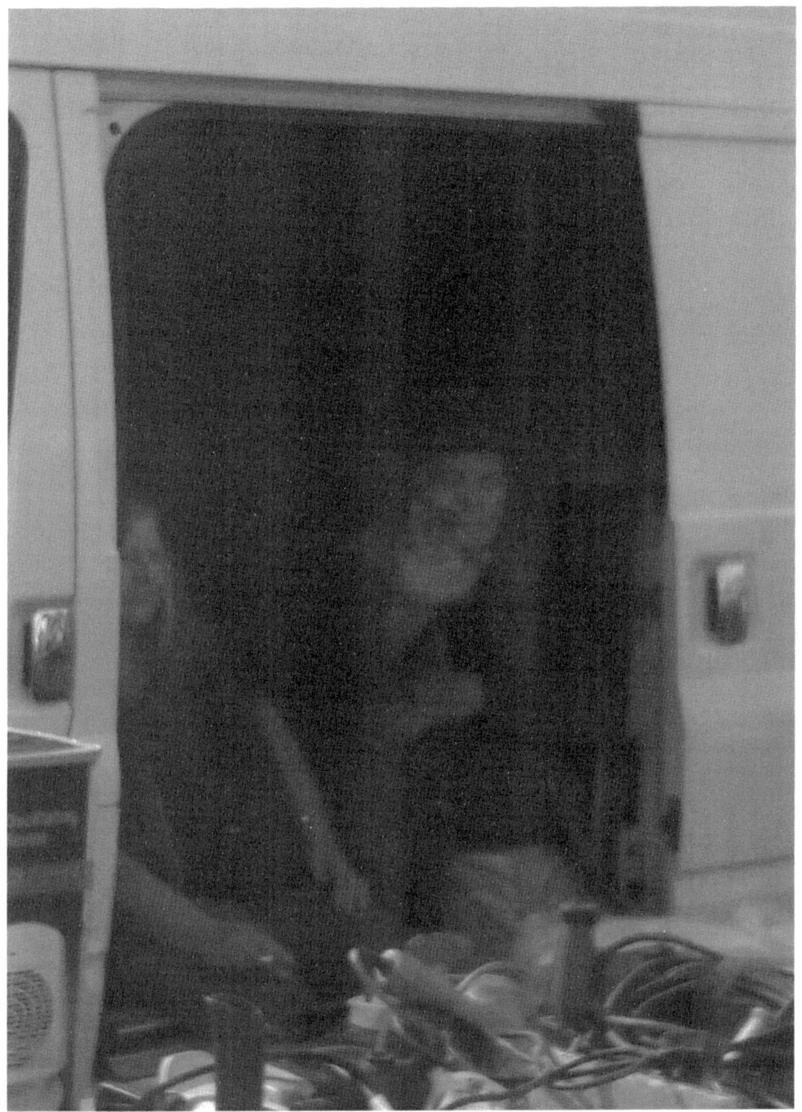

2017 after the decision not to charge Appleyard, the same day as he said "I'll fucking have ya.'" Appleyard waved condescendingly and said "See ya, go away little girl." When he was sentenced, I returned the sentiment and said "See ya!"

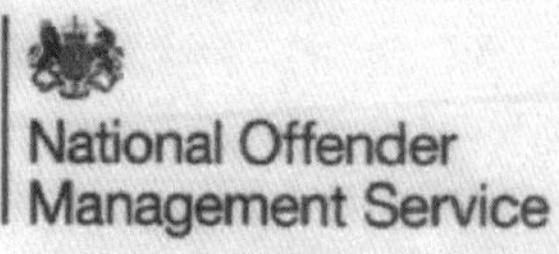

Kirklees & Wakefield Victim Services Unit
20/30 Lawefield Lane, Wakefield WF2 8SP
Victim Liaison Unit 01925 853309

VICTIM CONTACT REPORT

THIS REPORT AND THE INFORMATION CONTAINED HEREIN, IS STRICTLY CONFIDENTIAL AND MUST NOT BE DISCLOSED TO THE OFFENDER OR A THIRD PARTY WITHOUT THE PRIOR PERMISSION OF THE VICTIM

Victim Name: Carol Higgins	**Victim DOB:** 23.04.69
Date of Contact: 27.03.19	**VSU Ref. No:** 13KD0601916
Type of Contact: Home visit	**Names of people present & Relationship to Victim:** Carol Higgins
Victim Liaison Officer: Ruth Kerry	**VSU Contact Details:** 01924 853309

Offender Name: EA	**Offender DOB:** 29.06.47
Offence & Offence date: **Rape & USI btw 1982 -1985**	**Court:** Leeds Crown Court
Date of Sentence: 25.01.19	**Sentence:** 20 years custody
Offender Manager:	**OM Contact Details:**

INFORMATION CONVEYED TO THE VICTIM/VICTIMS FAMILY

Key Sentence Dates & Restrictions:

HDC	ACR	PED	NPD	LED	SED
N/A	January 2029	N/A	N/A	January 2039	January 2039

SOR: Yes
Judge ordered defendant may be placed on Barring List by the Disclosure and Barring Service, Sex Offender Register for Life.

Civil Order: Yes
Restraining Order (Protection from Harassment Act 1997 S5) Must not contact directly or indirectly Carol Higgins or Paul Appleyard. This order lasts until further order.

THE PURPOSE OF THE VICTIM CONTACT WAS TO:
The reason for the units contact was to inform the victim that she was entitled to receive information relating to the offender's sentence. To also take account of the impact of the offence and to have her views and concerns considered when decisions are being taken about the conditions to which the offender may be subject to on their release. Where appropriate and neccessary victim led licence conditions could be applied for.

Page 1 of my Victim Contact Report

CONFIDENTIALITY
Does the victim have any concerns about their views being communicated to the Offender? **Not now, however her views may change when the next report is completed.**

INFORMATION SHARED WITH THE VICTIM: (please check all those shared);

A copy of the Victim Contact scheme leaflet	x
A copy of the Area Complaints procedures leaflet	x
Sentence information card confirming key dates	x
Equal opportunities monitoring form	x
Victim satisfaction questionnaire	x
Information regarding other services available to victims	x

VICTIM PERSONAL STATEMENT:

Does this case fall within the criteria of making a Victim Personal Statement to the Parole Board **No**

CHILD PROTECTION:
Is the victim a child: No, Carol is now an adult, however she was a child at the time of the offence?

IMPACT/CONCERNS OF THE OFFENCE:

When I first visited Carol, it was clear that she needed to talk to me about how she felt she had been let down not only by her father, but also by the very Justice system who should have protected her.

Carol had a remarkable recall of the events spanning some 33 years and it was no wonder that having carried all this abuse and trauma with her for such a long period of time that she felt so hurt and damaged. Carol however showed extraordinary fortitude and her perseverance to get to the truth is truly amazing.

Carol is still in the process of unravelling the systematic failings of the West Yorkshire Police since initially reporting the index offence in 1982 to the present day. I therefore did not feel it was appropriate at this initial interview to ask Carol to quantify how this offence had impacted on her, there is still too much for Carol to process and to come to terms with, these offences have affected her both physically and emotionally, notwithstanding the devastating affect that this has had on her family unit.

To this end I will revisit with Carol later at which time she may feel more able to talk in detail about any concerns that she might have regarding the offender and the future.

MEDIA INTEREST:
Yes: This received coverage in the local media and the victim herself is very vocal on social media and has self-published regarding her experiences of abuse at the hands of the offender and what she sees as systematic failures of the Police.

RESTORATIVE INFORMATION:
It was not appropriate to discuss Restorative Justice at this point, however in the future it may be that this is something that can be explored with the victim.

RISK ASSESSMENT:
Does the victim know the offender? **Yes**
If Y: in what capacity: It is her father

Are there any mutual friends/relatives between the victim and offender: Yes, extended family?

Does the victim know if the offender is aware of where they live/work/go to school etc: Yes?

As previously stated this was a familial offence with there being extended family and close friends who are linked jointly to the offender in Denby Dale and Carol the victim, both now and in the past. Carol advised me that there was an occasion in recent years when the offender having attempted to obtain a restraining order against her, then chose to travel from Denby Dale to an area very close to where Carol lives in Ackworth to attend a car boot sale! It is of note that Denby Dale and Ackworth are some 18 miles apart, so this action by the offender is somewhat questionable!

How vulnerable is the victim?
Carol is vulnerable due to her fragile emotional state, which has fundamentally been caused by a combination of not only the index offence but the last 33 years of battling with the establishment to have her voice heard and ensure that justice is seen to have been served.

Is the victim frightened? Yes
While Carol is safe from any direct physical harm for the period that the offender remains incarcerated, she still struggles daily to manage the residual effects of the last 33 years. Carol remains anxious about her physical health and any long-term damage that may have been caused as a direct result of the offence and the ensuing anxiety that she must cope with daily.

Furthermore, although the offender has now been sentenced, she has no sense of closure and this is not something that she is likely to be able to achieve any time soon. There is also her emotional and mental health which is yet to be fully addressed, while the offender has received a significant custodial sentence this in no way will act as a panacea and instantly put right the harm caused by the actions of the offender and the West Yorkshire Police over last 33 years

Are any risks identified towards the offender from the victim? Nothing physical, although the offender may feel threatened about the disclosures that have subsequently been made in recent publications, where he is identified by name as responsible for abusing his daughter Carol.

LICENCE CONDITIONS REQUESTED:
Licence conditions were not discussed at this time, this is a long sentence and these will be addressed with the victim prior to any proposed release.

ARRANGEMENTS FOR FUTURE CONTACT:
I have arranged to contact the victim again in x 3 months at which time it is hoped that she will have some resolution from the IPCC and she will also have had settlement regarding her CICA.

THE VICTIM DOES WISH TO SEE A COPY OF THIS REPORT

DATE OF REPORT:	28 March 2019

EPILOGUE

Before the trial I thought I would begin to feel at peace with myself and have a sense of closure if my father was sent to prison. In 2016 I had made a complaint to the chief of West Yorkshire Police, Dee Collins about their conduct throughout the various investigations, or lack of them, regarding my case and the way I was being treated. I had been told this could not be pursued by Police Professional Standards whilst my father was being investigated because this would be subjudice. This could now go ahead. I also wanted to sue the police in a civil claim for their repeated serious systematic failings to investigate over thirty-five years. Such a claim under Article 3 of the Human Rights Act 1998 must be made within a year of the end of the trial. Consequently, I felt the pressure of meeting this deadline and finding a suitable solicitor to represent me.

Ruth, a Ministry of Justice probation officer, came to interview me once Appleyard had been sentenced, to complete a victim impact report to take account of the impact the offence had on my life. She concluded that I could not get closure due to the ongoing complaint and unresolved civil claim against West Yorkshire Police.

In this book I have begun to document some of the failings of the police and the CPS, however the main focus has been the trial. My next book in the trilogy will describe my continuous struggle to get the criminal case to trial and will explore in greater detail these repeated failings. The final book will describe further the impact familial rape (incest) has had on my life and how I am trying to raise awareness of this taboo subject.

I still need to tell my story in order for lessons to be learnt by the authorities who have failed and are still failing children today. There are also lessons for society and families and for people who work with victims and survivors. Safeguarding policies must be drawn up which take into account the voices of those who have been sexually abused, as recommended by the Independent Inquiry into Child Sexual Abuse (IICSA). This inquiry acknowledges institutional failings at the highest level. The police would do well to scrutinise their attitude towards victims, both current and historical, especially in light of the recent revelations about celebrities, politicians and other high-powered people involved in child sexual abuse. There are so many children who are afraid to speak up, who are scared of not being believed and who fear the justice system is likely to fail them. Boris Johnson likened investigating historical child sexual abuse to spaffing money up against the wall. This attitude needs to change. If I had not got justice my father would still be free to rape other children.

My search for healing continues and it took me years to understand that I was not to blame. I feel that the truth is still being covered up or ignored and I will not get closure until the truth comes to light. I stood for local election in May 2020 and when I was canvassing a retired police officer of thirty years' service, told me that the overall consensus of the police had been to "leave the little sluts and prostitutes alone." How can a child be a prostitute or a slut!

I grew up in a council house in Denby Dale and my dad rented land from retired Chief Inspector Richard Ellis, Judge James Pickles, Simon Walter Fraser from Cannon Hall Estates, Barnsley and from local farmers where he kept pigs. In this book you have heard the recording of my MP's office saying that everyone knew that Judge Pickles was a prolific and notorious leader of a paedophile ring but could do nothing about it. I want to expose who was in that ring and acknowledge those who suffered at their hands.

As a final thought, I want you to know that to have a chance at getting justice you have to record everything, even if it means installing a recording app on your phone like I did. You have to gather the evidence to bring your abuser to justice. If you don't, who will? I hope your truth will be your defence.

1

Carol.

You need to read this letter because it will be the last communication from me to you. Me writing this to you has played on my mind for quite a while, in fact before the court case and reading the book you wrote which the police have still got with all the lies you told in it the lighted. i cant take the fact you climbed that mountain was very coragueae. ~~You have forgotten to write in~~ your book about when i took you away from him. we had only moved to penistone a week when you started seing a boy call Craigh who lived accross from us and they used to take you to there caravan at week-ends. When we moved again to hinda's you soon started to go out with her son David and you were having sesc with him. And did you also forget to write in your book that behind my back you were meeting your father in Barnsley and he was buying you

Page 1 of the last communication from my mother.

2

things, you were always very materical mistic, like the times when you were living with me in Barnsley - you rang up in your lunch hour from work and asked me to lend you some money as they were having a sale on at your works at glents, i agreed and took the money to you and said if you see anything that might fit me you said that means one less thing i will be able to buy for you. I bet you did not think to write that in your book. And while we are talking about you living with me did you forget to say the times i sat with you trying to tell you it was not your fault and even got you councilling. By the way the person who was your councelor came to the house early and said she had done this because she told me that you would always ~~bad behaviour~~ blame what happened to you for your bad behavier and not to accept it. And you also forgot to put in the book of lies the time you told me you were thinking of moving

3

back to Denby dale, and i told you that you would be putting my grandchildren in danger, and if. you did this i would get in touch with Social Services. The last thing i am going to remind you that you did not put in your book of lies, the morning you rung me and told me that you had got cancer, i asked. where and how do you know you said you had seen a consultant, and in fact you were going to see him the next day regards your treatment, I said what time i will come over and give you some support - and what did you say - stop being a drama queen what a cruel thing to say to me - we have only ever had one drama queen in the family and that is you always you have been

Shame on you.

There is another thing you need to know i am not having a funeral when i go have arranged it; The one of the reason's is i dont want Grahams millie to be in ~~em~~ embaressed that my grand children will not be there as you and Paul have turned them against me, again Shame on you.

Page 3

4

Also there will be no grave, if i go before graham my ashes will be put with his - but he will have a funeral and a celebration of our life together, again you are not invited.

So please do not ring or write Nothing can ever erase what you have done. I love Jake & Ella it's a shame i cant love you.
Shame on you

Mum

Page 4

In life we encounter many mountains, we are overwhelmed by them. The choice is to fear them or conquer them. Throughout my life I have chosen to do the latter. For those who still seek justice my strength and love goes out to you all.

My mum won't talk to me and neither will my brother. He says that if I hadn't been my dad's girlfriend his dad would still be his hero. My sister, Donna, has sadly committed suicide because she couldn't cope with how cruel life had been to her. I am still trying to heal from a broken heart. This is the impact familial rape has on families. Writing this book has been one of the biggest mountains I have ever had to climb. But it is not the last...